T0339573

Routledge Handbook of Sports Journalism

The *Routledge Handbook of Sports Journalism* is a comprehensive and in-depth survey of the fast-moving and multifaceted world of sports journalism. Encompassing historical and contemporary analysis, and case studies exploring best practice as well as cutting edge themes and issues, the book also represents an impassioned defence of the skill and art of the trained journalist in an era of unmediated digital commentary.

With contributions from leading sports-media scholars and practising journalists, the book examines journalism across print, broadcast and digital media, exploring the everyday reality of working as a contemporary reporter, editor or sub-editor. It considers the organisations that shape output, from PR departments to press agencies, as well as the socio-political themes that influence both content and process, such as identity, race and gender. The book also includes interviews with, and biographies of, well-known journalists, as well as case studies looking at the way that some of the biggest names in world sport, from Lance Armstrong to Caster Semenya, have been reported.

This is essential reading for all students, researchers and professionals working in sports journalism, sports broadcasting, sports marketing and management, or the sociology or history of sport.

Rob Steen is an author, journalist and sportswriter, and former senior lecturer and co-leader of the BA (Hons) Sport Journalism course at the University of Brighton, UK. He has been cricket correspondent for the *Financial Times* and deputy sports editor for the *Sunday Times*. He has written for many other newspapers and magazines, including *The Guardian*, *The Independent* and *Independent on Sunday*, *The Daily* and *Sunday Telegraph*, *The Age* (Melbourne), *India Today* and *Hindustan Times*. He won the 1995 Cricket Society Literary Award, the UK section of the 2005 EU Journalism Award "for diversity, against discrimination", and has been shortlisted twice for the William Hill Sports Book of the Year award, and once for the Lord Aberdare Prize for Sports History.

Jed Novick is an author, journalist and sportswriter, as well as senior lecturer on the BA (Hons) Sport Journalism and Journalism courses at the University of Brighton, UK. He has written for *The Times* (sportswriter), *The Independent* (TV editor), *The Guardian* (arts writer), *The Observer* (deputy arts editor) and the *Daily Express* (arts editor), as well as a number of magazines and journals.

Huw Richards is a journalist and university teacher who is currently an Associate Lecturer at St Mary's University, Twickenham, UK. He has been rugby correspondent for the *Financial Times*, cricket correspondent for the *International Herald Tribune*, and a staff reporter for the *Times Higher Education Supplement*. He has also taught at London Metropolitan University and London College of Communication, UK, and been shortlisted for the William Hill Prize and the Lord Aberdare Prize for Sports History.

Routledge Handbook of Sports Journalism

Edited by Rob Steen,
Jed Novick and Huw Richards

LONDON AND NEW YORK

First published 2021
by Routledge
2 Park Square, Milton Park, Abingdon, Oxon OX14 4RN

and by Routledge
52 Vanderbilt Avenue, New York, NY 10017

Routledge is an imprint of the Taylor & Francis Group, an informa business

British Library Cataloguing-in-Publication Data
A catalogue record for this book is available from the British Library

Library of Congress Cataloging-in-Publication Data
Names: Steen, Rob, editor. | Novick, Jed, editor. | Richards, Huw, 1959- editor.
Title: Routledge handbook of sports journalism / edited by Rob Steen, Jed Novick and Huw Richards.
Other titles: Handbook of sports journalism
Description: First. | Abdingdon, Oxon ; New York, NY : Routledge, 2021. |
Series: Routledge international handbooks | Includes bibliographical references and index. |
Identifiers: LCCN 2020019957 | ISBN 9781138671874 (hardback) | ISBN 9781315616704 (ebook)
Subjects: LCSH: Sports journalism.
Classification: LCC PN4784.S6 R68 2021 | DDC 070.4/49796--dc23
LC record available at https://lccn.loc.gov/2020019957

ISBN: 978-1-138-67187-4 (hbk)
ISBN: 978-1-315-61670-4 (ebk)

Typeset in Bembo
by KnowledgeWorks Global Ltd.

This book is dedicated to the memory of Mike Marqusee, a campaigning journalist, author and tireless political activist who always upheld the principles of fair and fearless reporting, inspiring us in more ways than he could possibly have known.

Contents

List of contributors   x

Introduction   xv
Jed Novick

1 Why sports journalism matters   1
Rob Steen

PART I
The trade   **21**

2 Sport and journalism in the 18th and 19th centuries   23
Mike Huggins

3 The art of sportswriting   33
Rob Steen and Huw Richards

4 Newspapers   41
Guy Hodgson

5 Tabloids   51
Rob Shepherd

6 Agencies   61
John Mehaffey

7 Regional newspapers   71
Graham Hiley

8 Fanzines   83
Huw Richards

9 Multiplatform sports journalism   101
Mark Barden

Contents

10 Broadcasting: Interview with Martin Tyler   111
    Adrienne Rosen

11 Twitter   125
    Simon McEnnis

12 Public relations   135
    Owen Evans

13 The sports editor: Good cop or bad?   147
    Paul Weaver

14 The sub-editor   151
    Charles Morris

15 Humour   159
    Rob Steen

16 Statistics and records   173
    Huw Richards

17 When dreams fall apart   189
    Rob Steen

    Half-time interval: Interview with David Lacey and Patrick Barclay 195
    Rob Steen

PART II
Issues   **205**

18 Race   207
    Rob Steen and Jed Novick

19 Sexuality   223
    Neil Farrington

20 Homophobia: Interview with Alex Kay-Jelski   235
    Neil Farrington

21 Money   237
    Peter Berlin

22 National identity   251
    Peter English

23 The Olympics   261
    Gareth Edwards

24 Football hooliganism   273
    Roger Domeneghetti

25 Football managers and the press   281
    Stephen Wagg

26 Who owns the narrative?   295
    Sam Duncan and Ian Glenn

27 Caster Semenya   321
    John Price

28 Lance Armstrong   329
    Peter Bramham and Stephen Wagg

PART III
Trailblazers   **339**

29 Frank Keating   341
    Rob Steen

30 Hugh McIlvanney   345
    Kevin Mitchell

31 Vikki Orvice   347
    Steven Howard

32 John Samuel   351
    Matthew Engel

PART IV
The future   **353**

33 A new Golden Age?   355
    Raymond Boyle

34 Diversity   359
    Carrie Dunn

35 Reporting   367
    Toby Miller

Index   *377*

Contributors

Mark Barden is a senior lecturer in journalism at the London College of Communication, UK. He began his career in local newspapers before joining the BBC as an editorial publicity officer. He was also a publicist for BBC Sport before joining its website as a reporter ahead of its launch in 2000. Mark worked as a multi-platform news editor and sub-editor, and reported from numerous major sporting events. In 2011, he joined *Metro* newspaper as a digital sub-editor and began teaching journalism and sports journalism. He made the switch to full-time teaching at LCC in 2013.

Peter Berlin is a sports journalist based in London, UK. He started in local newspapers, then worked at *The Observer, Telegraph, Sunday Express, Evening Standard* and *Evening News* before settling at the *Financial Times*, primarily as sports editor. He moved to Paris to become sports editor of the *International Herald Tribune*, where he spent 15 years. He has also written for *Sports Illustrated, New York Times, The Independent* and *Washington Post*. He has covered five FIFA World Cups (four men's, one women's), six UEFA European Championships, four Olympics, five Rugby World Cups, Roland Garros, the Davis Cup, the athletics World Championships, the Super Bowl and the World Series. He is currently on the English-language sports desk at Agence France-Presse and teaches master's students at the Institut Pratique du Journalisme: Paris-Dauphine and at IESA, l'école internationale des métiers de la culture et du marché de l'art.

Raymond Boyle is Professor of Communications and Director of the Centre for Cultural Policy Research at the University of Glasgow, UK. He has been researching the relationship between media, journalism and sport for many years and has published widely in this area.

Peter Bramham was, until 2007, Reader in Leisure Studies and taught sport and leisure policy at Leeds Beckett University, UK. He was involved in the European Consortium for Leisure Studies and Research.

Roger Domeneghetti is a senior lecturer and programme leader in journalism at Northumbria University, UK. His research focuses on the societal history of sport media and the (re)presentation and negotiation of individual and collective identities therein. He has been shortlisted for the Lord Aberdare Literary Prize for Sports History. Prior to this he worked in print and online media for more than 20 years. He continues to write for a variety of publications including *The New European, The Blizzard* and *BBC History Magazine*.

Sam Duncan is the course leader and lecturer on Holmesglen's Sports Media and Sport Business degrees in Melbourne, Australia. His main research interests focus on play, sport and the media and the role of sport and media in shaping and influencing community, society and culture. Duncan is a passionate sports fan, published author and regular contributor to Australia's mainstream media, commenting on sport-related topics and issues for organisations including *The Age*, the *New Daily*, *Ten Daily* and *SEN*.

Carrie Dunn is a journalist. She has covered the last three Women's World Cups for *The Times* and Eurosport, and is a regular voice on radio, where she co-commentates for a variety of BBC stations.

Gareth Edwards is currently a lecturer in Sport Journalism at the University of the Arts in London, UK. He is also completing a PhD with De Montfort University, researching the history of sport on commercial television in the UK. He has published on the Olympics, capitalism and the birth of modern sport; physical culture after the Russian Revolution; and racism in English football. He blogs – very occasionally – at insideleft.org.

Matthew Engel landed his first journalistic job at his local paper, the *Northampton Chronicle*, progressed to Reuters, then covered sport and politics for *The Guardian* for 25 years (including the unique double of stints as cricket correspondent and Washington correspondent). He then became a columnist on the *Financial Times*. He has also served as arguably the most radical editor in the century-and-a-half history of *Wisden Cricketers' Almanack*. He was the 2011 Visiting Professor of Media at Oxford University.

Peter English is a lecturer in journalism at the University of the Sunshine Coast in Queensland, Australia. His research interests focus on sports and online journalism, with a particular emphasis on the media industry's changing demands on sports journalists. He has been a journalist for more than 15 years, writing for print and online titles in Australia, the United Kingdom and India.

Owen Evans is a sports business academic, BA Sport Journalism (Hons) course leader at the University of Brighton, UK, and a former sports journalist. He was editor of *SportBusiness International*, the oldest magazine covering the business of sport, and covered major events including the 2012 London Olympics and the 2015 Rugby World Cup. Before that, having gained a NCTJ pre-entry certificate, he was a news reporter with Northcliffe Media.

Neil Farrington worked as a sports journalist for regional and national newspapers in the UK for 18 years, which included spells as a chief sportswriter, sports editor and sports content editor. Having been nominated six times for UK regional sportswriter of the year awards, he took up a role as a Senior Lecturer at the University of Sunderland, UK, in 2010, and now leads teaching on the BA and MA Sports Journalism programmes there. He has co-authored a number of books and research papers, frequently focusing on the treatment, presentation – and sometimes the propagation – of racism in the sporting media.

Ian Glenn is Emeritus Professor of Media Studies at the University of Cape Town, South Africa, and a Research Associate in Communications Science at the University of the Free State, South Africa. He worked as a sports reporter during his undergraduate studies in Natal and covered the 1967 and 1970 South African victories over Australia at Kingsmead.

Graham Hiley is a lecturer in sports journalism at Solent University in Southampton, UK. He was previously Saints correspondent at the *Southern Daily Echo* from 1988 to 2001. He then joined Southampton FC, working as managing editor from 2001 to 2008 before becoming editor at Premierleague.com from 2008–2011.

Guy Hodgson was a journalist for more than 30 years, working on the staffs of the BBC and *The Independent* among others. He reported on many major sporting events, including two Olympic Games, one football World Cup and too many Open and Wimbledon championships to count, before becoming a lecturer. He was head of media at the University of Chester and now works at Liverpool John Moores University, UK where his research interests include sport, newspaper history and wartime journalism.

Steven Howard started his career at the *Salisbury Times and Journal* in 1970 and also worked for *Wimbledon News* and *South London Press*. He joined *The Sun* in 1978 as a sub-editor under Frank Nicklin – the sports editor who changed the face of tabloid coverage – and moved up to become sports news editor, sports feature writer, tennis correspondent, rugby correspondent, chief football writer and chief sports writer.

Mike Huggins is Emeritus Professor of Cultural History at the University of Cumbria, UK, and President of the European Committee of Sports Historians.

Simon McEnnis is a principal lecturer at the University of Brighton, UK and researches into sports journalism professionalism. His work has been published in academic journals including *Journalism, Journalism Practice, Ethical Space* and *Digital Journalism*. He worked as a sports journalist with *The Sun* for nine years, and his current industry involvement includes running a development programme for Sky Sports News journalists and chairing the sports journalism board for the National Council for the Training of Journalists (NCTJ).

John Mehaffey covered international sports for the Reuters news agency in London for more than 30 years after working as a general news and political reporter in New Zealand and Australia. He joined Reuters on the world desk in 1980 and switched to the sports desk in the following year, being appointed athletics correspondent in 1983 and chief sports reporter in 2000. John covered seven summer Olympics plus world championships in rugby, soccer, cricket, boxing and gymnastics, and also wrote features, interviews, profiles and sports news articles.

Toby Miller is Stuart Hall Professor of Cultural Studies, Universidad Autónoma Metropolitana-Cuajimalpa, Mexico; Research Professor of the Graduate Division, University of California, Riverside, USA; and Professor in the Institute for Media and Creative Industries, Loughborough University London, UK. He is President of the Cultural Studies Association (US).

Kevin Mitchell cut his journalistic teeth on the *Maitland Mercury* in New South Wales, the first step in an illustrious career that would encompass Hayters, the *London Daily News*, the *Sunday Times, The Observer*, where he was chief sports writer, and *The Guardian*, where, thanks to a predilection for *mano a mano* combat, he has performed the quite possibly unique dual role of tennis and boxing correspondent. He is a former Sports Journalist of the Year and Sports Features Writer of the Year.

Charles Morris has been a journalist all his working life, in particular on the *Financial Times,* for 28 years where he became sports editor. Since retiring, he has taught journalism at London

College of Communication, UK, and reading to primary school pupils, and he continues to write for the *Financial Times* and football magazine *When Saturday Comes*.

John Price is a senior lecturer in journalism and Programme Leader for BA (Hons) Sports Journalism at the University of Sunderland, UK. His previous research has focused on subjects such as racism in sports journalism, diversity in the sports media and football-related hate speech on social media. He is currently leading a Google DNI-funded research project which will create an online tool to help sports journalists research and report stories about social media abuse.

Adrienne Rosen has worked as a journalist for most of her career, beginning in newspapers and moving on to broadcast. She spent 12 years with the BBC, as a reporter and news editor in radio, before moving into TV as a correspondent. She also produced and presented a number of half-hour documentaries for the BBC. Beginning teaching at Bournemouth University, she took over the post graduate Broadcast course at Highbury College. She was course leader of the BA (Hons) Multimedia Broadcast Journalism degree at Brighton University and ran the media MA and BA programmes at the University for the Creative Arts.

Rob Shepherd has been chief football writer of *Today*, senior football writer at the *Daily Mail*, football and sports editor at the *Daily* and *Sunday Express* and football editor at the *News of the World*. He has also freelanced extensively for the *Sunday Times*, and as a presenter and pundit on Sky TV and talkSPORT.

Stephen Wagg is Honorary Research Fellow in the International Centre for Sports History and Culture at de Montfort University in Leicester, UK and Visiting Professor at the University of Newcastle, UK. He has written widely on the politics of sport, of childhood and of comedy.

Paul Weaver joined the *Sussex Express* in 1970, his first job in journalism, then worked for Hayters and the *Southend Evening Echo*, where he won a number of awards. He became cricket correspondent of the *News of the World* in 1979 and the *Daily Mirror* in 1986, before joining *Today* as senior sportswriter in 1989. He then joined *The Guardian*, spending 25 years there (1992–2016).

Introduction

Jed Novick

The bright blue court isn't so much a sporting venue as a gladiatorial arena. At one end stands the only man alive who could wear a dazzling fluorescent pink t-shirt and still look like a warrior. His shirt has no sleeves, possibly because there isn't enough bright fluorescent pink material in the world that could cover his biceps, and he starts his familiar ritual. He bounces the ball. He tweaks his shorts at the back. Adjusts the shoulders of the t-shirt. Pushes his hair behind his left ear, wipes the sweat from his nose, pushes the hair behind right ear. Then he starts bouncing the ball again. The concentration. The eyes. There's one thing in his eyes, one thing in his entire being.

"Freezing cold water. I do this before every match. It's the point before the point of no return. Under the cold shower I enter a new space in which I feel my power and resilience grow … I'm a different man when I emerge. I'm activated. I'm in 'the flow', as sports psychologists describe a state of alert concentration in which the body moves by pure instinct, like a fish in a current. Nothing else exists but the battle ahead."[1]

The day before, Roger Federer had saved seven match points to come through an almost four-hour match against the improbably named Tennys Sandgren. After having to leave the court due to a groin injury. At the age of 38. Marvel Comics? Pah.

These people, they're not like us. Watching them is our pleasure. And telling their stories is the work of the sports journalist. Work? Well, let's not worry about that word too much.

Sports journalists. We're storytellers. Yes, there's analysis and interpretation and reportage, but it all adds up to the same thing. Storytelling. And no area of life has better stories than sport because no area of life has better heroes than sport.

So often, our leaders seem to be trying too hard to prove that they're fallible humans. Our politicians are … no, let's not go there. Musicians, writers, artists. These people fill our hearts and feed our souls, but maybe the crucial difference between them and our sporting heroes is that their art is created in isolation and then presented to us. David Bowie never invited his fans into the Hansa Studios (which, in truth, is probably a good thing), but when Federer⋆ hits that one-handed backhand and creates art, we watch it happen. He does, we watch, and – and this is the crucial detail – no one knows what will happen. What drama. What pressure. What tension. What stories.

And what a privilege to be the teller of those stories. There's a story, probably apocryphal, about Geoffrey Green, chief football writer for *The Times* during an age (the third quarter of the 20th century) when reporters went nameless, credited merely as "Our Correspondent". Green, the story goes, kept a Christmas tree in his office because, as a sports journalist every day is Christmas. I'm not sure everyone would want more than one Christmas a year, but it's a potent idea. (Guy Hodgson elaborates on this story in his chapter.)

As time has moved on and life has evolved, the job has changed, of course. The ever-increasing demand for coverage, and the array of technological advances and progressions, the gadgets and the gizmos, the platforms and the apps … these things haven't quite yet usurped paper and pen – not for want of trying – but everything has multiplied. Deadlines are squeezed. No, deadlines are constant. Post, file, Tweet. What's your Insta profile looking like? How many followers have you got? Sports journalists have never had to work as hard as they do now.

And as the platforms have multiplied, so have the obstacles. Gatekeepers and agents and PR managers lurk around every corner.

Once upon a time in what now seems like a far, faraway land, a young cub reporter went to interview Glenn Hoddle, the then Chelsea manager. The reporter was new to the game and didn't have any contacts, so found out the number for "Chelsea FC", called up and said:

"Can I speak to Glenn Hoddle please?"

"Of course," came the reply from the lady on the switchboard, and the reporter was put through to Hoddle's PA.

"Hello. I'm a young cub reporter and I'd like to interview Glenn Hoddle," he said.

"OK, let me see. Can you come to the training ground next Tuesday for 11 am?" the PA said and gave the reporter the address.

That was then, this is now. Now, if the cub reporter called up, they'd be listening to menu after menu ("… and press 4 for catering") before eventually dying of cold and hunger. "Please hold the line. Your call is important to us."

Now Chelsea isn't a football club. It's a brand. And Glenn Hoddle wouldn't just be a manager, he'd be considered an asset, an asset to be protected. Control the asset, control the brand. The brand must be protected because if the wrong message leaks out, that could have consequences. Like us fans – and, at heart, that's what we all are – the brand cares about points, but the points the brand cares about are those on the Stock Market Index, not the league table.

Protecting the brand has evolved into an artform. Reporters are routinely banned from grounds for not toeing the line. PR departments dictate the news agenda, and access to the movers and shakers is strictly rationed.

Where does this leave the sports journalist? It leaves us in exactly the same place as we've always been. We tell the stories. It's our challenge is to be both truth-teller and storyteller, campaigner and painter; to care enough about our subject's value to society to convey the beastly as well as the beauty.

Where does this leave the sports journalist? It leaves us in exactly the same place, still in awe of Nadal, still mesmerised by Federer, still thinking "I should really like Djokovic more" … And still smiling inside at the joy of it all.

WHAT IS A SPORTS JOURNALIST? Who is a sports journalist? Why is a sports journalist? This book, we trust, answers those questions. We've endeavoured to cover the past, present and the (possible) future of our world. In the "Trade" section, we look at the component parts of sports journalism from grassroots fanzines to regional papers to the nationals, from multiplatform to social media and public relations. We look at how stories are made and recorded, the role of the practitioners from sports editors to sub-editors. Or should that be the other way around?

But sport is life and life is sport, and things aren't always how we'd like them to be. There's still racism and sexism, homophobia and violence. There's the good, but there's also the bad and the ugly. There's no point in shying away from that truth, and we don't. It's the way of life. You can't have the Beauty if you don't have the Beast.

Life has changed since we started writing this book. Originally, we had planned a much thicker volume, incorporating a broader international spectrum and range of voices. Female voices are scarce (albeit an accurate reflection of the enduring gender bias on sports desks the world over). And while there are chapters from contributors residing in Mexico, France, Australia, New Zealand, South Africa and the US, the perspective is primarily English and white. On the other hand, given that England is home to what has long been considered the planet's most viciously competitive newspaper market, that den of inquisition and iniquity formerly known as Fleet Street, this does not strike us as an insuperable shortcoming.

And when all's said and done, keep your eye on the beauty and remember why we're here. As Raymond Boyle says in the "A new Golden Age?" chapter: "Post and pre-sports event chatter may have become more accessible (if at times less restrained), yet journalists writing about sport and the events and circumstances it creates and represents will remain important cultural intermediaries in the process of creating the myths, values and narratives that make sport such an important cultural form. Don't be surprised if future generations look back at this moment and reach for the label 'Golden Age'."

(★ Delete and insert the name of your hero as applicable)

Why sports journalism matters by Rob Steen

"Sports journalism matters because sport matters, for better and worse. And because sport has two faces. And because it encompasses society's basest urges and noblest aspirations, and occasionally teaches it a trick or two. Nobody, moreover, is better equipped than a journalist to capture the heroic and the villainous, the exhilaration, the contradictions, the communality and the fellowship, and of course all those crimes and misdemeanours. We should have the words, the professional discipline, the nose for a story, the ear for a key quote and a telling line – and, ideally, a symbiotic, clearly demarcated working relationship with the people we are reporting on. But our duty to our readers and watchers is to be informants as well as celebrants, and that means fulfilling the journalist's prime function: holding power to account, telling hard truths about uncomfortable subjects."

Sport and journalism in the 18th and 19th centuries by Mike Huggins

"The press helped to make sport a popular spectacle and a commercial success. *The Sporting Magazine* (1792–1870) was England's first magazine expressedly for the sportsman, with a largely rural country gentleman readership. It covered 'the turf, the chase and every other diversion interesting to the man of pleasure, enterprize and spirit'. A significant proportion of the articles were written by readers and correspondents. By 1819 foxhunting was gaining a substantial readership. To increase circulation the magazine employed an early journalistic hunting specialist, Charles Apperley (Nimrod), from 1822 to 1827, which doubled sales. The magazine's approach was copied by other monthlies such as *The New Sporting Magazine* (from 1831) and *The Sporting Review* (from 1839)."

The art of sportswriting by Rob Steen and Huw Richards

"The essential difference between good journalism and good sports journalism is that while both must inform, the latter, because of its traditionally lighter, fluffier, more celebratory nature, often demands an ability to entertain. By the same token, not all the best sportswriters achieve this blend, a reflection of the increasingly serious and complex issues that were largely ignored before newspapers began expanding sports coverage in the 1970s but now find unprecedented space in print and on the web. This chapter unashamedly celebrates the cornerstones of good sportswriting: art, craft, wit, passion, proportion, commitment, honesty, wisdom and vision."

Newspapers by Guy Hodgson

"Sport has been one of the success stories of the printed newspaper over the last three decades, and without it there are grounds for believing more publications would have followed the online-only route in recent years. 'Unlike hard news, where the impact of TV and the internet appears to have eroded sales, sport tends to boost readership,' Roy Greenslade, formerly editor of the *Daily Mirror*, wrote, and this was in 2005. The importance of sport in newspapers has not diminished since."

Tabloids by Rob Shepherd

"It's not often an England football manager tells you to 'F.k off out of the country'. But that's what happened to me in November 1993 as the so-called 'Tabloid War' was at its height in Fleet Street, the bullets were flying and the bombs exploding with ferocity. The back pages had become one of the main battlegrounds and the then England boss Graham Taylor had become the prime target. I was dragged into the crossfire by accident, although maybe on reflection, by design on his part."

Agencies by John Mehaffey

"Tell what happened in that first paragraph and tell it quickly – who won, the time, the round, the fatal punch, the crowd, the gate – and get emotional and literary afterwards. Tell the yarn dramatically if you can and make it live, but above all tell it and feed those machines. You cannot sell papers that aren't on the street even if you are Bernard Shaw, Ring Lardner and Tolstoy all rolled into one. The media world has changed out of all recognition, but speed, accuracy and coherence remain essential to Thomson Reuters, the AP and AFP, plus the national news agencies and the specialist sports agencies such as Sportsbeat in Britain and Sport-Informations-Dienst (SID) in Germany."

Regional newspapers by Graham Hiley

"Manchester had *The Pink*; Sheffield was known for its *Green 'Un*. Coventry, Newcastle and Southampton were Pink ... Aberdeen and Hull were green. Every major regional newspaper printed its own Saturday night sports edition, mostly on the colour newsprint which gave them their distinctive names, which became almost synonymous with the cities and towns of their home."

Fanzines by Huw Richards

"What seems odd now is its complete novelty then. The surprise is not, though, that football fans developed their own independent media in the second half of the 1980s, but that groups with a strong collective sense of identity had not done so before."

Multiplatform sports journalism by Mark Barden

"The widespread availability of the internet by the mid-1990s significantly altered the working practices of many sports journalists. Those in newspapers and magazines were no longer limited by print deadlines and the availability of space on any given page of their publications. They were now serving two masters: print and online, and the move towards genuinely multiplatform sports journalism had begun – but it took a while in many places.'

Broadcasting: Interview with Martin Tyler by Adrienne Rosen

"He's known as The Voice and it is, of course, perfect for broadcast – clear, sonorous and expressive – but nothing quite prepares you for two other aspects of the man: his majestic height and his disarming modesty. Even when Martin Tyler was voted Premier League Commentator of the Decade in 2003, he declared the award to be as much for his colleagues as himself."

Twitter by Simon McEnnis

"Sports journalism and Twitter have emerged as particularly close bedfellows because of the way that, as Umberto Eco pointed out, sport lends itself to chatter. If Twitter is a conversation, then sport is inevitably going to be at the heart of it."

Public relations by Owen Evans

"The increase in sport's professionalism has coincided with the global embrace of celebrity culture and the two – money and celebrity – make a potent mix. And that is where the world of PR comes in. Players – and managers and coaches – are public figures with profiles to match. No longer can a 19-year-old footballer get drunk on holiday. He's a commodity to be protected, a product whose public face cannot be dirtied. He cannot be too outspoken, let off the leash or allowed to act naturally. He needs gatekeepers to protect his image."

The sports editor – good cop or bad? by Paul Weaver

"The sports editor, ideally, is something of a polymath. He or she must have a sound knowledge of production, a flair for presentation, be able to combine the skills of a copy-taster with those of a sub-editor, have a basic knowledge of all major sports and the political skill to lead a team while compromising with the editor and performing a PR shift with important figures outside the newspaper office."

The sub-editor by Charles Morris

"After a dash from the press seats and briefly into the sunlight across the walkway to the adjacent media centre, I began hammering away at my computer keyboard and eventually filed my report with just a few minutes to spare. My haste at the end of the match, however, led to an error. I had failed to register in my notes that Nadal had held his serve in the penultimate game to gain his third game of that set, and in striving to meet the deadline I forgot this fact. My report consequently credited him with one fewer, recording the score as 6-2 in the final set. At this point only two people could prevent my error going into print: the sports editor, who would read it, and the sub-editor, who would also edit it and place it on the page."

Humour by Rob Steen

"To steal shamelessly from Martin Mull, writing seriously about comical writing may well be even less enlightening than dancing about architecture, but this chapter will not shrink from its obligations."

Statistics and records by Huw Richards

"Every cricket fan knows cricket's greatest statistical phenomenon: 'Bradman needed only four more runs to achieve a total of 7,000 runs in Test cricket. Furthermore, his Test average, when the last Test started, was 101.39 [runs per innings]. He needed only to score those four runs to keep that average above 100, a record never achieved before or since.'"

Failure by Rob Steen

"Journalists rarely admit to such vanity, of course, but find me one who doesn't hoard a stack or two of yellowing cuttings in a cardboard box … and I'll show you a dissatisfied journalist. Some, indeed, serve as bracing reminders of both personal failure and the precarious nature of our trade. I maintain two piles in that final category. One comprises contributions to the *London Daily News*, the other my work for *Full Time*. The former, an evening London-centric title owned by the media magnate Robert Maxwell, debuted in February 1987 but expired within six months, the victim of its proprietor's vaingloriousness. The latter, a Saturday evening football classified paper set up by a pair of similarly dodgy entrepreneurs, was dead by its seventh week. As co-editor, while there were alibis aplenty, its failure hurt considerably more."

Interview with David Lacey and Patrick Barclay by Rob Steen

"I wanted to be a footballer – no chance. Then I wanted to be [commentator] Kenneth Wolstenholme – no chance: there was only one job like that. So I walked from the playground into DC Thomson's offices and got a job as a trainee. I wanted to travel. I became a *Guardian* sub in Manchester in 1966 and when the editorial operation was centralised in London and someone was made redundant in 1976 I applied for a job as sports sub there."

Race by Jed Novick and Rob Steen

"It surely says much that, in 2015, the player chosen for the cover of the 154th edition of *Wisden Cricketers' Almanack* was Moeen Ali, the rising England all-rounder and a proud Muslim brave enough to play in a Test match wearing wristbands proclaiming 'Free Palestine' and 'Free Gaza'. Even those – not exclusively Jews – who saw this gesture as one-eyed and/or foolhardy found cause to cheer: here was a British Asian whose racial origins and religious faith had proved no bar whatsoever to becoming a national hero."

Sexuality by Neil Farrington

"Thomas Hitzlsperger likes men. I like women – and football and the occasional beer in the pub and a ride on my new bike. Sounds quite dull when it's put that way. And that's precisely how it should be. Why on earth has a large proportion of the football news agenda been given up this week to Hitzlsperger 'outing' himself?"

Homophobia: Interview with Alex Kay-Jelski by Neil Farrington

"His rise through the ranks at the *Daily Mail*, moving from lowly sub-editor to the top job on the sports desk in barely seven years, revealing his sexuality along the way, offers a compelling case study in an era when the media narrative regarding LGBT athletes is under ever-increasing scrutiny."

Money by Peter Berlin

"For most of the population, money rivals sex as an overriding daily preoccupation. Yet, as with sex, a willingness to understand what's going on in finance is not simply a matter of technical expertise. Sport, and the boys who cover it, remained for a long time in the thrall of the Victorian idea that money, like sex, was a subject not to be discussed."

National identity by Peter English

"So much of sports reporting centres on scores, but international contests also contain elements magnifying issues beyond the on-field results. Consider the importance in an Asian context whenever India and Pakistan 'play'. Particularly in cricket, where the rivalry is at its most fierce, the stakes are sky-high between nations often in dispute – and the audience figures nudge one billion."

The Olympics by Gareth Edwards

"The Olympics are the biggest sporting event in the world, all but unrivalled in terms of scale, profitability and global reach. The trappings of the Olympic brand – the five rings of the Olympic flag, the torch relay, the opening and closing ceremonies – are instantly recognisable, even to those who would normally claim little interest in sport. As Joseph Maguire has noted, the Olympics are 'not merely of supreme significance in the world of sports, but as a carrier of cultural meanings which are almost uniquely available to vast international audiences'."

Football hooliganism by Roger Domeneghetti

"It was quickly shown that organised Russian gangs were indiscriminately targeting English fans and, furthermore, that violence did not only happen where the English went. In fact, Euro 2016 was marred by trouble in seven different host cities involving followers of at least 11 countries other than England. In Lille, German and Ukrainian fans fought each other; in Nice, French and Northern Irish fans clashed; in Paris, French hooligans attacked Turkish fans and there were also fights between French and Portuguese fans; in Cologne, Spanish tourists were attacked by Russian hooligans; in Saint-Etienne, there was violence during the match between the Czech Republic and Croatia; in Lyon, there were clashes between Albanian and Romanian fans; in Marseille, Hungarian fans clashed with stadium stewards."

Football managers and the press by Stephen Wagg

"The manager is now, effectively, a paradigm, within which explanations for team performance are now commonly sought; that's to say it's become virtually impossible to discuss the outcome of contemporary elite football matches without citing team managers as the key variable."

Who owns the narrative? by Sam Duncan and Ian Glenn

"Setting the sports news agenda and owning the narrative was once a battle between the traditional media and sporting organisations. Historically, traditional media set the agenda and, largely, also set the tone of the broader discussion around the issue. During times of controversy and crisis, sporting organisations would try to manage the message, control the narrative and, in doing so, limit the damage to their organisation. Thus, forming strong relationships with news organisations, reporters and journalists was vitally important for sporting bodies. However, this process has changed."

Caster Semenya by John Price

"The case of Caster Semenya is an interesting one as it raises questions about some of the fundamentals of sport, such as: What is fair competition? Can sport ever be a level playing field? And, who should compete against who?"

Lance Armstrong by Peter Bramham and Stephen Wagg

"In the world of cycling journalism, David Walsh, who, when working for the British *Sunday Times*, became Armstrong's chief inquisitor, has suggested that there are many media journalists who, often travelling in convoy with the riders, behave like 'fans with typewriters'."

Frank Keating by Rob Steen

"Will another writer ever be so willing, without a scintilla of bashfulness, to salute the awe and the ooh and the aah of sport, the electricity and the humanity – the way, even now, even in the age of naked professionalism, it celebrates courage, invention and style, mateship and manners, self-sacrifice and honour?"

Hugh McIlvanney by Kevin Mitchell

"Hugh McIlvanney's life as a sports journalist resembled one of his perfectly crafted sentences: long, lyrical and rich with surprises. He was a scrupulous and perceptive witness to what he regarded with reverence as the 'magnificent triviality' of sport, and his death, at the age of 84, will be the more keenly felt in a climate of concern about the dwindling integrity of the printed word. He leaves behind a fading image of an era that was more forgiving of boisterous behaviour than the one from which he retired in 2016 after nearly 60 years of excellence."

Vikki Orvice by Steven Howard

"Her all-round talent was quickly recognised, and she would soon become the paper's athletics correspondent, a role which she relished – covering all of Usain Bolt's world records – and in which she would prosper."

John Samuel by Matthew Engel

"Samuel presided over the operation like an impresario running a music-hall troupe. Detail was never his forte: there was little point because his era coincided with the peak of the paper's

Grauniad years when misprints were a speciality and pictures often resembled inky smudges. But he had a knack for attracting talented performers and allowing them to get on with it."

A new Golden Age? by Raymond Boyle

"The 'Golden Age' of any cultural form tends to always be in the past. We can live through these times and be blissfully unaware that some future generation will ascribe this title to a moment in history, that for those who lived through it, may have felt very much less than golden. In the middle of a maelstrom it's often difficult to chart a course or to see the true direction of travel you may be undertaking. For some, the Golden Age of sports journalism, and journalism per se, lies in the past".

Diversity by Carrie Dunn

"The part of the book where the only balls that count are made of crystal. If we were writing this on 20 March 2006 and we said that in the near future a new website would be launched, a website that would only allow you to write 'articles' of no more than 140 characters and we said that it would revolutionise the way we communicate, you'd be well within your rights to question our judgement."

Reporting by Toby Miller

"We cannot credibly predict the future without some knowledge of history and contemporaneity. So following a discussion of journalism in particular, and its historic role and its place in the current conjuncture, this chapter examines some key aspects of football journalism's possible future. The topics are nationalism, gender/race and technology/labour. But first – what is football journalism for? What does it do, and what should it do?"

Reference

1. Rafael Nadal and John Carlin, *Rafa: My Story*, Hachette Books, London 2011.

Why sports journalism matters

Rob Steen

Why does sports journalism matter? The short, incontrovertibly correct answer requires just three words: because sport matters. The full, strictly personal answer runs to rather more (rest assured: the other editors have approved it for taste and factual accuracy, been mightily indulgent on the word count, and send profuse apologies for the innumerable references to my favourite sporting fix, cricket, a game whose lexicon might prove occasionally challenging for some).

Once upon a very recent time there was a place called Great Britain, a small but exceedingly wealthy island that had recently ruled a third of the planet and thoroughly justified more than half its name (albeit only because empire-building was once regarded as an unavoidable and acceptable fact of life). Its name concealed multiple identities – English, Scottish, Welsh and two kinds of Irishes – not to mention confusing alternatives such as the United Kingdom, Britain and the British Isles, the last "a term", as Matthew Engel would point out in 2014, "now increasingly considered politically incorrect, some pedants preferring 'North-west European Archipalego' or 'Islands of the North Atlantic'".[1] Fear, loathing, stupidity and nostalgia reigned. Enmeshed in the near-pitiable chaos of exit from the European Union, aka Brexit, with xenophobia, inequality, zero-hours contracts, online teenage suicide notes, homelessness and food banks soaring, here was a small patch of land mired in the past and growing ever more divided by the day. A patch renowned for its sense of humour where, in its northern climes, the surrealist Swedish comedian Olaf Falafel (in a show entitled It's One Leek for Mankind) had just won the award for the funniest joke of the Edinburgh Festival Fringe for a look-how-daring-I-am slice of wordplay mocking victims of Tourette's Syndrome. For those grateful for any reason to be cheerful, the dizzying weekend of 24–25 August 2019 offered relief, however brief.

For one thing, it was blissfully and ceaselessly sunny, though even the most ardent Extinction Rebellion activists would not have relished the latest hottest Bank Holiday in the annals of an island where fair weather had historically been as commonplace as equitable income distribution. Meanwhile, at Headingley, home to Yorkshire County Cricket Club, the England men's team, drawn from a multi-ethnic pool of talent encompassing players of Asian origin as well as the sons of Ireland, Barbados, Zimbabwe, South Africa and New Zealand, won a match they had no earthly – or even "solar systemy" – right to win.

An historic, hypnotic, magical, mystical and occasionally hysterical passage of bat-and-balling at Headingley began at 11am on the Saturday and ended more than twelve playing hours later

(29 in real time, pausing only for two ritual lunches, drinks breaks and a tea-break, breakfast, dinner and a few thin hours of sleep). For the final hour, the clock, perversely for a sporting contest, was utterly and gloriously irrelevant: there was still another full day scheduled. In the Age of Instant Gratification, slow eating was one of the latest, hippest health fads in Notting Hill and Hampstead; could slow sport yet catch on?

The occupants of the press box, for whom time is never a friend, especially in the claustrophobic age of tweeting and blogging, knew the feeling all too well. "The messiest corner of any sportswriter's life is their waste-paper bin," admitted Andy Bull in *The Guardian*. "A lot of the time print deadlines are so tight that most of the writing is done live while the match happens, and since sport has an unfortunate way of throwing up all these late twists you end up often throwing half of it away. This is the stuff that does not even get to be the next day's fish and chip paper, intros undone by late winners, articles discarded because of last-wicket partnerships, rough first drafts of the history that almost was."[2]

When the end finally came, England had beaten Australia in a manner unseen – and wholly unforeseen – since the nations first met on a cricket field in 1877 to kick off the longest-running major international sporting soap opera of them all. The Headingley contest was the third in a five-chapter series, the prize for the duellists "The Ashes", a tiny terracotta urn first presented in 1882, its contents still unconfirmed (they've been identified, variously, as the remains of a cricket bail, a cricket stump, the cover of a ball and even a bride's veil). At three stages in a match they could not afford to lose, the home team had been bereft of realistic hope; as the crescendo beckoned, Australian nerves frayed and umpires erred, they were indebted thrice more to that most indispensable of sporting gifts, luck.

The odds against England winning, given the circumstances, are best conveyed by history and statistical probability: in 1,013 previous Test matches spanning 142 years, they had never totalled 359 runs to win in the fourth and final innings, their target that afternoon. The closest they had come had been at the dawn of the Great Depression. When the ninth wicket (of ten) fell, bringing Ben Stokes and Jack Leach together, 73 more runs were required. Only once in 2,358 Test matches – by Sri Lanka earlier in 2019, as it happened – had a side's last available partnership ever conquered such a mountain. England's entire batting order, furthermore, had been whistled out in their first innings for 67, their lowest total against Australia since 1948. In *The Guardian* came further context from Geoff Lemon, the estimable Australian cricket writer: "Three teams previously have been rolled for such a low score and won: all of those cases were in the 1800s, when a hard day's bowling was probably attended to by medicinal leeches or a sacrifice to the Sun God. Then there was this, the summer of 2019, which makes sense given the darkly absurd timeline that our world appears to have lurched down."[3] Perhaps the most priceless of Test cricket's virtues remains its structure: two innings per side can mean, for all 22 players, a second chance.

But still, cricket is a trivial pursuit, one of the more moth-eaten members of the newspaper toy department. Far newsier news abounded. The apparently unavoidable divorce from the EU was threatening even darker economic gloom, even the very existence of the United Kingdom. Seeking to suppress opposition to his pursuit of a no-deal Brexit, Alexander Boris de Pfeffel Johnson was about to suspend Parliament, an act that would have been unconstitutional had there been such a thing as a written, legally binding British constitution. Nicola Sturgeon, Scotland's First Minister, would declare it "the day any semblance of British democracy died"; Simon Jenkins, a former editor of *The Times*, compared the new prime minister to F. Scott's Fitzgerald's Jazz Age anti-hero: "There is a Gatsby quality to him, of rich people having a good time as they 'smashed up things and creatures and let other people clean up the mess they had made'. That is the fate of all nations that put their faith in unwritten constitutions. They are vulnerable to rogues."[4] A letter to *The Guardian* from Dr Mike Addison underlined the depth of disbelief: "My mother, an Austrian refugee, used to tell her children that Hitler could never have risen to power in the UK because of the existence and power of the monarch. [Johnson] proved this argument false". Perhaps the most plaintive view came from another *Guardian* reader, Fiona Black: "I am a mother of four who grew up in Northern Ireland. I live in fear of a no-deal Brexit. Not because of trade or finances but because of the return to violence which a hard border will bring with it. Every day of my childhood was spent hearing of people being killed by bombs and bullets. I lived in fear that I, my siblings or parents would be next. Is this what we want for our children?"[5]

Other reasons to be fearful and furious were queuing up: Prince Andrew's connections with the billionaire Jeffrey Epstein, the American paedophile, sex trafficker and friend to presidents who had recently committed suicide in jail under deeply suspicious circumstances, were growing ever shadier and shabbier. A crucial G7 meeting of world leaders was in progress in Biarritz, where No. 10 Downing Street's truth-allergic stand-up comic of a new president had been warning his new best buddy Donald Trump that a trade war with China would result in a global recession. Unenlightened populist despots ruled the roost in the United States, India, Brazil, Hungary, Syria, Saudi Arabia and too many other places besides. The Amazon rainforests were ablaze, the havoc ordered by Brazil's prime minister, a man who deserves only that his name should be expunged from memory with indecent speed and extreme prejudice. Riots had returned to the streets of Hong Kong. In Lancashire, after 135 years as an integral part of the local community, one of the lesser latter-day cogs in the football business, Bury, was about to go out of business, the first club to be expelled from the English Football League since Leeds City during the 1919–1920 season.

Nothing, though, could stop each and every one of Monday's nine daily national newspapers leading their front pages with a photograph of Stokes at the moment of victory, arms at ten-past-ten, roaring his delight. Even the *Financial Times*. And all this for a sport struggling to stay relevant in its cradle, an activity and entertainment so un-21st century that a match could still consume 30 hours without yielding a winner.

What was that about the media being experts solely in the art of packaging bad news? Here's a taste of the reaction:

Best Summer's Day Ever
Daily Express headline
Boris Johnson promises Ashes star Ben Stokes 'Dukedom'
The Mirror headline
U Must Be Stoking
The Sun headline
Land Of Heat And Glory!
Daily Mail headline
I have no sister but if I did I'd want her to marry Ben Stokes.
Tweet by Graeme Swann, ex-England colleague of Stokes

The more considered verdicts, from Englishmen and Australians alike, seem no less worthy of reproduction (for those unfamiliar with cricketese, please forgive the terminological complexities of the first):

Upon reaching his 100, the best of his career, [Stokes] did not celebrate. That was not his goal. Next Stokes took 17 runs from a Hazlewood over, pull shots, drives and legside flicks, which magically just managed to keep finding or clearing the boundary. A half-chance flew to Marcus Harris at third man but he could not quite cling on as he dived forward. This was beyond Roy of the Rovers.[6]

Vic Marks, *The Guardian*

To be a young cricket addict watching the 1981 Ashes was to be struck with awe, [Ian Botham's] belligerent swagger felt thrillingly un-English. To me, aged 12, he was a superhero. Perhaps the very best thing about Stokes yesterday was to feel, even in middle-age, that same wonderment – and see it in the faces of three generations gathered together. The very best of sport, and the very best of athletes, draw the world in communal joy. You look at each other, with crazy grins, and ask "how is that even possible?"[7]

Matt Dickinson, *The Times*

Utterly, cruelly, wonderfully fair. Even in this age, obsessed with precision and quantity, the rational and the logical, there remains in cricket an abiding belief in the rub of the green, which Stokes had by then mightily earned.[8]

Gideon Haigh, *The Times*

Call off Test cricket now. In fact, call off all cricket. Not because it could never get any worse than this, but because how could it ever be better, surely? That's talking as a cricket fan and connoisseur of the incomparable drama of sports, not as an Australian partisan. Let's all die happy now, or only a little bit sad, and permanently awe-struck.[9]

Greg Baum, *Sydney Morning Herald*

Oh hell, just call it off now. Forget the Premier League, cancel the Rugby World Cup, bin the world athletics championship and whatever else we're supposed to get excited about in the coming weeks and months. They'll all pale after this Headingley Test, when Ben Stokes, that most unlikely saint, worked the second of the two miracles he needs for his canonisation.[10]

Andy Bull, *The Guardian*

The most surprising comeback since the first boomerang.

Mick Beeby, letter to *The Guardian*

If we can beat Australia despite the experts writing us off, surviving Boris Johnson will be a breeze as long as we all keep our nerve.

Frederick Cantrell, letter to *The Guardian*

And then there was this:

England cricket: an apology from *The Times*

We may have given the impression in Saturday's Times that Joe Root's England side had "No fight, no idea, no hope" after they were bowled out for a dismal 67 in their first innings.

We now recognise that they are among the finest, battling sides this country has ever produced. We are happy to make this clear.[11]

The heroes, as befits those truly worthy of that oft-abused word, were human beings of rare drive and resilience. The first was Stokes, a towering physical specimen of Maori ancestry. Having spent the first 12 years of his life in New Zealand, he had migrated to north-east England with his steely, never-knowingly-cowed father. A professional rugby league player and coach, Ged Stokes was committed to that ubiquitous mantra about there being no "I" in "team" (as well as the lesser-known one about there almost always being an "I" in "failure"). He once sacrificed a finger to the greater cause, bidding a doctor to cut a damaged one off, thus hastening his return to action. It took a broken neck to persuade him to retire.

Lovingly nurtured, Ben's talent for those apparent polar opposites rugby and cricket was unmissable. Athleticism, power, hand-eye coordination, ferocious commitment and a lifetime membership of the "Who Dares Wins" school of philosophy; he had it all. Better yet, he far preferred team sport to individual sport because it tapped into his yearning for collective endeavour and mateship. But despite that paternal influence, cricket – where he excelled in all three departments, as batsman, bowler and fielder – snared his ambition.

The inner fire was no less in-your-face. Ginger of hair, even the most skilful understaters could not accuse him of being gingerly. On the field, he was the walking definition of a captain-in-the-making: the ideal team leader, both exemplar and enabler. Only those perennial burdens – as a three-in-one master of all the game's trades – could stop him from ascending the throne occupied by the England cricket captain, the most demanding public post in the land not to include the words "prime" and "minister" in its job description (at least the England football manager doesn't have to tackle a rival centre-back or risk a broken shin). Opponents who bested Stokes, however temporary their superiority, would mimic and taunt. Failure fired fury, almost always self-directed. During a match in Antigua in 2014, it spurred him to punch a dressing-room locker, busting a wrist – one of the most debilitating injuries a cricketer can sustain.

In Kolkata two years later, the pain was infinitely greater: watched by an estimated global audience of more than a billion (the cumulative home viewership in India alone was 730 million), [12] Stokes – the clever, canny, pacy Stokes – was the bowler entrusted with completing England's seemingly inevitable triumph in the World T20 final; but he fluffed his lines, conceding four consecutive sixes – aka "maximums", as contemporary parlance has it – to an unheralded West Indian hulk, Carlos Brathwaite. "I couldn't believe it," the loser sputtered in the soul-freezing, brain-chilling draught of bitter, unexpected defeat, echoing every watcher from Zanzibar to Ashby de la Zouch. "I didn't know what to do. It took me so long to get back on my feet. I didn't want to get back up. It was like the whole world had come down on me. It was just complete devastation." Management denied threatening to subject him to anger management classes, but few doubted the logic.

Just over a year later, in September 2017, having recovered his equilibrium enough to become England's vice-captain, Stokes hurt himself again, and even more grievously. In 2013 he had been sent home from an England A tour of Australia after a brace of nocturnal drinking sessions; on this occasion, having elected to spend an unsober evening at a Bristol nightclub after helping England beat the West Indies, a richly earned break beckoning after 25 sapping games for his country in nine months, he was filmed (fuzzily) outside the premises, laying wobble-legged waste to a pair of locals with those brickish fists. Both were left unconscious, one with a broken eye socket.

At the time Stokes claimed he had been defending two other young men from homophobic abuse. While both publicly thanked him, neither was asked to give evidence at the trial the following August; instead, he was the one thus accused. Amid the ill-focused footage of the beatings, you can just make out the panicky voice of Alex Hales, the similarly built and still more foolhardy England teammate who had accompanied him during his staggering journey to eruption. (Although he and Stokes would be charged with bringing the game of cricket into disrepute, Hales, remarkably, would go uncharged, but would risk his future even more senselessly, above all selection for the 2019 World Cup squad, by failing back-to-back recreational drug tests.) "Stokes, Stokes," he urges in the recording, "That's enough."

The prosecution case was that Stokes had been the aggressor, having become "enraged" after a doorman barred him and Hales from entering the club. At the 11th-and-a-half hour, Nicholas

Corsellis requested permission to add two counts of assault to the indictment but was turned down on the not unreasonable basis that this would penalise the defence, who had prepared for a different case. After six days of testimony and front-page news, Stokes was cleared. For many, the temptation to suspect that a lesser-known figure would have been found guilty was irresistible.

"In the scrap folder of my laptop," wrote Bull, "I have a copy of Stokes's career obituary, written in the winter of 2017 [when he was awaiting trial]. Like a lot of writers, I had one ready in case he was found guilty. Mine started with an anecdote from his autobiography, *Firestarter*. It was from December 2015, right after England's short tour of Sri Lanka. He had barely made a run all winter and was so dejected that when he got home to his family he turned around and went right back out again to go and play drinking games with three of his teammates. It's what happened next that made the story worth repeating. He 'red-carded himself', went home at half one in the morning, got into the shower and then broke down in tears. It never seems to occur to him that, the way he tells it, he sounds a lot like a man who was drinking to self-medicate a depression."[13]

Suspended from national duty from the day after the Bristol incident until the trial finished a year later, Stokes redeemed himself, professionally at least, at the 2019 World Cup, where the hosts finally landed the game's biggest prize at the 12th attempt. England's most consistent force in the tournament, he almost singlehandedly inspired victory over, of all opponents, New Zealand, in a breathless, freakish, unforgettable final. (That he repeatedly scorned any mention of the word "redemption" says everything for his enviable ability to block out and survive the past.) He was even nominated as New Zealander of the Year, seemingly out of admiration as much as bruised sarcasm. How could he ever top that? That he did so a mere six weeks later was the single most improbable aspect of Headingley '19.

Granted, there have been parallels – Brian Lara broke cricket's Test and first-class records for an individual innings within six weeks in 1994; Ian Botham won man-of-the-match awards in three consecutive Ashes Tests for England in 1981; Johnny Vander Meer pitched consecutive no-hitters for the Cincinnati Reds in 1938 – but not so many that one's breath could be easily contained. In the process, Stokes submitted for our edification an exposition of sporting craft that can rarely have been matched. When defence was the watchword he was a rock in a hard place, repulsing 73 deliveries and contenting himself with just three runs; when attack was the only option he pulled out every shot in the textbook and beyond: driving, cutting, uppercutting, gliding, hooking, sweeping, reverse-sweeping, over-the-shoulder-flipping. The result was 74 runs off 47 deliveries, a change of gear that left the opposition frozen and unconscious once more. Many sages, senior as well as junior, have since hailed it as the most resplendent exhibition of batsmanship they have ever witnessed. A *Guardian* editorial went further still, describing it as "one of the most extraordinary demonstrations of sporting excellence of the past 50 years."[14]

Among the dissenters and the patriotic alike there were mildly affronted, polite murmurs. The feats of a Sri Lankan, Kusal Perera, were proffered as the equal of Stokes', and not exclusively by Sri Lankans. In leading his country to an equally astonishing victory in Durban, as recently as February 2019, Perera had contributed a far greater share of his side's runs (50.7 per cent to Stokes' 37.6 per cent) while sharing a last-ditch partnership worth even more than that shared by the English pair (78 to 76). Unlike Stokes, given that Sri Lanka had been universally written off before the match against South Africa began, Perera had barely felt a gramme of pressure on his shoulders aside from the imagined howls of his benighted countrymen. Nor can it have hurt that the stands at the Kingsmead Stadium, in stark contrast to those at Headingley, were virtually empty. Unlike Perera, who was playing in the opening Test of a series, Stokes knew that defeat was not an option. Stokes also had to bear the weight of history, the burden of those 142 years of Anglo–Australian conflict. Case closed.

"Stokes is allergic to defeat," attested *The Observer's* Rob Smyth, one of the best cricket journalists to emerge this millennium. "His true superpower, the thing that has enabled his twin miracles this summer, is his will. He belongs to that rare group of all-action sporting heroes who believe they can climb Everest with a hangover . Stokes did not just bring England back from the dead last Sunday; he brought them back from a cremation. But trying to assess his impact through statistics is like trying to quantify love."

"Armchair psychoanalysis is a dubious exercise but Bristol does seem to have made Stokes a wiser, warier man. He will never be perfect on or off the field but he has developed into a different kind of hero – a superstar with no side to him, and with little discernible ego."[15]

High praise indeed, yet the most cherishable tribute, so far as Stokes was concerned, can only have been this, courtesy of a teammate, Stuart Broad, one of England's all-time bowling champions: "Everything he does is for the team. He is the perfect teammate. He didn't celebrate his fifty; he didn't celebrate his hundred. He deserves everything that comes his way because he's an incredible cricketer and an even better bloke."[16]

The other hero of 24–25 August 2019 was Matthew Jack Leach, Jack to one and all, a jack of precious few trades. The staunch, modest ally without whom Stokes' efforts would have been in vain. Primarily one of the most vulnerable of cricket beings, a slow bowler, his job was to spin the ball, his trustiest weapons being sturdy, flexible fingers; guile; deception; temptation; and optimism. He was also Stokes' spiritual and physical opposite. As naked of head as he is of pretension, as fire-red of beard as Stokes but wide-eyed and infinitely more innocent of bearing, he looked like an accountant in the middle of a midlife crisis. Outwardly gentle and gawky, struggling to locate the competitive growl within the artist that Stokes, the personification of the athlete–warrior, could find with every breath, Leach was also one of the few successful ballplayers to take the field in prescription glasses. Not exactly an insurance policy when facing 90 mph bowlers. Good fortune, however, had hitherto made strenuous efforts to avoid this genial, faintly comical West Countryman.

In 2015, while he was establishing himself as a professional, he fainted in the bathroom, hit his head on the sink and suffered a fractured skull. The next year, his bowling action was declared illegal, the most egregious of cricketing crimes, a crime not judged by intent but by mechanics and degrees of flexion. A crime that, in the most controversial, arguably racist case, blinded so many to the genius of the Sri Lankan sorcerer of spin, Muttiah Muralitharan, the Tamil titan who amassed more Test wickets – 800 – than anyone will almost certainly ever grab; a maestro of art, science, defiance and resolve whose feats united a nation engulfed in civil war, and whose bowling action brought personal persecution and a major rule-change, and directly stemmed from a birth defect that had left him with a right arm he couldn't straighten. Extensive and difficult remodelling ensued for Leach, career on indefinite hold. Branded across that dome-ish forehead, so far as cricket was concerned, was the most damning word employed in the game's extensive array of character assassinations: "chucker". Even more damning than "cheat", because, in most cases, to chuck – especially as a fast bowler, who can hence generate extra pace and venom – is to cheat *and* to threaten physical harm. (Technical note: to chuck is to hurl or throw, as baseball pitchers do, not bowl, which demands a straight arm at the point of release.)

Hovering in the background, as it had done since Leach was 14, was Crohn's disease, a chronic inflammatory bowel condition with a range of debilitating symptoms. Living with Crohn's, according to a close friend long plagued by bowel disorder, means living with recurring flare-ups which cause, among other things, severe abdominal pain, diarrhoea, extreme fatigue and weight loss. "Apart from the obvious physical effects," she said, "the condition can have a significant life impact both practically and emotionally."

Each and every obstacle was overcome with the noiseless drive that propels the least likely winners. "[Crohn's is] something I'm always battling with a little bit, even if I am very lucky to not be affected as badly as some people can be," said Leach, by now a master of un-Machiavellian understatement, when interviewed by the BBC a month before that imperishable Yorkshire Sunday. Half a year earlier he had been a major architect of a historic England series victory in Sri Lanka, beguiling and bamboozling the locals, whose own slow bowlers had been expected to dominate. "Going out to places like Sri Lanka, I need to be extra careful. If I was having a bad day with the ball, it would be nice to be able to blame it on the Crohn's, but I've never done that. If there's a day when I'm struggling, I know how to fight through. If I was in the middle of a big flare-up, I would feel at a physical disadvantage compared to other players, but I haven't had one of those since I was about 16."[17] Leach endured his first "flare-up" as a professional cricketer during the summer of 2018, though he was adamant that his bowling was unaffected. However, since stress is known to trigger the symptoms of Crohn's, he did concede that the emotion of playing his maiden Test in New Zealand a few months earlier, followed swiftly by a stint on the injured list, may have played a part.

Undaunted, he underlined his mettle at Headingley. With bat, not ball. While Stokes was outdoing himself with a fusillade of audacious shots underpinned by an unfathomable serenity, Leach kept him company, rigidly resisting Australia's trio of marauding fast bowlers for a full hour. The last elastic, spine-prickling hour. One error, one piece of Australian competence and/or the tiniest intrusion by our wilful frenemy Dame Fortune, and the game would be lost. Time and again, Leach annoyed the Australians, bringing play to a halt to wipe his glasses, fogged as they were by the heat and tension. As the suspense reached its improbably sustained peak, whenever Leach was batting, Stokes, on his haunches at the other end of the pitch in apparent prayer, averted his eyes.

Then, in a sudden, surreal, adrenaline-stoppering, slow-motion rush towards both glory and normality, came resolution. Steeled by those long battles with adversity and rejection and Dame Fortune's sniggers, Leach, now outstripping Stokes for outer and inner calm, tucked away the run that ensured his team could not be beaten, scampering those 22 yards like a spindle-legged deer warming up for a frolic. Sixty seconds later, he hugged and kissed Stokes after the latter had thrashed the winning shot in the manner of a king personally beheading every plotter and pretender with a single swing of his axe. A cult hero had been born. "That's nice," responded Leach. "I don't really know what that is. It's probably because I look like a village cricketer out there with my glasses, the bald head and many people think: 'That could be me.'"[18]

That scampered run proved to be his sole contribution to scoreboard and scorecard, the records and the stats; Stokes netted 135. The previous month, batting at the top of the order in an emergency stint as the sacrificial lamb-cum-protector known universally as the "nightwatch-man", humiliating his betters and sparing their blushes, Leach had top-scored against mightless Ireland, sparing English shame; how gleefully he would have traded those 92 runs for that solitary, stoical single. "Jack has got some serious bollocks," avowed Stokes. "We can confirm we will offer Jack Leach free glasses for life," tweeted Specsavers, the optical retail chain.

Two contrasting heroes. So many reasons to be cheerful – even for Australians. Sky Sports replayed the highlights on a loop for the next 24 hours: just the ticket, not only for those who hadn't been among the enraptured 20,000-strong crowd and had missed the live broadcast, but for those of us who needed regular reminders that our eyes hadn't been lying.

Inevitably, as is the way of all sport, historical comparisons flowed like water from Victoria Falls. One, though, was missed. The best way to translate all this gobbledygook if you are a baseball fan and/or cricket virgin? [1]Try this. Nine days later and an ocean away, in Washington, DC, the Washington Nationals would beat the New York Mets 11-10, scoring six runs in the bottom of the ninth inning to mock precedent: in 274 games that season wherein a team had been faced with such a task, precisely none had won. Not since the Nationals joined the Major League Baseball ranks 50 years earlier had the franchise ever mounted such a rally. "Stuff like that is not supposed to happen," said one of the breathless winners, Ryan Zimmerman. "It's a crazy sport. Crazy things happen."[19] Allowing as we must for the vicissitudes of hyperbole and brand-projection, the headline on the official Major League Baseball website said it all: "Nats pull off 'the craziest' walkoff." Now multiply "craziest" by 10.

The comparisons, made and not made, led, inevitably, to The Great Coincidence (or was it more?). In the same Headingley arena 38 years earlier, during the previous angst-ridden summer for British self-esteem, identity and unity, Ian Botham and Bob Willis had pre-empted Stokes and Leach, conjuring victory from the precipice of defeat, a victory so timely and unimagined that readers of *The Observer* were still dazzled enough to vote it their favourite British Sporting Moment two decades later. Ahead of the 1966 FIFA World Cup final.

The gods of coincidence did not stop there. In 1981 as in 2019, Australia had been poised to take a 2-0 lead in the series, an advantage only once squandered in Test history, by England against Australia in 1937. Again, the odds on precedent being spot on were not so much prohibitive as silly. England had been quoted at 500-1 against after day three, though as Matthew Engel asserted in *The Guardian*, "that was more PR stunt than serious assessment";[20] this time, Bet fair had England at 35-1 on the final day, still gast-flabbering for a two-horse race. Then there was Botham, the prototype Stokes. Another bold, aggressive all-rounder drunk on self-belief and the loin-charging wonders of competition. Another overgrown boy whose off-duty behaviour made him problematic for those who delude themselves that young people who make a living from their body should be uniformly lionised, and crucified, for their imposed obligation to be "role models".

In 2000 Alastair McLellan and I co-wrote a book about that first match, *500-1: The Miracle of Headingley 1981*. Inconceivably, for myself and innumerable others, even the men whose feats had demanded that a book be published for the 20th anniversary, and whose lives had been defined by that match, Headingley 2019 trumped it instantly. Some went even further. "I've seen some remarkable cricket moments in my life," tweeted Geoff Boycott, another member of England's Headingley 1981 XI, an accomplished tease and curmudgeon, "but that is the best I've seen in over 50 years."

"For its twists, turns and thrills and its collective and individual sense of redemption," rejoiced Engel, formerly editor of cricket's annual bible, *Wisden Cricketers' Almanack*, the world's longest-running series of annual sporting books, "Headingley '19 may be the best of them all."[21] Neither Botham nor Willis begged to differ. What the Headingley '81 duo didn't say, and possibly didn't realise or remember, was that it meant even more to their countrymen. As much as the British – and especially the English – needed an injection of escapism, fantasy and jubilation in July 1981, we needed a whole lot more perking up in August 2019.

When the shot hits the fan

And yet and yet. The Miracle of Headingley II could neither suppress nor disguise the often dispiriting complexities of the sporting context. Beneath the glory lay the Sisyphean struggle to secure cricket's future as England's summer game, not to mention the future of the five-day Test match. Ever-conscious of its inescapable anachronism, cricket has survived, most obviously because South Asians are addicted to it. (To cite merely the most obvious examples, India is the game's economic powerhouse while Pakistan's prime minister as I write is Imran Khan, Oxford graduate, erstwhile Mayfair playboy and the best cricket captain that the accursed, misunderstood, mismanaged and bewildering land has ever had.) Credit, nevertheless, must also go to the administrators who have been "woke" enough to devise shorter, faster formats that can be played after rather than during the working day. The ever-nagging fear, festering and rising for more than half a century, is that the whizz-bang, profit-boosting alternatives, distinguished by brevity (a result in a day!), customer-friendlier kick-off times and the colour of the ball used (white for the cartoons, red for the Test theatrics), will make the more searching, more versatile contests redundant. As it is, the newer kids in town have underwritten the still-vibrant pensioner. Not that there was much of a choice. No major spectator sport, it must be stressed, has had to be more creative in defying the march of time and the shrinking of attention spans by the black-widow seductiveness of the World Wide Web, nor ready to strike compromise between past and future, tradition and progress, money and love, authenticity and credibility.

But worse, and far more complex, was the battle being fought for the lesser-spotted soul of the team game most commonly associated, justly *and* ludicrously, with fair play.

A few hours before Stokes and Leach started flexing their wands, the *Sunday Times* ran an article headlined "Less than five years since the tragic death of Phillip Hughes, bowlers are still being lauded for launching 96 mph missiles at their rivals' heads." The author was David Walsh, the sportswriter widely acclaimed for exposing Lance Armstrong's lies. (To be fair, his colleague, the former cyclist Paul Kimmage and the Frenchman Pierre Balester warranted equal billing.) Walsh had been driven to put forefinger to keyboard by an incident during the Lord's Test the previous Saturday, one that had seen England defuse the threat of Steve Smith, the most prolific batsman international cricket had seen for nearly three-quarters of a century.

The bomb-disposal expert chosen was Jofra Archer, a chillingly quick fast bowler making his Test debut, already feared globally after two magnificent seasons in the Indian Premier League and a score of wickets during that victorious World Cup campaign: vindication indeed for the unprincipled officials who had changed the eligibility rules specifically to ensure he would be available for England. (Barbados had been his home until the end of his teens, though he had a British passport thanks to his English father.) Come the end of his first 17 matches for England, Archer had also accumulated more than a score of felled opponents. Not bad for a non-contact sport.

Smith was in the form of his life, but speed, controlled and disciplined, is the most priceless asset a bowler can have; after all, since the heyday of the military cannon, no ball has had quite the capacity for violence as the leather-cork beast deployed in cricket. A baseball, admittedly, comes mighty close. Slightly heavier (163 g to 149 g) and marginally smaller (9 ins to 9.25 ins), the cricketing missile packs more danger into a tighter package. According to the blogger Math-spig, attempting to calculate which is the more dangerous by using ballistic measures, the impact (mass × velocity) of a cricket ball is greater: 9.6 kilogram-metres per second to 8.4. And it is the impact, the change in momentum, that does the physical damage.[22]

In both sports, batters/batsmen wear helmets, though cricket waited a couple of centuries before formally accepting the need, a need that anyone with an ounce of compassion had worked out long before 1978. Baseball's physical threat is more persistent because the pitchers target the batter's body more directly; in cricket, almost every ball bowled bounces before it reaches the batsman, purposefully and in order to satisfy the rules, allowing a few milliseconds more time. Bowling actions, moreover, are more complex, and involve a run-up of up to 40 yards. As I write, only one bowler has ever been officially timed at 100 mph in a professional cricket match, in 2003; in 2016, 31 major league pitchers attained or exceeded 100 mph (curiously, as of August 2019, the league record, 108.5 mph, stood precisely where it had since 1974). At the time of writing, only one major leaguer, Ray Chapman, had ever been killed by a ball while batting, in 1920. In 2014, Phillip Hughes, an Australian Test regular of no little repute, became the first full-time professional batsman to suffer that sickening fate. Struck in the back of the neck trying to evade a steeply bouncing delivery, he died two days later. Now all helmets made in Australia are equipped with a neck-guard, and wearing them is mandatory. When he faced Archer, Smith, citing claustrophobia, refused to wear one.

Fortunately for Smith, Archer's bouncer struck him in the front of the neck. Compelled to "retire hurt", concussion regulations were waived and he was allowed, unthinkably, to resume his innings shortly afterwards; evidently out of sorts, he didn't last long. Delayed concussion was diagnosed and, quite properly, he was ruled out of the Headingley match, scheduled to start four days later. "He should not [have] put himself back in immediate danger," said Luke Briggs, deputy chief executive of Headway, a brain injury charity. "The reaction time of a batsman facing a 90 mph-plus delivery is incredibly small and concussion leads to delayed reaction times so makes that just incredibly dangerous."[23] When Smith fell forward on to his face after being hit, he recalled, the ghost of Hughes hovered over him: "That was probably the first thing I thought about."[24]

"I don't think I've ever played in a series where so many people have been hit in the head," Broad would reflect before the fourth Ashes Test of 2019. "It feels like the doctors are running out every 10 overs, doesn't it? But that's part of Test cricket. You bowl a bouncer not to hit someone in the head, you bowl a bouncer to manoeuvre footwork and change momentum of body weight. But your best bouncer is directed over leg stump and at the head, unfortunately. If it hits, fortunately the helmets have got really good. They are much better now."[25]

Over the four days that separated Headingley and the unintentional brutalising of Smith, I exchanged a flurry of texts with Jed Novick, another of this book's co-editors, about the morality of it all. Another journalist-turned-academic, he loves football and tennis but keeps an amused eye on cricket, which he plays, inefficiently but exuberantly, rather than watches. On the evening before the Headingley match, we continued our respectfully impassioned debate over pizza. The only subject we had ever hitherto disagreed about is Israel.

Jed's stance was unequivocal: he could find no justification whatsoever in what he saw as Archer's assault. I defended Archer, cricket and competitive sport to the hilt. Only one of us had forged a career from knowing that, in the southern hemisphere summer of 2013–2014, Australia's Mitchell Johnson had so terrorised England's batsmen that some had vomited before facing him. That Australia's Jeff Thomson, a twinkle in his icy eyes, had baldly stated on the eve of the 1974–1975 Ashes series that he was partial to seeing blood on the pitch. That the most torrid, tempestuous and divisive Ashes series of them all, the 1932–1933 encounter, was played out against the backdrop of the Great Depression that had so depleted Australians and seen their plight exacerbated by the oppressive and unreasonable economic demands made by their colonial rulers. That an almighty row had erupted over what became immortalised as "Bodyline": a name drummed up on deadline by a reporter, it referred to a strategy instigated by the visiting team and devised by their pragmatic patrician captain Douglas Jardine, who despised Australians, to neutralise the Steve Smith of his day, Don Bradman. Bradman's phenomenal insatiability and influence was curbed, humanised, the Ashes easily won and crushingly lost. Means and ends. The wider upshot was crowd riots, a fractured skull for Australia's Bert Oldfield and a rare loss of temper from his captain, the devoutly Christian Bill Woodfull. Struck over the heart and retreating to the dressing-room for treatment, Woodfull said to the England manager, "Plum" Warner: "There are two teams playing out there. One is trying to play cricket and one is not." The dressing-down was meant to be private but was rightly and properly leaked to the press. The anger and ethical discord spread from Adelaide to Whitehall: diplomatic relations between coloniser and colony came closer than they ever have to divorce.

Few of those who comprehend cricket would deny that Jardine's target was the greatest sportsperson ever to confine his genius to a single ballgame. Bradman was a small, indifferently built arch-competitor with astonishing hand-eye co-ordination who had the additional handicap of carrying a young nation's hopes for global respect on his back. Crowned "The Don" more than 40 years before *The Godfather*, he reigned unchallenged between 1930 and 1948, ensuring Australia won the Ashes six times out of eight. Despite his slightness he was freakishly indomitable, almost always at ease with the searing pressure as expectation rose. His statistics were off the chart – his Test batting average, 99.94, was more than 60 per cent higher than anyone else had ever compiled, a margin of superiority unglimpsed in the competitive arts; they remain unthreatened, untouchable.

To regain that tiny urn, England had to stop him somehow. Thus it was that, in the southern hemisphere summer of 1932–1933, Jardine, aided by his executioner-in-chief, a miner from Nottinghamshire, Harold Larwood, adapted a popular English tactic designed to stifle runscoring – leg theory – into something terrifying. Both had been roused by the memory of the final Ashes Test of 1930, when Larwood had occasionally made Bradman, fresh from "smithereening" virtually every significant batting record in the book, hurry, hop and flinch. The stumps were not the target in 1932–1933, the body was; Bradman's body first, last and pretty much everything. He survived serious injury because, well, he was The Don, and no batsman has ever thought quicker or reacted quicker than The Don. Lesser mortals were the casualties of this "war minus the shooting", the deathless phrase George Orwell used to characterise, and declare war on, international sport.

The scars ran deep, and took time to heal. Predictably, while Jardine was acclaimed for his captaincy and remained in office until he voluntarily bowed out, Larwood, the dispensable working-class scapegoat, found himself shunned when the next Ashes series was held in England in 1934, his Test career over. It says so much for the fellowship of sportsfolk that, not long after the end of the Second World War, Jack Fingleton, another of the Nottinghamshire bullet's targets, was the man who helped Larwood emigrate to Sydney, where he lived in peace for the rest of his days, appreciated more by Australians than Englishmen.

"Not cricket" is a phrase waved all over the world, the very definition of unfair play, understood and wielded even by those who have no interest in sport, let alone any comprehension of cricket (the game rather than the noisy insect). As Woodfull implied, Bodyline was definitively "not cricket". And physical violence, above all sins, had always been "not cricket". Yet many Englishmen were ashamed, and not every Australian was aghast and aggrieved; more than one respected former Test star felt embarrassed by what they saw as whingeing (losing badly, a Pommy trait by tradition). Eighty-five years later, this time on an English stage, Smith played Bradman while Archer stood in for Larwood. And while Bradman's Fred-and-Ginger footwork saved him from harm, Smith's fractionally less twinkly toes could not. And Archer might well have been bowling a knot faster than Larwood.

The debate continued. I trotted out the time-honoured line: eliminate the danger, that omnipresent threat of physical pain, and cricket would not only be competitively diluted, tilting the balance between batsman and bowler even further askew than it has always been; it would cease to exist as popular entertainment and culture-shaper. So too, among others, would both rugby codes, the myriad football variants, baseball, sailing, motorsports, equestrianism and cycling, let alone boxing, the one game you can never "play" but still the biggest money-spinner on Planet Sport (which it seems fairly reasonable to assume is the only remaining legitimate venue in the known solar system where life can be at stake in a game played for the purposes of public entertainment). From the gladiators and chariot racers and lions of Rome to Ben Chapman and Phillip Hughes, the sombre, deadly song remains the same. In 1931, John Thomson, the

Glasgow Celtic goalkeeper and so-called "Prince of men", died after suffering a head injury diving at the feet of a Glasgow Rangers striker (Sam English, the accidental killer, played on for seven years but found the remainder of his career "joyless"). In 2017, the Rangers fan group, Real Rangers Men, unfurled a risibly provocative banner at Ibrox Park that converted the ghosts of English – and, by implicit extension, Thomson – into firearms in the endless displaced Irish Protestant (Rangers) v. Irish Catholic (Celtic) conflict, the sporting answer to The Troubles that had disgraced Scottish football and turned Glaswegians into "90-minute patriots" for more than a century: "He was a proud young Protestant – Sam English 1908 to 1967."[26]

To cite the most needless and excessive waste of humanhood, the annual Tourist Trophy (TT) motorcycle races have been conducted since 1908 amid the petite, pretty, perennially peaceful environs of Douglas, capital of that tax-shelter par excellence, the Isle of Man. The original circuit was the "Four-Inch Course". On winding, undulating, narrow roads long-since relocated and rebranded, rather more portentously, as the "Mountain Course", each lap is a 37.73-mile ordeal with 219 turns that have seen riders exceed speeds of 200 mph; the bodies have piled up at an average rate closer to three per year than two. In 1970, improved roads claimed a record six riders. In 2016 the count was five. By 24–25 August 2019, the weekend that gave us The Miracle of Headingley II, if we combine the races (the TT, Classic TT and Manx Grand Prix), the parade laps and testing, and throw in the 14 other fatalities involving paraders, unofficial testers, officials, spectators and even bystanders, sport had become a 274-time serial killer.[27]

After Dale Mathison had become the 259th rider to fall prey to the Mountain Course in June 2019, Ben Hunt, commenting for *The Sun*, insisted, bloodlessly, that the show should go on, could only go on; as, the previous June, had the 2018 Senior TT winner, Peter Hickman, whose material reward, given the monumental extent of the inherent risks, had been a relatively piffling £20,000. The money, both were adamant, ran a distant second to the thrill of the risk and the urge to conquer. "That statistic [Mathison being the 259th victim] alone should have Health and Safety chiefs flocking to Douglas in a clamour with their clipboards demanding that the race be shut down," wrote Hunt, sarcasm dripping from his keyboard. "It is after all, understandably dangerous and involves motorsport and, as we know in this snowflake world, neither of the two are tolerated." At the head of the page ran the headline: "RIDE ON: Isle of Man TT racers know they are dicing with death – it's their choice and snowflakes should never be allowed to stop it."[28]

The sub-editor responsible for that dismissive summary did not bother to remind readers what a snowflake was when it wasn't falling from the skies; there was no need. "Timid" was the kind and gentle interpretation. The 2019 Oxford Dictionary definition of its 21st-century derogatory meaning was: "An overly sensitive or easily offended person, or one who believes they are entitled to special treatment on account of their supposedly unique characteristics."[29] Merriam-Webster was both more succinct and accurate in quoting this sentence: "One side derides the youth driving the movement as *snowflakes* and social justice warriors, too sensitive and too politically correct."[30] Political correctness, it always bears reiterating, is a vice invented by those immutable naysayers, the politically incorrect, those staunch conservatives who resist social change, above all the cause of economic, sexual and racial equality: a cynically invented, twisted, perpetually misrepresented vice whose name allows the politically incorrect to decry and deride and subdue those they fear.

Perhaps the most challenging episode in the history of sporting violence came at Edgbaston, a leafy, quiet, amply-heeled suburb just outside Birmingham, England's so-called "Second City", in the summer of 1978. The victim was Iqbal Qasim: a Pakistani left-arm slow bowler like Leach, a sometime nightwatchman like Leach, another "tailender" of moderate batting technique and pedigree. And he wasn't protected by a helmet because batsmen had only just been permitted to wear them and the specialists, almost exclusively, were the early adopters. Two years earlier, it had been agreed that opposing international captains would draw up informal lists of lower-order batsmen who would not be subjected to bouncers at the start of a series. "In reality it made little difference," acknowledged ESPNCricinfo.com's eminent historian–journalist, Martin Williamson, "and the sight of fast bowlers peppering batsmen with seemingly endless 'chin music' became the norm. Cynics noted those making the most noise in protest tended to come from countries without their own battery of quick men."[31]

David Frith remains the game's foremost historian to this day; as editor of the then 57-year-old *The Cricketer*, its most durable magazine and defender, his warning was that of a man sickened by what had happened to his beloved obsession: "the physical threat to batsmen has spread like acid".[32] In March 1977, the Centenary Test had packed Melbourne Cricket Ground, the game's most capacious venue, for a lavish, celebratory one-off, an emotional reunion for past and present antagonists in Anglo–Australian exchanges; long before lunch on day one, Bob Willis broke Rick McCosker's unprotected jaw. Before the year was out, Australians were shuddering in unison as another bouncer, this time from the Antiguan hitman, Andy Roberts, struck David Hookes, the latest "new Bradman". He'd taken the precaution of ramming on a motorcycle crash helmet, but his jaw, too, was broken. Nerves rattled, the South Australian buccaneer never fulfilled his vaunted promise.

Qasim had previously aggregated a pitiful 29 runs in a dozen Test innings, yet now he kept England at bay for 40 minutes, annoyingly at first, before growing in assurance, prodding and provoking the home team into opting for the solution of last resort. Their captain, Mike Brearley, urged Willis, the fastest, most dangerous bowler on the field by far, to bounce him out. A Cambridge classics scholar who had travelled widely to support human rights, Brearley was a good batsman promoted beyond his capabilities; he had secured his selection almost exclusively by dint of his leadership acumen. Here was an enabler without historical peer. A man of peace and a sportsman of integrity. The man who would draw the best from Botham and Willis three years later – the brains behind The Miracle of Headingley '81. Willis, not a violent man by any means, struck Qasim a sickening blow in the face, then strode back to the end of his run-up, ignoring the collapsed batsman. Spitting blood, Qasim had to be helped from the field and was unable to resume. Nuisance neutralised: job done. The Test and County Cricket Board, the governing body of the English game, issued a statement of profound regret and reminded Brearley of his responsibilities. Thrown a juicy morality-infused bone, the media had a field day for weeks.

Brearley had been one of the first to arm himself with the new insurance policy, designing and donning his own skeleton helmet, a padded skullcap with earflaps worn under his cap. He remains the most revered of cricket captains and one of the two wisest players ever to helm a professional sporting team. His only equal is another cricketer, the Lord David Sheppard, Bishop of Liverpool, the selfless, tireless humanitarian whose refusal to bat against the all-white 1960 South African XI, whom he rightly regarded as standard-bearers-cum-propagandists for Apartheid, helped dig the roots for the sporting boycott that would result in the pariah republic being progressively banned from major events until Nelson Mandela became president, more than three decades later. Brearley, too, was a leading figure amid cricket's sluggish contributions to the campaign to bring human rights to impoverished black Africans, a boycott that Mandela would credit with helping to end Apartheid. On this occasion, however, his ethics, and morals, came under scrutiny as never before or since.

In the 1988 edition of his oft-reprinted book, *The Art of Captaincy*, a seminal exploration of sporting leadership originally published seven years after that alarming Qasim episode, Brearley – evidently a sceptic when it came to the game's self-anointed, exaggerated, jealously guarded and always laughable reputation for nobility – claimed that he regretted nothing. Long before the reinvention of the snowflake, the opening statement for the defence was unexpectedly flippant and cold: "The irrational furore [over the injury to Qasim] had led to an undue namby-pambiness about bouncers being bowled at tail-enders."[33]

Bouncers are addressed repeatedly throughout Brearley's book, leading to a magisterial summing-up that incorporates impeccable logic and apt historical comparison while being undermined by what some might regard as hair-splitting: "I think that umpires have the main responsibility for taking a firm line too much short-pitched bowling, and I favour the rule that restricts a bowler to one each over. Captains, too, should not allow their fast bowlers to resort to viciousness. In my opinion, they should instruct them not to bowl out-and-out bouncers at those who are unable to defend themselves. However, bouncers are a physical threat to *any* batsman, and I see no reason why a tail-ender should specifically be protected from them. I welcome the availability of helmets, which make bouncers into tactical rather than physical weapons. I have, as I have said, no regrets [about Qasim], especially as he had come in as nightwatchman. England's 'Bodyline' bowling in 1932–1933 was another matter. Not only was the batsman's body systematically used as a target; but also the placing of six or seven fielders on the legside, on top of bowling short outside the leg-stump strikes me as going way beyond what is acceptable."[34] Come 2020, Brearley had not changed his tune, recalling the criticism of the Qasim incident as "fatuous".[35]

There have been calls for the bouncer to be outlawed, which is why it is worth reflecting on the most notorious, reverberant chapter in the seamy annals of chucking. Touring the Caribbean in 1962, Nari Contractor, the Indian batsman, came close to death after having his skull fractured by a rapid short-pitcher from Charlie Griffith, a growling, glowering, likeable bear of a bowler from rural Barbados whose action would thereafter be questioned by opponents, some would argue, on racist grounds. (Admittedly, one deceptive freeze-frame of his open-chested delivery did suggest he was trying out for a darts team.) When, shortly after, Contractor was rushed to hospital, the Bajan paceman was no-balled for throwing (he claimed it was his slower ball) and the link between illegality, intent and near-fatality was cynically forged by the press. Indian administrators wanted bouncers banned and held the Barbados Cricket Association culpable for Contractor's injury because, as Griffith put it, "they had encouraged the players 'to play the game in an unfair manner'. To this accusation, the Board replied that there had been no suspicion about my action before the tour began".[36] Indeed, Cortez Jordan, the first umpire to no-ball Griffith for chucking, had previously overseen his work on several occasions and never found fault. Never did he do so again. Only on two other occasions did anyone else. It should be added that advances in camera technology have meant that the degree of flexion by fast bowlers of the past has been found to be greater than imagined, sparking a change in regulations.

Griffith had to be persuaded not to retire by teammates, and found form and devil increasingly elusive after 1963. "For days after Nari Contractor had been injured," he reflected ruefully in his aptly titled autobiography, *Chucked Around*, "I was sick to death of cricket. I was ready to surrender."[37] What made it all the worse, he bemoaned, deeply hurt, was the sense of betrayal: "The rumours that I was a bogeyman who did not play according to the rules, started in Barbados, my own home."[38] Doctors advised Contractor to retire, and he did, then launched a futile comeback. Shortly before he was allowed to fly home from hospital, Contractor called his wife and told her, "Charlie is not to blame." Contractor, indeed, was reluctant to join the ensuing chorus demanding the extinction of the bouncer. "I wouldn't like to create a situation that would allow anybody to point a finger at me and say, 'Because he was hit, he is a crybaby.' If the ICC [Imperial Cricket Conference, then the game's global governing body] decide to ban or curb the bouncer, let them do so. But let them do it because they think it is good for cricket. I don't want to end my career in a mess of complaints."[39]

Whether you forgive or damn Griffith, or hail, accept or scorn Brearley's analysis, it is difficult to draw a definitive conclusion, except this. Even the fairest-minded sage, given time to reflect, can be shaky in the witness box when defending themselves against the charge of enabling violence.

The crucial difference between the daredevil risk-junkies who get their kicks challenging the Mountain Course and the game played by Archer and Smith is that the latter, in their different ways, are not unhappy hurting each other. Smith was doing his level-best to destroy Archer's ego; Archer was prepared to injure Smith if that was the price of inducing an error. It's also a question of intent. Archer is a decent, intelligent, respectable and respected young man. He wasn't trying to hit Smith; he was trying to unsettle him, provoke misjudgement. Jed shot back a right hook with the i-word: intimidation. Cue much ducking and weaving. Parroting Brearley, the laws of cricket, I said, are there to help the umpires interpret whether a bowler is guilty of intentional intimidation, and bouncer-limits are enforced, but the line between a fair ball and an intentionally intimidating one is slim to invisible. Risk, I added, was part of life, the quintessential path to reward. Not once did I let my conscience out of its underground cell. Not for a nanosecond did I convince myself I was in the right.

On the fourth and final morning of Headingley '19, Jed texted me a photo of Walsh's article and a message: "I think Walsh must have been sitting behind me in that pizza place." The opening paragraphs certainly suggested as much:

> Back in primary school, the subject wasn't called "Religious Studies" or "Christian Doctrine" but "catechism". We're talking a long time ago and it was our introduction to the sacraments. At some point, cricket was mentioned and then explained. "The English", we were told, "not being a very spiritual race, conceived the game of cricket to give them some concept of eternity."
>
> So, you will legitimately ask, what would he know? How can he understand? The truth is I don't. Not really. I don't understand how hurling a rock-hard ball at 96 mph in such a way that it will take one bounce and then rise towards an opponent's head is considered good sport. Not only acceptable, but the contest at its most compelling. The ultimate test.[40]

At bottom, though, the debate with Jed was less about sport's inherent violence and physical risk than its wider ugliness. If spectator sport is modern society's most unkickable drug, we seem quite prepared to accept that the toxicity is worth it because the highs are so high. Heroin for those who prefer alcohol to temperance.

In sport as in life, beauty has always co-existed with the beastly. In the good corner lie good health, elation, thrills, drama, artistry, innovation, skill, bravery, intelligence, determination, patience, mental strength, collectivism, fairness, fortitude, fellowship and the capacity to learn even more from failure than success. In the bad corner: violence, dishonesty, cheating, corruption, misogyny, racism, inequality, injustice, ruthless competitiveness, incompetence, greed and the latest demonic threat to fair play, sportswashing (c. Adolf Hitler). All of human life is here. Sport has long shone the way for wider society in terms of fostering peaceful co-existence, battling racism, misogyny and religious intolerance, improving workers' rights. Megan Rapinoe, Frank Worrell, Muhammad Ali, Cathy Freeman and Arthur Ashe; Tommie Smith, Peter Norman, John Carlos and Martina Navratilova; Colin Kaepernick, Raheem Sterling, Billie-Jean King, Curt Flood and Jackie Robinson: these are sport's greatest champions, not for the records they broke but for the minds and hearts they changed.

Professionalism, broadcasting deals and unimaginable rewards have only raised the stakes, intensifying the addiction. And so we watch on. Boats against the current. Borne back ceaselessly into the past – and the future.[2]

Call to arms

But back to the title of this chapter and thus conclude with that time-honoured journalistic ploy of circularity: ending as we began. And a clarion call to arms.

Sports journalism matters because sport matters, for better *and* worse. And because sport has two faces. And because it encompasses society's basest urges and noblest aspirations, and occasionally teaches it a trick or two. Nobody, moreover, is better equipped than a journalist to capture the heroic and the villainous, the exhilaration, the contradictions, the communality and the fellowship, and of course all those crimes and misdemeanours. We should have the words, the professional discipline, the nose for a story, the ear for a key quote and a telling line – and, ideally, a symbiotic, clearly demarcated working relationship with the people we are reporting on. But our duty to our readers and watchers is to be informers as well as celebrants, and that means fulfilling the journalist's prime function: holding power to account, telling hard truths about uncomfortable subjects.

For far too many decades, sports editors ignored the socio-political context, but the deeper coverage afforded by increased pagination and the internet has bred a welcome change of tack. Ballester, Kimmage and Walsh are far from being lone keyboard warrior–rangers, following in the bold traditions set by, for instance, John Arlott, the broadcaster and journalist who, in 1960, smoothed a path into English cricket for Basil D'Oliveira, the Cape Coloured South African who had been denied professional status in his own country and went on to become the most enduring sporting symbol of the Anti-Apartheid movement. As radical composers of journalism-as-first-draft-of-history, the likes of Roger Kahn, Lester Rodney, Wendell Smith and Dave Zirin have also been critical in addressing racism. So, too, has Peter Oborne, a staunch Tory and longtime *Daily Mail* columnist who has written compelling book-length studies of D'Oliveira and Pakistani cricket. No less vital has been Daniel Taylor, the football correspondent whose reports on sexual abuse for *The Guardian* have emboldened so many other silent, shamed, long-troubled victims to come forward. Laurels, too, to Heidi Blake, Jonathan Calvert and the rest of the *Sunday Times* Insight team that exposed the debauched financial chicanery of FIFA, building on the inexhaustible, irreverent, old-fashioned door-stepping toils of Andrew Jennings, the man who exposed similarly arrogant bribers within the Olympic movement for the *Daily Mail* and *Panorama*. Likewise the more cerebral but no less driven Howard Bryant, the African American sportswriter (still not a sub-clause that can yet be typed with any frequency): his book dissecting steroid abuse in baseball, *Juicing the Game: Drugs, Power, and the Fight for the Soul of Major League Baseball*, is another gleaming monument to investigative reporting. (Editors' note: how reporting can ever *not* be investigative has always been utterly beyond us.)

Yes, priorities lie elsewhere. Spending an open-ended stretch of time on a single story is seldom cost-effective, and in an era of declining newspaper circulations across the world, money has never been more intrinsic to editorial decision-making. How much cheaper, not to say simpler and safer, to pump out a glut of football match reports. Yet with broadcasting rights soaring and interest in its plotlines never wider or more avid, spectator sport, the Great Intoxicant, matters more than ever; the same, by logical extension and necessity, can therefore be said of sports journalism. Its responsibilities, furthermore, have never been clearer, or more onerous.

Still, let's conclude with a time-honoured sports page standby

What happened next

The Ashes Roadshow resumed at The Other Old Trafford, the original Old Trafford (the cricketing castle opened for business in 1857, the noisier palace across the road in 1910). Steve Smith was back for Australia, and picked up where he had left off before Jofra Archer battered him into submission. Under-par, short of pace and hampered by a docile pitch, Archer pinged down a few short ones but found his arrows returned with swagbags of interest. The records continued to topple. On day one Smith became the first man to score 50 runs in eight consecutive Tests; when a beach ball blew onto the field he swept it away as if it was a strand of pollen. Throughout his innings he had been treating the smaller, harder, fiercer red ball as if it was an inflated lump of plastic: as a metaphor for his dominance, what could be finer than the snap of Smith dismissing the beach ball from his presence that graced the back page of the next morning's *The Guardian*?

On day two he climbed to 200, becoming the third Ashes combatant ever to rack up three double-centuries (though that still left him a way to go to overhaul The Don's eight). By the time he was sated, he had amassed 589 runs in the incomplete series (at the satisfyingly Bradmanesque average of 147.25): no colleague had totted up even half that many. For England to be "bowling at my head", mused a seemingly amused Smith, ruled out two of the most trusted methods of getting him out. "It softens the ball up as well so it played into our hands."[41]

For the heroes of Headingley, the game started with a whimper and never really recovered. The outrageous, faintly embarrassing luck they had enjoyed on 25 August was in severe debit by 4 September. Stokes soon left the field with a bad back. Leach endured the numbing, humbling experience of ejecting Smith shortly after he'd reached his first 100, only for the batsman to be recalled when TV replays showed that the bowler had delivered the ball illegally. This time it was not about chucking but unprofessionalism: his rear heel had strayed millimetres beyond the thin white line separating fair from foul, an offence his career average insisted he would commit once every thousand balls bowled. A no-ball by a slow bowler for overstepping? Sport doesn't get much dafter than that.

And anti-climaxes don't get much more deflating than Australia's eventual victory, which enabled them to retain the Ashes. On the other hand, despite the lack of free-to-air coverage of the encounter, a public vote saw Stokes fêted as the winner of the beauty contest otherwise known as BBC Sports Personality of the Year, thrusting cricket ever more firmly, and improbably, back into the public eye.

Given that the runner-up was Lewis Hamilton, who had won his sixth Formula 1 title, many will doubtless raise a querulous eyebrow, reasoning, not unreasonably, that Stokes' heroics had been in vain – but only those who measure sport exclusively by the final score.

Notes

1. There is far more cross-fertilisation than you might imagine, but then cricket is best described to the baseball-fan-oblivious-to-cricket as baseball's bizarro twin. Uniting them are runs, outs, pitches, catches, fielders, descending batting orders arranged primarily in order of competence, unparalleled devotion to their own history and image and symbolic powers, in thrall to their own lofty uniqueness and sense of moral and ethical superiority. But runs are scarce in baseball, ten-a-penny in cricket; and while outs are cricket's holiest grail, they're baseball's loose change.
2. To mangle the immaculate prose poetry of F. Scott Fitzgerald, the real Gatsby.

References

1. Matthew Engel, *Engel's England: Thirty-nine Counties, One Capital and One Man*, Profile Books: London, 2014, p. xii.
2. Andy Bull, "Once troubled hero now has a summer he will always own", *The Guardian*, 27 August 2019, p. 42.
3. Geoff Lemon, "Tourists must reset after England's low point ends on a high", *The Guardian*, 26 August 2019, p. 46.
4. Simon Jenkins, "Only one person can avert a no-deal Brexit. And that's Boris Johnson", *The Guardian*, 30 August 2019, https://www.theguardian.com/commentisfree/2019/aug/29/no-deal-brexit-boris-johnson-parliament, accessed 23 January 2020.
5. Letter to *The Guardian*, 30 August 2019.
6. Vic Marks, "Stokes heroics hit new level to turn series on its head", *The Guardian*, 26 August 2019, p. 51.
7. Matt Dickinson, "True greats shape world around them", *The Times*, 26 August 2019, p. 7.
8. Gideon Haigh, "This was the kind of drama you can only get from a Test", *The Times*, 26 August 2019, p. 50–51.
9. Greg Baum, "We can all die happy now – cricket doesn't get any better than this", *Sydney Morning Herald*, 26 August 2019, https://www.smh.com.au/sport/cricket/we-can-all-die-happy-now-cricket-doesn-t-get-any-better-than-this-20190826-p52knk.html?fbclid=IwAR1aD_cvsP54xxZuedstA2n-NVSLxLJMogo2oSIKkmLmBXl-eug-AVVvukgw, accessed 24 January 2020.
10. Andy Bull, "Best innings since Botham puts all else in the shade", *The Guardian*, 26 August 2019.
11. Editorial, *The Times*, 26 August 2019.
12. icc-cricket.com, 18 April 2016, https://www.icc-cricket.com/news/183145
13. Andy Bull, "Once troubled hero now has a summer he will always own", *The Guardian*, 27 August 2019, p. 42.
14. Editorial, *The Guardian*, 27 August 2019.
15. Rob Smyth, "Hero of Headingley is England's humble buccaneering totem", *The Observer*, 1 September 2019, Sport, p. 18.
16. *The Cricketer*, 25 August 2019, https://www.thecricketer.com/Topics/news/england_ashes_lifeline_ben_stokes_stuart_broad_headingley.html, accessed 26 January 2020.
17. Stephan Shemilt, "Jack Leach on England, DJ-ing at Jos Buttler's wedding, Crohn's & trollies", *BBC Sport*, 25 July 2019, https://www.bbc.co.uk/sport/cricket/46046486, accessed 26 January 2020.
18. Vic Marks, "From 'village' cricketer to a cult hero: Leach relives his 17-ball epic", *The Guardian*, 27 August 2019, p. 43.
19. mlb.com, "Down 6 in 9th, Nats pull off 'the craziest' walk-off", 4 September 2019, https://www.mlb.com/news/nationals-score-seven-in-9th-to-walk-off-on-mets
20. Matthew Engel, "There have been 2,358 Tests since 1877 – and Headingley was the greatest of all", *The Guardian*, 28 August 2019, p. 44.
21. Ibid.
22. "Which sport is more DANGEROUS to play? Cricket or baseball?", *Mathspig Blog*, 4 September 2009, https://mathspig.wordpress.com/2009/09/04/which-sport-is-more-dangerous-to-play-cricket-ball-or-a-baseball/, accessed 26 January 2020.
23. Roderick Easdale, "Australia's double standards simply aren't cricket", *The Article*, 26 August 2019, https://www.thearticle.com/australias-double-standards-simply-arent-cricket, accessed 25 January 2020.
24. Lemon, "Smith: 'Archer's got the wood over me? He hasn't actually got me out …'", *The Guardian*, 29 August 2019, p. 44.
25. Ali Martin, "'It will be brutal' – Broad warns Smith to expect Archer barrage on return", *The Guardian*, 3 September 2019, p. 56.
26. IndyCelts.com, "Disgusting Rangers mock Sam English and John Thomson", 16 April 2017, https://www.indycelts.com/disgusting-rangers-mock-sam-english-and-john-thomson/, accessed 28 January 2020.
27. "List of Isle of Man TT Mountain Course fatalities", Wikipedia.com, https://en.wikipedia.org/wiki/List_of_Isle_of_Man_TT_Mountain_Course_fatalities, accessed 25 January 2020.

28. Ben Hunt, "RIDE ON: Isle of Man TT racers know they are dicing with death – it's their choice and snowflakes should never be allowed to stop it", *The Sun*, 6 June 2019, https://www.thesun.co.uk/sport/9226195/isle-of-man-dicing-death-snowflakes/, accessed 28 January 2020.

29. Lexico.com, https://www.lexico.com/en/definition/snowflake

30. merriam-webster.com, https://www.merriam-webster.com/dictionary/snowflake, accessed 27 January 2020.

31. Martin Williamson, "End of the innocence", ESPNcricinfo.com, 18 May 2013, http://www.espn-cricinfo.com/magazine/content/story/636540.html, accessed 25 January 2020.

32. Quoted in Williamson.

33. Mike Brearley, *The Art of Captaincy*, second impression, Coronet: London, 1988, p. 18.

34. Ibid, p. 239.

35. Mike Brearley, "'A quick wit and almost manic effervescence'", *The Cricketer*, February 2020, p. 37.

36. Charlie Griffith (with David Simmons), *Chucked Around*, London, Pelham, 1970, p. 52.

37. Ibid, p. 17.

38. Ibid, p. 54.

39. Martin Williamson, "The bouncer that ended a career", ESPNcricinfo.com, 6 December 2014, http://www.espncricinfo.com/magazine/content/story/807661.html

40. David Walsh, *Sunday Times*, 25 August 2019.

41. BBC Sport, "Ashes 2019: Steve Smith says England's tactics played into his hands at Old Trafford", 5 September 2019, https://www.bbc.co.uk/sport/cricket/49600408

Part I
The trade

2

Sport and journalism in the 18th and 19th centuries

Mike Huggins

Newspapers were already in circulation in Britain, America and elsewhere by the early 18th century. But across the 18th and 19th century as the developing nations experienced rapid social, economic and demographic growth, newspapers became a key communication form. Britain was ahead of many countries in its newspaper development, but its sports journalism was a major beneficiary, largely due to its sporting progress. Though there were very different models of "sport" across Europe at this time, elements of the British "sport model" were very influential, especially in the later 19th century, as competitions associated with British ball games such as rugby, soccer, golf and tennis diffused globally.

In Britain, early 18th century newspapers initially had little sporting news, but the organisers of forthcoming sporting events such as race meetings quickly recognised the benefits of advertising and providing post-event reports. By the 1740s, national and some regional papers had already recognised that sport aided their circulations. There were reports on a variety of sports, including horse racing, hunts, foot-races and matches, cock-fights, single-stick, pugilism and curling. Because of newspaper taxes, first levied in 1712, readership was largely drawn from the wealthy and middling classes. Gambling nourished the appetite for many sports at this period. There was sufficient interest in racing for Cheny, editor of an annual racing calendar, to start issuing a fortnightly sheet newspaper of advertisements and results in 1732, and this was continued by some other racing calendar publishers.

From the 1750s, as more turnpike sections of road began to be built, national newspapers, sporting news and sporting correspondence were distributed by the coaching services much more quickly. Metropolitan and provincial news became increasingly intertwined. There were 8.6 million newspapers sent out from London in 1798. Many weekly provincial papers merely copied sports results from London papers which they thought would interest readers.[1]

This more rapid news distribution fostered growing interest in sports material. Sport offered a diversion, a welcome distraction from the anxieties fostered by the popular revolution in France and political issues in Britain. There was a significant demand for horse racing and pugilistic intelligence. Journalists gained in popularity and influence. By the 1820s, provincial papers such as the *York Herald* or the *Manchester Mercury* had weekly racing reports. Journalists with inside knowledge of specific sports were sufficiently nationally known to add to newspapers' circulation, despite an 1815 Stamp Act tax and taxes on advertisements.

Rob Steen argues that "the status of sport as the people's opiate began to take shape in Britain after 1855", and most scholars of Victorian sport history adopt a similar chronology.[2] The press played a key role in this expansion, thanks to several key factors. Advances in rail transport allowed much more rapid conveyance of news and encouraged more sports spectatorship.[3] The lowering and, from 1855, abolition of the punitive Stamp Act allowed newspapers to be published far more cheaply, expanding their readership. A steady improvement in living standards and disposable incomes gave many time to play and watch growing numbers of sports and sporting events, most often held on Saturday afternoons or Mondays.

Rapid spread of the telegraph across Britain from the 1860s onwards provided more rapid results services than the use of rail transport or homing pigeons, though many local papers still used them to bring in results from surrounding games until the 20th century. The telegraph encouraged working-class betting, since results and short reports could be rapidly transmitted across Britain to newspaper editors. After the Post Office took over in 1868, the number of telegraphed press messages increased eightfold between 1870 and 1875.[4] In the 1890s, the telephone allowed reporters to dictate lengthier reports to a secretary and speeded reports. As early as March 1889 the *Sheffield Evening Telegraph* was able to boast that it had received the telephoned result of Sheffield Wednesday's away game against Wolverhampton Wanderers within four minutes of the final whistle and had copies on the street about three minutes later.

Increased educational opportunities and rising literacy rates created a larger literate public and further encouraged demand for sporting news, especially for racing. Many press agencies quickly saw opportunities. One of the largest, the Central Press, was founded in 1863 and became the Central News Agency in 1870. In 1872 it even sent cables to New York to keep Americans informed of a major international sculling race on the Thames, as well as sending material to newspapers throughout Britain.[5] The Press Association was founded in 1868 by a group of provincial newspaper proprietors and by 1870 was providing a London-based service of news-collecting and reporting from around the British Isles, initially providing rapid news on racing and cricket issues to the press and sporting clubs. According to the *Cambridge Chronicle* in 1872, "the gentleman who acts as sporting editor to the Press Association attends personally or sends his deputy to every race in the kingdom and has an income equal to that of many a West End physician".[6]

By the 1870s, betting on horse racing had become a key working-class leisure practice and cricket a major summer team game. More sports competed for coverage and the development of regular fixtures in many sports made sports editorship a legitimate news specialism, purveying more news to a mass audience. Sports journalism expanded in the next two decades. So too did the role of the sports reporter. Amongst winter games, soccer was initially rather less popular than rugby. Cup matches and derby games increased their popularity amongst their middle-class and artisan followers. Soccer quickly became more dominant, especially in the towns of the industrial North and Midlands, following growing professionalism and the introduction of leagues from 1889 onwards. Northern Rugby Football Union (rugby league) provided a popular semi-professional form of rugby from 1895. More and more readers were interested in sporting forecasts, match details and results.

There were technological innovations in newspaper production methods. From 1886 onwards, linotype web-fed rotary presses could produce 6,000 copies of a paper per minute, expanding the provincial daily and evening press. By 1892, there were 159 daily papers in the United Kingdom outside London, and 85 evening titles. By 1900, over 2,000 weekly papers were being published in England alone. The growth of the evening press facilitated interest in sport, and reaped the benefit of increased sales as it tailored edition times to the sporting calendar. Incoming racing results allowed several editions to be sold, fostering further growth in commercialised mass ready-money gambling culture despite its illegality.

Newspapers and sport

The press helped to make sport a popular spectacle and a commercial success. *The Sporting Magazine* (1792–1870) was England's first magazine expressedly for the sportsman, with a largely rural country gentleman readership. It covered "the turf, the chase and every other diversion interesting to the man of pleasure, enterprize and spirit". A significant proportion of the articles were written by readers and correspondents. By 1819, foxhunting was gaining a substantial readership. To increase circulation, the magazine employed an early journalistic hunting specialist, Charles Apperley (Nimrod), from 1822 to 1827, which doubled sales.[7] The magazine's approach was copied by other monthlies such as the *New Sporting Magazine* (from 1831) and the *Sporting Review* (from 1839).

The sixpenny weekly *Bell's Life in London and Sporting Chronicle* (1822–1866) was usually read by "gentlemen" but found widely in pubs and clubs. Significant coverage of racing and hunting, and mention of most other sports, ran alongside fashion, humour and high and low life in London.[8] Edited by Vincent Dowling from 1824 until 1852, it employed expert writers for particular sports, with horse racing its specialised field. It sent journalists to cover key events, alongside carefully checked material from freelance local writers. It became a leading authority on the early Victorian sporting world, including well-written, reliable reports from the industrial centres of Britain, especially Manchester and the North.[9] It reached a circulation of about 30,000 at its height and was widely trusted. Copies probably passed through many hands. But though *Bell's Life* journalists regularly discussed the regulation of sport in their columns, their actual influence on rules was limited and they were unable to exercise strong supervision of Victorian sporting life.

British developments encouraged overseas parallels. *Spirit of the Times: A Chronicle of the Turf, Agriculture, Field Sports, Literature and the Stage* aimed at an elite readership, was the most popular weekly in the United States by 1839. Its coverage of horse racing helped to standardise practice there. It had a West Coast competitor, *California Spirit of the Times*, in 1854. In Australia, *Bell's Life in Sydney* appeared in 1845, *Bell's Life in Victoria and Sporting Chronicle* in 1857 and *Bell's Life in Adelaide* in 1861. In France, Eugène Chapus and Napoléon de Saint-Albin's instigation of *Le Sport* in 1854 pioneered French sports journalism.[10] Chapus belonged to the literary, high-society and horse racing social circles of the French Second Empire (1852–1870), and this provided the matrix from which grew the French sporting press.

In Britain, as *Bell's Life* responded to growing "popular" interest in sport, *The Field* (1853–) moved in to provide a sixpenny weekly for country gentlemen. Its sporting coverage focused on hunting, shooting, outdoor sports, racing and more elite sporting activities such as yachting. *Bell's Life*'s "popular" market was challenged by the new "penny press", cheaper products like *Sporting Life* (1859–1998), dominated by horse racing, much written by racing expert "Augur" (Henry Feist).[11] It made betting on horse racing a key element in popular culture by providing training reports from the main training areas, possible runners and jockeys, betting odds and racing tips. In the 1870s, it provided starting prices, further encouraging illegal ready-money betting. Circulation soared. The paper was selling over 200,000 bi-weekly copies by 1876 and became a daily paper in 1883. It was joined in 1865 by *The Sportsman*, which had a cross-class appeal, making a commercial shift towards the working man. It covered a variety of traditional and modern sports, alongside extensive racing material.

The first widely circulated northern English racing paper, *Sporting Chronicle*, was published by Manchester press entrepreneurs Hulton and Bleackley from 1871. The same publishers brought out *The Athletic News*, a weekly paper, in 1875. It deliberately ignored horse racing, initially covering amateur sports and professional aspects of cricket. From 1885 onwards, it provided ever more extensive coverage of professional football with correspondents' reports from leading soccer regions from London to Scotland, as well as picking up on track and field athletics, cycling and rugby. America saw a similar expansion of sports reading culture in the 1850s and 1860s with the *New York Clipper* (1853), *Philadelphia Police Gazette and Sporting Chronicle* (1856), *Sportsman* (1863) and *New York Sportsman* (1865). Canada followed a similar trajectory, though in Montreal *Le Courier Athlétique*, the first ephemeral French-language sporting newspaper, only appeared in 1892.

The national "dailies" had always covered more nationally significant and elite sporting events and broadened their coverage alongside the wider growth in sport's popularity. In Britain, *The Times* had long reported on "The Turf" and had reports on 19 different sports by 1874. The "new journalism" of the 1880s saw sport becoming a larger ingredient in national newspaper coverage, with an increased emphasis on novelty, sensation, controversy and sporting celebrity. To boost circulation, the emerging popular press of the 1890s such as the *Morning Leader* (1892) or the *Daily Mail* (1896) devoted over 12 per cent of their column inches to sport. They also contributed to the "nationalisation" of sport reporting, since in their search for readers they often covered provincial as much as metropolitan events.

When local weekly and evening papers first began publishing soccer, rugby and cricket reports in the 1870s, reports of local events were typically brief, and, since usually written by club secretaries, were often biased and unreliable, though they provided a useful sports information service. Only a few regional papers, such as the *Northern Echo*, *Manchester Guardian* and *Leeds Mercury*, refused to provide racing results. As soccer's mass popularity boomed in the 1880s, some British papers began to publish Saturday evening "football specials", targeting soccer enthusiasts, providing results and much more opinionated comments on games and players. One of the first "specials" known was published in Birmingham in 1882, and the pattern quickly spread across the country – to become "a ubiquitous feature of Saturday-night urban life".[12] The pressures of inter-newspaper competition and rapid production by then placed heavy demands on newspapers with a shortage of specialist sports staff.

Up to the 1880s, periodicals on specific sports struggled to sustain readership in a highly competitive market, even from the committed. An analysis of Manchester's specialist sporting periodicals shows initial growth in the 1870s and "a more pronounced expansion in the 1880s".[13] Though many tried, most proved short-lived.[14] Nationally, the longer-lasting ones catered for a largely middle-class readership. The *Alpine Journal* (1863) catered for elite climbers; *Cricket* (1882) was the first to enjoy conspicuous cricket success; *Golf Illustrated* (1899) was the first golf periodical to sustain a lasting readership. In France, in 1903, sports daily *L'Auto* quickly became famous for its coverage of the Tour de France for bicycles and automobiles. Periodicals aimed at a female readership generally only began to cover sport in the 1890s,[15] though editors of more mainstream male-oriented newspapers slowly began to cater for growing upper and middle-class female interest from the 1880s. *The Illustrated Sporting and Dramatic News*, for example, had a "Sportswomen's Page" by the 1890s.

Sunday papers slowly began to cover sport. In the United States, William Cauldwell's *Sunday Mercury* was the first newspaper to regularly cover baseball, describing it as a "national pastime" in December 1856. In 1858, Cauldwell hired rising star Henry Chadwick, later dubbed the father of baseball, as a writer. In Britain, the *Sunday Times* included a page of sporting news by 1840, while specialist sport papers such as *The Referee* (1877), *The Umpire* (1884) and Manchester's the *Sunday Chronicle* (1885) later provided weekend sporting news. But even in 1890 national papers such as *The People*, *Weekly Dispatch* and *Reynolds Newspaper* all had less than 3.5 per cent of their columns covering sport, of which about half was racing news, though the *Weekly Times* and *News of the World* had more.[16]

The 1890s saw unprecedented expansion of coverage, as British Sunday papers increasingly specialised in sensation and sport for a largely working-class readership, though there was limited coverage of Saturday fixtures. Britain's imperial dominions often picked up on British models, though rather later. Sydney, Australia, for example, had its own *The Referee* in 1886, featuring personality profiles of leading sportsmen.

The sports journalist

From the early 19th century, it was the sports journalist, an often "obscure and yet consistently influential figure", who showed people what sport meant and helped to shape that meaning. Yet, as Tony Mason has noted, "little is known about most of the editors and writers who contributed to the Victorian sports periodical press".[17] Most sports reporters generally provided factual reports. It was columnists who had more scope for vivid description, comment and speculation. For leading figures, their by-line was a marketable product. Even in the 1890s, most wrote under pseudonyms and pen names that were well-known and respected.

As early as the 1820s, the pioneering British journalist Pierce Egan (1774–1849) was a key figure in developing sport as a distinctive area in journalism, especially in his *Life in London and Sporting Guide* newspaper (1824–1827). His journalism was shaped by the prevailing political culture of the Regency period in England and responded to early radical ideas of "British Liberty", through the defence of popular sports and through the assertion of "the people" and their "rights", attracting a readership across the social spectrum. He covered sports such as pugilism and horse racing, and with the inventive imagery of his sporting style and the exuberance of his sporting slang had an impact on subsequent sporting journalism.[18] In less-accomplished later hands, however, the style was laboured, extravagant and florid, with blow-by-blow descriptions and classical allusions, and came to be ridiculed.

Many of the better-known mid-century sportswriters wrote for several papers, and had expertise in racing, the prize ring, pedestrianism, athletics or cricket. T. Henry Hall Dixon (1822–1870), for example, "unrivalled as a sports journalist", wrote about racing for *Bell's Life* and the *Sporting Magazine*, as well as editing the *Doncaster Gazette*.[19] Dixon wrote as "The Druid".

Up to and beyond the 1860s, the term "sporting editor" was most often applied to the editor who managed a paper's racing results and betting information. By the 1880s, many newspapers employed a single full-time specialist sports editor, a role which often combined the writing of reports and specialist columns, the commissioning of articles, sifting of material from correspondents and sub-editing. It has been suggested that these multiple roles "secured a rate of pay above many in the industry", though mere sports reporters "would earn less than his colleagues covering news", and there was much competition for jobs.[20] In many daily papers sports editors enjoyed questionable status amongst editorial colleagues, though it was a demanding role. But it was sufficiently attractive that even in 1875 there were reportedly between 500 and 800 applications for the post of "sports editor" for the *Daily Telegraph*, including some titled and men of position, usually involved with the turf.[21] This competition for jobs in the industry, however, depressed wages.

By then editors and leading reporters were playing significant roles in the British sporting world. Their enthusiasms, editorial commentaries and more detailed reports and illustrations helped to shape sport, its progress and its multiple images. They affected public attitudes and created sports heroes. Letters to the paper helped indicate changing readership responses and orientations. Reporters were well-known inside sporting circles, which probably gave them a sense of status and esteem, of being part of a shared enterprise. While they helped to construct sporting knowledge, they also reflected dominant sporting community social understandings. Long-standing columnists helped create a shared history of sport.

Some of the leading editors and columnists had been (or continued to be) active as sports-men, officials and administrators. In 1869, FC Wilkinson, sporting editor of *The Field* and author of books of sporting rules, also acted as judge and referee at important athletic sports races. John Bentley, involved in *The Athletic News* as assistant editor from 1886, and later editor, was on the Football League management committee from its foundation. Charles W. Alcock, "father of modern sport" according to his biographer, was another leading journalist, editing the *Cricket* newspaper for many years.[22] He was a former FA Cup winner, England soccer international and referee, secretary of the English FA from 1870 to 1895, and also of Surrey County Cricket Club, an early advocate of the passing game, a leading supporter of the acceptance of soccer profes-sionalism in 1885, and arranged the first cricket "Test match" at The Oval in 1880. The *Glasgow Examiner's* reporter on its "Athletic Notes" in the 1890s was a leading Glasgow Celtic official. By contrast, Steve Tate's fascinating study of James Catton, the *Athletic News* editor from 1900, shows he was deeply involved in newspaper work from the age of 15, and built up a reputation as "the voice of football" without such close involvement.[23]

In the British press, leading papers adjudicated on sports rules in their columns and debated them in their editorials. They could help or hinder a sport's progress. Major sporting papers played a key role in promoting and sponsoring sports. They pushed for better facilities for spec-tators at sports grounds. They provided referees for judges. They created prizes and trophies, as indeed too did some of those regional papers who were increasingly providing coverage of sport in their locality. Early editors were often stakeholders for sporting challenges. *Bell's* editor Dowling began acting as a stakeholder as early as 1828 and by the 1830s was ever-increasingly publishing (at a price) challenges for money stakes, which increased the volume of sporting events. Dowling held stake money for some of these bare-knuckle prize fights, pedestrian events and bets, and was active as a sporting organiser.

The paper's very substantial correspondence section raised issues and disputes for which Dowling was soon trying to act as an expert decision-maker, and he became a major public figure in sporting circles. *Bell's Life* gave strong support to the prize ring until the late 1850s, but its corruption and attacks on its staff forced it to withdraw support in 1863. The same year a letter in its columns pressing for better regulation of the emerging game of football encouraged editorial interest and the meeting which created the English Football Association. By the 1860s, the *Sporting Life* editor was heavily involved in promoting pedestrianism. So too was the editor of the *Sheffield Daily Telegraph*. On the Tyne, in the 1860s the sporting editor of the *Newcastle Daily Journal* acted as stakeholder for a variety of matches and challenges, in sculling, dog racing, etc., and would choose a neutral referee if the sides could not agree.

Across the Atlantic, in the 1850s, as baseball developed, the press became a quasi-official source of information. The semi-structured nature and the changes occurring within organised baseball made it imperative for those interested in baseball to follow the game in its columns.[24] Henry Chadwick, a journalist with the *New York Times* from 1856, chaired the National Baseball Committee's discussion on rules in the 1860s and was credited with creating box scores and batting average statistics.[25] Richard Kyle Fox, editor of the *National Police Gazette* in New York, who reported on middle- and working-class sports through the lens of American masculinity, was also both a sports promoter and a purveyor of sporting goods, and created celebrities out of leading sportsmen such as boxer John L. Sullivan.[26]

In Melbourne, Australia, the sporting editor of *The Australasian* was a stakeholder for pedestrian events. In 1859, when possible rules for Australian football were discussed, WJ Hammersley, then known as "Longstop", the sporting editor of *The Australasian*, and JB Thompson, sportswriter for *The Argus*, took active roles. Hammersley was its first regular cricket writer, and under the pseudonym "Felix", Tom Horan used his experience as a former Victorian and Australian cricketer to provide informed comments. From 1870, "Peter Pindar" covered Australian football as its crowds grew.[27]

As Michael Oriard has emphasised in his reading of early American football as a cultural text, the ways in which the popular press interacted with sports created a number of dominant narratives, which could be read in different ways by different readers.[28] Each paper's editor privileged particular sports and linked sport to sets of values, masculinity, gender and class and racial attitudes. Some newspapers gave a substantial boost to some of the more commercial gambling sports such as pugilism, pedestrianism and racing.

It was the middle classes who ran and reported on many sports, so there was often a built-in bias against issues such as professionalism, or the place of gambling or drinking in working-class life.[29] Some editors saw professionalism and gambling very negatively, stressing their potential for corruption and result-fixing. They and their middle-class and elite readers sought magazines and newspapers which covered more "amateur" activities not associated with profiting from sporting involvement, and pushed health, morality and positive character values. The journalism in such papers boosted the increased divisions in sporting society. In 1850s, American writers such as Henry Chadwick had reported on early baseball clubs like the Knickerbockers with only limited details, stressing the game's positive effects upon physical fitness and character, but later in the century as the game became more professional, some journalists picked up reader concerns about professionalism, wanting baseball to be played for recreation and sheer enjoyment and not for financial gain. Different newspapers and different columnists might variously espouse "pure" amateurism, accept a measure of professionalism, criticise sham amateurism or willingly accept fully professionalised forms of sport. Philadelphia's *Sporting Life*, for example, first published in 1883, claimed to be a mouthpiece for "clean sport", of "moral uplift" and for "true sportsmen" everywhere.

Columnists took different attitudes to notions of "fair" and "unfair" play. There were debates in Britain in the early 1880s over soccer and rugby on-field "violence", and attempts by some newspaper editors to "clean up" such practice in American football in 1897. Attitudes to sporting behaviour in baseball likewise varied, and though clubs strengthening their teams with outsiders for specific games, players abandoning their sides for another offering more money, teams throwing games to gain through betting and players betting on their own games all attracted criticism, this criticism was sometimes strong, but sometimes little better than a mild rebuke.[30] In part they should be seen, as Oriard reminds us, in the context of "campaigns for circulation".[31] But for some writers they were probably genuinely felt.

Underpaid and unrespectable

Those entering journalism in the expanded sporting context of the late 19th century, especially those reporters on the weekly provincial press, had limited opportunities to escape the drudgery and repetition of compiling results, and this was even truer of the Saturday sports specials. Much work was casual, done in a rush by outsider correspondents, juniors and other low-status employees. Newcomers were often drawn from the lower reaches of the middle class, with limited educational attainments and financial support. Their wages and status were low. There was intense competition for each job and this depressed wage rates, though earnings could be increased on an extra linage basis.[32]

Sporting journalists were always seen by some as unrespectable, in part because of the wider content of sports papers and reporters' association with disreputable activities such as gambling, alcohol and the drink trade. In America, New York's sporting male weeklies of the 1840s included much about the theatre, prostitutes and ribald humour.[33] In Britain, journalists likewise always had a questionable status, partly because of their involvement in less respectable social life. To cite just one example, one of the *Sporting Times'* leading journalists in the 1880s and 1890s was Arthur Binstead, nicknamed "Pitcher" (1861–1914), who had first worked for a small sporting press agency, providing telegraphed reports and results for licenced clubs and the London and provincial press. He regularly wrote about the seamier side of racing, mixing with bookies' runners, tipsters and members of the race gangs as well as trainers and owners.[34]

An associational culture amongst sports journalists sometimes emerged asracing reporters often travelled together by train, stayed in the same hotels and socialised together, but was also limited by competition to be first with the news. Accommodation for journalists at many British sports stadia was uncomfortable and cramped, though larger county cricket grounds often had better facilities. In the 1890s, there was huge demand for space at major games. In 1899, over 180 journalists watched the England–Scotland match at Villa Park, and 150 watched the FA Cup final at Crystal Palace.

By the century's end, sports journalism was becoming a more coherent occupational grouping, though the job continued to face the problems of occupational strain and tension and often low pay early in the career. Sports journalism had moved from contrived description to a more opinionated and informed style, and its leading exponents had become widely known. From the 1870s onwards, as commercial and amateur sports became a key part of urban culture, sports reporting became a necessary and often key component of daily and evening newspapers, and ever-growing numbers of journalist catered for its needs. They, in turn, helped to shape the future pattern of sport.

References

1. Victoria EM Gardner, *The Business of News in England, 1760–1820*, Basingstoke, Palgrave Macmillan, 2016, provides useful examples.
2. Rob Steen, *Sports Journalism: A Multimedia Primer*, Abingdon, Routledge, 2008, p. 23. Key texts include Tony Mason, "Sporting News, 1860–1914" in Michael Harris, Alan J. Lee (eds), *The Press in English Society from the Seventeenth to Nineteenth Centuries*, London, Associated Universities Press, 1986, pp. 168–186; Mike Huggins, *The Victorians and Sport*, London, Hambledon, 2004, pp. 141–166.
3. John Tolson and Wray Vamplew, "Facilitation not revolution: railways and British flat racing 1830–1914", *Sport in History*, Volume 23, 2003, pp. 89–106.
4. Mike Huggins, *Flat Racing and British Society 1790–1914*, London, Frank Cass, 2000, p. 28.
5. *Pall Mall Gazette*, 11 June 1872.
6. *Cambridge Chronicle*, 31 August 1872.
7. Carl B. Cone (ed.), *Hounds in the Morning: Sundry Sports of Merry England*, Lexington, University Press of Kentucky, 1981.
8. For details of leading sports newspapers and journalists in Britain see Laurel Brake and Marysa Demoor (eds), *A Dictionary of Nineteenth-Century Journalism: The Press in Britain and Ireland, 1800–1900*, Ghent and London, Proquest, 2009.
9. Adrian Harvey, *The Beginnings of a Commercial Sporting Culture in Britain 1792–1850*, Aldershot, UK, Ashgate, 2004, pp. 31–62 has good material on *Bell's Life*.
10. Philippe Etart, "Entre sport, mondanités et dandysme: esquisse biographique d'Eugène Chapus. Partie 2: Chapus au temps du sport", *European Studies in Sport History*, Volume 9, 2016.
11. Matthew McIntire, "Odds, intelligence, and prophecies: racing news in the Penny Press, 1855–1914", *Victorian Periodicals Review*, Volume 41, Issue 4, 2008, pp. 352–357.
12. Dave Russell, *Football and the English: A Social History of Association Football in England 1863–1995*, Lancaster, Carnegie Publishing, 1997, p. 104. See Mason, "Sporting News", pp. 177–178.
13. Steven Tate, "The Professionalisation of Sports Journalism, 1850 to 1939, with Particular Reference to the Career of James Catton", Ph.D. thesis, 2007, University of Central Lancashire, pp. 40–43.

14. Huggins, *The Victorians and Sport*, pp. 152–153.

15. Hilary Fraser, Judith Johnston and Stephanie Green, *Gender and the Victorian Periodical*, Cambridge, UK, Cambridge University Press, 2003, pp. 211–227.

16. David Scott Kamper, "Popular Sunday newspapers, respectability and working-class culture" in Mike Huggins and JA Mangan (eds), *Disreputable Pleasures: Less Virtuous Victorians at Play*, Abingdon, UK, Frank Cass, 2004, p. 97; Mason, "Sporting News", p. 177.

17. Tony Mason, "Sport", in J. Don Vann and Rosemary T. VanArsdel (eds), *Victorian Periodicals and Victorian Society*, Toronto, Canada, University of Toronto Press, 1995, p. 297.

18. Keiko Ikeda, "Political analysis of the historical development of sports writing in Britain from the early radicals to the New Left", *International Journal of Eastern Sports & Physical Education*, Volume 4, Issue 1, 2006, pp. 201–209; David Snowden, *Writing the Prizefight: Pierce Egan's Boxiana World*, London, Peter Lang, 2013.

19. Brake and Demoor, *Nineteenth-Century Journalism*, p. 173.

20. Tate, *Professionalisation of Sports Journalism*, p. 100.

21. *Edinburgh Evening News*, 11 January 1875; *Sheffield Independent*, 16 January 1875.

22. Keith Booth, *The Father of Modern Sport: The Life and Times of Charles W. Alcock*, London, Parrs Wood Press, 2002.

23. Steve Tate, "James Catton, 'Tityrus' of *The Athletic News* (1860 to 1936): a biographical study", *Sport in History*, Volume 25, Issue 1, 2005, pp. 98–115.

24. R. Terry Furst, *Early Professional Baseball and the Sporting Press: Shaping the Image of the Game*, Jefferson, North Carolina, McFarland and Co, 2014, p. 9.

25. Andrew Schiff, *The Father of Baseball: A Biography of Henry Chadwick*, New York, McFarland and Co, 2008.

26. Guy Reel, *The National Police Gazette and the Making of the Modern American Man, 1879–1906*, New York, Palgrave Macmillan, 2006, pp. 177–196.

27. Robin Grow, "Nineteenth century football and the Melbourne Press", *Sporting Traditions*, Volume 3, Issue 1, 1986, pp. 23–37.

28. Michael Oriard, *Reading Football: How the Popular Press Created an American Spectacle*, Chapel Hill, North Carolina, University of North Carolina Press, 1993.

29. Pamela Dixon and Neal Garnham, "Drink and the professional footballer in 1890s England and Wales", *Sport in History*, Volume 25, Issue 3, 2005, pp. 375–389.

30. Furst, *Early Professional Baseball and the Sporting Press*, p. 99.

31. Oriard, *Reading Football*, p. 203; Huggins, *The Victorians and Sport*, pp. 76–77.

32. Tate, *The Professionalisation of Sports Journalism*, p. 363.

33. Patricia C. Cohen, Timothy J. Gilfoyle and Helen Lefkowitz, *American Antiquarian Society, The Flash Press: Sporting Male Weeklies in 1840s New York*, Urbana, Illinois, University of Chicago Press, 2008.

34. Arthur M. Binstead and Ernest Wells, *A Pink 'Un and a Pelican*, London, Bliss, Sands, 1898.

3

The art of sportswriting

Rob Steen and Huw Richards

When aspiring sports journalists seek guidance on how to improve their writing, we can be relied upon to reply with a four-letter word: read. When they ask how to improve their journalism, the recommendation is precisely the same. Given the intense subjectivity involved in assessing literary style, let alone the accuracy of the facts conveyed or the quality of views expressed, this is not necessarily straightforward.

While encouraging students to build an extensive vocabulary and vary the length of sentences to enhance rhythm, clarity and impact, personal experience dictates that any attempt to lay down rules beyond the barest necessities – never plagiarise, patronise, browbeat, hector, fabricate or miss a deadline – is doomed to confuse. Everything we've learned stems from appreciating, analysing and understanding the methods, tics, thought processes and (apparent) beliefs of those who were already doing the job we craved: bombarding readers with our –not-necessarily humble opinions on music, cinema or sport – ideally, all three.

The essential difference between good journalism and good sports journalism is that while both must inform, the latter, because of its traditionally lighter, fluffier, more celebratory nature, often demands an ability to entertain. By the same token, not all the best sportswriters achieve this blend, a reflection of the increasingly serious and complex issues that were largely ignored before newspapers began expanding sports coverage in the 1970s but now find unprecedented space in print and on the web. This chapter unashamedly celebrates the cornerstones of good sportswriting: art, craft, wit, passion, proportion, commitment, honesty, wisdom and vision.

Transatlantic connections

When Robin Daniels was writing his 2009 memoir of his fellow Lancastrian Sir Neville Cardus, renowned music and cricket correspondent for the *Manchester Guardian* from the 1920s until his death in 1975, the subtitle he finally plumped for was nothing if not apt – *Celebrant of Beauty*. Sportswriting's priorities have undergone enormous changes since Cardus's heyday, not least in the premium placed on reporting the politics and business of sport, but thanks to the trail blazed by Cardus as well as Americans such as Paul Gallico, Damon Runyon, Ring Lardner Sr. and Jr., sports journalism remains, for many, the most literary branch of the profession, concerned as it still is with celebrating human endeavour, teamwork and the art and craft of both competition and language.

Aside from a mutual fascination for bats, balls, nets and points, British and American sports-writers might appear, at first glance, to have precious little in common. Soccer, rugby and cricket are the focal points on this side of the Atlantic; baseball, basketball and American football on the opposite bank. American sport is largely insular, almost devoutly anti-internationalist (save when it comes to importing talent); Britain has been sending its representatives on tour since 1860. Indeed, cricket would die out as a desirable profession if it were purely a domestic activity.

Burrow a little further and the stereotypes become cloudy. While Americans may have per-fected the art of turning sport into a profitable industry, you won't find a vast sponsor's logo daubed into the middle of the field at Joe Robbie Stadium or Fenway Park, nor a sponsor's insignia emblazoned across a single player's shirt. America may be capitalism's citadel, but it is also the home of free agency, revenue-sharing, powerful unions, players' strikes and an unques-tioning insistence on the virtues of "competitive balance". Britons may be renowned for their steadfast adherence to tradition, but it is baseball that resists any attempts to abbreviate the game to suit modern attention spans. Moreover baseball's regard for its history has been enshrined since 1939 in its Hall of Fame.

In baseball and cricket, moreover, Americans and Britons are united by a common affliction. Both are strictly summer games. Both revolve around bats and balls, swings and hits, runs and outs, fielders and catchers. Both are besotted with records, statistics and decimal points, to an extent no other sport would dream of venturing. Both, more potently, are held up as symbols of their country of (purported) origin – or, rather, its finer traditions and nobler aspirations. Cricket stops for lunch and tea. Baseball games pause three-quarters of the way through, allowing the crowd to sing its song of praise, "Take Me Out to the Ballgame". For an Englishman, captaining a men's national cricket team on a losing streak can be akin to simultaneously taking on the posts of prime minister, ambassador to Russia, chairman of the BBC and National Scapegoat-in-Chief. Not so much because cricket is so crucial to the national identity – though the sport is still paraded, however erroneously, as the embodiment of Englishness – more so because the tasks he faces are so diverse and demanding. And in cricket, as in baseball, a reporter's duties are daily. Major League Baseball teams play a minimum of 162 games a season; their counterparts in county cricket are onstage for around 100 working days per summer, with winters to add. The microscope is accordingly intense.

While British sportswriters have long cast envious if not always appreciative glances at their peers and predecessors across the Atlantic, primarily for the greater freedom they have been afforded by editors, there are exceptions. "Only in America is it possible for earnest young men to major in journalism, whatever that means," claimed the late Ian Wooldridge, one of the most celebrated British sportswriters, ignoring the recent eruption of journalism degrees in his own country. "This explains why much American sportswriting, with a few formidable exceptions, reads as though it has been computed in a word-processing machine."[1] That last statement is not one with which I can concur.

Type until the blood seeps

One of Wooldridge's exceptions was Red Smith, droll yet incisive doyen of the *New York Herald Tribune*, and latterly the *New York Times*, for five decades spanning the Second World War and the Falklands War: an inspiration for several British sportswriters of my acquaintance. Once asked whether his "trade" (Wooldridge's words) was a taxing one, Smith responded with his customary blend of modesty, understatement and graphic description: "You merely sit there at a typewriter and think until the blood seeps out of the pores on your forehead."[2]

The ginger-mopped, peppery-witted Smith was once instructed by his sports editor, Stanley Woodward, to "stop Godding up those ball players." Of all the crimes a self-respecting journalist could be accused of, that of bowing and scraping to scantily educated, over-muscled oafs is arguably the most grievous. Unless it is to commit the opposite, as Smith did when he berated Muhammad Ali for taking his stand for Black America and the North Vietnamese ("Cassius makes himself as sorry a spectacle as those unwashed punks who picket and demonstrate against the war"[3]). For the most part, come adulation or ridicule, Smith subscribed to the Rhett Butler Theory: he didn't give a damn.

Smith was a master of the drop-intro, the delayed punchline. Wisecracks and perspicacity flowed in equal measure, underpinned by an innate grasp of rhythm. In 1956, he captured the often-contradictory essence of Connie Mack, one of baseball's greatest managers; the conscious repetition of the word "and" would have been indigestible in less capable or assured hands:

> As long as he was Connie Mack he was tough and human and clever. He was tough and warm and wonderful, kind and stubborn and courtly and unreasonable and generous and calculating and naïve and gentle and proud and humorous and demanding and unpredictable.
>
> Many people loved him and some feared him, everybody respected him and, as far as I know, nobody ever disliked him in the ninety-three years of his life. There may never have been a more truly successful man, for nobody ever won warmer or wider esteem and nobody ever relished it more.[4]

Another of Wooldridge's exceptions was his own journalistic hero, Paul Gallico, whose 14 years as a sportswriter in the 1920s and 1930s culminated in a revealing, humorous and often scathing collection-cum-memoir, *Farewell to Sport*, before he turned his hand to novel-writing. Witness his homage to Babe Ruth, baseball colossus and second, after WG Grace, as a trailblazer for global sporting celebrity. The accent is not on Ruth's prodigious skills but squarely, refreshingly, unabashedly, on his humanity and fallibility:

> I learned to love him because he was all man. In his early days before the great reformation he drank, he smoked, he cursed, he wenched, he indulged himself, he brawled and sulked, and got the swelled head and got over it. He was discovering, living and enjoying this wonderful thing called life with all of his senses, enjoying it more than anyone I have ever known.[5]

What Gallico and Smith had in common was a fondness for the colloquial and the conversational. Nick Pitt, a London-based sportswriter and former sports editor of the *Sunday Times*, once related that, when he sat down to write a story, he would write it as if telling the story to a friend in the pub. That, though, is far more the traditional American way.

Musical prose

Nearly half a century after his death, the most lauded English sportswriter remains Neville Cardus. A journalist as renowned for reviewing string quartets as cricket matches, he sought, and often attained, beauty; and he saw his job as locating and celebrating beauty. Which is why he thought nothing of heightening facts and embellishing reality.

Here, in a brief paragraph, Cardus expertly conveys the mentality of the sporting winner while distilling the importance to Australian cricket, and Australia in general, of Donald Bradman, who dominated the game between the World Wars to an extent no individual player has ever remotely managed in any other major sport.

> Once more Bradman was Australia's spinal column. Had he failed, the rubber would on the fourth evening have been in England's hands. He never fails when he knows a rubber depends on him. Bradman served the cause with an almost moral control of his customary avariciousness. He batted grammatically, committed no vanities. Only once did he attack, and that was while the English bowling temporarily lost certainty of touch.[6]

Note that consistency was a conspicuous asset. In 1934, he wrote of a Bradman inning thus: "Spirit lived in every stroke. Beauty that comes out of life at the crown of manhood." On another occasion he was almost contemptuous: "Bradman was the summing-up of the Efficient Age … Here was brilliance safe and sure, streamlined and seemingly without graceful impulse. Victor Trumper was the bird; Bradman, the aeroplane."[7]

Nobody took over Cardus' baton with greater gusto than Alan Ross, whose duties as cricket correspondent of *The Observer* in the third quarter of the 20th century also embraced poetry and travel writing. Witness this characteristic description of the Port of Spain ground in Trinidad:

> The enclosing mountains, densely wooded, of the Northern Range curve round ahead of the pavilion. The various stands are shaded by vast, scarlet-flowering tulip trees or overhung by the top-heavy filigree spread of samans, always, on account of their shallow roots and bulging superstructure, the first to be bowled over by heavy winds. An enormous, all-informing scoreboard, with COCA-COLA picked out in large letters above it, dominates the mountain end of the ground. But since the sponsors of Coca-Cola, at a reputed cost of $8,000, built the board and maintain it, who could demur at the disfigurement of natural beauties?[8]

Ross, though, was one of the last of his breed. Like Cardus and early 20th-century American sportswriters such as Heywood Broun and Grantland Rice, he inhabited press boxes before live television, before devoted sports channels and before the internet altered the landscape. He could proffer opinions and depict scenes with freedom and varying degrees of exaggeration, because he couldn't be second-guessed by sub-editors or readers.

Angell of the keys

More recently the style of Roger Angell and Hugh McIlvanney, in many eyes the best British sportswriter in the second half of the 20th century, stood in contrast with the more conversational style practised so eloquently from the early 1980s by the likes of Thomas Boswell and Matthew Engel, who built vividly on the legacy handed down by Gallico, Runyon and other Americans of the interwar years while curbing their excesses. Aided by the fact that neither was fettered by the tyrannies of the daily deadline – the American wrote for the weekly *New Yorker*, the Scotsman for Sunday papers – Angell and McIlvanney assembled articles as if they were constructing palaces to their erudition, or composing symphonies. Each word is a brick or note, each sentence individually designed and designated, each wholly interdependent.

Here, in the summer of 1981, Angell interviews the ageing Joe Wood, formerly known as "Smokey" Joe Wood, one of the greatest of all professional pitchers:

> The flow of recollection from Joe Wood was perhaps not as smooth and rivery as I have suggested here. For one thing, he spoke slowly and with care – not unlike the way he walked to the grandstand at Yale Field from the parking lot beyond left field, making his way along the grass firmly enough but looking where he was going, too, and helping himself a bit with his cane. Nothing infirm about him, but nothing hurrying or sprightly, either. For another, the game was well in progress by now, and its principals and sudden events kept interrupting our colloquy.[9]

More so even than Red Smith, Angell has won a number of awards for his writing, many of them from non-sporting panels, including a George Polk Award for Commentary, a Kenyon Review Award for Literary Achievement and the Michael Braude Award for Light Verse, presented by the American Academy of Arts and Letters. He is a Fellow of the American Academy of Arts and Sciences, and in 2011, with splendid aptness, was the inaugural winner of the PEN/ESPN Lifetime Achievement Award for Literary Sports Writing. In 2015, he won the National Magazine Award for Essays and Criticism for his piece on facing up to death, "This Old Man". The previous year, stirred by a photo of his boyhood self playing baseball with his mother, he wrote a brief memoir, "Olden Opener":

> I look more like a [centre] fielder trying to cut down a speeding baserunner at third base or home, but give me a break, guys. By the looks of me, I go about eighty-two pounds here, and the angle of my arm shows an instinctive understanding of the physics of the fling. Only the greatest athletes seem to have this somewhere within them, an elegant je ne sais quoi that marks the Mathewsons and Mayses of each era and warms the hearts of even the idlest, most distant onlooker.[10]

Just as the author's own liquid, vivid prose will, one can only trust, continue to warm the hearts of generations of sportswriters to come.

The art of writing for publication, to believe that in a competitive world one's words are particularly fit to be heard and heeded by large audiences, is by definition an act of ego and display. But as with all such matters, it is a question of how much.

The writers who dominate this chapter had more ego than most, not least because to write differently and originally requires the levels of self-confidence necessary to cope with the pushback they invariably receive from more conventionally minded editors and sub-editors. Along with this is the "sliver of ice" famously identified by Graham Greene, the attitude of mind that regards all things – and most of all people – as the material of writing before they are anything else.

These attitudes are recognisable to anyone who both possesses an element of self-awareness and writes for a living. Their downside, analogous to those studies of personality that show that many highly successful people are sociopaths, is that they are wont to be cited in mitigation by mediocrities who sow just as much collateral damage to others in their trajectories without offering any of the benefits.

Fine writing is not, though, the exclusive property of the human bulldozer. It can also be informed by empathy, compassion and a belief that the person you are writing about is much more than mere "material". It is found in many parts of the media jungle, nowhere more clearly than among cricket writers from the West of England.

It had particularly fine expression, on the radio rather than in print, at the England v. New Zealand test match at Lord's in 2004. Mark Richardson, a dour left-hander whose ungainly technique betrayed a tail-end past but whose durability epitomised New Zealand's unfailing gift for extracting the maximum from the talent available, was in the 90s and visibly uncomfortable. A learned discussion among the sages of *Test Match Special* concluded that he had "lost his off stump".

Following a change of commentator and summariser, Victor Marks appeared at the mic, and asked: "Is it just possible that he's close to a century at Lord's and might just be feeling a little nervous?", a consideration his colleagues had not voiced.

Marks (b 1954) sits firmly at the centre of one thread in British sportswriting, the manner in which the final trickle of Oxbridge cricket blues who played for England – himself, Michael Atherton, Derek Pringle, Mike Selvey and Steve James – graduated, almost to a man, to second careers as broadsheet cricket writers. Each has brought distinctive qualities to the role, notably Atherton's rigorous analytical intellect and Selvey's acute understanding of bowlers.

On the first Saturday of his first tour as a writer for the *Observer*, to the West Indies, Marks was scheduled to cover a one-day international. When it was called off, he learnt from his editors back in London that he was still expected to fill the allotted space. The competence with which this forbidding task was fulfilled boded well for the future.

Marks' most consistent quality was epitomised in that exchange with his TMS colleagues – the recognition that sport at any level is played by fallible human beings rather than automata. A former captain of Somerset, it places him firmly in the line of the West of England school of writers epitomised above all by David Foot (b 1929). He is not, as he has doubtless often had to point out, a member of the notable politico-literary clan, which has however produced its own distinguished sportswriter in the academic John Foot, author of notable studies of Italian cycling and football.

David Foot's own literary lineage is more one of association, as the son of the church warden who showed TS Eliot around East Coker church when the notably unsporty Anglo-American poet was working on *Four Quartets*.

In matters of reputation, Foot is wont to defer to his own hero, the Somerset fast bowler turned writer Raymond Robertson-Glasgow (1901–1963), seen at his best in the books of sketches which show an ability to vividly delineate what makes a cricketer distinctive in the space of a few hundred words.

Foot always gave the impression of regarding himself as an artisan – in his own self-description, a "jobbing journalist" rather than an artist in the Robertson-Glasgow mould. This is not mere self-deprecation. There is also a pride in the skills of the trade developed as a reporter on the *Western Gazette* and *Bristol Evening World*, times chronicled affectionately in his *Country Reporter* (1990). "Jobbing journalist" also expressed the reality of a working life around the theatres and sports grounds of the West of England and Midlands, weekly repertory rather than West End, county championship not rather than test matches.

It was a world in which his warmth and decency left a deep impression. Mike Averis, long-time *Guardian* sports editor but before (and after) that plougher of many of the same furrows, has spoken of the way other Guardian writers in the region came to expect welcomes in which warmth was tinged with disappointment. "Ah, you're from the Guardian. Terrific, good to have you. But does that mean David Foot won't be coming?"

Quite why Foot wasn't used for bigger events is a question only Averis and successive *Guardian* sports editors, none of them ill-served for talent, could answer. A personal memory is of meeting him at the West Indies v. Bristol World Cup match at Bristol in 1999. By some margin the most distinguished writer there, he was still excited at the prospect of reporting a World Cup match, something he had rarely done before.

But then his own interests and tastes tended to the human rather than the exalted. As he once explained, he would far rather interview a young player struggling to break into their county team than the captain of that team. So "jobbing journalist" is a reasonable description, albeit in the same sense that Roger Federer is a tennis pro or Eric Clapton a guitarist.

Mundane terminology does not exclude the sublime, offered by Foot in years of finely judged match reports, but to an even greater degree in a series of biographies which showed those underlying qualities of empathy, compassion and perception at much greater length. First came the unrelentingly grim *Harold Gimblett: Tortured Genius of Cricket* (1984), based on his recordings of conversation with the former Somerset opener and published after his death. A much more cheerful tone was set in *Cricket's Unholy Trinity* (1985), a study of three interwar cricketers – Charles Parker, Cecil Parkin and Jack MacBryan – whose careers were limited by obstreperous temperaments. *Wally Hammond: The Reasons Why* (2006), sought to find how a colossally talented, once fairly cheerful cricketer became a distinctly grim human being, and homed in on the character-changing qualities of the mercury treatment Gloucestershire's (and arguably England's) greatest cricketer since WG Grace received for a venereal disease contracted on tour.

There were also the two collections of short biographical essays, *With Bat and Ball* (1993) and *Fragments of Idolatry* (2001), which included a study of Robertson-Glasgow. All are scrupulously researched, beautifully written in a simple, unpretentious style wasting few words and sparing in flourishes, rooted in his deep affection for his native West Country and informed above all by his underlying empathy, compassion and perception. There is a consistent feeling for the underdog – while a man of peace, he leaves little doubt as to where his ultimate sympathies lie in the scene in *Unholy Trinity* where an exasperated Parker assaults Pelham Warner, the epitome of establishment hypocrisy, in a lift in a Bristol hotel.

If there is a unifying argument beyond a plea for human understanding, it is his contention that cricket, which is regularly cited as exposing personality, just as often conceals it. There was never a happier-looking cricketer than Gimblett at his most dashing, nor a county which has more consistently seemed expressive of the joys of the game than Somerset – Foot's own history of the county conveys this in its title, *Sunshine, Sixes and Cider* (1988). Yet the pleasure Gimblett gave to spectators was in inverse proportion to his own feelings about the game, and his name is just one among Somerset's disproportionate contribution to cricket's sad history of suicides, a list also including Robertson-Glasgow and Peter Roebuck.

The biographies came, in differing senses, both late and early for Foot. They were late in that the first of his major works, *Harold Gimblett*, was published when he was well into his 50s, but also too early in coming a little before the creation of the William Hill Prize in 1989. Had John Gaustad and Graham Sharpe had their brainwave a few years earlier, it seems entirely possible that Foot might have anticipated the triumphs of a similarly unpretentious writer, the regional paper veteran Duncan Hamilton.

To read Hamilton and Paul Edwards, the Lancashire-based ESPNCricinfo writer who offers perhaps the closest echo of Foot among the contemporary cricket press, is to wonder how many other sublimely gifted scribes worked for restricted regional audiences. And it is worth remembering that those qualities are not confined to cricket writers, or men. They are perhaps incarnated best in the contemporary *Guardian* by their north-eastern football writer, Louise Taylor.

While the north-east no longer produces steel, chemicals or ships as it once did, and the lessons offered by its football clubs have been almost entirely confined in recent years to "How not to" parables, it has at least continued to produce prime football writing talent. Jonathan Wilson is the game's leading historian of ideas and the Middlesbrough duo of John Nicholson and Harry Pearson respectively its most effective polemicist and most consistent humourist (albeit one with a serious side and a hinterland extending well beyond football expressed in fine studies of Learie Constantine and Belgian cycling).

Taylor, like Wilson from Sunderland, had to be durable in an era which routinely placed obstacles in the paths of female writers, and has survived on her considerable merits to reach what may be, because of her regular contributions to *The Guardian*, the largest audience of the four north-easterners. Her virtues were perhaps most obvious during periods when it was weighted with interminable transcriptions from press conferences at Man U and Arsenal, the paper's twin obsessions.

It could be argued that covering three major clubs freed Taylor from the Stockholm Syndrome risks endemic to those focused on a single club. But what really stood out was the knowledge of those clubs she had built up, at both institutional and individual level, over years of coverage; an eye for what really mattered; and a sympathy for the people involved and their aspirations. Where the Arsenal and Manchester United stories had quotes, Taylor's coverage of the north-east had people – recognisable, living, breathing human beings whose lives were entangled, whether by contract or allegiance, with the North-East's leading clubs. North-eastern football has been short on luck in recent years, with Newcastle and Sunderland particularly unfortunate in their ownership. But in this single aspect, at least – outstanding, sympathetic, thoughtful coverage in a national newspaper – it may count itself lucky.

If there is a lesson here for talent spotters, it is a simple one. Your next genius might just be the noisy iconoclast, proclaiming his own talent for all to hear and letting nothing stand in his way. Or it could be the quiet chap or girl in the corner, getting on with the cultivation of sources and getting from them the insights that nobody else quite seems to manage. The sporting world has need of them both.

References

1. Ian Wooldridge, *Searching for Heroes – Fifty Years of Sporting Encounters*, London, Hodder & Stoughton, 2007.
2. Ibid.
3. Quoted in "Ali's toughest foe: The Army", Bruce Lowitt, *St. Petersburg Times*, 30 December 1999, http://www.sptimes.com/News/123099/Sports/Ali_s_toughest_foe__t.shtml Accessed 25 May 2019
4. Red Smith, *Red Smith on Baseball*, Chicago, Illinois, Ivan R Dee, 2000.
5. Paul Gallico, *Farewell to Sport*, New York, AA Knopf, 1938.
6. Neville Cardus, *Australian Summer – England's Tour of Australia 1936/7*, London, Souvenir Press, 1937.
7. Robin Daniels, *Cardus – Celebrant of Beauty*, Lancaster, UK, Palatine Books, 2009.
8. Alan Ross, *Through the Caribbean – England in the West Indies 1960* (reprint), London, Pavilion Books, 1986.
9. Roger Angell, "The web of the game", *Late Innings*, New York, Simon & Schuster, 1972, reprinted in Roger Angell, *Once More Around The Park*, New York, Ballantine Books, 1991.
10. Roger Angell, "Olden Opener", *The New Yorker*, 2014, https://www.newyorker.com/sports/sporting-scene/olden-opener, accessed 16 December 2019.

4

Newspapers

Guy Hodgson

Henry Winter, the chief football writer for *The Times* as I write, tells a story that is indicative of what, for some, was the golden age of newspaper sports reporting: the 1950s and 1960s.

When a young reporter visited the home of Geoffrey Green, a veteran chronicler of events on sports fields, he was puzzled by one thing: why was there a Christmas tree heavy with decorations in the garden? The days were long and the temperature was far too clement for the festive season. Green, a sports correspondent for nearly 40 years for *The Times*, was amused that the young man seemed so bewildered. The tree was there all year, he explained, "because, when you are a football journalist, every day is Christmas".

The story, Winter concedes, may be apocryphal, but there is no reason to question the authenticity of the enjoyment that Green got from his work and can be summed up by his reaction to his winning an award late in his career. His peers waited for the usual words of thanks, but instead of making for the stage, Green sent forward a tape recorder. Perhaps he was too overcome to talk? Or he had lost his voice? The reason became clear when the recorder was switched on and Louis Armstrong began singing "It's a Wonderful World".

Green's career, which ended with his retirement in 1976, spanned the age when British football was played predominantly at 3 pm on a Saturday. Not 12 pm, 2 pm or 4 pm on a Sunday, nor Friday and Monday evenings, but at a time set in the early 20th century to accommodate workers whose shifts frequently finished on Saturday lunchtimes. There were midweek matches but they were restricted, almost without exception, to Tuesdays and Wednesdays and, until a Football Association ban on floodlit games was lifted in 1950, were played during the afternoon. Managers did not have press officers positioned to act as a barrier between themselves and reporters, and footballers, rather than avoid or, at best, tolerate journalists, would go drinking with them. The richer half of this social equation was the men (and it was almost invariably men) who described the action from the stands rather than those who performed centre stage.

Whether Green would now be digging up his tree, trashing his fairy lights and searching for a more world-weary track of music is debatable, but he would find a very different kind of sports journalism. It is now a craft where opinion and quotes are the main currency as newspaper reporters crave something different from what is being pumped into homes via the internet, Twitter and 24-hour news on television and radio. It is a world where sport events start at the behest of television companies, so the FA Cup final kicks off at a time that ensures many supporters miss their last train home. It is a profession where the journalist's most useful contact may not be a cricketer, athlete or racing driver, but his or her agent or public relations consultant. It is a lifestyle where you can report cricket at 9 pm, boxing at 4 am and football seven days a week, and you can have feedback berating your ability within seconds of posting your latest story on the web. And the sports people you publicise can earn twice your annual salary in a week.

This chapter will examine the evolution of sports reporting in newspapers. It will chart the journey where sport has gone from being the "toy department" to a key driver for attracting readers, whether it is to websites and apps (increasing) or print editions (decreasing). It will trace the increasing profile of sport in newspapers and look at changing writing styles and news values. It will also speculate as to the future of sports journalism in newspapers as circulation numbers for the printed editions dwindle and the industry strives to find a business model that works online.

Bigger, wider and less ink

On 26 March 2016, a significant milestone was reached in the history of the press in the UK. *The Independent* and *Independent on Sunday*, national newspapers that their founding editor described as "classic with a twist", stopped being printed after a 30-year run and instead became web-only publications.[1] They are unlikely to be the last. Newspaper circulations are falling; advertising, in the words of the late former *Guardian* editor Peter Preston, is taking "another cold bath"; and in September 2016 the owners of the *Daily Mail* announced 400 job cuts.[2] The future of newsprint newspapers is uncertain other than they are moving with greater pace towards their ultimate destination, the internet; what will happen to sports journalism is equally uncharted, but it can rest more easily because its future is secure. No matter what medium it appears on, there appears to be a market for reports on people chasing a ball, or racing each other. For example, the BBC achieved record viewing figures of 45.24 million for an overseas Olympics for the Rio de Janeiro Games in 2016, while the corporation's online coverage set new records, reaching 68.3 million devices in the United Kingdom, and 102.3 million globally.[3]

Sport has been one of the success stories of the printed newspaper over the last three decades, and without it there are grounds for believing more publications would have followed the online-only route in recent years. "Unlike hard news, where the impact of TV and the internet appears to have eroded sales, sport tends to boost readership," Roy Greenslade, formerly editor of the *Daily Mirror*, wrote, and this was in 2005.[4] The importance of sport in newspapers has not diminished since. Thus, while the provincial evening sports publications such as Manchester's *Sporting Pink* and Birmingham's *Sports Argus* fell victim around the turn of the century to the movement of big sports occasions from Saturday afternoon to Saturday night and Sunday, there was a corresponding boost to sports coverage in the national press. Between 1984 and 1994, almost every national newspaper in the UK increased its pagination by at least 50 per cent, the *Sunday Express* and *Mail on Sunday* tripling in size, but coverage of sport has increased in an even greater proportion and has been important in establishing brand identity. The *Daily Star* used the "Ooh, Ah" chant borrowed from football supporters extolling the virtues of Eric Cantona in the 1990s while *The Sun* and *The Times* paid £20m to broadcast Premier League highlights on tablets and phones for three years in 2013.

Raymond Boyle showed that sport took an increasing percentage of newspapers between 1974 and 2004, noting that in *The Times* it rose from 11 to 21 per cent, *The Guardian* 11 to 17 and the *Daily Telegraph* 18 to 30.[5] He looked at newspapers over the month of September while Hodgson's content analysis of the *Daily Mirror*'s 22 June editions of 1970 and 2005 showed that the sport section had a 16 per cent share of each, although their pagination had increased from 24 to 64 in the 35 years.[6] This would seem to contradict Boyle's findings until the rest of the 2005 edition was examined and the importance of sport was underlined. The front page was dominated by football with a picture of David Beckham and an unrelated lead story about allegations of sexual harassment at the Football Association. The latter was accompanied by a two-page spread on page four and five and a comment piece on page 11; Britain's Wimbledon hopes, Tim Henman and Andy Murray, filled page 9; photographs of the Beckhams on holiday comprised pages 12 and 13; and on page 16 the lead story was about an alleged rape involving Arsenal's Robin Van Persie. In terms of editorial, sport comprised 46 per cent of the edition. In terms of column inches, it made up more than 50 per cent.

For the purposes of this chapter, the 22 June 2016 edition of the *Daily Mirror* was analysed and confirmed the trend. Sport comprised 12 of the 60 pages in the newspaper proper, but there was also a 12-page supplement devoted to football's European Championships. A third of that supplement was made up of puzzles, horoscopes and cartoons, but it still meant that sport, football in particular, made up 28 per cent of the newspaper. The news pages were not dominated by sports-related stories as they had been in 2005, but, just as the edition of 11 years earlier may have been exceptional, circumstances in 2016 ensured that politics was predominant. The 22 June edition was printed the day before the UK's referendum on membership of the European Union (EU), and the agenda was framed by the *Mirror*'s backing for the Remain campaign. Sport was not entirely absent from the debate, however, as Beckham, one of the most enduring British sportsmen to be elevated by newspapers' culture of celebrity, was cited as being an advocate for staying in the EU.[7] Elsewhere in the news section there was a report on Russian athletes being banned from the Rio Olympics and a picture story of the England and Leicester City footballer Jamie Vardy playing golf.[8] Looking at the figures in purely quantitative terms, there was a decline in sport's proportion of the *Mirror* from 2005 to 2016, but once the news agenda is taken into account, the discrepancy is less pronounced. People can vote in British elections from 7 am, so 22 June was the last opportunity for the newspaper to try to influence all its readers' voting intentions and nine pages were devoted to the EU referendum. This for what was described as Britain's "most important decision in decades"; sport took up more than double that, 20 pages.[9]

If the same qualitative interpretation – analysing the coverage in the light of events around it – is applied to the 1970 and 2016 editions, the increase in the proportion of sport is emphasised. A news story intruded on the normal preserve of football, cricket, rugby union, etc. – the back page – on 22 June 1970, a piece previewing the first meeting of Edward Heath's newly elected Cabinet. This suggested that it had been a humdrum day on the world's sports fields, but this was not the case. Brazil, the version of which is repeatedly cited as the greatest national football team in history, won the World Cup in Mexico the day before, yet it was not even the principal sports story. That was claimed by the triumph in the US Open Golf Championship of Tony Jacklin, the first Briton to win the tournament in 50 years. Inside the edition, there were also events that would have merited the back page on lesser days: an England cricket Test and the Wimbledon tennis fortnight beginning that afternoon. It was an edition, in short, that chronicled two momentous events and offered the prospect of more, yet sport filled only 16 per cent of that 1970 edition while in its 2016 counterpart, on a day when Britain was on the eve of making its most important constitutional decision in 50 years, it made up 28 per cent. Bigger, wider and quicker; just like the participants, the coverage of sport in the UK has grown and shows no signs of diminishing.

Not a mere catalogue of hits

There may never have been a time when sports journalists habitually began their reports with "Yorkshire won the toss and elected to bat," but some came close. In 1895, Phillips' guide to becoming a newspaper journalist stated that a sports report should be "a word picture of what took place ... without the introduction of any expressions of opinion at all".[10] Contrarily, seven years later Pendleton quoted an editor who required a cricket reporter to cover Lancashire's matches at Old Trafford: "It is indispensable that the work should be done in a critical and picturesque style and not be a mere catalogue of hits."[11] Many journalists had a formula and stuck with it. The work of Bernard Darwin (golf), Neville Cardus (cricket) and others showed that an individual style could be executed with a flourish, but others followed a template that mixed a rigidly simple blow-by-blow account with journalese.[12] John Brierley, who, as "Perseus", reported sport for the *Lancashire Daily Post* from the 1890s, bemoaned the slack phraseology of some sports reports that lacked originality, thought or felicity of expression:

> We have thought and talked in terms of stupid hyperbole. We have a language of our own. We have alluded to the ball in football as the sphere, the leather, the inflated windbag, anything but what is, a ball.[13]

John Macadam, who was chief sports columnist for the *Daily Express* in the 1950s, had someone similar in mind when he described "Old Charlie", a permanent presence in a Midlands press box, who uncharacteristically arrived just after a match had begun. After a flustered squeeze along a row of fellow reporters to his seat and an extravagantly measured placement of notebook, programme and pencils, he turned to a neighbour: "Which side," he asked, "kicked off with a rush?" As Macadam noted: "Old Charlie – all the old Charlies – had been using the sacred soccer jargon for so long in his numerous reports that he even talked it."[14]

These reporters were writing in an age when the newspaper was the prime conveyor of news about sport, a point illustrated by a comparison between newspapers of different eras. Even half a century ago the imperative was a descriptive account of the action because the vast majority of the audience had not seen it. Now, with the internet, live television, highlights packages and sports news channels most goals, tries, wickets, controversial incidents, etc., have been viewed even before newspaper journalists have filed their copy. The reporter – and this applies beyond sport to across the newspaper spectrum – has to provide something different, and opinion has grown in volume and significance. Thus, in 1970 Ken Jones, writing from Mexico City, could begin his World Cup final report with a simple statement of fact: "Brazil reclaimed the World Cup here today and with their third success made the Jules Rimet Trophy their own."[15] In 2016, Dave Kidd's report on England's European Championships defeat by Iceland was much more opinionated and made assumptions about the reader's knowledge. His opening two paragraphs read:

> And so, in keeping with recent events, an England without a functioning government, opposition, nor any future plan, no longer has a manager for its football team either.
>
> Roy Hodgson will go down in history as the man who led England to their most humiliating result of all time, having already piloted their worst-ever World Cup campaign.[16]

This is not to decry Jones, who was one of the best sportswriters of his generation and who proved he could blend comment and sophisticated language with the best of them as the inaugural chief sportswriter for *The Independent* in the 1980s and 1990s. He was doing what was required of him, just as Kidd was. The latter makes assumptions about Hodgson's reputation and brandishes questionable assertions (England's football team that included Tom Finney, Wilf Mannion and Stan Mortensen lost to the part-timers of the United States in 1950, and the worst-ever World Cup campaigns must surely include 1974 and 1978 when they failed to qualify for the finals), but that was the point. He wanted his readers to argue with him. Most of them had watched the match on ITV the previous night so a simple match report would not have registered. He wanted a debate via the internet forums that online newspapers encourage: clickbait. Paul Newman, the tennis correspondent and former sports editor of *The Independent*, wrote: "The written media have had to become more analytical, more informative and more entertaining."[17] He could have added: more provocative.

Another change is an emphasis on quotes. In 1970, there were some but not many – only a four-centimetre sidebar accompanied Jones's report on the World Cup final – while now the comments of the protagonists usually outweigh their actions. That, however, creates conflicts. Sportsmen, frequently inarticulate, soon learn that a careless remark can be magnified into something it was never meant to be, and they become wary. Comments become blander, and reporters are frequently required to build stories by using anodyne quotes made spicier by the language around them. This was embodied by Alan Shearer, who resembled a policeman giving stilted evidence in court when he spoke to the media as a footballer for England, Southampton, Blackburn Rovers and Newcastle United, because he was too intimidated by the potential consequences to say anything above the obvious. Now, underlining how much he reined in himself as a player, he has in retirement become an articulate, intelligent and humorous commentator on the game for the BBC's *Match of the Day*.

This is fine when, like Shearer, you know the rules (many sports figures, including those in authority such as Sir Alex Ferguson, have used the media for their own agendas); it is only when someone who does not know these parameters is exposed to this treatment that the practice is revealed in its full shabbiness.

Carlos Alberto was a much-respected figure in football. He captained the Brazil side of 1970, was the man presented with the World Cup that June afternoon and scored the sublime fourth goal in the 4-1 win over Italy. He also managed Azerbaijan, who played England in April 2005, and was astonished by what he had read in British newspapers. In the build-up to the match against opponents who had been beaten 8-0 by Poland a few days earlier, Michael Owen had been asked by journalists whether he would like to move closer to Bobby Charlton's England scoring record by equalling or bettering Malcolm Macdonald's mark of five goals in a single international. As a striker, Owen had little option but to say yes, because any other answer would have betrayed lack of ambition. But he was careful to avoid predictions, and anyone who has observed his modest demeanour would know that the bragging headlines that followed the next day – "We'll Thrash Them!" was one – were the over-egged product of sub-editors. Except that Carlos Alberto did not know Owen or understand the machinations of newspapers. "I have 45 years in this game and I have not known anything like this," Carlos Alberto said in the aftermath of a 2-0 defeat in which Azerbaijan, relative minnows in world football, had performed creditably. "Who is … what is his name? Owen is a nobody." He went on to describe the England vice-captain as a midget who had done nothing in the game and a shoddy creature who should learn respect.

Richard Williams, then chief sportswriter of *The Guardian*, watched this outburst, embarrassed by a misunderstanding that was pitting one generation of footballers against another. "Not one of us in the room," he wrote, "had the guts to stand up and tell Carlos Alberto that he had got it wrong, that he had been deceived by a grotesque distortion of Owen's words." Williams described it as a sort of distortion – "an example of twisting or spinning, or 'twirling' in the latest euphemism designed to reduce its toxicity still further" – that is commonplace in English newspapers and is recognised as such by politicians and celebrities in the UK as well as by footballers and their managers. It is accepted as part of the game.

> But here was an outsider, ignorant of the arcane and highly specialised rules, taking it at face value. Who would expect Carlos Alberto to comprehend the circulation battle between the English newspapers, and their need for ever more hysterical stories and headlines to retain the attention of their readers?[18]

This was sports newspaper journalism in its least flattering light, but there have been instances where quotes have been changed to protect the reputation of the speaker. Bob Paisley, one of the greatest builders of British football teams, was not a natural orator and would frequently forget names. Journalists would listen to the Liverpool manager refer to "doings" in midfield or defence, and then hold a mini-conference among themselves afterwards to work out which player he was referring to. Had reporters quoted him verbatim, he would have been open to ridicule, and Paisley was happy with the unspoken contract between himself and reporters that allowed the latter to enhance his phraseology. Bobby Robson, the former England manager, was equally forgetful, but was revered in football circles partly because of his malapropisms, while one of the sadder sights in a post-match press conference was Malcolm Allison, a brilliant and innovative coach in the 1970s and 1980s, giving full vent as Bristol Rovers manager in the 1990s about two penalty claims that no one else in the room had seen. Maybe only a former professional footballer could have spotted the alleged infringements, but conversations afterwards with the players who had been on the pitch were not supportive of that theory. To their credit, not a single reporter that day quoted anything that would have suggested any of Allison's words had come from a befuddled mind.

Looking forward

To guess where you are going, it is helpful to chart your previous direction, and examining the 30 years of *The Independent* from cradle to print grave is informative. The first edition, 6 October 1986, comprised 32 pages, only four of which belonged to sport, three pages of reports and another carrying racing cards and results. Yet this was an expansion on the norm. Charlie Burgess, the newspaper's first sports editor, was tasked with filling three broadsheet pages in midweek and four on Saturday and Monday, and described it as a "daunting". He added: "You rarely saw big features or interviews, but suddenly we were regularly offering our readers big, 1,000-word pieces."

Soon the sports section expanded and by 2016 was offering three times as much sport in its printed editions than it was in 1986. This conforms to the pattern of expansion drawn earlier, but the content has also changed. The early editions of *The Independent* carried hockey reports every Saturday and Monday, and there were weekly columns on sailing, squash, rowing, judo, table tennis and fishing. There were reports from at least three of cricket's County Championship matches every day in the summer (weather permitting), and boxing was considered so important that Ken Jones would perform a round-by-round runner from even British title fights. Now many of these sports receive coverage only during Olympic and Commonwealth Games. Just like *The Independent*, coverage of "minor" sports has gone online so enthusiasts can find results and statistics from, for example, motorsport's world rally championship, as the events are taking place. Newspapers now follow the higher echelons of sport so that there will be three or four reports from England cricket Test matches while the County Championship is creeping slowly away from the printed page.

It is football that dominates. In 1986, *The Independent* could afford to ignore some First Division matches and not risk the wrath of its readers because other newspapers did the same. Imagine now if there was no report on Liverpool, Arsenal or Manchester United? The effigies of sports editors might not be burned, but the modern equivalent of masses surrounding newspaper offices with pitchforks and flaming torches would materialise via internet chatrooms. The turning point was the formation of the Premier League in 1992 and the realisation by Sky that football was more likely than anything else to win customers to its satellite broadcast system. If the public are prepared to pay around £40 a month for the full Sky Sports Package, then newspapers could hardly ignore the Premier League; every match is reported by every national newspaper, and the more important matches frequently generate several reports.[19] *The Times* had one journalist, Green, and one report on the 1976 FA Cup final; 50 years later the same newspaper had five reporters and a former referee writing about the match. And this for a competition that has declined in prestige since the advent of the European Champions League.

Television, paradoxically, has proved to be a twin-edged sword. While football's growth in financial and cultural worth has an undeniable link to pay-per-view broadcasting, other sports have taken the satellite shilling and suffered a decline in profile, a process that has, in turn, reduced the coverage in newspapers. Cricket is the classic case. It reached oxygen-requiring heights in terms of national consciousness when England defeated Australia to win the Ashes in 2005, yet a decade and a half on, even established players are not household names. Often the game goes unnoticed, a prime example being Yorkshire's Joe Root, an exception in terms of recognition, who failed to be listed as a contender for the BBC Sports Personality of the Year in 2015 despite scoring more than 2,000 runs at an average of 50-plus; in 1975, David Steele won the prize for scoring 250 runs in three Tests.

Context and the number of alternatives play their part in all awards, but other sports have noticed declines. Boxing has reduced in significance in terms of newspaper coverage, partly because the decision to eschew selling rights to free-to-air broadcasters has left its fighters out of sight and mind; speedway has virtually disappeared; interest in Formula One may be waning; and membership secretaries in golf clubhouses are nervously pondering the potential effects of golf's major championships moving from terrestrial television. Cricket and boxing have moved inwards from the back pages of newspapers; motor racing and golf may follow.

Horse-racing, meanwhile, is televised via a hybrid of free-to-air, satellite and internet broadcasters, and is showing mixed results. The National Hunt Festival at Cheltenham has grown to become a major fixture in the UK sports calendar, but while Lester Piggott and Willie Carson's fame stretched far beyond the turf, only Frankie Dettori could claim the same now. Racecards, too, a staple page-filler in newspapers of the 1980s and 1990s – *The Independent* carried four in its first edition – frequently simply do not appear. The big races are still there, but a dedicated punter often needs specialised publications to find out which horses are running in the 15.30 at Plumpton. Newman wrote that it took sports editors a long time to accept that racing merits limited space, his newspaper being the first to drop racecards. "We did so with great trepidation, but there was not much negative reaction from readers."[20]

Looking forward, newspapers no longer have their fate or their content in their own hands. Television has changed the nature of press reports and has an effect on the popularity of sports and their participants, swings in sentiment that the printed press has to follow. The next big thing might be bowls or rugby union, but it will be the broadcast coverage that decides it. Yet, just as newspapers have had to alter, so have TV broadcasters as the public have changed their viewing habits away from the traditional channels and onto the web via computers, tablets and phones.

That change is unstoppable, the only contention being the way the internet platform delivers the content. News as a print form will survive electronically, and it is a question of whether established brands such as the *Daily Mail* or specialist websites will provide that service.

There will be a market for intelligent, opinionated and entertaining reports about sport – the launch of the UK version of *The Athletic* in 2019 reinforced that – but the writer will live on with growing demands on his or her time, as Mark Barden examines within these pages in his chapter on multiplatform journalism. "Whether it is a story, blog post, tweet, or video clip, the reporters interviewed are being asked to produce much more content than they were even a decade ago."[21] The concept of a deadline is also disappearing. That used to mean "on the whistle" with a rewrite needed an hour after the game ended; now, sports reporters are always on deadline, always filing information. Equipment and communication have improved dramatically, and there is no reason to expect a slowing down of that impetus; technology has also meant that scores and results no longer have to be laboriously phoned to copy-takers, but can be sent automatically with the barest of human intervention. The reverse of this, however, is that it has cost the jobs of hundreds of freelance reporters, who used to rely on the small, but regular, fees that came from events that were important for newspapers to cover, but not significant enough to send a staff reporter.

There is also far more interaction between newspaper sports reporters and their consumers, a trend that will grow. When Green was working, his reports were largely a one-way process that only deviated when readers were engaged sufficiently to write, post and pay for the postage of a letter. It was the classic top-down model of communication that allowed very little leeway for a conversation. Now there is a very quick response via newspaper websites and social media. At their best, these sites can enhance the communication model between the correspondent and the readers, particularly Twitter, which not only allows the reporter to provide a service beyond the match report, but is now an indispensable reporting tool. Roberts and Emmons wrote:

> Because Twitter is particularly effective on the smaller screens of smartphones, sports journalists can provide news and information to fans attending events, where replays and updated information may be lacking, and fans can gather electronically during events and respond to sports events in real time.[22]

They also noted that sports journalists are providing statistics and performance information, and they engage with fans who query them or respond to observations. This is the ideal world. The internet has also given a near-anonymous platform to trolls, and even the interventions of moderators removing comments that infringe on the editorial guidelines of websites offer no protection when it comes to uncensored tweets. Swimmer Rebecca Adlington, an Olympic gold medallist in 2008, was accused of letting down Britain when she gained "only" a bronze four years later. "I couldn't get my head around why someone would go to the effort of looking someone up, and then sending them a nasty tweet. I still can't really," she said. "What's going on in those people's lives?"[23] If a woman who is a sporting inspiration can attract abuse, then reporters draw it like magnets. "I get death threats," Winter wrote, "but also marriage proposals."[24]

References

1. Andreas Whittam Smith, *The Independent*, 7 October 1986, p. 2.
2. Peter Preston, "Even proprietors are finding it hard to sell newspapers", *The Guardian*, 9 October 2016. https://www.theguardian.com/media/2016/oct/09/proprietors-find-it-hard-sell-newspapers-media-ownership, accessed 28 November 2019.

3. BBC, "Rio Olympics 2016: BBC achieves record television and digital audiences", 22 August 2016. http://www.bbc.co.uk/sport/olympics/37156975, accessed 28 November 2019.

4. Roy Greenslade, "The transfer season opens", *The Guardian*, 1 August 2005, Media Section, pp. 6–7.

5. Raymond Boyle, *Sports Journalism*, London, Sage, 2014, p. 50.

6. Guy Hodgson, "The changing face of sports journalism and its relationship with hard news" in Peter J. Anderson and Geoff Ward (eds), *The Future of Journalism in the Advanced Democracies*, Aldershot, UK, Ashgate, 2007, pp. 157–171.

7. Ben Glaze, "Becks leads sports stars with plea for UK not to go it alone", *Daily Mirror*, 22 June 2016, p. 4.

8. Jeremy Armstrong, "Jump and extra hurdle if you want to come to Rio", *Daily Mirror*, 22 June 2016, p. 17; "Up for another round, Jamie?", *Daily Mirror*, 22 June 2016, p. 18.

9. "For the sake of our great nation's future … We must not leave", *Daily Mirror*, 22 June 2016, pp. 2–3.

10. Ernest Phillips, *How to Become a Journalist. A Practical Guide to Newspaper Work*, London, Sampson Low, Marston, p. 83.

11. John Pendleton, *How to Succeed as a Journalist*, London, Grant Richards, 1902, pp. 48–49.

12. Cardus's style did not please everyone. In a memo his editor, WP Crozier described his writing as "too copious and luxuriant for my fancy" (*The Guardian* Archive, Crozier to Bone, 1942).

13. JA Brierley, "The sports writer and his job", *The Journalist*, 1929, p. 3.

14. John Macadam, *The Macadam Road*, London, Jarrolds, 1955, pp.130–131.

15. Ken Jones, "Brazil Sunday punch does it", *Daily Mirror*, 22 June 1970, p. 24.

16. Dave Kidd, "Ice, ice, bye-bye", *Daily Mirror*, 28 June 2016, pp. 50–51.

17. Paul Newman, "Thirty years of sport … and how reporting has evolved", *The Independent*, 26 March 2016, Sport section, pp. 10–11.

18. Richard Williams, "Twisted media culture to blame for Carlos Alberto's rant at Owen", *The Guardian*, 1 April 2005, www.theguardian.com/football/2005/apr/01/sport.comment2, accessed 28 November 2016.

19. Sky Sports, www.sky.com/shop/tv/sports?DCMP=bac-SS.com/GSS-na-BAU-Nav, accessed 29 October 2016.

20. Newman, "Thirty years of sport", p. 11.

21. Brian Mortiz, "The story versus the stream: digital media's influence on newspaper sports journalism", *International Journal of Sport Communication*, Volume 8, Issue 4, 2015, p. 403.

22. Chris Roberts and Betsy Emmons, "Twitter in the press box: how a new technology affects game-day routines of print-focused sports journalists", *International Journal of Sport Communication*, Volume 9, Issue 1, 2016, p. 100.

23. Alexandra Topping, "I still get abuse from Twitter trolls, says Olympic swimmer Rebecca Adlington", *The Guardian*, 6 June 2014, www.theguardian.com/media/2014/jun/06/twitter-trolls-abuse-olympic-swimmer-rebecca-adlington, accessed 28 November 2019.

24. News UK, www.news.co.uk/who-we-are/toptalent/henry-winter/, accessed 29 October 2016.

5
Tabloids

Rob Shepherd

It's not often an England football manager tells you to "F★k off out of the country". But that's what happened to me in November 1993 as the so-called "Tabloid War" was at its height in Fleet Street, the bullets were flying and the bombs exploding with ferocity. The back pages had become one of the main battlegrounds and the then England boss Graham Taylor had become the prime target. I was dragged into the crossfire by accident, although maybe on reflection, by design on his part.

In a pre-match conference ahead of England's decisive World Cup qualifier against Holland I had questioned Taylor's team selection and tactics, suggesting he was in danger of making the same mistakes that had seen England slump to defeat earlier in the year against Norway in Oslo, a resounding 2-0 defeat which had made the match in the Netherlands a game they could not lose if they were to qualify for the 1994 World Cup in the USA.

My questions, and "worried" demeanour were based on sound journalism. Tabloid journalism, where "the story" – telling readers something they did not know – was the goal, not just reporting the matches. That morning I had run an exclusive tale, based on contacts close to the England squad (two players I knew well who couldn't believe what Taylor was doing), naming the team that would play against the Dutch.

From a journalistic point of view, I was relieved that my back-page splash revealing the lineup, which had seemed a bit left-field, was confirmed as Taylor announced his team at the press conference. After all, I was merely the chief football writer of the now-defunct *Today*, a midmarket tabloid that did not have the bark or the bite of two tabloid "Red Tops", *The Sun* and *Daily Mirror*. These two rather vicious and at times vindictive papers often set the agenda, but on this occasion *Today*, still part of the circus, had. But this time the Red Tops had been "scooped".

Even when you are convinced a story is right, you may have been dropped a dummy by contacts or things can change even overnight, and you are left holding sackcloth and ashes. And often, even when you get a story spot-on, it can initially be knocked down or denied outright. Or if the source or information is wrong, despite your confidence, then you are made to look stupid, or worse, face legal action, even though many think all newspapers work under relatively strict laws under the notion of a "free press". This story was hardly Watergate, but at the time it was a big story as the nation awaited England's World Cup fate. In football that is big news.

There was a tense, almost bewildered atmosphere in the room as the press corps started to fire the questions at Taylor. Indeed, even some of the usually more measured broadsheet writers, often reluctant to stick out their necks on hard news, if not opinion, weighed in.

Why was Ian Wright, who was on fire for Arsenal at the time, not starting? How could he justify selecting Carlton Palmer and Lee Sharpe in odd roles against a technically gifted Dutch team?

But it was the confrontation I had with Taylor that became one of the "highlights" of what would become perhaps the best-ever fly-on-the-wall football documentary, initially aired on Channel Four, a year after my spat with Taylor, by which time he had resigned. *Graham Taylor: The Impossible Job* was subsequently reissued on DVD as *Do I Not Like That*, one of the many manic phrases that jumped off the screen in the hour-long doc. It went "feral" back then. In the digital age it remains a YouTube "hit". In a sports context it was a cross between Spinal Tap and Monty Python.

After an exchange of views, Taylor, who had spotted me shaking my head in dismay as he engaged with a couple of stunned journalists, then turned on me, went on a rant then sighed (and I paraphrase): "You might worry, Rob, but don't make the rest of us worry ... if you were one of my players with an attitude I'd tell you to f...k off out of the country ... rise yourself, man ... put a smile on your face, we are here for business."

I disengaged and did smile. The spat was then defused with nervous laughter. The confrontation made a bit of a stir on the day. I was grilled by Jimmy Hill on lunchtime radio, but it was all forgotten after the events of the following day; or so we thought.

You see, none of us in the "hack pack" who followed England at the time — in the pre-internet, pre-social media age there was a hard core of print, radio and TV correspondents which ranged between 10 and 50 depending on the size of the assignment, not the multimedia, TV-dominated circus that exists now — knew that a documentary was being filmed by a covert crew. But Taylor did.

Why on earth did he allow such access? I felt then — I still do — that it was an attempt to prove a point, that he was not "Taylor the Turnip", as he had been depicted on the front page of *The Sun* after England were humbled at the 1992 European Championship finals in Sweden. It was his fightback against the tabloid tsunami. At the time it backfired spectacularly. What he had hoped would be a monument to his coaching prowess became an epitaph to his career as England manager.

Eighteen months earlier, Taylor had been pilloried in *The Sun* by a morphed image of his head fused with a turnip. Why? It was on the back of one of the immortal tabloid headlines: "Swedes 2 Turnips 1". The simplicity was stunning. England's chaotic Euro '92 adventure had ended in abject failure when Taylor's team were eliminated in the final match of the group phase by hosts Sweden, who came from behind to win 2-1. After all, Taylor had inherited the nucleus of an England team from Bobby Robson — who had suffered plenty of tabloid flak but somehow managed to come through relatively unscathed (he was pilloried as a "plonker") — that had reached the semi-finals of the 1990 World Cup and only lost to West Germany on penalties. By comparison, England's tournament in Sweden had been a shambles, defined best by Taylor's ludicrous decision to take off Gary Lineker and replace him with Alan Smith as England chased the game. It might have seemed a bit crass, but "Swedes 2 Turnips 1" summed up the ire of the nation, if not the crass photoshopped image on the back page.

As the son of a provincial journalist, Taylor had thought he could cajole, or at least appease, the press with a combination of bravado and bonhomie. But this was England not Watford, where he had been so successful at turning pigs' ears into to silk purses in the late 1970s and 1980s, nor Aston Villa.

Shocked by the intensity and cruelty of the backlash, Taylor decided he needed to adopt a PR strategy. And so he agreed to allow a TV crew unprecedented access for a warts-and-all documentary. He felt this would be the way to get his revenge. It was a way to prove he was the best man to manage England. This way, he could be perceived as a Pied Piper leading England's merry men to the World Cup in the US. Not a man with the intellect of a root vegetable. And this was the way to turn the tables and make the media men, especially from the tabloids, look like melons.

Taylor also had an advantage. He knew the cameras were rolling. We didn't. Neither did the players, well, at least for a while, by which time they had allowed themselves to be filmed in some embarrassing scenes that made Taylor's England set-up look a bit like away days for Boy Scouts. This contributed to him "losing" some of the dressing room. But he hadn't accounted for the, er, turn-up.

After only drawing against Norway and Holland at Wembley, England's World Cup campaign was suddenly on the back foot. They were playing catch-up. Then, when England lost to Norway after Taylor had made disastrous tactical and team selections, it became do-or-die when England faced Holland in Rotterdam. Indeed, after that defeat in Oslo, the *Daily Mirror* had attempted to score points over *The Sun* with an even cruder back page of Taylor morphed into a dollop of horse droppings with the headline "Norse Manure".

But the shit had already hit the fan, so to speak. A few days prior to that game in Norway in the spring of 1993, England had chiselled out a scrappy 1-1 draw in Poland which had put the campaign back on track. Yet afterwards Taylor, on a mission to woo the papers, had called an impromptu meet with the written press in the team dressing room after the game. The players had left for the team bus to ferry them to the airport, but the kit was still strewn around. The heady smell of liniment was strong. But not as heated as Taylor's invective in a lobby-style briefing. Such huddles no longer happen in an age where most interaction with the media is stage-managed.

Seemingly to deflect any of his own failings, he heaped blame on the players. When we arrived at a hotel in Oslo that night, Wright, who had scored the late equaliser in Katowice, and Paul Ince saw me in the foyer, beckoned me over and asked what Taylor had said to the press. When I told them he had described them as "headless chickens" and that that would be the next day's headlines in most of the of the tabloid press, they were not happy, to say the least.

Neither was Paul Gascoigne a day later when, at a more formal press conference, Taylor made a coded speech about Gazza's "refuelling habits". All the tabloids had a field day speculating on what Taylor was really getting at – obvious with hindsight – and even the broadsheets were dragged into all the tabloid tittle-tattle.

In a couple of days Taylor, in an attempt to appease the press, had lost significant parts of the dressing room. With team spirit undermined, the side, forced into bizarre tactical and personnel changes, played like strangers in that pivotal 2-0 defeat by the Norwegians.

The heat was on, but spirits were raised in the autumn when England playing with – as Wright put it – "the bulldog spirit, man" (thanks for the headline), crushed Poland 3-0 at Wembley. But then to Rotterdam.

"The referee has got me the sack"

England didn't fall apart quite as they had done in Norway. Indeed, they had suffered some bad luck and questionable refereeing. Nevertheless, the images in the documentary of sending Wright on as a substitute, to chase what would be a 2-1 defeat, were poignant. Evidence that Taylor had lost the plot were enhanced with the comedic footage of him stalking the touchline and ranting at the referee and rowing with the fourth official. "The referee has got me the sack … thank him ever so much from me," said Taylor, who perhaps had the next day's headlines whizzing through his head. On that rant, his instincts were right, of course.

Despite a 7-1 win in San Marino a month later, that defeat meant England would not go to World Cup, and it was all put down to Taylor. All sorts of stories spilled out onto the back pages of the tabloids, on and off the record, and Taylor was forced to resign before he was pushed. He hadn't so much reached the end of a road as fallen off a cliff.

It took Taylor, who died too young at the age of 72 in 2017, some time to repair the damage, but he did revive his career at various clubs and, ironically, in the media, and it must be said that he was a thoroughly decent person and a true football man. Strange as it may seem, I retained a decent relationship with him because he did have some grasp, perhaps a naïve one, of the strange alchemy between the football world and the press. There was a mutual working respect between us and many other reporters on the circuit, but he did have a bitterness about the excesses of the Red Tops and in many respects with good reason.

When Taylor resigned, our headline at *Today* was "They think it's all over … it is now", an ironic play on Ken Wolstenholme's sign-off when Geoff Hurst completed his hat-trick to ensure England won the World Cup in 1966. But *The Sun*, still sticking the knife in, revived that morphed "Turnip head" image under the banner of "That's your Allotment" – this time on the front page.

Things have changed massively since then, of course. Thanks to the internet and social media, being a sportswriter involves far more heavy lifting than it did when I started out: more deadlines, more white space to fill. Editors, it scarce needs adding, are also under unprecedented pressure, and the increasingly overbearing influence of agents, media offices and lawyers dissuades risk-taking. It's extremely difficult to imagine even a tabloid newspaper doing to the current England manager what *The Sun* did to Taylor.

And because of that pressure, editors simply don't have time to read what they are supposedly authorising remotely as thoroughly as they would wish. Their authority is undermined, furthermore, by the power of the big-money writers, some of whom not only have a Twitter following larger than the paper's circulation but pull in salaries in excess of £400,000 – this at a time when there are very many proficient and able, albeit young, writers down the food chain earning £25,000 a year, and many excellent freelancers are lucky to pick up more than a plumber's half-day pay for covering a down-table Premier League game. The top dogs, furthermore, can insist on a clause in their contract whereby their work cannot be altered without their permission. Talk about fuelling egos. Libel writs are more likely in this upside-down world. Among the many issues – tabloids, midmarket titles and broadsheets address – this strikes me as one of the most pressing.

A pit bull with a bone

I worked for four tabloids – *Today*, *Daily Mail*, *The Express* and *News of the World* – but turned down several offers from *The Sun* and *The Daily Mirror* because I couldn't stomach the extremity of the daily onslaughts. Once they had it in for someone, usually England managers, it was like a pit bull with a bone.

Often it left their reporters in the field embarrassed, and sometimes angry, when their honest endeavours were embellished once the copy was back in the office at the hands of rottweilers on the sports and news desks who had no qualms about stretching a good story beyond its limits to get the spiciest, sometimes nastiest, headlines they could dream up, in the belief that by dumbing things down it would appeal to their target audience. One may reflect that such a technique became part of the strategy of the Trump election campaign in the US in 2016, then the Conservatives in the UK in 2019. But that's another story.

One editor I worked under regarded the sports department, thus upholding the cliché, as "the Toy Department". So it was often seen as open season for a "bit of fun", even if the outcome often wasn't very funny given the prevalence of sixth-form humour. Yet sport, especially football, had always sold tabloid newspapers. Their circulation demise has not just been down to the advent of digital and social media, but because they didn't take coverage of football seriously enough, while the broadsheets – I have also written for the *Sunday Times* – often took the game too seriously.

Perhaps the greatest British broadsheet sports scribe of the last 50 years or so was Hugh McIlvanney. Yet he always regarded himself as a reporter rather than a writer, even though he was revered as a wordsmith. Hughie, who passed away in 2019, didn't have much time for "luvvies", as he saw some of his broadsheet rivals, believing they wrote from ivory towers. He preferred to hunt with the tabloid "hack pack" and then at the end of the week in *The Observer* – and later the *Sunday Times* – added some authority to a subject with colourful but rarely complicated prose. He also had excellent contacts who helped underpin his erudite words.

When I started out in Fleet Street – as it still was at the start of the 1980s – the legendary boss of the sports reporting agency Hayters, Reg Hayter, imposed on me, as he had others before and after, some fundamentals beyond the "tell 'em what they don't know" ethic: "Contacts, Contacts, Contacts"; "Keep it simple, keep it snappy"; "Comment is free, fact is sacred"; "Whatever you do make sure you hit the bloody deadline". These adages informed my every move, and McIlvanney respected that. He had the power to opine as much as he wished but preferred to shore up his thoughts and theories by checking things out with those who could offer an inside track. He had the utmost respect for those of us who would break the story or crash out the nuts and bolts of a live event – as he could also do when required – on a daily basis to make sure the next day's back pages were filled.

Perhaps I can best illustrate this with two examples of what a tabloid football writer is about beyond the features and opinion columns that are also required.

The man who succeeded Graham Taylor as England manager was Terry Venables. I first met Terry when he was heading towards the sack as Barcelona manager in 1987. I interviewed El Tel, his tabloid moniker (as he had become known in Spain), on the eve of his dismissal, writing a story that he would return to England and take over at Tottenham, which he did. I then struck up a professional rapport based on trust and mutual respect with three key elements: "On the record", so he could be quoted about any given issue; "off the record", information given to write a story but no quotes (or "nannies" as we hacks called them; "nanny goats" is rhyming slang for quotes); and "off limits", information that could not be used until the time was right. The last category was, and still is, tricky, and I lost the scoop that he would be buying a then-stricken Spurs in 1991 with Alan Sugar, a story that was broken via sources from the other end, so to speak, and in a rival newspaper. But then sometimes it was better to let a story get away than ruin a relationship with a contact – as long as the office didn't know.

Then, during what would become the Venables–Sugar battle after their briefly friendly take-over of Tottenham, I became a conduit for stories to support Venables in what would become fodder for a daily tabloid battle. But the trust garnered meant I would eventually get the story that Venables, who by then had departed Spurs in acrimonious circumstances with Sugar, would accept the job to take over from Taylor as England boss.

Prior to Euro '96 I was given the heads-up to break the story that Venables would quit as England boss whatever the outcome of the tournament because the Football Association were stalling on a new contract. Obviously, to this day I can't reveal my sources on that "exclusive".

Secondly, to the 1999 Champions League final between Manchester United and Barcelona.

All night games require a "runner" – copy filed in stages and stacked up during the game to make sure the pages are set for the first editions with a short intro "on the whistle". This is so far-flung reaches of the UK, for sometimes ridiculous production and distribution purposes, actually get a copy of the paper because the rest of the paper is "put to bed" by 7 pm only to be updated if there is a huge breaking news story or the front page is holding back an exclusive.

With a few minutes left, United were trailing 1-0, the bulk of my copy had been sent and it was going to be another of those glorious failure reports, all too familiar for English football back then. Even George Best, one of United's guests of honour in the VIP box, had given up the ghost and left to make sure he was first at the bar for the post-match wake at the team hotel.

Then boom, Teddy Sheringham equalised. Then boom boom, Ole Gunnar Soljskaer steered in the winner. Everything I had written made no sense. The comment was redundant, the facts were sacred. Now it was "glory glory Man United". I rang the office and told them to spike all my original running copy. "Only if you can refile within 20 minutes before the presses roll," I was told.

It was then that I remembered something I had been told by one of the great tabloid football writers from the heydays of tabloid papers in the 1950s, '60s and '70s, before some of the gruesome excess of the '80s took over, back when I was a young messenger boy in the late '70s, before I had ever penned a word in print. In the days before the laptop there was something called a typewriter, and as a teenager, working for Hayters, I had the job of reading over running copy of various writers over landlines as they built their pieces bit by bit, ripping pages off the machine. On big nights I often used to do so for Frank McGhee of the *Daily Mirror* to ensure his words were on the desk on time. He once told me: "Son, if you want to get into this game, then report what you see, keep it simple, keep it sharp, make it as good as you can but most importantly make sure you getting the f…ing words over in time for the desk to hit presses. Hit the deadline. The subs [sub-editors] can sort out any mess and do the rest. They can't work with a blank sheet. You will get a bollocking for crap copy but you will be hung from the highest lamppost in Fleet Street if you don't file on time. And if you can't write it out then get on the blower and ad lib to the copytakers. Just get it over."

So that's what I did. I shut the lid of the laptop, picked up my somewhat primitive mobile and got hold of the quickest copytaker – touch typists and steeped in sport – the paper, the *Daily Express*, had. Sadly, that profession no longer exists. The tabloids are the poorer for losing the spontaneous, adrenaline-filled copy that paints the colourful context of an occasion that often TV still can't convey.

Within 15 minutes, and before the trophy had been lifted, I had sent over the required 1,200 words while some others around me were floundering to rework their reports and unable to make the press conference downstairs for the back-page splash.

When he came in to speak to the media, Manchester United manager Sir Alex Ferguson's first words were: "Football, Bloody Hell". "Fergie", who had a fierce and frank love–hate relationship with the press – especially the tabloids (like Venables, he knew, though, how to work the media when it suited, a skill Taylor had failed to grasp) – had delivered not only one of football's great stories but one of the most powerful tabloid back-page headlines.

Those were still the days when the tabloid stories and headlines, however extreme, were governed ultimately by what happened on the pitch. The main protagonists, the players, the managers, even the owners, can all write their own headlines. Still can. Despite what people think, success sells better than failure, which maybe is why when things go wrong the tabloids ramp things up to the extreme in order to attract attention.

For me the best part of the job was always the white-knuckle ride of reporting succinctly on big match days – 600–800-word reports could often suffice – where ultimately there are clear adjudicators of the headline: the result, then, either the hero or the villain. But there are plenty of non-match days – or there were back then before wall-to-wall TV coverage – to fill the back pages.

Over the years there were inevitably highs and lows. It goes with the territory of a career on a rollercoaster. In that respect, many of the emotions mirrored those of the players and bosses.

I guess that's why strong bonds and confidences existed – when the men in muddy boots empathised to a degree with the men with inky fingers. An age before the game in all aspects became more cosmopolitan, certainly before the players became multimillion-pound brands, when even if a tabloid hack could cut to the bone one day he could be a confidante the next, a conduit to get a player's perspective across in print or even the catalyst for a transfer before the rise of the powerbroker agent.

I'm often still asked by those intrigued by the strange machinations between the tabloid press and players – what is the story I'm most proud of and the one which embarrasses the most? Some of my colleagues were quick to acclaim the obituary I wrote – ad-libbed off the top of my head to make the edition – when the news broke of Bobby Moore's death in February 1993. A scathing column I wrote comparing Sven-Göran Eriksson to Peter Sellers' Chauncey Gardiner in the film *Being There* as it became clear – although not soon enough to a commercially blinded Football Association – that he was wasting England's Golden Generation of players, gave me a strange sense of satisfaction but also angst-ridden frustration.

But from a pure story point of view it was that genuine exclusive (a tagline too often used cheaply and erroneously in tabloids) that Terry Venables would quit as England boss, accompanied by chapter and verse quotes plus follow-ups. It was a bolt from the blue not only to newspaper rivals, but also his employers at the FA. In tabloid terms pretty high on the Richter Scale, then.

And the most embarrassing? Well, pretty early in my career I was duped by one of the fore-runner super agents, Eric Hall. I was still cutting my teeth working for the aforementioned agency Hayters, but by then was being "farmed out" on a regular basis to the *News of the World*. It was 1984 (was this a sign of things to come?) and "The Screws" was then at the height of its powers before it descended into a sleazy sewer. That too is another story.

For so many – it had a circulation back then of over four million – it was the go-to paper for football. Even those who didn't like the "kiss 'n' tell" stories and showbiz schmaltz at the front end of the book "took" the *NOW* alongside the *Sunday Times* or even *The Observer*. A *NOW* back page was a really big thing and had to pass the demanding litmus test of one of the great sports editors, the late Bill Bateson. But it was Bill who took me under his wing, who asked me to speak to Hall because he had been in touch with office promising a "Monster, Monster" story. Eric, who had moved from the music business into football, loved that self-coined phrase.

So the exclusive story Eric landed in my lap was that Luton's young striker Paul Walsh would be joining Real Madrid for the considerable fee of £400,000 the following week. Bang: the back-page splash. A "world exclusive" with all the trimmings. Hall was Walsh's agent. It was from the horse's mouth. Or so it seemed. Two days later I might as well have had a horse's head in my bed when I awoke to find out that Walsh had joined Liverpool for £440,000 and on bigger wages than my first real scoop. It could have been game over. But Bill knew the background and the game.

For all their faults as far as people in the game were concerned, tabloids can often help their own agendas. Bill just adopted the "chip paper" theory and helped guide me into my career as a fully fledged reporter. But it was a lesson learned along the lines of *Timeo Danaos et dona ferentes* – beware Greeks bearing gifts.

Before he opened the floodgates to fully fledged showbiz-style agents into the game, Eric had worked with Frank Sinatra and Elton John, as well as plugging "Bohemian Rhapsody" when an A & R man, and still has a laugh about that one when we talk from time to time. And, to be fair, he made it up to me over the years with some priceless information without asking for the usual "buy-up fee" that tabloids often splashed out to agents and players to secure a scoop.

The players and agents no longer need such financial incentives, another change in dynamic of the tabloids' power in the football world and a further aspect of the demise in circulation.

But the story that still haunts me is one which was run on the back of the *Daily Mail* in the mid-1990s under the headline "Wright: Pleat is a Pervert".

After a game where the Arsenal striker Ian Wright had pulled the dreadlocks of Sheffield Wednesday winger Regi Blinker, captured on camera by one of the "Smudgers" (sports photographers – they called us hacks "Blunts", as in, not very sharp pencils), Pleat, then Wednesday manager, castigated Wright.

A few days later, after a flight back from a European tie in Austria, Wright was happy to talk with four of us tabloid hacks at the carousel at Luton airport in the early hours. He was incandescent at Pleat's comment and went on a rant about aspects of Pleat's life that had led to his dismissal as Tottenham manager in the late 1980s.

Now a top media pundit, Wright's comments on tape were volunteered and clear. Indeed, at the end of the interview, he said: "And I want you guys to print that." As it turned out, even the sports and news desks of *The Sun*, *The Daily Mirror* and *Daily Star* decided not to. But the *Daily Mail*, on reflection starting to change direction under its relatively new editor Paul Dacre, decided the story and headline were justified.

In the cold light of day, the headline the following morning looked awful. Wright was soon on the phone to me ranting and raving. So was his agent.

I felt terrible, not least because I had known Wright from his Crystal Palace days and even been round to his house for a party. That's how much he trusted me. But now we had fallen out big time. We made up a few years later, and when I bump into him from to time we laugh about it along the lines of "It's only a game."

Sometimes that philosophy is the only way a tabloid football writer, just as much as a footballer, can stay sane in the rat race that is print circulation or soccer success.

Steve Curry RIP[1]

Steve Curry could have been a Shakespearian actor. He often recited soliloquies and speeches from Henry V to Macbeth – via *Coronation Street* – word-perfect and with a pitch that would have satisfied Richard Burton from erudite lips poised above a Kirk Douglas chin. There was a bit of Falstaff about Steve, although his joie de vivre and self-effacing humour sometimes resembled a lovable pantomime dame.

Growing up in Clitheroe, Lancashire, the son of a schoolmaster, the world revolved around the working man's theatre – football. Steve was good at it. He made it to Bolton reserves, but a broken leg brought that career path to an end. As it turned out, the initial pain opened a colourful highway to the printed heights of what was then known as The People's Game.

The pen rather than muddy boots became Steve's sword.

Treading the boards, he rose through the old school ranks of local papers, made it to the sports desk of the *Daily Express*'s then-thriving Manchester office, then on to Fleet Street, where the shackles of being a sub-editor were fully taken off and Steve was able display his considerable all-round skills as a chief football writer and reporter, most notably for the *Express*, over three decades, in the days when it was the "go-to paper" for British sport.

Steve was also proud of his "elder statesman stints" with the *Sunday Telegraph, Sunday Times* and *Daily Mail*. He also became a highly opinionated and recognisable pundit on Sky and TalkSPORT. He was one of the best in the business. It was football writers like Steve, Jeff Powell and Alex Montgomery who inspired me to have a shot at being a soccer scribe.

Over the years, Steve and I became particularly close despite the 20-year age gap. He was like a favourite, sometimes fussy, uncle to me. There are so many stories about him on and off the pitch. It's fair to say he was what is now termed "old-school; worked hard, played hard. After the copy had been filed, he was a wonderfully convivial social animal. A favoured phrase of Steve's to a waiter at dinner tables around the world, after the job had been done, was, "Pour till you get tired."

Steve smelled the game as well as the vino. Aside from his considerable football writing skills, knowledge and thespian attributes, Steve could also sing well, especially on the back of a bus transporting the "troops" from the stadium on the way to an airport in the early hours after England and club games in a far-flung places. He could do a really decent Elvis or Sinatra, but his forte was Dean Martin's "Little Old Wine Drinker Me".

He was a fine wordsmith, top-notch reporter and, as a consequence of his gregarious character, a first-rate contacts man when contacts rather than computers were regarded as prime tools of the trade for pressman. A mighty Colossus.

Steve knew the great, the good and even the bad and the ugly. If they weren't around a dinner table or a bar, where Steve was a terrific storyteller and raconteur – a Bard of Banter if you like – they were only a telephone call away.

If one vignette sums Steve up then it was during the 1990 World Cup. The day after England had drawn 0-0 with Holland – a game that changed not only the direction of Italia '90 for England but the future of English football – Bobby Robson, a firm friend of Steve's, had given the players a "day off". Some had joined Aston Villa chairman Doug Ellis and Tranmere owner Peter Johnson for a party on a yacht which was anchored just off the Forte Village in Sardinia, where most of the English press corps were camped. These were the days the press had better accommodation than the players, so another section of the squad decided to partake of the facilities of the Forte Village.

I was walking from my bungalow on the way to the beach having filed several follow-ups when I stumbled upon a small group huddled in one of the snug bars. Sitting there knocking back a few beers were the injured Bryan Robson, Terry Butcher, Chris Waddle and, lose of course, Steve Curry alongside his main running mate of the time, Colin Gibson – Gibbo – of the *Telegraph*. Steve summoned me to join the company.

Talk about being in the company of giants. But of course it was Steve who was holding court, despite the fact the "Gang of Three" players were explaining, with the use of beer mats and pepper pots, how they had persuaded Bobby Robson to change tactics and adopt a sweeper system in order the get the best out of Paul Gascoigne, who eventually turned up dripping wet, having swum to shore from the boat party.

It was all off the record, of course – especially after Gazza seconded a bike, then went "missing" for a few hours (now that's another story) – but the players were happy for that story to be run as long as they were not quoted and it was portrayed more as a revolution than a revolt. And we kept quiet about Gazza. It made the back page "exclusive" splash the next day for those of us in the circle. It's how it worked back then and Steve, with certain other doyens of that era, had long been a master of that form of journalism.

In 2019, shortly after Steve's beloved son Mike – who became a TV producer for Sky Sports – rang me to tell me of Steve's death, I rang Bryan Robson – or Robbo, as he was happy for us to call him – albeit only once some tears had subsided.

Now while Steve was weaned on the Busby Babes and often cited Duncan Edwards as his hero – Tom Finney too – he adored Bryan Robson, aka Captain Marvel. Bryan was genuinely shocked and saddened. "Steve was one of the great troopers," he told me. "Aye, there were ups and downs between us players and the press boys back in those days but with Steve, along with some others, we knew he was passionate, genuine and honest. There was respect. So sorry to hear: I'll ring and tell gaffer." The gaffer, of course, being Alex Ferguson.

"Fergie told me" was one of Steve's many memorable phrases, up there with "Now let me tell you," or, "By the way." Steve had a great working relationship with Sir Alex, as he did with so many players and managers down the years – Moore, Best, Law, Ramsey, Robson (both Bryan and Bobby) all the way through to Lineker and Beckham.

Peter Reid was another. After speaking to Robbo, I rang Reidy to inform him of Steve's death. "Gutted to hear that, pal", he said. "I knew Steve since I was a baby. Aye, he never tired of telling me of his Bolton days as a player. He was one of the good guys. Great lad, him." Sam Allerdyce and Harry Redknapp expressed similar sentiments.

On the Sunday before he died, Steve watched his beloved Manchester United beat Chelsea 4-0 on the opening day of the new season at his local cricket club in Weybridge, Surrey. There was, of course, chardonnay on hand and an audience eager to hear Steve's opinions and anecdotes. A few hours later he suffered a massive neurological trauma, and after being rushed to hospital soon passed away peacefully. In a sense this lovely, generous man, who was proud of his roots, not ashamed to admit he went to school in clogs, died with his boots on.

For so many in and round the football and media world, he will be sorely missed but never forgotten. It was Ken Bates, the former Chelsea and Leeds United chairman, who perhaps summed up it best when I broke the news to him while he was having dinner in Monaco with his wife Susannah – both great friends of Steve and his partner Carol. Ken said: "So sad, upset, but I'll tell you this, the world was a better place for Steve moving through it."

Conclusion

It's often said by those who run tabloids, when defending their excesses in news, politics, showbiz and sport, that they are merely serving up what the readers want. Or to quote Paul Weller, "The public gets what the public wants." Having spent over 30 years in the game, I'm not convinced. Judging by the slump in sales, neither are many readers.

Then again, perhaps the public are. They have just gone underground, lapping up vast chunks of unregulated tabloid bytes of football reports, stories and rumours online with constant TV action and YouTube footage to go alongside. And it's often free. Plus, reporters no longer have the unique access to the players and managers they once had. Back in the day, despite the friction, the reporters would often speak on a regular basis to the protagonists on the phone, or even socialise with them. Such relationships helped me get the story that lit the blue touchpaper with Taylor. Now, in a more sanitised world, they are cocooned by a raft of agents and advisers. Many tabloid reporters simply rely on Twitter and other social media, thus losing what is now termed the "USP" – the unique selling-point – or, in old money, an exclusive.

Maybe, then, that Taylor documentary was a tipping-point, a moment when the tabloid excesses were portrayed as rather grotesque, the moment when Video Killed the Tabloid Star.

Note

1. This section is a revised version of a tribute to Steve Curry originally published by the Football Writers' Association on 16 February 2019.

6

Agencies

John Mehaffey

Roger Kahn, author of the 1972 baseball classic *The Boys of Summer* retained throughout a long and distinguished career the lessons he absorbed while writing American college football reports for the Associated Press (AP) at the weekend during his apprentice days at the *New York Herald Tribune* in the early 1950s. The AP is one of three major international news agencies, along with Thomson Reuters and Agence France-Presse (AFP), which supply a constant stream of news stories from all parts of the globe, including politics, finance and sport, to their clients throughout the world.

"The essentials of Associated Press dispatches are speed, simplicity and artless, necessary organisation," Kahn wrote. "Each story is transmitted to hundreds of newspapers. A few may print all. Most carry a fragment. The same AP dispatch that runs 150 words in the *Philadelphia Bulletin* may run 75 words in the *Camden Courier-Post* and 50 words in the *Hartford Times*. Readers of each newspaper are equally entitled to coherence. These conditions require a story to begin with the names of the teams, an indication of the sport in question, a mention of the final score and, if possible, the winning play. One devotes succeeding paragraphs to significant moments, in the order of their importance and, when space is so tight that real description is impossible, pertinent statistics."

"The AP considers that it has beaten rival news services when its dispatch is used, and experience indicates that on a busy Saturday of college football, sports departments select the first story that arrives, regardless of merit."

Kahn was instructed to file his story no more than 15 minutes after the final whistle. "John Keats is said to have written 'I stood tiptoe upon a hill' in 20 minutes. He and Leigh Hunt were holding a sonnet-writing race, which Keats won both in elapsed time and in lyricism. There was no prohibition against lyric writing at the Associated Press. If in 15 minutes a man was able to compress the facts of a football game *and* compose lyrically, he was welcome to go ahead."

"At the AP you learned formula and developed speed. The first is antithetic to creative writing and the second is largely irrelevant, but both are critical to the confidence of every newspaperman. There is never a working day when the guillotine of deadline does not hang above one's neck. It is a comfort beyond prayer to realise when sweeter muses are struck dumb one can always write a variation of AP Formula One, 'A fourth quarter scoring pass from Chris Kartalis to Whitey Drown' and neither win a prize or utterly fail."[1]

A generation earlier, Paul Gallico, who covered sport for the *New York Daily News* before quitting to write short stories and novels, filed under similar pressures in a fiercely competitive New York newspaper world. At the big fights, which would stop the nation during the 1920s and '30s, Gallico typed his copy round-by-round and passed it to a teletype operator who transmitted it to his newspaper's office where it was set in type as the fight progressed. He would then file an instant story, as soon as the referee had announced the winner, praying that the score he had written at the end of each take - to indicate to the sub-editors how he thought the fight was progressing, allow them to prepare a headline in advance and get the presses rumbling, before their competitors had accurately predicted the result.

"Tell what happened in that first paragraph and tell it quickly – who won, the time, the round, the fatal punch, the crowd, the gate – and get emotional and literary afterwards. Tell the yarn dramatically if you can and make it live but above all *tell* it and feed those machines. You cannot sell papers that aren't on the street even if you are Bernard Shaw, Ring Lardner and Tolstoy all rolled into one."[2]

The media world has changed out of all recognition since Kahn and Gallico learned their trade. But speed, accuracy and coherence remain essential to Thomson Reuters, the AP and AFP, plus the national news agencies and the specialist sports agencies such as Sportsbeat in Britain and Sport-Informations-Dienst (SID) in Germany.

Steve Wilson held the post of International Sports Editor at the AP, responsible for all sports coverage outside the United States, for a quarter of a century before quitting at the end of 2016 to pursue other interests. "Accuracy was drilled into me from day one," said Wilson. "Being first and fast was important, but not at the expense of being wrong. There was also an emphasis on clarity, brevity and concise writing. Purple prose was frowned upon. The other thing was being fair and balanced, giving both sides of the story. That was part of the ethos, being fair and balanced and impartial."[3]

Olaf Brockmann, born in East Germany and brought up in the West, worked at SID as a schoolboy. He joined the agency full-time in Duesseldorf in 1972 at the age of 18 in time to help cover the 1972 Munich Olympics. Subsequently, Brockmann has attended every summer Olympics, apart from the 1976 Montreal Games, as well as every outdoor and indoor World Athletics Championships. Also a specialist in swimming and table tennis, he has reported on sports from 84 countries. "The main goal was to get the information to the clients as quickly as possible," he said. "I was told to put all the information in the first paragraph: Who? Where? When? What? And from the beginning I was told to separate news from comment."[4]

At Thomson Reuters, the style guide recommends, "short and direct words phrases and sentences rather than long ones", not least because the wire is translated into several languages.[5] The final point is stressed in the sport style guide written by the late Steve Parry, the agency's sports editor from 1982 to 2000. "Colour and informed interpretation are essential ingredients in the well-written sports report. Sports writing seeks more frequently than general news to entertain as well as inform the reader. In the context of sports writing, colour, authority and interpretation can usually be linked to two basic requirements – a reasonable grasp of the technicalities of the sport and adequate background knowledge of the people involved. Correspondents attempting to bring colour and flair to descriptive sports reporting must be aware of using terms or phrases which will not translate easily into other languages."[6]

Mike Collett, who worked as a staffer for United Press International (UPI) and Thomson Reuters as well as covering the summer Olympics and the Commonwealth Games for AFP and the AP respectively as a freelance joined UPI's London desk in 1980 after a year on the Press Association's (PA) news desk. "The requirements were very clearly laid out. You had to report the facts in a manner that was of relevance to a news agency, the copy had to be clear and clean, quick, accurate. There was a real urgency to make sure it was accurate, make sure it was right, get it out quick."[7]

David Clough works on the PA's racing desk after travelling the world covering the England cricket side. He joined the PA from the *Portsmouth Evening News*. "Not much changed in terms of the writing style. I've got quite a simple way of going about things, fairly basic, which is what agencies want. The time element was similar in that we used to have a pink sports newspaper on a Saturday afternoon down in Portsmouth and that was obviously quite full on. You're always on deadline in an agency so it's kind of like having Saturdays all week."

Filing by phone

When Wilson started at the AP in 1979, reporters still filed their stories over the telephone. One of his early chores was to guard the agency's phone at the finish of the Boston marathon when the reporters poured off the bus which had been following the runners to file their stories, which they had been scribbling in notebooks during the race. The procedure was similar in each of the international agencies, with reporters either typing their stories and handing them to telex operators or phoning them to copytakers.

Wilson recalls sitting next to the AP sportswriter while he was dictating his story to the Boston office. "I would sit and listen to him in silence. It was wonderful as he did this. He could watch the game and pick up the phone and dictate a perfect story off the top of his head. As baseball can change in the last innings he would say 'Okay' and start over without taking a note. I would watch and observe and he would barely talk to me but I knew what I would do. I would go down to the locker room at the end of the seventh inning, the game would end and I would go in with the rest of the journalists and get the quotes from the manager and the players. I would come back and give him my notes and quotes and he would use them in his follow-up stories."

Jon Henderson, who covered England cricket tours for Thomson Reuters in the 1970s and ran the agency's Wimbledon operation throughout the '70s and '80s, said the telex machine "was king on overseas assignments". "The memories from India on the 1972–1973 and 1976–1977 tours: taking a motor rickshaw from the ground in Ahmedabad to our hotel, where there was one of the only telexes in town, at lunch, tea and close, punching out scores and leads myself on perforated tape, feeding the tape through the telex and then returning to the ground where the next session of play was almost over, walking down the main street in Gauhati in Assam the day before the match there started in desperate search of a business that had a telex, which I eventually found

"And then the Test match in Calcutta where the dilatory Indian telex operator responded to my telling him that my copy had to be in London in five minutes by musing: 'What is five minutes against eternity?'

"For most of the 1970s, the Wimbledon copy was filed from a small office, totally isolated from the rest of the media, under the slope of the old number one stand. We telephoned our copy through to copytakers in the head office. In those days at major events such as World Cups and Olympic Games, Reuters made a fair bit of money as a communications hub used by numerous newspaper and magazine journalists."[8]

For the first part of Wilson's career, the AP, a co-operative of US newspapers and broadcasters, was engaged in a fierce domestic battle with UPI, founded by newspaper publisher Edwards Willis Scripps in 1907. "My focus was always on beating UPI. I can remember at events, running to the phone to try to beat the UPI guy. That was the culture of the time. It was a major rival and we were out to beat each other," said Wilson. "Eventually UPI died out, but when I was there it was still a big, big thing."

Collett retains vivid memories of his UPI days after joining the scrappy outsiders who had taken on the might of the AP establishment and established an enduring reputation on 22 November 1963, when White House reporter Merriman Smith grabbed the sole mobile radio telephone in the press limousine after hearing gunshots while following President John Kennedy's motor cavalcade in Dallas. Smith held on to the phone to dictate his first bulletins while his AP rival tried vainly to wrestle it from his grasp.[9]

"It was my first full-time sports job but I didn't know a lot about UPI, apart from the fact that they got the scoop on President Kennedy's assassination, because I like newspaper and journalism history," Collett said. "I knew the story of Merriman Smith. I think the most interesting thing looking back was that I was totally unaware that UPI was nearly going bust and in real financial trouble. But it has to be said that none of those problems ever stopped us working at events, travelling to the continent and staying in some of the finest hotels you could possibly stay and travelling first-class.

"It was drummed into you from day one that UPI was smaller than the AP and Reuters and that UPI were the outlaws of the big three. AFP didn't come into the reckoning because they were French. AP and Reuters were seen very much as the opposition and my brief at UPI was to write different, more colourful copy to differentiate from what was perceived at the time to be straight up-and-down agency journalism of both the AP and Reuters."

Brockmann's initial brief was to serve 120 West German newspapers plus radio and television stations, exchange news with international news agencies and supply copy to some international newspapers. "Our first demand was for reports and results plus features and commentaries. The main demand from the clients was to receive the information as quickly as possible. Of course, we had to give the results of top German athletes and, sometimes, there was a special request from local newspapers to receive results of their local heroes. If possible, we fulfilled this request. And often local newspapers asked us to get a contact number for where their local heroes were staying."

Wilson took up his post as AP international sports editor in London in 1991 after stints on general news in India and Italy. "Reuters internationally was regarded as the big rival in news. In sports it was more widespread: there was Reuters, still UPI and, of course, AFP. My brief when I started was to cover the Olympics and the International Olympic Committee (IOC). I sat on the IOC press committee, there was a representative from all the agencies.

"The US bosses wanted Wimbledon, they loved Wimbledon. Wimbledon resonates in America like very few other sports. The big things they wanted was anything about the Olympics, anything to do about Wimbledon, the British Open golf, the Ryder Cup, any US angle, a US basketball player making a splash in Italy, and of course any US teams playing overseas."

Ed Osmond, who now works for Thomson Reuters, was one of a trio asked to set up a European sports desk for the US financial data news agency, Bloomberg, in 1994 to supplement an American desk in Princeton. "Tennis was big and the Americans loved Wimbledon so they were always happy for us to go down to Wimbledon. They loved the stories about strawberries and cream and all that kind of stuff.

"Football, or soccer as we had to call it, was king. But we had a hell of a job persuading the powers that be that cricket merited serious coverage. We had to explain a lot of terminology so lbw [leg before wicket] would be seen by one of the American chiefs in New York who would ring me up and say 'What is lbw? I don't know lbw.'

"Clearly most people reading a report would know lbw but we had to put 'lbw, stands for leg before wicket, which means the ball hits the batsman's pads and would have gone to hit the wicket'. It makes the copy somewhat clumsy and hard to read but it is difficult to explain that to an American editor. We gradually wore them down, we did manage to convince them that we didn't have to do it every time, but it was a battle and one that we weren't going to win completely.

"We were not allowed to use many adjectives and were very stringently watched by the powers that be in New York. So it became kind of a running battle to how far we could push it in terms of trying to write stories in a way that sports fans want to read them rather than this very rigid Bloomberg style. Having said that, it was a very good grounding for me and I learned a lot of things about good writing; a lot of the Bloomberg rules I've kept with me throughout the rest of my career. Show, don't tell, nut grafs (an American term for a paragraph near the top of a story telling the reader why the story matters), not just giving a straight list of quotes but trying to add value and your expertise and experience. Bloomberg stopped covering sport about four years ago when they decided they couldn't compete with the AP."[10]

Bizarrely, cricket is one of the strengths of the AFP sports file as Guy Jackson, editor of the French's agency's English language sports file, explains. "AFP is a slightly unusual beast in that it is the main domestic agency for France. It's the Press Association for France and it has an international operation alongside it. The French sports service's first market is the French regional daily papers. The English service's main thrust is Asia for general news and sports and our biggest clients are in Japan. The main clients are MSN and Yahoo. Yahoo with all their regional variants: Singapore Yahoo, Asia Yahoo, Australia Yahoo.

"I think it's an irony and a fantastic quirk of sports agency journalism that Agence France-Presse, in a country where cricket is considered an oddity, has a worldwide reputation for cricket coverage. If that isn't a perfect illustration of sports agency journalism's strangeness, I think that's the biggest one. We are part state-funded, we are the French national news agency and yet the sports side is why we are well known in India and Pakistan."[11]

Team play at big events

Kahn's "artless, necessary organisation" remains essential to news agency sports journalism, and the bigger the event, the more necessary it becomes. A World Cup football final or the 100 metres finals at the summer Olympics, events staffed by more than 100 people, including journalists, photographers and technicians at the three big agencies, are cases in point.

At Thomson Reuters a sub-editor in the media centre will transmit a snap (one line in capital letters) giving the result of the football or the winner of the race. The first will be followed by an immediate update with the scorers and the second with the names of the top three and their times. By this time the reporter in the stadium will have had sufficient time to file a self-contained four- to six-paragraph story which will be updated with extra details, colour and quotes – first from the television, then from the mixed zone where journalists can speak to the athletes after their events and, finally, from the formal media conference. Other reporters will contribute sidebars from the media conference and there will be "factboxes" giving extra information, such as all the previous World Cup champions or 100-metres gold medallists.

Day-to-day agency sports writing is less frantic but no less demanding. It is commonplace in the business that agency journalists are first to arrive at the event and the last to leave, as Clough recalls of a typical day at a cricket Test.

Clough would arrive 90 minutes before the start of play on the first day and make sure the communications were working. "We used to have two people cover every home Test but over the past 10 years that has pretty much disappeared, it's a one-man job but we are more or less doing what two men used to do. On day one, toss copy, copy after maybe half an hour of play, the lead at lunch time with the latest state of play, maybe a few running pages if something ridiculous happens like a hat-trick or what have you, just file immediately. The same thing through the afternoon, the night lead report (for evening papers) to go. It probably wouldn't matter if it was 10 minutes after the close of play but if you left it 10 minutes after play you've missed the press conference. So realistically it has to go after they walk off, which can be quite a test because obviously you're trying to write for all sorts of different people.

"It's needed immediately by some people, outlets who will only take the top two or three paragraphs anyway. Some of them might be audio, they just want you as a cue. On the other hand, it will be printed in regional morning papers the next day. So sometimes it can be quite tricky to get your thoughts together and put the day into sort of perspective, literally as they're walking off the field, especially if something has just happened off the last ball of play, literally – Alastair Cook out off the last ball, you need to change what you are writing about. There's that, then dash to the press conference.

"Usually it's not written down but the agency tends to get the press conference rolling, or that used to be my job, so you can ask some pretty lame question to start with, then get a couple more in then let the press conference develop. Get back, write up the quotes night lead, which is a separate piece, it has to stand alone. Some customers will only use that and won't use the match report so all the elements that you thought you put in the math report need to be referred to. And then we have a thing called an 0430, which is more or less rewriting the copy that you have just written as a night lead, subbing it down and just kind of taking it on to the next day, taking a slightly different angle on it. That's before Twitter started, which never finishes, but in the old days that would be the end of the day around eight o'clock.

"The quotes piece will just be someone's take, someone who was directly involved at the press conference, their take on the day. So whereas the papers will often write a second piece which will be themed and will be on a particular player, what he's done that day, my piece won't quite be like that unless someone has had an utterly exceptional day, it will be just someone's take on the day's play. Of course they could be reflecting on their own performance beyond everything else if they've done particularly well."

Clough has straddled the generations who started their careers filing match reports and sports news stories from laptops to newspapers and radio and television stations when there were only a handful of news feeds, and the information explosion since the advent of the internet. Sport is now a vastly lucrative business with an increasingly crowded calendar since the IOC finally decided, in 1988, to allow professionals to the summer and winter Olympics, and today every agency is struggling to adjust to the flood of information available from a bewildering number of sources and transmitted to a variety of platforms.

Thomson Reuters sports editor Ossian Shine says the agency's newspaper clients, the traditional base of the news, finance and sports wire, also now have different demands. "Even those big print customers are themselves gambling their future on multimedia," Shine said. "Because we are, in theory, all things to all men there is a market, that does require a standard match report. At the same time we've got customers who don't want a match report because their view is anyone who cares about have either watched it or followed it closely on any other digital or social platform. Our first story in some respects is almost the next day story. There's an assumption that today's new is old news. The news cycle has massively overtaken everyone in terms of what we're chasing and we're now looking at the next day's story or the story after that. At Reuters, because we've got such a broad spectrum of customers and so many of them, we still have to cater for both. The question is finding a way of doing the basic match reports, but still allowing ourselves enough space to throw the story forward."[12]

Jackson concurs. "We're trying to move to a shorter match report and a separate story complementing it. We are thinking of people seeing it on a mobile phone, shorter stories, in theory, shorter headlines. My 16-year-old son has seen virtually every bit of sports news that I might cover, certainly in football. He's seen it if not before me than a minute or two after on Instagram or one of these websites. I don't know where these people even are. Everyone in the world sees a World Cup rugby final. The added value is the quotes after it and, more and more, the controversial episode.

"Now we're doing multimedia, we can put photographs into the story now. When we do a story we can choose where that story goes. So you've got the classic wire clients who get the text of the wire and get the photographs on the photo wire, and increasingly we got what we call multimedia clients – we send a story and the photographs and graphics are in the story. So you are clicking on a story and you've got a photo slideshow or graphics, whatever.

"We can influence where those multimedia stories go. I would say the overall rule in the English service of AFP is that everything goes to everywhere. We are finding that sports news in Africa, because of the Asian-Chinese investment in Africa now, there is cross-fertilisation because of Chinese interest in Asia. The English sports service is commercially important in Asia because, you won't be surprised to learn, of English Premier League football. Premier League football is very much the big product for Asian clients. And we've got clients in South Africa as well. The sports editor at the *Strait Times* was asked, 'What are your five priorities sports-wise?' And he said: 'Premier League, Premier League, Premier League, Premier League and Premier League'."

Clough experienced the changes first hand with the arrival of Twitter when a single tweet from the controversial cricketer Kevin Pietersen instantly became the story. "It's not just reacting to social media posts, but generating them. If I were to go an England practice day and not send a quick video of whoever England's current injury victim is, either non-netting or netting, they would say, 'you're not doing your job anymore'. Point the phone, try to get it in frame, hope nobody swears when you are doing then tweet it. If we need it branded with the PA logo it's another 10 or 15 steps. It's all time not watching what you should be watching or speaking to whom you should be speaking and finding out the real story, but on the other hand it's priorities isn't it?

"If you go racing, if we don't have a staff photographer, it's absolutely critical that after a race has finished I get myself down to the winner's enclosure as quick as possible to get a picture of the jockey coming in on the horse, tweet that or send that to the office. You get the quotes and then, just literally, send the quotes to the office. Quite often I'll find I don't write the copy on the feature race but I'll write copy later on the scorecard and the office will write the feature race and put my name on."

Wilson said the shift away from match reports had freed agency journalists to become more like their newspaper contemporaries. "There's so many different angles you can take on sport, the athlete, the drama. Over time agency sports writing changed. We were not only encouraged but required to follow a conventional lead with an optional lead, a softer lead, or a different lead, or a non-conventional approach to the story. In the first few minutes after the match you would have who scored and won, the basic agency account. Then we would have to come back with an alternative lead.

"We got used to that so you almost started writing the optional way. No more of the straight leads, you almost got straight into the optional lead. Everyone knew the basics already so give them something different, something they didn't see. It gave sportswriting a whole new breath of fresh air. As a writer you have much more freedom to write the story a different way, to put different information into it, and I thought it was great. That grew into further changes up until today. It's more about narrative and storytelling."

Shine said Thomson Reuters reporters have "to be a lot more nimble".

"I remember the days when it hadn't happened unless we had said it. Now it's all over Twitter even before you have fired up your laptops. Your value isn't just breaking news any more, you need to figure out what your value is. We now have to think, or try to think, about the end customers' need. We have to think really carefully about how we shall tell this story. What's the best format? Is it better told in a video? Is it better told in text? If we have a factbox, what kind of factbox? We are far more nimble now because we get so much more information. So we can attack it in a slightly different way.

"We used to set the agenda, not only for our customers but for other journalists. Now the agenda is constantly and fluidly set by random characters, by the key players themselves. It's quite a thin line to tread because you don't want to join in all the froth but at the same time you don't want to be known as the slowest player in town and suddenly become irrelevant."

Worlds apart

In 1987, two reporters from Thomson Reuters covered the first rugby union World Cup final in Auckland between New Zealand and France, one for the world wire and the other for the French service. The copy for the world wire report was dictated from Eden Park to a staffer in Sydney and edited by the general news desk in Hong Kong. There was a quick report, followed by an update with quotes and, finally, an overnight story, dictated to London from the reporter's hotel room. Two photographers were assigned to the tournament.

Thirty-two years on, Shine outlined the Thomson Reuters coverage for the 2019 final. "We started first thing in the morning with a live TV feed. We had booked a hotel opposite the Yokohama Stadium in a high room and had a live feed going out that people could switch to. At half past eight in the morning, you've got fans arriving. We then did vox pops [informal interviews] for TV with fans arriving. We put in that into a text story and there were still pictures as well all the time. We updated that throughout the day with more fans arriving. We then updated it on text when the teams were announced, unchanged and updated it again at kick-off. Our next update was half-time. Still pictures were going out throughout the game. Then, as we always used to do, at the final whistle we snapped the result, then four pars, 14 or 15 pars within five minutes. The snap and the first quick story were sent ahead of time to the desk and we confirmed it with them when the final whistle went. We had quotes from Siya Kolisi and Eddie Jones in the trunk [the main story] and we were updating it regularly. We then had separate sidebars from the press conferences as is traditional. Then a slightly softer overall broad brush piece which went out about 25 minutes to half an hour after the final trunk had gone out. Thomson Reuters had five reporters at the match and two photographers."

James Toney is the co-founder and managing editor of the British sports agency Sportsbeat, which is also exploring previously uncharted territory. "Journalism is about telling a story, isn't it?" Toney said at Sportsbeat's London office in Twickenham. The agency has another office in Manchester. "But I think our ways about telling stories and the clients we tell them to are different.

"I would say our client base falls into three parts. First, it's traditional media clients. It's having an arrangement to supply 100 Olympic sports stories to the Eurosport website. It's having an arrangement to produce content for the old Yahoo website. It's on a Saturday covering about 400-plus rugby games and we do lots of page production here. That's what I would call our traditional agency work. We don't have newspaper saying, 'Can we pay you x number of pounds to turn up to a press conference?' It's impossible to budget for that for you don't know if one month is going to be good and one month is going to be bad. All of our traditional agency work sits within contracts.

"And then other people come to us and ask us for editorial feeds. That could be everyone from a betting company that might want a feed for their website. It might be an outdoor advertising agency who want content that shows on the screens as you're on the London underground. But we also work with lots of associations and teams and events. They will ask us to run their content strategy and that can be anything from their official publications to their website, to their social media, to their YouTube channel management, and they'll come to us and say, 'Look we've got content, but we want a specialist to produce that content.'

"The Six Nations website is exclusively Sportsbeat content. We produce in three different languages, their social channels are all us, so that can be everything from producing graphics, animations for videos. The same for Pro-14 rugby, the same for the Gallagher Premiership, the same for Team GB, the same for Paralympics GB, the same for the Open golf.

"And then you'll have another element of the business which is where you'll work maybe with a brand. Sport is a whole myriad of sponsors who pay a lot of money. When they take that sponsorship on it's about much more than having a bit of perimeter advertising and the logo on their product. They will usually say, 'Well what's our strategy behind it?' The brands are much more into the storytelling.

"Another part of our company is journalism training. On another floor of this building we've got a floor of trainees and I always say to them that journalism is the ultimate team sport. And that's one of the things that I love about going to the Olympics. We will send six or seven people to Tokyo next year and you work together in a team, you back each other up. When the guy or the girl finishes at the athletics you'd hope they would just go, 'Does anybody need a help anywhere?' And someone will go, 'Someone needs to help me with these quotes, I need to do a preview for the swimming.' And I think that's quite unique. I do think the very best place to learn your trade is in an agency. I look at our guys here and they'll be doing a story for the print edition of a regional newspaper and then they'll do something for digital, and then they've got to think how they'll push that through for social media."[13]

As Toney indicates, the relentless deadline pressure faced by news agency reporters is accompanied by a camaraderie rare in a competitive, ego-driven trade. "The pressure was huge," says Brockmann. "Day by day. At a world championships or Olympic Games, the pressure was to be quicker than Reuters, AFP or AP. A kind of a fight against the other agencies. We compared the minutes when we sent the flashes, sometimes, very rarely, even the seconds. But I always liked the pressure. I loved what I was doing for SID."

Wilson said he still has nightmares about being in a foreign land and unable to find a phone. "It's a cliché but there's a deadline every minute. It's literally 24/7, you're competing against a lot of others and you had to get it right and you had to get it first."

Clough concurs. "It's got to be right and it's got to be quick. I was on a beach in St Kitts and I got a call from a colleague who said, 'David, [Pakistan cricket coach] Bob Woolmer has been murdered.' I said, 'What?' 'Bob Woolmer was murdered.'. Then he had to file along those lines. At which point I was the nearest that the Press Association had to the event even though I was 1,000 miles away."

The rewards, says Collett, ultimately outweighed the endless days and perpetual deadlines. "I was blessed to have the career I had. I once added up that I had worked in something like 45 or 50 countries. I saw some of the greatest sports events of the last 30 years. It was an amazing life. There was a camaraderie. We know in our agency world, once the day's work is done, we could go out with the guys from AP, with Reuters, with UPI and have an absolutely fantastic time and no one was scoring points as long as we produced, and that's why we did it year after year."

References

1. Roger Kahn, *The Boys of Summer*, Harper & Row: New York, 1972, pp. 74–75.
2. Paul Gallico, *Farewell to Sport*, Simon & Schuster: New York, 1988, copyright Paul Gallico 1937, 1938, p. 258.
3. Interview, 16 October 2019.
4. Interview, 8 October 2019.
5. Ian Macdowall, *Reuters Style Guide*, London, April 1991. Updated September 1995.
6. Stephen Parry, *Reuters Sports Guide*, 1988.
7. Interview, 17 September 2019.
8. Interview, 17 September 2019.
9. Gregory Gordon and Ronald E. Cohen, *Down to the Wire: UPI's Fight for Survival*, McGraw Hill Publishing Company: New York, 1990, p. 21.
10. Interview, 26 September 2019.
11. Interview, 29 October 2019.
12. Interview, 30 September 2019.
13. Interview, 28 September 2019.

7

Regional newspapers

Graham Hiley

Regional sports papers were not just a British institution, they were a community. For football fans growing up before the advent of the internet, these brightly coloured treasures were a way of life.

Manchester had *The Pink*; Sheffield was known for its *Green 'Un*. Coventry, Newcastle and Southampton were Pink; Aberdeen and Hull were green. Every major regional newspaper printed its own Saturday night sports edition, mostly on the colour newsprint which gave them their distinctive names, which became almost synonymous with the cities and towns of their home.

The usual explanation for using pink or green paper was to make it stand out on the shelves – even though they rarely stayed on the counter long enough to be moved. The more popular theory was that it was cheaper – and football fans didn't need to see things in black and white, as their views were already coloured. It became a standing joke. "Why on earth do you buy the Pink?" "I've got a pink toilet."

But fans did buy it. Every Saturday; in their thousands. Strange as it may seem in days of instant access to news, punters would queue outside newsagents in their own mini-community talking about that afternoon's game, whether a new striker was needed and anything else football-related. It was the forerunner to the football forums or phone-ins but face-to-face as people chatted, asked about each other and cared. It was more than just information, it was a tradition. For decades it was part of the fabric of life.

If it was raining, the claustrophobic interior of the newsagents would be packed. Woe betide any housewife who decided that 5.45 pm on a Saturday was a good time to pop in for a pint of milk. If it was dry, fans would wait on the pavement in order to get their hands on a paper more quickly. They had already handed over their copper coins and the community spirit ensured they were trusted to take just the copy they had paid for.

Most weeks they would stand for up to half an hour awaiting the screeching arrival of the newsvan, which barely even stopped. Often a door would simply slide open and a bundle of papers would be hurled onto the pavement to be seized upon as though it were a food aid parcel. That may seem an exaggeration, but football fans in the 1950s, '60s and '70s – even the '80s – were starved of information.

Southampton FC programme curator Chris Tuck recalls: "It is still one of my strongest child-hood memories, walking to Whites newsagents with my dad and trying to guess what the front page headline would be. When we got there, there were always a dozen or so other people wait-ing and we would chat about the game or the club until the van arrived. The papers would be hurled out and someone would cut the plastic ties and we would dive in and grab a copy.

"I would buy it every week, win, lose or draw. It was the only way to find out the other scores and the first chance to see the league table to see how close Saints were to that line above the bottom three … or two as it was for so many years. I would read the headline and intro then go straight to the other scores and then devour every word of the match reports. I don't know how they got it produced so quickly but it was the same process across the country. When I began going to away games I would always pick up the local Green or Pink.

"The *Echo* and *Sports Echo* were really invaluable sources of information with reports and features on non-league as well as professional teams. There was so much in it; it was fantastic value for money – though in the end not enough to keep people buying it once the internet took over.

"Nowadays it is really hard to get youngsters to pick up a newspaper at all and it is so sad they will never get to enjoy that kind of childhood memory of waiting for the Pink to arrive."[1]

It is hard to explain to Millennials just how much of a lifeline these papers were – and that in itself is a reason for their demise. In an era where scores can be obtained with a swift swipe, there is simply no need to wait to find out how your team have got on. More than that, the huge strides in technology now mean fans can even view the goals on their phones well before the old sports papers would have been loaded onto the fleets of vans entrusted to dispatch such precious cargo. Today, it is taken for granted that you can find out a score and every match detail at the touch of a screen. Heaven help the Wi-Fi provider who makes a consumer endure a time lag of more than a second for a page to load.

Contrast that with the patient wait for information as fans craned their necks for a distant glimpse of a distinctive van while speculating about how their rivals might have got on. Across the country, the contents would be eagerly devoured with strangers not just permitted but often encouraged to share a glimpse over a shoulder. Copies were passed round pubs and then posted to those who no longer lived in the circulation area.

Southampton FC official historian Duncan Holley notes: "I always remember hanging around newsagents waiting for the van to pull up at exactly five to six. That habit began when I used to wait with my father and for nine pence he could get his bus-fare, admission to the match, a programme, a copy of the *Football Echo* and fish and chips. If we won, it was a perfect day.

"It was a real part of the matchday experience. Nowadays the information is all there on a screen but back then it was the only way to find out the other scores. If you missed them on the radio at 5 pm, there was no other way of learning the results that night.

"There would be reports on Saints Reserves, even if they were away from home. And the coverage of non-league football was in-depth so you read about your own team and see how your mates had got on. It was like a football Facebook.

"Even when I no longer lived in Southampton, I would time my departure to coincide with the *Football Echo* being delivered so I could read it on the train. And when I moved abroad, my grandmother would post it every week. It was the only way ex-pats could keep in touch with the club at the time.

"That was how we got news. The local reporter was the only way we learned of transfers and injuries etc. It was a huge responsibility."[2]

The only other way to find out scores was to take a radio to the game – a trend which became more popular in the 1960s and 1970s as the invention of the transistor made it possible to fit in a pocket rather than a suitcase. The BBC's *Sports Report* would broadcast results at the final whistle but there were no live updates during play. Half-time scores were delivered by physically posting numbers against letters on the perimeter boards along the touchlines. Fans had to buy a matchday programme to see which games corresponded to which letters. The trusted – and often only – source for full-time results was the local paper.

Most would print a late-night final of their news edition with a Stop Press column which would give the half-time scores. But if fans wanted the full set of results, they had to wait for the bundle of green or pink pages to thud onto the pavement. Even then, they would not contain up-to-date league tables – at least not until the technology became available in the late 1970s to amend them by computer. Until then, sports papers would publish the tables at the start of play and leave readers to work out for themselves how many places their team had moved up or down – not easy in the days of goal average rather than the much simpler goal difference.

Any matches requiring more than a few minutes of injury-time would have that most frustrating of letters against them – L, to denote late result. Sometimes the game would finish just in time to squeeze the final score into the Stop Press; other times, fans would be left wondering about the outcome until the Sunday papers were delivered.

It had been that way pretty much since the first sports paper was published way back in 1895, when the *Newcastle Chronicle* launched its Saturday Football Final, which became *The Pink* in 1963. It was followed in 1897 in Birmingham by the *Sports Argus*, which for many years was the largest-selling sports paper in Britain until it closed on 13 May 2006.

Its final edition, ironically, showed exactly why Saturday night sports papers had become a dying breed. The front-page lead was the FA Cup final between Liverpool and West Ham, which went to extra-time. Deadlines were set in stone, van was at the ready, staff were on standby; the paper had to go to print at 90 minutes, without the final score. Sub-editors carefully hedged their bets with the headline "Nailbiter", but by the time the paper hit the shops, everyone knew the result and the report was well out of date.

And there it was, the very reason this glorious British tradition had run its course. Regardless of whether the paper was pink or green, it was faded to black in the eyes of the readers.

Immense power

Yet it was not always so. At the dawn of the 20th century, that is all there was. The sole source of football information came from newspapers – and the "local rag" was the main messenger.

It placed a huge responsibility and burden of trust on the chief football writer, initially hidden behind such quaint pseudonyms as "Observer", "Goalpost", "Full-back" or "Spectator". The local reporter – or football correspondent – became a key middleman with the unenviable task of writing honestly for the fans but without alienating the club contacts on whom he depended for copy. He – in those days, a woman writing about football would have been unthinkable – wielded immense power. His words were the only source of information the fans could access. His view was the only view. And it mattered.

That gave rise to a new breed of columnists who no longer simply reported the action in a staid and starchy style; suddenly there was opinion. The first recognised columnist hid behind the name "Off-Side", his true identity never coming to light during his three years on the Darlington-based *Northern Echo*, a respected halfpenny broadsheet where the sports news was buried on the back page just above the shipping forecast. Victorian historian EA Freeman rated it as "The best paper in Europe".[3]

Writing in Issue 7 of *The Blizzard*, Paul Brown notes that Off-Side immediately set out his "intention to be a fair-minded advocate for football". Writing in an introduction to his Football Notes column, Off-Side pledged: "The object of the writer will be raising the status of the game. A main feature of the notes will be their thorough independence. There will be no trucking to this club or to that. Everyone will be treated alike. This is the most important point and the general public can depend on it being observed. The writer is not officially connected with any club and will not sing the praises of one club at the expense of all the rest."

It was a significant time for football as the game was eased from the elite and passed to the working man. Public school sides like Wanderers, Old Carthusians and Old Etonians found themselves eclipsed by upstarts such as Aston Villa, Blackburn Rovers and Preston North End. As Brown notes: "This power shift led the Football Association to legalise professionalism in 1885 and would also lead to the formation of the Football League."

Even so, football coverage remained thin, with national newspapers in the 1880s preferring to focus on horse racing along with rowing, pigeon shooting and even pedestrianism.

Brown acknowledges:

> Spectators were becoming supporters and developing strong affinities for their local teams. *The Times* and *Daily News* covered selected FA Cup ties and international matches and weeklies such as *Bell's Life* in London and *the Athletic News* provided more comprehensive coverage of other high-profile matches but, in general, supporters had to rely on their regional paper for regular up-to-date coverage of their team's fortunes.
>
> By placing commentary alongside reporting, the *Echo*'s influential young editor W. T. Stead (who would later go down with The Titanic) had created a distinctive and lively paper that, it was said, could appeal to pitmen and dukes alike.[4]

Previously the paper's sports coverage had been basic, fitting expectations of the time. While papers in Blackburn, Glasgow and Birmingham published Saturday sports editions, *The Echo* listed the region's results and gave basic details each Monday. Their compromise was to have results telegraphed to their office on the final whistle. Brown notes that these were posted in the front window for anyone interested to view. Mostly, the reports printed on a Monday were submitted by club secretaries and were therefore brief, unreliable and often biased. It is a system which local newspapers continue to use to this day – though no longer with professional football.

With staffing levels being ruthlessly cut almost beyond bare bones, local newspapers depend more than ever on club or league secretaries to send in results and details. For years it would be the job of the most junior reporter – and more latterly anyone on work experience – to re-write these.

In *Making the Local News*, Rod Pilling writes:

> Trainees, who do much of the reporting for the local press, typically conduct the greater part of that work in the office. One is quoted as remarking: "Being tied to an office because there aren't enough staff for you to go out, is the antithesis of what reporting should be." Editors listed handout rewriting as the most essential competence required of trainees of six months standing. The dangers of this reliance on press releases have been well rehearsed elsewhere. They skew the local news agenda and give a promotional advantage to those organisations with sufficient resources to provide them. Rewritten, or worse merely inserted verbatim, they threaten – even eliminate – journalistic independence. They do however fill space quickly and cheaply and provide an informational subsidy to the local press – mainly from public corporate bodies keen to "manage" the news about themselves.[5]

For a local paper, though, these match reports and results would be a godsend. Pre-internet, they would be scrawled, hard to read and very often long and rambling – yet still missing key details, particularly anything which might reflect badly on the club or organisation. In times where football is a global industry raking in billions of pounds, dollars and euros, it is hard to fathom how top-flight match reports could consist of basic details sent in by a club secretary.

"Off-Side changed that, introducing insight and opinion to the back page," says Brown. "In his new column he criticised tactics and training regimes, waded into rows between clubs and spectators and traded blows with correspondents who challenged his views. He campaigned against disorganisation in the game, including the lax rules of local associations and the tendency of clubs to pull out of fixtures at late notice. However, he turned his nose up at the creeping nuisance of professionalism and shook his head when clubs and players pursued 'the shekels'.

"Much of Off-Side's criticism was reserved for clubs and administrators whose incompetence he felt inhibited the growth of the game. Clubs would be chastised for poor organisation and the problem of teams failing to turn up for fixtures became a regular theme. 'This conduct cannot be too strongly condemned,' he wrote. 'And as a punishment, means should be adopted for making the club in default pay the expenses which have been incurred.' As his column became established Off-Side began to occupy a position of some influence and was able to compel clubs and associations to account for their actions. He would criticise them in print and demand answers which he would print the following week. Correspondence was a major feature of the column which became a valuable forum for football discussion. Rules were debated, best practice was deliberated and arguments were settled with Off-Side becoming an unofficial arbitrator of football-related disputes."[6]

While these are all integral and essential elements of the game's wall-to-wall coverage today, back in 1885 they revolutionised reporting, and the club columnist became a key man for local papers.

"White Rose" took up the fight for the *Leeds Mercury*, while "Full-Back" wrote for the *Hull Packet*. Brown reveals that a rare exception to the trend for anonymity was Tityrus at the *Nottingham Daily Guardian*. His identity was revealed as James Catton. With no other way of learning information on their teams' fortunes, fans became increasingly engaged with the local paper as the sole source of both news and comment. The football correspondent's opinions were respected and eagerly anticipated. Fans would eagerly turn to the Monday verdict to find out if the reporter's outrage matched their own. Similarly, they would wait impatiently for the Pink (or Green) sports paper to arrive, giving them not only the other scores but also a detailed blow-by-blow account of the game.

With no television replays to help them, no internet and no mobile phones, reporters would cram into tight press boxes with just a clunky handset and a telephone line booked thorough a local news agency. At the other end was a copytaker who would patiently type out the report dictated by often stressed and demanding journalists who were trying to watch the game, write notes, dictate copy and gather their thoughts all at the same time.

Phil Andrews notes: "Running copy (often referred to by journalists as a 'runner') involves filing copy in a series of takes, originally by telephone to a copytaker but now more likely from a laptop straight into a newspaper's computer system. If a reporter is asked to write a 550-word runner on a soccer match, for instance, he or she will be expected to file the first take of 250 words at half-time, the second take of 250 words 10 minutes from the end and a final take of 50 words together with the scoreline, the moment the referee blows the whistle at the end of the game.

"An even more extreme example of this is the report written for the Saturday afternoon sports paper printed within minutes of games ending so they can be sold to fans as they go home from matches. The reporters involved are in constant telephone contact with their offices and report the game incident by incident as it happens. (This process has now been adopted by websites which produce minute-by-minute reports which can be read on a variety of mobile devices."[7]

Time was of the essence as the paper had to be subbed, typeset, printed and distributed to local shops within an hour of the final whistle – so injury-time and late goals became the stuff of nightmares. The regular formula would be 20 paragraphs on the first half, 14 on the second and the opening three paragraphs would be dictated before the final whistle in the hope that nobody scored. If all went well, the reporter would be off the phone by 4.45 pm and heading for the press conference, where he would often remain strangely silent before being granted a one-on-one interview with the manager, provided there was trust on both sides.

As the thirst for information grew, the newspaper's chief football writer became almost a part of the club, afforded privileged access and even travelling with the team. In the foreword to *The Day Two Teams Died*, a tribute to the journalists who died at Munich, using their reports and articles to chronicle the story of the Busby Babes, *Daily Mirror* sports editor David Walker notes: "Sixty years ago the social strata linking players, football management and the media was very different. It was the *Daily Mirror*'s Archie Ledbrooke who lived in leafy Bramhall while Matt Busby and his players lived around Chorlton-cum-Hardy and the inner city."[8]

Their names became as well-known around town as those of the players. Mostly old-school in the best possible way, they were the journalistic equivalents of Shankly, Busby, Bill Nicholson et al. Few ever relinquished such a prized position willingly.

Newcastle had Alan Oliver and John Gibson while Liverpool boasted Ken Rogers and Phil McNulty, now chief football correspondent at BBC Online. The new Off-Side at the *Northern Echo* was Eric Paylor. Portsmouth had Mike Neasom, Ipswich Dave Allard and Sheffield Paul Thomson (Wednesday) and Tony Pritchett (United). Brian Swain seemed to be at Luton for ever; Brian Hayward and Bob Brunskell preceded the author of this chapter at Southampton.

And then there was the doyen of them all, David Meek, who covered Manchester United for the *Manchester Evening News* from 1958 until his retirement in 1996. He died in October 2018. He took over the role in tragic circumstances, succeeding Tom Jackson, who was killed in the Munich Air Disaster, one of eight journalists to perish on the runway in the snow. In *The Day Two Teams Died*, author Roy Cavanagh recalled: "Back in 1958 people were reliant on newspaper journalists to tell them what was really happening in the world. Those journalists killed and badly injured at Munich were literally the voice of sport for the masses."[9]

At the time Meek was a political journalist and leader writer but, as the paper's most capable reporter, he was asked to switch and fill in. He said: "It was not something I had previously considered, but in an emergency you do whatever you can to help. Over time I got to quite like the job. I did it for 37 years."

Despite his status as one of the most recognisable faces at Old Trafford outside a red shirt, Meek always had time to help others, especially up-and-coming journalists trying to make their way in the industry. He said: "Reporting on your local football club is a huge privilege but it should never be abused. Be honest, be true to yourself and to your readers. The local paper is effectively a gateway linking the fans to the club they adore. It is part of the community. You are the prime source of information so think carefully about every word you write in case it can be misinterpreted by the fans or the club. If you upset both in equal measure then you are probably getting it about right!"[10]

Those principles of building trust helped Meek forge a strong bond with the club's notoriously feisty manager Sir Alex Ferguson, who was won over when the writer refused to back his editor's call for a campaign to oust the boss during his early days in charge. A specially commissioned poll had concluded that United should sack the Scot, but Meek wrote a typically balanced article saying he should be given more time – and casting suspicions that the vote may have been hijacked by mischievous Manchester City supporters. He reaped the rewards of his support many times over as Ferguson went on to establish a silver-laden dynasty at Old Trafford with Meek trusted to tag along for the glory ride.

It was a similar story in other cities, with the local paper's main man developing a mutually beneficial bond with the manager, though perhaps not always to the extent of *Southern Evening Echo* (as it was then) correspondent Brian Hayward and Southampton boss Ted Bates.

Hayward delighted in recounting the story of how he arrived at The Dell armed with his notebook and pen only for Bates to say: "I'm sorry, I've got absolutely nothing for you." Hayward told him he had a page to fill and desperately needed a story, so Bates picked up the phone and called his Everton counterpart to ask: "Would you be interested in selling Joe Royle … No? Ok … thanks." He turned to the reporter with an impish grin and said: "There you go, you can write that I have enquired about Joe Royle!"[11]

Done right, that rapport would work both ways. The manager could feed out stories he wanted in the public domain and the journalist could write with greater insight and accuracy to enlighten the fans while still retaining the necessary objectivity; the umbrella term for the role was a critical friend. So it was that reporters would often travel with the team, not just on foreign trips as a cost-saving measure to the club but frequently on the team coach, enabling them to build up trust and a rapport with the players – even joining their post-match (sometimes pre-) drinking sessions.

As long as they did not overstep the mark, the local paper had pretty much free rein when it came to getting copy. It was the norm for the local reporter to drive to the training ground, watch the players preparing and then grab them for interviews as they headed for the dressing rooms. The training ground was accessible to fans, who could often watch the players or at least wait for autographs in the car park – at least until the advent of social media, which saw team line-ups and tactics revealed by those desperate to show they were in the know. Experienced and trusted reporters like David Meek would know what to say and when to hold back, ensuring they delivered the most insightful content for the readers but without ever abusing their access.

Even going into the 1980s, the local newspaper was still seen as the font of all knowledge when it came to the club, though technology and an increasing thirst for news were about to change a system largely undisturbed for a century.

In 1983, ITV broadcast the first live league game – discounting their aborted attempt to launch it in 1960 with Blackpool against Bolton kicking off at 6.50 pm on a Saturday night and the cameras allowed to go live only at 7.30 pm. Unsurprisingly, it was not a hit with viewers or fans, with just 17,000 scattered around a stadium which could have easily accommodated as many again.

After a wait of 23 years to show live league football, ITV and the BBC were granted five each. The Beeb opted to screen their allocation on a Friday night while ITV went for a Sunday afternoon match between Tottenham and Nottingham Forest at White Hart Lane. This time, the perceived threat to attendances failed to materialise as the clash drew the biggest crowd of the weekend, even if it was just for novelty value, or the chance to see Chas 'n' Dave. Far from tempting fans to stay at home, the easy access to the game sparked a huge surge in interest and local newspapers had to react. In the mid-1980s, the *Southern Evening Echo* took the revolutionary step of finally putting sport on the back page; previously, a Saints signing would have had to compete with crime and council stories for that kind of prominence.

Despite the advent of television and a certain amount of radio, newspapers still ruled supreme when it came to the dissemination of information. Radio stations, on a tight budget, would manage to send a man to pre-match press conferences; local TV followed suit. But it was still the local newspaper reporter who led the way, getting irate when answers to his questions were broadcast on the airwaves before the next day's edition had gone to print. A sign of the times – and a forewarning of what was to come.

The next threat to local newspapers came in 1986 with the brash upstart that was Clubcall, a service which charged fans 50p a minute for breaking news about their favourite team. Very often these exclusives were thin and offered little new, if anything. But every story was sensationalised and strung out, starting with teasers to draw in the unsuspecting punter and keep them hanging on until some tiny nuggets of information were finally offered up once the listener's patience – and wallet – had been drained.

Another issue was the rise of free newspapers, which impacted heavily on regionals, hitting their revenue and consequently their willingness to invest in quality journalism in both news and sport. Brian McNair argued in 2009: "The growth of the free newspaper has added further to the challenges facing the traditional print journalism industry in the UK and is certainly a factor in the declining circulation for paid-for newspapers, especially those in the regions.

"The online revolution has had an impact on the local newspaper sector as much as, if not more than, the national press, reducing circulation and advertising revenue as readers slowly but steadily migrate to the web. Technology-led trends have led to the competitive pressures caused by an expanding 'freesheet' sector. Free newspapers, distributed to commuters on trains and buses, have grown substantially in number and readership ... to the point, where in the view of some observers, they threaten the very viability of the paid-for regional press and the quality of the journalism it produces.

"The regional press enjoys a distinctive and important role in British journalism, supplying local communities with news and information in a way that no other medium can. One observer defined it thus: 'It's a good pub landlord. It should make people feel that they belong, that they are valued and their lives have some significance. People need to feel, from the paper, that their community is being noted and celebrated.'

"Regional titles have the inherent advantage of being first and arguably best in their reportage of local stories. They can also boast a high degree of reader loyalty. Freesheets, it is argued by their detractors, are reluctant to invest in editorial resources, and more likely to produce the kind of standard content that Bob Franklin and others have called McJournalism."[12]

In the same chapter of McNair's book, Patrick Barkham observed: "Investigative journalism takes time and money. Scrutinising government and town halls may not produce the sexy copy the free papers crave. Some believe that councils can get away with almost anything in areas served only by poorly resourced free papers. The fourth estate's powers of scrutiny and accountability are diminished: local and national democracy is weakened. As more and more media content is made available free of charge, the paid-for regional newspaper is now an endangered species."[13]

Regional newspapers attempted to rein in costs at the expense of quality content, many taking the view that extended shelf-life would lead to increased sales. As a result, they printed much earlier in the day, offering readers the previous day's news instead of a "late night final" with more up-to-date content.

Andrews notes: "The regional daily press in the United Kingdom has been contracting for many years ... most just one title, now normally published fairly early in the day to give them more time on newsagents' shelves, but still referred to as an evening newspaper. These try to appeal across the social-economic spectrum and are pitched somewhere between the mid-market and down-market tabloids."[14]

That view is backed up by Bob Franklin and David Murphy:

> The push to tabloid seems to have been driven by the wholly untested belief, which seems prevalent in many parts of the newspaper industry, that the way to keep readers or even enhance circulation is to "go downmarket" editorially. The strategy offers obvious financial as well as those presumed marketing advantages; the provision of infotainment is considerably less demanding on editorial resources than investigative journalism or hard political news.
>
> The prospect for the local press as investigators and informers of the public in the process of local democracy looks even bleaker than that for the democratic process itself.[15]

The biggest change came in 1992 with the formation of the Premier League, hand-in-hand with Sky, who paid £304 million for the rights to screen games live. It was the beginning of the end for local newspapers and not just because of the increased competition and the advent of the internet. Suddenly a huge number of games were no longer being played at the traditional slot of three o'clock on a Saturday.

Traditionally sales were greatest if the local team won away from home and lowest with a home defeat. But they hit a new low if the side weren't playing at all. Coupled with fans' increased access to information, it was a losing battle. The *Coventry Telegraph*'s Pink closed in 2004 after 58 years on the streets. The *Newcastle Chronicle*'s Pink ran for 110 years before winding up in 2005. The *Birmingham Sports Argus* went in 2006 after 109 years in existence; the *Manchester Evening News* Pink switched to a Sunday version in 2000 and closed in 2007. Sheffield's *Green 'Un* died in 2013.

Curiously, while the northern football powerhouses' publications went under, two remained on the south coast. The *Portsmouth Sports Mail* ran from 1903 until 2012 but was then revived as a Sunday paper in October 2016. That left Southampton's Pink as the last Saturday sports paper until it too was killed off on 9 December 2017.

Saints official historian Duncan Holley notes: "The *Football Echo* was first published in 1898 to coincide with the opening of The Dell. It is interesting to look back and see how the sports coverage kept increasing in the ordinary paper until it was felt there was a need for a sports version. The club was selling the paper. Back then it was huge, almost three feet high"

"The local paper was always the lifeblood of the community. Even now the older generation still hold it in esteem even though so many staff have been made redundant and the coverage is much more sparse. They seem to be staffed now by youngsters with laptops who do not have the contacts or the in-depth knowledge of the city or the people. It is a real shame because the local paper is there to help with democracy and act as a watchdog, to investigate and hold wrong-doers to account.

"I know when the author of this chapter left the *Southern Daily Echo* in 2001, there was a sports desk of 12 at the paper and he was the only member of the club media team doing the whole of the website, the whole of the matchday programme and acting as press officer. Now it has gone full circle. The *Echo* has a sports desk of just three and the club has a media team of around 15."[16]

Even small non-league sides now have their own website or at least a Facebook page, while top Premier League clubs have a media team bigger than many lower-level playing squads. Their priority is not just to disseminate information but to spin it and protect the brand while driving traffic away from traditional media – including the local paper, which has lost its privileged seat at the table and now has to make do with occasional scraps.

In *Digital Sports Journalism*, Charles M Lambert writes: "In the 1990s sport began to appreciate the growing commercial value of its product. British football started receiving tens (later hundreds) of millions of pounds from BSkyB television and the big clubs became global brands with supporters in every corner of the planet. So, there was more demand for stories about these clubs and more openings to write about sport. The new fans, many of whom might not ever visit their club's home ground, had an insatiable appetite for stories. And, when there weren't any stories to be had, they would happily make do with opinions, discussion and prediction.

"At the end of the last century, relatively few football clubs outside the Premier League had a media team. Requests for interviews or match passes and news about the signing or release of players were all conducted through the club secretaries or by a direct phone call to the manager if they'd given reporters their phone numbers (which they usually did). By 2005 most league clubs had at least one employee to deal with the press. We [journalists] started taking most of our stories from the club website. It was quicker than calling the manager who, of course, was very busy. But, of course, if we could get the news from the club website, so could fans. We were adding very little to what was already publicly available.

"Clubs wanted to take control of how they were represented in the wider world. A club like Liverpool boasts as many fans in America or south-east Asia as in the United Kingdom, so why allow journalists based in the north-west of England to remain as its principal channel of communication?"[17]

"Like losing a friend"

While young football fans once dreamed of writing for the local sports paper, many now aspire to being a club journalist – even at the expense of traditional journalistic integrity and independence.

Recalls Holley: "The *Sports Echo*, or *The Pink*, was a huge part of this city. The paper even used to post the latest Saints score on a noticeboard on its balcony on a Saturday afternoon. It was such a shame when it closed, the last one in the country to go. It felt like losing a friend. It was all very sudden and it just went out with a whimper after more than 100 years. It has left a huge hole in my life."[18]

Regional sports papers are now treasured artefacts. For historians like Holley, they remain invaluable tools for research; for fans who enjoy wallowing in nostalgia, they are stored away in lofts and garages to be produced for threads and reminiscences on social media. But for all the hankering for the good old days, it seems unthinkable that regional sports papers could ever be sufficiently financially viable to make a comeback when competing against the speed of the internet.

As Anton Rippon wrote for the Sports Journalists Association in May 2019: "To think I once had to wait until the Midday Edition of the *Derby Evening Telegraph* to find out how Derby County had gone on at Leyton Orient the night before. No internet and no local radio, and the national papers for our neck of the woods had gone to bed before the game ended.

"That was back in September 1963 but it could have been any midweek game right up to the early 1970s. And not just The Rams. Supporters of most clubs had to wait until the following day to learn how their favourites had fared in a midweek away game.

"And as lovely as it is to remember those cold Saturday teatimes when there was a crowd outside the newsagent's waiting for the van to pull up and drop a bundle of Green 'Uns or Pinks 'Uns on the pavement, it isn't going to happen again. What would be the point? There would be no one to greet it. Everyone would be at home looking at the TV or scanning their computer screens for the latest tweets from sports journalists on the spot. You may as well hope that tomorrow morning you might hear the clip-clop of the milkman's horse coming down your street".[19]

References

1. Interview with Chris Tuck, 8 July 2019.
2. Interview with Duncan Holley, 9 July 2019.
3. Paul Brown, "The first columnist", *The Blizzard*, Issue 7, 1 December 2012, pp. 51–54.
4. Ibid.
5. Rod Pilling, "The changing role of the local journalist: from faithful chronicler of the parish pump to multiskilled compiler of an electronic database", in Bob Franklin and Brian Murphy (eds), *Making the Local News*, Routledge: London and New York, 1998, p. 185.
6. Brown, *The Blizzard*.
7. Phil Andrews, *Sports Journalism – A Practical Introduction*, Sage: London, 2005, pp. 59–60.
8. David Walker quoted in Roy Cavanagh, *The Day Two Teams Died*, CreateSpace Independent Publishing: London, 2018, p. 9.
9. Cavanagh, p. 11.
10. Personal information, conversation with David Meek, 19 November 1988.
11. Personal information, conversation with Brian Hayward, 1 August 1988.
12. Brian McNair, *News and Journalism in the UK*, Routledge: Abingdon, UK, 2009, pp. 169–172.
13. Ibid., p. 8, 158, 169, 172 (Barkham).
14. Andrews, p. 14.
15. Franklin and Murphy, p. 18.
16. Holley interview.
17. Charles M. Lambert, *Digital Sports Journalism*, Routledge: Abingdon, UK, 2019, p. 7, 126 and 127.
18. Holley interview.
19. Anton Rippon, *Newsletter of the Sports Journalists Association*, May 2019.

8

Fanzines

Huw Richards

"Fanzines are an idea whose time has come", wrote sports journalist Phil Shaw in 1989.[1] Three decades later some might argue that it has long gone, a football phenomenon of the late 20th century as transient as clothing fashions or musical sub-cultures. They certainly no longer exist in the number, or sell as well, as in their heyday. They are now most likely to make news when some long-established title such as *The Oatcake*, which bowed out in September 2019 after 653 issues devoted to Stoke City, closes.[2]

Any novelty provokes questions about its durability. John Gaustad, whose *Sportspages* bookshop was both showcase and clearing house for a huge range of fanzines, observed as early as 1995, "If there's a trend at all it is slightly downward."[3]

Three years earlier *The Absolute Game* - which captured the acid wit, linguistic vigour and capacity for invective of Scottish terrace discourse - had asked whether fanzines were "still a vital outlet for the concerns of supporters or well past their sell-by date?"[4] A year after that Bill Brewster of *When Saturday Comes* (*WSC*) reckoned "The standard has gone down a little. It's like punk in 1979 – a lot of the original people have moved on, and the imitators aren't quite as good."[5]

Gaustad and *The Absolute Game*'s Archie MacGregor were both speaking in terms of quality and vitality rather than technology. Then came the internet. As Tom Davies, in 1986 a founder of *Leyton Orientear*, pointed out in 2011, "The Web negated the need to knock out 40 pages of A5 every month or two," along with other demands such as physical printing and distribution, while offering a potential global audience and interactivity.[6]

Yet the fanzine lives on. Davies was writing for *WSC*'s 25th anniversary issue. *Orientear* has celebrated its 33rd. *STANDamf*'s list of existing fanzines, apparently last updated in 2015, referred to a "dying art". Yet it cited 10 survivors from the 1980s, including *WSC*, *Orientear* and *City Gent*, and 20 founded since 2010, suggesting a new wave.[7]

The list of just under 50 titles omitted both *The Oatcake* and the Middlesbrough-focused *Fly Me To The Moon*, reckoned by *Oatcake* editors as their closest challenger for the record number of issues. It included the Wolves fanzine *A Load of Bull*, which closed in 2012. An informal exercise, it aimed to help fanzines and potential readers but did not pretend to be exhaustive: "We've probably missed some out."[8]

But it illustrates some difficulties concerning fanzines. There are uncertainties of definition, of determining how many there were in total, or at any particular time. They were, and are, inherently informal. They network. Whether titles were founded in 1986 or 2017, editors talk of exchanging information, advice and copies with other titles. But there was never a formal Fanzine Publishers' Association with a membership list to provide a sense of definition and numbers.

When Saturday Comes, best known and arguably most influential of the genre, described by academic Richard Haynes as a "symbolic trade mark", illustrates some of the issues.[9] Shaw noted astutely in 1989 that it never called itself a fanzine – billing itself as "The half-decent football magazine". Andy Lyons, co-founder with Mike Ticher in March 1986 and editor since Ticher moved to Australia in the late 1980s, says that "If we used [the term] now it would only be facetiously".

There are points at which it can be argued to have crossed the line dividing fanzines from commercial magazines. Staff were first paid in the late 1980s, albeit initially the modest stipends permitted under the Thatcher government's Enterprise Allowance Scheme; they accepted advertising from April 1990 and in recent years have paid contributors. Some writers suspected a scam in emails from "Rich Guy" offering back payments, before remembering that *WSC's* publisher was, and in 2020 still is Richard Guy. But as Lyons says, "We've never really drawn the distinction."[10]

Not least of its contribution to publications which unquestionably were fanzines was the monthly directory listing them, with addresses and prices. Likened by *The Guardian's* Barney Ronay to "a secret tour of the country" and "a slightly angry version of the Shipping Forecast", the list provides a rough barometer for fanzine numbers – 22 in January 1988, 215 a year later. From 1990 the list split across three issues and by the mid-1990s numbered around 370.[11]

While more authoritative than the *STANDamf* listing, it was more indicative than definitive. It depended on titles contacting *WSC* and while inclusive by practice and instinct, listing was not a given. Much as it still excludes MK Dons from pre-season surveys in protest against the manner of the club's formation, in 1991 it dropped the Manchester United fanzine *Red Issue* – among the best-selling club fanzines with average sales reckoned to be around 10,000. Lyons said that its stereotype-based abuse of Liverpool fans was "not something we want to be associated with".[12]

These were often ephemeral, mostly locally circulating, publications. Haynes recorded that "Every month *WSC* can list over ten new titles, with as many becoming defunct," and reckoned that by January 1992 more than 600 had come and, in many cases, gone.[13] The historic list maintained by memorabilia website Footybits.co.uk records more than 900, with Chelsea (18) the single club leader followed by Newcastle (17), Hearts (17) and Brighton (16), although the truly eye-catching number is five devoted to Chesham United.[14]

Further definitional issues occur with the coming of the Internet and its proliferation of message boards, blogs and websites. *The Guardian* blurred the lines in a six month-long weekly series in the first half of 2001, mixing established print fanzines such as *King of the Kippax* (Manchester City) and *No-One Likes Us* (Millwall) with websites such as www.cardiffcity.com and OneValefan.co.uk (Port Vale) and some, including *GMK* (Coventry City) and *Rage On* (Oxford United), which did both. In the same spirit, Tim Gentles of the Football Fans Census, sponsor of the Zine Awards for 2007–2008, argued that "websites and blogs are certainly a continuation of the original culture and they'll be central to its future". He was contradicted by a prizewinner, *City Gent* editor Mike Harrison, who questioned the inclusion of websites, arguing that they were "entirely different animals".[15]

Nor, thanks perhaps to this ephemerality, is there a wealth of serious studies. Haynes's *The Football Imagination* (1995) is the one book-length examination. There were anthologies edited by Shaw, John Robinson and Martin Lacey, a chapter in Anthony King's *The End of the Terraces* (2002), a smattering of academic articles and passing references elsewhere.[16]

Peter Millward argued (2008) that they offer a fertile source for scholarly examination, but as Kevin Dixon (2018) has pointed out, this has yet to happen, even if club case-histories have been suggested as an ideal topic for MBA students interested in the value of being "first mover". That all three anthologies were published in 1989, with *Best of the Fanzines* clearly intended as first of a series, shows how attention peaked early and was not maintained.[17]

So any account is necessarily selective and anecdotal. This one recognises that websites such as codalmighty.com, a Grimsby site whose match reporter Tony Butcher is credited by the journalist Phil Ball with "combining obscure musical references with effortless and witty metaphor that has been the unofficial dialect of the club", and Jason McKeown's Bradford City site widthofapost.com more than fulfil the hopes Gentles expressed in 2008 for electronic fan media, but focuses largely on printed titles.[18] It also concentrates on football, although the shelves at *Sportspages* carried titles devoted to other sports. Shaw in 1989 noted four from rugby league, closest in fan culture to football.[19]

Punk inspiration

Good ideas seem obvious in retrospect. As Ronay has written: "What seems odd now is its complete novelty then."[20] The surprise is not, though, that football fans developed their own independent media in the second half of the 1980s, but that groups with a strong collective sense of identity had not done so before.

Technology was undoubtedly a factor. Football's fanzine pioneers had access to means of production – photocopying, neighbourhood print shops, word processing and desktop publishing – not available to earlier generations. But other groups got there earlier. That the *Oxford English Dictionary* defines "fanzine" as "a magazine for fans esp. those of science fiction" reflects that American sci-fi enthusiasts started their own magazines in the 1930s. *The Comet*, started in May 1930, is reckoned to be the first. While the OED's earliest citation is from *New Republic* in 1949, the coinage appears to date to Louis Russell Chauvenet writing in *Detours Magazine* in October 1940: "We hereby protest against the un-euphonious word 'fanmag' and announce our intention to plug fanzine as the best short form of 'fan magazine'."[21]

In the UK, music launched the concept in the 1970s with publications echoing punk rock's noisy anarchism and rejection of traditional production values. As Shaw noted, it redefined fanzines as "by and for fans", expressing punk's "do it yourself" mentality.[22] Martin Lacey recalled: "In the beginning there was *Sniffin' Glue*, the archetypal fanzine channelling the punk explosion of 1976–7." It was "badly written, badly laid out and overpriced" and lasted only a dozen issues. Short lives were the norm. Lacey noted that 24 issues over three and a half years made his own *New Musical Excess* "a real veteran among fanzines", reflecting an audience who were "cynical, apathetic, like to think that they've seen it all before even if they haven't and would probably rather spend their last 50 pence on drink".[23]

The model was there for young men with an enthusiasm, and the 20 issues of the Liverpool-based *The End* published between 1981 and 1988 have been cited as the bridge between music and football. John Peel, the broadcaster and Liverpool fan, described it as being "about music, beer and football, the very stuff of life itself".[24] "By young men, for young men," it was "a diary of underground Liverpool in the 1980s", couched in Scouse vernacular and "full of street attitude, humour and graphics". While editor Peter Hooton recalled it as "not really a football fanzine", the football component grew steadily. His objective was "to give a platform to people who really didn't have access to the media … in those days to get stuff into print was a lot more difficult. It was an opportunity for people to express themselves".[25]

Haynes argued that the influence of *The End* "can easily be overstated".[26] There were also sporting forerunners. The better known was *Foul*, "Football's Alternative Paper", published from 1972 to 1976. Started by Cambridge graduates, among whom Steve Tongue went on to a notable career in the mainstream football media, its resemblance in style and outlook to *Private Eye* was accentuated from Issue 10 onwards when it was typeset and distributed by the same firm. Its critique of the game, according to contributor Chris Lightbown, later of the *Sunday Times*, was that "football had simply not assimilated any of the social or cultural changes of the sixties. It was in a complete time warp". Targets included the grim football of the time, reactionary administrators and the quality and values of the media, getting it sued by one tabloid writer.[27]

Foul was funded in its later stages by the Broadway and Hollywood lyricist Tim Rice, and is reckoned the only thing he ever lost money on. It is credited by the OED with, in 1975, the earliest use in print of "bonk" as an idiom for sexual intercourse.[28] Contributor Stan Hey recalled it capitalising on "a lot of material that the mainstream press didn't really touch", but it "gradually ran out of money and the mood changed – people fell out of love with football when we didn't qualify for two World Cups in the 1970s", and closed after 34 issues.[29]

Less noticed because it covered another sport, and rapidly evolved into looking nothing like a fanzine, was *Open Rugby*, devoted to rugby league. Started by Cumbrian Harry Edgar in Oxford in 1976 as a "bi-monthly news sheet of comment and opinion for all rugby league people", it argued on a first front page which mixed type with (neat) handwriting that "On the field of play it can't be beat, but off it has suffered from such an appalling lack of good publicity", attributing this in part to "a smear campaign from a few sick-minded patrons of a rival rugby code" but also to "its own inability to promote its own assets".[30]

That sense of injustice, critique of officialdom and affection for the game's heritage anticipated key fanzine themes. They remained staples though 22 years and 208 issues before *Open Rugby* joined the mainstream, was sold to League Publications and revamped as *Rugby League World*. The fanzine look was short-lived with glossy covers from September 1979 and full colour from May 1980, rebranding as "The International Rugby League magazine". It took adverts and employed full-time staff, including Peter Deakin, perhaps the most gifted British marketeer of either rugby code. Yet, like *WSC* in later years, it remained outside the mainstream. Steve Wagg has pointed to the "professional identity" of journalists reflected in bodies like the Football Writers' Association. Edgar, arguably the most influential league writer of his era, was immune to journalistic clubbability. *Independent* writer Dave Hadfield caught both influence and detachment in jokingly describing him as "widely believed to be one of the most shadowy, sinister figures on the face of the earth" in *XIII Winters*, rugby league's equivalent of the *WSC* publication *My Favourite Year*.[31]

Yet the first football fanzine wave waited nearly a decade from the demise of *Foul* and launch of *Open Rugby*, appearing uncoincidentally as Football League gates hit a post-war low below 16.5 million in 1985–1986. The game's troubles can be exaggerated, Lyons rightly pointing out that far from being the basket case which, according to some influential narratives, was rescued by Sky Sports and the Premier League in 1992, it was "struggling along as the most popular game in the world". Fanzines formed part of what Chris Stride, Nick Catley and Joe Headland have characterised as "the oft-ignored late 1980s/pre-Premier league revival in football's fortunes."[32]

But the game, and in particular supporters, had reason to feel under attack. It was characterised largely in terms of hooliganism, and a snobbery typified by the *Sunday Times* description in mid-1985 of a "Slum sport played in slum stadiums, and increasingly watched by slum people, who deter decent people from turning up".[33] Such attitudes fed the Thatcher government's plan, in 1988, to counter hooliganism by requiring identity cards for admission to matches.

Football fans have been grumbling since the first one paid for admission, but this was rather different. Under attack, they needed and found voices. The Football Supporters' Association (FSA) was founded in 1985 to give fans a more vigorous voice than official supporters clubs and their National Federation, bodies whose deferential ineffectiveness have their definitive chronicle in Rogan Taylor's *Football and Its Fans* (1992), but were never more effectively captured than in a description from JL Carr's *How Steeple Sinderby Wanderers Won the FA Cup* (1975) of a team whose finances were "largely provided by the Supporters Club, who ran a football pool, the admin. complexities of which, in recent years, had put two treasurers in jail and another in a mental home. The Supporters Club had no representative on the Board, but was invited to the Annual General Meeting".[34]

Many early fanzines voiced fan resistance. *Off the Ball*, a short-lived Birmingham-based fanzine, was a hugely influential exemplar for others in the mid-1980s, defining many issues in its first editorial:

> We won't be treated like idiots any more. We being "ordinary" supporters of mainly ordinary clubs, who are sick of being portrayed as morons in the press, tired of being patronised by television's lifeless coverage of a great sport, and most of all angry at being manipulated by tyrannical directors and administrators who in their eagerness to "modernise our game" show all the rationality of headless chickens.[35]

Among those they inspired were Lyons and Ticher, who worked together in a London record shop. They knew nothing of *Foul*, but saw *Off the Ball* at an FSA meeting, while Ticher had contributed to a music fanzine called *Snipe*. Lyons recalls:

> Fans had a bad image, and were increasingly written about and treated as if they were all hooligans. We needed something to redress that balance because we thought that there were probably quite a lot of people who shared our outlook, but no magazine which reflected it or gave them an outlet.[36]

The first issue of *WSC*, with some content – such as a feature on Fulham as "The Boys Next Door" – reflecting Ticher's Chelsea affiliation, was published as an offshoot of *Snipe*, but before long superseded it.[37]

While *Off the Ball* and *WSC* considered the game as a whole, many more titles focused on single clubs. A Leicester University survey found that many wanted an alternative to existing media, and in particular match programmes, that fitted Davies's characterisation of mainstream football writing in 1986 as "stultifyingly one-paced and unquestioning".[38] Two young Bradford City fans, John Dewhirst and Brian Fox created what became the longest-running club fanzine, *City Gent*, in 1984. Dewhirst recalls:

> We'd seen two supporter magazines, Wondrous World at Bolton and Terrace Talk at York, and thought "we could do that". We were also both programme collectors and very aware of the deficiencies of our own clubs, which was an embarrassment. It wasn't a matter of wanting to replace the programme, but of providing the things we'd like to read – gossip, a certain amount of critical observation and history among them.[39]

Both were recent university graduates, Dewhirst from Oxford and Fox from Durham. Dewhirst, training as an accountant, recalls missing the intellectual challenge of university while Fox had journalistic ambitions but was unemployed. While in contrast to terraces still largely occupied by manual workers, this was typical of fanzine editors. Students, accountants, civil servants, social workers and clerical officers were the largest groups in the admittedly small sample, around 25, surveyed in 1989 by Martin Lacey. Far from waiting to be invented by Nick Hornby's *Fever Pitch* (1992), the middle-class football fan was waiting for Hornby, the invention more than anything of the upward social mobility associated with the 1944 Education Act and the Robbins Report. They were also ready for fanzines, confident with the written word and, in the 1980s, much likelier to be unemployed like Fox, or under-stimulated like Dewhirst, than earlier cohorts who graduated into full employment.[40]

If the "I can do that" uttered by Alan Bleasdale's creation Yosser Hughes in his *Boys from the Black Stuff* (1982) – a series incorporating a character named Dixie Dean and cameos by Liverpool players Sammy Lee and Graeme Souness – was among the catchphrases of the unemployment-blighted 1980s, its spirit of emulation was evident in fanzines. Just as *City Gent*'s founders saw other club fanzines, *Leyton Orientear* can trace its origins to social worker Dave Knight seeing *Off the Ball* and *Eagle Eye* (Crystal Palace) editor Dave Ellis – who recalled that "I really wanted to write, but found I could only write about Palace" – reading *Off the Ball* and *WSC*.[41]

If emulation was common, so was discovering a previously unsatisfied demand for what they were doing, with numerous stories of instantaneous interest. The *Arsenal Echo Echo* recollection of selling only 12 copies outside Highbury, then "squeezing the remaining 687 through the turnstiles", is a comparative rarity.[42] Dave Wallace of *King of the Kippax* (Manchester City) "Nearly bottled out from selling … I sold 80 on the first day. Wow! It was off the ground", while the first *City Gent* printing of 200–300 copies "sold out in about 15 minutes" on a midweek night at Valley Parade.[43] *Orientear* sold out around 100, and *WSC*'s reward for sending its first issue to Phil Shaw at *The Guardian* was a mention in a football diary which prompted "200 letters in the post. We had to do a second printing."[44]

Lacey, who edited and printed music and football titles, contrasted cynical, apathetic music aficionados with football fans who were "Just that – *fanatics* – and if somebody's taken the trouble to write about their team they'll buy it, and if it is any good – most fanzines are – they'll come back for more".[45]

With cut and paste – one unquestionable connection with punk – the main means of production, entry costs were low, although technological issues did impinge. Rob Nicholls of *Fly Me to the Moon* doubtless gave thanks that Middlesbrough contracts to "Boro" after producing early issues on "a typewriter with a dodgy vowel key. I tried to avoid any word with a 'u' in it".[46] Matt Johnstone became editor of Motherwell fanzine *One Step Beyond* in 1995, "basically because I was the only one with a computer".[47]

Football continued to throw up motivating issues. Charlton's exile to groundshare with Crystal Palace led Rick Everitt to start *Voice of the Valley*, driving a campaign whose success was built on initiatives such as running "Valley Party" candidates, who won 14,838 votes at London Borough of Greenwich elections in 1990, unseating the chair of planning. The identity card scheme was dropped only after the Hillsborough disaster, the product of ill-conceived policing rooted in the assumption that most irked many fanzine pioneers – that "all fans are hooligans".[48]

"Translating articulate spectator opinion"

By December 1989, the *WSC* listings showed that 71 out of 92 Football League clubs had fanzines. A year later only five – Rotherham and Southend United in Division Three and Blackpool,

Scarborough and Stockport County in the Fourth – remained unrepresented, suggesting that seaside resorts and communities close to major conurbations were likeliest to remain immune. Only one was fanzine-less by the time Vic Duke attempted to define "A Research Agenda for Football" in 1991. Larger clubs were better represented in absolute terms, Duke finding that in December 1990 First Division clubs had on average 2.9 titles, compared to 2.2 in Division Two, 1.33 in the Third and 1.25 in the Fourth. Six titles covered Leeds in December 1990, and five apiece Manchester United, Sunderland and Norwich, all First Division clubs. But the Leeds sextet competed among an average home gate of 29,312, with Manchester United's five titles serving more than 43,000. The 2,946 still sustaining Fourth Division Cardiff City had a choice of four titles.[49]

Their role was defined by Jory, Horne and Bucke as "translating articulate football spectator opinion from an unwritten culture to an immensely lively, engaging and persuasive written form", while Haynes perceived "a novel, irreverent gaze upon the world of football contributing to a wider oral tradition of talking about the game either at the match, the pub or the workplace".[50] Lacey and Robinson's anthologies offered both a sample of these forms and pointers to longer-term themes.

Humour rooted in matchday experience was an essential element. Some observed archetypes such as "The Tranny Man" from *The Absolute Game* and a series on "Really Annoying People You Meet at Football" from *Brian* (Nottingham Forest). Black humour expressed through mordant recall of club misfortunes has remained a staple, expressed early on through the *Chelsea Independent*'s series of "Great Own Goals" and *Sing When We Fishing*'s chronicle of bad Grimsby signings as "Blundell Blunders".[51] Steve Nicholson of *Rub of the Greens* (Plymouth Argyle) in 2001 cited the "morbid sense of humour" common to many Argyle fans and reflected that "the low points for a fanzine editor are often the high points for a club … sales are much better if the team is doing badly".[52]

The *Arsenal Echo Echo* column purportedly written by pre-war manager Herbert Chapman was a libel on a historic innovator, but an effective satire of old school attitudes and writing styles, while *Leyton Orientear* made a cult figure out of the "Fat Fryer" presiding over a Brisbane Road burger stall. *Orientear* also fielded a contributor called "Sid the Surrealist", and *War of the Monster Trucks* (Sheffield Wednesday) later claimed to be edited by a labrador retriever called Sir Stanley Headfire.[53]

History and heritage were *City Gent* staples, also figuring in *Chairboy Gas* (Wycombe Wanderers) through reminiscences of lost grounds at Ilford and Leytonstone and, much more grimly, in *Light at the End of the Tunnel*'s (Dartford) recall of "Highgate Cup Horror", the 1967 Amateur Cup tie during which Highgate United's Tony Allden was killed by lightning.[54]

No theme has been more central than critiques of club managements such as *Tired and Weary*'s (Birmingham City) view of owner Ken Wheldon that "Men like him are the reason football fanzines are born".[55] Paul O'Dowd reflected in 2017 that "Some of the best fanzines have some of the worst owners", citing as a high-point in 28 years of *The Square Ball* (Leeds United) the "Kenopoly" issue devoted to chairman Ken Bates.[56]

Robinson's selections also included *Voice of the Valley*'s blow-by-blow account of its campaign to return, a two-page *Off the Ball* demolition of the identity card scheme ending with advice to "Visit your MP, sign FSA petitions, get yourself on local radio, TV etc." and *WSC*'s four pages of reaction, plus a memorable cover, to Hillsborough. *WSC* co-editor John Duncan's two-page analysis of press coverage began "In media terms, tragedy is the best news …" and finished with Anthony Burgess in the *Daily Telegraph*, who "typified much of the media coverage … he knew nothing and cared less". If less grievous, an episode of ITV police soap *The Bill* was reviewed by *Wise Men Say* (Sunderland) as "seeming to have been written by [unpopular sports minister]

Colin Moynihan under the influences of repeated showings of *West Side Story*", with the address of the Independent Broadcasting Authority appended for letters of complaint.[57]

Jory, Horne and Bucke identified fanzines as "a case of successful cultural contestation" waged by titles "united in the view that the game is, or rather ought to be, theirs, not the private property of businessmen and remote administrators, or the playthings of press and television or police and politicians", but they were not wholly homogenous.[58] Anthony King identified *WSC*'s falling-out with *Red Issue* as symptomatic of a class and culture division between "club fanzines produced by and for the lads, articulating masculine understandings and publications such as *When Saturday Comes* which are produced and read principally by educated members of the professional public sector middle classes".[59]

That masculine understandings were fundamental is not in doubt. Haynes argued: "While not openly sexist, male subjectivity is inscribed into the *When Saturday Comes* text and football fanzines in general, offer a subtle brand of male bonding."[60] A 1992 readership survey found that *WSC* readership was 97 per cent male. Female participation was unusual. The Leicester survey found that roughly one in five titles had some female involvement. *Orientear* stood out among pioneers for the contributions of Sarah Tabor, while Sue Wallace drew cartoons for *King of the Kippax*. From 1990, *Born Kicking*, edited by Jane Pardon, provided an outlet for both female voices and the women's game. More recently Hazel Potter of *The Second of May* (Bristol Rovers) stood out as a very rare female fanzine editor, while Tom Hudson, editor of *Black Watch* (Everton), founded in 2017, confessed disappointment at not having female contributors.[61]

Although Lacey's questionnaire for fanzine editors found 14 declaring themselves left-of-centre politically, six located themselves on the right or centre-right, Dewhirst's (presumably) satirical self-designation as "Socialist Unity Party of East Germany" defying classification. King saw some contradiction in many fanzine critiques of the commercialisation of football, given the entrepreneurialism essential to their existence. Kevin Dixon's chronicling of *The Mag*'s initially enthusiastic support for John Hall's ousting of the McKeag dynasty from Newcastle United shows a degree of complicity with his commercially driven agenda followed by progressive recognition of the "double-bind" that Hall's policies would marginalise some supporters and affect fan experience – eventually evoking Orwell's *Animal Farm* with McKeag as Farmer Jones and Hall's Magpie Group the animal revolutionaries eventually indistinguishable from their human predecessors.[62]

Forming what Adam Brown has described as a "culture of dissent" made relationships with the establishment represented by clubs and mainstream media inherently tense. *City Gent* was less oppositional than some titles, an attitude reinforced by the shared horror of the Valley Parade fire in 1985: "We felt that in relations with the club we had to stand by it. We were critical, but positive and constructive in our criticism," recalls Dewhirst, who as editor from 1986 to 1988 defined their outlook as "Bantam Progressivism".[63] In 1989, they told Lacey that the club had been "surprised at its popularity" and that "directors and management showed they were prepared to co-operate". But their experience, along with *Heartbeat* (Heart of Midlothian) – which told Lacey that it had "nothing but help and encouragement from the club and players" – and *The Flashing Blade* (Sheffield United), recipient of "a letter of encouragement and thanks", was something of a rarity.[64] The 1988 Leicester survey found only seven per cent of fanzines reckoned their clubs "strongly supportive".[65]

Thirty-four per cent described club attitudes as "opposed".[66] Some, like Crewe and Grimsby, saw fanzines as pirate programmes. Lacey's own *Elmslie Ender* (Wealdstone) claimed to be "Britain's Most Banned Football Magazine". It fell out with Wealdstone, which demanded that the official Supporters Club take it over, then a complaint from a Dagenham fan led the GM Vauxhall Conference (now National League) to ban it from all 22 grounds, plus 190 in feeder leagues.[67] Arsenal did *Echo Echo* a huge, ham-fisted PR favour, stopping the editor from selling outside Highbury and escorting him to the club offices were he was told the title was banned for life, "which didn't seem very long". Issue number 3, headlined "Editor Arrested", attracted widespread media attention. "The press loved it," including an appearance on ITV, "admittedly at 3.30 am".[68]

Elsewhere wariness was tempered by some acceptance. Leyton Orient's mid-1980s struggles lent themselves, Davies recalls, to a critical stance which for *Orientear* has "dictated the tone a little ever since", but by 1989 they reported a club attitude of "resigned tolerance", although sales were still prohibited in the ground, club shop and bar. Relations at Notts County were characterised as "up and down".[69] Although *The Pie* donated all profits to the club, it was in and out of the club shop, one issue so upsetting some players that they insisted that "the club should not be associated with us". At Crystal Palace, initial hostility to *Eagle Eye* had given way to "taking more and more notice and beginning to accept that we are not hooligans, but a group of people worth listening to".[70]

For mainstream journalists, fanzines were intruders at the gate of the trade, critiquing their output and challenging their monopoly of interpretation. Haynes perceived a generational element, with writers closer in age to youthful fanzine contributors – the Leicester survey found that 79 per cent were 30 or younger – more sympathetic. *The Guardian*, shown in a 1992 readership survey to be the favoured paper of *WSC* readers, reflected this. Shaw gave important initial publicity to both *Off the Ball*, and *WSC* and his colleague Stephen Bierley wrote in 1989 of fanzines as "one of the delights of football in the past four years, glorious pulsating beacons of irreverence, wit and real information". Lyons recalls David Lacey, the highly respected football correspondent, as less responsive.[71]

Gaustad, a perceptive and sympathetic observer, noted "some journalists who are dismissive of fanzines, who choose to focus just on the ones that use swear words all the time and present them as being the essence of fanzine culture".[72] Nor were local papers invariably supportive. When Swindon Town's *The 69er* and Oxford United's *Raging Bull* collaborated to try to reduce crowd trouble at their derby in 1996, BBC and commercial local radio provided coverage within 24 hours, but the Swindon *Evening Advertiser* failed to respond to a letter and 17 phone calls. *The 69er*'s Richard Parkin noted that it and the *Oxford Mail* had been conducting a "civic slanging match" for several months.[73]

Yet relationships changed over time. Clubs recognised that fanzine contributors represented a rich seam of enthusiasm and talent. Many, including *City Gent* editor Matt Dickinson, became match programme columnists. Shaw had presciently suggested in 1989 that Bradford City "do the decent thing and hand over to their erudite followers".[74] Dewhirst records that "there were overtures. But were we aware that football club regimes are here today, gone tomorrow – a year or two and they might drop you – and preferred to keep our independence".[75] Charlton were sufficiently impressed by *Voice of the Valley*'s Rick Everitt to first ask him to devise new ticket schemes and then, from 1998, to join full-time, running a new commercial department. *Dial M for Merthyr*'s Mark Evans joined the Football Association of Wales staff under comic circumstances: "I went to interview Alun Evans, the FAW secretary, and he thought I'd applied for a job there." It was, he recalls "only as an office boy", but the error had a happy ending – he is still there 30 years later as the FAW's International Officer.[76]

There was parallel recognition by mainstream journalism that fanzine editors had roles as news sources and spokesmen, and possibly also journalistic talent. Tom Davies recalls of his time as *Orientear* editor from 1993 to 1996 that "the phone rang all the time".[77] Some fanzine writers entered the journalistic mainstream. Everitt joined the *South London* Mercury, and Davies has been on *The Guardian* sports staff since 2007. Davies, a Leeds University politics graduate, has no doubt that "working on *Orientear* gave me the confidence to push ahead with journalism": he entered the graduate training course at Harlow College before working on local papers in East London. But, being the son of a journalist, he might have followed the same path anyway.[78]

The same "what if?" proposition applies to many notable writers. *WSC* gave early opportunities to the diverse talents of Barney Ronay, Harry Pearson and David Conn, who all graduated to *The Guardian*, while the formidable knowledge of all things Arsenal that made Amy Lawrence invaluable to first *The Observer* and *The Guardian* and, since autumn 2019, *The Athletic* was first expressed in fanzines. *The Guardian* cartoonist Dave Squires did his earliest work for Swindon fanzines in the 1990s, "which I should probably stop mentioning because someone might see them and they might be awful", and contributed to *WSC* before moving to Australia.[79] Adrian Goldberg, editor of *Off the Ball,* has had a notably versatile BBC radio career while Phil Ball, author of the "Blundell Blunders" feature from *Sing When You're Fishing* anthologised by Robinson, moved from Grimsby to a long career chronicling Spanish football from San Sebastian. But active or aspiring journalists were always a significant element in fanzines, the 1988 Leicester survey finding that just under one in five contributors had had some journalism training. One reason why journalism is more trade than the profession it often claims to be is that – unlike law, medicine, accountancy or teaching – it has never been confined to the formally trained. It has gatekeepers, many highly vigilant, but multiple gates.[80]

Davies, Ronay and Gaustad have all suggested that the impact of fanzines on the commercial mainstream was as much in style and outlook as personnel. Ronay in 2019 cited *WSC*'s style as "the voice that every publication uses to talk about sport and culture now, to make sport fun and funny", while noting its impact on the coverage of issues:

> *WSC* has tended to be first with so many things … on the issues too. Pick one and *WSC* is likely to have been there for some time. Racism in football for example. *WSC* was covering this, accepting that racism was about structure and subtext and what happens in the boardroom, when most were telling themselves it had disappeared.[81]

Davies's comment in 2011 that they "undoubtedly helped broaden how the game was written about" echoes Gaustad's observation 16 years earlier that:

> Fanzines have had a profound impact on the broadsheet press both in terms of the style of writing and in affecting their point of view. It has meant that there are certain stories they wouldn't now write, and they don't go about it in the old-fashioned way. They can no longer pretend they can't find a representative fan to ask for a quote when something happens at a club.[82]

They also alerted the book trade to a potential market. Michael Parkinson's *Football Mad*, drawing on his *Sunday Times* columns, pioneered portrayal of fan experience but was reminiscent, an affectionate recall of Barnsley FC in the decade after the Second World War, rather than current. The breakthrough was novelist Pete Davies's *All Played Out*, focused on the 1990 World Cup. Its misfortune was to have been John the Baptist to Hornby's *Fever Pitch*, but as Gaustad recalled in 1995, it was "really important because it spoke directly to fans", doing so in a way that exposed the gap between them and the mainstream football media: "Journalists hated it and used to say things like 'there he was, in this brilliant position with access to all the players and he didn't know what the right questions were'. And I used to wonder if they'd read the same book."[83]

A further novelty was the *Complete Record* club histories published by Derby-based Breedon Books, starting with Derby County in 1984. While paralleling fanzines in offering fans something new, they are closer in spirit to Alan Sutton's photographic history imprints, both reflecting real-isation that while books about communities such as towns and football clubs are unlikely ever to become national bestsellers, strong localised loyalties make them commercially viable. In other media, perhaps the purest exposition of fanzine style – critiquing authority while celebrating the idiosyncrasies of football culture – was probably the first, Danny Baker-hosted incarnation of BBC radio sports phone-in *606*. BBC2 television's *Fantasy Football League,* hosted by comedians Frank Skinner and David Baddiel in the mid-1990s, also offered echoes. In 2019, fanzine idiom still echoed in *The Guardian*'s daily *Fiver* mailing and *Football365*'s forensic dissection of (mostly) tabloid idiocies in *Mediawatch*.[84]

Fanzines and trusts

If *Voice of the Valley* was the clearest example of fanzine influence, a natural affinity with the independent supporters movement represented by the FSA created what Haynes called "an alternative football fan network".[85] Rob Nicholls of *Fly Me To The Moon* recalls early fanzines as "cheek by jowl with the FSA".[86] Relations with official supporter organisations could be frostier. Mike Kelly, editor of *Blue Print* (Manchester City), reported that the chairman of the Supporters' Club "walked into our meeting with an air of indifference, barely looking at us and stating after a couple of minutes of his valuable time that he could never support it as it might criticise the club".[87]

The alliance survives, but is not unconditional. Lyons recalls: "We broadly supported the FSA, but didn't want to do the same issues every month, and they did their own magazine, which wasn't always very good. After the merger to form the FSF they became a more mainstream body and gave a lot of focus to England and things like fan embassies."[88] But there is little doubt that the fanzine contribution to raising fan awareness contributed to the rise of Supporter Trusts, which by another "so simple it was obvious in retrospect" device – organising fans collectively to buy shares in clubs – ended the ineffectuality chronicled by Taylor.

Rob Marshall, editor of *What a Load of Cobblers,* was among the Northampton Town fans who called the meeting in January 1992 which set up the first Supporters' Trust.[89] As expressions of fan activism, fanzines and trusts were natural allies. But just as trust officers became an alternative to, and in time supplanted, fanzine editors as the mainstream media's go-to voice of fans, it seems reasonable to assume that for later generations some of the energy which in the 1980s had gone into fanzines migrated to the Trust movement.

The mainstream football print media also diversified. One element in *WSC*'s peak sale approaching 40,000 was the absence of alternatives for those seeking anything more sophisticated than *Shoot!* or *Match*, both aimed at the none-too-enquiring teenager. The arrival in 1994 of *FourFourTwo* signalled commercial publishing's belated acceptance of one clear fanzine lesson, that some fans wanted magazines which treated them as adults. Other publishers responded. One asked the *WSC* team whether they were interested in relaunching as a glossy. Lyons remembers: "We didn't think we were the right people to do a glossy, and we fairly sure that our core readership did not want one." The publishers went elsewhere, and their title was short-lived. Nevertheless, the market was more crowded than before.[90]

Running a fanzine took time and energy – Dewhirst called *City Gent* "A baby which grew into a time-consuming monster".[91] The median age of editors surveyed by Lacey in 1989 was 27, the youngest (Davies) 18. By 2000 all but two had reached 30 and the median was 38, with the life-changes that implies. Evans recalls in *Dial M for Merthyr* that "Life got in the way. People had kids and other commitments. We kept going for a while doing a couple of issues a year, but it more or less petered out in around 2001."[92]

On top of this came technological change. As Raymond Boyle and Richard Haynes pointed out in 2004: "Website production is relatively easy. All it takes is some basic knowledge of using an .html editor, access to a host server and know-how to transfer the files from a personal computer to a server."[93] Steve Kelly, editor of *Through the Wind and Rain* (Liverpool), told Millward that "Before the internet, fanzines were the only outlet for fans to 'mouth off' in any way they choose. The web gave some people the chance to do it at that very moment and not have to wait months for a new issue." In a much more competitive environment, sales fell and titles closed. Millward cites peak sales of *Through the Wind and Rain* and the Oldham title *Beyond the Boundary* as 6,500 and 5,000 respectively. By 2004, these numbers were 1600 and 450, and by 2009 both had gone.[94]

FSF chairman Malcolm Clarke is hardly alone in his reflection, in 2017, that "In some ways I'm surprised they've survived. You might have thought that with the rise of social media and the internet they would have vanished years ago, but they haven't".[95] But, as Millward points out, development has been neither wholly linear nor solely determined by technology. Webzines, he argued, were as much continuity with as replacement for fanzines. A number of print fanzines, including some pioneers, will survive into the third decade of the 21st century.[96]

When Saturday Comes now sells around half of its peak circulation, and much of its readership has aged with the magazine. In late 2019 it launched a Supporters' Club to generate extra funding, telling readers, "*WSC* as a print magazine is no longer self-sustaining."[97] Yet, as Lyons points out, its circulation decline is slower than the average for an embattled magazine sector. Crises have been to do with distribution rather than sales. Takeover offers were resisted in the prosperous 1990s, and Lyons' policy of "trusting our own judgment" has steered a course between the twin traps of drifting into the mainstream or angry sectarianism.[98]

City Gent is, Dewhirst thinks, now seen as an "old man's magazine" by the bulk of Bradford City supporters. But it is "something of a Valley Parade institution" with a clear place among media devoted to the club, its early strength such that it never had a serious fanzine challenger. Individuals, as ever, are crucial. Dewhirst points to "A sense of responsibility to keep it going. Nobody wants to be the one who has to close it down", with Harrison seventh and longest-standing in line.[99]

Orientear too exists amid a range of club-related media, but Davies says: "It is still where you go for a 700-word think-piece about the future of the club." The death in September 2019 of founding father Dave Knight, whose kitchen table was the production plant for early issues, might have threatened a less solidly established title. But their notable success has been finding new generations of editors and contributors. "The last three editors have all been in their 30s," says Davies, who points to *Orientear*'s football team as a source of renewal, some contributors starting as players before gravitating to writing or editing.[100]

Common to all three is that the print edition remains central. Web and social media presences are an add-on which assists rather than rivals hard copy. Each has maintained a consistency of tone and, in some cases, personnel. Clarke acknowledged that survivals were "partly in some cases a sense of brand loyalty … but also because some have very high quality writing".[101] Match-going fans are, Dewhirst points out, "creatures of habit and ritual. They like to go through the same routines, and buying and reading the fanzine is a part of that".[102] Along with credibility, good fanzines build up knowledge and expertise. Chris Atton pointed to a Nicholls interview in 2005 with Middlesbrough's commercial manager for *Fly Me to the Moon* as:

> More an occasion to provide discursive and detailed analysis of the club's finances and future prospects. Here we see the coming together of the fanzine writer's own expertise and knowledge with the access to sources and journalistic skills we would normally associate with the professional local sports journalist.[103]

Survivors have been supplemented by revivals. *Voice of the Valley* ceased print publication in 2001, but returned in 2013. Everitt, sacked following a power struggle at the club, resumed his role as an energetic critic, powers of invective similarly undiminished if a denunciation of the "egotistical, erratic and incompetent stewardship" of owner Roland Duchatalet in August 2019 is any guide.[104]

Dial M for Merthyr also reappeared amid the crisis in 2010 that led to Merthyr Tydfil's rebirth as fan-owned Merthyr Town, its name as a League club in the 1920s. Evans found a new niche created by the disintegration of the local press:

> Nobody writes much about Merthyr, the club or the town, now. We're lucky to get a match report. The fanzine fills that gap. It's a small club, so we all know each other, so there can be a lot of in-jokes. But we also write about the town, its issues and its history.

While seeking younger contributors, it is largely run by veterans of the earlier *Dial M*. Fan ownership changes its role: "I'm an owner now, like everyone else. We're not railing against an absentee owner anymore." With a regular sale around 200, half the average home crowd, it asks questions and sets agendas: "We try to pose the unthinkable questions, such as whether we should leave the English pyramid and join the Welsh system."[105]

Both revived titles also reflect the broadly left-of-centre sympathies of most fanzines – in 2019 Everitt, a former parliamentary candidate, led the Labour group on Thanet District Council while Evans was Plaid Cymru candidate for Merthyr Tydfil and Rhymney Valley at the general election in December.[106]

There has also been an authentic new wave. The West Ham title *Blowing Bubbles Monthly* started online, but an experimental print edition in 2012 proved so popular that it persisted through the move from Upton Park to become a matchday fixture at the Olympic Stadium. A new generation of editors has emerged whose earliest football memories are not of smoky terraces but the post-1992 world of the Premier League, replica shirts as leisure wear and all-seater (if far from all-sitting) stadia.

Tom Hudson, a lecturer in geography and planning at Liverpool University, started *The Black Watch* (Everton) in 2017:

> I started buying fanzines such as *When Skies Are Grey* in about 2001 when I was 16, I've been a fanzine reader ever since and I enjoy writing. It was a disappointment to me when I came back to Liverpool that there was no print fanzine for Everton and while there are podcasts, they've become quite professional and are close to the club. There was nobody doing what *When Skies Are Grey* was doing in 2001, something which was independent, and much less concerned with tactics or signings than with the lived experience of being an Evertonian.[107]

The start-up was triggered by wanting to write about the pre-season tour of Tanzania in 2017 in a less ephemeral medium than a website: "I like print and feel a commitment to it." He found other fanzine editors happy to offer advice, a Blackburn title recommending a printer. He produced the first issue by himself, and continues to do most match-day selling, getting a sense of his audience: "There's a mix, a lot of people who remember *When Skies Are Grey* but a fair few in their 20s who seem to enjoy it. I recognise a lot of the faces now." A rhythm of eight issues per season has been established, and a writing team. Each edition sells a few hundred copies, with occasional mishaps recognisable to earlier generations: "We printed 550 before a match against Man City, it rained and we were left with rather more copies than we had hoped."[108]

He sees subtle differences between the pioneers and the second wave: "A common factor among the second wave is an affection for the style of the platform, for print and the physical object of a fanzine. It is perhaps less driven by the sense of grievance there was in the eighties, but there is still a feeling of wanting to offer a counterweight to established narratives."[109]

That affection for the physical object is echoed by Ian Hanahoe, editor of *Ewe Tea Bee,* which started chronicling North London non-leaguers Haringey Borough in 2019. Hanahoe, 31, works for a software company and differs from the "lifelong fan" model of most club fanzine editors – he comes from Wrexham, but first watched Haringey in 2011 and has been a regular since moving to the district in 2016. "I've always enjoyed fanzines. I also enjoy making things and the feel of having created a physical object, and I like writing and having a platform for it."[110]

Sales of the first two editions were in three figures, at a club whose average home gate rose in 2019 to 300-plus: "There's a great deal to be positive about this club and my aim is to have a broadly positive attitude. At the same time you need to have a critical perspective and a certain amount of irreverence is built into the idea of a fanzine." A team of four contributors produces items such as Issue number 2's imaginative take on club history, a walking tour of various sites of importance in a past incorporating the genealogy of name and ground changes and mergers common to London non-league clubs.[111]

His affection for print is reinforced by its advantages over websites: "A website is very immediate, and you have the pressure to keep it going, so that it can become a chore. With print there's a burst of effort, but without that need to keep ticking over there's more to chance to think things through, and for better writing."[112]

There is, Hudson acknowledges, some parallel between fanzines and the revival of music delivered via vinyl rather than download, although as Davies says with wry affection, it represents "a slightly scruffier, more downmarket demographic".[113]

Diversity the key

The football world has changed enormously in the half-lifetime since the oldest surviving fanzines were launched. Once an endangered sub-culture, the game has become so pervasive that the regular *WSC* feature documenting "Football's bid for world domination" is only half, if that, joking. Where Mrs Thatcher apparently hoped to strangle the last football fan with the entrails of the last sociologist, subsequent Premiers and party leaders have felt compelled to proclaim an allegiance (genuinely in the cases of Michael Howard, Gordon Brown and Jeremy Corbyn), even if some had difficulty remembering what it was.

Nor are the inauthentic protestations of smooth centrist politicians all there is to dislike. Few fanzines ever asked for galloping competitive inequality, ever-increasing corporatisation, gentrification, rocketing ticket prices, television-dictated scheduling or the tribalism that has recast some followers of traditionally amiably self-aware Manchester City as defenders of the social order in hereditary Middle Eastern dictatorships. As Hudson, made peculiarly aware of such issues by Everton's tantalising position as historic giants just outside the oligarchy, says: "There are a lot of fans whose reaction to anything in football is 'what's in it for us?'. If we're in, we're for it, if we're not we're against." He can imagine circumstances, particularly those involving European Super Leagues, which might prompt him to "Sack it all off and start watching Prescot Cables instead".[114]

But if fanzines are now merely one voice among many, that diversity of fan outlets – for which they were both forerunner and catalyst – is welcome. They helped create the conditions in which fan participation became a serious alternative to the inherently unstable "rich man's toy" ownership model, and while this has mostly been in lower leagues, a major trophy – Swansea City's League Cup in 2013 – has been won by a club part-owned by fans. And, if they had done nothing else, good writing and (mostly) innocent entertainment has transformed a once-barren environment.

Written in 2011, Tom Davies' verdict still holds good:

> Ultimately, the anger that fuelled the fanzine boom still exists. Many threats to the game have receded, but plenty of the problems that worried us then have got worse since. So though we cracked some bad jokes, got our spellings wrong, couldn't lay a page out in a straight line and were a bit full of ourselves at times, when it came to the fundamentals, we were right about a lot of this stuff.[115]

References

1. Phil Shaw (ed.), *Whose Game Is It Anyway? The Book of the Football Fanzines*, Argus: Hemel Hempstead, UK, 1989 (pages not numbered).
2. stokesentinel.co.uk/sport/football/football-news/stoke-city-final-last-oatcake-3141924, 3 August 2019.
3. *When Saturday Comes*, No. 105, November 1995.
4. *TAG* cited in Richard Haynes, *The Football Imagination: The Rise of Football Fanzine Culture*, Arena: Aldershot, UK, 1995, p. 66.
5. Brewster quoted in Nick Hornby, "Kick up the Grass", *New Statesman and Society*, 13 August 1993.
6. *WSC* 290, April 2011. Interview with Tom Davies 27 September 2019.
7. Standamf.com/a-to-zine-the-stand-fanzine-directory n.d Accessed 24 July 2019
8. Ibid., stokesentinel.co.uk, 3 August 2019; birminghammail.co.uk/sport/football/football-news/wolves-fanzine-a-load-of-bull-waves-182184, 30 March 2012.
9. Haynes, p. 79.
10. Shaw; Interview with Andy Lyons, 22 August 2019.
11. Barney Ronay, "When Saturday comes still shooting from the football fringes", *The Guardian* football blog, 11 March 2016; Haynes, p. 61; University of Leicester Department of Sociology Sports Resources Fact Sheet No. 7: Fan Power and Democracy, www.le.ac.uk/so/css/resources/factsheets/fs7.html, 24 July 2019
12. Haynes, pp. 74–75; Anthony King, *The End of the Terraces*, Leicester University Press: Leicester, UK, revised edition, 2002, pp. 170–171.
13. Haynes, p. 62.
14. Footybits.co.uk/information.php?info_id=12 Accessed 30 July 2019.
15. Guardian.com, 18 January 2001 (introduction), 24 January 2001 (Cardiff City), 3 February 2001 (GMK), 7 February 2001 (Rage On), 22 March 2001 (King of the Kippax), 29 March 2001 (No-One Likes Us), 25 March 2001 (OneValefan); *WSC* 257, July 2008.
16. Haynes; King; Shaw; Martin Lacey (ed.), *El Tel Was a Space Alien*, Juma: Sheffield, UK, 1989; John Robinson (ed.), *Best of the Football Fanzines*, Fanzine Publishing: Cleethorpes, 1989; "Cultural Aspects of Football", *Sociological Review*, Volume 39, Issue 3, April 1991.
17. Peter Millward, "Return of the football fanzine", *Journal of Sport and Society*, Volume 32, Issue 3, August 2008; Kevin Dixon, "Demand and the reduction of consumer power in english football, a historical case study of Newcastle United fanzine *The Mag* 1988–1999", *Soccer and Society*, published online 12 December 2018; theafterword.co.uk/when-Saturday-comes-and-football-fanzines, 25 April 2016, 18 July 2019; Haynes, Lacey, Robinson.
18. *WSC* 391, November 2019, codalmighty.com/site/ca.php?/article=494; Interview with John Dewhirst, 12 September 2019.
19. Shaw.
20. Ronay, *The Guardian* football blog, 11 March 2016.

21. *The New Shorter Oxford English Dictionary*, Oxford University Press: Oxford, UK, 1993 edition, Volume 1, p. 916; *SFE,* The Encyclopedia of Science Fiction, sf/encyclopedia.com/entry/fanzine, 12 June 2019, www.Oed.com/view/Entry/68126?redirectedFrom=Fanine#eid; *Science Fiction Citations*, jessesword.com/sf/view/186 Accessed 30 July 2019

22. Shaw.

23. Shaw; Lacey; Haynes, pp. 40–41.

24. Roger Domeneghetti, *From the Back Page to the Front Room*, Ockley Books: Huddersfield, UK, 2014, p. 180.

25. Jenny Coleman, "How a Liverpool football fanzine inspired a generation", bbc.co.uk/news/uk-england-merseyside-15821361, 30 July 2019

26. Haynes, p. 45.

27. Domeneghetti, p. 177; Andy Lyons and Barney Ronay (eds.), *When Saturday Comes: The Half-Decent Football Book*, Penguin Reference: Harmondsworth, UK, 2005, p. 138.

28. Domeneghetti, pp. 177–178, www.oed.com/view/Entry/21345?rskey=3FXtGS&result=1#eid, 30 July 2019

29. Domeneghetti, p. 178.

30. *Open Rugby*, No. 1, May 1976, sourced via totalrl.com/rugby-league-world-covers/, 22 July 2019

31. totalrl.com; Wagg cited in Haynes, p. 27; Dave Hadfield (ed.), *XIII Winters*, Mainstream: Edinburgh, 1994, p. 127.

32. Attendances listed in *Football Yearbook 2018–2019*, Headline: London, p. 567; Christopher Stride, Nick Catley and Joe Headland, "Shirt tales: How adults adopted the replica football kit", *Sport in History*, 2019, DOI: 10.1080/17460263.2019.1578255, 3 August 2019

33. *Sunday Times*, 18 June 1985.

34. Rogan Taylor, *Football and Its Fans: Supporters and Their Relations with the Game*, Leicester University Press: Leicester, UK, 1992. JL Carr, *How Steeple Sinderby Wanderers Won the FA Cup*, London Magazine Editions: London, 1975, Grafton pbk, 1986, p. 59.

35. *Off the Ball*, No. 1, January 1986, cited in Haynes, p. 50.

36. Andy Lyons interview.

37. *WSC* 1, March 1986, reprinted in Issue 350, April 2016.

38. Tom Davies, "The publishing boom", *WSC* 290, April 2011.

39. Liverpool survey cited in David Jory, John Horne and Tom Bucke, "Football 'fanzines' and football culture, a case of successful cultural contestation", *Sociological Review*, Volume 39, Issue 3, August 1991, p. 589; Dewhirst interview; Lacey.

40. Dewhirst, Lyons interviews; Lacey; Jory, Horne and Bucke, p. 588.

41. Ellis quote from Lacey; Dewhirst, Davies interviews.

42. *Echo Echo* quote from Lacey.

43. *King of the Kippax* from *The Guardian*, 22 March 2001; Dewhirst interview.

44. Davies, Lyons interviews.

45. Lacey.

46. BBC Sport, "Fanzines in the digital age", bbc.co.uk/sport/av/football/27293994, 6 May 2014.

47. Matt Johnstone, *Extended Highlights (The Life of a Fanzine Editor)*, Motherwell Daft Productions: Motherwell, UK, 2006, p. 9.

48. *Voice of the Valley*, No. 153, October 2019. Votvonline.com/history/, 3 August 2019

49. Vic Duke, "The sociology of football: A research agenda for the 1990s", *Sociological Review*, Volume 39, Issue 3. Accessed 3 August 2019

50. Jory, Horne and Bucke, p. 590. Haynes, p. 152.

51. Robinson, p. 13 (Tranny Man); p. 17 (Blundell Blunders); p. 27 (Really Annoying People); other 1989 examples from Lacey.

52. *The Guardian*, 14 March 2001 (Plymouth).

53. Lacey; *The Guardian*, 20 November 2001 (Sheffield Wednesday).

54. Robinson, p. 12 (*Chairboys Gas*); p. 32 (*Highgate Cup Horror*); Lacey; Dewhirst interview.

55. Lacey.

56. bbc.co.uk/news/uk-england-41149738, 25 November 2017 (Square Ball).

57. Robinson, p. 28–30 (Voice of the Valley); p. 31 (The Bill); pp. 36–39 (Hillsborough, *WSC* 28); p. 40–41 (ID cards); others from Lacey.

58. Jory, Horne and Bucke; p. 581, 584.

59. King, p. 170.

60. Haynes, p. 121.

61. King, p. 178 re. *WSC* readership; Lacey; Jory, Horne and Bucke, p. 587 re. female participation; *WSC* 180, February 2002; Interview with Mark Evans 20 September 2019 re. Hazel Potter; Interview with Tom Hudson 4 October 2019.

62. Jory, Horne and Bucke, p. 588; Lacey; King, pp. 172–173; Dixon.

63. Dewhirst interview.

64. Adam Brown (ed.), *Fanatics: Power, Identity and Fandom in Football*, Routledge: London, 1998, p. 52; Lacey.

65. Jory, Horne and Bucke, p. 584.

66. Lacey.

67. Shaw (Grimsby); *The Guardian*, 8 March 2001 (Crewe); Lacey re. *Elmslie Ender*.

68. Lacey.

69. Davies interview; Lacey.

70. Lacey.

71. Haynes, p. 76; Jory, Horne and Bucke, p. 587 re. fanzine contributor ages; King, p. 178 re. *WSC* readers; Shaw; Lyons interview.

72. *WSC* 105, November 1995.

73. *WSC* 111, May 1996.

74. Shaw.

75. Dewhirst interview.

76. Evans interview; votvonline.com/the2019-20-blogs/13-8-yes-there-s-an-agenda-and-it-s-all-about-charlton/, 3 August 2019

77. Davies interview.

78. Ibid.

79. Nick Miller interview with Squires, TheSetPieces.com/interviews/vox-box-guardian-cartoonist-david-squires/, April 2016., 24 July 2019

80. Davies, Lyons interviews; Jory, Horne and Bucke, p. 588.

81. Barney Ronay, "When Saturday comes in Peril should bother everyone who cares about football", *The Guardian*, 17 November 2019.

82. Davies, *WSC* 290, April 2011; Gaustad, *WSC* 105, November 1995.

83. Gaustad; Michael Parkinson, *Football Daft*, Stanley Paul: London, 1968; Pete Davies, *All Played Out*, Heinemann: London, 1990; Nick Hornby, *Fever Pitch*, Gollancz: London, 1992.

84. Peter J. Seddon (ed.), *A Football Compendium*, The British Library: Boston Spa, UK, 1995 p. 55.

85. Haynes, p. 57.

86. Domeneghetti, p. 184.

87. Lacey.

88. Lyons interview.

89. Brian Lomax, "Democracy and fandom: Developing a supporter trust at Northampton Town FC", *Sport and Society*, Volume 1, Issue 1, pp. 79–87, DOI: 10.1080/146609700087221250

90. Lyons interview.

91. John Dewhirst, *A History of Bradford City AFC in Objects*, Bantam Press: Shipley, UK, 2014, p. 332.

92. Evans interview.

93. Ray Boyle and Richard Haynes, *Football in the New Media Age*, Routledge: Abingdon, UK, 2004, p. 141.

94. Peter Millward (ed.), "Football and social media", in J. Hughson, K. Moore, R. Spaaij and J. Maguire, *The Routledge Handbook of Football Studies*, Routledge: London, p. 191, 198.

95. Calum McKenzie, "I'm surprised that football fanzines have survived", bbc.co.uk/news/uk-england-41149738, 25 November 2017. Accessed 3 Aug 2019

96. Millward.

97. *WSC* 393, December 2019.

98. Lyons interview.

99. Dewhirst interview; *A History of Bradford City*, p. 332.

100. Davies interview.

101. McKenzie, bbc.co.uk, 25 November 2017.

102. Dewhirst interview.

103. Chris Atton, "Football Fanzines and local news", in Bob Franklin (ed.), *Local Journalism and Local Media: Making the Local News*, Routledge: Abingdon, UK, 2006, p. 287.

104. votvonline.com/the2019-20-blogs/13-8 loc cit votvonline.com/about-us/, 3 August 2019

105. Evans interview.

106. votvonline.com/about-us Accessed 3 Aug 2019. Merthyr Tydfil and Rhymey Valley PlaidCymru Twitter account : MT&ChR@PlaidMTchR, 6 November 2019.

107. Interview with Tom Hudson, 4 October 2019.

108. Ibid.

109. Ibid.

110. Interview with Ian Hanahoe, 19, 22 October 2019.

111. Ibid.

112. Ibid.

113. Davies, Hudson interviews.

114. Hudson interview.

115. *WSC* 290, April 2011.

9

Multiplatform sports journalism

Mark Barden

Although there are earlier examples, particularly in relation to cricket, horse racing and prize fighting, the development of sports reporting as a distinct branch of journalism serving mass audiences was driven by the codification and professionalisation of sport in the Victorian era. And for the best part of a century, sports journalism was delivered to those audiences via a single platform – print.

Newspapers and periodicals enjoyed a monopoly that remained unchallenged until the development of radio broadcasting, and the advent of newsreels, in the early decades of the 20th century. The former enabled pioneering radio stations in Europe and North America to take their first steps in offering live coverage of sport, while the latter captured it on film to be screened a few days later in short news and current affairs digests in cinemas.

By the 1960s, the newsreel had been rendered obsolete by television, which gave viewers the chance to watch regular news programming in the comfort of their own homes. The same applied to major sports events, initially shown mainly via recorded highlights packages but (as broadcast technology improved and became more reliable) increasingly as they happened, although many sports governing bodies were initially reluctant partners, fearing the impact of live coverage on attendances and gate receipts.

Thus, by the mid-20th century, sports journalism was disseminated across multiple media platforms, but it was not truly *multiplatform*. Newspapers and magazines, radio stations and TV broadcasters remained largely separate and siloed, certainly in editorial and commercial terms, if not in relation to their overall ownership. Even in those instances where they had the latter in common, rival platforms resolutely did their own thing and regarded each other with suspicion, liberally laced with contempt, hostility and a generous dash of envy.

For aspiring sports journalists, and in the absence of specialist broadcast courses at higher education level, local newspapers remained the most likely entry point into the media industry. Some would then switch to radio, from where a move into TV was a logical next step, but many stayed in the print sector, which had its own established progression routes via larger city/regional newspapers and news agencies to national newspaper sports desks.

The point being: if you wrote about sport for a living, you tended not to also report on it via radio or television. If you ended up in one of the broadcast media, you were unlikely to also write about sport for print. TV had the lure of generally being better paid than print or radio (with the added attraction of its showbiz associations), but jobs were more plentiful in print and, to some extent, radio, and less concentrated in certain cities.

Thus, most sports journalists spent their careers working in one medium, and the majority of them in print due to the scale of the newspaper industry (with a title in every town). There was little, if anything, that was truly multiplatform about either the jobs they did or the outlets for which they worked. By the 1990s, however, the established structures of sports journalism were about to be blown out of the water by a combination of game-changing developments.

Internet game-changer

In the words of Bradley Shultz and Ed Arke: "The emphasis today is on doing more with less and having reporters that work on a variety of platforms – a consequence of both economic realities and growth in new technologies."[1]

The widespread availability of the internet by the mid-1990s significantly altered the working practices of many sports journalists. Those in newspapers and magazines were no longer limited by print deadlines and the availability of space on any given page of their publications. They were now serving two masters: print and online, and the move towards genuinely multiplatform sports journalism had begun – but it took a while in many places.

An example from my own career. In 2000, I joined the fledgling BBC Sport website as a reporter. After a few months, our team was relocated to another part of BBC TV Centre in west London along with colleagues producing the sports pages for Ceefax, the BBC's text-based TV service, which was still using technology developed in the 1970s. For some time, the web and text teams continued to create their own versions of the same stories for the two platforms: a frankly insane duplication which wasted time, effort and resources.

It did not take long for a fix to be found whereby stories were written to be used on both platforms, with the top four paragraphs (80–90 words) fitting a Ceefax template and then allowed to "run on" beneath these for the web version. Thus, the skill of capturing the essence of the most complex sports news story, or an incident-packed live event, migrated from text to the web, and our now-combined team became multiplatform sports journalism practitioners.

Elsewhere, newspapers, radio stations and TV channels were making decisions about how to embrace this first digital revolution. All of them wanted their own website, but the commercial potential of online remained unclear. In fact, some in the print media predicted their industry's ultimate demise at its hands. If content was offered at no direct cost to consumers, was not limited by space constraints and could be updated at any time, why pay for print titles at all?

Sure enough, UK national newspaper sales fell by 19.7 per cent between 2000 and 2009[2] and continued to decline. When it comes to local newspapers, for so long a major employer of sports journalists, 245 titles have closed in the UK since 2005.[3] Others are now produced from labour-saving editorial hubs, where one team of reporters works on several titles. Meanwhile the web's potential for expanding the audience for (and shelf-life of) radio and TV content began to be realised via technological advances which enabled platforms such as the BBC's iPlayer (2007) and ITV Hub (2008) to be launched.

Whatever the misgivings or optimism, the Pandora's box containing the internet has been opened, and there's no going back, particularly for sports journalism and broadcasting which, together with feature films, were an early driver of domestic satellite and then cable TV services. According to Schultz and Arke: "Demand for sports content has always been strong, but as technology improves and offers more options, demand noticeably increases."[4]

The anecdote about BBC Sport's web/text solution hints at the profound impact these technological developments have had on not just sports journalism but the wider news media industry in the past 25–30 years. The internet, and the rapid development of its associated digital technologies, have given organisations the chance to streamline their operations and workflows via the process of convergence.

Petros Iosifidis claims that: "Over the last three decades or so, convergence has been most manifest in the digital communications environment with the merging of the computing (information technology), broadcasting, print and telecommunications sectors."[5]

As the above quotation suggests, this "interconnection of information and communication technologies, computer networks and media content"[6] is by no means an entirely new phenomenon – plus, businesses have always sought to become more profitable by growing in order to dominate established markets and position themselves to tap into fresh ones. However, the speed of technological advances in the media sector in recent years has served to accelerate matters, tearing down the traditional boundaries between "old" and "new" media platforms. It has led to consolidations, takeovers, mergers and the creation of super-companies, many operating in global markets, whose activities span and link a huge range of content outlets, including those that were once, as noted earlier, separate and siloed.

In relation to the sports media, Raymond Boyle summarises the situation: "At the core of the relationship between the media and sport are three key factors that are shaping its development. These are: the marketisation of the media (and sport); the evolution of a digital landscape; and the globalisation of labour, economy and aspects of cultural practice and identity. The marketisation of media and sport, and indeed the internationalisation of sports and media cultures are in themselves not new. You could also substitute the term technology for digitalisation and again argue that this has always been a central component of the historical relationship between the media and sport. However, it is the scale, scope and pace with which these differing forces are impacting on the sports and media industries which has become increasingly significant."[7]

"Working harder and longer"

At the level of the individual journalist, this rapidly-evolving media landscape has created employment opportunities, new ways of sharing content with audiences, a need for new skills and the ability to work more efficiently. It has also created more work. Ask any mid-career journalist in 2019 what working across multiple platforms involves, particularly in the sports news/ live sports environment, and the stock answer will be "working harder and longer".

Newspaper sports journalists can no longer afford to relax once the day's final print deadline has passed; there are always extra stories to be written and additional content generated for the internet. Breaking news updates can be delivered at any time on the web, radio and via the 24/7 TV news channels facilitated by advances in broadcast technology. New technology creates new posts, but it is equally true to say that efficiencies invariably lead to job cuts, and this adds to the workload of remaining staff (or freelancers – they are cheaper, after all).

Tom Fordyce has worked for the BBC Sport website since 2000, having begun his career in the mid-1990s writing for *Match* magazine. He combines being the site's chief sportswriter with a variety of work for BBC Radio 5 Live, including his role as co-host of the hugely popular *That Peter Crouch Podcast*, and is also no stranger to being on camera. Multiplatform working can be, Fordyce believes, both a boon and bane for sports journalists.

"It creates some great opportunities, but it's also effectively a way of getting people to do more for less. There's definitely an economic imperative, and that's what drives it to a certain extent. It can also be totally relentless. Yes, being immersed in it is great, but it's impossible to switch off now. There's always something happening; you feel like you should always be on your phone, and people assume you are always available. Everyone is working more than they used to, and you do need to fight for that mental space – to take step back and come up with fresh ideas – because it isn't there like it used to be."[8]

Thus, a national newspaper sportswriter may now also host a weekly podcast, or be on camera for a live online debate show. They may conduct video interviews but also transcribe them for written content. They are expected to be active across the most popular social media channels, and navigate the potential pitfalls of interacting with readers/users. They must know how to maximise social media's potential in terms of promoting content – and what kind of content works best on it. We shall return to the subject of social media shortly, but for now it is clear that the direction of travel in multiplatform sports journalism makes it no country for old men (or women) – or at least for those who are not prepared to adapt and learn new tricks.

As Boyle puts it: "While some old-school sports journalists have never totally embraced the technology side of modern journalism … the reality is that contemporary sports journalism now often stretches beyond the confines of the game itself, so the modern sports journalist requires a breadth and range of skills that digital technology can help to facilitate … A new generation of more technologically-oriented journalists is entering the field."[9]

Fordyce concurs: "You definitely need more than one string to your bow these days, whether it's live blogging, podcasting, going on the radio to talk about a story, or interacting on social media. With the latter, certainly some older sports journalists, who really weren't used to receiving feedback, struggled with it. That whole idea that we are the gatekeepers whose knowledge is not to be questioned has gone. There are people out there who will know more than you do, so sometimes you have to see it as a collaborative thing, and if someone points out something you've missed, you just have to say 'thank you'. Ultimately, you've just got to embrace it all because if you don't, you risk being overtaken, not just by other people, but by the technology itself. Things are moving so quickly."[10]

Of course, specialist roles will continue to be needed in sports journalism and broadcasting – not everybody can do everything well. But universities and other educational/training organisations make a virtue of the multimedia nature of their sports journalism offerings. There are some 25 higher education institutions alone offering a wide variety of such courses in the UK at present, with the aim of turning out competently multi-skilled practitioners.

These courses are able to exist and attract students because of the explosion in the amount of sports news and coverage across all media platforms in recent years. Now in my mid-50s, television in the UK has, in my own lifetime, gone from being characterised by its lack of sports programming to a point where a host of dedicated channels deliver hundreds of hours every day. Digital broadcaster Sky Sports alone has 11. The BBC can now stream live coverage from every court at Wimbledon, and allow consumers to follow the sport of their choice at the Olympic Games.

The monetisation conundrum

This increase, and the proliferation of sports-based websites, digital radio stations, standalone podcasts, YouTube channels, etc., has clearly created many jobs in the sports media field. However, in relation to the internet, how to monetise clicks, views, follows, likes and shares continues to frustrate some of the finest minds in the wider media industry. For example, *The Guardian* had an audited daily circulation of less than 133,000 in July 2019,[11] but its website was ranked 10th in a global list of news sites, with 42 million monthly unique users.[12] And yet, stories on its site are accompanied by pop-up pleas for financial support from readers.

At the same time, *The Guardian* makes a virtue of the fact that its online content is entirely free, not hidden behind a paywall and only accessible to subscribers. The debate over whether to charge or not to charge consumers for online sports content continues unabated, and new entrants join the fray optimistically believing sports fans can be persuaded to pay for "quality". Summer 2019 saw the launch of the UK version of *The Athletic*, a subscription-based, American-owned website which promises users the best sportswriting, with no advertisements and therefore zero need for the kind of shallow or sensationalist "clickbait" stories churned out by many sports sites in their ceaseless drive for higher usage "traffic".

Adam Hansmann, *The Athletic*'s co-founder and chief operating officer, told *The Financial Times*: "It's a pretty contrarian idea that people would pay for sports content when there is so much out there [for free]. But fans really took to the model of an ad-free reading experience."[13] The company had reached 500,000 subscribers in North America by July 2019, with 80 per cent of them opting to renew. In the UK, the subscription rate at launch was £9.99 per month (soon reduced, inauspiciously, to £1.99), or £59.99 per year. The same *FT* article reported that the site was spending an initial £10 million in the UK, hiring more than 50 established sportswriters, with a focus on being "the new home of football writing" and aiming to attract 100,000 subscribers.

The Athletic's appeal is built on the premise that, in the words of Shultz and Arke: "TV, radio, magazines, newspapers and the web all need great storytellers who can captivate an audience and bring them back on a consistent basis."[14] This has been a media industry mantra since those earliest days of sports reporting mentioned at the start of this chapter, and continues to manifest itself in all sorts of ways, from *The Athletic* hiring only the cream of UK football writers on the web, to TV and radio paying big money for presenters who "really connect" with viewers/listeners, and national newspapers promoting their "big name" columnists.

At the same time, today's sports fans (thanks to the internet, including wider availability of sports-related stats/data and multiplatform sports journalism itself) are better informed than ever before, more eager to share and promote their own opinions (or see them highlighted as user-generated content), and far less in thrall to any notion of a gatekeeping sports media elite than previous generations. How could this not be so, given the radical changes to the ways in which we access and consume sports content?

So, while *The Athletic* set out in summer 2019 to persuade 100,000 paying customers to sign up in the UK, Arsenal TV – the YouTube channel "set up by Arsenal Fans for Arsenal Fans" – celebrated notching up its one millionth (non-paying) subscriber, with more than 662 million views of its videos since launching in October 2012 (as of August 2019). It also has a sizeable presence on other social media platforms, including Instagram (661,000 followers) and Twitter (317,800), and is essentially a self-created, full-time sports media job for founder Robbie Lyle.

Purists might say, "He's a disaffected fan, not a journalist," and they would be right – but also wrong, because the inexorable direction of travel in sports journalism is surely towards greater engagement with consumers via social media platforms. Fordyce recalls: "About seven or eight years ago, James Brown [former editor of *Loaded* and *GQ* magazines] said the future of journalism is no longer websites, it's social media. I remember thinking, 'Hang on, we've only just established websites as the successor to print,' but he was right."[15]

Increasingly, social media is being harnessed for the creation and promotion of bespoke content guided by commercially led strategies, offering a reminder that the primary purpose of sports journalism has always been to make money. It is used to create loyal customers and drive sales (including the take-up of the latest TV, broadband and mobile phone technology); it sells ad space and airtime slots. Latterly, it has offered advertisers, sponsors and other commercial entities, including sports rights-holders, the potential to build more meaningful relationships with consumers and engage with them in ways which feel more organic and less corporate.

Social media platforms, especially when accessed via mobile phones, are key to those business interests in terms of connecting with younger consumers. Those in the 18–34 demographic generally do not buy print products. They may have sat in front of the TV a lot as small children, but increasingly watch programming via apps on hand-held devices. They also either skip the advertisements or pay more for an ad-free service. Those apps also allow them to listen to radio stations without ever turning on a radio, although many prefer to access their favourite music via streaming platforms such as Spotify. In short, the best way to reach consumers – including sports fans – is increasingly via the multiple media platforms carried on their personal screens.

As Boyle states:

> We are moving to an age where debates about old and new media are becoming outdated and the new paradigm is one that places the relationship between content and screens at its core. By this we mean an age where technology allows screens to be held in your hand, be on your work desk, be in any room of your home and increasingly occupy public spaces from shopping malls to airports. The debate will be about how we pull content down onto these screens and how money is made from this transaction.[16]

A 2018 study in the United States found that 88 per cent of 18–29 year olds in America use social media; 94 per cent of those aged 18–24 watch YouTube; 78 per cent are active on instant messaging platform Snapchat; 71 per cent use Instagram; 45 per cent use Twitter. Nearly 70 per cent of all American adults use Facebook. Want to reach female consumers in the United States? Over 40 per cent of them are on Pinterest. College graduates? Fifty per cent use the professional networking and jobs platform LinkedIn.[17] It is clear that, in particular, our mobile phones – once just simple devices for making telephone calls – are now a vital conduit through which we engage with the world, and increasingly how sport and business engage with us.

This can be in the direct form of sport itself being made available via apps and social media platforms. Thus, if you are a Sky TV subscriber paying the necessary amount, live coverage of Premier League matches can be streamed to your smartphone via the Sky Sports app (and maybe your phone contract is with Sky Mobile). In 2016, Twitter acquired the rights to live stream the NFL's Thursday night games. A year later, it lost that 10-match package to Amazon Prime, who reportedly also fought off rival bids from YouTube and Facebook. In 2019, "alternate camera angle" live second-half streaming of 20 NBA games was unveiled by Twitter.

Sport has long been commodified in this way, but what is unique to today's multiplatform media age is just how subdivided the rights to broadcast it have become. The kind of exclusivity once sought by broadcasters when doing deals with sports rights-holders is fast disappearing. Sky held the exclusive UK live rights for the Premier League from 1992 to 2007 but now shares the available packages of games for the 2019–2022 seasons with BT Sport and Amazon. Those rights-holders, in the form of leagues, governing bodies and tournaments, increasingly seek to maximise the value of their "product" by doing different deals with multiple partners – and often in multiple markets around the world. This has served to increase the number of jobs in the sports production sector, but also created ancillary employment in web and social media roles, and in associated programme-making companies.

Thus, BT Sport – launched as a UK rival to Sky in 2013 – carries live and recorded sport across four channels; has a website team creating news, features and content which promotes the sports it screens; and commissions documentaries and other shows to complement its live sport offering. Not forgetting that all of these activities require social media planning and execution across various platforms to ensure the organisation engages with its key target audiences.

The new breed

Although the traditional business of the sports media – that is, the coverage of live events – will always be at its heart, it strikes me that this latter point touches on the direction in which multiplatform sports journalism is heading in the third decade of the 21st century. In an age of information overload, endless choices and the resulting scramble to get (and then hold) people's attention, a different kind of multiplatform sports practitioner is on the rise.

This new breed is best understood via the work companies such as Livewire Sport, an award-winning digital sports consultancy and content agency whose roll call of clients includes the Premier League, Wimbledon, the Football Association, World Rugby, the International Cricket Council, Formula 1 and the National Football League among many others. It was founded in 2011 by five colleagues from the BBC Sport website who saw a potentially lucrative gap in the market as broadcasters, brands and federations pondered how to maximise and monetise their digital media activities.

One of those co-founders, Pranav Soneji, admits there is an obvious difference between working *on* sport (to deliver coverage of it in the traditional sense) and working *for* sport (that is, in a business relationship with sport itself). "It's creating content to serve a [commercial] purpose, it's not sports journalism as it's traditionally been understood. It's not journalism in terms of scrutiny, it's not impartial, it's not the fourth estate.

"We're a strange organisation because we're not journalists, we're not working for the media, but we're a media company working on behalf of some of the biggest rights-holders and brands in the world, so we still need to have journalistic integrity to be able to make the right editorial calls." So, Livewire employs old-school sports journalism values? "But in a completely new set-up. That's effectively the best way to describe it."[18]

The company initially majored in providing live text commentaries on sports events for sports governing bodies and their commercial partners, but quickly saw their clients were engaged in a more fundamental struggle to realise the multiplatform potential of their "product". This was particularly true of the various social media channels on which many consumers (and especially sports fans) were spending an increasing amount of their time. How best to tap into these growing levels of digital engagement – and possibly make money from doing so?

Soneji recalls: "We began to realise that people [increasingly] weren't going to sit around for ages reading live blogs, or articles. It's all about creating stuff that captures the attention quickly, gets the message across, because many of us are time-poor but technology-rich, and how can we maximise the impact of what we're trying to do for our clients?

"Digital is always on, so we need to be able to create content regularly for audiences and ensure that our messages are relevant, and the objectives they serve are being met. But there has been a big change in terms of how people used to view the potential of digital to how it's viewed now. How do we get the most out of the various platforms that are available? How can that potential be monetised? How do we get our brands out there to reach the people they want to reach in order to achieve their business objectives?"

Thus, from initially hiring staff and freelancers with skills broadly aligned to written sports journalism, the company moved towards recruiting people with a wider range of abilities (or at least the desire and determination to master new ones), as well as for newly created specialist roles, particularly in relation to creating video content for use across various outlets. Moreover, these new multiplatform practitioners must have a critical awareness, in the words of Shultz and Arke, that: "It's best to understand today's sports media as the intersection of money, technology and culture, with each element influencing the other two."[19]

The "money" aspect of this tripartite relationship is something which, in truth, seldom bothered most sports journalists in the pre-digital age. Business considerations were for the board and advertising department; sport's commercial tie-ins were viewed as a necessary evil (but with occasional perks); governing bodies organised events and were not multimedia entities in their own right, while athletes (and their sponsors) relied on the sports media to connect with fans.

All this has changed. Sports journalists now need an appreciation of what content "works" (both editorially and commercially) on the multiple platforms they serve. Governing bodies, clubs and sport's business partners now employ their own sophisticated multimedia strategies to deliver measurable key performance indicators and tangible returns on investment for their brands. Many of these strategies feature sportspeople and utilise their appeal on social media, while other athletes use their status and digital profile for their own commercial purposes.

Livewire Sport has become a notable player in this new sports media landscape by expanding its activities into the "four Cs" – consultancy, creative, content and commercial – and these priorities shape its recruitment. Adaptability and a good understanding of sport's place in today's digital world, allied with strong editorial judgement, are the key qualities sought.

Echoing the words of Tom Fordyce, Soneji says: "You need to be able to show you can expand your skills into different areas, and that's how we expect people to develop their careers. They may be better at editing video, or as someone who edits social channels. We also expect our senior social managers to liaise directly with clients, and that in itself is a skill they need to develop. As that trust grows, we want to be able to give people more responsibility. So, there are lots of different ways to develop your career, but it depends on the individual and where they want to go."

There will, at least for some time to come, be jobs in sports journalism where commercial inputs and outcomes are not integral. Companies such as Livewire Sport will continue to sit alongside more "traditional" providers of sports news, features and coverage. Young sports journalists can still aspire to being the next Tom Fordyce, Anna Kessel or Henry Winter. But with the average salary of journalists in the UK static at £27,500 between 2012 and 2018,[20] other sports media-related career paths may seem more attractive to the next generation.

The other thing, as Soneji points out, is that the chances of anyone becoming the next Fordyce, Kessel or Winter are slim. "If you are making your way in the industry, at the start of your career, digital is so pluralised, with so many ways of delivering content to audiences, that your first job is probably going to be within our sector. Opportunities to join what were seen as the established media companies are probably two to three per cent of the [new jobs] total these days. You really have to make your own luck with the newer type of media companies which need people with the skills we've mentioned."

For Soneji, the "four Cs" which encapsulate Livewire's work are the way forward for the next generation of sports media practitioners. "Taking an idea from inception through to delivery, reporting back, being able to justify bigger budgets to create more commercial opportunities by using content effectively. We are content experts, but that still requires editorial integrity and judgement. A more independent way of working is crucial, as is being self-sufficient and self-motivated. People who are self-starters, who will take ownership of a project, they are the future of multiplatform working in the sports world."

References

1. Brad Schultz and Ed Arke, *Sports Media: Reporting, Producing and Planning* (3rd ed.), Focal Press: New York, 2016, p. 8.
2. "Newspaper sales plunge over the decade", *The Guardian*, 14 December 2009, https://www.theguardian.com/media/2009/dec/14/national-newspapers-sales-decade, accessed 12 December 2019.

3. "National newsbrands ABCs: Sundays hit by biggest circulation drops", *Press Gazette*, 13 June 2019, https://www.pressgazette.co.uk/national-newsbrand-abcs-sunday-newspapers-hit-by-biggest-circulation-drops/, accessed 12 December 2019.

4. Schultz and Arke, p. 6.

5. Petros Iosifidis, "The convergence phenomenon in media and communications", in *Global Media and Communication Policy, Palgrave Global Media Policy and Business*, Palgrave Macmillan: London, 2011.

6. Terry Flew, "Media Convergence", *Encyclopedia Britannica*, https://www.britannica.com/topic/media-convergence, accessed 12 December 2019.

7. Raymond Boyle, "Sport and the media in the UK: the long revolution?", *Sport in Society*, Volume 13, Issue 9, 2010.

8. Interview with Tom Fordyce, 15 August 2019.

9. Raymond Boyle, *Sports Journalism: Context & Issues*, Sage: London, 2006, p. 139.

10. Interview with Tom Fordyce.

11. "National newsbrands ABCs: Sundays hit by biggest circulation drops", *Press Gazette*, June 2019.

12. ebizmba.com, http://www.ebizmba.com/articles/news-websites, accessed 12 December 2019.

13. "US sports site *The Athletic* spends £10m to attract UK readers", *Financial Times*, August 2019, https://www.ft.com/content/8dc7ec28-b531-11e9-bec9-fdcab53d6959, accessed 12 December 2019

14. Schultz and Arke, p. xi.

15. Interview with Tom Fordyce.

16. Raymond Boyle, "Sport and the media in the UK: the long revolution?", 2010.

17. "Social media use: a majority of Americans use Facebook and YouTube, but young adults are especially heavy users of Snapchat and Instagram", *Pew Research Center*, March 2018, https://www.pewinternet.org/2018/03/01/social-media-use-in-2018/, accessed 12 December 2019.

18. Interview with Pranav Soneji, 5 June 2019.

19. Schultz and Arke, p. 2.

20. "'Real terms' wages drop for journalists as average salary in 2018 same as six years ago", *Press Gazette*, 1 November 2018, https://www.pressgazette.co.uk/number-of-uk-journalists-climbs-to-73000-but-fewer-work-in-newspapers-and-magazines-major-new-survey-shows/, accessed 12 December 2019.

10

Broadcasting: Interview with Martin Tyler

Adrienne Rosen

He's known as The Voice and it is, of course, perfect for broadcast – clear, sonorous and expressive – but nothing quite prepares you for two other aspects of the man: his majestic height and his disarming modesty. Even when Martin Tyler was voted Premier League Commentator of the Decade in 2003, he declared the award to be as much for his colleagues as himself.

For generations of fans he has been known as the voice of English football, leading Sky Sports' coverage of the Premier League since 1991. But it was the previous decade that firmly established him as a commentator, when he worked for ITV behind Brian Moore, attending the 1978, 1982 and 1986 World Cups and leading the team at the 1984 European Championships. In 1990, he moved to what was then British Satellite Broadcasting. Even now, at 72 years old and with 43 years of commentating to his name, he humbly refers to his career as "shouting 'goal' for a living".

But one of his most fulfilling moments has nothing to do with commentating, awards or notoriety. It's his proud admission that he's gone full circle and become assistant manager of his club – Woking.

Martin came into the television studio at the University for the Creative Arts in Farnham in 2018 to meet Adrienne Rosen and, as he took his seat next to the microphone, declared that he was rather looking forward to the interview and it was another opportunity he owed to the "beautiful game".

AR: So first of all I wanted to ask you about your own aspirations as a footballer. Has that somehow aided your ability to commentate?

MT: I wanted to play football for England, and for Woking particularly, because that was my club, that was where I went when I was eight years old to see my first live game, thanks to the boy next door who was one of six kids living in a bungalow. My dad had a shop in West Byfleet. I was born in Chester actually, which was on my mother's side of the family, and that's where most of the sport came from. My uncles and my grandfather and my great-uncle all played cricket for Cheshire and it was a very good standard and I learned a lot from them about how to behave in sport and how to win with dignity and lose with dignity, from when I was very young.

Football was odd because there was no organised football then – football came from me kicking a ball around in the local recreation ground. Our bungalow backed onto a school playing field which we weren't supposed to use, but we used to climb over the fence and use it until we got run out of it. So I used to whack a ball against the fence and my dad hated that because it would damage the fence. The hockey goals were quite good for little kids, so that all sort of fell into place really, and then I went to Woking football club at eight years old, December 1953. This 12-year-old neighbour took me on the bus, and Woking won 4-1 against Kingstonian, the club I later coached. I won't say the rest is history, but it sort of fell into place.

I played football until I was 27, 28 at a reasonable level for Corinthian Casuals – actually I've gone back to it now. I'm speaking to you this morning off the back of winning a playoff game last night at the club I coach, Hampton and Richmond Borough. We're trying to get out of the National League South into the National League, which would be a real commitment. It's the fifth division of English football, and we had a great win last night in extra-time. So I didn't get home until 1 am!

So it's still there, the active football side of my life. I look back on it in different ways, really. I was pleased to have played at the level I played, and although I wasn't particularly good, I played against some really good players who went on to play [professionally], and some of them I commentated on, which was nice. I didn't get trained as a broadcaster, so I guess the football side got me through those early tentative commentaries, and I love being in football company. I'm very comfortable being around football people, which strangely enough I don't think all commentators are, but they also have many other skills. They are much more trained in the use of their voice and maybe more. Journalistically I'm probably not great, but football journalistically I think I'm alright because I grew up reading all the newspapers, as you did in those days.

There wasn't much to watch on television – I heard a lot of radio. Radio was very big when I was growing up for football. I heard my first mention of football clubs on the radio. There was always a game. They used to broadcast the second half live of a match on a Saturday, and they couldn't tell you what it was. They were very petrified that you were going to hear it on the radio and you wouldn't go. I didn't ever quite follow that logic, but so we were told. I was still not going to football myself. I was six, seven years old, we were told at some point on the Saturday afternoon what the game was, and these were mystical places – Blackburn and Bristol and Middlesbrough. So I sort of fell in love with it very young, and I've tried to be involved in it all the way through and in different ways. Playing was one, obviously being a fan was one. And being a commentator has been an amazingly durable part of it.

AR: **Did you ever had any kind of training? Because I know some places like the BBC, it doesn't matter how senior or how good you are, you still get trained in voice coaching.**

MT: The only coaching I ever had with voice was when I would have been in my late 40s, early 50s. I went through a spell when my voice started to struggle towards the end of commentaries, and I got some advice. Funnily enough, there was an item about voice on *News at 10*, and someone pointed me in the direction of a specialist. I saw her once, and she said, "Oh you're at an age. You've never been trained, have you?" And I said no. She said, "You're still speaking with the voice coming in on the breath, not going out." I had one session, she gave me a cassette – that tells you how long ago it was – and told me how to count ONE, TWO, THREE, FOUR on the out breath. I've still got the cassette. I don't think I've got anything to play it on now! But I was very grateful to her, it was just a little hiatus and it could have got worse.

So no, it's all come from listening to other commentators, I suppose, and being absolutely in love with the game. It's never been boring or repetitive, which people might think my work is, but it's never repetitive for me. No two games are ever the same, and no two games are ever any more important than the other. I keep getting asked about the most important games – as you know from live broadcasting, only the next one is important. When I get asked about the past, it's quite difficult. I can do it, but I'm always looking forward. As soon as one game is finished, the next game is the one. I tend to do a lot of the same clubs, so I'm automatically updating what's happened in that game in my mind, and then because I'm doing them again in two weeks' time or something like that.

AR: **What sort of preparation do you do before a game?**

MT: I call it getting the smell of the fixture. What does it mean at this particular point in time, on this day when I go live, when we go live as broadcasters, what's the story? Sometimes that's very obvious, sometimes it's harder to create. Last week we had Man United and Arsenal, Arsène Wenger's last match at Old Trafford. It wasn't grand for the scheme of the match, but getting the Wenger shots walking out was important. You have to think about timing, and you've got a presentation and you've got a limited amount of time to do that, and hitting the right moments is important. It was not as intense as Man United games have been against Arsenal in the past, because Arsenal aren't doing particularly well at the moment. Manchester United are locked into second place and not likely to finish anywhere else.

First of all you have to know what the players look like. You can't hide on television. I know there are famous stories of radio commentators even missing goals, and then the next time there's a bit of cheering and shouting GOAL when it wasn't a goal because they caught up, if you like! Nobody knew any different but I think those days are long gone. The radio commentators are very good now. You have to identify the players and you have a certain amount of information, which is the hard skill really, to equate the information to the moment. You might be desperate to say something about somebody and you want to do it, and if you force it then suddenly the ball is in the net at the other end and you're left holding a sentence that you should never have started!

So that's part of the fun of it because you can never get that right. You know it's just that you're seeking perfection, perfection you can never attain, but it doesn't stop you trying.

AR: **So what kind of cribbing goes on? Do you have some kind of crib sheets – do you have photographs that you're able to refer to or is that all locked in your memory?**

MT: The identification, obviously, week-in week-out in English football is very easy. You know everybody really, though occasionally they throw a new one at you and we would have access sometimes. We would ask – can I have a look at him? They might bring the player to ask a question about the pronunciation of a name – you want to get it from the player not the club; it's quite a new phenomenon, really. Obviously, everybody knew how to pronounce all the players for the first 20 years I was commentating, because they were all British. I remember having a big discussion with a couple of players in the early 1980s who were Chris and Michael, and one wanted to be called

Michael because his mum called him Michael and another one was Mick, or Mickey or Mike. You know you want to get those right, the little subtleties. As a fraternity we have conversations about how to pronounce names. Certainly Sky ask me, if Sky Sports News have a problem with a new player, "what would you say?" The match is like an exam of your preparation, but it also has a life of its own of course. My biggest advice to young commentators is a simple one – watch the game. It sounds very obvious, but watch what happens. Don't pre-judge it just because you've done stacks of notes on something, watch what happens and react to that. It's more a reactive job, but you want to be propped up I suppose by all the prep.

AR: **Have you ever had a daft moment, an embarrassing moment, something you regret?**

MT: They're all immediately syphoned out of my brain, you can't sleep if not. Every time I do something that I don't like, whether it's wrong or just a grey area of being wrong, I know how to deal with it. I know I won't sleep, I know when I wake up in the morning it will be the first thing I think about and I know in two days' time I'll be better again. But the only way I get better again is to forget about it.

I think you always learn, there's always something that comes up when you think, "Oh I've done everything," and something happens in a game where you go, "Oh I've never seen that before, ever." That's why football is continually stimulating. Yes, you're in possession of the knowledge of both teams and you know what the strategies are, then you watch it unfold, which is an amazing privilege to have, really, and it has an outcome you can't predict. But you can't do too much prep, I don't think. I do write it out a page for each team as to what is relevant and a page for each team's players, so I have four pages of notes, plus the opening is always scripted because we have so little time, but that may not be scripted until 45 minutes before kick-off.

The only time I stop is when I get to a point where my brain won't do it anymore, so I know I have to stop, but mostly if I've got three weeks between games – which doesn't happen very often – I take three weeks prepping. If I have got three hours, I'll take three hours. At the World Cup, where you do get games back to back, you can't carry too much information about the second game before you've done the first. But as soon as the first is over, all you think about is the second. When the second is over all you think about is the third and it constantly goes on like that. I'm not saying I speak for every commentator but that's the way it works for me.

AR: **Do you think that is something to do with the nature of broadcasting though, because there is the idea that if you blink you'll miss it, whereas if you're writing something for print or writing something online, it's quite different?**

MT: I used to do match reports for *The Times* when I was obviously trying to get into journalism any which way. Yeah, I love the immediacy of it. I always read the papers the next day to see whether the print journalists have seen it the way I've seen it, or what lines they've taken from the game. It's more difficult now as there's so much online stuff.

Most of the football I did for the first twenty years was recorded highlights, because there wasn't so much live football. So for me it's always a special buzz when it's live and on the occasional occasion I get asked to do a recording that's only for highlights, I find it very hard, much harder than I thought I would to reach the "live-ness" of it. It's what lifts you.

You wait for the red light to go on and if I don't think I've got the energy, or I've got the flu, and I wonder how I am going to get through the next two hours, and then the red light comes on and two hours later you've done it. You stagger back to your car, but the adrenaline gets you through. It's a wonderful experience – really it's amazing how it conquers all.

AR: **Do you think football is particularly suited to the spoken word – that almost interactive nature of broadcasting – rather than reading about it the following morning in the papers?**

MT: I'm a consumer as well as a broadcaster so I want to see it while it's happening, but as a consumer it's hard to do that, so sometimes I would record a game and not find out about it, like the famous episode of the 1970s comedy series *Whatever Happened to The Likely Lads*. James Bolam and Rodney Bewes were two Geordie boys who were trying to get through the evening before the highlights of an England international came on TV because they felt it would ruin the whole enjoyment of watching. Sport is unscripted, hopefully. Maybe not always, sadly but that's another story.

Television is having its own difficulties at the moment because it's a different kind of vision. People still want vision, they want access to it, but they want a different kind of vision. They want access to it, but they don't want to necessarily sit down on a Sunday at 4 pm and watch a whole game. The younger generation will have it on their devices and we now offer goals as soon as they've happened on an app. We're having to move with the times, and I do things now like Facebook Live and Twitter interviews before the game that go out on our website, and they are really important to building up the whole package. One thing I've learned is that I have to be, despite my advancing years, on this modern page, and I enjoy it, to be honest. I don't participate in social media myself, but that's a different principle really. But I understand why the company does, so I'm always up for doing these extra little bits. I think you just have to learn a new language and learn the new technology, because it's constantly changing and television has changed a lot during my 40 years of broadcasting.

What hasn't really changed is my job in the match. I still identify the players, I still add the information and I still try to tell the story. I've still got almost the same piece of equipment, the lip mic. They tried the headsets but they don't work so well, but that lip mic, which was invented by the BBC back in the 1940s, I used on the first game I did back in 1974 and the last one I did last Sunday, and I think that's amazing really. With all the better cameras, the different lineage on the pictures and the whole analogue digital stuff and I still use the same lip mic! Not exactly the same one, but made by the same design.

AR: **Have you had to adapt your style in any way given the kind of devices that most people will watch or listen to commentary on?**

MT: I don't think so. The one thing that has changed in my time is having the co-commentator. When you did recorded games, there wasn't room for two. It was hard to edit two voices, so there was only one voice. Funnily enough, I'm going to the World Cup live for Australian television and I'll be on my own. It will be strange because the conversational style that has come in through a two-handed commentary is the biggest change in my time. I would say it's like a couple of mates going to a game with a microphone. You've got to have a bit more responsibility than the two mates. There are laws of the land that you can't infringe and language barriers too, but that's what it's like, and I really enjoy the camaraderie of a two-handed broadcast.

People always say, "Who is your favourite?", but they're all part of my flock, so to speak. I want it to work for them. I'm not a trained broadcaster, but I am an experienced broadcaster. Ex-players are either inexperienced or often not trained when they come out of football to sit alongside the commentator, so I try to work really hard to make them comfortable because I know it's for the better of the broadcaster, and therefore the broadcast. And I'm part of that so you get a bit of reflected glory if they're good. You have to sort of guide them along really, so that's a big change.

The other thing about relating to young people is that I do voiceover commentary for a computer game called FIFA. I've done it for 10–12 years, and that resonates with the very small and up to teenage years, so you might find me at my local football club at a game after I've been coaching, sitting and talking to a group of eight-year-olds thinking "What's going on here?" And they'll be quizzing me about the computer game and telling me what it lacks is this, this and this, and they're brilliant. It's fascinating, I suppose. It is extraordinarily humbling to find you go to the World Cup in Brazil and there's a kid from Ecuador who's eight years old and knows your voice.

AR: What did being voted commentator of the 1990s mean to you?

MT: What it did make me realise was that Sky Sports had had a fantastic decade and I was the main voice on Sky Sports, so it's very nice to have the trophy and it's on my mantelpiece at home. But I think if I hadn't got it, I wouldn't be sitting here talking to you now. Because I had the responsibility of carrying many of the main matches through that decade for Sky, and Sky had a huge impact on change. The Premier League was new – satellite television, as it was called then, was new. We used to go up and down on the train to our games and look at all the cities we would go through and see how many satellite dishes there were.

Television is a team game, just like football, and to be honest with you I don't really approve of the individual awards for footballers because it's the team and none of them can do it without the team. I feel the same about anything I've had, really, that I'm representing an amazing sense of broadcasting. Where Sky came from, people forget what it was like before sports channels started.

I shared a flat in the early 1970s with a very young and promising cricketer called Bob Willis, who was out of work in the English winter, but he'd been mentioned in despatches as a candidate for the England tour to Australia. Back then, the only coverage of the Test matches out there was half an hour of BBC highlights per day, which we watched together even though they were broadcast while the next day's play was in progress. Anyway, in the middle of November, Bob got a call and he was hustled out to Australia to play for England as a replacement, so by the time the third Test came around I'm sitting in this little flat in Streatham looking at the same television and the guy who was sitting next to me a week earlier is on the screen playing for England. An extraordinary experience.

The BBC and ITV were multi-purpose broadcasters, and back then sport had to go where it could, and it was a nuisance sometimes for the schedulers, *Coronation Street* being moved, things like that. So a sports channel was an amazing thing to happen for all sports lovers, and of course suddenly everything was live. England cricket matches have all been broadcast live since Sky entered the picture, and nobody would ever broadcast anything 24 hours later except a repeat of a live show. I was lucky because I'd had 17 years at ITV and I'd learnt my trade, and I was just about the right age and had the right amount of experience. I wasn't the first choice – I don't even know how many choices I was down the line. I know the risk of moving from a secure terrestrial television commentary job to something that could have folded in six months would have been too much for some people.

AR: **Why wasn't it too much for you?**

MT: It was to start with, but in 1982 I did the World Cup final for ITV, which was a really big thing in my career. I'd only been a commentator for seven or eight years, so to do a live World Cup final up against the BBC was an amazing bit of fortune, and then I did the 1986 World Cup. I was down to do the 1990 World Cup, but I wasn't going to do so much because Brian Moore presented and commentated and he was going to do more commentating. So I was down the pecking order, but I still had a job.

I know two or three people definitely turned Sky down for reasons of insecurity, and it came my way. I had an interview in January 1990 and I loved the idea of an all-sport channel. This was when it was British Satellite Broadcasting. A lot of ex-BBC people, such as Nick Hunter, Mark Pearman and Mark Schofield, came across. I still wasn't going to do it, and then a guy who was looking after me, my agent John Hockey, sat me down and said, "Look, you should do this. You're not going to get that much more at ITV as Brian is doing all the commentating and he's going to get all the big games." I said, "But no-one will watch it." He said everybody in football will watch it because it was live, and I went, "Where do I sign?" I realised then that the people I wanted to show my worth to was the football community that I loved and respected. I thought, "They will watch, they will find a way." So yeah, I made a big jump and happily the landing was a nice soft one.

AR: **How important is the producer to you in the whole process? Is there somebody you have particularly enjoyed working with?**

MT: I can't tell you people I don't want to work with for sure.

AR: **Are there some?**

MT: I probably felt a bit like that in ITV terms because they weren't sports specialists. I can remember doing a game in the 1980s where I heard the director say to the camera operator, "I want a shot of Kenny Dalglish," who was a superstar. The camera operator said, "Which one is he?" and I go, "Well, what chance have we got?" So when you get to work with the specialists, everyone is in it because they love the sport.

It's a demanding job working for a 24/7 sports channel. It's more the match director who would oversee what I do and point out various things for structure, where the commercial breaks were, things like that, but the match director is the important one because we're working very closely with the pictures, and the truth is the picture is miles more important than the words. Miles. Honestly, I'm not just being super silly modest here, it's about the pictures, and if I can find some words that marry up to pictures then I'm doing my job.

I get linked – I'm not unhappy about it – with the Sergio Aguero goal in 2012 which won Manchester City the Premier League title with the last kick, but nobody talks about Tony Mills the director when they show it, and the shots are amazing. He's got a shot of Joe Hart, the City goalkeeper, who is in total disbelief. They needed to score two in added time to win the league, and if they didn't, they would have lost the league from a position where they should have won it, and, more than that, Manchester United, their biggest rivals, would have won it. If you'd made it a movie, people would have laughed. I was with Tony and we had a split screen, and Manchester United had finished their game – their players were watching our monitor at Sunderland – so we split the screen and the game was still going on in front of us. As the screen went back to its fullness and they got rid of the Man United stuff, they won the ball and City had scored the goal within 10 seconds, and then this shot of Joe Hart running around not knowing how to celebrate. It's just a wonderful piece of television and I get asked about every third day about it. People still ask me about it, and I always say, "Look at the pictures, turn the sound down and look at the pictures." The pictures are amazing, and that's the joy of it.

I've done a little bit of radio since being a commentator, but I was maybe slightly different from the other commentators. They all came through a radio background. It's much easier to get a chance in radio than on TV, especially when I started, so I'm a sort of freak, really. I'm a football person of not very high stock as a player, but somebody who had been coached by good people and played against good people, and who managed to find a voice in the midst of it.

AR: Do you adapt your style for different broadcasters, or do you find that the reason they want to work with you is because you have this very individual style?

MT: I don't know what my style is. What I would say about commentating is you have to be yourself. You might ham it up a bit, you know what I mean. You might accentuate it, but it is essentially yourself, and if you try to be somebody else you're not going to get very far because it's unscripted. If you're given a script you could be an actor, but if you're not given a script you have to be the best improv person ever to do that for 90 minutes, three times a week, so you have to be yourself. I've worked for the Americans, I've worked for Australia and I've worked for world feeds. I do that quite a lot now. I did a thing for the World Cup for the USA for ESPN in 2010, and the terminology is different – for instance, they don't have "draws", they have "ties". To them, a draw is something you put your clothes in. And there are various other differences, but we came to the conclusion to use the English terminology. I would never call it soccer, never, ever. We did have quite a brainstorm on what was best to do and the agreement was to do what you do naturally, so being what you are is important. I couldn't change too much. In fact, I've got to do a promo for Sky, and they've said on my behalf, because it's an outside contractor, that you can't get him to say anything he wouldn't say normally.

AR: What kind of things might they try to get you to say?

MT: Just use of words probably, or maybe a level of shrieking that I wouldn't do. People say, "What do you do?" when they don't know me, and I say, "I shout GOAL for a living," and that's what I do. If there is a tombstone, which can't be that far away now, I would be quite happy for that to go on … he shouted GOAL for a living for 40 years!

AR: Was it harder for you commentating on your own team, Woking?

MT: I've only commentated on Woking about four times, and it wasn't hard at all. It's just another game. Afterwards you've got more of an interest in it, but, no, in fact if anything you probably make sure that people know that that is your team. I'm very lucky because most commentators support a Premier League team. The thing you can't change, it's the world that we live in, is I get accused, "Ohm you support them, you hate them, etc." That's why I'm not on social media because I would spend my whole life going, "I'm a Woking fan tweet, tweet. I'm not a Liverpool fan, I'm not a Man United fan, I'm not an Arsenal fan …" "Oh, you must be, you said this." So for a total clear conscience, I have no allegiance to anybody and I haven't commentated on Woking for a long time. I did do a couple of games where they had quite good wins, because they're a non-league team and we were covering the [FA] Cup, but nobody doped me out on it. I have to go to the manager of the other team and I have to say, "Can you tell me how your team is going to play?" and

I have to have that trust, so that's been quite easy, but I do know some of the others have quite dedicated followers of big teams and we chuckle about it. They've had a moment where their team have lost a game, but it's only banter. But the public don't know. The public think they would recognise a bias in you, but I can't stop that. They are entitled to their opinion, but I can tell you with a total clear conscience that the only team I support is Woking.

AR: **What about covering England international matches. Is that any harder for you?**

MT: That's a good question because I've always taken the view that there are two teams on the pitch. I've never called England "we", and when I left ITV in 1990 I'd done the 1978 World Cup which England weren't in; the 1982 World Cup where I did all the England games; the 1986 World Cup where I did all the England games, and I still wouldn't say "we". Now I know the current commentators for BBC and ITV feel a bit differently to that, but every World Cup I've done since I left ITV from 1990 up to this one I just got my visa for. I've been doing it for another country, so I can't say "we" when I'm on Australian television. By the time this interview gets to print, I will have done 300 England games. It sort of felt at the start like you get picked to play in your own job. I remember my first one in 1982 and I was down to do the World Cup in 1982, and I said, "Thank you so much for picking me to do the England game," but I haven't done one yet. Don't you think I should do one first? And they played Holland, as we called them in those days, in the May of 1982, and I did that one. I also did a home international in Cardiff against Wales. I also count one appearance as a substitute. I was working for ITV in 1985, and England were on tour in Mexico before the Mexico World Cup in 1986, and Brian Moore went out to commentate. We have a backup in the studio if the sound doesn't come through, and when England played Italy in Mexico the sound didn't work so I got on for the first 20 minutes from London pretending I was in Mexico, so that counts.

AR: **Is there any commentator whose style you have particularly admired or who influenced you?**

MT: I admire everybody who earns a living doing it because it's not easy to get going. It's a little bit easier when you've done a few years, because the familiarity of the voice is important and I think once you become a familiar voice, a recognisable voice, you're more likely to be indulged if you get things wrong or let off if you make a mistake. People would, I think, be a bit more sympathetic. I would say I do around a hundred games a season, but I would say I'm pleased with four of them.

AR: **Are you too hard on yourself?**

MT: I don't think so, no. I've been constantly looking to get it right. People always say, "Have a good one, good luck," and I say, "I'm due one," or, "I'll keep trying and I'll get it right one day." You just can't get it to the point of perfection. There will be something in the broadcast where you'll go, "Why did I say that?" or "Why didn't I say that?" or "Why did I pause?" or "That seemed like an odd gap." It doesn't happen so much now, but it used to happen. I've been lucky, I haven't had to change my pace for television. I've never done radio except for the odd time when I've been asked to help out, and I'm no good at it as you have to talk all the time. You might think it's odd, because I'm talking all the time today, but you have to understand all the elements that go into it. It's only complex to the commentators – that's why we all get on very well together, that's why I admire everybody who has a job in it. And I try to encourage them and help them, but I've just been doing it longer and you can't really understand it unless you do it, and that's hard for the producers because they don't do it. If you have a producer who has been a commentator, you're quids in because you can have a conversation about the minutiae of it, but they will ask why didn't you do a particular thing or why are you a bit flat today. Maybe the game was flat, maybe you're right, maybe I was.

So it's weird because it's both completely different and somewhat repetitive because of the dynamics of it. Occasionally something might happen. I had poor Ryan Mason, who had to finish his career with an injury [for which he received treatment] that lasted 15 minutes on the pitch, and you have to fill that amount of time. That's a different kind of day. Or in the old days of crowd trouble I was very lucky, I think, that I wasn't at Hillsborough. I wasn't at Heysel. I wasn't at the Bradford fire, and there are some amazing broadcasts of terrible events. The nearest I had was the England game in Dublin that got stopped after 27 minutes for crowd trouble in 1995. I had to fill a bit for that, but I was quite prepared because there was a bubbling-under feeling the day before that there might be trouble. I had some news stuff to back it up, but I haven't been forced into that. John Helm, a good friend of mine, how he did the Bradford fire I don't know, when it was all going on around him.

AR: **Maybe that was the secret, because it was going on around him and he's a broadcaster, he locked into professional mode and described the unfolding events. Some intensely moving journalism came out of that time. Still, it's every broadcaster's nightmare to hear in their earpiece the word "fill", especially as you have no idea for how long. How do you do it?**

MT: I've got a mate with me, a co-commentator, so we can talk to each other, and there are games where I think this is not going to be particularly dramatic. I've got to be interesting and I've got to have some things to talk about which are maybe not totally related to the game. I did a game at Wembley on Monday – maybe they are selling Wembley or not, maybe you know the story, so that's sort of up your sleeve. But when the game is going on, you have to do it carefully when the ball is out of play or there's an injury break.

It's my subject. I couldn't really fill on anything else, so I ought to be able to do it. I spend my whole life talking about it, there are always issues. I was actually thinking, coming here today, about the number of goals that Manchester City have scored this season: 129, I think. Liverpool scored two more last night, so they are well into over the hundreds, and there is something changing about football. These are new figures, so what's happening in football? Why are we not defending properly? Has the game been tilted in favour of the attackers by law changes, things like that? I'm thinking I'd better do a bit of work on that, because this game on Sunday that I'm doing against Huddersfield is only really being covered because at the end of it City are going to get the trophy, which they won two weeks ago. So we are only really there for that, although Huddersfield have to get some points, otherwise they might be relegated, so there will be an edge to it from their point of view. But if City are three-nil up and the result is in the bag, maybe I should be talking about what is happening, why we can't defend properly, why are so many goals being scored. There is always something to say.

AR: **Do you have a favourite co-commentator?**

MT: No, it's my job to make them all work and I like them all. I think I'm a little bit starstruck still. I'm wanting to be the kind of footballer that they are [or were]. I got close enough to know how much better they were at what I was trying to do. I wasn't just a park footballer. I played with people who then went on and played in the old First Division, so I could see why they were better than me, and then the guys I'm sitting with have been in the forefront of the game, so I can ask Gary Neville about winning the league with Manchester United, or I can talk to Alan Smith about scoring the goal at Anfield that helped Arsenal to that amazing title win in 1989. It's a privilege. I'm just somebody who would be watching it if I wasn't doing what I'm doing. I don't know what else I would have done. I went into market research when I left university and it was just horrendous. I would have been a white-collar worker somewhere watching football and wishing I could talk to these guys, and here is someone paying me to talk to these guys. So, happy days.

AR: **What has been the most memorable game for you – Manchester City beating QPR with two goals in the last minute to win the Premier League?**

MT: That's what everybody says. In fact, my favourite game was a match in 1996 between Liverpool and Newcastle. Both teams were going for the title in April, and neither won it as it turned out. It finished 4-3 and it was a rollercoaster game played with wonderful attacking skills, and it did, in 90 minutes, sum up absolutely everything that you needed to become a football fan. Every ingredient about football was in there: an iconic ground, great clubs. Kevin Keegan was managing Newcastle and had played for Liverpool. There were a lot of connections between the clubs, and Liverpool scored after two minutes. Robbie Fowler scored two, Stan Collymore scored two, [David] Ginola, [Faustino] Asprilla and [Les] Ferdinand scored for Newcastle, famous players. It was a stellar cast, and it was a midweek game, actually, which we broadcast live, and we didn't want to leave the ground. We were in the presence of greatness and we didn't want to go! They had to virtually tell us to get out of the ground. We were all going back to parts of the Midlands and me to London, and we stopped at a pub on the Liverpool ring road – and I'm one of these people, that if I drive you to Newcastle from here, we ain't stopping unless you have to go to the loo. So I would be normally getting in the car at Anfield and driving straight home as quickly as possible. But that night we stopped and talked and talked about it – and there are nine minutes on YouTube if you want to understand what it's about. A spellbinding game.

AR: **I'm intrigued about how you stop some bias from creeping in. Because of course the beauty of television, as you said, is being able to use the words that go with the pictures, but at the same time your tone of voice can give away a great deal. So how do you stop that bias?**

MT: The difficult part about being objective is of course you get to know some of the players better. There was a player, Mervyn Day, who played for West Ham, Aston Villa and Leeds. He had a long career, and I'm godfather to his daughter. He's a goalkeeper, and if he makes a mistake as a goalkeeper it usually leads to a goal, so those kind of things, personal things, are a little bit more challenging. Gareth Southgate is manager of England now. He is a very well-balanced guy and a very likeable man, and he was playing for Aston Villa, a game against Chelsea, and Chelsea won 3-0 and two of the goals were down to Gareth. Well, Gareth was playing for England a few weeks later, and I said, "I'm sorry to go to town a bit on those goals," and he said, "You wouldn't have been doing your job if you didn't," and maybe not everybody is quite as mature as that.

I expect my broadcasts to be criticised by the television critics and on social media, I just expect it. Nobody likes to be told they're rubbish, but the truth is that if you put your head above the parapet, people have a right to have a pot shot at it. And as broadcasters, we do. Maybe it took me a while to come to terms with that. It's not nice when you start. You're always looking for compliments, particularly because people who are going to employ you are going to read the papers. Now it just comes with the territory. You can't please everybody all the time, and all you try to do is be journalistically objective, be fair. Yes, as lead commentator we do criticise, but the co-commentator has a more critical role. If you say, "That's a terrible foul," or whatever, you know you can't not be judgemental. But I'm not there to be the judge, the judge is alongside me. I might be somebody who can suggest rather than actually nail down some heavy stuff.

I very rarely disagree with the people we have, who are very good, but occasionally I will disagree. Take the Arsène Wenger thing. Alan Smith played for Arsenal but not for Wenger, but he thought it was time for a change of manager. It was a big day at Old Trafford, and I basically said, "It's a sentimental day today, you're not really into being sentimental like that?" and he said, "No, I suppose not," and afterwards he said, "Did you put me on the spot then?" and I said, "No, I know you, I know what you want to say and I know you can handle it." We want it to work. I would say everything in sport is a team – the officials are the teams, the players are the teams, the management have a team. I'm part of the management team at a non-league club, and I know exactly what it's like. Television is nothing if it's not a team, it just can't exist, and in 25 years that team at Sky has grown from being a small team with very big ambitions, but plenty of times we looked as though it wasn't going to quite happen. Now I go in there and it's a mega campus. It's unbelievable, absolutely unbelievable, and I have a little chuckle and go, "If it wasn't for football this never would have happened."

AR: So what about the next step on your journey? Are there any personal aspirations you still have?

MT: Apart from being able to say, "England have won the World Cup," no. I've achieved far more than I ever thought. I like kicking a ball about a park, and it seems like only yesterday, really, because life does go fast when you're having fun, and I've had a hell of a lot of fun. I would like to continue doing it. I'm very aware that I'm at an age where – nothing to do with ability, just the physiology of the human species – I'm at some point going to say that's it. I've got a wonderful optician. I think I should be sponsored by Ellis & Thompson of Cobham because eyesight is really important, just as important as your voice, really. With some of the grounds now like the London Stadium, the commentary position is a really long way away. I've done about 10 in there this season, and you just come away thinking, "Oh thank god I've survived it."

There have been many changes for the better. Identification is always a bit worse in the bad weather. When there's no mud, that is a great help for commentators because all the pitches were muddy when I started. You soon got [players] caked in mud and there were no distinctive hairstyles, and if shirt numbers were covered in mud that made it really quite difficult. The floodlights are much better. In the early years – they'd been going 20-odd years when I started – they weren't fantastic, but the lux has to be a certain level, so we get a lot of help in that sense. When the teams were all numbered 1–11 you went by the teamsheet, but if somebody decided they wanted to wear the number eight and swapped with a teammate, if you didn't know the players, you would just be going off the numbers. Now of course they have a number for the season, so that has been a great boon for the commentators. I always believe survival equals success, and I'd like to survive for a bit longer.

AR: What about the somewhat male world that you inhabit? Are you seeing that change?

MT: You're right to ask the question, because it was just the way the world was and football has always reflected the world. Maybe towards more recent times it's had more power to change the world. I think it can be a real force for good. There are certain things that I'm trying to be involved in where football might help. There's a lot of good work done by football that doesn't get perhaps as much credit. They've got so much money that they should be doing this. People make good decisions and, as an example, Sky and the Premier League were doing this joint promotion about single water bottles instead of plastic bottles. This is a save the planet scheme, and I was able to give that a bit of a push for a worldwide audience so there are a lot of good things that go on. Diversity is very important, and I think football has been excellent there. There is very little racism on the pitch. My first fellow forward when I joined a football club after university was an African called Dougal Alvarenga. He was fantastic, and he took me into his world. I was 22 years old and he was 19, we became really good mates. Football has carried on a path of diversity and there are more players from diverse ethnicity now, it's fantastic. Colour of skin is nothing to do with football – you're either good enough or you're not. The club that I coach at, we have got all sorts of different backgrounds, London in particular. It's great, and I think the world is catching up a bit on that.

We are playing catch-up a bit on the diversity issue with women, but now my daughter's best friend's sister is Vicky Sparks, who is commentating on *Match of the Day*, and she is really good. She is very lucky, because she has a slightly deeper voice, and I think you do have to have a bit of resonance in your voice. I worked with Alex Scott, and she played for England a hundred times and she's working at Sky on a lot of matches now. We are probably a bit behind, but it is getting there. I do think now, "I can talk football to ladies," which perhaps 30 years ago I wouldn't have had much opportunity to. And, of course, women watch Sky. What they don't do is send fan mail to commentators, which is a great shame. It's always been a real curse in my life. I met somebody who said, "My wife is big fan of yours," and I said, "I've been doing it 32 years and that's the first lady who has become a fan." I would like a few more lady fans!

11

Twitter

Simon McEnnis

If a new platform provides the opportunity to mass-communicate with audiences, then journalists do not generally miss out. Journalism responds to the advent of a new social media network by instantly establishing a presence. Facebook, then Twitter and, more recently, Instagram are prime examples. Newsrooms have developed multi-platform strategies that are designed to reach fragmented audiences. Sports journalism and Twitter have emerged as particularly close bedfellows because of the way that, as Umberto Eco pointed out,[1] sport lends itself to chatter. If Twitter is a conversation, then sport is inevitably going to be at the heart of it.

Twitter's emphasis on real-time communication neatly complements sports journalism's emphasis on live event reporting. Twitter also lends itself to snippets of opinion – an important norm in sports journalism. As a consequence, Twitter has intensified the daily work routines of sports journalists, who must curate and regularly update their personal Twitter accounts in addition to their core practice of sourcing and writing stories.

Twitter was launched in 2006 but not widely used in sports journalism practice until 2009.[2] Elite sports journalists working for national newspapers found they were quickly able to develop significant followings augmented by television and radio appearances. Initially, sports journalists were not entirely sure how to use Twitter, not helped by the lack of clear advice and guidance from newsrooms.[3] Further, younger journalists adapted and embraced Twitter quicker than older journalists entrenched in traditional ways of working.[4] Newsrooms were uncertain whether Twitter was a fleeting trend or a new world order.[5] After all, social media networks such as Friends Reunited, MySpace and Bebo were in decline by 2009. We now know that Twitter has shown resilience as an important platform for digital communication within journalism. However, while other digital media corporations such as Google, Facebook and Amazon continue to grow, Twitter has struggled to both make money and grow its user base.[6] Uncertainty persists around its future, although the general view from within the media industry is that the disruption and innovation it has created is here to stay and will only evolve.

Sports journalism's relationship with Twitter has attracted significant interest within both the academy and industry. These analyses tend to focus on the ways in which sports journalists use Twitter and the following themes have emerged: publishing platform, source for stories, user interactions and news/opinion. Studies in this field have yielded interesting findings

– for instance, that there is a discrepancy between how sports journalists view their Twitter use (breaking news) and what they actually post (opinion).[7]

My interest in the Twitter–sports journalism relationship is how these shifts in practice have impacted on the professional identity of sports journalists. I explored how professional sports journalists articulate their occupational distinctiveness when confronted with fans and athletes posting their own news and opinions on Twitter.[8] I found that sports journalists considered their experience in attending sports events to be vital in the development of expertise while their privileged access to the professional sports environment led to the accumulation of exclusive information that could be packaged as breaking news. Sports journalists thought these insights into professional sports infused their tweets with considerable cultural value.

However, the sports journalists interviewed also spoke about Twitter as a source of professional uncertainty in their attempts to maintain ethical standards. They also spoke of experiencing anxiety in the way that Twitter was reshaping their lived experience, particularly their "real-life" human interactions. There is also a need, then, to analyse how Twitter has disrupted sports journalists' professional conditions. Sports journalists must still ultimately strive to be professional and be recognisably so to outsiders, regardless of the technological circumstances of their practice. What has Twitter meant for sports journalists' ethical standards? What new market-driven pressures are in play? How has Twitter redefined sports journalists' professional relations inside and outside the newsroom? This chapter will mainly focus on the UK, as my research is situated within this particular national context, and will predominantly reference football due to its prominence in UK sports journalists' use of Twitter.

Thirsting to be first

Twitter has hastened the urgency to break a story, partially arising from newsroom paranoia that someone either within or outside the profession will tweet it first. Journalism as a profession has always been obsessed with exclusives as a form of competitive advantage over a commercial rival. However, newsrooms have no inkling over who else has access to that same information.

Sports journalists are in danger of sacrificing speed for accuracy due to the pressures of instant publication. "Breaking news" tweets may not properly be verified, and sports journalists may be tempted to share and retweet second-hand information without checking it themselves. Rumour can spread like wildfire on Twitter. In 2011, French footballer Steed Malbranque was thought to have prematurely ended his contract with Saint-Étienne in order to look after his four-year old son, who had been diagnosed with cancer. Premier League footballers including Wayne Rooney, Joey Barton and Rio Ferdinand tweeted their sympathy and support. However, Malbranque's solicitors revealed that the story was not true – not only did the player not have a four-year-old son with cancer but he did not have a four-year-old son at all. Also, Malbranque had no plans to retire from football or terminate his contract at Saint-Étienne.[9] This example shows the importance of sports journalists remaining vigilant, to do their own primary checks on stories, and not rely on second-hand information. Journalists certainly find truthfulness more difficult to achieve in the Twittersphere.

Further, sports journalists must also make difficult, almost unfathomable, calculations over whether a story is likely to hold until the next day's newspaper or if it is likely to be scooped if they wait that long, in which case they tweet the news and upload the story to the website.[10] Journalists are reminded by their employers that Twitter does not generate money for news organisations through advertising revenue, so they must use the platform to attract traffic to the newspaper website.

Twitter has also stimulated a more complex relationship between journalists and transparency. On the one hand, journalists experience immense pressure from their news editors to provide a constant supply of content for websites, which can lead to under-developed stories. This changing dynamic has led to greater secrecy and distrust within newsrooms. Journalists may conceal stories in progress and only inform their editors when they are ready for publication. On the other hand, Twitter has forced journalists to acknowledge rumour and speculation, particularly around big, breaking news stories. Audiences now expect journalists to be that authoritative voice in confirming facts around the initial fog of confusion. Journalists, who have historically been notoriously secretive in revealing their story-gathering processes, must tell readers on live blogs how they are seeking to verify the rumours that are swirling around on social media.

Decisions on what to tweet and when to tweet can also bring sports journalists into conflict with senior managers. Editors no longer have complete control over information that is generated from within their own newsrooms. News organisations have drafted social media policies and guidelines, but tensions remain between editors and reporters over Twitter behaviour and conduct. Editors can become mistrustful of reporters' motives behind tweeting, with suspicions that they are looking to promote their own individual brand. As a result, senior managers are fearful that their employers may attempt to seek personal glory by claiming the scoop for themselves on Twitter rather than going through the official, revenue-generating lines of publishing on the newspaper website. In April 2017, *The Sun*'s deputy head of sport Dean Scoggins reacted to news that Cornwall's *Sunday Independent* in the south-west of England was to close after 200 years[11] by tweeting: "Another one goes. Please buy a paper. And if you're one of the journalists who gives stories away for free for Twitter-follower ego, stop it." However, reporters point to the fact that tweeting has now become an expectation among senior managers as a way of boosting the news organisation's profile, reputation and audience reach. Twitter has led to a blurring of their work and leisure time without any recognition of this shift in their employment and pay conditions. Twitter has led to an intensification of sports journalists' daily work routines, commonly without additional financial or professional recognition.

Twitter also has created problems for 24-hour rolling broadcast news. Richard Sambrook, a former director of global news at the BBC, and Sean McGuire, former head of strategy at BBC News, have stated: "If we want it [news] now, we will go online and get it instantly. Twitter – and increasingly live blogs of breaking news events – consistently beat 24-hour TV channels."[12] This disruption for broadcast news also extends to journalistic relations in the professional football environment. The broadcast media had the advantage of publishing content from press conferences and media briefings quickest, which meant that print journalists would not be able to provide their audiences with original content, leaving them at a commercial disadvantage. However, the roles are now reversed. Twitter has meant that print sports journalists can instantly tweet soundbites and snippets. TV journalists complain that they are now being placed at a commercial disadvantage by the behaviour of print journalists.

Reliable or unreliable sources?

Twitter has proved highly disruptive to journalists' attempts to control the flow of news. Traditional sources, such as athletes and coaches, can cut out the middlemen of journalists and tweet their own exclusive, newsworthy information. Sports journalists therefore often ask sources not to tweet details of their interviews and conversations and hence protect the story. However, professional sports insiders recognise that by bypassing the mainstream media they have greater control over what information does and does not find its way into the public domain. They can also determine how that message is delivered and can avoid any difficult questions from journalists.

So Twitter has created a situation whereby traditional sources feel less reliant on journalists for publicity. As a result, journalists can find it much harder to arrange interviews and thus generate original, first-hand stories.

Journalists also react to Twitter as not only a source where news breaks, but where news is generated. And what rich pickings it has yielded. Examples of big sports stories in the UK originating from Twitter include Aston Villa defender Joleon Lescott tweeting a picture of an expensive car soon after his club had suffered a resounding 6-0 defeat by Liverpool, which he later claimed was an accident (thus providing sports journalists with the opportunity to run another, follow-up story).[13] Also, footballers are increasingly finding themselves on disciplinary charges, as Liverpool's Ryan Babel found out in 2011 when he hinted at official bias by posting a mock-up photo of referee Howard Webb wearing a Manchester United shirt. BBC Sport journalist Ben Dirs argues that Twitter has provided sports journalists with story opportunities that did not use to exist:

> An irony for sports journalists is that while it has never been more difficult to pin down sport's biggest names and wring anything vaguely interesting from them, along comes Twitter and all of a sudden they are splattering the minutiae of their lives across the internet for all to see. Not only that, they are letting slip things they would never in a million years reveal in a controlled interview situation.[14]

However, the new types of stories that Twitter generates tend to appeal to the more sensationalist and gossip-fuelled reaches of the sports journalism spectrum. Further, sports desks have recognised that stories from Twitter can be easily and cheaply produced by young, casualised, office-based shift workers. This realisation has led to far more stories being sourced from Twitter than can be considered remotely healthy for the profession. In any case, media managers' concerted efforts to educate professional sports insiders on delivering anodyne, PR-friendly tweets rather than drawing attention to themselves may lead to a dwindling supply of juicy morsels for journalists to feast upon.

Further, discourses around "lazy" sports journalism frequently involve reporters finding stories from Twitter rather than speaking to "real people". For instance, in 2016, television pundit Gary Neville – rather ironically – tweeted his disgust ("Print Journalism is becoming really shit!!") that the *Daily Mirror* had produced a story on the basis of one of his tweets. Neville, a former England footballer, asserted his belief that European commitments were to blame for Manchester United's poor start to the season by tweeting: "That EL (Europa League) is a killer!! Always has been and always will … Twitter please educate me on a team that's excelled in the league and been in it." The *Daily Mirror* based an entire story around this tweet headlined: "Gary Neville makes excuse for Jose Mourinho as Manchester United labour to draw against West Ham."[15] Neville later agreed to appear on a TV show with leading UK sports journalists to debate his claims.

In addition, sports journalists can never be certain if Twitter accounts are genuine or if tweets are actually written by the sportsperson. Sports journalists' failure to get this area right can lead to massive embarrassment for their news organisation and a serious undermining of their professional credibility and reputation. Fake and parody accounts of athletes and coaches complicate the Twittersphere. UK broadcaster Channel 4 apologised in 2013 after sports reporter Jordan Jarrett-Bryan mentioned on air a tweet from a spoof account that he believed belonged to Manchester City striker Mario Balotelli during a news item about how the player had been involved in a training-ground confrontation with his club manager Roberto Mancini.[16] The parody Twitter account holder posted a picture of the altercation with the words "Me and Mancini auditioning for Strictly Come Dancing". Jarrett-Bryan told viewers how Balotelli was making light of the incident on Twitter. Similar occurrences have happened elsewhere. For instance, in the United States, an NFL fan deceived ESPN in 2016 into believing defensive end Olivier Vernon had signed a new contract with the Jacksonville Jaguars.[17]

In a further twist, sports journalists may have to contend with being the subject of a spoof Twitter account. For instance, Sky Sporfs News can easily be mistaken at a glance for Sky Sports News, which can be potentially damaging for reputation and credibility. There have also been interesting examples of media manager interventions on Premier League footballers' social media accounts that have been rather less than transparent. To give a sense of the professional challenges that sports journalists face in this regard, Sunderland striker Victor Anichebe took the advice he was given by a media manager a bit too literally when he tweeted in October 2016: "Can you tweet something like Unbelievable support yesterday and great effort by the lads! Hard result to take! But we go again!"[18] In September 2017, it was reported that Manchester City defender John Stones posted the seemingly bizarre message of support for title rivals Chelsea on Instagram: "Great win today and congratulations @alvaromorata on his hat-trick! #cfc.". However, it emerged that the words were meant for Chelsea defender Gary Gahill – an England teammate of Stones – and that a public relations company ran the accounts of both footballers.[19]

If sports journalists can successfully negotiate the fake accounts and the PR-infused tweets while surviving the parody accounts of themselves, then they can enhance their professional status as an important sober and reliable source of information over social media.

It's a game of opinions

To achieve objectivity, journalists must be distant from, and disinterested in, the stories they write. Journalists are only objective if both sides to every story are accurately and fairly presented without judgement or bias. This information must be properly verified by a reliable source acknowledging it as true. However, historically, sports journalists' relationship with objectivity has been problematic because sport lends itself to subjectivity and partisanship. Sports journalism has a "toy department" reputation within the newsroom for low professional standards due to a lack of distance from their sources and their focus on trivial subject matter in their stories.[20]

In this respect, Twitter has not done anything to enhance sports journalism's professional reputation. If anything, Twitter has led to an intensification of subjectivity and partisanship, as sports journalists tend to tweet opinion rather than facts from the press box.[21] Sports journalists are expected to send regular tweets from arenas and stadiums. Print sports journalists placed greater emphasis on opinion after radio displaced their core function of relaying description from sports events in the mid-20th century.[22] Factual description from sports journalists becomes increasingly redundant as the number of events made available to watch on television continues to rise. For instance, in 2017, the Premier League told the UK broadcast industry regulator Ofcom that it will hike the number of football games made available for TV companies to buy from 168 to 190 from the 2019–2020 season.[23] Sports journalists are therefore more likely to tweet opinion to complement the action their followers are already watching on televisions, tablets, phones or in public places such as bars and pubs.

As Twitter's architecture fosters interaction and conversation, sports journalists have never been more disconnected from objectivity. London School of Economics professor Charlie Beckett has argued that social media has played an important role in taking journalism down a more emotional, and therefore subjective, path.[24] Sport is particularly susceptible to this development because of the passions and emotions involved in fandom. Even the most objective sports journalism will usually be accompanied by the reporter's verdict on their own story. Broadcast news embarked on this route a while ago with conventions such as presenters having conversations with reporters. Print sports journalists have followed their lead on Twitter. Newspapers have always contained opinion-based columns or leaders in their pages on the big story or stories of the day. However, Twitter's conversational dynamics mean every story is commented on, usually by its author.

Twitter should also be seen as an important cog in a bigger wheel of social media strategies within newsrooms that, by definition, tend to lead to softer forms of content production. Sports journalists are expected to provide "added value" by posting video footage of their behind-the-scenes experiences (for example, travelling to sports events) on social media platforms such as Facebook Live or Periscope.[25] Here, sports journalists find that they can run into complex political and economic issues such as sports rights deals. For instance, in 2015, reporter Stephanie Wei lost her PGA Tour accreditation for the remainder of the season after using Periscope to show golfers on the practice facilities. Wei had earlier received a warning for posting a round by Tiger Woods at the Phoenix Open on Instagram. Wei attempted to convince the US Professional Golf Association of the promotional benefits of her actions, and that her footage did not replicate broadcast coverage:

> I understand the Tour has certain rules and regulations in place to protect their broadcast partners, but this was a Monday (which I also now understand is technically during the tournament week). However, I was unclear with whether it conflicted with broadcasting rights since the practice rounds (to my knowledge) are not televised, nor was the somewhat raw, alternative footage I was showing. It was truly meant to spread fanfare for the Tour, its players and the event.[26]

The Wei example demonstrates the challenges that sports journalists face in providing additional, behind-the-scenes content for social media. Further, sports journalists' attempts to provide multi-platform content can inadvertently become a distraction from exercising good journalism on a particular story. However, sports journalists can also use their privileged access to sports events to tweet insights from arenas and stadiums that are not shown on television. Examples of subject matter include managers' orders to players from the sidelines and fan songs/chants from the stands. Print sports journalists are also well placed to tweet events that broadcasters are less likely to point cameras at because of the conflicts of interest inherent in multi-billion-pound rights partnerships with leagues and governing bodies. For instance, in 2015, Crystal Palace fans launched a protest against the Premier League for rising ticket prices despite agreeing a £5 billion domestic TV rights deal with Sky and BT Sport. One banner read: "£5 billion in the trough yet supporters still exploited. Share the wealth, pigs."[27]

Closer to the fans?

The early optimism that sports journalists would interact with audiences in meaningful ways over digital networks has long been abandoned given the antagonistic and acrimonious nature of Twitter as a forum for communication, often referred to as "trolling". Sports journalists' attempts at effective communication are particularly hampered by the tension that has historically existed with fans. Sports journalists occupy a paradoxical position in this respect. On the one hand, fans avidly follow sports journalists for the latest news, gossip and information. Fans also like to compare their own observations and experiences of sports events with "expert" professional sports journalists. However, sports fans are also highly critical of their professional standards and often accuse them of bias towards particular clubs and managers. These contradictions play out on Twitter in that sports journalists at national news organisations can attract abuse and criticism from their sizeable followings.

Sports journalists believe that their privileged access to the professional sports environment gives them rare insight and knowledge of behind-the-scenes information that supporters value. However, fans consider journalists to be an integral part of the commercialised sports environment, and therefore their ethics and motivations are questioned. Far from developing a reputation as a watchdog on the corridors of power, sports journalism was viewed with suspicion as entering into commercial and collusive relationships with the elite. The historical development of sports journalism is closely entwined with the growing commercialisation of the professional sports environment. For instance, the advent of the Premier League and Sky Sports broadcasting deal in 1992 led to a growth in sports pages and pull-out sections in national newspapers in the UK.[28]

Sports journalists consider themselves to be more knowledgeable than the average football fan, which rankles among supporters – particularly those who attend their club's matches regularly. Audiences can get frustrated with, and sceptical over, sports journalism conventions such as transfer/trading rumour stories. The transfer market is considered to be the pinnacle of unprofessional behaviour, with rumour and speculation rife. Sports journalists demonstrate an astonishing lack of transparency in the linking of sportspeople with moves to other clubs and organisations. Stories are often attributed to unnamed sources, and player agents are always kept anonymous to safeguard their commercial and business interests. Yet the occupational principle of protecting sources is generally meant to guarantee the personal safety of whistleblowers in possession of highly sensitive information in the public interest. There is significant scepticism among sports fans around the transparency, accountability and accuracy of such stories (many claims do not actually materialise), and it is therefore unsurprising that they lead to trust issues.

Resilience and persistence have always been important character traits for journalists in ensuring that they can find truth in places where it is carefully concealed. However, sports journalists have had to develop a thicker skin for different reasons in the Twitter age – in order to withstand vitriolic abuse and criticism. I have interviewed sports journalists who admitted that the online comments that they receive are a source of anxiety and despondency that they never used to have to deal with on such a consistent basis. In some cases, this abuse is directed by professional sport insiders themselves. Then-*Daily Mirror* chief sports writer Oliver Holt claimed he was called "a fat prick" by Manchester United defender Rio Ferdinand over Twitter's direct message (DM) function in 2013.[29] It is a far cry from the letters page – and even then readers' input was selected and filtered by professional journalists.

Sports journalists also now have to make decisions on whether or not to reply to tweets, which ones to reply to and how to reply to them. Reporters embroiled in Twitter spats is never edifying and tramples on the professional code that journalists should never be the story (see the previous Holt-Ferdinand example). Ultimately, Twitter certainly does not seem to be an arena in which sports journalists and fans can exchange knowledge and move towards more collaborative, public journalism models.

Nonetheless, at a basic level, Twitter is an interesting barometer of the popularity of sports journalists in society – even if users may not be choosing to follow for entirely constructive reasons. Professional sports journalists continue to attract thousands of followers on Twitter, demonstrating that, irrespective of their professional standards and veracity coming into question, they continue to be of continuing fascination and importance to fans. Sports journalists provide a useful stimulus for chatter, and Twitter exchanges can get heated due to the passions and emotions inherent in sport. *The Times* chief sportswriter Henry Winter could boast 1.24 million Twitter followers as of 3 November 2017 – more than his print title's print and digital sales combined. *The Times'* newspaper circulation at the time stood at 446,463[30] while its digital subscribers were estimated at 413,600.[31]

Twitter has not changed what it *means* to be a professional in that traditional expectations of sports journalism standards and behaviour persist. Research has found that sports journalists use Twitter within existing norms such as news or opinion. However, sports journalists face new considerations and challenges in their attempts *to be* professional.

Sports journalists are confronted by new ethical and decision-making considerations over Twitter. They have been able to raise their popularity levels using the social media platform, but it provides a fraught, crisis-prone environment in the maintenance of professional standards. Also, it is important to consider how Twitter has impacted sports journalism not solely in terms of its direct use as a tool for digital communication. Twitter has also disrupted sports journalists' lived experiences of human relationships within both newsroom and commercialised sports environments. Twitter has redefined sports journalists' internal relations with their senior managers and their external dealings within the professional sports environment. Sports journalists have therefore seen Twitter has a comprehensive and far-reaching impact on their professional conditions.

Twitter should be understood within a broader context of digital transformation within journalism practice. Sports journalists have been confronted with new ethical challenges in the digital age that may not necessarily be exclusive and specific to Twitter but are certainly commonly encountered on the platform. Sports journalists are experiencing general concern over verification, transparency and reliability in their new digital surroundings. For instance, interactivity with audiences can also take place in the below-the-line comments on web articles or on other social media platforms. Twitter is therefore a useful focal point for identifying these shifts in that it has become an important digital tool in the daily work routines of professional sports journalists.

Twitter has been game-changing not only for the journalism profession but for other professional fields such as public relations and marketing. Yet sports journalism is a particularly important case study because of sport's prominence in Twitter conversation and journalism's central role in providing information, analysis and opinion. Sport's significance in social media was both recognised and reinforced in Twitter's acquisition of 10 NFL Thursday Night Football games in 2016.[32] Digital media giants are increasingly turning to live sports content to drive subscriber and user growth, with Amazon's UK rights deal to show the ATP men's tennis World Tour providing another relevant example.[33] With that in mind, it does not look like journalism's integral role in sports chatter on social media is likely to end any time soon.

References

1. Umberto Eco, *Faith in Fakes: Travels in Hyperreality*, Vintage: London, 1998, pp. 159–167.
2. Kyle Sears, "Twitter's Impact on Sports Journalism Practice", Georgia State University: Thesis, 2011, p. 9.
3. John Price, Neil Farrington and Lee Hall, "Tweeting with the enemy", *Journalism Education*, Volume 1, Issue 1, 2012, pp. 9–20.
4. Brad Schultz and Mary Lou Sheffer, "An exploratory study of how Twitter is affecting sports journalism", *International Journal of Sport Communication*, Volume 3, Issue 2, 2010, pp. 226–239.
5. Mary Lou Sheffer and Brad Schultz, "Paradigm shift or passing fad? Twitter and sports journalism", *International Journal of Sport Communication*, Volume 3, Issue 4, 2010, pp. 472–484.
6. Rani Molla, "Jack Dorsey's two-year anniversary of Twitter CEO in charts", Recode, 4 October 2017, https://www.recode.net/2017/10/4/16384672/jack-dorsey-two-year-twitter-anniversary-charts-timeline, accessed 13 December 2019.

7. Sheffer and Schultz, pp. 472–484.

8. Simon McEnnis, "Raising our game: effects of citizen journalism on Twitter for professional identity and working practices of British sport journalists", *International Journal of Sport Communication*, Volume 6, Issue 4, 2013, pp. 423–433.

9. G Anderson, "Steed Malbranque: No truth in these sick rumours", 6 September 2011, http://www.sunderlandecho.com/sport/football/sunderland-afc/steed-malbranque-no-truth-in-these-sick-rumours-1-3745754

10. Peter English, "Twitter's diffusion in sports journalism: Role models, laggards and followers of the social media innovation", *New Media & Society*, Volume 18, Issue 3, 2016, pp. 484–501.

11. Freddy Mayhew, "Cornwall's Sunday Independent closes after 200 years in print with 20 journalism jobs to go", 5 April 2017, http://www.pressgazette.co.uk/cornwalls-sunday-independent-closes-after-200-years-in-print-with-20-journalism-jobs-to-go/, accessed 13 December 2019.

12. Richard Sambrook and Sean McGuire, "Have 24-hour TV news channels had their day?", in Stephen Cushion and Richard Sambrook (eds.), *The future of 24-hour news: New directions, new challenges*, Peter Lang: New York, 2016, pp. 16–17.

13. Simon Rice, "Joleon Lescott tweet: Aston Villa player claims car picture was 'tweeted by accident' as fans rage", *The Independent*, 15 February 2016, http://www.independent.co.uk/sport/football/premier-league/joleon-lescott-tweet-aston-villa-player-claims-car-picture-was-tweeted-by-accident-as-fans-fume-a6874611.html, accessed 13 December 2019.

14. Ben Dirs, "How Twitter changed the rules", BBC Sport, 17 January 2011, http://www.bbc.co.uk/blogs/bendirs/2011/01/twitter_blog.html, accessed 13 December 2019.

15. Jack Rathborn, "Gary Neville makes excuse for Jose Mourinho as Manchester United Labour to draw against West Ham", *Daily Mirror*, 27 November 2016, http://www.mirror.co.uk/sport/football/news/neville-manchester-united-mourinho-europa-9349043

16. Paul Byrne, "Channel 4 apologises after being fooled by tweet from Mario Balotelli parody account", *Daily Mirror*, 5 January 2013, http://www.mirror.co.uk/tv/tv-news/mario-balotelli-channel-4-apologises-1519102

17. Zac Wassink, "The best Twitter trolls and satirical accounts in sports media", 23 March 2016, http://bleacherreport.com/articles/2626773-the-best-twitter-trolls-and-satirical-accounts-in-sports-media, accessed 13 December 2019.

18. Callum Davis, "Victor Anichebe suffers embarrassing Twitter howler following Sunderland's last minute defeat to West Ham", *Daily Telegraph*, 23 October 2016, http://www.telegraph.co.uk/football/2016/10/23/victor-anichebe-suffers-embarrassing-twitter-howler-following-su/, accessed 13 December 2019.

19. Mark Jones, "Gary Cahill and John Stones involved in Instagram mix-up after Chelsea and Manchester City Victories", *Daily Mirror*, 23 September 2017, http://www.mirror.co.uk/sport/football/news/gary-cahill-john-stones-instagram-11226310

20. David Rowe, *Sport, culture and media: The unruly trinity*, Open University Press: Maidenhead, UK, 2004.

21. Chris Roberts and Betsy Emmons, "Twitter in the press box: How a new technology affects game routines of print-focused sports journalists", *International Journal of Sport Communication*, Volume 9, Issue 1, 2016, pp. 97–115.

22. Rob Steen and Jed Novick, "Texting and tweeting: How social media has changed news gathering" in Andrew Billings and Marie Hardin (eds.), *Routledge handbook of sport and new media*, Routledge: Abingdon, UK, 2014, p. 121.

23. Matt Slater, "Premier league set to sell even more games to broadcasters with extra matches set to be televised from 2019", *Daily Mail*, 9 June 2017, http://www.dailymail.co.uk/sport/football/article-4589000/Premier-League-set-sell-games-broadcasters.html, accessed 13 December 2019.

24. Charlie Beckett, "How journalism is turning emotional and what that might mean for news", LSE Polis, 10 September 2015, http://blogs.lse.ac.uk/polis/2015/09/10/how-journalism-is-turning-emotional-and-what-that-might-mean-for-news/, accessed 13 December 2019.

25. Periscope is a video-streaming app that was acquired by Twitter before its launch in 2015. In the context of this chapter, Periscope is accommodated within a broader interpretation of Twitter.

26. Samer Kalaf, "PGA Tour yanks reporter's credential after she live-streams practice", *Deadspin*, 4 May 2015, https://deadspin.com/pga-yanks-reporters-credential-after-she-live-streams-p-1702080600, accessed 13 December 2019.

27. Vaishali Bhardwaj, "Crystal Palace fans protest against new Premier League deal with banner hitting out at 'pigs' before Arsenal game", *Metro*, 21 February 2015, http://metro.co.uk/2015/02/21/crystal-palace-fans-protest-against-rising-ticket-prices-with-banner-hitting-out-at-pigs-before-arsenal-game-5073254/, accessed 13 December 2019.

28. Raymond Boyle and Richard Haynes, *Power play: Sport, the media and popular culture*, Edinburgh University Press: Edinburgh, UK, 2009.

29. Gordon Tynan, "Ferdinand caught up in furious row on Twitter", *The Independent*, 7 June 2011, http://www.independent.co.uk/sport/football/news-and-comment/ferdinand-caught-up-in-furious-row-on-twitter-2294434.html, accessed 13 December 2019.

30. Dominic Ponsford, "National newspaper ABCs: Bulks helped times and *Daily Telegraph* boost print circulations in September", 19 October 2017, http://www.pressgazette.co.uk/national-newspaper-abcs-bulks-helped-times-and-daily-telegraph-boost-print-circulations-in-september/

31. Freddy Mayhew, "Times titles claim boost to subscriber numbers after move away from breaking news online", 27 March 2017, http://www.pressgazette.co.uk/times-titles-claim-boost-to-subscriber-numbers-after-move-away-from-breaking-news-online/

32. Jasper Jackson, "Twitter to live stream NFL's Thursday night football", *The Guardian*, 5 April 2016, https://www.theguardian.com/media/2016/apr/05/twitter-stream-nfl-thursday-night-football, accessed 13 December 2013.

33. Mark Sweney, "Amazon outbids Sky to win exclusive ATP tour tennis rights", *The Guardian*, 1 August 2017, https://www.theguardian.com/media/2017/aug/01/amazon-outbids-sky-to-win-exclusive-atp-tour-tennis-rights, accessed 13 December 2019.

12

Public relations

Owen Evans

As sporting teams continually invest to grow their in-house media teams, the career ambitions of trainee sports journalists are evolving to match the changing media market. The opportunity for access to the biggest press boxes and brightest stars in sport has meant club media experience has superseded a fortnight on a newspaper's sports desk for many trainees, but at what cost?

Roles listed as "in-house journalist" and "editorial assistant" attract aspiring reporters on paper, but often the reality is work akin to public relations and marketing due to the pressure to produce subjective, sanitised copy.

The increase in sport's professionalism has coincided with the global embrace of celebrity culture, and the two – money and celebrity – make a potent mix. And that is where the world of PR comes in. Players – and managers and coaches – are public figures with profiles to match. No longer can a 19-year-old footballer get drunk on holiday. He's a commodity to be protected, a product whose public face cannot be dirtied. He cannot be too outspoken, let off the leash or allowed to act naturally. He needs gatekeepers to protect his image. Just as he needs a coach to tell him how to kick the ball, he needs a PR manager to tell him how to answer those all-important post-match questions.

For the sports journalist, this presents a problem. How to get to the real story rather than the story they want you to see? The age of journalists having players' phone numbers, of hanging out together in pubs and after-hours drinking clubs, has largely gone. Relationships – who you know – still hold the key to good journalism, but more and more the relationship is with the press officer rather than the player.

This chapter looks at those relationships and how life now works, the rise of club media and if a solution to an increasingly influential public-relations sector is on the horizon.

The invisible hand: Sport media's puppetmasters

One of the most influential figures in global sport died on 8 September 2018.[1] However, the average football fan would struggle to pick him out from a two-man wall.

Mike Lee OBE helped bring the Olympic Games to London, Rio and Paris, turned rugby union into an Olympic sport, Lord Sebastian Coe into International Association of Athletics Federations (IAAF) president and, most controversially, the 2022 FIFA World Cup to Qatar.

He was a political strategist with the Premier League and media adviser for UEFA before he became communications director for London's victorious bid to host the 2012 Olympics. Afterwards he founded Vero Communications, a company that would go on to influence the biggest sports stories across the world, from Olympic bidding wars to FIFA presidential campaigns.

The contrast between Lee's anonymity with the general public and his omnipresence with the consultants, city strategists, journalists and rights-holders who felt his wrath underlines the fundamental premise of the modern-day PR expert – you have to be everywhere and nowhere at once. Creating, but never becoming the next big story.

Playing the role of the invisible hand is the daily remit for any aspiring PR professional in sports media. Whether it's a Premier League-winning captain's wife selling the sports desk bad blood – or Tour de France winners caught using it – the guardian at the gates when the scandal breaks is the communications specialist. However, the rise to prominence of the likes of Lee and other influential communications experts should also act as a warning for the future of independent sport journalism.

The battleground for information throughout sports media is increasingly dominated by public-relations specialists, in-house journalists and communications consultants. The potential consequence of this media land grab not only threatens regional sports desks of newspapers up and down the UK, but also the authenticity of the industry itself. A dominant, self-censored flow of communication coming from clubs and athletes – bypassing reporters and going straight to the audience – means an independent sports press is more important now than ever before.

The hundred-year war

The first influential PR footprints into journalism's territory can be traced back to World War I, when a "system of supplying newspapers with publicity and propaganda in the guise of news became so popular that a census of accredited press agents was carried out" (Park, 1927). Over the past century that influence has grown rapidly, with the pair becoming uneasy bedfellows in the media landscape.

Despite opposing ideological differences (Reich, 2009), the exponential growth of the media industry means interaction is inevitable. With the increasingly blurred lines between journalism and PR, an uneasy alliance has formed as "beat reporters are drawn into a symbiotic relationship of mutual obligation with their sources, which both facilitates and complicates their work" (Gans, 1980) across crime, entertainment, news, politics and lifestyle desks.

From a journalistic perspective, though, familiarity has bred contempt. According to Macnamara (2016) the "strained bed fellowship" between the two trades was a result of journalists often having a negative perception of their PR counterparts. That difficult partnership has come under the greatest scrutiny on the sports desk. Rowe (1999) stated that "it is no exaggeration to see some forms of sport journalism as the compromised ally of the sport and entertainment business rather than as a legitimate arm of the news media", and embroiled in "circuits of promotion" with media partners (Whitson, 1998).

The crux of the issue lies within the proximity between PR professional and sports reporter. More than 50 years ago, Arthur Hopcraft described it as a "co-operative, collusive relationship [that] existed between the football world and the press with a cast of local reporters in constant relaxed contact with the clubs, a relationship based upon a combination of day-to-day friendliness and professional ingratiation" (Hopcraft, 1967), and that relationship has become cosier in the digital age, with newspapers dependent on clubs and players for 24/7 coverage.

Sports journalists live in fear of "being frozen out, particularly at local level" (Rowe, 2005) due to their dependency on their club for stories and interviews. Formal and informal sources of information are freely gifted and include media packs, press releases, news conferences, organising committee databases, wire services and other published media (Sugden and Tomlinson, 2007).

Then there is the issue of accessibility, with numerous examples in recent years of clubs banning local media for not complying with the company line as their respective media teams grow stronger. In December 2018, Bolton Wanderers banned the *Bolton News*[2] reporter Marc Iles for a post on social media covering the story that the club's players and staff had not been paid. His news editor, Karl Holbrook, responded by saying: "We will press on with our independent coverage no matter what. We answer to the fans, not the chairman."

As Sugden and Tomlinson (2007) observed, it is the "carrot of accreditation alongside the stick of excommunication" that is the daily dilemma for the contemporary sports journalist when dealing with their PR counterparts. Nowhere is this seen in greater focus than the weekly press briefing. The staged conference, the controlled spaces and access – all of these escalate the scale of the mediation process, and consolidate the control, flow and direction of information in the interests of the organising and official bodies (see Case Study Two).

The rise of PR in sports media means that dealing with a communications specialist is now part and parcel of any reporter's beat. Access is everything, and the days of having the phone numbers of footballers disappeared with the advent of social media, so now every interview request goes via the gatekeeper. But the extent of the sports PR professional's power does not end in the press room.

The rise of club media

The sports media landscape is experiencing a major power shift that is fundamentally changing the relationship between reporters and their PR counterparts.

Football clubs such as Real Madrid and Chelsea no longer see themselves as the "utility maximisers" (Sloane, 1971) they once were, serving at the heart of a community and prioritising people over profit. Instead, they are reinventing themselves as "content creators"[9] with global audiences hungry for 24/7 content across traditional and social media platforms.

More than a few eyebrows were raised in 2018 after Manchester United claimed they had 659 million fans across the world,[10] but the Old Trafford executives were happy to take on the fans' mirth – their opinion is becoming increasingly irrelevant to the boardrooms of major football clubs – as the real audience was the blue-chip companies who would traditionally advertise with media giants such as beIN Sports and ESPN.

Clubs as content producers is a major threat to independent sport journalism. The current power shift has the potential to not only marginalise the independent sports press, but also to lower the overall quality of stories published due to self-censorship. It's the blurred line between sport journalism and public relations, with in-house "reporters" peddling the company line for their respective clubs in return for access. It's a threat those working at the top of football journalism know all too well.

During the 2018 Manchester Football Writing Festival at the National Football Museum, panellists[11] Rory Smith (chief football writer, *New York Times*), Miguel Delaney (chief football writer, *The Independent*), Jonathan Northcroft (chief football writer, *Sunday Times*) and Jonathan Wilson (author, *The Guardian* columnist and editor of *The Blizzard*) all warned how the rise of club media is forcing the traditional football press into a corner.

"Football clubs are becoming more and more sophisticated and targeted with regard to working with particular journalists that they know are going to be good for them and their message," Northcroft said. "This has always gone on at a local level, but I believe they [clubs] are becoming a lot more strategic now at picking certain groups of people who they know

Box 12.1 Five candidates, one kingmaker

One of the best examples of the growing influence was seen in the race for football's top job in 2015: president of the game's governing body, FIFA. Sepp Blatter, despite consistently courting allegations of corruption throughout his tenure, was running for re-election at the 65th FIFA Congress that May.

After David Ginola's bookmaker-backed, short-lived publicity[3] stunt and former FIFA presidential advisor Jerome Champagne's failure[4] to get sufficient support from national associations, the candidates tasked with stopping the 78-year-old Blatter securing a fifth term were: 2000 Balon D'Or winner Luis Figo, Dutch administrator Michael van Praag and Jordanian Prince Ali Bin Hussein.

For those not conversant with power systems in sport's biggest governing bodies, the chief driver behind electoral success is not former glory on the pitch or royal patronage, but influence on the ballot blocks. Blatter moving the World Cup into Africa (2010) and the Middle East (2022) for the first time was in no small part motivated by the knowledge that he would gain substantial voting influence from FIFA members in both regions.

The 2015 presidential election required a two-thirds majority in the first round, and if this was not achieved, a simple majority in the second. Any candidate coming into the race to challenge Blatter knew he already had significant support from two of FIFA's six major confederations.

That was the task facing Lee's aforementioned Vero at the start of 2015. First up was Prince Ali, who was president of the Jordan Football Association (JFA) at the time. Sujit Jasani, a Vero director, set up interviews to start pushing Ali's manifesto to the international sports press.[5] A few days later, another call came through from Vero. This time one of Jasani's colleagues at his office invited the same journalists to Wembley to hear about rival Luis Figo's headline-grabbing $3.5 billion giveaway manifesto. The candidates were just window-dressing. The real presidential race was Blatter versus Lee.

Lee's monopoly on communications inevitably led to rumours regarding vote-trading between Vero's stable of candidates, depending on who came out of the campaign period the strongest. All of this with everyone's favourite outsider in the race, UEFA president Michel Platini, waiting in the wings, watching the early running before submitting an expected bid for presidency closer to the election. Lee and Platini knew each other well from the former's time working at European football's governing body as a media adviser. In the end it wasn't enough: despite throwing all their weight behind Ali after Figo withdrew and Platini being too busy with other issues to stand, the Jordanian and Vero lost out in the second round of voting, as Blatter's Asian and African backing saw him through.[6]

It was a short-lived victory for Blatter, though. The FBI's raid[7] at the congress ultimately led to his resignation days later, and by February 2016 former UEFA general secretary Gianni Infantino had been elected as the new president of FIFA.

Infantino's PR partner in the successful presidential campaign? Mike Lee & Vero Communications.[8]

will be on-message and appear to be pseudo-independent voices. It's only happening at a very slow, drip-drip level, but it's certainly a big change I've noticed in the last couple of years. It's almost like we've gone back to local hacks and away from national media and the idea of an independent journalist that covers an entire competition.

"You've already seen this with the rise of the local reporter that is so close they often cannot see anything beyond the club's message. I think we're at a real crossroads now for the industry where independent journalism has got to fight against this sort of insidious stuff. I also think fans quite like the club message, and maybe it's up to journalists to be so good that they force a different narrative. It does worry me how that part of the industry is changing."

In 2018, Amazon released *All or Nothing*, an eight-part fly-on-the-wall documentary about Manchester City's record-breaking 2017–2018 campaign[12] offering insights from within the Premier League champions' dressing room. Despite the fanfare on its release, the £10 million series received mixed reviews, with some critics pointing towards an unsatisfying end product due to the overly orchestrated structure.

"It's interesting that *All or Nothing* was brilliantly made television, but not necessarily brilliant television," said Northcroft. "It seems to be the best example of a wider issue happening in the industry now, which is almost a fake confessional, inside view, which takes you behind-the-scenes but only to the limit where the individuals concerned want you to go."

Delaney added: "What clubs are trying now – and you can especially see this with the Man City documentary – is to reinvent themselves as content producers, which puts them into direct competition with the media. There's one major club in the past season (2017–2018) who don't give journalists one-to-one interviews anymore as they see it as content exclusive to them. That kind of direct access has been completely cut off."

At the beginning of the 2018–2019 season, fan channel Arsenal Fan TV had over 800,000 subscribers on YouTube, pitching its audience somewhere between the readerships of the highest-selling English tabloid *The Sun* (1.411 million) and broadsheet *The Times* (418,000).[13] As a result, clubs and national teams are targeting these fan channels when putting out new stories, ahead of the press pack from the traditional sports desks.

"I'd been asked to the Nigeria and England [2018 World Cup] kit launch as I write for *Sports Illustrated* and got an invite through them," said Wilson. "I turned up thinking it was going to be the usual event where various players would be booked for me and other national journalists so we could have our nice and cosy 10-minute chats so we can get quotes that will give us five days' worth of copy. I get there, look around, and literally do not recognise anybody. The vast majority of people there were YouTubers with cameras filming stuff. That was a shock to me, that Nike would launch the England kit without inviting any national journalists. I'm sure they did their research and decided this was the best way to do a launch now to get the message out there, but it did suggest to me a loss of the old model of journalism."

However, despite the loss of access, Delaney believes this new dynamic could shake the independent sports press out of their comfort zone and spur them back to finding the stories their club does not want them to find out. "We've all been invited to those kit launches where you get access to a player for 10 minutes of anodyne quotes. To be honest it's just filling space that we shouldn't be doing. That's one example of what clubs are doing now, though. By targeting specific YouTube accounts and bloggers for that type of event, they are bypassing the traditional media. Journalism in the truest sense of the word – information that people don't want you to find out – will always travel better."

It's not just the clubs cutting out the national media. High-profile players with huge social media fanbases are shunning national press and their own club media directly via their own channels. During the 2018 World Cup, a number of first-person pieces published on *The Players' Tribune* gained significant attention online, with the sports press extracting stories out of the headline quotes.

"There was a series of fantastic pieces from *The Players' Tribune*, from the likes of Raheem Sterling[14] and Romelu Lukaku,"[15] Northcroft added. "Excellent pieces that looked at their back stories and were really quite personal. They were fantastic but they only told you what they wanted you to know. You got the sense they were opening up, but in reality it was only what they wanted you to know."

Box 12.2 Controlling the narrative

In December 2018, the assembled press gathered at Tottenham's pre-match press conference for the forthcoming trip to Everton. Just three days earlier, Manchester United had sacked manager José Mourinho, and Tottenham's Mauricio Pochettino was the bookmaker's favourite to replace him.

In the end, neither the press nor Pochettino dictated the story. Instead, the club's head of communications, Simon Felstein,[16] took centre stage.

Dharmesh Sheth (DS): "It won't have escaped your attention that there's a lot of talk at the moment about yourself [Pochettino] and Manchester United. Now, the former technical director of Southampton, Les Reed…"

Simon Felstein (SF): "We've gone over Manchester United and the manager [vacancy] before. No. Anything to do with Manchester United we dealt with 48 hours ago… we had the same conversations… the manager's answered, I'm not prepared to have another press conference dominated by this."

DS: "It's not being dominated by it, I have to ask the question…"

SF: "Well your man was here on Tuesday and asked the same questions, I'm not prepared to have it again, so I'd ask you to move it on".

DS: "With respect, everybody is talking about this…"

SF: "Okay, with respect, I'd say move it on because we invite you here to preview a football match and you're coming in and asking our manager about another job."

DS: "It works both ways, though. There are other occasions where you say 'let's not talk about the football match because you want to get something else out'. It works both ways."

SF: "No."

DS: "Surely?"

SF: "No. Move it on please."

DS: "Can I ask, in that case, [with] everything that's happening at the moment, I just want to tell you what Les Reed [technical director, FA] has said…"

SF: "No."

DS: "What?!"

SF: "No, no, no. I've said."

Mauricio Pochettino (MP): "[to Felstein] You're going to be the star of the press conference. It's nice."

SF: "I know, I know. Don't worry… move it on please, Dharmesh."

DS: "What I am saying is, this is going to carry on for months…"

SF: "Okay fine, let people speculate. We're not going to have our press conferences dominated by it. There's plenty else to talk about…"

At this point, Felstein requested the cameras be turned off so he could underline his point to the rest of the journalists before restarting the conference, but within hours the clip of the national journalist being kept at arm's length by a club PR officer had been viewed more than 100,000 times on Twitter.

Felstein had shifted from invisible hand to visible gatekeeper, with his actions name-checked in reports across *The Telegraph*, *BBC*, *The Guardian* and beyond. However, whereas previously having been seen as breaking the cardinal sin of any PR professional, the reaction from outside Fleet Street on social media was that this type of control of the narrative was a welcome development to fans and fellow PR professionals. A sign that clubs could fight back against the media. An ominous flashpoint for those banking on an independent sports press in the future.

Fan club or Fourth Estate?

A 2017 University of Loughborough study into the communication practices of 25 current and former Premier League clubs found that just seven were still pursuing professional relationships with the mainstream press.

The study found that "the rise of social media has shifted the focus of clubs away from traditional media channels and instead towards in-house publications, such as magazines, television channels and online". More worryingly, the report found that three of the clubs admitted using their channel to limit their relationship with the independent sports press, which was described as "a lost cause" (Manoli, 2017).

On the back of these findings, the University of Brighton carried out a study at the culmination of the 2017–2018 season with current students and alumni who had worked on the exclusive paid partnerships with Arsenal and Brighton and Hove Albion FC. The structure of the paid internships sees final-year sports journalists audition for club media roles, which sees them working on match days with the first team and providing content for the clubs' various platforms.[17]

One of the attractions in club media for aspiring sports reporters is prestige branding. The opportunity to leverage the team's social media presence to pursue celebrity sport reporter status. Modern sports journalists "need to have social following to be taken seriously, and by working in club media you can use the prestige to get the followers. The older form of written press isn't really seen as a preferential option for us now, as most of our news and sources come straight from social media" (Sugden and Tomlinson, 2007).

A review of the responses showed a collective suspension of ethical values that the candidates had learned through their degree through awareness of adapted professional identity. In particular, the interviews revealed concerns about the paradox of power for the trainees where "free" journalists fall into the hands of censuring commercial and corporate elites (Hargreaves, 2003). Due to being constrained by control of club media, reporters self-censor (Rowe, 2005).

There were times when I was frustrated knowing that I could not write the best story. During one match I interviewed a player in the mixed zone after he was sent off. His quotes were amazing, really emotive. I sent them up to the desk and was told they wouldn't be used as they were too controversial. I think it [the club journalist role] was closer to public relations. I know I had to promote the club first and foremost, and put a positive spin on everything I filed, even if that didn't reflect what actually happened. For instance, the 'Five things we learned' article published on the club website in March 2018. The five sub-headings were: Record breaker, Strength in depth, Murray back in the goals, Impressive Izzy and Landmarks for experienced Seagulls… Brighton lost 5-1.

BHAFC interviewee

Many of the interns described the difficulty they had in separating the emotive behaviour of the fan in a professional context (Rowe, 2005), and they were ethically compromised when reporting on their own teams – such as the Manchester United example below – which invariably led to self-censorship and diluted journalistic practice (Boyle, 2000).

> I was really nervous going into the Manchester United game. All day I was trying to think up a safe question for [José] Mourinho, so it would be a nice experience and memory to look back on. I didn't want him [Mourinho] to mug me off as [Manchester] United are my team.
>
> *BHAFC interviewee*

> I remember being really nervous before speaking to [Liverpool manager] Jurgen Klopp. I have to admit that when the Liverpool goals were going in, I was celebrating under the [press box] desk.
>
> *Arsenal interviewee*

However, one common theme was the overriding benefit of positive experiential learning, and the confidence that comes from working with high-profile managers and players from the Premier League.

> I won't pretend that a lot of my job involved journalism. Through my training, I've learned that journalism is about reporting without bias and investigating. However, a real positive is the confidence you get from speaking to high-profile managers, players and sports journalists. I remember the first time I interviewed Phil Neville, I came back and half my face was in blotches as I was so nervous. I know people criticise club media for not being proper journalism, but just look at the industry. I've done shifts and placements at *The Express* and *The Independent*, and so much of the work is just re-nosing other papers' stories. That's not journalism either. Given the choice of the two, there's no doubt which one has made me a better sports journalist.
>
> *BHAFC interviewee*

Fast changes, slow future?

Throughout this chapter we have described how an increasingly influential public relations sector is casting a shadow over the independent sports press. Combined with the rapid rise of a self-censored club media and greater collusion between reporters and PR professionals, and the fear is editorial standards will slip even further for the sake of accessibility.

However, in August 2019, the football journalism industry experienced one of the most seismic shifts for a generation. *The Athletic*, a US-owned subscription-based platform, persuaded 57 journalists from national and regional sports desks to join *The Athletic UK*, including *The Guardian*'s chief football writer Daniel Taylor. The list also included the leading reporters from regional sports desks at the *Liverpool Echo, Yorkshire Evening Post* and *The Argus* – the same local reporters that *Sunday Times'* Jonathan Northcroft feared had become too close to the clubs they report on.

Despite its impact, *The Athletic* had received a cautious reception from the industry. *Buzzfeed* and *Vice Sports* – once heralded as the catalysts for change in football journalism in the digital era – proved to be false dawns with record job cuts in the first six months of 2019.[18] It also received a lukewarm reception from regional and national sports desks in the UK. Not only for coming in and luring away their best reporters, but also for CEO Alex Mather's claim that *The Athletic* will "wait every local paper out and let them continuously bleed, until we are the last ones standing."[19]

Aside from the increased pay packets, why did many of the leading sport journalists in the country leave prestigious titles such as *The Times* and *The Guardian* to gamble on a subscription-based future? One major motivation brings us back to the crux of this chapter: control.

Whenever a new reporter signs for *The Athletic*, their first task is to write a "Why I Joined…" essay – where the writers describe how they perceive themselves and the industry. According to Gravengaard (2012), the five metaphors journalists use to define their work is "selection, construction, a race, trading and the power game". With all five of these metaphors directly threatened by an increasingly powerful public relations industry, it's easy to see why a new model offering greater control – or at least the illusion of that – would be attractive. As Andy Naylor, who joined *The Athletic* after spending more than three decades on *The Argus*'s sports desk, said: "To be frank, this 55-year-old was becoming increasingly disenchanted with certain aspects of an industry… while churning out copy for both paper and website."[20]

Whether a futuristic sport journalism industry based on old-school values combined with subscription-based websites helps reporters take back control remains to be seen, and will no doubt be a subject for further academic study, as no matter the publication format, the media teams, press officers and communications specialists will continue to guard the gates of accessibility. Ultimately, it will be the reader who decides what is acceptable quality regarding the stories coming out of their favourite teams and athletes – and if that does not come up to standard, how much they are willing to pay for better value.

References

1. "Mike Lee Obituary", *The Times*, https://www.thetimes.co.uk/article/mike-lee-obituary-nht27jd80, 27th July 2020
2. "This is what led to Bolton wanderers banning The Bolton News reporter from stadium", *The Bolton News*, https://www.theboltonnews.co.uk/news/17299432.this-is-what-led-to-bolton-wanderers-banning-the-bolton-news-reporter-from-stadium/
3. "Ginola set to run for FIFA presidency", *BBC*, https://www.bbc.co.uk/sport/av/football/30849269
4. "Jérôme Champagne withdraws from FIFA presidential race", *The Guardian*, https://www.theguardian.com/football/2015/feb/02/jerome-champagne-withdraws-fifa-president
5. "Jordan's Prince Ali announces intention to stand for FIFA presidency", *The Guardian*, https://www.theguardian.com/football/2015/jan/06/jordan-prince-ali-fifa-presidency
6. "Sepp Blatter re-elected as FIFA president for fifth term", *The Guardian*, https://www.theguardian.com/football/2015/may/29/sepp-blatter-reelected-fifa-president-fifth-term
7. "FIFA officials arrested on corruption charges as World Cup inquiry launched", *The Guardian*, https://www.theguardian.com/football/2015/may/27/several-top-fifa-officials-arrested
8. "How Infantino won the FIFA presidency – and what next?", *Around the Rings*, http://aroundtherings.com/site/A__54944/Title__Op-Ed--How-Infantino-Won-the-FIFA-Presidency--and-What-Next/292/Articles
9. "How global sports brands like Real Madrid are learning to think like digital media companies", *Business Insider*, https://www.businessinsider.com/how-teams-like-real-madrid-are-emulating-digital-media-companies-2017-10?r=US&IR=T
10. "Why Manchester United's reputed global fan base of 659 million is more urban myth than fact", *Forbes*, https://www.forbes.com/sites/bobbymcmahon/2018/12/18/why-manchester-united-reputed-global-fan-base-of-659m-is-more-urban-myth-than-fact/#52f06a1610d6
11. 2018 Football Writing Festival: The Blizzard, Live! August 30, 2018.
12. "Amazon dips into UK soccer market with Manchester City series", *Bloomberg*, https://www.bloomberg.com/news/articles/2017-11-09/amazon-dips-into-u-k-soccer-market-with-manchester-city-series

13. "National newspaper ABCS: Mail titles see slower year-on-year circulation decline as bulk sales distortion ends", *Press Gazette*, https://www.pressgazette.co.uk/national-newspaper-abcs-mail-titles-see-year-on-year-circulation-lift-as-bulk-sales-distortion-ends/

14. "It was all a dream", *The Players' Tribune*, https://www.theplayerstribune.com/en-us/articles/raheem-sterling-england-it-was-all-a-dream

15. "I've got some things to say", *The Players' Tribune*, https://www.theplayerstribune.com/en-us/articles/romelu-lukaku-ive-got-some-things-to-say

16. "Tottenham media chief prevents Mauricio Pochettino from answering questions on Manchester United links", *The Telegraph*, https://www.telegraph.co.uk/football/2018/12/20/tottenham-media-chief-prevents-mauricio-pochettino-answering/

17. *Blurred Lines: How the rise of in-house media is impacting upon the ethical values of trainee sport journalists* presented at the 2018 Association of Journalism Education conference, Canterbury Christ Church University. This study carried out semi-structured interviews with 10 sport journalism trainees whose identities have been removed to protect the quality of the data.

18. "Journalism job cuts haven't been this bad since the recession", *Bloomberg*, https://www.bloomberg.com/news/articles/2019-07-01/journalism-layoffs-are-at-the-highest-level-since-last-recession

19. "Why *The Athletic* wants to pillage newspapers", *The New York Times*, https://www.nytimes.com/2017/10/23/sports/the-athletic-newspapers.html

20. "Andy Naylor: Reporting on the twists and turns of Brighton for more than 25 years has kept me sane", *The Athletic*, *https://theathletic.com/1089265/2019/08/05/andy-naylor-reporting-on-the-twists-and-turns-of-brighton-for-more-than-25-years-has-kept-me-sane/*

For further reading

- K. Blessing and K. Marren, "Is the PR-ization of media… B.S.?", *Media Ethics*, Volume 24, Issue 2, 2013.
- R. Boyle, *Power Play: Sport, the Media and Popular Culture*, Longman: London, 2000.
- J. Curran, "The future of journalism", *Journalism Studies*, Volume 11, Issue 4, 2010, pp. 464–476.
- DE DeLorme and F. Fedler, "Journalists' hostility toward public relations: An historical analysis", *Public Relations Review*, Volume 29, Issue 2, 2003, pp. 99–124.
- HJ Gans, *Deciding What's News: A Study of CBS Evening News, NBC Nightly News, Newsweek, and Time*, Constable: London, 1980.
- G. Gravengaard, "The metaphors journalists live by: Journalists' conceptualisation of newswork", *Journalism*, Volume 13, Issue 8, 2012, pp. 1064–1082.
- I. Hargreaves, *Journalism: Truth or Dare?* Oxford University Press: Oxford, 2003.
- A. Hopcraft, *The Football Man: People & Passions in Soccer*, Aurum: London, 1967.
- J. Lewis, A. Williams and B. Franklin, "A compromised Fourth Estate? UK news journalism, public relations and news sources", *Journalism Studies*, Volume 9, Issue 1, 2008, pp. 1–20.
- A. Marr, *My Trade: A Short History of British Journalism*, Pan Books: London, 2015.
- J. Macnamara, "Journalism–PR relations revisited: The good news, the bad news, and insights into tomorrow's news", *Public Relations Review*, Volume 40, Issue 5, 2014, pp. 739–750.
- J. Macnamara, "The continuing convergence of journalism and PR: New insights for ethical practice from a three-country study of senior practitioners", *Journalism and Mass Communication Quarterly*, Volume 93, Issue 1, 2016, pp. 118–141.
- E.A. Manoli, "New goals: The changing face of media relations in the Premier League", https://www.lboro.ac.uk/news-events/news/2017/august/changing-face-of-communications-in-premier-league-, 22 August 2017.
- R.E. Park, "Main currents in the history of American journalism. William Grosvenor Bleyer", *American Journal of Sociology*, Volume 33, Issue 2, 1927, pp. 291–293.
- Z. Reich, Sourcing the news: Key issues in journalism – an innovative study of the Israeli press, 2009.
- D. Rowe, *Sport, Culture and the Media: An Unruly Trinity*, Open University Press: Buckingham, UK, 1999.

- D. Rowe, "Fourth Estate or Fan Club? Sports journalism engages in the popular", in S. Allan (ed.), *Journalism: Critical Issues*, Open University Press: Maidenhead, UK, 2005, pp. 125–136.
- P. Sloane, "Economics of professional football – football club as a utility maximise", *Scottish Journal of Political Economy*, Volume 18, Issue 2, 1971, pp. 121–146.
- J. Sugden, and A. Tomlinson, "Stories from planet football and sportsworld: Source relations and collusion in sport journalism", *Journalism Practice*, Volume 1, Issue 1, 2007, pp. 44–61.
- D. Whitson, "Circuits of promotion: Media, marketing and the globalisation of sport", in A. Wenner (ed.), *Circuits of Promotion: Media, Marketing and the Globalisation of Sport*, Routledge: London, 1998, pp. 57–72.

13

The sports editor: Good cop or bad?

Paul Weaver

The sports editor, ideally, is something of a polymath. He or she must have a sound knowledge of production, a flair for presentation, be able to combine the skills of a copy-taster with those of a sub-editor, have a basic knowledge of all major sports and the political skill to lead a team while compromising with the editor and performing a PR shift with important figures outside the newspaper office.

Considering the many demands made upon him or her, it's hardly surprising that there aren't many very good ones. Their most common failing, in my experience, is in the area of man-management. Papers should invest more in teaching people skills to potential executives. But they don't. So resentment is often needlessly created when the important thing is to build a good team spirit. The newspaper reporter, remember, is so often asked to go the extra mile, to work well beyond their basic terms of reference. It is not a nine-to-five job. So morale is important, and a little mutual give and take and generous handling are required.

If you're lucky you will get someone who will improve your all-round game. My favourite sports editor was Bill Bateson at the *News of the World*, the paper I joined as cricket correspondent in 1979; it was my first job in Fleet Street.

Bill had a rare, Brian Clough-like talent. He was so well respected by his workforce that we were desperately keen to please him – though we didn't fear him, as so many of Clough's players did. Bateson was a Falstaffian figure with a great sense of humour, but also a demanding boss whose approval felt like a journalistic imprimatur.

For Bill to say, "Well done with that – come on, I'll buy you a pint," was to feel a rush of elation. And when Bill bought you a pint – at a time when Fleet Street resembled a river of alcohol – it didn't stop at one. Bill was a big man, and usually very thirsty. The first time we went drinking I attempted to curry favour by proving my own prowess with the dimpled glass. I feel a little queasy now just thinking about it. I was a decent cruiserweight taking on a champion heavyweight.

After eight pints, knocked back at a tempo quicker than I felt comfortable with (on local papers you cannot afford to drink so quickly), I had to proffer my excuses and stumbled from the bar and into the late night air of Fleet Street. Taking deep breaths, I hailed a taxi for my Crouch End home in north London. Then, to my embarrassment, I threw up inside the cab.

"That's the end of work for me for the evening," said the driver. I tipped him heavily and still had to find another taxi to take me home. I was more wary of attempting to match Bill drink for drink after that.

One Tuesday morning, which was when we made out our expenses claims, he said: "Right chaps, the editor has decided to have a clampdown on expenses and told me I must cut £10 from each claim. So when you do your exes add an extra £10 which I can cut." It was a typical ploy, showing you at once his loyalty and his sense of humour.

That loyalty inspired the same quality in his staff. In my days at the paper I toured with the England cricket team, with players such as Ian Botham, David Gower, Allan Lamb and Bob Willis, players whose enjoyment of life was not necessarily confined to their achievements on the field of play.

But while some sportswriters are – most unfairly at times – asked to write about events off the field, that was never the case with Bill. If the news editor ever wanted me for anything he always had to go through Bill. "I want you out there drinking and socialising with the players," he would say. "And you can't do that if you are reporting on their misbehaviours." The *News of the World* had an immense reputation for its sports coverage; the paper was nicknamed "The Screws of the World" but the tittle-tattle was to be found on other pages.

"What's occurring?" Bill would ask on a daily basis, and you had to give him a précis of developments in your particular sport. You didn't have to wear a tie in those days. But you always had to carry one in your pocket. "Just in case I ask you to go off and interview the Queen," Bill said. Every Tuesday lunchtime he would take his team to Ye Olde Cock Tavern, high up in Fleet Street, near The Strand. And we would talk sport. Often, on that opening day of the working week, we would stay there, drinking from 12 noon until 8 pm when the pub, like so many in that part of London, closed. By that time we were making little sense. But for the first three or four hours we would thrash out the stories and features for that weekend's paper, dutifully jotted down by Bill's deputy.

There was a strong drinking culture in the old Fleet Street, helped by generous expenses. I was delighted to experience the end of it before Rupert Murdoch led the departure of newspapers from there in 1986, to escape the print unions. Seven years of pounding my liver was probably enough.

Every newspaper had its own pub, but the most famous drinking establishment in Fleet Street was El Vino. The great playwright and novelist Michael Frayn, who came to London EC4 from the *Manchester Guardian*, tells a nice story in Tony Gray's delightful 1990 book *Fleet Street Remembered*.[1] Frayn says: "I don't know whether I should mention his name, but what the hell, he won't care. It was Henry Fairlie. And he'd been assigned to cover the summit conference in Paris. By this time Henry had been employed by almost every publication in Fleet Street. He was a brilliant journalist, but he did have this very bad habit of running up enormous bills and consequently a lot of the newspapers in Fleet Street found it too expensive to employ him.

He finally ended up at the *Daily Mail* and they had arranged to send him to this vital summit conference in Paris. Henry managed to draw a huge advance on his expenses and he got as far as El Vino, and there he stuck. He covered the entire conference by telephone, from El Vino. And the funny thing is that his coverage of the conference was perfectly satisfactory. In fact some of the stories he got on the phone were a lot better than the rest of them were able to get over there in Paris."

The worst sports editor? There was one who wasn't just bad – he was awful. He was a one-eyed Arsenal supporter and when his beloved Gunners defeated north London rivals Spurs one evening, he allegedly jumped on top of the subs' table, opened his flies and pissed all over a Tottenham supporter. And, no, I don't know how he kept his job.

He used to write headlines before you had filed your copy. Once, before leaving the office for his habitual long lunch, he told his cricket correspondent to include in his report that John Emburey, the England off-spinner, had been born in Peckham, south London. The headline the following day ran: "What a bunch of plonkers," using one of Del Boy's favourite lines from the BBC sitcom *Only Fools and Horses*.

Choosing your editor

Sports editors tend to choose their writers, more than the other way around, which is a shame. It would be nice to pick them because, as with football managers and cricket coaches, they have a profound effect on the development of their charges.

But you can, if you're pig-headed enough, choose your own, and with outrageous good fortune and a very thick skin I managed to do this on a few occasions. So if you don't happen to be as brilliant as Ian Wooldridge, and newspapers are not beating a path to your door, you can sometimes do it the other way round.

When I left school my parents pushed me into the Civil Service, with the encouraging words: "They will never fire you there." They were right, to a certain point. Once you become "established" in the Civil Service, which happened to me after about a year, you are almost sack-proof. But working for the Inland Revenue at a rudimentary level was deadly dull. Besides, at 18 I had decided I wanted to become a sportswriter. So every week, and every day for some weeks, I besieged the offices of the *Sussex Express* in Lewes. It was about a decade before Alan Bleasdale's *Boys from the Blackstuff* was aired on BBC, with Yosser Hughes, close to insanity because of his inability to find a job, pleading "Gizza job!" to any potential employer. I was equally demented with the weekly *Sussex Express*. "But I'm afraid we don't have any vacancies," said editor Les Lacey – father of the famous *Guardian* football writer, David, back in 1970. "My son, Jerry, is the sports editor and he's a one-man band, I'm afraid. He writes a lot of it himself and the rest comes from outside contributions." That was the way with most small weeklies.

But it didn't put me off. I bombarded the paper with pieces, some of which were published. "Can you give me a job now, please?" I pleaded. Eventually, to keep this nuisance quiet, they relented and took me on as a junior reporter, covering general news but also writing on Sussex cricket and writing about Brighton and Hove Albion.

A few months later I almost brought the *Sussex Express* to a standstill. Standing in for Jerry Lacey on the stone of the hot metal paper (a surviving practice from the 19th century) in Hastings, where it was printed, I picked up and moved some typeface. Suddenly, there was a terrible silence. What I had done was against print union rules. "Do that again and everyone here walks out," said one gruff "inkie".

Then, in about 1990 and unhappy at the *Daily Mirror* for reasons already touched on, I "invented" a job for myself at the midmarket tabloid newspaper *Today*, which was owned by Murdoch. I wrote to the editor, David Montgomery, pointing out that while they had a chief sportswriter they didn't – like the *Daily Mail* and *Daily Express* – have a No. 2, a "chief sports feature writer". And I suggested I was the man for the job. Amazingly, Montgomery rewarded my effrontery by giving me the job.

My third target was Mike Averis, the sports editor of *The Guardian* in 1992, when I decided to move from tabloids to a broadsheet. *The Guardian* had always been my favourite paper. But they didn't have a vacancy. And they weren't offering me a job. So I sent off a feature on [the cricketer] David Gower, which they used. They then gave me a five-days-a-week freelance contract in 1993, followed by a staff job a little later. I wouldn't have the nerve to behave like that now. Besides, staff jobs are even more difficult to come by.

Averis was a good man to work for, and he knew his cricket and rugby. But he was also a notorious non-delegator. I remember going into the paper's old offices in Farringdon Road one evening. I had been covering Wimbledon tennis. It was also the time of the 1998 football World Cup in France. Mike was hectically running around the office, picking up all the ringing phones, while other subs sat idly by, watching the football on TV. But when it came to changing a page at short notice, ripping up the first edition to make way for breaking news, Mike was one of the best.

I enjoyed 25 years with *The Guardian*, and they were the happiest of my career. But those formative, bad and bawdy days in Fleet Street are the ones I remember most vividly.

Reference

1. Tony Gray, *Fleet Street Remembered*, William Heinemann: London, 1990.

14

The sub-editor

Charles Morris

As the sun lowered over Wimbledon's Centre Court on 9 July 2006, I was sitting in the pressbox as the men's singles final was reaching its denouement. In a long contest of swinging fortunes, defending champion Roger Federer was leading 6-0, 7-6, 6-7, 5-3 against Rafael Nadal, and Federer was serving for the match. My pulse was racing, partly because of the scintillating quality and tension of the tennis. In my subsequent report for the *Financial Times,* I wrote: "Both men were moving beautifully, like skaters gliding on ice. Rarely can there have been a more aesthetically pleasing final."[1]

The main reason for my pounding pulse, however, was that the first edition deadline for the *FT*'s sports page was just over an hour away, and in that time I had to write some 650 words to fill the empty space on the page. The longer the match continued, the more my anxiety increased over the writing time available. Sports reporting is often a rushed job, but now every minute was counting against me. Fortunately, Federer's trusty serve came to his, and my, rescue as he duly won the game to love, to claim his fourth consecutive Wimbledon championship.

After a dash from the press seats and briefly into the sunlight across the walkway to the adjacent media centre, I began hammering away at my computer keyboard and eventually filed my report with just a few minutes to spare. My haste at the end of the match, however, led to an error. I had failed to register in my notes that Nadal had held his serve in the penultimate game to gain his third game of that set, and in striving to meet the deadline I forgot this fact. My report consequently credited him with one fewer, recording the score as 6-2 in the final set.

At this point only two people could prevent my error going into print: the sports editor, who would read it, and the sub-editor, who would also edit it and place it on the page. Given the little time they had to work on the article, the odds were against them noticing it – and neither did. I attach no blame to them; the mistake was entirely mine. One of them, however, spotted it later and it was at least rectified for the second edition.

An incorrect score is a cardinal error in sports reporting. Although being one game out in a four-set tennis match is a lesser of such offences, it nevertheless left me mortified and feeling unprofessional. Howlers, however, can happen when human beings are involved. The *Scotland on Sunday* newspaper in the mid-1990s printed an incorrect score for, of all things, the Edinburgh football derby, Hibernian v. Heart of Midlothian, a match right in the centre of its main sales area of eastern Scotland. This was the equivalent of the London *Evening Standard* publishing an incorrect score for an Arsenal v. Tottenham Hotspur game. Again, the gaffe was spotted in time for the second edition, and its effects were mitigated since the first edition was distributed only to London and other fringe circulation areas.

Such stories illustrate the most important role of editing in sports and any kind of journalism: identifying mistakes and doing everything to ensure accuracy. Truth is the *sine qua non* of the trade – and should be even more so in an era of so-called "fake news" and "alternative facts". Nothing damages a publication's credibility more than getting basic facts wrong. People, no matter how punctilious, can make mistakes. So a second pair of eyes is essential in the presentation of any information. Writers should strive to their utmost for the truth, and their editing colleagues are the extra filter through which their reports must pass to assist in this aim.

Stereotyped by Hollywood

The popular historical view of journalists, however, tended to skirt over this quest for accuracy. The public perspective was heavily influenced, as in so many cases, by Hollywood. In this regard, the 1931 film *The Front Page* and its various later versions provide an illuminating and significant thread. Based originally on a stage comedy written by former reporters Ben Hecht and Charles MacArthur, and produced by Howard Hughes, the film became a box-office hit that garnered three Academy Award nominations. The plot involves a fearsome Chicago newspaper editor trying to hang on to his star reporter, who wants to leave to get married and enjoy a quieter life. Meanwhile, a massive scoop falls into their lap involving an escaped accused murderer, who they attempt to hide while the police and rival newspapers search for him. The play was also adapted for American radio and for director Howard Hawks' brilliant comic film *His Girl Friday* in 1940, which starred Cary Grant and Rosalind Russell. A popular remake of *The Front Page* emerged in 1974, directed by Billy Wilder and starring Jack Lemmon, Walter Matthau and Susan Sarandon, and a further broadcasting version appeared in 1988 titled *Switching Channels*, with Burt Reynolds, Kathleen Turner and Christopher Reeve.

This sequence of plays and films, together with others about journalism, established a public image, or even stereotype, of journalists. Ruthless editors were seen barking down the phone at glamorous reporters with a press card in their hat band and a cigarette in the corner of their mouth. These reporters, using quick wits and animal cunning, would do almost anything for a good story. Such portraits of colourful characters operating on the fringes of society's seedier side enticed many youngsters, myself included, to take up the profession.

The films also established a profile of the least-known and least-glamorous of journalists: the sub-editor. He – and in pre- and immediate post-war days that was predominantly the case – was depicted as a middle-aged man sitting around a table with several colleagues. Jackets off, pencils in hand and wearing visors to protect their eyes from overhead lights, they would be furiously editing articles fresh from reporters' typewriters amid clouds of cigarette smoke.

Hollywood might not have emphasised the search for journalistic accuracy until later films such as *All the President's Men* (1976), but it did faithfully depict the sequence of newspaper production in those earlier days of hot-metal printing that helped achieve it. In the sports department, the day began with the sports editor and his lieutenants holding a conference to discuss the events they would cover that day, what news stories were expected and the feature articles they also planned to publish. Based on these conference decisions, page designers among the sub-editing team would draw page plans on paper. The best stories would "lead" the various pages and the remaining, lesser ones given a prominence elsewhere relative to their significance.

Reporters, meanwhile, went off and compiled their stories, which would be read by the sports editor or his/her deputy. They checked if they were up to standard, had no obvious errors and fulfilled the brief requested. If they had any queries about the content they would contact the writer. Having cleared these hurdles, the article, or "copy" as it was called, would be passed to the sub-editing desk to be placed on the page. The sub-editors, or "subs" as they became known in Britain, would edit and cut them to the length allocated on the page plan, and also write a headline.

This process has remained largely unchanged since computerisation of the industry, which began in the 1970s and was firmly established in the Western world by the end of the next decade. The differences in today's internet age are that stories are produced for print editions and/or websites, and the subs perform, in addition to their previous tasks of copy editing, those formerly done by printers: typesetting, or putting the story in the correct typeface and point size; reading for spelling and punctuation errors; and composition, putting the page together according to the design plan.

Great page design is as much an art as a science, as a glance at the best magazines will testify. Its twin aims should be to catch the reader's eye, lure them into the page, while making the reading experience as easy as possible. Striking photographs are particularly enticing, and perhaps the most useful basic advice of page design is: "Build a page around your best picture." And here sports journalism is rich indeed. Sport, by its sheer physicality, provides spectacular, dramatic and at times beautiful photographs. Who could forget, for instance, the image of Muhammad Ali standing over a prone Sonny Liston after knocking him out in their 1965 world heavyweight boxing title bout, snarling at him to "Get up and fight like a man!"; Bob Beamon flying through the thin air of Mexico City during his world record long jump of 8.9 m at the 1968 Olympics, or sprinters Tommie Smith and John Carlos raising their black-gloved fists on the podium as a display of black pride and unity at the same Games? Some might want to forget the extraordinary picture of prop forward Fran Cotton literally caked in mud from head to toe during the British Lions tour of New Zealand in 1977, but not Kelly Holmes' wide-eyed look of joyous disbelief after winning the 800 m gold medal at the 2004 Olympic Games in Athens.

The shape of your chosen picture – landscape or portrait – and the crop and size required to display it effectively will dictate how the lead and subsidiary stories are presented around it in a newspaper. The lead story will command the headline with the largest point size, and other headlines will descend in size down the page. One exception will be if a reasonably lengthy "basement" article is used across most columns at the bottom of the page, which will command a point size higher than some above it. On facing pages, a long single-column story on the right edge of the left-hand page will provide a useful visual boundary or break, to prevent headlines running into each other across the two pages. Another, smaller picture or two further down the page will offer visual balance and prevent large "grey" areas of print only.

Another boon for sports journalism was the improved printing and reproduction technology that enabled colour photographs to become the norm in the late 1970s, giving the printed form added zest after a predominantly black-and-white century. A more recent development has been the increased use of graphics and tables, and the ubiquitous data of sport provides fascinating material for this alternative visual tool.

Despite such enhancements to the overall product that sub-editors can produce, their basic and most important role remains the same – thorough copy editing. On receiving a story, the sub will read it through once for "sense" – to understand what it is about and whether it flows coherently. Serious editing begins with the second reading. Now the sub is looking closely for errors, whether factual, grammatical or in spelling and punctuation. It helps tremendously, and is usually the case, if the sub is a sports fan with a general knowledge of the most popular sports, enabling him or her to identify blunders or be suspicious enough to check a less obvious potential mistake. This task has been made much simpler and quicker by the internet. Occasionally photographs of the match being reported can also help in this regard. I remember once correcting a description of a catch in a cricket Test match. The reporter had written that the fielder caught the ball in his left hand but the photograph of the incident before me on the desk, which was being used to illustrate the report, showed him using his right.

Armstrong v. *The Sunday Times*

Potential libels should also be foremost in a sub's mind if the story concerns sensitive matters. Their occurrence is perhaps less likely in sports journalism than in general news reporting, but certain subjects should be eyed warily. Stories about performance-enhancing drug-taking, corruption by players and officials or the recent child abuse scandal in British football, for instance, should set a sub's antennae twitching. Is there a balancing comment from the accused? If they have denied the accusations, has this been included in the story? Is any criticism malicious in nature? If there is the slightest doubt, the story should be referred to the publication's lawyer for checking. By doing so, publishers are saved extensive legal entanglements and costs.

This point is illustrated comprehensively by the long saga of the *Sunday Times* and its allegations of drug use against Lance Armstrong, the American cyclist who "won" the Tour de France seven times. David Walsh, the paper's chief sports reporter, became particularly suspicious of Armstrong in 1999 after he had remonstrated with French cyclist Christophe Bassons, who had written a column suggesting that Tour riders used drugs. Bassons was drummed out of the race because of Armstrong and other riders' antipathy towards him.

"If Armstrong was anti-doping, Christophe Bassons would have been his friend not his enemy," explained Walsh in a 2014 lecture at the London College of Communication. "Why bully him?"[2]

The mounting evidence Walsh gained about Armstrong resulted in him co-writing a book, *LA Confidential*, in 2004. The American subsequently sued the *Sunday Times* over a related article by another journalist, and in 2006 the newspaper reached an out-of-court libel settlement with the rider. Walsh and the newspaper, however, continued to raise questions about Armstrong and were eventually vindicated in 2012, when the United States Anti-Doping Agency found him guilty of drug use. He was subsequently stripped of his Tour De France titles and banned from the sport for life. The newspaper also sought to recover its reported 2006 libel settlement of £300,000 plus £720,000 costs, and reached an agreement with Armstrong on this in 2013.[3]

Throughout Walsh's 13-year pursuit of Armstrong, the editing of his numerous articles would have involved rigorous checking for potential libels, particularly after the 2006 case and Armstrong's litigious nature. Incidentally, it is to the eternal credit of Walsh and the *Sunday Times* that they persevered with their investigations for so long when many other reporters and publications were deterred by a potential loss of access to the icon Armstrong then was, and his legal threats. Walsh himself pithily highlighted the dangers to journalism and sport of this safety-first approach when he described it as journalists acting "like fans with typewriters".[4]

The importance of flow

In addition to looking for errors or libels, the sub-editor will also be cutting the story to the correct length for the page slot – or conversely adding extra background material from previous articles or press agency stories if the copy comes up short. Cutting a story adroitly also demands a certain artistry. Anyone can simply remove sentences from the bottom of a sports news story, but deft surgery throughout – the odd word here and there, or substitution of one word where three or four have been used – can retain information that would otherwise have been lost. Economy of words is almost a religion for the diligent and effective sub.

Editing is also concerned with a story's content and flow. The classic structure for a news story is that of an inverted pyramid: the main bulk of information at the top and then tapering down to the least important details or background information. It begins with an introductory paragraph that aims to summarise the news in question in as dramatic and enticing a way as possible. Writing a good first paragraph, or "intro" as it is known, involves employing the "WH" formula: it should include the Who, What, Where, When, Why and How of the story. For example: "Steve Smith (Who) scored a second century (What) on his return to Test cricket at Edgbaston (Where) yesterday (When), with an innings of grit and class (How) to put Australia in a commanding position (Why)." Not every intro has to include all of these facets, and particularly the "how" and "why" are often unnecessary or follow later. The story's subsequent paragraphs then expand on the intro, with the most newsworthy facts following in rational order. Hence, if the print deadline is imminent, the quickest method of cutting it would be to remove the last paragraph or two.

The sub-editor has to decide whether the story has been written not only in accordance with this formula but also in the most readable, interesting and clearest manner. His or her priority at this point are the readers – that they receive the information in the most accessible and interesting form possible. So could the intro be improved by making its wording more dramatic? A young, inexperienced reporter might even have misjudged the most salient fact of the story and included it further down, rather than in the introduction. Similarly, sometimes important subsidiary facts are placed too low in a story, and merely lifting a paragraph or two further up can improve matters hugely, or make the flow of information more logical. A sub should also be checking that the words employed carry the intended meaning, or if they might create an ambiguity. For example, to state that "Bill Bloggs has doubled his batting average this season" raises the question of whether this is in comparison with last season only or with his entire professional career. Such queries should be put to the reporter to check his or her intended meaning and ensure accuracy.

The flow of a story is particularly important for a feature article. If you expect readers to tackle 1,000 words or more, they need to have an easy ride. The various themes and parts of the feature need to follow logically and smoothly from one to the other using linking sentences. A feature is topped and tailed by introductory paragraphs that draw one in, and a clear, satisfying ending in which a "pay-off" line is often employed. There is no set formula for a feature as with a news story, but a common structure is to have a few alluring introductory paragraphs – a fascinating anecdote relating to the subject in question, for example – and then an "establishing" paragraph, which summarises what the article is about and why it is being written now.

This structure was used, for instance, in a feature about Colin Kaepernick, the San Francisco 49ers quarterback who in 2016 first sat, and then kneeled, on the pitch during the US national anthem before National Football League games as a protest against police violence against black people. The article however, begins with a few paragraphs about another player, Kenny Stills of the Miami Dolphins, and his subsequent strong campaigning against racial injustice. These lead into and culminate with a quote from Stills, saying how Kaepernick's actions had "played a really big part in helping open my eyes". Then comes the establishing paragraph, which sets down the article's subject and explains why it is being written:

> Last week marked three years since Kaepernick first brought attention to police brutality against people of colour by sitting during the national anthem, a protest that ultimately led to the former San Francisco 49ers quarterback's athletic exile.[5]

The feature goes on to explain that Kaepernick's protests have cost him his career, but also how he has influenced other athletes to follow in his footsteps. It also seeks to identify his place among leading sports personalities who have used their status for political and social causes. Smith and Carlos are, of course, notable examples, as was Muhammad Ali in his refusal to fight in the Vietnam War. The careers of each was either ended prematurely or affected temporarily, yet all were eventually lauded for actions that were initially castigated by sporting and other authorities.

Visual aids

Once satisfied that the flow of a story is satisfactory and all other editing functions have been fulfilled, all that remains for the sub is to write a caption for any accompanying photograph and a headline. A headline's function is to persuade readers, as their eyes scan a newspaper or the home and section pages of a website, to read the story. It must summarise the essence of it while seeking to be as enticing as possible through the use of active, dramatic or witty words. For instance, "Smith caps triumphant return with second century" would suffice for the example of an article's introduction used above. While good headline writing can be taught and achieved with experience, the best exponents just seem to have a natural flair for it. Tabloid newspapers place a particular emphasis on it, and will even redesign a page layout to accommodate a dynamic headline. That would certainly have been the case when *The Sun* came up with an unforgettable headline in 2000 after Inverness Caledonian Thistle had caused one of the biggest shocks in Scottish Cup history, beating Celtic 3-1 at Parkhead: "SUPER CALEY GO BALLISTIC, CELTIC ARE ATROCIOUS".[6] This, of course, was a wonderfully witty pun on the song *Supercalifragilisticexpialidocious,* sung by Julie Andrews and Dick Van Dyke in the 1964 film musical *Mary Poppins.* What reader could fail to be amused or resist it? Perhaps *The Sun* should not have all the credit, however, since I have read that the *Liverpool Echo* got there first when headlining an outstanding performance by Liverpool's Ian Callaghan in the 1970s against Queens Park Rangers: "SUPER CALLY GOES BALLISTIC, QPR ATROCIOUS".[7]

Headlines have a lexicon of their own to a certain extent, resulting from the lack of space often afforded to the sub-editor. Single-column headlines pose the most difficult challenge. Hence the use of short words rarely encountered in everyday speech, such as "rap" meaning to reprimand, "axe" as a verb for being dropped from a team or sacked from a job, or "eye" in the sense of anticipating something or considering an action. Whatever the words used, however, they must reflect the story accurately. Headlines that distort or oversell a story will soon irritate readers when they realise the deception. The racier sections of internet publishing tend to feature such "clickbait" headlines, but it is a policy of diminishing returns.

One final action before releasing a story for publication should be to run a spellcheck, to catch an error you might have missed. These software tools, however, are not foolproof, and in some cases there is just no substitute for the human eye and being a dab hand at spelling bees. Take, for instance, the words "prey" and "pray", or "feint" and "faint". A sports journalist might employ the following phrase when reporting on a cricket match: "Six English batsmen fell prey to Nathan Lyon's devastating off-spin." If the journalist mistakenly used "pray" instead of "prey", this would not be revealed by a spellcheck because "pray" is a word in its own right. Equally, erroneously using "fainted" instead of "feinted" would describe a rugby player collapsing on the ground rather than using a deceptive movement to go past a defender. Again, the spellcheck would not be of assistance.

This whole editing process applies just as much to website production as it does to print journalism. An advantage of the world wide web (WWW) is that it allows more space for articles, indeed an almost infinite length at the extreme, but good editing includes judging correct length. Every story, no matter how strong, has a sensible length in terms of its interest and content. Step over this mark and you begin to bore readers with unnecessary information. Another hugely significant benefit of the web is the ability to link directly to related stories from the one being read – a tremendous bonus for anyone with an avid interest in the subject in question. A mass of information is just a few clicks away, unlike with a newspaper or magazine. The use of photographs, however, often remains more limited on the internet to set template sizes, but technology on this front will doubtless keep improving. Websites have also learnt to replicate the serendipitous element of newspapers – that when scanning your eyes over pages they are caught by a headline that intrigues you, often about a subject beyond your normal interests. Hence home pages and section home pages, such as sport, tend to be packed with headlines and photographs, offering a cornucopia of stories.

Do no harm

The task of editing is so varied and, to an extent, subjective in nature that it is difficult to identify one overall, summarising phrase of advice to an aspiring sub-editor. The best such mantra I can come up with is: "Do no harm." Yes, ruthlessly hunt down and correct errors and libels, and ensure the writing and form are of the standard demanded by the publication, but do not rewrite for the sake of it. As well as wasting time and discouraging the reporter, it is also likely, ironically, to lead to the sub-editor inserting mistakes in the story not there in the first place. Any serious rewrite should be checked with the writer. Editing is about making a badly written article respectable or turning an average one into a good piece – but leaving the well-written story alone.

While mentioning the inserting of mistakes, it would be egregious to infer that sub-editors are somehow beyond error. These guardians against mistakes are of course human, too. Seared in my memory is a gaffe from my early subbing days on the *Northern Echo* during the early 1980s. I edited a picture story about a village barber retiring after some 40 years of cutting the locals' hair, and in what I can only put down to a brainstorm gave him a different first name in the headline. I cannot recall the names, either his or the incorrect one I used, but the headline was something like: "Bob makes his final cut after 40 years." By inserting the wrong name, I cast a shadow over this largely unsung man's one public moment in the sun. Looking back, I can try to rationalise matters and ease my guilt by reflecting that the vast majority of the countless articles I have edited have been improved by my attentions. Yet the memory of this barber lingers – and yes, I did get a rollicking from the night editor.

It is in the improving of a story that lies the pleasure of editing. The best reporters rightly gain the industry's garlands and public recognition, but the least glamorous arm of the profession nevertheless takes enormous satisfaction from designing a striking page, choosing a stunning photograph and cropping it effectively, or turning a mediocre article into a good one and writing a zinger of a headline.

Publishers over the years have been tempted to reduce the sub-editing element, or even tried to remove the middle men and women of the production process entirely, to save money. In the nascent stages of computerisation at the *Financial Times* during the early 1990s, management researched the idea of reporters writing to fit certain-sized templates to match the newsworthiness of their story, and a software program then writing a headline based on the key words of the first paragraph. Unsurprisingly, nothing ever came of this given its optimistic assumption that every reporter could always be relied on to produce error- and libel-free stories in perfect journalistic prose.

There was a similar temptation among the wider industry to ditch the sub-editing process at the onset of website publishing. But if owners and managers wish to maintain a publication's reputation for credibility and accuracy, that second pair of eyes will always be necessary. And furthermore, in my defence of the sub-editor, what computer could ever come up with "SUPER CALEY GO BALLISTIC, CELTIC ARE ATROCIOUS"? I rest my case.

References

1. Charles Morris, "Federer too strong as spirited Nadal falters", *Financial Times,* 10 July 2006.
2. Roy Greenslade, "*How I brought down drug-taking Lance Armstrong*, by David Walsh", *The Guardian*, 28 January 2014.
3. Telegraph Sport and Agencies, "Lance Armstrong settles with Sunday Times", *The Telegraph*, 25 August 2013.
4. Andrew Pugh, "David Walsh: 'It was obvious to me Lance Armstrong was doping'", *Press Gazette*, 11 October, 2012.
5. Patrick Hruby, "Three years in the NFL wilderness: What Colin Kaepernick lost – and won", *The Guardian*, 19 August 2019.
6. Rodger Baillie, "SUPER CALEY GO BALLISTIC, CELTIC ARE ATROCIOUS", *The Sun*, 9 February 2000.
7. Scott Murray, "The joy of six: Great football headlines", *The Guardian*, 12 December 2008.

15
Humour

Rob Steen

Some of the wittiest sportswriting has seldom been read on a published page. Plays such as David Storey's salute to rugby league in Yorkshire, *The Changing Room* (1971), all brittle masculinity and ludicrous Russo-phobia, and Richard Greenberg's *Take Me Out* (2002), where homophobia meets xenophobia in a baseball locker room. Movies such as *Horse Feathers* (1932), a Marx Brothers showcase whose co-authors included the inimitable SJ Perelman; *The Bad News Bears* (1976), written by Burt Lancaster's son Bill and good enough to be remade in 2005, and Bill Forsyth's enchanting homage to football and first love, *Gregory's Girl* (1981). Billy Wilder and IAL Diamond supplied some of the silver screen's most quotable lines, yet few were saltier than the one in *Some Like It Hot*, a 1959 recreation of Chicago in 1929, when Tony Curtis swats away Jack Lemmon's aversion to risk with a list of imponderable improbables: "Suppose you got hit by a truck. Suppose the stock market crashes. Suppose Mary Pickford divorces Douglas Fairbanks. Suppose the Dodgers leave Brooklyn!" The Dodgers left Brooklyn in 1958.

Standing tallest, for this observer, is *Bull Durham* (1988), the first of a string of perceptive and often riotously funny sporting films written and directed by Ron Shelton, a former minor league baseball player. Mind you, the most enduring quip, Shelton assured me, was the brainchild of its star, Kevin Costner: "You couldn't hit water," his character, Crash Davis, tells the wild young pitcher Nuke Laloush, "if you fell out of a boat."[1]

There have been books aplenty, too, such as PG Wodehouse's *The Clicking of Cuthbert* (1922) and *The Heart of a Goof* (1926), WP Kinsella's *Box Socials* (1996), Marcus Berkmann's *Rain Men* (1995) and Harry Pearson's *Slipless in Strettle* (2010). The spotlight here, though, is on the full-timers, those employed to cover sport by newspapers, magazines and even the classier websites, and hence entitled to call themselves sportswriters. Regrettably, due to the author's almost enviable mastery of mono-linguistics, that spotlight is confined to those working in the English language.

One further *mea culpa*. If this chapter suffers from excessive nostalgia, please forgive it. While it would be imprudent to propose that the golden age of sporting wit has passed (has there ever been such a glorious era, and if so, how can we measure it?), the transformation from pastime to global profit machine-cum-social barometer has bred a more scathing press and a graver, shriller tone, a necessary if not necessarily conscious counterpoint to the incessant cheerleading of the broadcasters and PR teams. That there is more space devoted to the wrongs is to be applauded, unstintingly, but the upshot has been a reduction in levity.

Legitimised by the boundary-free excesses of social media, witty reporting is harder to find than masterclasses in sneering, sarcasm and histrionics. So long the main event around which everything else revolved, the games themselves have become a distraction from the serious, often ugly business that spectator sport, so long covered chiefly as a source of daily cheer, has so visibly become. This has left less room for proportion let alone warmth, and much more for a cold, scathing brand of wit. With salaries for athletes soaring and press barons slashing not only wages but jobs, it is not difficult to see resentment and envy as spurs. That chuckles are now largely the province of fringe players, the TV sport columnists and (often unpaid) bloggers, does not feel coincidental either.

To steal shamelessly from Martin Mull, writing seriously about comical writing may well be even less enlightening than dancing about architecture, but this chapter will not shrink from its obligations.

Ringing the changes

As coverage of boxing, ballgames and horse-racing began to take wing in the 19th century, the desire to be taken seriously bred over-compensation; witness the over-excitability, excessive gravitas and cringe-inducing grandiosity of the early sportswriters. Even now, several decades after the *New York Daily News* and *New York Post* columnist Jimmy Cannon (1909–1973) was purportedly the first to celebrate sport as "the toy department of life", the newspaper sports desk, source of some of the most avidly consumed pages, print and web, is still regarded as such in some haughty quarters, distortedly and demeaningly so.

It is not insignificant that North American newspapers are city-based and state-centred while the best-selling English titles are national organs and were variously known, even after they began dispersing to Wapping and Canary Wharf in the 1980s, as a collective – "Fleet Street", "Grub Street" and "The Street of Shame". In theory, this made it easier for reporters to poke fun rather than concern themselves with maintaining good relations with their subjects. "I belonged to the gee-whiz group of sportswriters," reflected Paul Gallico, who gee-whizzed for the *New York Daily News* from 1923 to 1936 before bidding adieu with *Farewell to Sport* – a compendium of his columns – then making the relatively short if usually prohibitive hop to best-selling novelist. To be an American sportswriter between the World Wars, he contended, was to be guilty of habitual exaggeration, overt patriotism and even xenophobia:

> We had an overwhelming innocence… we were so naïve. Not only we sportswriters but the whole country… Everybody was happy… You could let yourself go on sports. A heavyweight championship fight, the build-up… was like the Israeli-Arab war… your side and their side. The goodies and the baddies. When Helen Wills played Suzanne Lenglen, when they met for the first time, you would have thought the world was coming to an end if our fine American girl got licked by this dreadful frog, this awful Frenchwoman.[2]

The backlash was inevitable. While Fleet Street's finest were more dispassionate, more driven to asserting their intellectual superiority (witness Pierce Egan, the journalist and satirist whose musings on horse-racing and bare-knuckle boxing in the 1810s made him the first sportswriter of consequence), their counterparts were louder and showier. Thus it was that the first influential seeds of waggish, critical, even cynical sportswriting were sown by Americans, albeit primarily syndicated columnists ranging across a number of sports and working for publications read overseas as well as nationwide. Most prominent were Ring Lardner (*The Sporting News*, *Chicago Tribune*), Red Smith (*New York Herald Tribune*) and Lardner's son John, aka Ring Jr. (*Herald Tribune*,

Newsweek, The New Yorker, The Saturday Evening Post). In the estimation of Cannon, who was himself once toasted as "the most distinctive sportswriter of his time":[3] "Sportswriting survived because of the guys who don't cheer."[4]

Ringgold Wilmer "Ring" Lardner cheered the little guy. Graduating from baseball reporter to eminent and sometimes wicked satirist, his breakthrough work was *You Know Me Al*, a novel comprising a series of letters home from a baseball player adjusting to life as major leaguer, originally published in the *Saturday Evening Post* in 1914 and between hard covers two years later, drawing plaudits from the high-minded likes of Virginia Woolf. He also co-wrote a hit Broadway comedy with George S. Kauffman, contributed sketches and lyrics to the Ziegfeld Follies, and was admired by aspiring writers such as Hemingway as well as proven ones, including Fitzgerald (Ring, it has been claimed, was the model for the tragic Abe North in *Tender Is The Night*). Groucho Marx, too, was a fervent fan. "I was always crazy about Lardner," he declaimed on the *Dick Cavett Show* while he and Truman Capote were discussing whether Ring's work was comedic or dramatic.[5] On a glummer if more important note, Lardner helped break the 1919 World Series "fix" story that robbed his country of what remained of its sporting innocence.

"It is commonly argued that Mark Twain taught American writers how to write in the way Americans speak," said Jonathan Yardley, Pulitzer Prize-winning *Washington Post* book critic and author of *Ring: A Biography of Ring Lardner*. "But if you look at *The Adventures of Tom Sawyer* and *The Adventures of Huckleberry Finn*, the dialogue is incredibly stilted. Lardner, on the other hand, who was a gifted musician, had a perfect ear. You can read the best of the short stories and the chatter between husbands and wives and between ballplayers and other ballplayers; it's perfect."[6] Like Twain, noted Liebenson, "the Michigan-born Lardner's most memorable stories were grounded in his Midwestern sensibility and were devastating, character-driven exposés of the hypocrisies and blithe cruelties of life not only in the big cities but in small-town America as well".[7]

"It was in an effort to turn out seven columns a week [for the *Chicago Tribune*]," warranted his anonymous obituarist in the *New York Times*, "that Lardner hit upon the method which was to make him famous. In hotel lobbies, clubhouses, dugouts, he had been listening to talk among the ball players – using slang and singular nouns and plural verbs mixed together. One day in an effort to fill out his piece he wrote a short dialogue supposedly between two players engaged in a Pullman car poker game... with shrewd touches of character and the natural speech of the lowbrow."[8]

The strategy worked. Readers lapped it up. For that season's World Series, he invented a left-handed pitcher for the New York Giants, who reported the games in Lardner's style. This fondness for the "lowbrow" bloomed in *You Know Me Al*, where Lardner combined that ear for vernacular chatter with an edgy whimsy. By today's standards, he might easily be accused of being haughty and patronising, but the compassion shone through:

> The hotel here is a great big place and got good eats. We got in at breakfast time and I made a B line for the dining room. Kid Gleason who is a kind of asst. manager to Callahan come in and sat down with me. He says Leave something for the rest of the boys because they will be just as hungry as you. He says Ain't you afraid you will cut your throat with that knife. He says There ain't no extra charge for using the forks. He says You shouldn't ought to eat so much because you're overweight now. I says You may think I am fat, but it's all solid bone and muscle. He says Yes I suppose it's all solid bone from the neck up. I guess he thought I would get sore but I will let them kid me now because they will take off their hats to me when they see me work.[9]

It is possible, nonetheless, to propose that son outstripped father. John Lardner certainly defied F. Scott Fitzgerald's best-known assertion, that there are no second acts in American lives, more efficiently than most. One of the "Hollywood 10" blacklisted by the House Un-American Activities Committee, he was reborn as an Oscar-winner for his adapted screenplay for Robert Altman's satirical *M*A*S*H* (1970). As a sportswriter, he was the consummate snook-cocker. You don't have to be a baseball junkie to enjoy "The World's Richest Problem Child", a column about Ted Williams, the prickly, controversial Boston Red Sox colossus of the 1940s and 1950s. Mind you, it does help to know that a batting average of .340 is exceptional and one of .406 extraordinary:

> Many students of human mentality (most of them play the same instrument that I do, the typewriter, and have learned psychology by close observation of the bartender at the water hole around the corner from the office) have been saying for years that Mr. Williams has a complex. They watch him with honest pity as he gropes his way through the shadowland between .340 and .406. They agree with a sigh that he is the strongest lefthand-hitting neurotic they have ever seen. A few weeks ago, Thomas A. Yawkey, the Red Sox owner, took cognizance of Ted's condition and tried the cure I spoke of. It is a form of shock treatment. The subject is pelted softly but firmly with handfuls of green banknotes in large denominations. The size of the dose varies with the individual. Mr. Yawkey might still be showering his patient with engravings of General Grant had not Williams, rising from the couch when the total reached $125,000, remarked, by way of small talk, that he was satisfied.[10]

Lardner could also be winningly self-deprecating. "The stuff in this book," he nudge-nudged in a collection of his *Newsweek* columns, "was carefully checked for accuracy like Louella O. Parsons's, and, like Gibbon's *Decline and Fall of the Roman Empire*, it contains many a dry chuckle. The publisher of [my first book] rang up the sales total on his fingers and toes, of which he had the normal compliment."[11]

"A little pleasure, a little entertainment"

Walter "Red" Smith wrote irreverently insightful daily dispatches during the second and third quarters of the 20th century, mostly for the *New York Herald Tribune* and, latterly, the *New York Times*. He was Ernest Hemingway's favourite sportswriter.[12] Even in his ninth decade, the twinkle never left those impish blue eyes.

"I like to report on the scene around me, on the little piece of the world as I see it," he once explained. "And I like to do it in a way that gives the reader a little pleasure, a little entertainment. I've always had the notion that people go to spectator sports to have fun and then grab the paper to read about it and have fun again. I've always tried to remember – and this is an old line – that [sport] isn't Armageddon. These are just little games that little boys can play, and it really isn't important to the future of civilisation whether the Athletics or the Browns win. If you accept it as entertainment, and write it as entertainment, then I think that's what spectator sports are meant to be."[13] Like the Lardners, Smith probably went too far in emphasising sport's trivial sheen, and the fact that he objected long and hard to baseball's racial integration suggests this hampered his perspective, blinding him to sport's impact on wider society. Not that that cooled the affections of the illustrious panel commissioned by *Editor and Publisher*, the so-called "bible" of North American print journalism, to nominate the 25 most influential newspaper folk of the 20th century: Smith was the lone sportswriter.

He was a master of the drop-intro, the postponed punchline. Take this report of a World Series game in 1947:

> In 1942 the president of the Dodgers, whose name is lost in antiquity, hired Louis Norman Newsom as pennant security. Mr. Newsom, one of the most distinguished of latter-day poets, responded with a telegram:
> "Have no fear
> Bobo is here."
> Brooklyn didn't win in 1942, but Bobo Newsom is a man of honour, to whom a promise is a gilt-edged bond. Yesterday he put the Dodgers into a World Series. He did it belatedly and not altogether voluntarily, but when he had pitched an inning and two-thirds for the Yankees in their third and most sordid encounter with Brooklyn, the Dodgers were on their way to victory, 9 to 8.[14]

How can you not find something to delight in somewhere in those paragraphs? The sly opening that glosses disdainfully over the name of a bumptious administrator; the easy flow of nimble sentences; the light but precise choice of words; the spry, spare, understated asides ("not altogether voluntarily"); and above all the artfully delayed, somewhat surprising fact that Newsom – so far as his teammates, employers and most of the Bronx were concerned – turned out to be the villain.

The sly winker

The first sportswriter to make me laugh was Michael Parkinson. Whether in his columns for *The Sunday Times* or books such as *Football Daft* (1968) and *Cricket Mad* (1969), he captured the fun and the ridiculousness. Drawing on his Yorkshire roots and experiences as a reporter for the *Barnsley Chronicle* and the *South Yorkshire Times*, he mimicked the players tenderly but also took them mercilessly to task:

> We've received a letter which will be of interest to anyone who believes in paying money for old rope. It is from Mr Bobby Moncur, the captain of Newcastle United Football Club, setting out a scale of charges for any newspaper wanting to interview himself or members of his team between now and the Cup final... I wouldn't mind if we got something original for the money, but it is always the same dreary, predictable pap. Chewing-gum for the mind. It is so predictable that I am going into business with my All-Purpose Pre-Wembley Kit for Newspapers.
> No kit would be complete without a Soccer Star's Superstition interview, which goes: "When I go out into the white-hot cauldron which will be Wembley tomorrow, I shall not have picked my nose for 10 days/I shall be wearing two left-boots/I shall be carrying my wife's lucky handbag/I shall be wearing my grandfather's vest. It is my lucky charm. It might seem silly but it is going to put Liverpool/Newcastle out of the Cup."
> I know my all-purpose kit is bound to be unpopular with the players, who will accuse me of taking the bread from their mouths. As a journalist, I can only reply that this is infinitely preferable to their habit of lifting the bread from our wallets.[15]

Initially, Parkinson was inspired by American sportswriters in general and Gallico in particular:

> What intrigued me was that the Americans, unlike the British, didn't look down on sportswriting as a second division occupation. I began reading Gallico, and doing so convinced

me I shouldn't be shy about wanting to write about sport. There was a humour about sport that got me – there had to be when you watched Barnsley play football. And the postwar period was a great time to be watching football because clubs were much closer to their community than they are now. You shared their ambitions and shared their humour. Then there was the way humour enhances cricket. Having played in the Yorkshire leagues myself, and played against the great fast bowler Fred Trueman, who was such a one-off, you needed a sense of humour.[16]

Cannon's "hilarious" book about the endearingly incompetent New York Mets, *Can't Anyone Here Play This Game?*, was another influence, Lardner's *You Know Me Al* still more so:

I began experimenting in that kind of genre, and plagiarised the great Americans shamelessly. One of them once said you could find both the worst and the best newspaper writing on the sports pages and I agree: Hugh McIlvanney at *The Observer* is one example, so was Neville Cardus on *The Guardian*.[17]

The first sportswriter who made me want to tickle others was Matthew Engel, who openly acknowledges the debt he owed Parkinson. The latter returns the compliment, describing Engel as "the complete writer – perceptive and funny".[18]

In all probability, Engel is unique in having reported from Olympic Games, World Cups, general elections, battlefields, the South Pole and Northampton County Cricket Ground. He has also written titter-strewn yet illuminating books about hardy British institutions: the tabloid newspaper, the second-class railway carriage and the English county. He is probably best-known, all the same, for his musings on cricket: as chief correspondent for *The Guardian* and editor of *Wisden Cricketers' Almanack* he flung open the doors, daring cricket writers, traditionally a flowery but stuffy breed, not only to embrace the 20th century but to laugh at its more straitlaced and po-faced customs. Until he first came to prominence in the late 1970s, the game was almost always reported with a snobbish reverence bordering on religious obeisance; thereafter, poking fun at the game's radical reinvention and outmoded ruling class became increasingly *de rigeur*.

"I always knew," he told me, "that I wanted to be funny."[19] Few, certainly, have better combined trenchant comment with the winking one-liner, an especially potent combination as cricket finally deigned to embrace commerce: "The presentation ceremony had to go ahead and since the litany for that includes the phrase 'Cornhill Insurance' [name of sponsor] repeated several times, it had to go on television, which could not happen for another five minutes, until *Neighbours* had concluded on BBC 1. That is the channel without advertising."[20]

Conversational English may not work for everyone, but in Engel's case, a very English form of chattiness, underpinned by mischievous understatement, were, and remain, perpetual assets, notably in this waspish dig at the stern resistance of cricket's most famous club, the MCC, to a loosening of its ancient rules governing attire: "The Lord's seagulls hovered as though expecting Middlesex blood; one made as if to dive-bomb a lady in the Warner Stand. They are getting noisier and cheekier. By next year they will be throwing cushions and trying to get in the pavilion without a tie."[21]

Nor did age temper that acerbic fire, as testified by a 2014 article for *The Oldie* bemoaning the state of his erstwhile trade:

One can sense ground authorities in the major sports eyeing up the press seats and wondering if they could be monetised, maybe by charging the hacks admission or revamping the space to create more hospitality boxes. In football, critics are regularly banned by disgruntled owners and managers: a journalist who has not yet been barred from Newcastle United's ground probably isn't doing his job.[22]

The stand-up sportswriter

After Paul Blair hit an unexpected home run during the 1966 World Series, one reporter noted, "If the Oriole centerfielder's grin had been any broader he would have swallowed his own ears."[23] After the same game, after Lou Johnson, distrusting the porous glove of Willie Davis, had cut in front of the LA Dodgers centerfielder to pilfer a catch, Jim Murray regaled readers of the *Los Angeles Times* with an even more liberal dose of purposeful exaggeration. "Lou came and caught a ball that was not only in dead [centre] but two cabs and a shuttle bus from where Lou plays. It was so far that Lou didn't get back to left field til the fourth innings."[24]

Twenty years later, as a new contender swelled England's daily broadsheet market from four to five, *The Independent* brought to wider attention Martin Johnson, whose command of exaggeration would see him give cricket and rugby followers, in particular, plenty to giggle about over breakfast. He had much in common with Engel, whom he had met in pressboxes at Northampton and Leicester during the mid-1970s while they were working, respectively, for the *Leicester Mercury* and the *Northampton Chronicle*. *The Independent* sports editor, Charlie Burgess, who had worked with Engel at *The Guardian* and wanted him to reprise his job at the new rival title, originally saw Johnson as his rugby union correspondent. Cricket, its traditionally oh-so-serious journalism above all, benefited enormously.

Covering the mostly hapless England team during the mid-1980s may not have been a job for a patriot, but it was well-nigh perfect for a master of gallows humour. Always a better read when the national side were losing, Johnson's mocking was also nourished by the soap opera surrounding Ian Botham, a great player hampered by back troubles, tabloid exposés and a penchant for forging relationships with the wrong people.

Johnson started as he meant to go on. Before the first Test against Australia at Brisbane in November 1986, he dipped his typing fingers in vinegar: "There are only three things wrong with this England team – they can't bat, can't bowl and can't field." That England won the match, and went on to regain The Ashes, ensured that a single sentence came to define the author. In 2012, he looked back, typically, in neither anger nor anguish:

> When England went to Australia their early form (in the days when they played a full month of proper warm-up matches) was so desperate that they appeared to have as much chance of coming home with the Ashes as a Mablethorpe beach donkey of winning the Derby.
>
> We all wrote them off, with the sole exception of the shrewd correspondent of *The Independent*, who prudently pointed out to the doom and gloom merchants that there were only three real areas of complete incompetence. However, as these were batting, bowling and fielding, even he was forced to acknowledge the ghastly probability of Australian journalists crowing – and if crowing was an Olympic sport, believe me they'd win the gold every time – for the entire four-month tour.
>
> So what happened? England not only spanked Australia in the Test series, but also won both of their triangular one-day international tournaments. None of the English journalists were in danger of getting sunburned on that trip, largely because the amount of egg on their faces made it impossible for the UVC rays to get through.[25]

Phrases such as "appeared to have as much chance of" and "largely because" were intrinsic to Johnson's schtick, the hallmarks of a stand-up comic. Punchlines are preceded by tried and trusted set-ups. Addressing the thorny issue of cheating and dissent, for instance, he offered a variation on that "has about as much chance as" trope:

> One day, perhaps, bats will be wired up to detect edges in the same way as fencers' foils at the Olympics, which brings to mind a competitor by the name of Boris Onischenko, who was thrown out of a Games for devising a way of making his blade light up at will.
>
> Sadly, modern-day cricket is sufficiently well populated by adherents of the Boris philosophy of fair play to place Sir Richard Hadlee's wicket-taking record in less danger of falling to a wizard of pace and swing, than to a graduate from an MI5 electronic bugging course.[26]

And oh, how he could tease. In 1993, after Shane Warne had flummoxed the stocky Mike Gatting with a delivery often if casually described as "the ball of the century", Johnson had a cosily familiar and irresistible target: "How anyone can spin a ball the width of Gatting boggles the mind." Still, like all proficient clowns, behind the smirking could also lurk serious intent. "Fifty-over cricket is like some ageing Hollywood actress, forever trying to revive interest with regular nips, tucks and injections of Botox. It works for a while but eventually the skin reverts from baby's bottom to dried-up riverbed and off you go again to the plastic surgeon".[27]

Does humour travel?

Not withstanding the American fondness for reworking British sitcoms for their own market – witness *Steptoe and Son/Sanford and Son*, *'Til Death Us Do Part/All in the Family* and even *The Fall and Rise of Reginald Perrin/Reggie* – the global success of *Monty Python's Flying Circus*, *Friends* and *Cheers* have all shown that humour can not only travel well but survive translation. Humorous sportswriting is more complex. Association football aside, few nations share precisely the same fondness for the same sports, and in any case, the knowledge required to get the most out of a particular sportswriter may be beyond all but the most wide-ranging of readers.

Sadly, to fully appreciate the wisdom of Thomas Boswell's decision to attend a Test match between England and West Indies at Lord's in 1984, familiarity with baseball is imperative, and baseball terminology in particular. As Boswell himself puts it, "Cricket, in many ways, is baseball raised to the nth degree." But to reap the maximum fruits from the following one needs to know (a) that cricket is baseball in reverse, with wickets/outs far more valuable than runs, (b) that a bullpen is the collective term for relief pitchers and (c) that in 1984 George Steinbrenner was the impatient, imprudent owner of the (then) success-starved New York Yankees. Ignorance, nonetheless, should not prevent a chuckle or two:

> England took a 342-run lead into the final inning today at Lord's Cricket Ground.
> And lost.
> Talk about a bad bullpen.
> It's a good thing George Steinbrenner doesn't own England.
> England hasn't had many days worse than this, inflicted at the hands of her children of Empire, since the Battle of Yorktown…

In almost every way, this day and this place and this particular match were a suitable introduction to a Yank at his first cricket match. I came with an open mind but a suspicion that I would despise the world's slowest team sport. After all, where else does it take five days and thirty hours of play to read, in many cases, a tie?

> However, instead of coming away a mocker, I now suspect it's lucky for me that I don't live in England. There's a cricket nut trapped somewhere deep inside me; stop me before I become addicted again.[28]

An all-rounder who joined *The Post* in 1969, Boswell has expended most of his energies on baseball, basketball, boxing, golf, tennis and the Olympics. Doubling as chief baseball and golf correspondent, his reports on Planet Sport's most staid spectator sport stand out for their unfashionable insistence that, on its most stirring days, there can be none more vibrant. "One thing elevates golf from the realm of games to the world of sports. The choke factor. Of all our American sports, golf is most humiliating for its stars. As Tom Watson once said: 'We all choke. You just try to choke last.' What happened [in 1989] to Scott Hoch at the Masters, Tom Kite at the US Open, Greg Norman at the British Open and Mike Reid at the PGA Championship – suffering a totally humiliating, self-inflicted collapse under pressure – is what makes golf a legitimate, big-time, big-money sport, rather than a tofu-and-quiche pastime for yuppies."[29] Baseball, though, was his first and most lasting love, and often inspired his most vivid and memorable work.

Boswell's jocularity works because, as with Engel, his style is so intimate. Here is high(ish)-brow journalism rendered digestible to different intellects and tastes by a reporter who achieves an unusual balance between profundity and tabloid immediacy, adept, like Engel, at convincing the reader that he is talking directly to them. Savour a taste of a delicious piece he composed for *The Post*, "99 Reasons Why Baseball Is So Much Better Than Football", the somewhat contrary quantity dictated by a weakness for subversion.

> Some people say football's the best game in America. Others say baseball.
> Some people are really dumb.
> Some people say all this is just a matter of taste. Others know better.
> Some people can't wait for next Sunday's Super Bowl. Others wonder why.
> Pro football is a great game. Compared with hockey. After all, you've gotta do something when the wind chill is zero and your curveball won't break.
> But let's not be silly. Compare the games? It's a one-sided laugher. Here are the first 99 reasons why baseball is better than football. (More after lunch).[30]

The ensuing reasons ranged from the deceptively skittish (the first three are "Bands", "Half time with bands" and "Cheerleaders at half time with bands") and the romantic ("Baseball has Blue Moon, Catfish, Spaceman and The Sugar Bear. Football has Lester the Molester, Too Mean and The Assassin") to the sneering ("Big league baseball players chew tobacco. Pro football line-men chew on each other") and the downright acidic ("The best football announcer ever was Howard Cosell"; "The worst baseball announcer ever was Howard Cosell"). Perhaps the most compelling reason was No. 20: "Eighty degrees, a cold beer and a short-sleeve shirt is better than 30 degrees, a hip flask and six layers of clothes under a lap blanket. Take your pick: suntan or frostbite."

At his sharpest, Boswell offered a blend of joshing, graphic images and acute perceptiveness – and he found the perfect subject in Bill Veeck, club owner, huckster par excellence and to most eyes baseball's ultimate salesman. "Veeck's whole body seems hyper-sensitised, almost overloaded with stimuli. He seems larger than his six feet because his gestures are so expansive. His short, frizzy hair seems like a million raw nerve ends trying to make their great escape from his scalp.

His fingers are always doodling, touching, examining – when they're not drumming painfully hard against the gristle of his large floppy ears, as if to awaken them."[31]

His intros are models of concision. Leading off a profile of the self-admiring baseball star Reggie Jackson came the following gem: "Mark Twain said that politicians, old buildings, and prostitutes become respectable with age. Reggie Jackson would like to make it a foursome."[32] Not that there was ever any danger of anti-climax. "He can mix hokum and genuine insight, subtle phrasing and pathetic bombast like no other star. Few men can match his knack for having a good idea, then mopping the floor with it. If Jackson discussed the Bill of Rights long enough, he'd make you want to repeal it."[33]

Boxing clever

In the 1990s, as television spread its tentacles and proved that watching sport was no longer necessarily about "being there", so emerged a new breed of journalistic funnymen (and they were almost invariably men): the TV Sport columnist. Chained to their armchairs, here were observers who had more in common with their readers than did the colleagues who crammed into pressboxes. Significantly, they focused less on the players than on the commentators and pundits. Open goals abounded. Into this genre surged several wordsmiths, of whom the most successful, helpfully, had little or no experience of life on the sporting road. Helpfully, because they owed no loyalty to anyone but their readers.

Two of the sharpest practitioners have been such outsiders: Martin Kelner (*The Guardian*), a lively radio broadcaster, and Giles Smith (*The Times*), who had spent decades as a music critic. Both would readily acknowledge a sizeable debt to David Coleman, the BBC TV commentator whose colourful phrasing and verbal misadventures enlivened most of the second half of the 20th century (viz. "Juantorena opens his legs and shows his class") and prompted *Private Eye*'s "Colemanballs", a column devoted to the un-*bon mots* of the sporting fraternity.

Unsurprisingly for a broadcaster, Kelner is a terrific raconteur. Not unhelpfully, like Engel and the ESPNCricinfo columnist-cum-stand-up comic Andy Zaltzman, another infectious non-travelling observer, he is Jewish. Unlike them, he sounds it. In his history of sport on TV, *Sit Down and Cheer*, he lays out his qualifications as if impersonating Woody Allen's formative routines in the Catskills:

> The trouble with most histories of sport is that they are written by people who were there. Any idiot with a press card – don't get me wrong, many of these idiots I count as personal friends – can tell you what the atmosphere is like on a big night of European Cup football in the San Siro… But to chronicle the last sixty colourful, tempestuous years of sport through the eyes of those who were present at its epoch-making events is to ignore a multi-channel elephant in the corner of the room. Because without the unholy union between sport and television, the sporting landscape we look out on today would be unrecognisable. The story of sport needs to be written by someone who stayed at home and watched, and my credentials to be its author are impeccable.[34]

Smith's act is droller, subtler, gentler. The title of a collection of his columns, *Midnight in the Garden of Evil Knievel* (2000), speaks volumes. Consider his list of "The 5 best sports television theme tunes", in particular No. 5:

> BBC golf: Woozy, swishy, apparently performed on early-adopted synthesizer technology, and sounding like the cinema's Pearl & Dean theme, but heard under heavy sedation. Yet,

like golf, strangely quickening. At my aunt's funeral, the coffin was borne in to this. It worked very well, and would have worked even better if she had had even the remotest interest in golf. (That's a joke. She loved golf.)[35]

If ever a sport-related television programme invited ridicule it is surely the BBC's long-running *Sports Personality of the Year*, an award decided by viewers' votes that seldom actually measures or even rewards personality; Smith skewers it with delicate precision as well as an atypical dollop of outright sarcasm:

Sporting action? Not so much. You could have counted on the paws of [Lewis] Hamilton's pooch the number of times a moment of sport was shown in real time and lasted more than two and a half seconds. Clips were slowed, chopped, tweaked, glammed-up, frenetically montaged, rendered incomprehensible as sport. Hamilton's film, in which he casually strolled between flaming engines, could have been an advert for a perfume or a pricey watch. One for the floating voter, most certainly… The future of the SPOTY show is, surely, as a sport-inflected version of ITV's Pride of Britain awards. Either that or follow right through and make it a singing contest. We can't have too many of those.[36]

Now savour this mock-serious response to the surreal revelation by Chelsea FC (his lifelong sporting passion) that their French defender, William Gallas, had threatened to score an own-goal if he was not released from his contract:

[This] raises numerous urgent questions, not least among them, what kind of own goal did Gallas have in mind? A scruffy and seemingly accidental deflection from a corner at some random moment in the second half, or a first-minute, 45-yard solo run through a baffled defence, rounding the goalkeeper and tucking the ball into the bottom corner, before wheeling away in the direction of the Chelsea bench with his finger over his lips? I'm thinking the latter. Gallas was, after all, and by all accounts, very keen to move. Either way, this affair clearly has repercussions way beyond the small cast of people involved. Straight away it casts into suspicion, both in the future and retrospectively, all own goals.[37]

The distinction "between basic incompetence and a desire for regular first-team football under Arsène Wenger", he concluded, "is suddenly a very hard one to draw". While my own near-hysterical response to that "very" might stupefy those unversed in the self-satirising solemnity of broadcasting-speak, the natural comic's sense of rhythm and timing seems unmissable. The gang's all here: the delicious subversion of cliché ("and by all accounts"); the skilful use of both understatement ("keen") and exaggeration ("numerous urgent questions"); best of all, the mock grandiosity ("both in the future and retrospectively") that so exquisitely skewers the near-universal tendency to invest sport with a surfeit of seriousness.

Smith's route to his current role began in the early 1990s, when he was music editor of *The Independent* and author of *Lost in Music*, a gentle rib-tickling memoir of his years as an aspiring popstar. "The satellite sports channels were getting properly underway and dishes were beginning to dot the skyline," he recalls. "Simon Kelner, then the sports editor of the *Independent on Sunday*, invited me to write a weekly television review which only featured sports programming, or programmes with sportspeople in them. There just seemed to be an awful lot of it about, and it seemed to be getting more important to people, and much of it was new, and therefore necessarily tentative and experimental in its tone and conduct, so the whole thing loaned itself to reporting."[38]

The late Clive James, an esteemed, innovative and singular TV critic for *The Observer*, was a formative favourite. "As a teenager, I used to cut out and keep [his] reviews. I remember, in particular, clipping the one that included the simile about Barbara Cartland ('Twin miracles of mascara, her eyes looked like the corpses of two small crows that had crashed into a chalk cliff') which has since gone into the language. Everything I have ever written for publication has been a failed attempt to create a comic impact equivalent to the one in that sentence. James wrote about television generally, of course, but his pieces on Wimbledon are among the funniest things he, or anyone else, ever wrote for a newspaper and, again, hugely inspiring. I was also very taken with something the late, great [TV darts commentator] Sid Waddell once pointed out, which is that trade names are normally funny and always more colourful – e.g. always write 'Ginger Nuts' instead of 'biscuits'.

"Someone I came across later, and still hugely admire, is Rick Reilly of *Sports Illustrated* and latterly of ESPN, who, on form, can be gut-bustingly funny. A website has recently taken great pleasure in demonstrating the extent to which he has been guilty of self-plagiarism, but some writers earn the right to replay their greatest hits and, frankly, I would be disappointed if he didn't. [He called one of his books] *Tiger, Meet My Sister… And Other Things I Probably Shouldn't Have Said*, which pretty much sums it up."[39]

Where some writers create an on-page character at odds with their true selves, the tenderness and compassion that suffuse Smith's mockery are of a piece with his character. "I'm not a particularly opinionated person. In fact, I find opinions quite hard to come by (or certainly to hold), so I was probably never going to be one of those journalists who rips things apart with their teeth. In any case, most of the time there would be something a bit inappropriate about getting properly barbed and confrontational over something as ultimately unimportant and intrinsically beside-the-point as, say, an Andy Townsend co-commentary. Plus, I have always admired the *New Yorker* approach – a single eyebrow, raised quizzically – and tend to think that better, or certainly more sustainable, comic writing arises from that rather than from the bulging-eyeball treatment."[40]

All the same, he freely admits to causing offence. Indeed, he welcomes correctives: "It's not a bad thing to be reminded every now and again that there are sentient human beings on the other end of your dashed-off gags. I had a small run-in with [ITV football commentator] Clive Tyldesley once after Bill McLaren had refused an honorary Scotland rugby cap on the grounds that such things were for players only, an act of humility which prompted me to suggest (in passing, I thought) that if you dangled such a thing in front of the ITV football commentary team, their hands would be in the air like a shot. Tyldesley felt this was a personal remark and that, as I didn't know any of the team personally, out of order. He had a point. Ian Darke, now of BT Sport but then of Sky, once rang to dispute my sense that, during a particular pay-per-view boxing broadcast, he had essentially been reduced to the role of door-to-door salesman on behalf of his employer. He, also, had a point. Barry Davies [BBC] has taken the trouble to put me right on some factual points regarding his commentaries. And I once had to ring up Robbie Savage and apologise to him after being unacceptably satirical (just plain mean, really) about his honorary degree from Wrexham University. But otherwise, no. I suppose it would be nice to have some battle-stories about getting rabbit-punched in a car park by Sue Barker. But the single raised eyebrow will generally keep you out of the nastier kinds of trouble."[41]

Parkinson, however, fears for the future.

Martin Johnson is still very funny, as is Giles Smith (although I really think he should report more, because he's a very good at observation), but I wonder if the papers still have an appetite for humour. It's not the industry it was. I hesitate to say drinking habits helped, but it used to be vigorous, robust, raffish. Now we have the rule of the mob, as witnessed in the Ched Evans [rape] saga, which dissuades people from expressing themselves.[42]

References

1. Rob Steen, "Hollywood rediscovers kick flicks and big hits", *The Guardian*, 4 March 2000, http://www.theguardian.com/film/2000/mar/04/sport.news, accessed 16 December 2019.
2. Paul Gallico quoted in Jerome Holtzman, *No Cheering in the Press Box*, Holt, Rinehart and Winston: Austin, TX, 1974.
3. Ibid., p. 273.
4. Ibid., p. 276.
5. *The Dick Cavett Show*, 25 May 1971, https://www.youtube.com/watch?v=3M5opTy7tco, accessed 16 December 2019.
6. Donald Liebenson, "Ring Lardner's work on display in 'Stories & Other Writings'", *Chicago Tribune*, 30 August 2013, http://articles.chicagotribune.com/2013-08-30/features/ct-prj-0901-ring-lardner-ian-frazier-20130830_1_ring-lardner-alibi-ike-printers-row-journal, accessed 16 December 2019.
7. Ibid.
8. Anonymous, "Ring Lardner dies; noted as writer", *New York Times*, 26 September 1933, http://www.nytimes.com/learning/general/onthisday/bday/0306.html, accessed 2 December 2014.
9. Ring Lardner Jr., *You Know Me Al*, Scribner's: New York, 1916, http://www.ibiblio.org/eldritch/rl/unomeal.htm, accessed 16 December 2019.
10. John Lardner, *Strong Cigars and Lovely Women*, Funk & Wagnalls: New York, 1951, pp. 99–100.
11. Ibid., p. xi.
12. Holtzman, p. 244.
13. Holtzman, p. 245.
14. Red Smith, *Red Smith on Baseball*, Ivan R. Dee: New York, 2000.
15. Michael Parkinson, "Cup Final fever or how to sell a load of old rope", *Sunday Times*, 28 April 1974.
16. Michael Parkinson, interview with author, 9 January 2015.
17. Ibid.
18. Ibid.
19. Matthew Engel, interview with author, 10 February 2015.
20. Matthew Engel, "Everything stops for lunch", *The Guardian*, 31 August 1988, reprinted in Engel, *Sportswriter's Eye: An Anthology*, Macdonald Queen Anne Press: London, 1989, pp. 105–106.
21. Matthew Engel, "The fastest waiter in Worcester", *The Guardian*, 7 June 1981, reprinted in Engel, *Sportswriter's Eye*, p. 14.
22. Matthew Engel, "The death of the sportswriter", *The Oldie*, 12 November 2014 (copy supplied by author).
23. Tom Adelman, *Black and Blue: The Golden Arm, the Robinson Boys, and the 1966 World Series That Stunned America*, Little, Brown: New York, 2006, p. 183.
24. Ibid., p. 179.
25. Martin Johnson, "The meerkat solution to watching England", Thecricketer.com, 7 March 2012, http://blog.thecricketer.com/?p=37067#sthash.pFWLfQ3M.dpuf, accessed 3 December 2014.
26. Martin Johnson, "Dissent driving umpires out of the game", *The Independent*, 22 July 1992, http://www.independent.co.uk/sport/cricket-dissent-driving-umpires-out-of-the-game-martin-johnson-cricket-correspondent-reports-how-a-deterioration-in-player-attitudes-has-led-to-the-current-crisis-in-test-cricket-1534826.html, accessed 16 December 2019.
27. Martin Johnson, "Nips and tucks do little good", *The Sunday Times*, 20 January 2013, https://www.thetimes.co.uk/article/nips-and-tucks-do-little-good-786hdnzd6xk, accessed 16 December 2019.
28. Thomas Boswell, "It's cricket", in *The Heart of the Order*, Penguin: New York, 1990, pp. 254–255.
29. Thomas Boswell, "The year of the gag", *Washington Post*, reprinted in Boswell, *Game Day: Sports Writings 1970–1990*, Penguin: New York, 1990, p. 248.
30. Thomas Boswell, "99 reasons why baseball is much better than football", *Washington Post*, 18 January 1987, http://articles.latimes.com/1987-01-18/sports/sp-5548_1_pro-football-game, accessed 16 December 2019.
31. Thomas Boswell, "Always leave 'em laughing", in *How Life Imitates the World Series*, Penguin: New York, 1983, p. 284.

32. Ibid., p. 257.
33. Ibid., p. 259.
34. Martin Kelner, *Sit Down and Cheer: A History of Sport on TV*, Bloomsbury: London, 2012, p. 1.
35. Giles Smith, "The 5 best sports television theme tunes", *The Times Magazine*, 6 December 2014, p. 36.
36. Giles Smith, "Hamilton burns off his rivals but Lineker produces real show of hoarse power", *The Times*, 16 December 2014, p. 61.
37. Giles Smith, "The moving stories that opened a can of worms, itching powder, stink bombs…", *The Times*, 9 September 2006, http://www.thetimes.co.uk/tto/sport/columnists/gilessmith/article2388628.ece, accessed 16 December 2019.
38. Giles Smith, interview with author, 10 January 2015.
39. Ibid.
40. Ibid.
41. Ibid.
42. Michael Parkinson, interview with author.

16

Statistics and records

Huw Richards

When Alastair Cook, on 75 in his final innings as a Test cricketer in 2018, edged through mid-wicket for a single, the electronic scoreboard at The Oval sprang into action, informing spectators that this made him the fifth-highest run-scorer in Test history and triggering yet another of the day's many ovations. It was the latest in The Oval's litany of farewells, accompaniment to its traditional role as host to the last Test of the English summer, inevitably provoking thoughts of the most famous of all, Donald Bradman in 1948.

Every cricket fan knows that one and its context, summed up by Charles Williams in perhaps the best biography of Bradman, cricket's greatest statistical phenomenon: "It was not just a matter of farewells. Bradman needed only four more runs to achieve a total of 7,000 runs in Test cricket. Furthermore his Test average, when the last Test started, was 101.39 [runs per innings]. He needed only to score those four runs to keep that average above 100, a record never achieved before or since."[1]

And what happened next is equally well-known – Bradman bowled second ball for nought – a duck, in cricket parlance – by veteran leg-spinner Eric Hollies, leaving him forever those four runs short, his batting average 99.94 (which is still more than half as high as the next most prolific batsman).

Sir Donald's duck is the most recalled moment of that relentlessly achieving 20-year Test career, the number it created invariably cited to illustrate his greatness. It made him, to Ayaz Menon, "the only player who can be defined by a statistic", to the website *Cricket Country* simply "the 99.94 dude".[2]

It has few rivals as the most famous number in cricket, as Gideon Haigh wrote, "the one batting average that nobody ever need look up".[3] It reaches beyond the game in Australia, where Paul Kelly argued that it "equates with the Prime Ministership and the great Australian novel in the antipodean cultural imagination".[4] The decimal point is silent, but the reference evident, in the Australian Broadcasting Company's PO Box 9994.

"That must have caused a fuss" was the understandable reaction of a Sports Journalism student, told of Bradman's duck and its statistical consequences nearly 70 years later, in a lecture room a bare mile from The Oval.[5]

It did, but not in the terms we understand now. The pathos of the duck and its incongruity with the rest of Bradman's career were well understood. But this was not a world in which career milestones were transmitted to spectators within seconds, or cricket fans around the world could know, as they did in 2007, that Inzamam ul-Haq needed 20 runs in his final Test to equal Javed Miandad as Pakistan's highest all-time run-scorer, or be informed in moments via a mass of multimedia when he fell three short.

Perhaps the most evocative account of Bradman's farewell is John Arlott's commentary for BBC radio:

> It's rather good to be here when Don Bradman comes into bat in his last Test. And now here's Hollies to bowl to him from the Vauxhall End. He bowls, Bradman goes back across his wicket and pushes the ball gently in the direction of the Houses of Parliament which are out beyond mid-off. It doesn't go that far, merely to Watkins at silly mid-off. No run, still 117 for 1. Two slips, a silly mid-off and a forward short-leg close to him. Hollies pitches the ball up slowly … and he's bowled …
>
> Bradman, bowled Hollies, nought. And what do you say under these circumstances? I wonder if you see the ball very clearly, on your last Test in England, on a ground where you've played some of your biggest cricket of your life and where the opposing team have stood around and given you three cheers and the crowd has clapped you all the way to the wicket. I wonder if you see the ball at all.[6]

Not a mention of career aggregates or batting averages. This was of course Arlott the poet, more interested in humanity than numbers, and grasping Bradman's state of mind. Bradman himself subsequently confirmed that he might not have been seeing with his usual clarity.

A 40-second pause between "and he's bowled …" and "Bradman, bowled Hollies …" was filled with the initial roar and subsequent applause from the crowd. Arlott, even without pictures and in only his third year of radio commentary, grasped the lesson – lost on many modern commentators (and still more by stadium announcers) – that you say nothing when the story is being told for you.

As well as being adept in the professional disciplines of the broadcaster, Arlott was too good a journalist to ignore the story of a great batsman falling just short of a truly extraordinary lifetime achievement, had he known it. But Arlott did not know. Nor did Bradman, the England team or hardly anyone else in a huge crowd.

Importance of records

This was not a world unaware of, or lacking an appetite for, cricket statistics. Records are, as historian Allen Guttmann argued in *From Ritual to Record*, part of what separates modern sport from its predecessors.[7] The Greeks kept lists of champions, but were not terribly concerned whether the winner of the javelin had thrown further than his predecessors. Modern sport, and its fans, want to know both.

Cricket, oldest of organised modern team sports, was quick on the uptake. Peter Wynne-Thomas in his *Cricket Historians* notes that averages were recorded as early as the 1790s, and *Bell's Life* listed seasonal averages by the 1840s. *Wisden* introduced seasonal averages in 1887 and "Some Cricket Records" in 1889. Frederick Ashley-Cooper's revision had by 1906, Wynne-Thomas records, produced a 23-page records section which "set the standard which in essence remains in the almanack to this day".[8]

Statistics were sufficiently well-established by the inter-war years to attract the satirical attention of Herbert Farjeon. He told, in an article which appears to date from the late 1920s, of watching a Surrey v. Middlesex match punctuated continuously by mysterious applause, all explained by the omniscient youth sat next to him:

It appears that if you really understand the finer points of the game, you can find a thrill in every ball, for every ball sets up a record of some kind.

Now Hobbs had run out his thousandth victim. Tremendous sensation.

Now a stolen single had brought the total number of runs scored by Middlesex that season up to exactly five thousand, five hundred. This sent the crowd perfectly delirious.

Not a single point escaped the boy at my side. Every one escaped me. By lunch-time he had become so patronising that he was explaining to me exactly what was meant by a recurring decimal.[9]

This was not to every taste. Readers of the 1948 *Playfair Cricket Annual* were treated to vintage harrumphing from EW Swanton of *The Telegraph*, at 42 already adept at sounding 30 years older: "With those whose knowledge of the game derives largely from what they read in the press, averages and records hold a position quite disproportionate to their true place in the scheme of things."[10]

Yet there were clear limits to the statistics available at the time. As Anthony Weigall wrote in November 1945 to *The Cricketer*, whose letters section was the main forum for statistical debate, there was as yet "no reliable list in evidence showing the total batting and bowling figures of our leading cricketers, both past and present".[11] That letter helped prompt the creation that year of the Society of Cricket Statisticians (since 1950 the Cricket Society).

A partial answer to Weigall's plea came in 1947 with the publication of Ernest Roberts' *Test Match Cavalcade 1877–1946*, which boasted: "Hitherto there has been no single book in which all the 277 Tests played during the last 70 years can be seen as a connected story." Roberts also tabulated every player's career records and listed the highest aggregates, led on 1 September 1946 by Walter Hammond with 7,002 runs at an average of 60.88, followed by Jack Hobbs with 5,410 at 56.94 and Bradman on 5,093, average 97.94.[12]

One reason for this "connected story" taking so long to tell was that statisticians had none of the electronic resources now taken for granted. Scores had to be transcribed and totalled up manually from *Wisden*, newspaper reports or scorebooks.

Another reason may have been the very limited scope of Test cricket. Of the 277 matches chronicled by Roberts, more than half – 143 – were between England and Australia. England had played in 246, and Australia 29 of the remaining 31, leaving the two-match meeting of New Zealand and South Africa in 1931–1932 the sole exception. Not until India entertained West Indies in November 1948 was there a Test involving neither England nor the "white dominions".

Ashes cricket – England v. Australia – was well-chronicled and both nations still wont to dismiss anything else as second-class. Brian Chapman of the *Daily Express* wrote the week before Bradman's fateful innings of the selection of the England party for that winter's visit to South Africa to play for "the Gold Dust, or whatever passes for the Ashes in those parts".[13]

Wisden Cricketers' Almanack reflected this outlook. The 1948 edition, primary point of reference for most writers covering that summer's Tests, split its usual records section into two. An enhanced 21-page Ashes section included summarised scores from the 148 matches so far, lists of centuries and other statistics. It showed that Bradman, with 4,520 runs at an average of 92.24 and a highest score of 334, was comfortably top scorer. The main 31-page section remained as before, with no aggregated Test career records.[14]

There were references to Bradman's career Test average in the summer's pocket annuals. Roy Webber in *Playfair* gave his current record as 6,488 runs at 102.93, while the *News Chronicle Annual* agreed on runs, but miscalculated the average as 104.64.[15] But these were mentioned in passing, buried amid other detail rather than headlined.

So a statistically alert journalist might have been aware of Bradman's record, provided he had either read Roberts and added on his subsequent performance against England and India in Australia's two home summers, or had picked up and read in detail either of the pocket annuals. Maybe some did, but the evidence suggests otherwise.

Newsprint rationing

Those writers had other constraints. English newspapers were being read in unprecedented numbers, with the *Daily Mirror* and *Daily Express* – billed on its masthead as the "greatest newspaper in the world" – both selling more than four million copies daily, but were (and would be until 1955) subject to newsprint rationing. Papers were limited to four or six pages, so previews and match reports which would once have flowed over multiple columns had become matters of concision, perhaps 10 to 15 paragraphs amounting to 250 to 400 words. Australian papers were less constrained for space, but transmitting copy from Britain remained expensive. It created an economy of style in writing, but enforced concentration on immediate events rather than broader analysis.

Nor was the Ashes the only major sporting event competing for space that summer. The Headingley Test, famed for Australia chasing down 404 to win in the fourth innings, ended on 27 July, while The Oval match began on 14 August. London's second Olympic Games filled the interim, running from 29 July to 14 August.

Most English papers devoted their previews to uncertain prospects of play on the opening day, a Saturday, although one *Daily Graphic* columnist wrote that "To write the story of Bradman's cricket career would be to write down all the numbers you can think of", and the *Express* ran Australian former spin bowler Bill O'Reilly's syndicated column noting that by captaining Australia against England for the 19th time Bradman was overtaking Joe Darling's record.[16]

Australian papers showed more interest in Bradman's other numbers. The *Sydney Morning Herald* recorded that he needed 674 runs in his remaining first-class matches in England to total 10,000 from his four visits, while the *Western Australian* noted the 83 he needed for 2,000 on this trip. A frankly inexplicable *Melbourne Age* picture caption said that Bradman, who was playing his 52nd Test – and 37th against England – "will play his 24th – and last – Test Match at The Oval today".[17]

It took two small papers to mention the numbers which now dominate the record. On 12 August, the Perth *Western Mail* recorded that "Don Bradman has got a chance to cap his Farewell Test – the fifth at The Oval on Saturday – with the greatest record of all. He needs 254 more runs to break W. R. Hammond's record of 7,249 in Tests against all countries".

"Don's overall test average is overwhelmingly better, too," it added in a seeming afterthought, getting his innings and not outs slightly wrong in tabulating his record as 80-11-6996-101.3.[18]

The London *Daily Worker* offered a reminder that good sports writing is sometimes found just outside the mainstream, from writers and papers not constrained to follow packs. Its sports page on Friday 13 August was dominated by a preview from AA Thomas which paid full tribute to Bradman, examining his achievements back to his first visit to England in 1930 and drawing the parallel with the Test farewell of English batsman Jack Hobbs at The Oval in the same year. Thomas cited both his career record against England – 5,028 runs with 19 centuries and a highest score of 334 at an average of 91.41 – and, in a little less detail, his overall Test numbers: 6,488 runs at 101.39.[19]

Unfortunately, while nailing Bradman's record against England and career average, Thomas omitted to add to the Test tally the 508 runs he had scored so far in the series. Maybe this error stopped other writers taking more note. That both he and the Perth *Western Mail* writer made small factual mistakes says something about the fragility of statistics in an era of pen-and-paper calculation (as well, perhaps, as the carelessness of journalists at any time).

But the likelier explanation is that very few people saw what they had written. The *Western Mail* was a weekly recorded as "primarily created to provide farmers with up to date information" in a sparsely populated state, while the *Daily Worker* was the organ of the Communist Party of Great Britain. Among the journalists, EW Swanton's politics were less antediluvian than appearances suggest – 20 years later, he resoundingly denounced Enoch Powell's Rivers of Blood speech – but it is unlikely that the *Daily Worker* was regular reading for him or any other Fleet Street correspondent.

Bradman in the dark?

Nor, it seems clear, did Bradman know about his proximity to an average of 100. He was certainly not unaware of other numbers. Jack Fingleton, a career journalist who had opened the batting for Australia in the 1930s, tells in *Brightly Fades the Don* of Bradman's final innings of the tour at Scarborough, first rewarding his two worthiest adversaries of that summer by deliberately holing out to be caught Len Hutton bowled Alec Bedser 153, then telling his vice-captain Lindsay Hassett: "I worked out that to average a hundred for every innings I have had in England, I would have had to make about 500 not out and this game, you know, is limited to three days."[20]

"500 not out" sounds like a number summoned randomly for the purpose of anecdote. But if so, it was a fairly precise randomness. Finishing with 9,837 runs from 120 innings, 18 times not out, in four tours of England, Bradman needed either 516 or 416 not out at Scarborough to have averaged 100.

His definitive version of what he knew at The Oval was offered in 1996 in response to Ray Martin asking if he laughed at having made the most famous duck in Test history. Bradman replied:

> No, I didn't laugh much about it, because I'm very sorry that I made a duck and I would have been glad if I had made those four runs so I could finish with an average of a hundred.
> You didn't know that?
> No, I did not know at the time. I don't think that the Englishmen knew at the time or they might have let me get those four runs.[21]

Both Bedser and wicketkeeper Godfrey Evans subsequently confirmed that England did not know, and that each would have been inclined to let Bradman have the runs.[22] It is less clear whether Hollies, whose plan relied on bowling his best "googly" second ball, and is reputed to have said, "Best bloody ball I've bowled all summer, and they're applauding *him*," on hearing the subsequent ovation, would have felt so charitably inclined.[23]

The best-known press reaction to Bradman's duck is the mutual glee of O'Reilly and Fingleton, his adversaries in the Australian team's cultural conflicts of the 1930s.[24] But unless press boxes were then vastly different places, the main reaction will have been heartfelt cursing. The last thing any reporter wants, least of all those of 1948 with their abbreviated word counts and need to factor in time to dictate reports down a phone line, is something else newsworthy at the end of an eventful day.

Enter the Don

Bradman came in to bat at 5.50 pm, 40 minutes from close of play. And the day was already more than adequately eventful. England had been bowled out for 52, their lowest score at home since 1888, of which Hutton, first in and last out to a stunning leg-side catch by keeper Don Tallon, made 30. Arthur Morris and Sydney Barnes put on 117 for the first wicket, so that Australia had – as Denzil Batchelor reported in the *The Sydney Morning Herald* – made "more progress towards total victory than any side before has wrung out of a day's play in a Test Match".[25]

England's collapse inevitably dominated Sunday's reports, with Bradman's demise briefly shoehorned in at the end. The *Sunday Times* headlined "England's Deplorable Batting: Out For 52: Hutton Alone Defies Lindwall", Neville Cardus reporting that Bradman was "cheered generously by thousands who had more than ceremonial reasons for acclamation when Hollies defeated him second ball".[26]

Raymond Robertson-Glasgow in *The Observer* noted that "the business restarted" after England gave Bradman three cheers and found space near the start of eight paragraphs amounting to perhaps 400 words to comment that "leg spin bowling by Hollies, who at times reached greatness, alone saved England from total ignominy".[27]

The *News of the World*'s "Special Correspondent" blamed "sheer bad batting" for England's collapse, appending a brief description of Bradman's dismissal. Its *White Friar* gossip column offered what would now be recognised as classic "clickbait" with its headline "Was He Batting With Tears in his Eyes?" The answer offered in much smaller type, that there was "No truth in the rumour", has since been corroborated to the historian David Frith by the closest England fielders to Bradman, Evans and Allan Watkins, both incredulous at the thought, and a mildly nettled Bradman.[28]

Even Thomas of the *Worker,* of all writers present presumably the most aware of the statistical implications, clearly felt the pressure of deadlines and events to the extent that his report for the Sunday edition referred merely to "A half-hearted roar and plenty of what might be called sympathetic applause".[29]

More, perhaps, might have been expected in Monday's papers. With Sunday a rest day, daily paper writers needed to produce more than just a rehash of their Sunday colleagues' match reports. But their focus remained firmly on explaining England's disintegration, with Bradman little more than a footnote.

Crawford White might, as compiler of the *News Chronicle* annual, have been alert to statistical developments, but referred in that paper simply to the "anti-climax" which followed the cheering for Bradman.[30] Swanton in *The Telegraph* evoked parallels with Hobbs, and the *Daily Herald*'s Charles Bray reckoned, with a fine unconscious irony, that because of the match situation "personal failure did not matter this time".[31]

Bradman's failure had, of course, been in the first innings, leaving a second possible. Nobody had the ill-taste to speculate on the possibility of his concluding with the first "pair" (two ducks in a match) of his career, the far greater likelihood being, as Chapman pointed out in the *Express*, that "The England players chose wisely to give Bradman the three cheers in his first innings. The second opportunity may not arise."[32] And so it proved, as Australia drove home their advantage, further defiance by Hutton plus rain stretching the match just into a fourth day before they prevailed by an innings and 149 runs to take the series 4-0.

Writers chronicled these developments faithfully if matter-of-factly, making the most interesting news to the modern eye the reporting of the death on 15 August of the American baseball hero Babe Ruth. The rumbustious, hard-drinking and womanising Ruth was the strait-laced Bradman's temperamental and behavioural antithesis, team-mate Ping Bodie reporting a night-life so relentless that "I don't room with Babe Ruth. I room with his suitcase."[33] The one encounter between the two icons, when the Australians toured North America in 1932, was reportedly "a series of uncomfortable silences", although Bradman enjoyed New York precisely because nobody wanted an autograph, or even knew who he was.[34]

But Ruth was his cultural equivalent, a defining, dominant figure in his sport whose fame extended far beyond its usual boundaries. Allan Schwarz's verdict that Ruth "put up statistics so marvellous, so downright preposterous, year after mind-boggling year, that journalistic coverage of him shot off in a different direction" applies equally to Bradman.[35] Those numbers – the 60 home runs in 1927, 714 in his career, both in 1948 still unchallengeable all-time marks – were fully emphasised in the reports.

It would seem, unless there was some stats-smart writer toiling on an obscure paper uncatalogued by either the Australian National Library's invaluable *Trove* database or the British Library's main holdings, that the number which would become to Bradman what 60 and 714 were to Ruth finally reached the public domain in the *Brisbane Courier-Mail* of 18 August. This was the morning of the fourth day of play in England but – given the time difference – the evening of the third in Australia.

Lance Kearney, described when he died in 1952 as the "doyen of Queensland sports journalism", had been brought to Brisbane by legendary rugby league journalist Harry Sunderland in 1919. He was probably better known for writing about league, in which he was a leading referee either side of the First World War, and boxing. But he wrote about cricket, like any smart columnist was seeking a fresh angle and, from the far side of the world, had the arguable advantage of immunity from the preoccupations of the Oval press pack.

His column was headlined:

"Test Average 99.94: Don's Duck was Costly"

Kearney wrote:

> Don Bradman's duck on Saturday has robbed him of the distinction of being the first player to retire from Test cricket with a century batting average.
>
> In all Tests – against England, South Africa, West Indies and India – Bradman has averaged 99.94 runs an innings.
>
> Don also passes from the cricket scene with one honour still eluding him – Walter Hammond's all-tests aggregate of 7,170 runs. He needed 174 runs in the Fifth Test to equal the Englishman.

This last paragraph was inaccurate, since Hammond's final tally was 7,249. The source of the error was characteristically Australian, since it ignored New Zealand. Kearney stated that "Hammond closed his Test career against Australia in 1946–1947", omitting his 79 in the single Test at Wellington which concluded the tour.[36]

But the error has the virtue of marking a trail through other papers. The following day's *The Sydney Morning Herald* included, unattributed, a compressed version including both the 99.94 revelation and the error in its round-up of the now-completed series.[37] *Trove* records its passage to papers such as the *Balonne Beacon*, the *Newcastle Morning Herald and Miner's Advocate* and *The Scone Advocate*.[38]

The Herald made little of what looks to the modern eye like significant news. It was buried in a short item "below the fold" of page six, shorter and less prominent than either Tom Goodman's match report or O'Reilly's column, although it did specifically cite Bradman's final run tally of 6,996 and tabulate his record.[39]

Aside from reflecting possible embarrassment at the sharp (if hardly rare) practice of lifting without attribution, this was also in keeping with a generally low-key reaction. The average and number of runs were now part of the record, but as yet referred to in passing or in statistical tables, rather than headlines or page leads.

Chapman of the *Express* appears the one London-based writer to have offered a whiff of the story, reporting on the morning of the 18th that "Bradman, musing on the fourth morning, may well take a last lingering look at his total of runs in all Test matches and sigh, not too deeply, for the missed chance of scoring the last four runs needed to complete his seven thousand."[40] It seems unlikely, unless the *Express* had an unusually alert stringer in Brisbane, that Kearney's column had crossed the world in a few hours, not least because while emphasising Bradman's run total Chapman said nothing of his average. Nor does he seem to have regarded this as anything other than a space-filling aside in his report of a rain-affected day.

The following day Chapman listed his outstanding memories of the series, lauding Morris, Lindwall and the defiant batting of England tail-enders Bedser and Jim Laker. Bradman was there, but for his "ovation at Leeds and his match-winning 173 (this one was his real farewell)". In an accompanying piece, Bradman's Test record was tabulated by opponent with full totals and average in the bottom line, but with no comment.[41] Bradman's home-town paper, Sir Keith Murdoch's *Adelaide Advertiser*, found space amid its quest to locate a red under every Australian bed to headline "BRADMAN IN TESTS: Ends with 89.78 Average" – his record against England alone.[42]

Mass of numbers

The view that while 6,996 at 99.94 was worthy of note, or at least tabulation, it was just one more amid a mass of astonishing Bradman numbers was replicated in the subsequent crop of annuals and other books. First up, at least in cover date, was the *Daily Mail's 52 Years of Sport: Complete Sporting Record 1896–1948*, covering winners and records from angling through to yachting and promising "complete Bradman records" on its cover.

The unnamed compiler placed the first-class career numbers at the start of his three-page feature, and grasped what truly amazes about Bradman, that he maintained over a 20-year career standards that the best of the rest attain only fleetingly. Writing that the "most general point of interest is his astonishing average for 'All Matches', given as 667-107-50,648-90.44", he added that "the majority of even top-ranking batsmen would be glad, and few have contrived, to produce an average of over 90 runs an innings for a year, a Test series or even a month". The reference further down to his falling four short of averaging 100 in Tests merited an exclamation mark and bolstered the comment that "his constant brilliance reached its peak in test cricket".[43]

The cricket annuals were also either matter-of-fact or more interested in other numbers. Robertson-Glasgow made no mention of statistics in the *Wisden 1949* tribute, which famously called Bradman "a business-cricketer", but a listing of the main current numbers included, at the bottom of both tables and page, the 99.94 average. Neither Reg Hayter's account of the tour nor Hubert Preston's match report mentioned it.[44]

The *News Chronicle* annual placed its tabulation at the foot of an article focused on what became (with varying names) a running story: "Is Harvey Bradman's successor?"[45] *Cyril Washbrook's Cricket Annual*, a one-off in 1949, gave the Test average pride of place in tabulation but emphasised the first-class average.[46] So did the veteran Roberts in the *Cricketer* Spring Annual, calling his first-class average of 95.14 "the most amazing figure ever compiled by a run-getter" and noting the missing four runs.[47]

Perhaps most striking is that Bradman in his autobiography *Farewell to Cricket,* published in 1950, has so little to say about what was by then generally known. He is far from uninterested in numbers and averages, particularly when they can be used to make a point in a narrative which sometimes sounds like a speech for the defence. Yet the numbers 6,996 and 99.94 appear nowhere except in statistical tables at the back. His Oval account, describing Hollies' delivery as a "perfect length googly" and admitting that "In the midst of my great jubilation at our team's success, I had a rather sad heart about my own farewell," is most interesting when he quotes an London newspaper report which could be of his own innings, but is in fact of Hobbs' finale at the Oval in 1930, Bradman's first Test there.[48]

One is left to wonder if Bradman, in 1950 at least, considered the Ashes the only true Test cricket. His open Anglophilia, plus experience otherwise confined to three home series in which Australia won 13 matches out of 15, 9 by an innings, might easily inculcate such a view. It also made sense, when analysing the greatest players, to consider only those he had played with or against. But he wrote only about English and Australian players, admittedly those of whom he had most experience, and cited only their Ashes statistics. This excluded Herbie Taylor of South Africa, India's Vijay Hazare – scorer of a century in each innings at Adelaide in 1947 – and most glaringly the West Indian George Headley, confined to a single passing, if highly complimentary, reference.[49]

Enter Webber

The irony in the press pack's failure to recognise the implications of Bradman's duck is not only that there was somebody there who can be assumed to have known what it meant, but that he gave an interview published during the match. Roy Webber, "a bespectacled young man with a green trilby hat pushed on to the back of his head", a chartered accountant who only did "enough accountancy to keep the wolf from the door", was the subject of the *Bird's-Eye View* column by Pat Taylor which appeared alongside the *Mirror*'s report of the third day's play in the issue of 18 August.

While the publication date suggests that she could have talked to Webber on the Tuesday, references to England batsmen "trooping off in a procession of failure" and hopes that the diagrams he used to record play would "never record another 52 all out for England" point to Saturday. Taylor noted that "Roy Webber's records":

Reveal little insights like the fact that Yardley scores faster off Lindwall than anyone else; that Compton has aggregated 100 or more off each of Australia's leading bowlers – Lindwall, Johnston, Toshack and Johnson – just as he did last year off the South Africans; that Loxton is Australia's fastest scorer (66 runs off every 100 balls) and that Laker is England's with 54 runs off every 100 balls.

The Aussies are proud – and rightly so – of their boy prodigy, nineteen-year-old Neil Harvey. Great things are predicted of him.

But Roy's Charts suggest that young Harvey will have to get some more scoring shots. They show that out of his 112 in the Leeds Test, 43 came from square cuts.

If the interview was done on the Saturday, there is a simple explanation for Taylor's failure to ask about Bradman or, if she did, for Webber to say anything which demanded inclusion in the 10 paragraphs allotted her. Her description of Webber animatedly making notes while all around him mourned England's collapse implies strongly that they talked long before Bradman came in to bat at 5.50 pm. Neither had the simple means of follow-up now given to writers and interviewees by mobile phones, email and social media.

But if unlucky timing cost Webber his chance to be first to tell the world of the conjunction of 6,996 and 99.94, he made up for it over the next few years in three books. These were the fruition of work which he told Taylor had begun aged 14 at a match where his headmaster was two seats away: "As we were both playing truant, we just ignored each other."[50]

Irving Rosenwater, an acerbically demanding critic, recalls Webber as "The first man to bring cricket statistics from a cottage industry to national significance. Never a scholar, never a profound thinker, he nevertheless catered for a mass audience that in a way he was partially responsible for shaping".[51]

Wynne-Thomas, who shares Rosenwater's low tolerance for the slipshod or foolish, credits Webber with industry which "flowered into books that provided cricket followers with the basic statistics to be able to check new record as they occurred" and with building "the foundation on which later statisticians could expand".[52]

The first of his trio of books, the blue-bound 320-page *Playfair Book of Cricket Records*, focused on first-class cricket and explained that a companion volume on Tests was in preparation. So Bradman appears frequently, most strikingly in Webber's remark that if he had played as much as Hobbs, his first-class aggregate "might have been 115,961 runs and 453 centuries", but with no reference to his Test numbers.[53] Rosenwater records that the book "broke much fresh ground and established a basis for the future seeker of career records".[54]

It sold fast enough to demand a reprint within months, part of a wave of works whose success showed a previously unsatisfied demand for authoritative statistics and records. The "52 years" of the 1948 *Daily Mail* book looks odd, but resulted from the "gratifying success" of a predecessor published in 1946. The first *Baseball Encyclopedia* was published in 1951, interest receiving a further immense boost the following year when career records began to appear on the back of baseball cards. The first *Guinness Book of Records* appeared in 1955.

The Test volume became two, one covering Tests up to 1939 and the second the post-war game along with an extensive records section. They appeared in 1953. It was, Rosenwater records, "a landmark in the statistical recording of Test cricket … no previous volume had ever recorded the entire score of every Test played".[55]

Section VII of Volume II was devoted to career records. Bradman's appearance at the top of the averages, distantly followed by the New Zealander Stewie Dempster (65.72), Harvey (65.29), Frank Worrell of the West Indies (64.32), Headley (63.91), Barnes (63.05) and Everton Weekes of West Indies (62.33) – all careers either as yet incomplete or not even half the length of Bradman's 52 matches – and the first seriously comparable pursuer, England's Herbert Sutcliffe (60.83), underlined the stupefying extent of his superiority.[56]

In 1952, *Wisden* record-keeper Geoffrey Copinger had listed for the first time, by county, Test career aggregates of more than 1,500 runs or 75 wickets. It was a key moment in the gradual but steady expansion of the Test section which saw the introduction of most wickets in a match and slowest innings in 1953, wicketkeeping records in 1958, tabulation by country of all-time results in 1963 and partnerships in 1967.

Listing by country meant that Bradman's average and aggregate, though still more than double the second-placed Clem Hill's 3,412 runs at 39.21 for Australia, did not dominate as definitively as in Webber's listing for all players. But *Wisden*'s wider circulation and quasi-biblical role in cricket culture made 99.94 part of the game's furniture, and by some way its most arresting numerical item.

Around the same time it moved from the middle of the pack to first (and sometimes only) among the numbers attached by Australian writers to stories about Bradman. *Trove* offers an early example from *Truth* in March 1949, but the first significant cluster comes in *The Courier-Mail*, *The Sydney Morning Herald* and *Truth*'s coverage of his resignation as a selector for the Australian national team in August 1952 following his son John's diagnosis with polio. *The Courier-Mail* called him "The greatest run-getter of all time. In 80 innings he scored 6996 runs, averaging 99.94".[57]

This initiated a steady ascent, Bradman's most famous number taking on that role for cricket as a whole, becoming the game's most compelling example of the phenomenon observed in baseball by Schwarz, that "eventually the best of these numbers ascend to a meaning well above the simple digits which compose them".[58]

It is illustrated by the change between Hollies' autobiography in 1955 and a biography in 2001. In 1955, he, his publishers and any co-writer (none is acknowledged) could rely on the fame of 20 years at the top, more than 2,000 wickets and almost equal fame as a non-batsman in offering in *I'll Spin You A Yarn*, an almost entirely chronological run through his career, with one notable deviation. Aside from a knowingly glancing reference in the section on 1948 to his reluctance to play the match – "However the Warwickshire committee persuaded me to play. And Bradman did not get his hundred" – he provides a fine example of what journalists call a "delayed drop", keeping the reader waiting until four pages from the end, in *Googly Bowling*, last of four chapters on broader themes, for a fuller exposition.[59]

By 2001, the cruel but ineluctable process of anno domini, by which all but the very greatest fade from collective memory, had taken hold. How many of the players at The Oval in 1948 are now known, other than among the hardest-core cricket aficionados, by those not old enough for personal recall? A guess says Hutton, Denis Compton and maybe Bedser on the English side and, other than the obvious, Ray Lindwall, Keith Miller and perhaps Harvey (longevity rarely hurts) of the Australians. Hollies, wonderful bowler as he was, is not among them, except by association with that single moment.

So in 2001 Norman Rogers opened his life of Hollies with three pages on *The Ball that Bowled Bradman*, including an explanation of Bradman's Test average before and after.[60] He may, one suspects, have regretted that rumbustious Somerset paceman Bill Andrews and his co-writer, the incomparable David Foot, pre-empted *The Hand That Bowled Bradman* as a title in 1973.[61]

The rise of statisticians

Developments since the 1950s, both sporting and cultural, have served to preserve and further elevate 99.94. Continuing growth of interest in statistics prompted the formation in 1973 of the Association of Cricket Statisticians, aficionados whose work was before long vastly aided by the democratisation of computing and the spreadsheet. The pre-modern game of cricket proved peculiarly well-adapted to the post-modernity of the internet. It made Cricinfo briefly the biggest site on the web, and still the most-used devoted to a single sport, the interactivity of its statistics enabling instant reference and calculation, while Cricket Archive supplies a vast, more reflective resource.

There has been massive growth in 99.94's context, Test cricket. August 1948 is almost exactly halfway chronologically between the first Test in March 1877 and December 2019. But in terms of numbers, the Oval Test is pre-history, number 303 on the list. There have been more than 2,000 since. And Tests, marginal grouches over half-a-dozen matches played by Rest of the World and World XIs apart, have been happily immune to the theological debates endemic to historical statistics, which in cricket have focused most on which games count as first-class.

So as with baseball, with its still more robust long-term framework of 154- or 162-match regular seasons, playoffs and nine-man teams with fixed (give or take designated hitters) fielding positions, statisticians looking at Test cricket can feel they are comparing like with like, continuity and integrity supplied by sources like *Wisden*, Cricinfo and Cricket Archive.

How important this is can be seen from other sports. Football's statistics have been needlessly but deliberately corrupted by the rise of the "Premier League Record" and rugby league is handicapped by the absence of either a *Wisden*-like annual record or comprehensive website. Club Rugby Union outside France lacks longstanding competitive structures.

Ninety-nine-point-nine-four has not been placed wholly out of reach by changes in the game, as Jack Hobbs' 61,237 first-class runs, Wilfred Rhodes' 4187 wickets or Cy Young's 513 wins as a pitcher have been. It has not been overtaken, unlike Ruth's two iconic marks, Fred Trueman's 307 Test wickets and Hammond's 7,249 runs.

And it remains theoretically beatable, much like Joe di Maggio's 56-match hitting run in baseball. Adam Voges' average for a short, late-blooming Test career for Australia soared momentarily past 100 in 2016. Baseball hitters who get hits in more than 30 consecutive games start to attract media packs and to see in their sleep images of Marilyn Monroe accompanied by Simon and Garfunkel lyrics.

But it is in reality the most outlying of all outliers, calculated by Australian statistician Charles Davis as equating to a .392 lifetime baseball batting average (unmatched by any player in even a full single season since 1941), or Jack Nicklaus winning 25 golfing majors.[62]

Batting average also continues to be accepted as, over time, the best test of a batsman's quality. Its baseball equivalent is assailed by critics arguing *inter alia* that it is, like the standard box-score, a historical hangover from the 19th-century pioneering of Henry Chadwick, adopted from cricket and in reality more applicable to it. There are of course serious variables, such as the quality of opposition and the balance of bat and ball at different times. But when researchers at Calcutta's Institute of Management – presumably provoked by endless comparisons between Bradman and Sachin Tendulkar – in 2017 threw a range of variables into the Weibull distribution model, Bradman emerged with a recalculated average of 109.42, ahead of Tendulkar, Hutton, Ken Barrington and Jacques Kallis.[63]

"The greatest Australian"

Non-cricketing factors have also assisted. In Britain, Bradman's synonymity with Australia was never in doubt. The toy koala seated on the nearest shelf as I write, a present on my first Christmas in 1959, was christened Bradman, and it is inconceivable that my cricket-loving grandparents would have called something so patently Australian anything else.

The ascent at home to "greatest Australian" was more contentious, although never sufficient to justify the question "*Bradman*. Do you mean *Badman?*" proffered whimsically by an early search engine. This apotheosis was, as the rigorously analytical Gideon Haigh has written, enabled by copious retrofitting to various national myths and archetypes.[64] Some have detected a political agenda. The most sustained analysis, Brett Hutchins' *Donald Bradman: Challenging the Myth* is at least as much a polemic against then-Premier John Howard, noisiest and most influential of the idolaters.[65]

Bradman's renown sits oddly with the transformation of Australia, in 1948 an Anglo-Celtic society of some seven million afflicted by the "cultural cringe" bemoaned by Victor Courtney in the *Perth Times* on October 17 that year:

> For some misguided reason anything sporting that comes from Australia, be it on two legs or four, is fit to compete with the rest of the world. But literature, poetry, arts or fashion that originate in our country are always subject to cynicism.[66]

The modern multicultural society of around 25 million has few such insecurities. But Bradman retains a strong appeal to those uncomfortable with change, while his achievements fit a modernity that erects statues to athletes rather than soldiers, politicians or preachers and seeks secular alternatives to former religious certainties.

Among Australian historians Don Watson has described Bradman as a "God substitute" for his compatriots, while Carl Bridge saw something of a "secular shrine" in the Bradman Museum at Bowral.[67] The British writer Matthew Engel called him Australia's Churchill, and his ill-fated cosmopolitan compatriot Peter Roebuck argued that only Shakespeare has stood so far ahead of his peers.[68]

The record speaks to a word increasingly beguiled by numbers, however spurious. Marking footballers out of 10 has spread from the *Sunday People* to outlets who would once, rightly, have condemned it as the clickbaiting eccentricity of a lowest-common-denominator paper. The BBC's thoughtful, accomplished education correspondent Sean Coughlan in late 2018 debated the growing influence of university rankings, while confessing: "[P]ut things in a numbered list and we're all hypnotised. We've done plenty of ranking stories."

But 99.94 continues to represent real, remarkable achievement, as Rosenwater wrote: "The classic instance where numbers *do* mean something."[69] It is also perfect in a way that 100 could never have been. It tells a poignant, human story, of a falling just short. That .06 might be seen to represent the extent to which Bradman was subject to standard human fallibility. The four runs, that tantalising single shot, by which he fell short is the perfect margin. One or two would have been too ridiculously close, six – something he rarely hit – just too far.

It was a relief when Charles Davis, after suggesting that the missing runs might be located in an early-career partnership with Jack Ryder, dismissed its likelihood and pointed out that rigorous re-examination of every scorebook was as likely to reduce the final tally.[70]

So it is maybe as well that nobody seems to have known what it meant when the soon-to-be Sir Donald made his momentous duck at The Oval, a lifetime ago.

References

1. Charles Williams, *Bradman, an Australian Hero*, Little, Brown: London, 1996, p. 239.
2. Suresh Menon, *Deccan Chronicle*, 17 December 2017; *www.cricketcountry.com*, 27 August 2015.
3. *Wisden Cricketers Almanack 2002*, John Wisden: Alton, Hampshire, 2002, p. 95.
4. Brett Hutchins, *Don Bradman, Confronting the Myth*, Cambridge University Press: Cambridge, 2005, p. 3.
5. My thanks to Daniel Shalom for raising this question during an undergraduate seminar at the London College of Communication.
6. LP record: *Highlights from 21 Years of BBC's Sports Report*, BBC 1969.
7. Allen Guttmann, *From Ritual to Record*, Columbia University Press: New York, 1978, p. 15, 51.
8. Peter Wynne-Thomas, *Cricket's Historians*, Association of Cricket Statisticians: Cardiff, 2011, p. 12; Averages, (*Bell's Life*), p. 51, 53, 77 (Wisden).
9. Herbert Farjeon, *Cricket Bag*, Stanley Paul: London, 1969, pp. 57–59.

10. *Playfair Cricket Annual 1948*, Playfair: London, 1949, p. 39.
11. *The Cricketer,* November 1945.
12. Ernest Roberts, *Test Match Cavalcade 1877–1946*, Edward Arnold: London, 1947, p. xiii, 193.
13. *Daily Express,* 13 August 1948.
14. *Wisden Cricketers Almanack 1948*, Sporting Handbooks: London, pp. 93–113 (Ashes stats), 134–164 (Records).
15. *Playfair 1948*, p. 27; *News Chronicle Cricket Annual 1948*, News Chronicle: London, 1948, p. 4.
16. *Daily Graphic*, 14 August 1948; *Daily Express*, 14 August 1948.
17. *The Sydney Morning Herald*, 14 August 1948; *West Australian*, 14 August 1948; *Melbourne Age,* 14 August 1948.
18. Western Mail (Perth), 12 August 1948.
19. *Daily Worker*, 13 August 1948.
20. Jack Fingleton, *Brightly Fades the Don*, William Collins: London, 1949, p. 196.
21. Peter Allen (ed.), *Farewell to Bradman*, Bradman Museum: Bowral, NSW, 2001, p. 108.
22. Peter Allen (ed.), *The Invincibles: The Legend of Bradman's 1948 Australians*, Bradman Museum: Bowral, p. 96.
23. Irving Rosenwater, *Sir Donald Bradman, A Biography*, Batsford: London, 1978, p. 349.
24. Williams, p. 240.
25. *The Sydney Morning Herald*, 16 August 1948.
26. *Sunday Times*, 15 August 1948.
27. *The Observer*, 15 August 1948.
28. *News of the World*, 15 August 1948; Watkins, Evans quotes from Allen, *Invincibles*, p. 96, Bradman quote on p. 27.
29. *Daily Worker*, 15 August 1948.
30. *News Chronicle*, 16 August 1948.
31. *Daily Telegraph*, 16 August 1948; *Daily Herald*, 16 August 1948.
32. *Daily Express*, 16 August 1948.
33. Leigh Montville, *The Big Bam: The Life and Times of Babe Ruth*, Broadway: New York, 2006, p. 109.
34. Don Bradman, *Farewell to Cricket*, Hodder & Stoughton: London, 1950, p. 55; Williams, p. 206.
35. Allan Schwarz, *The Numbers Game*, Thomas Dunne: New York, 2004, p. 44.
36. *Brisbane Courier-Mail*, 18 August 1948, 6 September 1952 (Kearney obituary).
37. *The Sydney Morning Herald*, 19 August 1948.
38. *Balonne Record*, 19 August 1948; *Newcastle Morning News and Miners' Advocate*, 19 August 1948; *Scone Advocate*, 20 August 1948.
39. *The Sydney Morning Herald*, 19 August 1948.
40. *Daily Express*, 18 August 1948.
41. *Daily Express*, 19 August 1948.
42. *Adelaide Advertiser*, 19 August 1948.
43. *52 Years of Sport: Complete Sporting Record 1896–1948*, Daily Mail: London, 1948, pp. 621–625.
44. *Wisden Cricketers Almanack 1949*, Sporting Handbooks: London, 1949, p. 76 (Robertson-Glasgow), 81 (Bradman statistics), pp. 204–211 (Hayter), pp. 251–253 (match report).
45. *News Chronicle Cricket Annual 1949*, News Chronicle: London, p. 27.
46. *Cyril Washbrook's Cricket Annual 1949*, Sportsguide Publications: London, p. 29.
47. *The Cricketer*, Spring Annual, 1949.
48. Bradman, *Farewell to Cricket*, p. 211.
49. Ibid, p. 43.
50. *Daily Mirror*, 18 August 1948.
51. Irving Rosenwater, *Roy Webber, Statistician*, Christopher Saunders: Newnham-on-Severn, 2001.
52. Wynne-Thomas, p. 157.
53. Roy Webber, *The Playfair Book of Cricket Records*, Playfair: London, 1950, p. 209.
54. Rosenwater, *Roy Webber*.
55. Ibid.

56. Roy Webber, *The Playfair Book of Test Cricket Records, Volume II*, Playfair: London, 1953, p. 155.

57. *Truth*, 6 March 1949, 24 August 1952; *Brisbane Courier-Mail*, 19 August 1952; *The Sydney Morning Herald*, 24 August 1952.

58. Schwarz, p. xiii.

59. Eric Hollies, *I'll Spin You a Yarn*, Museum Press: London, p. 76, 141.

60. Norman Rogers, *Eric Hollies, The Peter Pan of Cricket*, Warwickshire Cricket Publications: Birmingham, UK, 2002, pp. 12–16.

61. Bill Andrews, *The Hand That Bowled Bradman*, MacDonald: London, 1973.

62. Allen, *Farewell to Bradman*, p. 31.

63. www.business-standard.com, 13 October 2017.

64. *Wisden Cricket Monthly*, November 1998; *Wisden 2002*, pp. 95–96.

65. Hutchins.

66. *Perth Times*, 17 October 1948.

67. Watson quote in Allen, *Farewell to Bradman*, p. 118; Bridge in *Wisden 2002*, p. 121.

68. Roebuck quote in *Farewell to Bradman*, p. 101, Engel, p. 267.

69. Rosenwater, *Bradman*, p. 365.

70. *Melbourne Age*, 23 August 2008.

17

When dreams fall apart

Rob Steen

Journalists rarely admit to such vanity, of course, but find me one who doesn't hoard a stack or two of yellowing cuttings in a cardboard box, seldom disturbed yet hopelessly undiscardable, and I'll show you a dissatisfied journalist. Not that all the items that survive house moves and partner changes are necessarily worthy of pride. Some capture the naivety of youth, some the stubborn bias of middle-age, all too many the ample dangers of instant, often hasty, judgement, or ill-informed reasoning. Some, indeed, serve as bracing reminders of both personal failure and the precarious nature of our trade.

I maintain two piles of cuttings in that final category. One comprises contributions to the *London Daily News*, the first newspaper I worked for full-time, the other my work for *FullTime*. The former, an evening (and briefly 24-hour) London-centric title owned by the media and publishing magnate Robert Maxwell, debuted in February 1987 but expired within six months, the victim of its proprietor's vaingloriousness. The latter, a Saturday evening football classified paper set up by a pair of similarly dodgy entrepreneurs, was dead by its seventh week. As co-editor, while there were alibis aplenty, its failure hurt considerably more.

Reversing the tide

Raynes Park, south London, August 1990. Opening day of the Football League season. In a spare office in the building housing the *Racing Post*, two 30-something men are hunched over a flatplan – pre-computer speak for pencil-strewn page designs. One question looms larger than any other, as it always does: how the flipping hell are we going to fill all that white space? In this case, though, the answer is unusually elusive.

Until the 1970s, Saturday classified football papers, whether in the shape of regional "Pink 'Uns" or monochrome editions of London evening titles such as the *Evening Standard* and the *Evening News*, were integral to the English weekend, supplying as they did match reports and results to supporters travelling home from games and those unable to attend. Persuading delivery drivers to work on Saturdays without additional payment became increasingly difficult, however, and as distribution became ever more fraught, the service ebbed away. *FullTime* was an attempt to reverse the tide.

According to the heavily scrawled "specimen copy", Steve Pinder and I had been working on the design and content since the final weekend of the previous League campaign in May. I certainly don't recall having that sort of preparatory time at our disposal, but then the entire experience flashed by with the sort of speed that compresses memories into glimmers, a series of freeze-framed shards. Yet despite this – or, more likely, because of it – those seven weeks remain the most exhilarating and treasurable period of my working life.

There's nothing quite like devising and launching a publication, be it newspaper, magazine or website. First, naturally, there's the challenge of coming up with a fresh concept. Then there's the opportunity to experiment – with design, fonts and headlines, with the balance between news and features, with the use of photographs and graphics. Then there's the invigorating and perversely satisfying debate over house style – should "Gypsy" have an initial capital... is it "The FA" or "the FA"; "judgement" or "judgment"; "10" or "ten"; "full-back", "fullback" or "full back"? If nothing else, once the style guide has been agreed, it permits a rare sense of order amid the chaos of preparing for the unknowable quantity that will forever be live sport.

Then there's the joy of making those ideas spring to life by way of printed mock-ups, where nonsensical or repetitious "dummy" copy and headlines briefly convince you that your worst fears will be unfounded and that those pages will be adequately filled. Admittedly, that soon pales as cuts and changes and second thoughts jostle to form a disorderly queue, but as the deadline for the first issue nears, so sap and anticipation rise, often to extraordinary and ludicrous flights of optimism. At their height, the self-delusion soars. "We're going to change the world," you can't help but imagine, "or at least this teeny little corner."

The economics, too, must be considered. Are the proprietors trustworthy? How committed are they? How long are they prepared to wait for whatever they deem to be success? Could it all be a tax dodge? What about a freelance budget? There was no doubt that Steve and I had been sweet-talked, but how could we resist the chance to create something of our own? No contract or employee rights were offered or granted, but at least the monthly cheque promised was eminently decent. Besides, running a weekly meant there was plenty of time to maintain other work commitments. Our gravest fear revolved around distribution. Given the problems encountered by the *Evening Standard* and the *Evening News*, how could we be sure our drivers would be able to deliver copies to all of London's mainline train stations, never mind all the host grounds, by 5.30 pm – 45 minutes after the chorus of final whistles? "Don't worry about that," we were assured. "We've got a crack team. Masters of the M25."

Timing, as ever with journalistic ventures, was critical. Helpfully, the omens were auspicious. In Italy just a few weeks earlier, England had progressed, however fortuitously, to the semi-finals of the World Cup for the first time since 1966 (nobody distinguished between the men's and women's tournament back then; after all, the latter, while quietly incepted in 1970, when there were just seven participants, did not air its second edition until 1991). The patriotism, the drama, the tension, the collectivism and the soapy operatics imbued the country with an unexpected but heady sense of well-being and optimism. A renewed love for the game – following mercifully hot on the heels of the tragedies of the Heysel (1985) and Hillsborough (1989) crowd disasters – would be witnessed at the turnstiles and, come 1992, in the advent of the Premier League. If ever there was a time to launch a new football-themed publication in London, especially one that filled a palpable void, this was it.

Establishing an identity

So on we marched. The first task was to work out how we would fulfil our overriding ambition: to run match reports for all the capital's League teams. A contract had been signed to receive the

Press Association (PA) wire, which meant we were guaranteed to be able to run a report from every venue in addition to photos from the main fixtures; our concern was whether the lower-division games would be covered in sufficient depth to fill the space allotted.

The next priority was to establish a *FullTime* identity. If every match report was to be, at best, a livelier rewrite of the PA feed, that would be exceedingly tricky, to say the least. Having been given a modest freelance budget, yes, we had room for bylined features, but given that the front page would carry a report from whatever we decided in advance was the most interesting match of the day, it seemed essential to have our own reporter on the beat.

Our choice was Rick Shearman, a former colleague at *City Limits*, the left-wing London listings magazine where Steve, then the sports editor, had handed me my first sportswriting commissions in 1983. Rick, whom Steve and I both regarded as the wittiest and most promising football reporter in the land, had graduated to the *Sunday Times* but elected to maintain his enthusiasm for the game by focusing on his day job as a solicitor. As much as he sought justice on the field, he preferred seeking it in court.

To dig out that first edition of *FullTime* and read Rick's report is to be reminded of the extent of journalism's loss. His task was to marry the eloquence of his *Sunday Times* reports to the constraints of a tabloid paper: shorter sentences, tighter paragraphs, chattier words and constructions, jauntier rhythms. Paul "Gazza" Gascoigne had become a nationwide cult figure after England almost reached the World Cup final; he may not have been playing for either Wimbledon or Arsenal in the match Rick was attending, but that didn't stop his being the name on everybody's lips, hence the following intro (it helps to know that "Gizza job!", which Rick subverted in the opening sentence, was the catchphrase of Yosser Hughes, the raging unemployed Liverpudlian at the heart of Alan Bleasedale's *The Boys From The Blackstuff*, a 1982 BBC TV series that captured the plight of England's working class in lacerating, heartrending fashion):

> Gazza break! Arsenal reminded one and all that there are two teams in North London and that they, without a single overweight Geordie in the side, will be the ones to watch out for in the championship this season.[1]

Deadline pressures notwithstanding, the next few paragraphs were assuredly no anti-climax:

> Post-World Cup euphoria ensured a packed house at Plough Lane, although the first half put things into perspective.
>
> No one in their right mind would readily compare either of these teams with Brazil, for instance, but it still looked ominous for the bright new season when Wimbledon passed back to their keeper directly from the kick-off.
>
> Things looked little better when Limpar, one of Arsenal's three summer signings, found himself booted up in the air in his first minute of English league football.
>
> If either team had absorbed anything from the World Cup, it seemed to be from a diet of Ireland v Egypt videos plus of course the law according to Jack Charlton, that the most attractive football doesn't win matches.[2]

Newsiness, concision, a keen grasp of the bigger picture, a pair of hobnail boots to lay into the game's uglier aspects, a compelling turn of phrase and a spoonful of wit: as we pored over our copies of the printed product later that evening like anxious parents, Steve and I felt thoroughly vindicated with our choice of standard bearer.

Fortunately, much of the copy had been written and filed earlier in the week. An "Also Inside" column listed women's football (an exceedingly rare sight in English papers back then), Italian football, athletics, cricket, a pools forecast, a Fans' Forum (another vogue-to-be) and a column by Alan Hudson, the Chelsea legend, in addition to a full results/tables service encompassing all four League divisions as well as the Scottish Premier League and the Conference. There was also room within those 20 pages for horse-racing, greyhounds, rugby league, basketball and fitness, not to mention a heartening host of adverts, including full-pagers for Sky TV, CBS Fox, Littlewoods Pools and Labatt's Canadian Lager, as well as sizeable spots for Virgin Atlantic, TCP ointment ("soothes painful piles") and the new Bruce Willis movie, *Die Hard 2: Die Harder*.

Lurking inside the cover lay the nightmares. On the first spread (pages 2 and 3), sponsored by Capital Radio, were nine football reports, all brief; that one (Ipswich 0 Sheffield Wednesday 2) featured neither a London club nor a First Division match-up sums up the technical complexities. The match Gascoigne not only played in but scored in (Tottenham 3 Manchester City 1) occupied less space than a Second Division affair (Charlton 1 Swindon 2). One headline – over a duller-than-ditchwater goalless draw between Middlesbrough and West Ham – ran to three decks (rows): further proof that our fears about the length and detail of the PA reports had been well and truly founded. Without being able to man all the matches we were covering with our own writers, and hence specify their word-counts, we were always going to be hostages to fortune.

Then there was the penultimate page (the entire back page, necessarily but shamefully, was an ad). Billed as "The Page Nineteen Round-Up", the all-so-knowing, clever-clogs irony of the header was almost certainly lost on 99 per cent of our readers. I can't recall whether it was a last-minute decision born of indecision or fully debated – sadly, Steve, who died in 2011, is no longer available to amplify my whispered memories – but, in hindsight, it jars horribly. As does the fact that, of the three matches covered, one held scant interest for the target audience (Sheffield United 1 Liverpool 3) and another catered for readers in Kent (York 0 Maidstone 1) – though, to be fair, we did list Maidstone in our London League table. Had there been more PA copy for the tiny sub-editing team to work with, Liverpool's win would not have been allocated a slot.

Still, the overall mood come Sunday was fairly buoyant: for all the uncertainties, "Issue No. 001" looked reasonably professional and contained all the most important information. Deadlines, better yet, had been hit. "On time, on sale" is the most important journalistic commandment, and we had fulfilled our half of the deal. The willingness and efficiency of the drivers, of course, was the great imponderable, but there was some feedback from readers, which suggested that copies had not only arrived at their destination but had been put where they were supposed to be put. However much we pestered the owners, nonetheless, sales figures would always be an enigma wrapped in a mystery encased in a riddle. Perhaps inevitably, rumours of the *Evening Standard* bribing the drivers not to work soon began to circulate.

Growing pains

Over the next six weeks, or so we liked to think, the growing pains eased and the palette broadened. In the fifth issue, the opening spread carried eight London games and one from Luton, which is a fair bit closer to the capital than Ipswich. The "Page Nineteen Round-Up" was now "North of the Gap", and featured games at Everton and Manchester United (well, there were plenty of Merseysiders and Mancunians living in Greater London). Boxing, rugby union and American football were accommodated, so too the following week's major fixtures, cinema, theatre and music listings.

There was also a selection of readers' letters, one of which coupled congratulations with a nudge about following the traditional lead of other Saturday classifieds and putting the League results on the front. "We feel the paper looks better with just one story on the front page," explained the editors, somewhat defensively, "and we wouldn't be able to put all the results and tables on the front page anyway; we feel they look good on page 4. However, what do other readers think?"[3] I don't recall any response. In fact, there is every chance that most of those "letters" were fabrications designed to demonstrate – in the absence of verifiable sales figures – that we had a readership. Hardly a novel journalistic gambit, so consciences were in no way troubled. Some of the bylines, dominated as they were by younger journalists eager to make their name and happy to wait patiently for whatever meagre payment they had accepted, now make decidedly gratifying reading: Owen Slot would go on to become a Sports Reporter of the Year and a splendid rugby union correspondent for *The Times*; Alex Spilius would rise to distinction as a tireless and worldly foreign correspondent for *The Telegraph* and *The Independent*.

Not that the going was ever smooth. It never is when the clock is the avowed enemy. Not only did we run a report without a final score (a late kick-off between Charlton and Millwall), we managed to type a headline over it that included a brand-new, as-yet untranslatable word – "miletone" instead of "milestone". As for the colour-drenched centre-spread, the nicest thing you could say about the quality of the photographic reproduction was that it was erratic: one shot of Crystal Palace's Ian Wright was as blurry and indistinct as a binge drinker's vision. Now happily a 50:50 split between editorial and advertising, the back page incorporated a half-time report from Gillingham v. Maidstone and a photo of Gascoigne from a match (Tottenham 1 Crystal Palace 1) for which there was no report anywhere in the paper. I cannot say for certain that this stemmed from panic-stricken oversight, but I can't summon, or even imagine, another credible alibi.

For Issue 007, shaken as well as stirred, we took the somewhat ambitious if pragmatic step of rebranding: our baby would henceforth be called *Full Time on Sunday* – mostly, if memory serves, because the distribution wasn't up to scratch. And although the paper would still be available on Saturday evenings, at least the deadlines wouldn't be quite so claustrophobic. "The Sports Paper For Londoners" proclaimed the subtitle – a sea-change from "London's Only Saturday Sports Classified". There was a commercial logic to the revamp: after all, the *Daily Telegraph* had only recently launched Fleet Street's first daily pullout sports section. Now there would be 28 pages, a 40 per cent increase.

Facilitated by the staff of the *Racing Post*, the racing page became a double-spread (there was also a preview of the Prix de L'Arc de Triomphe); a Third and Fourth Division round-up was accorded its own page, as did US sport (basketball, baseball and American football). Enhanced by the slightly later deadline, which enabled PA's later, more expansive bulletins to be adapted by the editors and subs, the match reports were longer, more colourful, more rounded. There were more, and bigger, photos, some of them reproduced handsomely, others – most embarrassingly a full-page, full Millwall squad lineup (one of our employers was a lifelong fan) – remained fuzzy. In all, there were four bylined reports, much the most encouraging development. At last: we had a team of reporters. Unfortunately, while Rick Shearman's offering was infinitely more entertaining than the match he watched (QPR 0 Tottenham 0), it extended on to the back page – never a good idea. Worse, despite the headline ("Gazza's wand lets him down"), there was no photo of Gazza.

Death of a newspaper

The end, when it came the following week, was simultaneously swift, shocking and profoundly unastonishing. Not unreasonably, Steve and I had anticipated that the rebranding would signify further investment, but those distribution migraines persisted. Deliveries were being missed; the owners had had enough. Faced with a seemingly insuperable obstacle (what's the point of being on time if you weren't on sale?), they lacked the depth of pocket, let alone the will or conviction, to carry on throwing good money after bad. Suffice to say, no effort at emulation has ever been made.

I say "throwing" money, but that isn't quite accurate. As is the way of such projects, the first casualties were the journalists, who were left bereft. Losing £2,500 apiece, even for two (as-yet) childless editors, was by no means easily absorbable. Even harder to stomach was being obliged to inform contributors, some of them eminent figures such as Kevin Mitchell (then with *The Observer*, later *The Guardian*), Mike Collett (UPI) and Huw Richards, that their work would go unrewarded. That they took it in such remarkably good heart made it all the harder to bear.

Yet regrets are non-existent. Steve and I would often reflect on those seven issues over the coming decades; never for an instant would we have swapped the experience for something safer. We took a chancy ride on an unproven horse, revelled in the thrills and accepted the spills. Being a journalist has never been about security, especially now, but maybe that's part of the appeal. Nothing in journalism can beat the rush of launching something new and different, of marching to your own drumbeat and playing your own power chords, of seeing the result of your sweat and nerves in hot, vigorous, dynamic print. Even when it's in a pile of unsold paper.

References

1. Rick Shearman, "Arsenal gun down Dons", *FullTime*, 25 August 1990.
2. Ibid.
3. Letters, *FullTime*, 22 September 1990.

Half-time interval: Interview with David Lacey and Patrick Barclay

Rob Steen

Langan's Brasserie, London, July 2011. Opened in 1976 by Peter Langan, the Irish restaurateur, in partnership with Sir Michael Caine and the Michelin star chef Richard Shepherd CBE, this Mayfair establishment has long been a favoured haunt for English footballers and media alike. In the twilight of their estimable careers, David Lacey and Patrick Barclay, once a venerated double act as football correspondents for *The Guardian*, are in splendid fettle.

Much unites them besides *The Guardian*. Both have won national reporter of the year awards. Both echo my scorn for the theory, expressed by that now-disgraced French maestro Michel Platini among others, that a perfect game would end 0-0. After all, this presupposes that all goals stem from errors. Both regard themselves as guardians of the game, as critics before reporters: Lacey brought humour to his trade; more of a purist, Barclay injected a reformer's zeal. Both revere Brian Glanville – for courage, knowledge, perceptiveness and use of language – as the most towering giant of their trade. Both laud George Best and Diego Maradona as his on-field counterparts.

Now strictly part-time – having retired as *The Guardian*'s chief football correspondent in 2002 – Lacey was still boyishly enthusiastic, still adoring the crowds and their impact. The younger Barclay, whose work has also regaled the pages of *Today*, *The Independent*, *The Observer*, the *Sunday Telegraph* and *The Times*, was "counting down" to retirement. In an email, he characterised Lacey's journalism thus: "Erudition, wit (not the sniggery crap that passes for it in most quarters), elegance of writing style and an ability to place occurrences in context. All are priceless."

Lacey's finest hour came at Belgium's Heysel Stadium in the immediate aftermath of the 1985 European Cup final between Liverpool and Juventus that saw 39 spectators killed after a wall collapsed during a crush caused by charging Liverpool supporters.

"There is bound to be talk," he reported, "of banning all English clubs from European competitions until our game puts itself in order. Yet only 24 hours earlier, members of the Football Association voted out a proposal to harden up the rules on club responsibility which would have fallen into line with Government thinking. After the Bradford fire [earlier in 1985], the cry went up: "Who pays?" In Brussels, last night there was only one answer, and they were lined up in a makeshift mortuary outside the Heysel Stadium.[1]"

Accompanying Lacey's match report was a commentary that brooked no doubt about where he felt the blame ultimately lay:

> When the authorities hold their inquiry they will need to ask about crowd segregation and the strength of the barriers that were meant to separate the fans. However, to judge by the empty and broken bottles in the centre of Brussels and on the outside the stadium, drink was again at the heart of the problem. While it is premature to lay the blame wholly at the door of the Liverpool supporters it must be said that before the disturbances there had been little, if any, sign of trouble on the terraces occupied by the Juventus fans.[2]

Where Lacey's fire simmered, Barclay's raged, his wit spikier. Take this coruscating attack on managers' treatment of referees, one that resonates as strongly now as it did when it was typed in 2008:

> Today's referee, whether you like him or not, knows the game better than any predecessor I can recall. It is the manager I worry about.
>
> Take the cases of Mark Hughes and Joe Kinnear. Hughes first, because, unlike Kinnear, he has no reputation for mischief. Last Sunday, while his Manchester City lost at home to Tottenham, he was a picture of frustration in the technical area, notably when Gelson Fernandes was sent off after a second yellow-card offence.
>
> I assumed his ire would be vented on the player. Instead he moaned about the referee, Mike Dean, whom he patronisingly accused of neglecting to take account of the slippery conditions, even though we could all see that neither of Gelson's foolish, ungainly and unprofessional offences involved a sliding tackle.
>
> Then there was Kinnear calling Martin Atkinson a "Mickey Mouse referee" on the grounds that he had missed a foul on the Newcastle defender Cacapa in the build-up to Andrew Johnson's second goal for Fulham. Again, he insulted our intelligence by implying it was a big mistake. There have been other occasions when we have wondered if managers know the game well enough to do their jobs, let alone justify their lavish salaries.
>
> Although the truth is that they are often speaking while the balance of their minds is temporarily disturbed by paranoia – you don't have to be a football manager to suffer from that – or lying in order to deflect attention from their team's shortcomings, it is annoying that they should even imagine our swallowing such guff.[3]

A Q&A seemed in order. References to FIFA aside – the controversies that removed Sepp Blatter et al. lay in the future – their views retain their relevance, not least when it comes to the vexed issue of video reviews, which was no more than a vague concept when we met.

Why football – parental or peer influence?

David Lacey: I was too slow to play – cricket was what I loved playing. I read Charles Buchan's Football Monthly and was devouring football books from the age of eight, when I read Allison Calling by George Allison, who succeeded Herbert Chapman [as manager] at Arsenal. I was intrigued by the pictures and became an Arsenal fan, saw the reserve team play at Hastings when I was 12, although I obviously followed Brighton too. My dad was a journalist [he edited the Sussex Express]. As an eight-year-old, I went to the Dripping Pan to watch Lewes and at 13, I was there dictating dad's copy to a Sunday paper – all 80 words of it! After 10 years doing National Service and general reporting for the *Brighton Argus* I joined *The Guardian* as a sub-editor through various slices of chance and luck. I'd never read the paper before – it was hard to get in Sussex. The incentive was that they gave sub-editors chances to write. Within a year I was covering a European Cup semi-final at the San Siro [Inter Milan v. Liverpool].

Patrick Barclay: Journalism and football came together. I was brought up in Dundee, which was a huge advantage – DC Thomson's offices were opposite my school. Charles Buchan's Football Monthly was my bible. In 1957, my grandfather told me all about the Dundee team who won the Scottish Cup in 1912 as he drove me to Dens Park – Dundee 1 Hibs 0. I fell completely in love with that dark-blue shirt with the white trim. I saw the 1960 European Cup final, the first to be shown on British TV and played at Hampden, which was wonderful. Then Dundee won the League in 1961–1962 and were drawn against Cologne in the European Cup. We thought we'd do well to get a draw at home, but we won 8-1 and got to the semi-finals. I thought it would always be like this!!

I wanted to be a footballer – no chance. Then I wanted to be [commentator] Kenneth Wolstenholme – no chance: there was only one job like that. So I walked from the playground into DC Thomson's offices and got a job as a trainee. I wanted to travel. I became a *Guardian* sub in Manchester in 1966, and when the editorial operation was centralised in London and someone was made redundant in 1976 I applied for a job as sports sub there. For my interview with Brian Redhead I bought a copy of the paper on the way in. It was the first time I'd read it. He asked me what I'd do to improve the paper and, rather flippantly, I suggested increasing the headline point size from 24 point, for more impact. As it happened, they decided to up it to 36 point shortly afterwards. As David says, the incentive was that *The Guardian* encouraged subs to write. Within two weeks I was covering Juventus v. Man United in Turin.

Being No. 2 to him [Lacey, at *The Guardian*] was the worst job imaginable! I don't think I ever didn't have a piece cut.

DL: John Samuel, the sports editor, was pressing for more space – he only had one and three-quarter pages a day and so much depended on the number and size of racecards. Why not editionalise them, I suggested? [They nod to each other in support and disbelief that this was never done.]

First hero, and why?

DL: As a kid, Denis Compton. He played cricket and football for England, did everything. When he injured his knee you agonised for him. But nothing quite beat George Best. When he was in town the crowd increased. No-one ever booed him.

PB: My favourite Dundee player – Alan Gilzean. I didn't know what cool was, but he was. As an adult, Rodney Marsh – glamorous, arrogant. Jim Baxter too, for the same reasons. I've been a bit sniffy about Ryan Giggs because he's not as good as Best, who was a poor team player but the most talented I've seen along with Maradona. I once saw him outjump big Ron Yeats for a defensive header!

DL: I remember the Scottish press applauding Best at Windsor Park in 1967.

PB: I remember Scottish fans booing when the home side had possession when Maradona made his first appearance in Britain in 1979. They wanted him to have the ball.

DL: I saw [Alfredo] Di Stefano at Wembley in the FA Centenary Match at Wembley in 1963, and also on TV in the 1960 European Cup final. Only then did you realise how much he did. He was everywhere.

Best team?

DL: Brazil in 1970 were the most complete team, and then came Barcelona in 2010–2011.

PB: Ditto. That Brazil side stands the test of time better than the Real Madrid of [Ferenc] Puskas and Di Stefano. But again, I'd also include Barca's team 2010–2011. The best performance I've ever seen was [Fabio] Capello's Milan in the 1993 Champions League final.

DL: Agreed.

Was there ever a time when you thought you didn't want to report on football for a living?

DL: After Heysel you kept thinking, not so much I should give up as "Why am I doing this?"

PB: I've always felt that I'm stuck with it. I'm an electrician – I can't be a plumber. I'm counting the days now. I'm not interested in transfers.

DL: When you read Daniel Levy continually saying [Luka] Modric isn't leaving, it's mad. Of course he is – he's just upping the price.

PB: Even more tedious is the crocodile tears school of journalism – "fans of [the team] deserve better …"

What difference has the extra space for the sports section made?

DL: When I started I had to write 400 words instead of 800, so you had to sort things out in your mind first.

PB: I've never had more fun than when I joined *The Independent* and tried to compete with David's Monday commentary piece.

DL: I was a *Telegraph* reader originally, because of their cricket coverage, and Donald Saunders wrote a Monday morning commentary – that's where I got the idea from. I got out of the habit of doing interviews – *The Guardian* didn't have the space until the Nineties and they used to hold [the interviews] over and over.

PB: I do a 700-word column now for a Monday and 800 for a Saturday. There's too much football writing now, too little back when I started, but the subject has broadened. It used to be that a man gets rich and invests in a club; now people get rich through football.

DL: So much has changed because of computers. Before, you wrote or typed a report then phoned it in. Once you were released from that it helped with the production process.

PB: Telephoning copy, to a copytaker who might know nothing about football or when phones were at a premium, was nerve-shredding – I once had to wait seven hours for a phone line in Turkey. But a computer can go wrong, hence my impotent rage.

DL: Computers are the greatest beneficial development during my career. The downside is the press officers and post-match press conferences. You used to wait outside the dressing room door and hope the manager was in a good mood. You got more of a gut reaction. Everyone gets the same quotes now. Roy Hodgson always offers good sense and Harry Redknapp good value, but there aren't many like them. Then again, I'm lazy and quite like the ease of knowing you'll get something.

Has Alex Ferguson gone too far in his criticism of referees?

PB: How many mind games did Matt Busby play with referees? Or Jock Stein, or Bill Shankly? I would like it to be mandatory for referees to sue if they're libelled or slandered by a manager – and the FA indemnify them against all costs. [José] Mourinho learned from Ferguson – Volker Roth called Mourinho the "enemy of football". I had to tone down some of my comments about Ferguson in my book about him.

DL: Back in Cloughie's day the media in general were not interested in managers – the change came with TV. In the 1960 European Cup final the commentator made hardly any mention of the referee or the managers. Wolstenholme was great because he knew when to keep quiet. Now we have Sky and far more people want a piece of the action, hence more interviews.

PB: The press wheedled away at Busby about Best until it was almost toxic. It's a sign of how important the game became in terms of newspaper circulation that whereas the back-page lead used to be a report of the event, now it's a quotes story. There's a demand for controversy and argument, and not just in the tabloids.

DL: I remember *The Guardian* putting sport on the back pages and when they saw a quote in my piece they'd shift it higher up.

PB: The attitude at *The Times* is "The tabs are going to big on this." So what?

What impact has the internet had?

PB: It's fragmented everything. Everything's in bite-sized chunks now – problem, analysis, solution. I enjoyed Carlton Cole's tweet about there being 20,000 Ghanaians at Wembley and that the immigration authorities ought to throw a net over them. Coming from someone of Ghanaian descent I thought it was very funny, but he got fined.

DL: Tweets are fine if they're invested with wit.

Are you relieved your career came when it did?

DL and PB (in unison): Absolutely.

PB: It's the easiest question you've asked!

DL: When I began the papers assumed readers were intelligent. Falling circulation has something to do with it – there has been a tendency to go downmarket. I devoured books – [Evelyn] Waugh, Somerset Maugham.

Why don't sportswriters have the same status in Britain as they do in the US?

DL: Football is still something the proles enjoy here.

PB: Do people know what good writing is? Simon Barnes is the best writer on *The Times*, on any subject. Matthew Syed's not a great writer, but you never get the impression anyone told him what to write – he has an independence of thought.

Who were the first football writers you noticed?

DL: Geoffrey Green, albeit more in books. And Glanville – I was always impressed by his use of language. He was very good at quotes, at capturing someone in what they say.

PB: Brian's got absolutely no snobbery. I couldn't believe how helpful he could be to a young reporter. I adore the elegance of his writing, and his judgement of footballers is fantastic.

DL: He's got an extraordinary memory.

PB: And even now, in his 80s, if he ever makes an error he beats himself up. His greatest asset is courage. He doesn't give a flying fuck. He's my absolute hero but I've been very lucky, too, to work with him [Lacey]. I've also been lucky to work alongside Ken Jones at *The Independent*, Hugh McIlvanney at *The Observer* and in pressboxes alongside James Lawton and Patrick Collins.

"The beautiful game"? I'm more inclined to compare it to the hard beauty of a woman with gorgeous eyes and mean, angular features

PB: Football reminds me of a bullfight – the bull is the left-back, the matador is the winger. I love it when beauty triumphs over physique.

DL: Football above all else has the knack of transmitting the game through the emotions of the crowd. You're never completely detached. When Maradona scored his second goal in the 1986 World Cup quarter-final against England 120,000 people stood up. It takes a lot to do that.

PB: Football has taken over from Hollywood. For 90 minutes, the good guy tries to take revenge on the bad guy, like a John Wayne movie being shown to 500,000 people at once. That's why Lionel Messi's second goal against Real Madrid at the Bernabau last season was doubly sweet, because Real had gone out to kick him out of the game. Isn't that what art is?

DL: What Mourinho did [telling his players to stop Barca playing] was a crime. I remember myself and a few other pressmen congratulating Ron Greenwood after West Ham drew against Eintracht Frankfurt in the European Cup-Winners' Cup. He wasn't flattered. "All we did," he said, "was stop a good team from playing."

PB: I would scrap extra-time and penalty shoot-outs and award victory to the team committing fewer fouls over 90 minutes. David thinks not because that would encourage diving, but that would be considered a foul, too.

DL: On TV, the Premier League is the most popular partly because there are so many mistakes. It's more intense. There's more action, maybe, but not more meaningful action. Spain were intriguing during the 2010 World Cup but boring on TV. Germany were more exciting.

PB: The Premier League is the most violent league and, I hate to say it, good box office. I think the referees have made a tacit agreement to go easy.

How does reporting on English football compare with what's on offer overseas?

DL: We've gone part of the way to the depth of coverage in Italy but not that far.

PB: In Italy, at a post-match press conference, they'll ask the manager if 4-3-2-1 was the right formation. We want soap opera.

DL: The first time I went to the Maracana in Rio, Frank McGhee [News of the World] took me to what I thought was a reception area, what with the marble floor and all. It was the Brazil dressing-room! In one corner it looked like a bloke was being attacked by 24 reporters – it was Claudio Coutinho, the manager.

In the press box, do you look at other reporters as colleagues or rivals?

DL: We're colleagues.

PB: Yes, we're mates.

DL: We see much more of our foreign colleagues now [because of the Champions League]. Some Dutch journos came over after Dennis Bergkamp joined Arsenal in the Nineties and said our football was refreshing because theirs was too perfect.

Are FIFA's tribulations significant?

DL: It's only important if you want something from them. They're relevant but not that important.

PB: I agree. They're not as important as they're made out to be. England are not the good guys – if we'd got the World Cup [hosting rights] would we have handed them back? We mustn't get holier than thou. What worries me is that we need to do something about referees and video replays, but it isn't even being addressed. Goal-line technology is a red herring and a terrible idea. It's a very expensive way of dealing with something that hardly happens – what we need is for referees to wear an earpiece connected to the fourth official. On the same day as Frank Lampard's "goal" against Germany [at the 2010 World Cup] Mexico fell foul of an offside ruling against Argentina. We need to have a TV for the fourth official for every televised match, and only for clear-cut decisions, with no right of appeal. It would restore the balance between the naked eye and what the spectator sees at home.

DL: Right, only on matters of fact – offside is a matter of opinion. Is the offside player interfering with play?

PB: FIFA are completely absorbed in FIFA matters, not the game itself. Mind you, you have to give Blatter and Platini credit for protecting players after the 1990 World Cup via the Task Force.

DL: That was the worst World Cup I've seen. But now the habit of fouling has largely gone out of the game. Claudio Gentile wouldn't get away with what he did to Maradona in 1982 now. He was a lazy player, not malicious. He did it without thinking.

PB: [Franco] Baresi thought it was an insult to his manhood to get beaten by a forward.

What journalistic memories do you most cherish?

PB: At one stage, in the late '80s probably, I went for the first time to the Berlin Wall, the Wailing Wall and Auschwitz in the space of three months. That sums up the privileges of the job for me. In terms of matches, the 1993 European Cup final was the best I'd seen until the final between Barcelona and Man United at Wembley in 2011, which offered football I never thought I'd see. I'd seen Barcelona produce a similar quality of play against Real Madrid six months earlier, but I wasn't sure whether Real had just played badly. At Wembley, United played quite well. It was great, great football.

DL: A couple of moments stand out. The 1970 World Cup final, when all the press bar the Italians wanted Brazil to win. After Italy equalised, Brazil were hanging on, then a flurry of passes found Gerson and he scored with a marvellous long-range drive – the good guys were going to win. The other came four days after [the] Hillsborough [disaster]. A few of us wanted to go to Milan, to the San Siro, to get away from it all. Ruud Gullit started and finished a wonderful movement, which restored faith. It was a time when you were embarrassed to say you worked in football, or even liked it, but the game was not so bad after all. Maybe, I thought, I'll carry on doing this for a while longer.

PB: I went too.

DL: Play stopped as a mark of respect for the Hillsborough victims, and the crowd sang, "You'll Never Walk Alone". There were a fair few lumps in throats.

Do you still follow your team's results?

PB: I still watch for Dundee's. I check the club website nearly every day and can name the team.

DL: I still support Brighton. I live in Cambridgeshire, but I might find an excuse to go to the new ground. When I worked for *The Argus*, Brighton were always in the Third Division [South]. In 1958 they played an evening match against Watford in front of 30,000-odd at the Goldstone Ground and I was fearing the worst, but they were five up by half-time and finally got promoted. People were wandering around in a daze.

PB: There always seems to be one huge debate going on. I got into journalism to end debates. But the popularity of the game makes it a privilege to work in. I like being recognised by strangers [because of appearances on TV].

Do you see yourself as a critic more than a reporter?

DL: Yes.

PB: Yes – I always liked giving constructive comment on people who were better than me. *The Times* try to separate opinion from news, but I prefer to weave them together.

Do football journalists command the respect they once did?

PB: The public don't read by-lines in the way I used to, though journos do.

DL: At school we'd quote Desmond Hackett [*Daily Express*] but now it's the TV pundits who get quoted.

PB: Online bloggers read and quote us.

DL: Readers want to be more involved in the process now. I don't get many abusive letters. They see more, know more.

PB: They're much more knowledgeable now. I date it back to Channel 4's coverage of Serie A [in the early 1990s]. Until 10 years ago I'd talk to a fan and say something like, "Sergio Aguero's a good player," and feel I was telling him something he didn't know, but now he'd know all the details. They know more than us.

How do you handle feedback from readers?

PB: I won't have rudeness. I ask them to rewrite if they're abusive. Actually, I don't read the comments, not even the constructive ones.

Do you see yourselves as guardians of the game?

PB: Yes. The thing I'm most proud of professionally is that I brought about a change in the offside rule, enabling a forward to be level with the last defender. Coming back from a Champions League game – almost certainly involving Milan – I met Ernie Walker, the then president of the Scottish FA, and suggested the change. He said: "I think you might be right – can you send it to me in writing?" The International Board put it through – with a slight adjustment – at their next meeting, as a Scottish proposal. Ernie sent me a letter afterwards, saying I should be proud. I'm much more interested in sticking my nose into the game than writing articles.

DL: John Charles and Ivor Allchurch once went to a coaching session in Wales where the teacher asked John where he would position himself for a corner. He gave his view and then the teacher chirped back, "Well, you see, John, that's where you're wrong."

PB: Glanville was the worst player you've ever seen. [Former England captain] Billy Wright once played for Chelsea Casuals, his team, and Glanville said afterwards, "The trouble is, he's not used to man-marking in a catenaccio system"!

A smile to cherish?

DL: England were playing in Turin in the '70s and there was a press match the night before the game. They slaughtered us. We went to drown our sorrows in a restaurant and a waiter came over with a plate with an orange on it, then proceeded to juggle it, as if to say, "And I'm only a waiter!"

References

1. David Lacey, "Liverpool fade into background", *The Guardian*, 30 May 1985, http://www.theguard-ian.com/football/1985/may/29/championsleague.sport, accessed 19 November 2019.
2. Ibid.
3. Patrick Barclay, "Football association and managers undermine respect campaign", *Daily Telegraph*, 15 November 2008, https://www.telegraph.co.uk/sport/football/3461089/Football-Association-and-managers-undermining-Respect-campaign-Football.html, accessed 19 November 2019.

Part II

Issues

18

Race

Rob Steen and Jed Novick

When *The Guardian* asked the writer JB Priestley to pay tribute to arguably the most renowned and influential sportswriter England has yet produced, he recalled how, on the final page of his autobiography, Neville Cardus had claimed that "it is only in the arts that I have found the only religion that is real and once found omnipresent". Priestley, whose love of football certainly did not blind him to its social context, took him to task:

> But while, God knows, I would not have had him waste a morning and a couple of paragraphs on party politics, he might have remembered that the arts do not exist in mid-air, that we have to give some thought to the society in which these arts flourish or wither. However deeply felt, the aesthetic creed is not enough.[1]

Sportswriters' priorities have undergone enormous changes since Cardus's time, due in good part to the expansion of newspaper pagination and the advent of the Internet, but also to a wider awareness of the folly inherent in the time-dishonoured view that their subject should be immune to political and social reality. It surely says much that, in 2015, the player chosen for the cover of the 154th edition of *Wisden Cricketers' Almanack* was Moeen Ali, the rising England all-rounder and a proud Muslim brave enough to play in a Test match wearing wristbands proclaiming "Free Palestine" and "Free Gaza". Even those – not exclusively Jews – who saw this gesture as one-eyed and/or foolhardy found cause to cheer: here was a British Asian whose racial origins and religious faith had proved no bar whatsoever to becoming a national hero. Amir Khan and Naseem Hamed had preceded Moeen into the British national consciousness but both were boxers, paths eased by the individualism of their sport. That said, Nasser Hussain, the cricketer who in 1999 became the first Asian immigrant to captain a British national team, was unlucky: *Wisden* had yet to introduce cover photographs when he was at his peak at the turn of the century as the man who rid the England XI of defeatism.

Similar progress has been witnessed elsewhere this young century. Those journalists fortunate to cover New Zealand's all-conquering rugby union teams could not care less whether victory emanates from the skill of a white man, a Maori or a Pacific Islander. The same goes for those reporting the comings and goings of the England cricket team, with its revolving mix of English, Irish, Scottish, Welsh, Southern African, Australian, Anglo-Caribbean and British Asian constituents. More complex have been the cases of Mo Farah and Mudhasen "Monty" Panesar. Farah, who left poverty in Somalia at the age of eight, was hailed unreservedly as a national hero in the media after winning the 2012 Olympic 5,000 m and 10,000 m in London; while a figure of fun owing to his lack of mobility and seemingly clueless batting, the spin bowler Panesar, a Sikh, became a folk hero without breaking a single significant record. In both cases, sadly, acclaim would be diluted: Farah's reputation was tarnished in 2015 by evidence that his coach, Alberto Salazar, had given his other clients performance-enhancing drugs; Panesar's painful divorce led to prolonged lapses in behaviour and form, and subsequent loss of employment. That the latter's precipitous decline may have been a consequence, at least in part, of trying to assimilate and adopt cultural norms, particularly in his consumption of alcohol, is a subtext that warrants further examination.

For far too long, the words "sport", "politics" and "race" never occupied the same sentence in a newspaper. Sport, or so the implicit reasoning went, occupied a parallel universe, untouched by such unpleasant considerations. Rare exceptions indeed were Jack Johnson, who became the first black world heavyweight champion in 1908, and Jim Thorpe, the unfeasibly talented Native American who won the pentathlon and decathlon at the 1912 Stockholm Olympics, sufficient for him to be named "The greatest sportsman of the 20th Century" by the *Wide World of Sports* TV show and "America's greatest sportsman of the 20th Century" by the US Congress. Both men, unsurprisingly, brought out the worst in racist reporters, Johnson especially. In spotlighting Nazism, antisemitism and the athletic virtuosity of an African-American, Jesse Owens, the 1936 Berlin Olympics, aka the "Propaganda Games", removed the first significant brick in a global, white-built wall. Moreover, as the Civil Rights and Anti-Apartheid movements gathered steam in the 25 years following the Second World War, it became ever harder for editors and reporters to keep their blinkers on.

Some of those praised, and properly so, for refusing to avert their gaze are those who identified most naturally with the cause: Shirley Povich, a Jewish reporter who covered the 1936 Olympics for the *Washington Post*; Wendell Smith, a black American sportswriter either side of the Second World War; CLR James, the illustrious Trinidadian Marxist who in 1960 spearheaded the campaign to install the West Indies cricket team's first full-time black captain and wrote *Beyond a Boundary*, which is still, more than half a century since its publication, the most resonant, influential and widely lauded book about sport and race. Today we are blessed with the likes of Howard Bryant, Smith's foremost heir, and by Asian, African and Caribbean cricket writers such as Sharda Ugra, Vaneisa Baksh, Firdose Moonda, Osman Samiuddin and Rahul Bhattacharya.

Given the racial origins of those writing the most influential sports pages, however, it was inevitable that attention to racial inequities should have been drawn primarily by white reporters, however reluctantly and belatedly. One obvious contemporary example can be found in the paltry number of non-white coaches and managers at the elite levels of association football in Britain and in American football. Before it was introduced, the Rooney Rule, a nod to affirmative action requiring all interviews for leading coaching positions to include a black candidate, was advocated by white journalists. Similarly, by dint of their platform, white journalists were at the forefront in the clamour for change that persuaded the Football League to announce in 2015 that it would follow suit.

This chapter, though, is concerned primarily with those who fought a lonelier battle in less enlightened times. Through the prism of civil rights in the United States, apartheid (and after) in South Africa and socio-economic advances in India, it focuses on sportswriters who have made a difference to a race other than their own.

"Press Box Red"

All too often neglected in discussions of Jackie Robinson's signing by the Brooklyn Dodgers in 1946, which led to him becoming North American baseball's first black major leaguer of the 20th century, is the role of the media. While Robinson was making his name with the Kansas City Monarchs in the Negro Leagues, Wendell Smith, his erstwhile roommate and confidant, by now a campaigning and resourceful black reporter with the *Pittsburgh Courier*, discovered that Isadore Muchnik, a liberal councillor in Boston, was pushing the city's major league teams, the Red Sox and the Braves, to integrate. Smith arranged a trial with the former for Robinson and two other leading black players, but it was never more than window-dressing; all left empty-handed. It seems more than coincidental that, while the Red Sox could have become the first major league team to integrate, they ultimately became the last.

Smith broke his homeward journey in New York to speak to Branch Rickey, president of the Brooklyn Dodgers and the visionary who had invented the farm system as a means of nurturing talent, suspecting he might be the likeliest executive to integrate baseball. Few knew this at the time, but Rickey, a conservative lawyer, had been concocting his own plan to do precisely that. His role in Robinson's breakthrough can never be overstated. Nor, therefore, can Smith's.

Yet while black journalists such as Smith were prominent in campaigning for an end to the colour bar, the best-remembered now, both perversely and inevitably, is Lester Rodney. Perversely, because Lester was white; inevitably, because white newspapers commanded so much more financial investment, and so many more readers, than their black-owned counterparts.

Motivation is crucial. In terms of political and social issues, Rodney, the subject of Irwin Silber's *Press Box Red* (2003), was arguably the first important campaigning sportswriter. As sports editor for the US Communist Party newspaper, the *Daily Worker*, from 1936 to 1958 (he resigned from the party once the scale of Stalin's murderous regime began to emerge in 1958), he launched the fight to integrate baseball in the 1930s. He was also the first writer to espy the promise of a second baseman named Jackie Robinson. "Lester Rodney was a communist," emphasised David Margolick, an author and, as we write, contributing editor of *Vanity Fair* magazine. "Whether because of that or in spite of that, he was also one of the most independent and courageous sportswriters of his day."[2]

One of his early priorities, though, was to change perceptions of sport as a fitting subject for the inquiring mind. "When I met my wife's father for the first time," he told his spiritual heir, Dave Zirin, in 2004, "he said, 'What do you do?' I said, 'I write sports.' He laughed uneasily and asked 'But what do you really do?' He couldn't grasp that his daughter was marrying someone who just wrote about games."[3]

At first, he told Zirin, "I didn't have a full realisation of what the meaning of sports could be." The 1938 heavyweight boxing fight between Joe Louis and Max Schmeling in New York City was a turning point.

> Abner Barry was a black columnist of the day and he … told how during the preparation for that fight and the fight itself, the streets were eerily deserted like a scene from after the atom bomb drops in a movie. The minute the fight was over people were teeming with people and young kids were laughing and giving the mock Hitler salute. And this was happening in every city in the country including Southern cities. In Knoxville [Tennessee] Blacks poured out into the streets and fought with the police who tried to keep them from marching. So you say there's no social meaning to Joe Louis? There was a young Black man being led to death row and he cried out "Save me Joe Louis!" It sounds corny and hokey, but it's true.[4]

Having established a niche for sport at the *Daily Worker* (albeit only a solitary page), Rodney set about addressing what he saw as a void. "It's amazing," he told Zirin.

> You go back and you read the great newspapers in the thirties, you'll find no editorials saying, "What's going on here? This is America, land of the free and people with the wrong pigmentation of skin can't play baseball?" Nothing like that. No challenges to the league, to the commissioner, to league presidents, no interviewing the managers, no talking about Satchel Paige and Josh Gibson who were obviously of superstar caliber. So it was this tremendous vacuum waiting. Anybody who became Sports Editor of the *Daily Worker* would have gone into this. It was too obvious. And some of the white comrades who had never paid attention to sports before began saying, "Is this an all-white sport?" People didn't think about it. It was the culture of the times and it was accepted.

While the major papers occasionally carried reports of Negro League games in 1936, recalled Rodney, there was "never a mention that these players were barred from advancing to the major or even the minor leagues. No incredulous editorials blasting this un-American discrimination, no investigative articles listing the qualified or over-qualified black players, no queries addressed to the commissioner, the league presidents, the team owners, the managers, and the white players. The conscience of American journalism on baseball's apartheid ban, sorry to say, was not in the hands of America's major daily newspapers."[5]

Satchel Paige – after whom Woody Allen named his first son – was one of those "over-qualified" players. One of the most compelling "what ifs" of American sporting history surrounds how Paige, a wily, virtually unhittable pitcher, would have fared against Babe Ruth. Sadly, by the time Paige finally signed a major league contract with the Cleveland Indians in 1948, he was 42, his best days behind him. Another over-qualified player was Josh Gibson, a troubled soul who didn't live long enough to follow Robinson into the major leagues. Gibson inspired the following tribute from one of the greatest pitchers of all time, Walter Johnson, published in the *Daily Worker* in 1939: "There is a catcher that any big league club would like to buy for $200,000 [an unthinkable fee at the time]. They call him 'Hoot' Gibson and he can do everything. He hits that ball a mile and he catches so easy he might just as well be in a rocking chair. Throws like a rocket."[6] Either Paige or Gibson could have been the first player to break the colour bar, but Robinson's character exerted a more profound influence than his athletic ability.

"It was not as though the worth of these African American athletes was unknown to the baseball establishment," reasons Silber. "Many a Big League manager knew but wouldn't say publicly that there at least several players of major-league calibre in the Negro Leagues they would be willing to bring to their clubs if the team owners would allow them to. Most owners knew it as well. But, as the 'bible' of Big League baseball, the [weekly] *Sporting News*, freely acknowledged in 1923, organised baseball had a 'tacit understanding that a player of Ethiopian descent is ineligible'. That 'understanding' prevailed for another twenty-two years."[7]

Rodney launched his campaign on 13 August 1936 with a dramatic announcement headlined "Outlawed by Baseball!" – followed by three subheadings worthy of *The Sun* on a good day:

> The Crime of the Big Leagues!
>   The newspapers have carefully hushed it up!
>   One of the most sordid stories in American sports!

Cue a call to arms:

> Though they win laurels for America in the Olympics – though they have proven them-
> selves outstanding baseball stars – Negroes have been placed beyond the pale of the Ameri-
> can and National Leagues.
> Read the truth about this carefully laid conspiracy.
> Beginning next Sunday, the Sunday Worker will rip the veil from the "Crime of the
> Big Leagues" – mentioning names, giving facts, sparing none of the most sacred figures in
> baseball officialdom.[8]

For the next three weeks, the sports page was not alone in trumpeting the promised exposé.
"Fans Ask End of Jim Crow Baseball" was one front-page headline, under which Rodney – in
an un-bylined piece – laid into what he characterised as "the un-American ... [and] invisible
barrier of race prejudice [that] keeps the Negro players on the sidelines. Fans, it's up to you. Tell
the big league magnates that you're sick of the poor pitching in the American League. You want
to see Satchel Paige out there on the mound. You're tired of a flop team in Boston, of the silly
Brooklyn Dodgers, of the inept Philadelphia Phillies and the semi-pro Athletics ... Demand
better ball. Demand Americanism in baseball, equal opportunities for Negro and white. Demand
the end of Jim Crow baseball!"[9]

In the wake of these and other articles, letters streamed into the offices of the *Daily Worker* –
overwhelmingly, notes Silber, in favour of removing the colour bar. Two of Rodney's aims were
to "shoot down the notion that the white players and managers wouldn't stand for it by directly
putting the question to them" and "put the league presidents and the commissioner on the spot
by challenging them to say whether there was an official ban, which they denied, of course".

> But maybe the most important was to generate fan participation in the campaign. Our
> biggest asset, though, was that the time was right. Black athletes had stolen the show at
> the 1936 Olympics in Berlin, especially Jesse Owens ... This was all over the newspapers,
> which had these marvellous pictures of black medal winners draped with the American
> flag. And Joe Louis was on his way to the heavyweight title, the first time there'd be a black
> heavyweight champion in more than twenty years. So it was a good time to say, "Why not
> in baseball?"[10]

The first manager Rodney spoke to was Burleigh Grimes of the Brooklyn Dodgers, the club
Rodney had supported as a boy, the club he was covering dutifully and avidly in the summer
of 1937. The men knew each other; Rodney knew Grimes respected him "because he knew
I didn't sensationalise things". The leading question was straightforward enough: "Burleigh,"
wondered Rodney, "how would you like to put a Dodger uniform on Satchel Paige and Josh
Gibson?" The response was not altogether surprising. "Well, he looks at me like I'd just hit him
over the head with a club," Rodney would recall. "You just didn't talk about those things then.
He stops for a minute. And then he begins to talk to me, patiently, like a father to a child." In
relating the story 60 years after the fact, Rodney realised he couldn't quote Grimes exactly, but
these, he insisted, were "almost" his exact words:

> "Lester," he says, "you're wasting your time. This'll never happen. Just think about the trains
> in the south. Think about the hotels. Think about the restaurants. How could it happen? It'll
> never happen." So I say, "Do you know some of the good black ballplayers?" And he says, "Of
> course I do. We all do. I know how good they are. But let's talk about something else. First,

it's never going to happen. And I don't wanna talk any more about it." "Burleigh," I say. "Can I at least write, 'I know how good they are – [says] Burleigh Grimes?' ..." Now he's almost livid. "No, no!" he says. "I'm not gonna stick my neck out!" He didn't want to be the first.[11]

Nor did anyone else. Nor, for that matter, was any major newspaper remotely interested in sticking its neck out. To Rodney, the media's complicity in the prolonging of the colour bar was beyond dispute. Take a story about the young Joe Di Maggio from that same summer. "We were in the dressing room at Yankee Stadium," recalled Rodney, "and somebody asked [him], 'Joe, who's the best pitcher you've faced?' And without hesitation young Joe said, 'Satchel Paige'. He didn't say 'Satchel Paige who ought to be in the big leagues', he just said Satchel Paige. So that was a huge headline in the next day's *Daily Worker* sports page in the biggest type I had: 'Paige best pitcher ever faced – DiMaggio'. No other paper reported that ... If the other reporters would hand that in, their editor would say, 'Come on, you're not stirring this thing up.' But we didn't see it as a virtue that we were the only people reporting on this. We wanted to broaden this thing and end the damned ban."[12]

When Lester first met Paige, in the latter's Harlem hotel during a trip to New York with the Kansas City Monarchs in 1937, the pitcher needed no invitation to express his disgruntlement. "He knew I was from the *Daily Worker*," remembered Rodney. "He knew my face because I had covered Negro League games and chatted with players. He was also aware of our campaign and even mentioned that he had read about it while playing in Puerto Rico ... While we talked he began to come up with ideas. Why don't they have a poll? Every Big League fan going into a game next year, just ask them yes or no, do you want coloured players in the Big Leagues. But he also had prepared one biggie in his mind beforehand. 'Let the winners of the World Series play an all-star Negro team just one game at Yankee Stadium,' he says, 'and if we don't beat them before a packed house they don't have to pay us a dime!'

"'Can I print that?' I ask. 'Absolutely,' [he replied]. He wanted this in the newspapers, but he hadn't gotten anywhere because the papers weren't paying any attention to him. He was an embarrassment to them. Like a bad conscience. How does somebody who works for a paper that doesn't mention the fact that blacks are banned interview Satchel Paige and come out with this challenge? He can't. But Satch knew that we would ... We played this up big. He loved it. He wanted ten copies. It created a stir. I mean, here was the most famous black player in the country challenging the ban publicly for the first time. The challenge was never accepted, of course. And none of the papers carried it."[13]

In June 1939, Wendell Smith began a series of eight articles in the *Pittsburgh Courier*, interviewing 40 players and, more illuminatingly and importantly, all but one of the nine National League managers in what the paper billed as "The Most Exclusive, Startling and Revealing Expose of the Attitude of the Major League Players and Managers Themselves Ever Written".[14] In virtually every case, the managers maintained the party line – there was no official ban – while shifting the responsibility, patronisingly, on to the white fans and the white players – it was they who were unready for such a revolution.

After digesting the start of the *Courier* series, Rodney rang Smith to congratulate him. From that arose an informal agreement whereby their papers could reprint each other's stories on the campaign. When the *Daily Worker* began giving space to his articles, Smith, in turn, wrote to Rodney, conveying his appreciation and solidarity. "Unfortunately," wrote Silber, "but undoubtedly in keeping with the times and the generally conservative views of his paper – and possibly in deference to the cooperation he was getting from the baseball establishment – Smith's admiration for Rodney's and the *Daily Worker*'s efforts did not find their way into the *Courier*'s own pages.[15]

"Nevertheless, tacit acknowledgement of the *Daily Worker*'s campaign … came from the baseball establishment itself. In a move reminiscent of charges by the defeated Confederates after the Civil War that northern 'carpetbaggers' were stirring up otherwise happy-go-lucky 'nigras', defenders of baseball's racial staus quo argued [that] there would be no problem with the racial state of baseball if it weren't for outside 'agitators' who, in the words of the *Sporting News*, 'have sought to force Negro players on the big leagues, not because it would help the game but because it gives them a chance to thrust themselves into the limelight as great crusaders in the guise of democracy … Some coloured people are not looking at the question from the broader point of view, or for the ultimate good of either the race or the individuals in it. They ought to concede their own people are now protected and that nothing is served by allowing agitators to make an issue of a question on which both sides prefer to be let alone'."[16]

Later in 1939 came the first chink of light for Rodney – the first even vaguely favourable comment he had gleaned from a club owner: William Benswanger of the Pittsburgh Pirates, mindful of Louis Armstrong, Duke Ellington and Billie Holiday, said he really didn't see why signing a black player "wouldn't be the same as having black musicians". Up to now, on this sensitive matter, even Leo "The Lip" Durocher, the cocky, outspoken manager who had replaced Grimes at the Dodgers, had refrained from airing his views. Now Benswanger had come out of the closet, Durocher felt emboldened. As Rodney stressed, he was unusually "sophisticated" for a manager. "Hell, yes!" Durocher replied upon being asked whether he would sign Paige or Gibson. "I'd sign them in a minute if I got permission from the big shots."[17]

Yet not for another three years, by when the Japanese had bombed Pearl Harbour and Rodney was in the army, did the *Daily Worker*'s histrionic, sneering, anti-communist rival the *Daily News*, then boasting the largest circulation of any US newspaper, make even a passing reference to Durocher's comments – and much the nicest thing you could say about that reference is that it was patronising. The even more influential *Herald-Tribune*, recalled Rodney, was even "snottier". As the tide began to turn, nonetheless, Durocher's bold statement would prove a significant milestone.

Arguably Rodney's most heartfelt, impassioned article was one that had no lasting impact whatsoever on its target, Judge Landis, the baseball commissioner who had so shrewdly maintained the strictly unofficial colour bar. It was published in the *Daily Worker* on 6 May 1942, in the form of an open letter, shortly before Rodney was drafted into the army, by when the major leagues, supported by President Roosevelt, had resolved that baseball should not be interrupted; amid such troubling times, it would serve an important function as a public diversion. "There can no longer be any excuse for your silence, Judge Landis," asserted Rodney.

"You are the one who, by your silence, is maintaining a relic of the slave market long repudiated in other American sports. You are the one refusing to say the word which would do more to justify baseball's existence in this year of war than any other single thing … It is a silence that hurts the war effort … America is against discrimination … There never was a greater ovation in America's greatest indoor sports arena than that which arose two months ago when Wendell Wilkie, standing in the middle of the Madison Square Garden ring, turned to Joe Louis and said, 'How can anyone looking at the example of this great American think in terms of discrimination for reasons of race, colour or creed?' Dorie Miller, who manned a machine gun at Pearl Harbour when he might have stayed below deck, has been honoured by a grateful people. The President of our country has called for an end to discrimination in all jobs. Your position as big man in our National Pastime carries a much greater responsibility this year than ever before and you can't meet it with your silence. The temper of the worker who goes to the ball games is not one to tolerate discrimination against 13 million Americans in this year of the grim fight against the biggest Jim Crower of all – Adolf Hitler. You haven't a leg to stand on."[18]

For two more seasons Landis did nothing – bar, that is, passing the buck, and the onus, to the club owners. Then, in November 1944, he died suddenly from a heart attack. Within a year, Silber recounts, Sgt Lester Rodney, then stationed with the 52nd Field Hospital on a remote island in the South Pacific, would receive a cablegram from New York sent by Nat Low, a fellow baseball integrationist: "Congratulations. Dodgers yesterday signed Jackie Robinson for [their] Montreal farm [team]. You did it!" Rodney was "stunned and elated".[19] As a childhood Dodgers fan, he was doubly delighted. "It completely united me. And it wouldn't have been the same if Cleveland or some other team had been the first."[20] Not until 1997, however, did Rodney receive his due.

"Something wonderful happened in the world of sports in 1997." Thus, in his foreword to *Press Box Red*, exulted Jules Tygiel, author of *Baseball's Great Experiment: Jackie Robinson and His Legacy* and just one of the scores of eminent American scholars who have not only adored baseball but seen it as an insight into American life. "Amid the hoopla and commercial sensationalism that characterised much of the fiftieth celebration of Jackie Robinson's historic debut with the Brooklyn Dodgers, Lester was rediscovered ... *The New York Times* praised his coverage of the Robinson story as among the most accurate of the era. Rodney even appeared on CNN ... and several times on ESPN."[21] This, Tygiel reasoned, was partly on account of Rodney's age – he was now in his 80s and had outlived most of his contemporaries – but primarily because he had been "a catalyst ... in the most significant sports story of the century".

Denial and complicity

Reporting a demonstration against South Africa's 1960 cricket tour of England, undertaken shortly after the Sharpeville massacre that had seen police shoot dead 69 protestors and injure 180, the cricket writer Charles Fortune described protesters as "no more than the cats-paws of certain churchmen who seized on the visit of the cricketers as an opportunity to gain for themselves some public notice".[22] Later a long-serving secretary of the South African Cricket Association, Fortune is most prominently commemorated these days by the name of the media centre at The Wanderers ground in Johannesburg. "Fortune was a conservative," declared his anonymous *Wisden* obituarist, "and appeared to take South Africa's exclusion from world cricket as something of a personal affront."[23]

In 2015, we asked Archie Henderson, not long retired as news editor of the South African *Sunday Times*, whether he could recall any white South African journalists taking issue with the way apartheid impacted on sport in the 1950s and 1960s.

> I can't think of anyone. Certainly not white. Terry Barron, who died homeless on the streets of Simonstown, tried to give the Peter Hain group a voice during the 1969–1970 South African rugby tour of the UK and was snubbed by the team. Marshall Lee, who was more a general news writer on the *Rand Daily Mail* in the 70s, would have fitted that category but he never wrote for the paper's sports pages.[24]

Nor, emphasised Henderson, did matters improve much. "Like many white sportswriters in the 1980s and onwards, the issue of segregated sport was anathema. But it took some of us longer to get round than others. Today of course I have many regrets. In my brief stint as sports editor of the Cape Times in the 70s I could have done more to publish the full scorecards of 'coloured' club cricket as we did religiously on a Monday with white cricket. I remember trying to assemble a network of stringers to do this, but without success. It seemed, too, there was a lot of politics behind this; if Hassan Howa [the founder member of the non-racial South

African Cricket Board of Control who led the campaign to boycott apartheid sport] did not like a particular stringer [freelancer], that person would be snubbed. The one big success was a bloke called Dickie Isaacs, who got around from club to club using the minibus taxi system. Sadly, he died in a taxi accident shortly before unification. One of the great unsung heroes of cricket journalism.

"There was another incident which I remember when I decided to lead the main sports (back) page with a thrilling tie in the SACBOC provincial championship between Western Province and Transvaal. I deliberately did not distinguish in the headline that it was the 'coloured' WP side as opposed to the white one, which got more prominent coverage. There was a complaint about 'misleading readers' from one big advertiser, but the editor, Tony Heard, discussed it with me and then dismissed the complaint.

"But you can safely say that, as there is no white person today who ever supported apartheid, there are no sports reporters in favour of segregated sport. Certainly it did not show in any of their reporting or commentaries until the 1990s. Now everyone claims struggle credentials. If there was a pioneer in this field (among the white sports journalists) it was Telford Vice, but at the time his writing did not get much play beyond the Eastern Cape where he was with the *Daily Dispatch* of East London. There were black journalists who were pushing for greater freedom in sport but they were few too; some collaborated with the establishment, which used its financial muscle to co-opt them. Others like Mogamad [Mo] Allie, who now reports for the BBC, was always firm and principled about his opposition to apartheid sport."[25]

Allie's memories chime with Henderson's: "As far as I could ascertain, there were no white sports writers who railed against the apartheid government. In fact, as late as the Mike Gatting rebel tour in 1990 the white media and sports journalists were still supporting tours like these while at the same time being scathing of the anti-apartheid movement's demonstrations and attempts to stop the tour. Not only did most of the white sportswriters do nothing, they were, in some cases, condescending of the activism of the non-racial movement.

"As for black writers, bearing in mind they had limited platforms at that time in our history, there were people like Abe Adams, later to become president of the anti-apartheid SA Council on Sport (Sacos), who had strong opinions against the regime. The late Dennis Brutus, a former Robben Island prisoner, although an academic, also campaigned strongly against the racist regime in the 1950s and 60s to the extent that he was forced out of the country and in 1962 set up the SA Non-Racial Olympic Committee (Sanroc) with the aim of isolating white SA from the Olympic movement."[26]

Nor did many visiting journalists rock the boat. RS Whitington, an Australian former first-class cricketer who had recently lived there, dedicated his account of Australia's 1966–1967 tour of South Africa to "the lonely land", yet not until Chapter 7 does he even mention the cause of the nation's isolation. Even then, forgivably, he takes on trust Prime Minister John Vorster's announcement, in April 1967, that "South African sportsmen could compete against non-white sportsmen abroad and that non-white sportsmen could be included in international teams making visits to South Africa." This proclamation seemingly cleared the way for D'Oliveira to tour his homeland with his new national team, England, two winters later. Whitington trumpeted it as "a triumph for quietly-conducted, well-reasoned argument and negotiation".[27] History begs to disagree.

A very small number of cricket writers were less easily or wilfully deluded than Whitington, less complicit than Fortune. On his first visit to South Africa in 1948–1949, John Arlott, a rising journalist and BBC radio broadcaster from Hampshire, stopped outside the Nationalist campaign HQ on the night Henrik Verwoerd came to power. Arlott's companion expressed his dismay, whereupon Afrikaner party supporters layered his car in spit.[28] Upon arrival in that benighted land, Arlott was asked what race he was; in silence, he completed the requisite form and, in the appropriate category, wrote "human". A few days later he asked a taxi driver to take him to a township: the poverty never left him.

In 1960, it was Arlott to whom Basil D'Oliveira, a Cape Coloured printer's assistant, wrote in search of employment in England, Arlott who befriended him, Arlott who recommended him to his first English club. D'Oliveira, the best coloured cricketer in South Africa, duly migrated to England in 1961 in search of reward for his skills and a better life for his family, wound up playing with distinction for England and became the principal symbol of the sporting boycott that would contribute to the downfall of apartheid in his native land.

Eight years later, during the so-called "D'Oliveira Affair", Arlott was angered by the all-rounder's exclusion from the England party to tour the Republic: to him, and many others besides, the reason was wholly political, a conviction supported by the clear desire of the Marylebone Cricket Club – which governed tour selection until the mid-1970s and under whose banner England teams still toured – to maintain good relations with South Africa, by the many former Conservative politicians who had served as the club's president, and by the right-leaning former public schoolboys who dominated the selection committee. Some weeks earlier, Arlott had informed the BBC he would on no account commentate on South Africa's scheduled 1970 tour of England. He explained his reasoning in *The Guardian*, inspiring the young Peter Hain, the mainspring behind the highly effective "Stop the 70 Tour" campaign. According to his son Timothy, Arlott had not wanted his friends "to wonder what side he was on":

> Apartheid is detestable to me, and I would always oppose it … a successful tour would offer comfort and confirmation to a completely evil regime … Commentary on any game depends, in my professional belief, on the ingredient of pleasure; it can only be satisfactorily broadcast in terms of shared enjoyment. This series cannot, in my mind, be enjoyable.[29]

D'Oliveira's subsequent inclusion in that 1968–1969 England party, which led the duplicitous Vorster to cancel the tour on the ground that this was "the team of the Anti-Apartheid movement", and in turn to South Africa being exiled from international cricket from 1970 to 1992, owed much to the public outcry that followed D'Oliveira's original omission. It would be wrong to propose that Arlott was alone in assailing the original selection: Peter Wilson in the *Daily Mirror* was equally appalled; even EW Swanton changed his tune, the same *Daily Telegraph* correspondent entrusted by the South Africans only weeks earlier as a go-between in an attempt to dissuade D'Oliveira from making himself available to tour – satisfyingly in vain. It would be no less incorrect to deny that Arlott's stance was the key catalyst in reframing and transforming the debate.

When Marx met Muhammad

Up to now, to ward off accusations of bias, we have resisted mentioning a friend of ours, yet omitting Mike Marqusee from this roll of honour would be entirely unjust: his death while we were researching this chapter supplied the saddest of justifications for a tribute.

Characterising himself as a "deracinated New York Marxist Jew", Mike moved to Sussex to study and never returned, his affection for England stirred in good part by a burgeoning love for cricket. As beautiful as he found the game's techniques and rhythms, conveyed memorably in his work for *The Hindu*, *Wisden Asia*, *Cricinfo Magazine*, the *Financial Times* and *The Guardian*, there was another irresistible attraction: here was a sport wherein racial divisions had long been entrenched – and occasionally healed. No other major team sport, furthermore, had seen black (in the guise of the West Indies teams from 1965 to 1995) repeatedly overtake white, on the field if not in the committee rooms. Instead, as he would chronicle with an enthusiasm that would gradually give way to considerable unease at the resulting corruption and greed, India would be the first nation to break the traditional Anglo-Australian stranglehold over how the game was run and monetised.

A co-founder of the pressure group Hit Racism For Six, Mike's immersion in the game of Empire can readily be appreciated in *War Minus The Shooting*, a wide-ranging, penetrating travelogue of the 1996 World Cup played in India, Pakistan and Sri Lanka, a volume that did much to combat racial stereotyping and promote the subcontinent as the epicentre of the game. A few years later, such was the respect and affection with which he was regarded in India – in contrast with the ludicrous lack of both in England, where Marxist cricket writers occupy a rung on the ladder of sports editors' preferences almost as high as that occupied by women rugby reporters – the news that he had been mugged made the front page. In February 2015, moreover, we discovered he had died via an email from Gulu Ezekiel, a journalist friend living in Delhi.

Mike's memorial celebration in London's Conway Hall in May 2015, attended by Arthur Scargill, the controversial former leader of the National Union of Miners and the then-much-admired Labour MP Jeremy Corbyn, who would assume the party leadership a few weeks later, found our friend and colleague Sharda Ugra, formerly sports editor of *India Today* and now editor of the immensely popular Indian arm of ESPNCricinfo.com, rendering her heartfelt thanks:

> Mike's engagement with South Asian cricket took place at a time when our writing in these parts was grappling between confidence in who we were and the conventional aspiration of wanting to be something else. Something maybe like England, with its well-nurtured traditions, or Australia and its hard-but-fair game centred around the mythology of mateship. Or the West Indies with its fast bowlers. In the 1990s, the cricket journalists of the world were, also largely divided between the haves and have-nots, or the north and the south, the developed and developing world. They were distanced from each other with very few exceptions from among the haves, who wanted to engage across cultures. Mike took to this scattered cricketing world, with curiosity, openness and energy. Not with orientalist wonder, but with objective and acute enquiry. It is why he was appreciated and befriended here.[30]

Yet Ugra was galvanised less by *War Minus the Shooting* than by *Anyone But England: Cricket and the National Malaise* (1994), Mike's first non-fiction cricket book (he had previously written a terrific cricket novel, *Slow Turn*). The first half of the title was a nod to Denis Skinner, an admirably principled Labour MP who, when asked which sporting team he supported, replied, "Anyone but England". Here, even more than Sir Derek Birley's myth-shattering *The Willow Wand* (1971), was the book that captured the so-called "gentleman's game" in its truest, most vivid and jaundiced colours. Most of the author's wryly eloquent disapproval was reserved for the way it was still run in his adopted home by, and for, the upper echelons of English society – which might well explain the subsequent reluctance of national newspaper sports editors to employ him.

"When we first heard about *Anyone But England*, even before we read it," recalled Ugra, "a younger generation of Indian cricket journalists wanted to run down the road, pumping fists. Mike had hacked through a jungle of cricket's historical fakery, kicked down the doors of its temple, challenged the game's conservative and controlled narrative, and given it a vital and largely ignored global context. It echoed what many of us felt at the time, giving us a loud and clear voice."[31]

Yet while Mike adored India, and never cheered a sporting triumph more resoundingly than when Sri Lanka overcame the odds in 1996, beating Australia to win the World Cup, he did not shrink from the geopolitical realities inherent in this relocation of the game's emotional and economic heartland. As Huw Richards put it in another tribute: "The secular internationalist in him disliked the growing evidence of Indian, in particular Hindu, nationalism, while the American anti-capitalist saw a growing affinity for becoming more like America."[32]

"So extreme had been the reactions to victory and defeat [in 1996]," noted Mike, observers had dubbed the cricket craziness of the subcontinent a psychosis. "Here was a global television spectacle which all three host nations hoped would boost their standing in the eyes of the world's financiers and investors. But the deep crises in all three societies kept erupting from under the glamour and hype. All three countries were opening their economies and following the well-worn IMF-charted path of privatisation, deregulation, cuts in public spending and encouragement of foreign investors. All three were building consumer sub-cultures in the midst of mass poverty. All three were racked with ethnic intolerance, and in all three the question of national identity was hotly contested. Not surprisingly, the World Cup raised yet again C. L. R. James's ever-pertinent question ['What do they know who only cricket know?']."[33]

Mike also wrote *Redemption Song: Muhammad Ali and the Spirit of the Sixties* (1999), a monumental work whose achievement can perhaps best be conveyed by the fact that it drew critical acclaim even though so many others had already sought to capture the essence and importance of Ali – and even despite being published nearly a decade after Thomas Hauser's purportedly definitive oral history-cum-biography, *Muhammad Ali: His Life and Times*. For the 2005 reprint, Marqusee added an Afterword that captures better than anyone, we would argue, what made Ali the most important sporting figure of all:

> Ali's real heroism lies in actions we can all emulate: in placing solidarity with human beings in remote lands above loyalty to any national government, in setting conscience before personal convenience. In the era of the war on terror, his example remains pertinent and powerful, but only if we retrieve the challenging historical reality that lies behind the harmless icon.[34]

Beyond apartheid

One of the neglected legacies of South African apartheid has been the fate of those who sought to emulate Basil D'Oliveira. Unlike black Africans, coloured South Africans from the Cape, some with Asian origins, have enjoyed widespread and conspicuous success in cricket, most notably Omar Henry, the first non-white player of the post-apartheid era to play Test cricket, Ashwell Prince, South Africa's first non-white captain, and the prolific medium-pace bowler Vernon Philander. In 2015, however, Telford Vice wrote an intensely moving and compassionate article about Henry Williams, the coloured fast bowler whose late-blooming international career entered rapid decline as soon as he agreed to bowl badly for money, having accepted a bribe from his corrupt white captain, Hansie Cronje. In the event, injury prevented him from carrying out what became known variously as a "micro-fix" or "spot-fix" – not engineering the result but, in his case, bowling wides. The King Commission into match-fixing did for him.

"Williams had been that rare thing – the coloured man nobody could argue did not deserve the chances he had earned," wrote Vice. "He worked hard, took his wickets graciously, did not let success go to his head, and knew that where he came from was where he was going back to, and he was happy with that. But now he had blown all that. As he sat there, he was, in the eyes of South African cricket, others like him and – most importantly – himself, just another scar of shame for coloured people. The slanting sun brought warmth into the room for most of us. For Henry Williams, it brought a cold, hard, ugly truth.

"In what must have seemed to him an aeon ago, he had been a proud and respected member of a community that is at once adored and distrusted in South Africa's cultural firmament. Coloured people, as they are called and call themselves, endure a slew of stereotypes – that their sense of humour is infallible, whatever the circumstances; that they are born soaked in alcohol and go through life topping themselves up; that every sentence they speak is shot through with profanities; that they are prone to being snared into criminal gangs whose currencies are drugs and knives.

"Closer to the truth is that coloureds were not white enough to enjoy the top tier of privilege in apartheid South Africa, and are not black enough to enjoy the sweetest fruits of democracy in the modern age. To be born coloured in South Africa is to be disregarded, except when someone needs to laugh or fancies a drink and a punch-up."[35]

Amid the difficulties of transition, no issue aroused more controversy than that of selection quotas, introduced in international and provincial cricket and rugby union to encourage black Africans to participate and hence undo the damage caused by the racist selection policies of the Apartheid era. Tristan Holme and Luke Alfred addressed the complexities with due sensitivity: "In a previous conversation, Thokozani Peter didn't want to talk about racial quotas in cricket. Asked for his thoughts on the subject, Peter, a 24-year-old fast bowler, shifted uncomfortably in his chair, drew air through his teeth, and said: 'I'm scared of answering that question.' Frankly, no one can blame him. Nothing divides the South African cricket community quite like quota policies because few issues define the country and its most pressing conversations quite like race.

"Rather than having open discussions that would encourage transparency, the issue is either forgotten or conveniently ignored – as it was in the debate around Ryan McLaren's exclusion from South Africa's [2015] World Cup squad. Commentators and journalists asked whether McLaren should have cracked the nod ahead of Farhaan Behardien or perhaps Wayne Parnell; the reality is that the selectors are committed to picking seven players of colour – including one black African – in a 15-man squad, and so McLaren's actual competition was among the eight white players selected.

"It was a symptom of confusion. The policies have changed many times over the years but have been hidden in phraseology, which created the quota debate's most public blowout in 2008. Mickey Arthur, the coach, was part of a selection committee that named just four players of colour in a 14-man squad; it was vetoed by Cricket South Africa's president Norman Arendse because the team was expected to have seven."[36]

South Africa's 2013–2014 season, recorded the statistician Andrew Samson, brought 308 appearances by black Africans out of a total of 1,926 in franchise cricket, and 919 out of 3,610 in the provincial game. Some clubs struggled to meet the requirements; others, as Holme and Alfred put it, were "positioned to take advantage of the financial incentives". Appearances by black Africans in franchise cricket (15.99 per cent) exceeded the quota (9.09 per cent). "Similarly, with some provincial sides already fielding a healthy number of black Africans, the percentage of appearances (25.45 per cent) exceeded the requirement (18.18 per cent)."[37]

The problem, conclude Home and Alfred, "is that the q-word has developed such a stigma that it is difficult to sit down and have an honest conversation about what it means for the players directly influenced by it and whether it is having the desired effect of uplifting a community that was deeply disadvantaged under apartheid …

"When the majority of black South Africa is growing up in poverty, it means that by the time most black players are exposed to a decent level of cricket they are profoundly disadvantaged compared to players from privileged schools. As much as CSA has tried through quota policies, no governing body can remould history into the ideal image of eight or nine black Proteas that easily, particularly after something as deeply divisive and traumatic as apartheid. On the one hand, the governing body deserves criticism because its attempts at transformation over the past two decades can be seen as nothing more than a design to show the country's politicians enough black faces in teams. This lack of spiritual commitment to genuine change is in turn played out at the franchises.

"On the other hand, CSA's mandate is to spread cricket; it is not tasked with building functional schools and ensuring that every young child who wants to play the game is adequately fed. As much as the politicians like to hold CSA to account in parliament, so the cricket body should be able to hold South Africa's incompetent and corrupt government to account on service delivery. Because the sad fact is that until South African society can be genuinely transformed, cricket will continue to lag behind in its own evolution."[38]

A version of this chapter was originally published in the Routledge Handbook of Race and Ethnicity and Sport, *2015.*

References

1. Quoted in Christopher Brookes, *His Own Man: The Life of Neville Cardus*, Methuen: London, 1985, p. 5.
2. David Margolick, quoted in Irwin Silber, *Press Box Red: The Story of Lester Rodney, the Communist Who Helped Break the Color Line in American Sports*, Temple University Press: Philadelphia, 2003 (back cover).
3. Dave Zirin, "Lester Speaks", Counterpunch, 3-5 April 2004, https://www.counterpunch.org/2004/04/03/an-interview-with-quot-red-quot-rodney/, accessed 24 August 2020.
4. Ibid.
5. Ibid., p. 50.
6. Ibid.
7. Ibid., p. 51.
8. Ibid., p. 53.
9. Ibid., pp. 53–54.
10. Ibid., pp. 55–56.
11. Ibid., p. 59.
12. Zirin, "Lester Speaks".
13. Silber, pp. 61–62.
14. Wendell Smith, *Pittsburgh Courier*, 15 July 1939, quoted in Silber, p. 67.
15. Silber, p. 68.
16. Robert Peterson, *Only the Ball Was White*, Gramercy: New York, 1970, quoted in Silber, p. 69.
17. Silber, p. 70.
18. Lester Rodney, *Daily Worker*, 6 May 1942, quoted in Silber, pp. 81–82.
19. Silber, p. 90.
20. Ibid., p. 28.
21. Silber, p. vii.
22. John Nauright, *Sport, Cultures, and Identities in South Africa*, Leicester University Press: Leicester, UK, 1997, p. 133.
23. Anonymous, in Matthew Engel (ed.), *Wisden Cricketers' Almanack 1995*, John Wisden & Co: Guildford, UK, p. 1384.
24. Email to author, 9 April 2015.
25. Emails to author, 9 April 2015 and 16 April 2015.
26. Email to author, 27 April 2015.
27. RS Whitington, *Simpson's Safari*, Heinemann: London, 1967, p. 133.
28. Timothy Arlott, *John Arlott – A Memoir*, Andre Deutsch: London, 1994, p. 71.
29. Ibid., pp. 166–167.

30. Email to author, 14 May 2015.
31. Ibid.
32. Huw Richards, "The transatlantic iconoclast", *The Nightwatchman*, Volume 10, Summer 2015, p. 60.
33. Mike Marqusee, *War Minus the Shooting: A Journey Through South Asia During Cricket's World Cup*, Heinemann: London, 1996, pp. 5–6.
34. Mike Marqusee, *Redemption Song: Muhammad Ali and the Spirit of the Sixties*, Verso: London, 2005 reprint, p. 314.
35. Telford Vice, "The coloured lie", The Cricket Monthly, ESPNcricinfo, January 2015, http://www.thecricketmonthly.com/story/816361/the-coloured-lie, accessed 15 December 2019.
36. Tristan Horne and Luke Alfred, "The faces of transition", The Cricket Monthly, ESPNcricinfo, May 2015, http://www.thecricketmonthly.com/story/863979/faces-of-transformation, accessed 15 December 2019.
37. Ibid.
38. Ibid.

19

Sexuality

Neil Farrington

Thomas Hitzlsperger likes men. I like women – and football and the occasional beer in the pub and a ride on my new bike. Sounds quite dull when it's put that way. And that's precisely how it should be. Why on earth has a large proportion of the football news agenda been given up this week to Hitzlsperger "outing" himself? I don't care who or what Thomas Hitzlsperger likes, be it men, women, the occasional beer in a pub or a ride on his new bike. It has not been the hot topic of discussion among my friends and contacts in the business. There has not been one sniggering remark made about Hitzlsperger's sexual preferences. Everyone read the story, rolled over and went back to sleep, or went out for a ride on their new bikes or maybe a beer in the pub.[1]

So wrote sports reporter Andrew Dillon in a leader column in response to the news in January 2014 that Thomas Hitzlsperger, a few months after retiring as a player, had become the first English Premier League footballer – past or present – to come out as gay. The polemic was headlined "Hitzlsperger is gay. So what? Who cares?"

It is a question good enough to sound rhetorical, and both the crux of Dillon's argument – that a footballer's sexuality is an irrelevance – and the prevailing positive tone of the tabloid coverage of Hitzlsperger's declaration were widely lauded. Indeed, veteran gay rights campaigner Peter Tatchell hailed them as a reflection of "the huge positive shift in public attitudes towards gay people".[2]

But it is a question which should really have been one asked of Dillon's employers. For while his editorial sat well with Tatchell and many right-minded others, how did it reconcile with the news of Hitzlsperger's outing – despite being news garnered second-hand from the German press rather than their own sources – having been splashed across the front pages of British tabloids five days earlier, front pages which included that of Dillon's own paper, *The Sun*?

So much for "So what? Who cares?"

Hitzlsperger later cited the "incredible" level of attention an active, high-profile player would "excite" as the biggest hurdle to a footballer coming out, and certainly nowhere was the "huge shift" described by Tatchell more essential than in the treatment of *The Sun* and its red-top tabloid competitors of a stubborn sporting "last taboo".[3] Equally certain is that nowhere has that shift occurred so belatedly. In short, when it comes to reporting on sexuality in sport, it has taken far too long for the UK's most populist, persuasive and, therefore, powerful newspapers to get their stories straight. Instead, they must answer an accusation of having maintained a narrative – anachronistic at best, homophobic at worst – which has done much, or arguably more than anything, to perpetuate an environment in which gay footballers *still* feel alien. Accept that the concept of "mediatization" first proffered by Kent Asp – in which politics "to a high degree is influenced by and adjusted to the demands of the mass media"[4] – applies to sport, and the gravity of that accusation becomes clear.

While it is beyond dispute that problematic narratives have been a common feature of press representations of sport generally, British sports media discourse appears not so much informed by as predicated on hegemonic masculinity, as first postulated by Connell[5] – "97 per cent of [UK newspaper] sport coverage a year after the [London 2012] Olympic Games was of men's sport"[6] – of which Donaldson notes that "Antagonism to gay men is a standard feature"[7] and, as Connell[8] posits, a footballer is a model. Thus, never mind how it reports the issue, the British press's arguable role in perpetuating the "last taboo" is an appropriate starting point for a discussion of sports journalism's treatment of sexuality per se.

Nancy boys, big poofs and dykes on bikes

In 2006, Peter Tatchell (and many others) called out *The Sun* for their description of Cristiano Ronaldo as a "nancy boy" and "pretty boy".[9] Such are certain wider traditional cultural narratives in the UK – "of saucy fun and bawdiness" which "are part of a wider tradition of English working-class humour" traceable back to the "theatrical innuendos of Victorian music hall ditties"[10] – that some might have quibbled when Tatchell accused *The Sun* of outright "homophobic sneers". However, in engaging a discourse of plain abuse, the newspaper surely went beyond the type of "sniggering remark" more recently proposed by Dillon, in *The Sun*, as a boundary of taste.

Yet more recently, the *Daily Star* pushed that traditional narrative of innuendo more clearly past a pejorative boundary in paraphrasing a film title to produce the headline "Beckham's a bender".[11] Some considered the ensuing story's focus on gay comedian Alan Carr's jokey suggestion that David Beckham was "a big poof" to be mitigation. However, Carr himself has been accused by some in the LGBT community of trading in the UK's historic comedic depiction of gay men as "one-dimensional, caricatured camp clowns",[12] and less than four months later, the *Daily Star* settled the debate decisively by again appropriating the film *Bend It Like Beckham* to produce the unequivocal "Benders ain't like Beckham" atop an article highlighting the virulent homophobia of Luciano Moggi, former chief managing director of Juventus, complete with his "Gays can't play football" barb in a sub-headline and prominent mention in the story proper of his reference to "post-match showers".[13]

In that context, the consequences – or lack of them – of *The Sun*'s decision to appropriate the same source material to apply a headline of "Bender it like Beckham"[14] to a story on the openly gay reality TV star Louie Spence – "Pineapple Dance Studios star Louie, or Louise as I like to call him" – attending a party thrown by David and Victoria Beckham, were informative. The article having prompted a complaint from a reader under Clause 12 of the UK's then Editors' Code of Practice compelling the press to "avoid prejudicial or pejorative reference to an individual's race, colour, religion, gender, sexual orientation or to any physical or mental illness or disability",[15] the then UK press watchdog, the Press Complaints Commission, refused to undertake any investigation because the complainant was not directly affected by the matters concerned. Challenged to at least issue guidance, if not censure, to newspapers on the use of words such as "bender" – on the grounds they are offensive to the LGBT community per se – the PCC did nothing.

Not so when sports broadcaster and former jockey Clare Balding's complaint to the PCC over being referred to as "the dyke on the bike" by AA Gill in the *Sunday Times*[16] (just three days before *The Sun's* "Bender…" headline) was upheld on the grounds that "dyke" was used as a "pejorative synonym relating to the complainant's sexuality". If that appears instructive again, the then *Sunday Times* editor John Witherow's response to an original letter of complaint he received from Balding was perhaps more so again. It read: "In my view some members of the gay community need to stop regarding themselves as having a special victim status and behave like any other sensible group that is accepted by society. Not having a privileged status means, of course, one must accept occasionally being the butt of jokes."[17]

In late 2009, Wales international Gareth Thomas became the first high-profile rugby player to come out as gay. The response, within rugby as well as without, was positive enough for him to play for another two years – the second of them in rugby league, which had become the first UK sport to sign up to Stonewall's campaign against homophobia, and promoting "lesbian, gay and bisexual equality"[18] in sport. Yes, in the same year that *Daily Star* sub-editors and reporters were having fun with football-informed "Bender" headlines and communal shower references, the governing body of English rugby league – a game "more usually associated with northern machismo and cauliflower ears" – made a stand for LGBT rights.

Emboldened by the RFL's stance and inspired by Thomas, Batley Bulldogs captain Keegan Hirst came out as gay in August 2015. He did so via a tabloid – the *Sunday Mirror* – and to an almost universally positive reception. However, *The Sun* and *Daily Star* would revert to grim type, publishing follow-up stories almost a year later – focusing on Hirst's appearance on a TV dating show – replete with such gratuitously, suspiciously lascivious comments from his supposed (and apparently snubbed) would-be paramour for the evening as "I feel like I've been taken for a ride – and not in a good way."[19]

So entrenched is the *Daily Star's* narrative on sexuality in sport that even when propagating a positive message – that gay footballers should be encouraged to come out – the connoted message, as delivered by "celebrity" columnist Gaz "Geordie Shore" Beadle in October 2016, remains squalid. "You can only do something about a s★★★ situation if you stand up against it and challenge it head-on (no pun intended)".[20]

Happily, the *Daily Star* apparently maintains minimal interest in the overwhelming majority of the near-300 sporting professionals, current or retired, to have disclosed they are LGBT – the large majority of them over the last decade. But then men's professional football has contributed just eight of that number, and five of those players only came out after retirement (although Robbie Rogers – having speculated on the media demands of an active footballer who has come out as being "interviews every day, where people are asking: 'So you're taking showers with guys – how's that?'",[21] resumed his career at US Major League Soccer's LA Galaxy three months after his announcement). Perhaps at least equally as significant is that none of those players did so while playing in top-division football – i.e., the British tabloids' sporting stock-in-trade.

Just how significant? Would that we could ask the highest-profile of those players, Justin Fashanu. Instead, the forlorn words of a man who was already a pioneer, as British football's maiden million-pound black player, when he became the first footballer to out himself (in an interview with *The Sun* in 1990) still echo – and, in this context, still jar – from beyond the grave.

"Many people thought I just did it for the money," he wrote in the mid-1990s. "I suppose they have never stopped to consider that my world is based around *Sun* and *Daily Star* readers… I genuinely thought that if I came out in the worst newspapers and remained strong and positive about being gay, there would be nothing more that they could say."[22]

Instead, Fashanu's reward was not a toast to his courage and a new era of enlightenment, but a large measure of moral opprobrium, and his playing career – albeit from an already downward trajectory – went into a tailspin before, in April 1998, he hanged himself in a lock-up garage in east London. Yes, the descent of both footballer and reputation – which hit terminal velocity when he was charged in February 1998 with the rape of an American teenager – was initially accelerated by Fashanu's own lurid claims of affairs with male MPs which quickly followed his coming out (they were later disavowed, and prompted many to depict him as arbiter of his own tragic destiny). However, that he resorted to such tawdriness says at least as much about the socio-cultural agendas of the day as it does about him. "In the Tory press he became a convenient scapegoat," asserted *The Independent*, "the black queer selling lies about government ministers, this week's tabloid target, a good man to take the flak off the government for a couple of days."[23]

Would, however, that it was just Britain's tabloids whose treatment of Fashanu crystallised a retrograde wider narrative regarding sexuality in sport. In the same 1994 profile, *The Independent* described the terrace chant of "Say ooh aah up yer arse" devoted to Fashanu by fans of his then-club Heart of Midlothian as "affectionate". Then, as late as 2009, and a full year after the launch of the Fashanu-inspired Justin Campaign to tackle homophobia in sport, fellow broadsheet *The Scotsman* felt comfortable in referring to him – again, regarding his spell in Edinburgh – as "Queen of Hearts"[24] in a headline.

Even less wonder, therefore, that an innuendo-free, unambiguously supportive editorial in *The Sun* should have been proclaimed as much a watershed as Hitzlsperger's revelation itself. Sadly, what was equally evident by January 2017[25] – indeed three years on almost to the day – is that the UK print media's gay footballer narrative, while – as indicated in another chapter in this book by *The Times* sports editor Alex Kay-Jelski – rarely still outright prurient in tone, can still be informed by a nudge, a wink and as rapacious a thirst for speculation as drives any transfer tittle-tattle.

Also pertinent, however, is whether those at the vanguard of the campaign to rid homophobia from football perceive the British press's still concomitant role in it. In a discussion arising from FA chairman Greg Clarke's suggestion in January 2017 that gay footballers should "synchronise" coming out to avoid the "significant abuse"[26] he had previously said they would attract, Professional Footballers' Association chairman Gordon Taylor spoke of having "hoped things would be so much better now",[27] and Ed Connell, chairman of the Gay Football Supporters' Network, said: "[Greg] Clarke was sadly right when he said the game wasn't ready yet for gay footballers... and until we eliminate gay banter among young players and to eliminate discrimination in club administration, and to even get rid of chanting – homophobic chanting – on the terraces, it simply isn't going to happen. We need to address the root problems before anybody is going to be interested at all in coming out." Neither man cited the UK media, and its intransigent discourse, as a root problem, despite quantitative research of English football supporters by Cashmore and Cleland producing compelling evidence of "rapidly decreasing homophobia within the culture of football fandom",[28] and the similar conclusions reached by the BBC in 2016[29] and *Sports Illustrated* in 2005, the latter interpreted by Kian as indicating that "sport fans and even pro athletes are more accepting of homosexuality than the reporters who cover those sports".[30]

However, while the bleak example of English men's football and indications of changing American attitudes – research by Nyland found "sufficient evidence to argue that homophobia is being confronted head-on"[31] by the US sports media – might suggest such prejudice now flowers more freely in Britain, the treatment of the few high-profile gay male athletes to have peered over the parapet of heterosexual hegemony in US sport suggests that, in practice, attitudes across the Atlantic also remain deep-rooted.

Bravest in the land of the brave?

Fashanu's story might resonate with Michael Sam, the first active, high-profile American Football player to come out as gay, in February 2014. Three months later, he was drafted by the NFL's St Louis Rams. But he quit the professional game less than a year later, citing mental health issues linked to his disclosure – and without having played a single NFL game. However, Sam was not quite akin to Fashanu as a pioneer. Ten months earlier, NBA basketball player Jason Collins had become the first active player in any of the US's "Big Four" sports to come out. The backlash against both men, although admittedly leavened by widespread messages of support, was heavier, more explicit – and more media-driven – than that faced by any openly gay sportsman in the UK.

Given the religious demographics of the US, with the stark contrast between its pan-denominational Christian conservatism and the increasing secularity of the UK, it is unsurprising that an evangelical zeal informed part of the negative reaction to Collins' landmark revelation. Of more pertinence and concern is that the mainstream US media not only provided a platform for that reaction, but made space on that platform for some of their very own.

Within hours of the publication of the *Sports Illustrated* interview in which Collins came out, he was denounced by ESPN senior writer/analyst and former *New York Times* sports reporter Chris Broussard as "walking in open rebellion to God" and "living in unrepentant sin".[32] Both Broussard's rant, which was broadcast on ESPN's *Outside the Lines* programme, and his later qualification of it were couched in theological terms. However, his multiple repetition of the word "openly" – e.g., "If you're openly living in unrepentant sin..." – more than suggested his biggest issue was not with Collins being gay, but having come out.

However, in a media context, a bigger issue still is that although ESPN apologised – albeit after a fashion, describing Broussard's comments as part of a "respectful discussion"[33] – and claimed to be "fully committed to diversity", they remained fully committed to Broussard, right up until offering him a new contract in 2016 in a failed attempt to prevent him from being headhunted by rival network Fox Sports. Among Broussard's new colleagues at Fox? Columnist Jason Whitlock, who said in March 2016: "Michael Sam was a stunt by the NFL. It was a play to the politically correct crowd."[34]

Sam himself cites that type of reaction – which followed a claim that the NFL had insisted the LA Rams draft him in exchange for the club not being featured on the warts-and-all HBO sports reality TV series *Hard Knocks*[35] – as pivotal to the failure of his career. "I think if I never would have came [sic] out, never would have said those words out to the public, I would still be currently in the NFL."[36] One common response to that statement sounded familiar: "This is really rich, considering we now know for a fact that the only reason Michael Sam was ever drafted into the league was because he was gay."[37]

Egg-chasing women

One arguable counterpoint to the practical struggle of the US press to reconcile male homosexuality with its propagation of what Young and Atkinson echoed Connell in describing as a "hegemonic brand of masculinity" which "legitimates the ascribed authority of a particular kind of male figure",[38] is the relatively enlightened, if still problematic, treatment of openly gay US sportswomen. While America's sports journalism establishment seems wedded to the "jock culture" which provides its male protagonists with what Kimmel and Aronson describe as "social privileges not only over women and gay men, but over other heterosexual men as well",[39] its attitude to openly gay female athletes appears at least nuanced, despite the observation made by Wright and Clarke, echoing many other scholars, that "print media representations of sport contribute to the denial of lesbian sexuality and social relations".[40]

All eight LGBT members of the 554-strong US 2016 Olympic team in Rio were women. At least seven players in the US's professional National Women's Soccer League are openly gay. Pertinently, given Jason Collins' experience, there are numerous acknowledged LGBT women's NBA basketball players, prompting media coverage which appears encouraging. "Less than a week after the subtle revelation that WNBA MVP Elena Delle Donne is gay – the third paragraph of an Aug. 4 story in Vogue magazine that didn't even mention the news in the headline – the story had all but died."[41] Moreover, more than three decades after Billie Jean King became the first female athlete in any discipline to come out (only because her partner filed a palimony lawsuit against her), there is a relatively healthy – if probably still not fully reflective – smattering of openly gay current female tennis pros, while in the UK, the arch-reactionary *Mail on Sunday* celebrated 2016 Olympic gold medallist hockey players Kate and Helen Richardson-Walsh as merely "Britain's first married winners since 1920".[42]

However, the wider sports media narrative regarding LGBTQ female athletes remains at best inconsistent, which itself has concomitant effects on men's sport. Notably, despite women's golf reputedly attracting a large LGBTQ following – as long ago as 2001, the Dinah Shore Classic tournament on the LGPA Tour was described as "a sapphic debauch writ large"[43] – no leading female professional player came out before the twilight of their career (Muffin Spencer-Devlin and Rosie Jones had been Tour pros for 17 years and 22 years respectively before they did so, and Sandra Haynie was effectively "outed" only by publicity surrounding her relationship with tennis legend Martina Navratilova) until Britain's Mel Reid announced her sexuality in December 2018. The fact that the last of Jones' 13 Ladies Professional Golf Association (LPGA) Tour titles came a year before her announcement is, as she has reflected, not coincidental. "Back then, the LPGA had a habit of protecting the brand because of the ever-present stigma of lesbians on our tour. And [that's] not to blame the LPGA, it was the sign of the times. The LPGA's first priority was to its entire membership and sponsors. Title sponsors and individual endorsements were hard to come by for women in general. It was even more difficult for those players who were thought to be gay."[44]

Such an example endorses Appleby and Foster, who argue that beyond "gender neutral" sports "such as soccer, tennis and swimming", gay female athletes still face being "consistently portrayed in overly (hetero)sexualized manners"[45] and, among many others, Lenskyj claims this "heteronormativity" has been "characterized in sport media for more than a century".[46]

Moreover, Appleby and Foster have observed that such "hetero-normative representations of [female] athletes" also impact male athletes. While female athletes must consistently display "feminine" behaviour to dissuade homophobic labelling, male athletes are always presumed to be heterosexual",[47] a point affirmed by tennis legend Martina Navratilova, who has said: "It hardly occurs to anyone that sportsmen are gay, but with women they almost have to prove they are straight. A journalist would never dare ask a male athlete, unless they were a figure skater, 'Are you gay?' But it is OK to ask a female tennis player."[48] In turn, the consensus view is that gay male athletes feel further compelled to keep their sexual identity secret from peers and public, and those who do still come out as gay meet more public hostility than female athletes who reveal they are lesbian.

But another widely experienced consequence of heteronormative sports (and sports media) discourse, is that the homophobic labelling or many of the assumptions to which LGBT female athletes are subjected can come from fellow women. The assertion by Navratilova – or "Martin", as Nyland[49] noted she was routinely referred to by CBS radio spots talk host Jim Rome – that there "is a kind of reverse homophobia with women… They are seen as dykes just because they play sports" may find particular resonance in women's rugby union, where LGBT stereotyping and "hegemonic notions of femininity and masculinity"[50] jar as sonorously as anywhere in sport.

While Burton-Nelson perceives that nowhere "are masculinity and misogyny so entwined as on the rugby field",[51] rugby union is inevitably "diametrically opposed in its style and purpose to everything that traditional society has encouraged women to be".[52] Conflate that paradox with Scrambler's view that "Sporting bodies are idealized in the media... the pressure for social conformity of the body has a greater impact on women than men",[53] and it is unsurprising if the potential offered by rugby to develop "an active, female physicality in contradistinction to the gender order" and "challenge hegemonic masculinity"[54] might be what "attracts them [women] to the game."[55]

This scenario is possibly particularly vivid in rugby, the nature of which arguably not merely precludes women players from acceding to the female athlete feminine "apologetic" as drawn by Rohrbaugh[56] and others, but which places them in happy opposition to what Messner identified as the threat of "the media framing of the female athlete... to subvert any counter-hegemonic potential posed by female athletes".[57]

Historically, however, pursuant to that "challenge" to hegemony has been a masculinised mediated depiction of women in rugby and other contact sports in the UK which has not only propagated tired gender stereotypes, in which "women who play are represented through 'fluff' pieces or photos that represent them in highly sexual and/or feminine poses or the opposite extreme",[58] but bordered on territory tawdrily comparative to that repeatedly revisited by *The Sun/Daily Star* regarding football.

> A few years ago there was a TV programme about the Harlequins women's rugby team, which showed their AGM in a private room at London's Sports Cafe. One of the girls went out to get the beers in, came back with a couple of foaming tankards and complained that some chauvinist pig had commented: "Nice jugs." It is time to admit that comment came from a group of sports journalists on a night out and that I was among that group. I apologise unreservedly, because they were very ordinary jugs and because women's rugby, like women's football or women's anything, is a serious sport.[59]

Moreover, for "Benders ain't like Beckham" read the *Daily Mirror*'s "Welsh girls on top in England"[60] or the *Sunday Mirror*'s headline – accompanying a feature interview with a rugby union player – of "Scrummy Kyra just loves her big hits."[61]

The rising popularity and profile of the women's rugby union World Cup, England's victory in the 2014 tournament – which "helped participation in the women's game in the country increase by more than 70%"[62] – and the Rugby Football Union's decision to award professional contracts (48 of them for the 2016–2017 season) to English players have contributed to the sport's decreasingly chauvinistic British media narrative in the decade and a half since *Mirror* newspapers dealt almost exclusively in double entendre. However, more recent research suggests that women's rugby's challenge to misogyny and hegemony is itself complicit – and not altogether unwittingly – in the prolongation of arguably similarly damaging mediated sexual stereotyping.

While Shockley found that female rugby players "actively create an important oppositional culture" to "regional norms of womanhood",[63] Carle and Nauright, Taylor and Fleming and others noted that said culture appears very closely related to that of men's rugby, as "women who play rugby draw on many of the heretofore masculine-only codes that have conditioned how rugby is played and interpreted",[64] resulting in a "play hard, party hard attitude"[65] of "post-game drink-ups complete with singing and socializing with the other team"[66] and a narrative arguably summated by "Women play hard in men's world".[67] Conflate those with the active promotion by some in the LGBT community of women's rugby as, if not quite a lesbian-only sport, then a "safe haven" for gay players, under headlines such as "Rugby's lesbian marketing officer wants you to play the field", and it is both arguably unsurprising that a study by Stubbs found that 18 per cent of female rugby players felt compelled to "embody the lesbian label"[68] by "embracing the stereotype through dress and behaviour", and inevitable that media discourse will remain informed by said stereotype.

Bindel, citing a Sport England-supported Women's Sport and Fitness Foundation study into poor female participation rates which reported that "some girls avoid certain sports for fear of being perceived as unfeminine or lesbian [while] some parents discourage their daughters from taking up sport",[69] framed that enduring discourse and its promulgation of "the sexist stereotype, that women wish to get hot and sweaty with other women on the pitch" as "Reverse homophobia", arguing: "Couple these attitudes with the fact that the majority of sports journalists and sports editors are men, and we have a double bind of sexism and anti-lesbian prejudice that prevent women from both participating and, if they are lesbian, coming out."

Conclusion

As indicated by *The Sun* leader column with which we began, and – crucially – as experienced by Alex Kay-Jelski during his career climb in UK sports journalism, contemporary sports journalists generally appear neither homophobic nor antipathetic to the principle of active gay athletes feeling emboldened to come out.

Gareth Thomas, the professional cricketer Steven Davies and Thomas Hitzlsperger are among professional sportsmen whose disclosure of their sexuality in the past decade has not prompted an explicitly pejorative UK media response as might have been expected – based on the examples from the 1990s and even the 2000s discussed – in previous decades. However, while any episode of outright homophobia in the British sports media would now be regarded as, at very best, anachronistic, we have clearly seen that the UK press *can* still retreat into damaging innuendo when reporting and discussing matters of sexuality in sport, resulting in discourse which promotes sexual and gender stereotyping, not least among football supporters whose speculated response to an active, high-profile player coming out is regarded by many observers as the foundation of British sport's so-called last taboo. Indeed, as Kay-Jelski acknowledges, the notion of outright enlightenment across all other UK sport is undermined by the non-emergence of the next Thomas or Davies, let alone an active successor to Hitzlsperger. Equally evident is that such stereotyping, while seemingly less egregious if sometimes still stigmatising in its effect on individual LGBT female athletes, exacts a significant toll on perceptions of – and, crucially, participation in – certain women's sports in the UK.

In terms of the way ahead, it is clear, not least from the former Press Complaints Commission's (at very best) disingenuous response to complaints over tabloid "bender" headlines, that it is incumbent on those policing the British print media to do as much to guard against the use of inimical language in sports discourse regarding sexuality as in matters of race and ethnicity. However, both the UK and US press must be proactive in pushing the issue of homosexuality in sport, rather than seek to justify maintaining a heteronormative narrative through long-held notions of the homophobia of their audience rendered largely redundant – in theory at least – by recent research by Cashmore and Cleland and others. While not guaranteeing that more high-profile LGBTQ athletes will emerge, for the industry to "absorb the fact that it might not be fear of fans' homophobia, but other concerns, that are stopping players from coming out"[70] would promise to at least add vital clarity to a still clouded issue.

In the United States, Christian conservatism would likely be widely cited as one of those "other concerns", as evidenced by the experience of Jason Collins. While the nation's sports media chooses to accommodate those who deal in fundamentalist, clearly homophobic discourse, excuses regarding the potential reaction of fans to openly gay athletes are specious, even in the era of Trump, Republican control of legislature and religious liberty appearing likely to be cherished far above LGBTQ rights.[71]

Factor in a dizzyingly fast-evolving mediated debate regarding the increasing success of transgender athletes, which has become polarised – specifically, regarding physiological issues such as testosterone levels and skeletal muscle mass – to the point that even some LGBTQ sporting trailblazers such as Navratilova stand improbably yet so squarely and vocally against transgender athletes that they are branded as transphobic, and the question must be asked as to what price the sports media's narrative on sexuality, no matter what recent progress has been made, yet taking an emphatic retrograde step.

References

1. John Dillon, "Hitzlsperger is gay. So what? Who cares?", *The Sun*, 9 January 2014.
2. Josh Halliday, "Peter Tatchell: Thomas Hitzlsperger may have turned tide of homophobia", *The Guardian*, 9 January 2014.
3. Alex Bryce, "Analysis: Gays – football's last taboo", *Pink News*, 27 April 2007.
4. Kent Asp, *Powerful Mass Media: Studies in Political Advocacy*, Goteborg Studies in Politics: Gothenburg, 1986.
5. Raewyn Connell, *Gender and Power*, Allen, Mercer and Unwin: Sydney, 1987.
6. Jane Martinson, "No increase in women's sport coverage since the 2012 Olympics", *The Guardian*, 13 March 2014, https://www.theguardian.com/lifeandstyle/womens-blog/2014/mar/13/womens-sport-newspaper-coverage-birmingham-university, accessed 13 December 2019.
7. Mike Donaldson, "What is hegemonic masculinity?", *Theory and Society*, Volume 22, Issue 5, 1993, pp. 643–657.
8. Raewyn Connell, "A whole new world: Remaking masculinity in the context of the environmental movement", *Gender and Society*, Volume 4, Issue 4, 1990, pp. 452–478.
9. Harry Deedes, "Ronaldo finds an unlikely defender in Peter Tatchell", *The Independent*, 5 July 2006, https://www.independent.co.uk/news/people/pandora/ronaldo-finds-an-unlikely-defender-in-peter-tatchell-1162810.html, accessed 13 December 2019.
10. Anita Bressi and Heather Nunn, *The Tabloid Culture Reader*, Open University Press: London, 2008.
11. Nigel Pauley, "Telly Alan: Beckham's a bender", *Daily Star*, 29 January 2008, https://www.dailystar.co.uk/news/latest-news/telly-alan-beckham-bender-18022038.amp, accessed 13 December 2019.
12. Owen Jones, "What Alan Carr taught me about gay men's homophobia", *The Guardian*, 20 April 2014.
13. Anonymous, "Benders ain't like Beckham", *Daily Star*, 23 April 2008.
14. Smart, "Bender it like Beckham: Pineapple Louie's 4am party with David", *The Sun*, 27 July 2010.
15. Anonymous, *PCC Editors' Code of Conduct*, 2008, http://www.pcc.org.uk/assets/696/Code_of_Practice_2012_A4.pdf
16. AA Gill, "Humping in tents: A great British tradition", *The Sunday Times*, 25 July 2010.
17. Caroline Davies, "Clare Balding complains to press watchdog over 'dyke' jibe", *The Guardian*, 30 July 2010.
18. Jenny Percival, "Rugby league to kick off anti-homophobia campaign", *The Guardian*, 28 November 2008.
19. Fay Strang, "NOT PLAYING BY THE RULES? Rugby star Keegan Hirst 'had secret boyfriend' when he filmed awkward first dates – claims ex wife", *The Sun*, 23 July 2016.
20. Gaz Beadle, "Gaz Beadle urges gay footballers to come out: 'What a misery it is to live a lie'", *Daily Star*, 27 October 2016.

21. Donald McRae, "Robbie Rogers: 'Why coming out as gay meant I had to leave football'", *The Guardian*, 29 March 2008.

22. Simon Garfield, "Gay sport special: The numbers game: Is anyone out there?", *Observer Sport Monthly*, 4 May 2003.

23. Anonymous, "Profile: The striker who didn't score: Justin Fashanu, dribbling round Westminster", *The Independent*, 12 February 1994.

24. Anonymous, "'Queen of Hearts' Justin Fashanu was never far from turmoil", *The Scotsman*, 5 August 2009, https://www.scotsman.com/lifestyle-2-15039/queen-of-hearts-justin-fashanu-was-never-far-from-turmoil-1-1214346, accessed 13 December 2019.

25. Sam Morgan, "'I've spoken to gay players' gay footballers in talks to come out together at the start of the season, FA boss reveals", *The Sun*, 9 January 2017.

26. David Kent, "FA chief Greg Clarke urges gay stars to come out together after player talks", *Daily Mail*, 9 January 2017.

27. *Drive*, BBC Radio 5 live, 9 January 2017, http://www.bbc.co.uk/programmes/b087spwh

28. Ellis Cashmore and John Cleland, "Fans, homophobia and masculinities in association football: Evidence of a more inclusive environment", *The British Journal of Sociology*, Volume 63, Issue 2, 2012.

29. Anonymous, "Homophobia in sport: Most fans 'would welcome gay players' – BBC survey", 26 October 2016, http://www.bbc.co.uk/sport/37760114, accessed 13 December 2019.

30. Edward Kian, "Sexuality in the mediation of sport", in Jennifer Hargreaves and Eric Anderson (eds.), *Routledge Handbook of Sport, Gender and Sexuality*, Routledge: London, 2014.

31. David Nyland, "Sports talk radio and masculinity", in Hargeaves and Anderson (eds.), *Routledge Handbook of Sport, Gender and Sexuality* 29 April 2016.

32. Chris Greenberg, "Chris Broussard, ESPN reporter, calls being gay an 'open rebellion to god'", *The Huffington Post*, 29 April 2013.

33. John Koblin, "ESPN says it regrets Chris Broussard's comments were 'a distraction'", *Deadspin*, 29 April 2013.

34. Trent Baker, "FS1's Whitlock: Michael Sam was a 'stunt' by the NFL to please PC crowd", *Breitbart*, 24 March 2016.

35. Matt Bonesteel, "Jeff Fisher denies that Rams picked Michael Sam to avoid 'Hard Knocks'", *Washington Post*, 24 March 2016.

36. Edge of Sports Podcast, 13 May 2016, http://www.edgeofsportspodcast.com/post/144306224535/michael-sam-the-first-openly-gay-man-in-the-nfl, accessed 13 December 2019.

37. Dylan Gwynn, "Michael Sam: If I had never come out, I'd still be in the NFL", *Newsbusters.org*, 6 May 2016.

38. Michael Atkinson and Kevin Young, *Deviance and Social Control in Sport*, Human Kinetics: Champaign, IL, 2008.

39. Michael Kimmel and Amy Aronson, *Men and Masculinities*, ABC–Clio Ltd: Santa Barbara, CA, 2003.

40. Jan Wright and Gill Clarke, "Sport, the media and the construction of compulsory heterosexuality", *International Review for the Sociology of Sport*, Volume 34, Issue 3, 1999, pp. 227–243.

41. Sam Amick, "Women's Olympic basketball players hope for more LGBT acceptance in NBA", *USA Today*, 14 August 2016.

42. Ian Gallagher, "Pictured: The wedding of hockey's golden couple as Britain's first married winners since 1920 say it was 'really special' to achieve victory standing next to each other'", *Mail on Sunday*, 20 August 2016.

43. Veronica Lee, "TEE PARTY: The LPGA won't admit it but the lesbian bars and clubs in Palm Springs tell the real story", *Observer Sport Monthly*, 6 May 2001.

44. Ron Sirak, "Mel Reid: 'This is who I am'", lpga.com, 22 March 2019, https://www.lpga.com/news/2019-mel-reid-sit-down-interview, accessed 21 December 2019.

45. Karen Appleby and Elaine Foster, "Gender and sport participation", in Emily Roper (ed.), *Gender Relations in Sport*, Sense Publishers: Rotterdam, 2014.

46. Helen Lenskyj, "Reflections on communication and sport: On heteronormativity and gender identities", *Communication and Sport*, Volume 1, Issue 1–2, 2013, pp. 136–150.

47. Ibid., p. 15.

48. Julie Bindel, "Sportswomen are stereotyped as gay – but that doesn't make coming out easy", *The Guardian*, 12 February 2014.

49. David Nylund, *Beer, Babes, and Balls: Masculinity and Sports Talk Radio*, State University of New York Press: Albany, NY, 2007.

50. Deborah Stevenson, "Women, sport, and globalization: Competing discourses of sexuality and nation", in *Journal of Sport and Social Issues*, Volume 26, Issue 2, 2002.

51. Mariah Burton-Nelson, *The Stronger Women Get, the More Men Love Football: Sexism and the Culture of Sport*, The Women's Press: London, 1996.

52. J. Potter, "Elegant violence", *Inside Rugby*, January 1999.

53. Graham Scrambler, "Sport and society: History", *Power and Culture*, Open University Press: London, 2005.

54. Ibid., p. 112.

55. David Howe, "Kicking stereotypes into touch: An ethnographic account of women's rugby", in Anne Bolin and Jane Granskog (eds.), *Athletic Intruders: Ethnographic Research on Women, Culture and Exercise*, State University of New York Press: Albany, NY, 2003, pp. 227–246.

56. Joanna Rohrbaugh, "Femininity on the line", *Psychology Today*, August 1979, pp. 31–33.

57. Michael Messner, "Sports and male domination: The female athlete as contested ideological terrain", *Sociology of Sport Journal*, Volume 5, Issue 3, 1988, pp. 197–211.

58. Alison Carle and John Nauright, "Women playing rugby union", in Chandler and Nauright (eds.), *Making the Rugby World: Race, Gender, Commerce*, London: Routledge, 1999, pp. 128–148.

59. Mick Dennis, "Women's rugby sent to try us!", *Daily Mirror*, 16 May 2002.

60. Anonymous, "Welsh girls on top in England", *Daily Mirror*, 13 April 2002.

61. Anthony Clavane, "Scrummy Kyra just loves her big hits", *Sunday Mirror*, 11 October 1998.

62. Anonymous, "*Women's rugby: England World Cup win boosts female participation*", 5 October 2016, http://www.bbc.co.uk/sport/rugby-union/37560447, accessed 13 December 2019.

63. Megan Shockley, "150 debutantes, brats and mayhem: Women's rugby and the creation of an oppositional culture in the south", *WSQ: Women's Studies Quarterly*, Volume 33, Issue 1/2, 2005.

64. Tony Chandler and John Nauright (eds.), *Making the Rugby World: Race, Gender, Commerce*, Routledge: London, 1999.

65. Anonymous, https://www.lsesu.com/activities/sports/clubs/7862/, accessed 13 December 2019.

66. Lucy Hallowell, "Rugby's lesbian marketing officer wants you to play the field", 2013, http://www.afterellen.com/general-news/106768-rugbys-lesbian-marketing-officer-wants-you-to-play-the-field, accessed 13 December 2019.

67. Beth Rose, "Women play hard in men's world", BBC Sport, 30 August 2007, http://www.bbc.co.uk/devon/content/articles/2007/08/29/womens_rugby_feature.shtml, accessed 13 December 2019.

68. Julie Stubbs, "'Lez' play rugby: Managing the lesbian stereotype on and off the rugby pitch", 2013, http://wheatoncollege.edu/academic-festival/files/2013/04/Stubbs-Lez-Play-Rugby.pdf

69. Anonymous, "Barriers to sports participation for women and girls", 2008, http://www.lrsport.org/uploads/barriers-to-sports-participation-for-women-girls-17.pdf, accessed 13 December 2019.

70. Tobin, Lucy, "Most football fans are not homophobic, says study", *The Guardian*, 21 September 2010.

71. Anon, "*Issues of Importance to Catholics*", 2016, https://www.donaldjtrump.com/press-releases/issues-of-importance-to-catholics

20

Homophobia: Interview with Alex Kay-Jelski

Neil Farrington

If anyone epitomises the UK media's journey – albeit incomplete – from the brand of homo-phobic sports discourse blamed for both the demonisation of football's first active openly gay player and the non-emergence of any successors, it is seemingly Alex Kay-Jelski.

Even if it had not happened at the newspaper "perceived as Britain's most homophobic",[1] Kay-Jelski's rapid rise to the position of Britain's first openly gay national sports editor might provide emphatic evidence of enlightenment at the heart of the sports journalism industry. As it is, his rise through the ranks at the *Daily Mail*, moving from lowly sub-editor to the top job on the sports desk in barely seven years, revealing his sexuality along the way, offers a compelling case study in an era when the media narrative regarding LGBT athletes is under ever-increasing scrutiny.

At the time of writing sports editor of *The Times*,[2] neither the significance of Kay-Jelski's role nor the fact that said narrative has failed to yet fully address fears of enduring homophobia in UK sport, are lost on him. However, he is adamant that significant progress has been made by the British press in its previously problematic – many would say pernicious – treatment of sexuality in sport, particularly in the last handful of years.

Asked if he has experienced homophobia, alienation or even innuendo and sarcasm since coming out "a few years after" starting work at the *Daily Mail*, Kay-Jelski says: "Absolutely not. I've never had any problems whatsoever. Most people just do not care. The UK sporting press is not homophobic. There has been nothing but support for people like [diver] Tom Daley, [cricketer] Steve Davies and [rugby union and league player] Gareth Thomas."[3]

Moreover, he insists that sexuality not being a factor in the sports journalism workplace is now being reflected in positive, innuendo-free reporting of sexuality in sport, adding: "Things have changed. Dramatically. LGBT stories are treated with respect and sensitivity. That language doesn't exist anymore, I don't think."[4]

Yet Kay-Jelski acknowledges that with that change comes paradox – in his belief that no active professional footballers will come out any time soon. Indeed, while others regard homosexuality in the so-called beautiful game as the last taboo, he suspects the ugly reality is that homophobia still extends across the range of major sports.

What he is *convinced* of is that the UK press are no longer driving that prejudice. "It [football] is a taboo. But let's not fool ourselves into thinking other sports are comfortable with gay players.

The one rugby and cricket players who came out did not lead to others following. Where are the openly gay British tennis players, jockeys and sprinters?"[5]

So how close may we be to seeing another footballer – or footballers, if Football Association chairman Greg Clarke, as revealed to Kay-Jelski's newspaper, has his way[6] – coming out? "Impossible to say really, but I'd imagine some way off. Dealing with fans' and team-mates' reactions would be really tough. But the media's response will be positive. That shouldn't be a worry in this scenario, and the media could influence the public – it does every day."[7]

For now, Kay-Jelski is reconciled to at least helping keep the issue on the sports news agenda. "It is important that it is still an issue. Openly gay footballers would send a message to in-the-closet people in all types of life that it's ok to be gay and that they shouldn't be scared."[8]

References

1. Paul Baker, "Fewer chances to disapprove? Tracking the *Daily Mail*'s changing representation of gay people" in Mark McGlashan (ed.), *Challenging Homophobia and Homophobic Bullying Through Children's Literature*, 2013, https://www.academia.edu/4196222/Challenging_Homophobia_and_Homophobic_Bullying_through_Children_s_Literature_-_Event_Programme, accessed 13 December 2019.
2. Kay-Jelski became editor-in-chief of *The Athletic* in 2019.
3. Interview with Alex Kay-Jelski, 24 January 2017.
4. Ibid.
5. Ibid.
6. Henry Winter, "FA chairman: I've spoken to gay players", *The Times*, 9 January 2017.
7. Ibid.
8. Ibid.

21

Money

Peter Berlin

For a long time, sports reporters took the lack of seriousness of their subject very seriously. They determinedly echoed the twin shibboleths of those who ran the leagues and tournaments they covered: sport and politics did not mix and, in polite society, one did not discuss money.

The news and financial departments reported the important events of the real world that had a tangible impact on the lives of readers; the arts section covered stuff that, in some mysterious way, was culturally significant; but sports journalists were boys (almost invariably boys) covering boys' games. They dealt in escapism, in noble athletes and their breathtaking feats, their redemptive triumphs and their heartbreaking losses, not hard news.

When the wider world encroached, sports journalists were, and still are, ambivalent. The government may be in chaos but let's cover the Ashes as if they are equally important. Sport is a refuge, and anyone who has worked on a sports desk will know the fury that can erupt if any member tries to turn the television to a speech by Boris Johnson while Steve Smith is batting.

Just because other journalists may unite in seeing sports reporting as frivolous, it does not mean there are not tensions elsewhere in the newsroom. Financial reporting is regarded with suspicion, even by financial journalists. Writing about the daily movements of the stock exchange, unpicking the obscure intricacies of company annual reports or explaining the nuances of a budget is not just highly technical; even those who do it often find it dull. Even though sports reporting usually requires a certain basic numeracy to interpret tables and team and player statistics, sports reporters happily subscribe to the general prejudice and plead incomprehension when confronted with a balance sheet.

For most of the population, money rivals sex as an overriding daily preoccupation. Yet, as with sex, a willingness to understand what's going on in finance is not simply a matter of technical expertise. Sport, and the boys who cover it, remained for a long time in the thrall of the Victorian idea that money, like sex, was a subject not to be discussed.

I apologise to any readers whose hopes had been raised, but journalism and sex is a subject for a different article. Let's talk about money, baby.

Money shapes sport

Reporting on money in sport is not simply financial journalism. As sport has evolved into a big business, understanding the annual figures of big clubs or the intricacies of player or sponsorship and broadcasting contracts has grown in importance. But at a broader level, money also shapes the way sport is organised, where and when it is played, the competitive balance and the accessibility to fans. It is also an ethical and political issue. For many sports journalists, and many fans and administrators, discussing the politics of sport remains distasteful.

Modern sports were born amateur. Sport rapidly begat sports journalism, which shared its suspicion of money. Mass sports and mass media were both products of the same changes that transformed Victorian society.

While football quickly bowed to Mammon and became a global game as a result, many in the game as well as fans and journalists remain suspicious of money. Other sports clung to amateurism far longer. Tennis went "open" in 1968; the Olympics embraced professionalism (for most sports) in 1986. Rugby union went professional in 1995.

Before the meeting at the Freemasons' Tavern on 26 October 1863 that created the Football Association (FA) and its first stab at the rules of its game, other sports had been organised in Britain. Boxing, cricket and horse-racing all had agreed sets of rules out of financial necessity. The aristocrats who bet on those sports wanted a level playing field.

As the men who had played differing versions of football at their public schools increasingly moved to rapidly growing London to run the Empire, they needed a common set of rules for sports that could be played over a defined time and in a small space. They wanted to play against their own class rather than against the great mass of ordinary people, but the same forces of urbanisation and industrialisation, as well as the Victorian belief in the virtues of team sports, meant that the populations of the fast-expanding cities and factory and mill towns across the country, who had long practised local variations of football, wanted to play too. They also wanted to watch others play, and the newspapers that were multiplying and growing to serve that increasingly literate and concentrated population began to cover the games.

While the founders of the FA, the Rugby Football Union, the Lawn Tennis Association and so on were clearly ferocious snobs desperate to keep the masses off their manicured and white-lined lawns, their obsession with the "purity" of sport was no doubt sincere. It is mirrored in the 21st century by the hostility of many, particularly worshippers of football as an expression of working-class community, to the corrupting influence of money on their sport.

In 1871, the FA, innovators again, created a cup competition. It was theoretically nationwide, but in the early seasons matches were played exclusively in the south-east of England, where the clubs where the public schoolboys played were based.

By 1882, the unwashed masses were at the gates. Blackburn Rovers became the first outsider club to reach the FA Cup final. Reduced to 10 men, they lost, 1-0, to the Old Etonians. Lord Arthur Kinnaird, the ultimate Victorian upper-class football man, reportedly celebrated his fifth winner's medal with a headstand.

The press was well-represented. *The Times*, *The Field*, *Bell's Life in London*, the *Sporting Life* and *The Sportsman* all carried reports,[1] but one indication that sports reporting was also in its infancy is that there was no agreement on who scored the only goal or in what minute they scored it.

The following year, the upstarts won. Blackburn Olympic beat the Old Etonians 2-1 after extra time. This time Kinnaird reportedly refused to shake hands after the final whistle. History had passed the Old Etonians by. None of the original aristocratic amateur clubs ever won the FA Cup again.

The press coverage showed that journalists were aware of the broader social significance but were divided on which side to take. Richard Sanders quotes, without naming either the writer or the publication, one journalist who portrayed the northerners as the underdogs:

"It was like a battle of the humble and weak, against the mighty and strong," the unnamed correspondent wrote. "They looked a tiny set. We should think the Olympic averaged about 5 ft 6 in and scaled about 10 and a half stones, while the Etonians were probably two to three inches taller and from a stone to 21lbs heavier per man."[2]

Other journalists repeated the long-held suspicion that northern clubs found ways to pay their players. They complained that Olympic had gone to Blackpool to train and asked how working men could afford the time or the expense. They also pointed out that some players had moved to Blackburn from clubs in other towns, notably Jack Hunter, who had moved from Sheffield to join the club.[3]

They had a point. The team contained mill workers, weavers, a plumber and an iron-moulder as well as a publican and a newsagent.[4] These were men for whom time off work to train and travel to games was a costly luxury. The rules stipulated that the FA Cup was still amateur, yet Olympic are widely regarded as the first professional winners.

The FA did not always turn a blind eye. In 1884, the FA did expel Preston North End from the competition after the Upton Park club complained, following a cup defeat, that the victors were professional. Preston threatened to break away and form a professional league. The FA formed a committee which backed down and, unlike rugby union, gave its blessing to the professionalism and the creation of the Football League.

Preston won the inaugural Football League title in 1888–1889. Upton Park represented Britain at the 1900 Olympics in Paris where, facing only a French amateur team, they won. The landscaped had changed.

Yet David Conn, who covered the changes in football in the 1990s with a sceptical eye, argues that those who oversaw the creation of football's first professional league were not entirely in love with money and saw that it presented dangers for their sport.

"The football authorities had looked at the professionalisation of the sport which they hadn't liked but had acceded to and they had thought: 'We don't want this sport of ours becoming part of entertainment industry.' They tried to institute a club ethos. There were historic rules in place to prevent the clubs just becoming companies that could be exploited for gain by the shareholders and they tried to implement a club ethos," Conn said in a wide-ranging telephone interview.[5]

That scepticism about money continues to inform much sports reporting.

1919 and all that

Money, unsurprisingly, brought neither happiness nor honesty.

The history of modern sport is spotted with financial scandals. The crimes cover almost every type of shady manifestation of greed. One month, October 1919, provides striking examples of two popular offences: fiddling the books to conceal payments to players and throwing matches at the behest of bookies.

It is possible to blame both the Leeds City and the Chicago "Black Sox" scandals on the meanness and dishonesty of team owners or the greed and dishonesty of some of their players. What is clear is that there are very few heroes in either tale.

In both cases, what is striking is the ferocity of the authorities in dealing with the scandals and the timidity of the press in covering them. While the Black Sox scandal did emerge through the wary reporting of a few journalists, the Leeds case completely blindsided the British press.

During the war, manager Herbert Chapman left second-division Leeds City to do his patriotic duty and manage a nearby munitions factory. He picked his assistant George Cripps to run the team, and Leeds attracted star players and won the unofficial wartime championship. The maximum player wage was £10 a week (during the season) and Leeds broke the rules. Cripps kept the paperwork.

When Chapman returned, the club was eager to get rid of Cripps, who seems to have been disliked. He reached a settlement with the club which apparently involved handing the papers to his lawyer James Bromley, who was supposed to pass them on to Leeds City.

They did not stay secret. It seems the culprit was Charlie Copeland, a disgruntled reserve-team full-back who was sent to Coventry City when he asked for a pay rise. He passed them not to the press but to the FA. It started an inquiry, and Bromley, himself a former Leeds director, also provided evidence. He later said that he had not passed the Cripps papers to the club because it had not made a requested £50 donation to Leeds Infirmary.

The FA asked Leeds City to explain by 6 October. The directors ignored the threat; after all, other clubs were doing the same thing. On 7 October, what seems to be the first newspaper report on the scandal appeared in the *Yorkshire Post* under the headline "SUSPENSION OF LEEDS CITY CLUB".[6]

The intro acknowledges that the newspaper had not been totally ignorant of the problem.

"The alarmist rumours which have been bruited abroad regarding the Leeds City Football Club have come to a head," it read. The paper, based in Leeds, made clear where its loyalties lay, and that it placed its faith in the local leadership, writing that: "There is a disposition in some quarters unfriendly to Leeds City to regard the club as already 'down and out'." But it also said the mayor of Leeds, Joseph Henry, "has great hopes of saving the club – and he is in a better position than anyone else at the moment to assess the club's prospects at their true value".[7]

That faith in the Lord Mayor was misplaced. Leeds were booted out of the league; four directors and Chapman were banned from football for life. The club's assets were sold off, including the player on 17 October at the Metropole Hotel. *The Yorkshire Evening Post* covered the sale of the players under the headline "THE LEEDS CITY TEAM 'GOING GOING GONE!'"[8] and ran the prices of every player "as if it were some livestock auction", observes the *ozwhitelufc* website.[9]

Port Vale took Leeds City's place in the league. Chapman argued, quite reasonably, that he had been managing a munitions factory at the time and was reinstated.

Those parts of the British sporting press that had allowed themselves to be, briefly distracted by the scandal, could return to writing about games.

The American way

Meanwhile, in the United States, the most notorious baseball World Series of all time was played from 1 October to 9 October 1919.

North America is the Galapagos Islands of sport. The traditional sports they played evolved differently, in part as a conscious expression of an American identity distinct from Britain. Rugby was transformed into American football. The first professional baseball club, the 1869 Cincinnati Red Stockings, was an offshoot of the local cricket club. Its manager, Harry Wright, was a Yorkshire-born former cricket pro and its star player was his brother George. The divide over money in American team sports was, from the start, between colleges and the pros. While the United States has had professional leagues for 150 years, the rigid opposition to paying "student athletes", even in "the revenue sports", only began to weaken in 2019 in the face of state legislation in California.[10]

Americans have long had a different attitude to money in sport and the relationship of clubs to their communities. When the novelty wore off in Cincinnati and the team stopped making money, the Wrights moved to Boston and changed their red stockings for red sox.

The potential conflict for club owners between improving the won-loss ratio or the profit-loss balance attracted American economists to sports in the 1950s. They found that US franchises were "profit maximising" businesses. When Peter J. Sloane, a British economist, repeated the analysis for British football clubs, he found that their boards were instead "utility maximisers". They were in it for something other than money. Utility maximisation, wrote Sloane, was "consistent with almost any type of behaviour".[11]

The Leeds City scandal involved a provincial second division team being thrown out of the league early in the season. The Black Sox scandal revolved around the pivotal event in the early 20th-century American sports calendar.

Gambling and match-rigging were a problem from baseball's earliest days. By 1903, a sport played only in the north-east quadrant of the United States had acquired a formal World Series. From early on, there were suspicions that some were rigged, although fans everywhere are prone to believe that they have been unjustly robbed when their team loses.

Yet for those who followed and covered "America's game" it was an article of faith that it displayed the special virtues of the republic. "The belief that baseball was honest and upright constituted an article of secular faith in the America," wrote Harold Seymour.[12] He quotes a *Chicago Tribune* editorial from October 1906 which argued that baseball "is one of the few sports which have not been contaminated by evil influences … And there is the belief everywhere that each player is Honest".

When Hugh Fullerton, who worked for the rival *Chicago Herald and Examiner*, heard rumours that the 1919 World Series was being fixed by gamblers, he wrote about it with caution. Fullerton, one of the first journalists to take a statistical approach to baseball, decided to count suspicious pays in the World Series. According to some modern sources, he was present following the deciding game when White Sox manager Kid Gleason told owner Charles Comiskey that some players had taken bribes.[13]

Fullerton might have known for sure, as might other reporters, but after the White Sox surprisingly lost five games to three to the supposedly inferior Cincinnati Reds, he was only prepared to write cryptically that the "unbeaten faction of the beaten White Sox did not quit", and also predicted that seven White Sox players would not be there "when the gong sounded next spring" and that some would not be in baseball.[14] In hinting at a scandal, he still went further than any of his peers.

The general reaction to Fullerton's insinuation in the rest of the US media was hostile. Yet the few reports that addressed the issue demonstrated, in retrospect, that journalists had a pretty good idea what had happened.

One response was to blame Jews for corrupting an honest American sport. In October, the *Sporting News* wrote: "There are no lengths to which the crop of lean-faced and long-nosed gamblers of these degenerate days will go." Later the same newspaper, for a long time the dominant sports publication in the United States, wrote that the problem was that "a lot of dirty, long-nosed, thick-lipped and strong-smelling gangsters butted into the World Series – an American event, by the way".[15]

In November, two newspapers in Fort Wayne, halfway between Chicago and Cincinnati, reported that gangsters had made money on the World Series. On November 10, the *Fort Wayne News-Sentinel* named Arnold Rothstein, a Jewish New York gangster.[16]

It was not until the following September that a grand jury was convened in Chicago and eight players, and several gamblers, were ordered to appear. A grand jury screens cases to see if they merit a proper trial. Evidence is kept secret. The jury decided there was no basis for an open trial, which meant the records remained sealed and journalists could not have access to what had been said, but they guessed. There is also a persistent story that the transcripts were then stolen, although others claim to have read them. The Society of American Baseball Research say that the case files "were in disarray", parts were missing and some names redacted.[17] All this only adds to the romance of the case and permits wild conspiracy theories and persistent disagreements over who were the true culprits.

In November 1920, in part as a consequence of the scandal, Judge Kenesaw Mountain Landis became the first baseball commissioner and quickly banned eight White Sox players for life. When the court records were later unsealed they showed that six (Eddie Cicotte, Lefty Williams, Chick Gandil, Swede Risberg, Happy Felsch and Fred McMullin) had made bad plays in exchange for money. The evidence is more ambiguous for the other two. Buck Weaver had refused the bribe and said he had told the White Sox. "Shoeless" Joe Jackson accepted the money but took it to the White Sox after the series ended and denied that he had played badly, a claim backed up by his outstanding statistics over the eight games.

That did not prevent Charley Owens of the *Chicago Daily News* writing that Jackson had confessed and describing an imaginary scene outside the Cook County courthouse that ran under a headline that remains one of the most famous lines in American sports journalism, even though Jackson never said it and the story did not, quite, contain it.

"When Jackson left the criminal court building in the custody of a sheriff after telling his story to the grand jury," wrote Owens, "one child stepped up to the outfielder, and, grabbing his coat sleeve, said:

"'It ain't true, is it, Joe?'

"'Yes, kid, I'm afraid it is,' Jackson replied."

The headline was: "Say it ain't so, Joe."

To paraphrase Mark Twain: it was good, but it wasn't true.

"The fake Series of 1919 produced some of the worst newspaper reporting that the American press ever has been guilty of and why all of us who were detailed to cover the show were not fired for missing the greatest sports story in 20 years is something I have never understood. We were terrible," wrote Westbrook Pegler in his syndicated column in 1932.

In 1919, Pegler had just returned from covering the First World War and taken up sports reporting. One can dislike Pegler's politics – in his later career, he used his column to attack the New Deal, the unions, the Supreme Court taxes and the Democrat presidents Franklin Delano Roosevelt, Harry Truman and John Kennedy – but on the coverage of the tainted World Series, he had a point.

The Black Sox scandal raises a perennial problem of reporting flawed heroes not just in sport, but in journalism.

In *Eight Men Out*, the 1988 film about the scandal, Fullerton (played by renowned Chicago broadcaster and historian Studs Terkel) counts suspicious plays with his protégé Ring Lardner (played by the film's director, John Sayles). It is a fiction. Fullerton shared the work with Christy Matthewson, who had been one of the game's greatest pitchers. Yet it attests to the perceived importance of American reporters as both truth-tellers and great writers. Lardner is a much-loved author of short stories.

One biographer, Sarah Bembrey, believed the scandal scarred him. "Ring was exceptionally close to the White Sox and felt he was betrayed by the team. After the scandal, Ring always wrote about sports as if there were some kink to the outcome," she wrote.[18]

This is not an isolated problem in reporting corruption in sport. When journalists discover that athletes they admired and praised never gave any hint in interviews that they were doping or taking bribes – the cases of American journalists and Lance Armstrong or cricket writers and Hansie Cronje are two examples – the initial reaction is often disbelief while the second is betrayal. The truth is painful, and many journalists, not just in sport, are loath to write it when they discover it.

Follow the money

In the 100 years since the Black Sox and Leeds City scandals, human nature has not changed, but sport has. Sports journalism has, sometimes reluctantly, followed.

The constants, and the changes, were summed halfway through the intervening century by Arthur Hopcraft, a football journalist who broke the traditional boundaries by writing a book, *The Football Man*, on the sport in 1968.[19] It included a chapter "Football and the Press".

"No newspaper can afford not to write about football," wrote Hopcraft but, he said, even those with "the resources and the ruthlessness" choose not "to dig up and overstress all kinds of little sins". He listed:

> Illicit payments to greedy players, sweetening of fathers in the bargaining for the signatures of promising boy-players, boardroom politics which squeeze out the directors who ask the awkward questions, rancour in the dressing room, players late nights and gambling debts.
> Sports staffs are in the main much more interested in the game.[20]

The sins remain the same, but they are no longer so little and, even though there are fewer professional media outlets with the resources to investigate stories, all those on his list are now staples of British football coverage. They include constant echoes of 1919. Betting and its inevitable bastard child match-fixing, as well as dodging contract rules and tax collectors, remain constants, just on a different scale.

Interpol issues a bi-weekly "Corruption in sport" report which lists cases where there have been fresh arrests, charges or convictions. Every month brings fresh sports and new nations in a global sporting crooks tour.[21] Even Esports are already struggling with match-rigging.[22]

The temptation has increased. The global sports betting industry is enormous, growing fast and defying accurate measurement. Estimates put the global value of online betting alone at somewhere between $46 billion in 2018 and a surprisingly precise $104.31 billion in 2017.[23]

The huge sums are also reflected in the cheating on player contracts and salaries. A string of star players and coaches have been fined for tax evasion in Spain, with Cristiano Ronaldo outscoring all his rivals by agreeing in January 2019 to pay the tax collectors €18.8 million.[24] Chelsea were caught trying to dodge rules intended to safeguard underage footballers and received a year-long transfer ban from FIFA in January 2019 after being found guilty of 150 rules breaches involving 69 under-18 players.[25]

Leagues, clubs, agents, sponsors and even national governments strive to conceal or suppress unfavourable stories in sport, just as those in power have always done. Yet, when cases are listed on the internet by Interpol or players, agents, coaches or clubs are dragged into court, the corruption becomes hard for the media to ignore. Furthermore, 150 rules breaches or

€18.8 million fines reveal industrial-scale cheating. Sport has become an industry and needs to be covered as an industry.

Over the past 50 years, the earning power of sport has been transformed by a collection of broader social, economic and technological changes. As in the old joke, when the traditional guardians of the Corinthian ethos of sport were presented with ever larger potential revenue, the only question they asked before abandoning their purity for money was: "how much?"

Where once it had been impolite to talk about money in sport, now it was a dominant topic. The discourse had changed. Just as journalists had learned the joys of talking about sex in public, so now they could openly discuss filthy lucre. Furthermore, the sums of money flowing through sport grew so large that sports desks on the more serious newspapers had little choice but to find writers who could follow.

"There's a time lag," said Conn. "Something happens, journalism scrambles to catch up."

US sports were quickest to exploit the "golden triangle" of television, advertising and sponsorship revenue. Internationally, the most spectacular example was the transformation of the earning capacity of the football World Cup under Joao Havelange, the president of FIFA from 1974 to 1998, with the encouragement of Adidas chairman Horst Dassler and sports marketing man Patrick Nally.

The tennis majors ended their "shamateur" era in 1968. The Olympics, which had always allowed professional fencers, began to open the doors further in 1988 and quickened the pace in the early 1990s. The first appearance of NBA players, led by the US "Dream Team", at the 1992 Games in Barcelona signalled an irrevocable break with amateur tradition while enhancing the value of the broadcast rights for American network NBC, which had paid a record $401 million despite poor ratings for the 1988 Games in Seoul.[26]

In 1992, the European Cup was rebranded the Champions League, allowing the countries with the most valuable television audiences more teams. Meanwhile, two broadcasters recently established by Rupert Murdoch used sports rights to buy audience. In England, BSkyB, created in 1989 and struggling to attract subscribers, bid £304 million for five years of exclusive live rights to the breakaway Premier League (although, in the end it only paid £190 million).[27]

The following year in the United States, Fox – launched in 1988 as a rival to the traditional Big Three national networks but struggling to attract local affiliates – paid over $1.1 billion to wrest four years of National Football Conference rights from CBS. (In contrast, NBC retained the AFC rights for $880 million.)[28]

As channels multiplied, the guaranteed audiences live sport could deliver, generally too small when there were just two or three channels, became increasingly valuable. In 2019, TV rights in the United States alone were worth $22.42 billion, and globally they were worth around $50 billion. That is a big business.[29]

In the UK, football enjoyed a brief flirtation with the stock markets. Tottenham Hotspur were the first to float on the London Stock Exchange in 1983. The fashion caught on from 1995 to 1997, when 15 football clubs floated, raising, as Bill Gerrard has calculated, £150 million.[30] While the experiment was not a success it moved football into the eyeline of financial reporters. It also meant clubs were obliged to publish annual figures, giving access to previously unavailable information.

For Conn, the naïve reporting on those flotations, particularly that of Newcastle in 1997, remains a source of irritation. "It was covered as funny and quirky and the stockbrokers were wearing black and white shirts. 'Isn't it funny that a football club are floating on the Stock Exchange?' It wasn't funny. It was a carve-up of our national game that had very important consequences. It should have been covered more critically."

In 1995, the Bosman ruling transformed the rights of professionals in European team sports.

The same year, rugby union, which exactly 100 years earlier had tied its identity to amateurism, officially went professional.

Mihir Bose, another of those who started covering sports and money in the 1990s, said that the Bosman ruling, ushering in free agency two decades after US baseball, was also not covered sufficiently seriously. "Before the Bosman ruling came down, it was very difficult to convince people this could be very crucial," he said in a telephone interview, adding that the insularity of the British sports journalists was partly to blame.[31]

"Most people were not interested in the European Union and the fact that the European Union could have an impact on English football was considered very odd," Bose said.

Huge deals, stock-market listings, contract litigation: these were all subjects that financial desks traditionally covered. As Bose said, one sport drove that change: "We're talking about football because football is the one that became a commercial game."

Bose, a trained accountant who was already covering football and cricket matches for *The Sunday Times*, began to report on what was happening in club boardrooms starting in 1991 when, as he explained, "Robert Maxwell fell off a boat. He owned Derby County and the whole Derby County ownership became an issue."

In 1995, the *Financial Times* asked Patrick Harverson, an LSE graduate who had been covering markets and economics for the paper since 1988, to add sport to a wider portfolio of business sectors he covered.[32]

Conn, a former commercial lawyer, began working as a freelance "after the Sky deal (in May 1992) and breakaway when clubs started to float". He found receptive sports editors at first *The Telegraph* and *The Independent* and then at *The Guardian*.

"The emergence of pay television exponentially increased the sport's capacity to charge for television," Conn said. Bose agreed. "Editors started noticing money," he said, even those working for newspapers whose owners had stakes in the new deal.

The Fox and Sky deals also helped reconfigure the broadcast media, and Murdoch also owned the *New York Post* and *The Times*, *The Sunday Times*, *The Sun* and the *News of the World* in the UK. "Sky had come in. I was working for Rupert Murdoch. And I asked: 'why did this happen?'" said Bose.

Conn also found Sky changed editorial attitudes. "There was a receptiveness to the subject because the money, especially in football, increased exponentially with the first Sky deal, and was in people's faces and the media did realise they needed to cover it but didn't know how to cover it."

In the United States, Richard Sandomir started writing the TV Sports column for the *New York Times* as a freelancer in 1991. And, he said in an email exchange in September 2019, that when he joined the staff full-time in 1993 he was told "that I had to spread out to do sports business".

"Fox's bold entrance into the United States sports television market, starting with the NFL, added a lot of excitement to the coverage of the beat," said Sandomir, who also judged their coverage as the sports TV reviewer. "It was technically innovative."

When Harverson started covering sport, he would joke that even the biggest football club in the UK, Manchester United, had the annual revenues of a medium-sized supermarket. By 1997, the industry had already grown enough for Harverson to become the *FT*'s full-time sports correspondent.

Although their experiences and explanations differ, both Conn and Bose found traditional sports journalists hostile to covering the business side of sport as a business. Conn believes that from the start other football writers were sympathetic, but found finance too technical and dull and also felt that, he said, "this isn't right for the game".

"A lot of the sports football journalists are not very interested in that, and it isn't very interesting. They're resistant to it because it doesn't feel right and I totally agree with that. They would probably admit they didn't understand it either because their training had not prepared them for it."

He said that journalists had good reason to view money in football with distaste. "Sports journalists who loved sport shared the amateur-type ethos. Obviously [football] had been professional for 100 years but [they believed] that the ethos of sport should still be about love of the game and love of the clubs and not to do with anybody on the ownership side trying to make money. Of course, the players had to be paid."

Bose, who was born in India, was attuned to hostility from other sports journalists at football matches. "I'm not saying they were racist, but they had never seen a non-white person reporting on football. The idea that someone from India should know about football was very strange."

He said he was therefore attuned and inured when he started covering corruption in football and faced similar hostility. He recalls the response after he wrote about bungs and George Graham, who was the Tottenham manager at the time. "I remember that Saturday going to Tottenham Hotspur to report a football match and all the other journalists looked at me and said, 'Hmm, I don't know what you're writing this all about.' Being the 'other' and to go from that 'other' as a football reporter to being the 'other' as a football business reporter was a very easy step for me to take."

For both Conn and Bose, that other traditionally taboo subject on the sport pages, politics, was a natural extension of their beats, though, again, they view it differently. For Bose, the politics of sport was another under-covered area to write about. For Conn, the changes money wrought in sport were part of a bigger political picture.

"Sports politics hadn't been covered," said Bose, pointing out that the International Olympic Committee had been the responsibility of the athletics correspondent at the *Sunday Times*.

"I started going to FIFA meetings, UEFA meetings, later on IOC meetings. Journalists who went to Olympic events, they didn't go to the meetings beforehand." He said that other papers largely ignored the meetings in Lausanne in early 1999 at which the IOC addressed the breaking Salt Lake City scandal. "I was given an open field. Even I could not miss an open goal."

Conn said he writes "Not just [about] money in sport but social justice issues, legal issues. Investigative journalism". Yet investigative reporting is a challenge in an increasingly resource-poor industry.

"Other journalists have limitations because they have to write every day. For investigative stuff you have to find time and space," said Bose.

Sport has grown wealthier just as news organisations have increasingly struggled for money.

As football grew into a big business, it focused more on controlling its image. One symbol of the change was Harverson's move from the *Financial Times* in 2000 to become communications director at Manchester United. This being football, rather than any other business, one of his qualifications was that United was one of the clubs he supported. Moving into public relations is a traditional, and respectable, career switch for financial reporters. And even though he was moving from one of more financially robust Fleet Street newspapers, and from being an observer to a participant in a sport he loved, it was also a change from a declining industry to a rapidly growing one.

One accusation levelled at sports journalists is, as Hopcraft, thinking principally of provincial reporters who cover only the local club, wrote, "there are some reporters who are much more like public relations officers". Yet the fear of losing access is a perennial problem in all forms of journalism. On the other hand, successful reporters tend to bridle at the suggestion that they cannot unearth the facts. Conn and Bose both say that, at the start at least, they gained good access to club officials.

"I started talking to the chief executives of the clubs, or the secretaries of the clubs or the chairmen of the clubs," said Bose. "And I found that many of them were willing to talk to me. The people in suits determine the conditions in which the men in shorts play."

"I found them very approachable. Nobody else had talked to them before," continued Bose before adding a couple of caveats. "If you strike up a friendship and you feel you are giving them a fair run, they will tell you stories. They won't tell you stories against themselves but they will tell you stories against other people." But he adds that, at the highest level, access has become more limited. "[Roman] Abramovich has not given an interview. Sheikh Mansour at Manchester City has never given a single interview."

Where Bose is professionally neutral on the impact of money, Conn is known to be hostile, yet he believes that journalists can make sport's investment in public relations work for them.

"All clubs have PR and press comms departments at now. It's a great resource for us. Most of them are decent people. They're not always spinning us a line. They know we're not idiots."

Bose said he felt the attitude of the clubs to him was: "However critical his pieces might be, we can see that he understands it and that he was doing the work properly."

The clubs will continue to give a journalist access, Bose said, "If you're nice, if you're polite, if they can see that you are a decent person and you reflect their perspective in the balance of the piece. When you don't give their perspective, that's when people get upset. It's fair. You need to put balance in".

At the *New York Times*, Sandomir enjoyed dealing with the man who initially ran the operation for Murdoch and had a product to sell. "At the top of Fox Sports was David Hill, a funny, creative Australian producer who was accessible, witty and open – qualities that made it easier to cover Fox."

Murdoch's gamble on sport with Fox and Sky succeeded. Even though Sky moved live football behind a paywall, the transformation in the amount of sport shown and the relentless marketing push from broadcasters, sponsors and sportswear makers helped convert sport into an even more central element of modern life. They transformed not only the role of sport but, as Sandomir pointed out, the way it was covered. They had an impact on sports journalism everywhere.

For newspapers and websites, sport draws readers and drives clicks. In a politically refracted media market, it is one area where people of wildly differing political views come together. Fox News viewers may avoid reading the *New York Times* and its readers, but both will watch the NFL and consume reporting on it in media they would normally avoid.

Fox and Sky sprinkled celebrity stardust on their coverage by hiring former players and coaches, rather than journalists, as analysts. Other media followed suit. This implies that those who had been involved in the sport offered better coverage than professional journalists who had not. It has had a particular impact in Britain where, more than in the United States or continental Europe, journalists seem particularly insecure when confronted with the argument that if you have not done it you cannot understand it.

Conn and Bose also point out that journalists are further intimidated by their own lack of expertise when it comes to covering sport finance. Indeed, Bose says his training as an accountant has been a help. He knows that auditors hide the unpleasant details in their notes and he knows how to decode them.

Yet money is an inescapable topic in football reporting. Football fans detest profit-maximising owners, often American, such as the Glazers at Manchester United; they also dislike the billionaire utility maximisers, such as Abramovich at Chelsea, Sheikh Mansour at Manchester

City and Qatari Sports Investment at Paris Saint-Germain, who can use their own money to outspend rival clubs. Before a modern football writer can cover Manchester City or PSG playing in the Champions League, she or he has to report on their struggles to avoid being banned from the competition under UEFA's – so far toothless – Financial Fair Play rules.

Fans care about sport sponsorship and broadcasting deals, club takeovers and the behaviour of their owners, the size of club revenues and how much they pay coaches, players and agents because they know that these things shape the chances of their teams.

The football transfer market is now an important beat, and one of the most-retweeted practitioners is David Ornstein, himself a transfer target when he moved from the BBC to *The Athletic*.

A reflection of sport's growing importance is that the *Wall Street Journal*, traditionally even more of a purist financial daily than the *FT*, has even built a sports desk. Conn says he is no longer covering a lonely beat and lists the members of what he calls the Sports News Lobby: Martyn Ziegler at *The Times*; Daniel King, football correspondent, and Martin Lipton, deputy head of sport, both at *The Sun*; Matt Lawton, chief sports correspondent at *The Times*; Rob Harris, the global sport writer at the *Associated Press*; Matt Slater, staff writer at *The Athletic* UK; and London-based journalist Tariq Panja, formerly of financial wire *Bloomberg*, the global sportswriter at the *New York Times*. What is striking is that none of these have the word "financial" in their job titles. Money, so long a taboo subject, is now part of a sports reporter's beat.

Challenging environment

Where once sports journalism despised and distrusted money, it now respects it not just as a subject to cover but because more than ever the profession is hobbled by a lack of it. The money in and around the sport industry is keeping sports reporting healthy, at a national level at least.

Sport was also particularly well-placed to adapt to the new technology that might ultimately kill professional journalism. "The metabolism of sports and the metabolism of the Web always seemed like a good match," said Jim Brady, in 1995 one of the first sports editors of Washingtonpost.com, told the *Columbia Journalism Review*. "You have horrible deadlines, things that change at the last minute, a lot of ups and downs."[33] Yet the changing financial and technological environment remain a threat to sport, as they do to all forms of reporting.

In the introduction to his 2018 autobiography *Reporter*, Seymour Hersh, the veteran award-winning American investigative journalist, laments the state of the profession. While old age often brings a belief that everything is going to pot, and Hersh turned 82 in 2019, many of his points ring true.

He is nostalgic for "The golden age of journalism, when reporters for daily newspapers did not have to compete with the twenty-four-hour cable news cycle, when newspapers were flush with cash.[34]

"There was sufficient time for reporting on a breaking news story without having to constantly relay what was being learned on the newspaper's web page. We are sodden with fake news, hyped-up and incomplete information, and false assertions delivered non-stop by our daily newspapers, our televisions, our online news agencies, our social media, and our President.

"The mainstream newspapers, magazines, and television networks will continue to lay off reporters, reduce staff, and squeeze the funds available for good reporting, and especially for investigative reporting, with its high cost, unpredictable results, and its capacity for angering readers and attracting expensive lawsuits."

For those attempting to properly cover the activities of the rich and the powerful in sport, as much as in any other form of journalism, the words describe an increasingly grim future.

Just as sports journalists have developed an appetite for covering money, they might find they no longer have the resources to do it.

References

1. Keith Warsop, *The Early FA Cup Finals: And the Southern Amateurs, a Who's Who and Match Facts 1872 to 1883*, Self-published, Nottingham, UK, 2004.
2. Richard Sanders, *Beastly Fury: The Strange Birth of British Football*, Bantam Books: New York, 2009, p. 88.
3. Graham Phythian, *Shooting Stars: The Brief and Glorious History of Blackburn Olympic 1878–1889*, Tony Brown: Nottingham, 2007, cited in Sanders.
4. Sanders, pp. 87–88.
5. All quotes from David Conn come from a telephone interview conducted on 18 October 2019.
6. Anonymous, *Leeds United F.C. History*, in *The History of Leeds City Football Club*, http://www.ozwhitelufc.net.au/leeds_city_history/, accessed 5 December 2019.
7. Article reproduced at http://www.ozwhitelufc.net.au/leeds_city_history/, accessed 6 December 2019. It is also cited by Dave Tomlinson, *Leeds United: A History*, Amberley Publishing: Gloucestershire, UK, 2015. Gary Edwards, *Every Cloud: The Story of How Leeds City Became Leeds United*, Pitch Publishing: Sussex, 2019, also has an account.
8. Headline reproduced at http://www.mightyleeds.co.uk/history/scandal19.htm 8 December 2019,
9. Ibid.
10. Sean Gregory, "How California's historic NCAA fair pay law will change college sports for the better", *Time*, 1 October 2019, https://time.com/5689548/california-ncaa-law/, accessed 5 December 2019.
11. Peter J. Sloane, "The economics of professional football: The football club as a utility maximiser", *Scottish Journal of Political Economy*, Vol. 18, No. 2, pp. 121–146, February 1971.
12. Harold Seymour, *Baseball: The Golden Age*, Oxford University Press: New York, 1971, p. 14.
13. Mark Klein Steven, *Hugh S. Fullerton, the Black Sox Scandal, and the Ethical Impulse in Sports Writing*, MA Journalism thesis, Michigan State University, May 1997, p. 40, citing G. Edward White, *Creating the National Pastime 1903–1953*, Princeton University Press: Princeton, NJ, 1996.
14. Hugh Fullerton, *Chicago Herald-Examiner*, 10 October 2019.
15. Cited in, inter alia, Daniel A. Nathan, *Saying It's So: A Cultural History of the Black Sox Scandal*, University of Illinois Press: Champaign, IL, 2005, pp. 32–33.
16. *Stuart Dezenhall Newspaper Coverage of the 1919 Black Sox Scandal*, The Shirley Povich Center for Sports Journalism, undated, http://povichcenter.org/newspaper-coverage-of-the-1919-black-sox-scandal/, accessed 6 December 2019.
17. William F. Lamb, *The Black Sox Scandal*, Society for American Baseball Research. 2015. https://sabr.org/research/black-sox-scandal-bill-lamb, accessed 6 December 2019
18. Sarah Bembrey (ed.), *Ring Lardner Sr.: The Lardner Dynasty*, Interactive Media Lab: University of Florida, Gainesville, FL 1999.
19. Arthur Hopcraft, *The Football Man*, 1968, revised edition, Aurum Sports Classics: London, 2006.
20. Ibid, p. 209.
21. "Corruption in sport", https://www.interpol.int/en/Crimes/Corruption/Corruption-in-sport, accessed 5 December 2019.
22. John Holden, "The cautionary tale for US sports betting in Esports match-fixing struggles", *Legal Sports Report*, 23 September 2019, https://www.legalsportsreport.com/35511/esports-match-fixing-us-sports-betting/, accessed 5 December 2019.
23. Zion Market Research, report abstract, 21 December 2018, https://www.zionmarketresearch.com/report/sports-betting-market, accessed 5 December 2019; Statista, *Size of the online gambling market in 2017 and 2024*, abstract, 23 September 2019, https://www.statista.com/statistics/270728/market-volume-of-online-gaming-worldwide/, accessed 5 December 2019.
24. BBC, "Ronaldo fined €18.8m over tax evasion", 22 January 2019, https://www.bbc.com/news/world-europe-46957605, accessed 5 December 2019.

25. BBC, "Chelsea transfer ban: FIFA punishment 'after 150 rule breaches involving 69 academy players'", 1 November 2019, https://www.bbc.com/sport/football/50261117, accessed 5 December 2019.

26. Gerald Eskenazi, "NBC wins rights to '92 Olympics'", *The New York Times*, 2 December 1988, https://www.nytimes.com/1988/12/02/sports/nbc-wins-rights-to-92-olympics.html, accessed 5 December 2019 (paywall).

27. "A history of TV football rights", 25 February 2003, *The Guardian*, https://www.theguardian.com/media/2003/feb/25/broadcasting3, accessed 5 December 2019.

28. Jim Benson, "NBC, NFL shut out CBS", *Variety*, 20 December 1993, https://variety.com/1993/tv/news/nbc-nfl-shut-out-cbs-116661/, accessed 5 December 2019.

29. Sport Business report, "US sports media market will be worth $22.42bn in 2019 according to latest SportBusiness Global Media Report", London, 7 February 2019, https://media.sportbusiness.com/2019/02/the-us-media-rights-market-2018-global-media-report-extract/, accessed 5 December 2019.

30. Bill Gerrard and Wladimir Andreff, Stefan Szymanski (eds.), *Handbook on the Economics of Sport*, p. 710, Edward Elgar Publishing: Cheltenham, UK, 2006.

31. All quotes from Mihir Bose come from a telephone interview on 27 September 2019.

32. In the interests of transparency: I was sports editor of the *FT* at the time Paddy formally began covering sports finance.

33. Sara Morrison, "The toy department shall lead us. Why sports media have always been newsroom innovators", *Columbia Journalism Review*, New York, July/August 2014, https://archives.cjr.org/reports/the_toy_department_shall_lead.php, accessed 5 December 2019.

34. Seymour M. Hersh, *Reporter: A Memoir*, Penguin: New York, 2018, introduction (unnumbered pages).

22

National identity

Peter English

International sport dominates global calendars, and the widespread media reporting of these contests can highlight aspects of national identity through descriptions of matches and players. While these fixtures involve battles over on-field trophies and confrontations, they often form the backdrop to issues ranging from political or economic concerns, to a country's collective pride, and minor matters such as supporters having bragging rights over friends. Sport's importance is often dismissed, particularly in journalism,[1] but the exposure generated through bulging fixture lists and the subsequent mass media coverage underlines its value.

So much of sports reporting centres on scores, but international contests also contain elements magnifying issues beyond the on-field results. Consider the importance in an Asian context whenever India and Pakistan "play". Particularly in cricket, where the rivalry is at its most fierce, the stakes are sky-high between nations often in dispute – and audience figures nudge one billion.[2] In a more trivial case, think of the ribbing endured by Australian supporters during 2016, a year in which the cricket team lost five Test matches in a row, the Wallabies rugby union side was defeated on four consecutive occasions by England and the Olympic team underperformed in Rio.[3]

In international sport, each match is reported on by groups of journalists and the coverage has been found to highlight stereotypes, ideologies and "us against them" narratives.[4] In this context, this chapter examines national identity in sports journalism using the 2014–2015 Australia–India Test cricket series as a platform. A content analysis of 1,265 articles across eight newspapers in Australia and India was undertaken in conjunction with 18 interviews with newspaper cricket journalists. The results provide a valuable overview of elements of national identity in contemporary media.

Sport and national identity

A country's sporting team means many things to supporters, including providing a reflection of their nation.[5] These outfits are therefore responsible for providing collective self-esteem, with broadcast and print publications having an influential role in this process. Billings et al. note how boosting national pride in media is widespread.[6] Vincent and Kian highlight the complexity of national identity and sport,[7] but conclude the media are key figures in reinforcing ideologies:[8]

"Media coverage of major international sport generates particular narratives or preferred readings about collective national identity at the expense of alternative, subordinated articulations."[9] Further, Boyle and Haynes state sport is easily employed as "an indicator of certain national characteristics", and therefore representative of national identity. They provide the example of cricket and its Englishness.[10] In more specific cricket terms in relation to attitudes on the field, England are often considered to display a more conservative approach, Australian teams are aggressive and experts at sledging (verbally abusing) opponents, and India are formidable at home while being easybeats away. These often-casual media observations can develop into national sporting stereotypes.[11]

Boyle and Haynes recognise how the success of sporting teams, particularly at global events such as the Olympics, can operate as a "barometer" of a nation's position in the world.[12] An example of this was Australia's substandard performance in swimming, cycling and sailing at the Rio Olympics, and questions over funding models to improve for Tokyo 2020.[13] *The Courier-Mail*'s Mike Colman complained that the days of Australians teasing the British about their poor Olympic performances have gone.[14] The gloomy review in Australia was in contrast to the buoyant reporting of Great Britain's results.[15]

Hutchins and Rowe state watching national teams and athletes compete on the international stage is one of the key reasons people spectate, and it offers "cherished shared moments where partisan fans" cheer the contests and themselves.[16] Through this, they also note the power of nationalism through the media. Hundley and Billings argue that nationalism and team colours can be the main reason for people being interested in a match or event, whether they know about the sport or not.[17] Bairner states sport is associated with constructing national identities, but nationalism can rely too heavily on myths.[18] Vincent and Kian discuss how media invent traditions, and also utilise athletes as "symbolic national warriors" when competing on an international stage.[19] The invented tradition was evident in the commemorating of Phillip Hughes, the Australian cricketer who died two days after being struck by a ball during a match in Sydney in 2014, the first professional batsman to die in such a fashion since the 19th century.[20] The Australia–India Test series, for which Hughes had been on the verge of being selected, was delayed to allow players to attend his funeral. When the first Test began there was significant mourning, which included the inventing of traditions. This was particularly noticeable in the way numbers relevant to Hughes's life, such as 63 not out – his score when hit – and 408 – his Australian Test number – were remembered by the players and mentioned regularly in the media.

While national identity links with invented traditions, myths and stereotypes in the media, it can also provide an "us against them" mentality that drives audience engagement.[21] These narratives are likely to emerge in broadcast and print particularly in international contests or major events.[22] Vincent and Kian note how "we" and "our" are used in newspaper reports in comparisons with other nations, in order to generate "interest, unity and patriotism".[23] In examining the Olympics, Billings et al. state that home commentators are more likely to focus on local athletes, describing their courage or composure depending on the results.[24] This type of coverage is also evident in media cheerleading. I have highlighted the criticism of sports journalists for their supportive coverage of the home team or nation.[25] However, in a study combining interviews with sports journalists and a content analysis, I found more reports of a critical nature than those including cheerleading aspects. Previous research has also indicated that when audiences are unhappy with media coverage, they can redirect their emotion towards them. As Butterworth argues, when redemption is required "we may either look inwardly for a corrective, or we may seek a scapegoat".[26] In sporting terms, this can apply when a team is being criticised, and rather than attack the star athletes, supporters find fault with the media highlighting the issue. This is an extension of the "us versus them" narrative of sporting coverage, and will be examined in this study.

Cricket and national identity

With its focus on the 2014–2015 Test series between Australia and India, this study analyses the media coverage of two teams from Commonwealth nations with strong sporting links. Cricket is considered the national game in Australia and a religion in India.[27] Nationalism and imperialism factors have been noted in other international sporting contests.[28] Hutchins argues that cricket has been important in developing national identity in Australia, where it is a traditional, masculine, Anglo sport.[29] He states that Australian cricketers are "steely-eyed" like Steve Waugh and "rugged" like David Boon.[30] These descriptions fit with the narrative of Australian players being aggressive. India, in contrast, has crowds that are passionate, volatile and colourful.[31] Ugra notes how cricket's symbolic importance has "intensified" in the "New India" environment.[32] Writing before the advent in 2008 of the Indian Premier League, which increased the profile of franchises, she highlighted the impact of the national side: "Cricket has become a motif of a modern Indian identity but one that is completely at the mercy of many notions of nationalism."[33] A decade later, India's rivalry with Australia is considered in some media as being bigger than the Ashes contest between Australia and England.[34] Crucially in this setting, Vincent and Kian argue that the widespread appeal of international sport provides an important base for analysis of national identity.[35] Therefore, this series is a valuable platform for an analysis of national identity in the media.

Method

International sport is consumed through mass media, and in this study newspaper journalists and their publications are the units of analysis. A multi-method approach is utilised, combining a content analysis of 1,265 newspaper articles focusing on the four-Test series between Australia and India with in-depth interviews of 18 journalists covering the matches. The content analysis was employed to determine how many reports included aspects of national identity. Stories were collected from eight newspapers, four each from Australia and India (see Table 22.1). The sample was determined to provide publications across broadsheet and tabloid titles, taking into consideration national, metropolitan and circulation characteristics to ensure equivalence.[36] Articles were collected from 8 December 2014 to 10 January 2015 to cover the length of the series. Only stories from Monday to Saturday editions were included, and all articles related

Table 22.1 Descriptions of national identity in cricket articles

	Articles containing elements of national identity	%	Total stories
The Australian	46	28.2	163
The Sydney Morning Herald	59	24.5	241
Herald Sun	47	21.7	217
The West Australian	18	22.8	79
Australia	**170**	**24.3**	**700**
The Times of India	35	19.6	179
Hindustan Times	32	19.5	164
Mumbai Mirror	13	17.8	73
Mid-day	26	17.4	149
India	**106**	**18.8**	**565**
Total	276	21.8	1,265

specifically to coverage of the series in the sport and news sections of the newspapers. Each article was coded using SPSS and was specifically focused on answering the following questions: are descriptions of national identity evident? How is national identify evident? And which nation's national identity is being mentioned?

To complete the data collection, in-depth interviews were undertaken with nine journalists from each nation in the media centres of the Brisbane and Sydney venues during the second and fourth Test matches. The interviews were conducted between 15 December 2014 and 6 January 2015, averaging 25 minutes. Eleven of the sports journalists were from broadsheet/quality publications, and seven were from tabloid titles. The average age of the respondents was 43, and they had worked for an average of 15 years in cricket journalism. Respondents, who were guaranteed anonymity, were asked whether national identity influenced their writing during a major international event; whether they were expected to support their national team through their stories; and what happened if they wrote critically of their national team?

Results and discussion

In the content analysis, articles with mentions of national identity aspects were present in 276 of the 1,265 (21.8 per cent) stories in the sample. A story was coded as including national identity elements if it contained national, location or team characteristics or descriptions. In Australian terms, for example, this included mentions of mateship, toughness,[37] players being aggressive or sledging and symbols such as the side's baggy green cap. Specifically Indian traits included aspects such as cricket being a religion, the team having expert spin bowlers or struggling away from home, players and supporters being passionate and mentions of Team India.[38] Pride, uniforms, badges and flags were also coded as containing national identity elements, along with characteristics of the nations, cities or grounds hosting the contests. This series was played less than two weeks after the death of Hughes. Tributes to Hughes were particularly prevalent in the first Test in Adelaide, with key aspects being his Test number (408) and references to 63 not out, the score he was on when struck. These figures quickly became part of the national identity of Australian cricket, linking with the inventing of traditions outlined by Vincent and Kian,[39] and were coded in this way.

Australia had a higher proportion of national identity aspects in stories, with these mentions in 24.3 per cent of articles, compared with 18.8 per cent in the Indian publications. As the host, Australia had more local issues for the print journalists to focus on, and won the four-match series 2-0. The results, along with the focus generated by the commemoration of Hughes,[40] may have contributed to the higher proportion of national identity aspects in the Australian coverage. In relation to the individual newspapers, there were similarities between the publications in their own nations. *The Australian* had the highest number of stories with national identity elements (28.2 per cent) while the *Herald Sun* had the fewest (21.7 per cent). In India, there was an even smaller range, with the *Times of India* having the highest proportion (19.6 per cent) and *Mid-day* the lowest (17.4 per cent).

Articles mentioning national identity were examined further to place them into specific categories. These included team stereotypes, national pride, location and mentions of Hughes. Due to the high number of articles initially coded under team stereotypes (162 of 276 stories; 58.7 per cent), this category was re-coded to create another of aggression, which included elements of sledging and toughness. Team stereotypes included, for example, India's opposition to the Decision Review System for contentious umpiring, or being poor performers away from home, or the Australian players being good mates. National pride included mentions of

Australia's baggy green cap or Team India; location involved national, city or ground characteristics. Stories were coded in the Hughes category if they mentioned 63 not out, 408 or tributes.

Aggression was the most prevalent category, particularly in relation to Australia's behaviour, including their sledging. There were 99 articles in the 276 national identity stories (35.9 per cent), with a greater focus on these identity aspects in the Indian publications (38.7 per cent) than in Australia (34.1 per cent). This indicates that the issues of aggression and sledging are slightly more newsworthy to the visiting media. In Australia, reporting these aspects could be considered normalised as part of the team's and nation's identity through its masculine, tough approach.[41] The second-largest category was team stereotypes (22.8 per cent). Indian publications again had the larger proportion of stories (26.4 per cent) compared to Australia (20.6 per cent).

The Hughes and location categories both received 14.9 per cent of mentions. Hughes stories were more than twice as likely to appear in Australian publications (19.4 per cent) than in India (7.5 per cent), which was unsurprising given that Hughes was a former Australian player and there was widespread mourning across the nation.[42] It was also unsurprising that the touring Indian journalists were more likely to mention location characteristics (23.6 per cent) than the Australians (9.4 per cent), given the hosts' familiarity with conditions and landmarks. National pride elements made up 11.6 per cent of the sample, with all but four of the mentions appearing in the 28 articles in Australian publications. This result suggests a relationship with cheerleading aspects,[43] such as a greater promotion of national pride when a team is playing – and winning – at home.

In this analysis, it is also relevant to examine who is writing about the national identity elements to understand whether the focus is on the home or away team. This can provide an indication of "us versus them" coverage.[44] Articles were coded to determine whether a story was detailing national identity aspects of the publication's own nation, or the other nation. The majority of stories mentioning national identity were focused on the publication's own nation, but this was due to the high proportion of Australian content (see Table 22.2).

Australian publications were predominantly focused on the national identity of their own team, including these descriptions in 81.8 per cent of stories compared with 32.1 per cent in India. Interestingly, Indian publications were more likely to mention national identity characteristics of Australia, with these elements appearing in 67.9 per cent of articles. One of the aspects of touring journalists is to find local angles and report on novel issues for readers. This could

Table 22.2 National identity aspects in articles by nation of publication

	Own nation	% of own nation	Other nation	% of other nation	Total national identity articles
The Australian	38	82.6	8	17.4	46
The Sydney Morning Herald	48	81.4	11	18.6	59
Herald Sun	39	83.0	8	17.0	47
The West Australian	14	77.8	4	22.2	18
Australia	**139**	**81.8**	**31**	**18.2**	**170**
The Times of India	12	34.3	23	65.7	35
Hindustan Times	12	37.5	20	62.5	32
Mumbai Mirror	3	23.1	10	76.9	13
Mid-day	7	26.9	19	73.1	26
India	**34**	**32.1**	**72**	**67.9**	**106**
Total	173	62.7	103	37.3	276

occur in relation to behaviour or location characteristics, as well as the emphasis on Hughes. In Australia, the results indicate that the identity of the Australian team is more important to their publications and, by extension, their audience. The *Herald Sun* was the most focused on Australian identity (83.0 per cent) but the amounts were again relatively similar among Australian publications. There were broader differences in the Indian titles, with the tabloid titles *Mumbai Mirror* and *Mid-day* less focused on Indian elements of identity than their counterparts. Overall, the national identity of Australia was more newsworthy in the coverage of both nations. Billings et al. found a greater focus on home athletes, including to produce more audience engagement, and the "us versus them" approach has also been recognised.[45] In these results, the focus on "us" is certainly reflected in the Australian publications but, unusually, in the Indian newspapers the "them" of Australia was considered more newsworthy.

In-depth interview analysis

The influence of national identity in relation to cricket was evident in the interview responses of both nations' sports journalists, although it applied in different ways. In setting the scene, an Australian tabloid journalist said that while there were multiple football codes in Australia, there was only one national cricket side. "The national identity of the Aussie cricket team is a big deal and I think people share a sense of ownership. If you win the World Cup, and if you don't win it, they share a sense of what the hell is going on with these players" This national background influenced the way stories were covered, especially during matches in Australia, where the audience expected the team to win. This aspect links with the national pride category in the content analysis. While this category had a relatively small amount in the content analysis at 11.6 per cent, its stories were published almost exclusively in the Australian newspapers. Analytics and audience feedback were also likely to influence the types of stories being produced. A broadsheet journalist said it was unfortunate that "Australian readers were more interested in Australia in stories". This meant he – and other journalists in the study – had to produce more content on the local team than the touring side. While these comments are not as direct as in previous research, they link with the "us and them" coverage in sport.[46] The perception that local content is more important than opposition material means there will be a greater focus on the traits of the country's own sportspeople – the "us" rather than the "them". These comments align with the Australian results of the content analysis in relation to national identity, with these publications focusing predominantly on their own country and team characteristics. Previous research from these interviews revealed an Australian journalist saying he looked at everything through "Australian eyes" because that suited his audience; as a result, his coverage was "slanted in that direction".[47] However, support of the home side was not generally required – or desired – by the Australian journalists. One reporter said he never felt he had to support the home team, but did feel the pull of his nationality occasionally: "Of course we're all seduced at times by patriotic tendencies, you have a stirring for Australia when you know you're an Australian." Another said that in more than a decade and a half of reporting on Australia he had never hoped they would win. Almost all of the Australian reporters indicated they were attempting to remain detached.

In contrast, many of the Indian journalists felt closer to the players and passionate about their nation. A broadsheet journalist argued that there were journalists who covered the Indian team who were proud of their connections: "It's kind of engrained in our system so when people become journalists they want to be seen with cricketers and they take great pride in knowing cricketers." He said that when journalists started to call players their friends, it put pressure on their coverage. Other respondents described their relationship with players in the squad as friendships. Patriotic feelings of the reporters towards the team were also on display in some responses. An Indian tabloid journalist said being a follower of the nation brought strong emotions: "At the end of the day, everybody's passionate about his country." Further, a broadsheet journalist recognised how passion may emerge in reports, and that it was difficult to maintain objectivity at times. A reporter for a vernacular paper said having readers who were so passionate meant writing in support of India. However, a broadsheet journalist said he would only "support with the truth" in his reports. Ugra noted the passion of the Indian fans[48] and the nationalistic elements involved in the game, which in this study are evident in the perceptions of some of the newspaper journalists. When the interview responses are compared with the content analysis, it is interesting to note how in terms of national identity the Indian journalists were more likely to write about Australian traits than those of their own team. This was despite the close ties with players and the audience's India-centric focus.

The narrative of national identity can be threatened when the media reports critically on their national team, stepping away from what Vincent and Kian describe as the preferred readings.[49] Journalists from both nations outlined occasions when they or their colleagues had been targeted through feedback in letters, emails, social media and fan forums. As a senior Australian tabloid journalist said: "You've got to have a crocodile skin and just get on with life, and you've got to accept that there's about four days a year which I call 'flak jacket days'." One broadsheet reporter noted how journalists received "some pretty firm bounce-back" if they criticised players. In India, multiple journalists agreed that targeting the superstar players would create a widespread, negative response. An Indian broadsheet writer said readers "do not take it kindly" when India – or a key player – is criticised: "The moment you write something against a star cricketer you know you will be fighting a lonely battle and you know you must be prepared for it." This was because the cricket followers put the players "on a pedestal and they cannot accept criticism". These responses link with Butterworth's argument that in times when redemption is required people look for a scapegoat.[50] With audience feedback, the anger directed at the journalists appears to be readers looking for targets when their favourite players are under attack for performing poorly.

Alternatively, many journalists in both nations said their readers expected them to highlight poor team or individual performances. In India, it was considered "okay" to criticise the team if they played badly and the readers would "expect" that type of coverage. One Indian broadsheet journalist noted how there were different expectations when India was playing away from home "because India never do well outside". This approach fits within the team stereotypes category of the content analysis, in which Indian publications had a higher proportion of articles. Another broadsheet journalist said the Indian readers could object, but they were more likely to have a problem if the journalists were "praising the team too much or defending the team too much". This trait was also recognised by some of the Australian journalists. As a tabloid journalist said: "You find that for a lot of people you're not critical enough of the Australian team or particular Australian players." A senior broadsheet journalist said a critical eye was expected: "People don't want cheerleading, they want news and analysis." This comment supports the findings of English, who highlighted more reports in this Australia–India series that were critical than those considered cheerleading.[51] The responses from the journalists regarding national identity narratives highlight an "us versus them" approach in some cases, especially in India with star players, but in other responses there is an expectation that the journalists are critical of their team. In these cases, it's "us against us", but only when the journalists consider it necessary.

National identity in media coverage can provide revealing elements in the reporting of matches and players, with these aspects also situated into broader narratives within individual, community and international contexts. While results, quotes and key moments often dominate coverage of sporting fixtures, there is space for descriptions relating to broader perceptions of athletes, teams and their countries. This may develop into an "us against them" storyline or include myths, stereotypes or invented traditions.[52]

National identity elements were prominent in both methods of this study into newspaper coverage of the 2014–2015 Australia–India Test series, although not always in expected ways. Descriptions of these traits were clear in the content analysis, where almost a quarter of stories in Australia, and almost one in five articles in India, contained these types of descriptions. However, the results were contrasting when focusing on whether the national identity content focused on "us" or "them". Australian publications looked predominantly at their own team, whereas the Indian titles were considerably more interested in Australia. This finding goes against previous home-team research,[53] although the current study is concerned specifically with national identity aspects and not broader types of coverage, such as the number of articles and subjects of stories. The in-depth interviews also reflected the influence of national identity on reporting. In Australia, the responses aligned with the content analysis in terms of the home focus. However, in India the audience demands, personal friendships and patriotic tendencies could lead to more support of their side. These findings are valuable in an international media context, but it is important to note they are based on one cricket series between two nations. Further research examining global contests, such as the Olympics or World Cup formats, would be beneficial in providing a comprehensive overview of national identity in contemporary sports reporting.

References

1. Marie Hardin, Bu Zhong and Erin Whiteside, "Sports coverage: 'Toy department' or public-service journalism? The relationship between reporters' ethics and attitudes toward the profession", *International Journal of Sport Communication*, Volume 2, 2009, pp. 319–339; David Rowe, "Still the 'toy department' of the news media?", *Journalism*, Volume 8, Issue 4, 2007, pp. 385–405.

2. Ravi Agrawal, "India vs. Pakistan: How a great cricketing rivalry matured", CNN.com, 15 February 2015, https://edition.cnn.com/2015/02/15/intl_opinion/india-pakistan-cricket-world-cup/index.html, accessed 11 December 2019; *The Economist*, "India and Pakistan's cricketing rivalry has always been about more than sport", March 2016, http://www.economist.com/blogs/gametheory/2016/03/not-just-game, accessed 11 December 2019.

3. See Paul Connolly, "Australia's well-planned, well-funded Olympic over-achievement is finished", *The Guardian*, 22 August 2016, https://www.theguardian.com/sport/2016/aug/22/australias-well-planned-well-funded-olympic-over-achievement-is-finished.

4. Andrew Billings, James Angelini and Dan Wu, "Nationalistic notions of the superpowers: Comparative analyses of the American and Chinese telecasts in the 2008 Beijing Olympiad", *Journal of Broadcasting & Electronic Media*, Volume 55, Issue 2, 2011, pp. 251–66; Michael Butterworth, "Do you believe in nationalism?", in Heather Hundley and Andrew Billings (eds.), *Examining Identity in Sports Media*, SAGE Publications: Los Angeles, CA, 2010, pp. 133–152; Jon Garland and Mike Rowe, "War minus the shooting? Jingoism, the English press, and Euro '96", *Journal of Sport & Social Issues*, Volume 23, Issue 1, 1999, pp. 80–95; John Vincent and Edward Kian, "Sport, new media, and national identity", in Andrew Billings and Marie Hardin (eds.), *Routledge Handbook of Sport and New Media*, Routledge: Abingdon, UK, 2013, pp. 299–310.

5. Raymond Boyle and Richard Haynes, *Power Play: Sport, the Media and Popular Culture* (2nd ed.), Edinburgh University Press: Edinburgh, UK, 2009; Brett Hutchins, "Unity, difference and the 'national game': Cricket and Australian national identity", in Stephen Wagg (ed.), *Cricket and National Identity in the Postcolonial Age*, Routledge: London, 2005, pp. 9–27; Brett Hutchins and David Rowe, *Sport Beyond Television: The Internet, Digital Media and the Rise of Networked Media Sport*, Routledge: New York, 2012; Sharda Ugra, "Play together, live apart: Religion, politics and markets in Indian cricket since 1947", in Stephen Wagg (ed.), *Cricket and National Identity in the Postcolonial Age*, Routledge: London, 2005, pp. 77–93.

6. Billings et al. 2011.

7. See also Hutchins and Rowe 2012.

8. Kian and Vincent 2013.

9. Kian and Vincent 2013, p. 307.

10. Haynes and Boyle 2009, p. 144; see also Stephen Wagg (ed.), *Cricket and National Identity in the Postcolonial Age*, Routledge: London, 2005.

11. See Garland and Rowe 1999.

12. Haynes and Boyle 2009, p. 145.

13. Connolly 2016.

14. Mike Colman, "Great Britain has obliterated Australia at the 2016 Rio Olympics", *The Courier-Mail*, 20 August 2016, http://www.couriermail.com.au/sport/olympics-2016/great-britain-has-obliterated-australia-at-the-2016-rio-olympics/news-story/3acd66f9bee3dfac46003d3c3fe302d2, accessed 11 December 2019.

15. For an example, see Owen Gibson, "Team GB's Olympic success: Five factors behind their Rio medal rush", *The Guardian*, 15 August 2016, https://www.theguardian.com/sport/blog/2016/aug/15/five-factors-team-gb-olympic-success-medal-rush, accessed 11 December 2019.

16. Rowe and Hutchins 2012, p. 122.

17. Heather Hundley and Andrew Billings (eds.), *Examining Identity in Sports Media*, SAGE Publications: Los Angeles, CA, 2010.

18. Alan Bairner, *Sport, Nationalization, and Globalization: European and North American Perspectives*, SUNY Press: Albany, NY, 2001.

19. Vincent and Kian 2013, p. 302.

20. Peter English, "The death of Phillip Hughes: Ccommemorative journalism and the cricket community", *Communication & Sport*, 2015, pp. 1–15. doi: 10.1177/2167479515597656

21. Billings et al. 2011; Butterworth 2010; Vincent and Kian 2013.

22. Andrew Billings, "Clocking gender differences: Televised Olympic clock time in the 1996–2006 summer and winter Olympics", *Television & New Media*, Volume 9, Issue 5, 2008, pp. 429–441.

23. Vincent and Kian 2013, p. 302.

24. Billings et al. 2011.

25. Peter English, "Cheerleaders or critics? Australian and Indian sports journalists in the contemporary age", *Digital Journalism*, 2016. doi: 10.1080/21670811.2016.1209082; see also Hardin et al. 2009; Rowe 2007.

26. Butterworth 2010, p. 148.

27. Hutchins 2005; Ugra 2005.

28. For an example, see Rob Steen, "Uneasy Ryder: The Ryder Cup, anti-Americanism and the 'Yoo-rop' phenomenon", *Sport in Society*, Volume 18, Issue 3, 2015, pp. 347–363.

29. Hutchins 2005.

30. Hutchins 2005, p. 13.

31. Urga 2005; see also Manu Madan, "It's not just cricket", *Journal of Sport and Social Issues*, Volume 24, Issue 1, 2000, pp. 24–35.

32. Ugra 2005, p. 79.

33. Ugra 2005, p. 92.

34. Amin Ali, "Australia–India cricket rivalry has even bettered Ashes: John Harnden", *The Times of India*, 30 June 2014, http://timesofindia.indiatimes.com/interviews/Australia-India-cricket-rivalry-has-even-bettered-Ashes-John-Harnden/articleshow/37477233.cms, accessed 11 December 2019.

35. Vincent and Kian 2013.

36. Patrick Rössler, "Comparative content analysis", in Frank Esser and Thomas Hanitzsch (eds.), *The Handbook of Comparative Communication Research*, Routledge: New York, 2012, pp. 459–468.

37. See Hutchins 2005.

38. See Madan 2000; Urga 2005.

39. Vincent and Kian 2013.

40. See English 2015.

41. See Hutchins 2005.
42. Ibid.
43. See English 2016; Hardin et al. 2009; Rowe 2007.
44. Billings et al. 2011; Butterworth 2010; Vincent and Kian 2013.
45. Ibid.
46. Ibid.
47. English 2016, p. 8.
48. Ugra 2005; see also Madan 2000.
49. Vincent and Kian 2013.
50. Butterworth 2010.
51. English 2016.
52. Billings et al. 2011; Butterworth 2010; Garland and Rowe 1999; Vincent and Kian 2013.
53. See Billings et al. 2011.

23

The Olympics

Gareth Edwards

The Olympics are the biggest sporting event in the world, all but unrivalled in terms of scale, profitability and global reach. The trappings of the Olympic brand – the five rings of the Olympic flag, the torch relay, the opening and closing ceremonies – are instantly recognisable, even to those who would normally claim little interest in sport. As Joseph Maguire has noted, the Olympics are "not merely of supreme significance in the world of sports, but as a carrier of cultural meanings which are almost uniquely available to vast international audiences".[1]

More than this, the Games have become, in Garry Whannel's oft-quoted phrase, "the ultimate media festival".[2] Television, rather than attendance, is the main way in which the Olympics are now experienced. Coverage of the Games through various mediums – television, radio, print and, increasingly, online – is consumed by billions of people the world over. This media attention has helped "to transform the nature, scale and interest" in the Olympics, making it the sporting phenomenon we see today.[3]

From curiosity to global spectacle

The driving force behind the renovation of the ancient Greek Olympics was Baron Pierre de Coubertin, a French aristocrat and Hellenophile, who believed sport could be harnessed for the good of the world.[4] Coubertin envisaged a sporting festival that not only celebrated athletic excellence but would also help to "[g]radually efface the peoples' ignorance of things which concern them all, an ignorance which feeds hatreds, accumulated misunderstandings and hurtles events along a barbarous path towards a merciless conflict".[5]

Little about the first modern Olympiad, staged by Athens in 1896, matched the lofty ambitions and noble ideals of the Baron. Instead the Games have been characterised as "happily chaotic".[6] Spread over 10 days, 241 athletes from 14 nations (the vast majority of whom were Greek) took part in nine sports, and the general standard of competition was poor. One Olympic historian has suggested most of the "English [athletes] were there by accident, and the Americans were there to have a good time".[7] The Irishman, John Pius Boland, who had travelled to Greece as a tourist, won both the singles and doubles tennis competitions after being entered into the draw by a friend.

While the renovated Olympics received a degree of interest from the British press, reporting was sparse, and, at times, disdainful – an editorial in *The Spectator* dismissed the event as mere "athletic whim".[8] Letters appeared in *The Times* prior to the Games doubting venues would be completed on time or value for money. Charles Waldstein, who would compete in Greece, felt compelled to rebut suggestions that preparation "was not progressing favourably; that the site and buildings could not be completed before the games began; and that the whole celebration was not likely to be a success".[9]

The *Manchester Guardian* did carry some limited reports of sporting events, with progress of the lawn tennis, cycling and swimming competitions appearing courtesy of telegrams from Reuters, the international news organisation. Interestingly, the paper also reported that foreign correspondents and representatives of the local press were guests at a luncheon hosted by the Greek royal family, an early example of the Games being used as political capital.[10]

The Athens Olympics may represent relatively humble beginnings, but the Games have subsequently grown from "fin-de-siècle curiosity into an international cultural performance of global proportions".[11] Today the Olympics offer an unparalleled sporting spectacle, an exemplar of what Maurice Roche has described as a "mega-event", defined as "large scale cultural events which have a dramatic character, mass popular appeal and international significance".[12] The 2016 Summer Games, held in Rio, saw more than 11,000 athletes from over 200 countries compete in 306 separate events spread across 26 sports.[13] The estimated global television audience was in excess of 3.5 billion.

In addition, more than 25,000 media personnel from across the globe were present, more than double the number of competitors. It is the continuation of a trend, beginning at the Barcelona Olympics in 1992, whereby the "total number of accredited press at the Games has exceeded the number of athletes".[14] The purpose-built media facilities in the Brazilian capital accounted for a reported $942 million, out of a total cost of $16.7 billion.[15] The level of media attention ensured Rio was, in the words of International Olympic Committee (IOC) President Thomas Bach, "the most consumed Olympic Games ever".[16]

The continued popularity of the Olympic Games is, in some ways, difficult to explain. Many of the world's most watched sports (cricket, American football, motor racing in its various incarnations) do not feature in the Olympics programme at all, while others do so in a particular format (Under-23 football, rugby sevens). Even so, the Olympics, with its motto *Citius, Altius, Fortius* (Faster, Higher, Stronger), have become a byword for athletic excellence, much as Coubertin had hoped, and mere participation represents the pinnacle of a sporting career for many athletes.

The American sports journalist Dave Zirin has suggested part of the Olympics' popularity rests on it being "one of the few times when women athletes get to have the highest possible stage".[17] London 2012 was the first Olympiad in which women competed in every sport, comprising 44 per cent of all participants. Saudi Arabia's decision to send two female athletes, Wojdan Shaherkani and Sarah Attar, meant the London Games were also the first in which no countries excluded women competitors.[18] One might also argue that, by showcasing a range of sports, including a number that might be described as "niche", it offers a welcome change of pace for both the casual and dedicated fan alike.

Sport alone cannot fully explain the popularity of the Olympics. It is clear that people are drawn to the Games as a vehicle for expressions of nationalism, despite the proclamations of the Olympic Charter, which states that the "Games are competitions between athletes in individual or team events and not between countries".[19] Contradictorily, the appeal of the Olympics also lies in its message of global cultural exchange and peaceful competition – the strand of Coubertin's thought that John Hoberman identified as "idealistic internationalism".[20]

The attraction of the Olympic Games, therefore, does not rest on a single premise, but on a multiplicity of factors: the diversity of sports and athletes showcased, the promise of athletic excellence, national pride and a sense of peaceful internationalism. This, in turn, begins to explain the appeal of the Games to the media. As Dick Ebersol, one-time NBC Sports President, has argued, the primary value of the Olympics is in being "the only thing in all of television guaranteed to put the whole family in front of the TV set".[21]

The success and popularity of the men's football World Cup means that Ebersol's observation, made more than two decades ago, needs a little revision. The Olympic Games may still retain its appeal across all sections of society, but FIFA's tournament has become an equally grandiose affair. The 2018 World Cup, staged in Russia, was watched by more than 3 billion people, with the final reaching an estimated live audience of more than 1.1 billion.[22] Although sponsorship revenue was down, broadcast rights for the 2015–2018 cycle accounted for more than $3 billion, and total profits were buoyed by the sale of marketing rights and the licensing rights to the EA Sports *FIFA* video game franchise.[23] As such, the examples of both the Olympics and the World Cup show the potential for television to turn sport "into a set of commodified global spectacles, producing huge audiences and massive new sources of income".[24]

The sporting triangle

The Olympics, alongside the FIFA World Cup, are one of the most high-profile examples of the "sporting triangle", the three-way relationship between sport, the media and sponsorship.[25] Barry Smart has succinctly summarised this relationship: "Sport offers commercial companies the prospect of world-wide television exposure for their products and services. The money from the sale of television and marketing rights in turn has transformed sport."[26] Similar connections are to be found throughout professional sports but, by virtue of their status and popularity, the "Olympics stand at the apex of global sports and provide a model for other sports providers".[27] As such, it is worth taking a moment to establish the size and scale of the connections between the Games, their sponsors and the media.

That corporations wish to associate themselves with the Olympics, either through spot advertising or via official partnerships with the IOC, is unsurprising. In addition to the extraordinary reach of the Games, multinationals desire proximity to the Olympic brand itself. This, according to market research carried out on behalf of the IOC in the 1990s, is comprised of four key elements: hope, dreams and inspiration, friendship and fair play, and joy in effort.[28] As Michael Payne, formerly the head of the IOC's marketing division, stated: "It became clear that non-commercial values provided the Olympic brand with its true commercial value to the marketing partners."[29]

The "commercial value" of the Olympics is evident in the joint-sponsorship deal signed between the IOC and Coca-Cola and the Chinese firm Mengniu Dairy. Worth more than $3 billion, it guarantees exclusive Olympic rights from 2021 until 2032 and is one of the most expensive sponsorship deals in the history of sport.[30] Having entered into such lucrative sponsorship agreements, the IOC is as keen to police the integrity of its brand as it is the integrity of sport, and media guidelines are produced which explain in detail how the five rings of the Olympic logo are to be used.[31]

Broadcasters are similarly drawn to the promise of large Olympic audiences and, in the case of commercial networks, the accompanying advertising revenue. While the accuracy of viewing figures has been questioned, it has not stopped networks renewing their Olympic broadcast deals.[32] In 2014, the American broadcaster NBC paid $7.5 billion to secure the rights of every Olympiad until 2032.[33] The sale of television rights remains the single most important income stream for the IOC: in 2018, the IOC recorded revenue in excess of $5 billion, with the sale of broadcasting rights accounting for 73 per cent of this figure.[34]

The sporting triangle is more than a description of financial transactions: it also functions as a framework for understanding how sport – especially televised sport – is shaped by wider forces. The US media, in particular, has exercised considerable influence over Olympic scheduling. The Calgary Winter Games in 1988 were "stretched to three weekends as a condition of the $309 million ABC Television contract for North American rights".[35] The finals of both the gymnastics and swimming competitions at the Beijing Olympics were rescheduled so as to synchronise with primetime in the United States.[36]

The responsibility for the production of live television, radio and digital coverage of the Games actually lies with the Olympic Broadcasting Services (OBS). Its content is subsequently distributed to Rights Holding Broadcasters (RHBs) around the globe. In the case of Rio 2016, OBS deployed more than a thousand cameras to generate over 7,000 hours of content, shown in 200 countries and territories. OBS stress their coverage "is neutral, favouring no particular country or athlete".[37] Yet this basic footage is only the raw material for a Rights Host Broadcaster. The final Olympic programme remains, as with all televised sport, the result of editorial choices:

> Television does not simply relay sport to us. It presents a particular view of sport, framed by its own selection of shots and the addition of its own commentary. It is a particular view, inviting us to look at events in a particular way. The attempt to reach, through entertainment values, a large audience means a constant attempt to forge links with that audience, to establish points of identification.[38]

Televised sport is, therefore, a highly mediated product, and the Olympic Games are no exception. As Michael Real has so eruditely noted, "no two countries see the same Olympics".[39] Traditionally, with only one or two channels available, RHBs have been forced to "make overt choices about what to show (selection), what to show a lot (emphasis) and what to avoid (exclusion) within a given telecast".[40] Sports broadcasting naturally gravitates towards action, drama and human interest stories. But network decisions over which sports and personalities to feature prominently are the result of a number of additional considerations.

Most obviously, RHBs tend to prioritise athletes from their home countries, particularly those with the possibility of a medal, no matter which sport. There is also an informal hierarchy of sports at the Olympics (athletics features more heavily than fencing, for example), national and personal rivalries are given exposure and there is a focus on the global sports star (Usain Bolt, Michael Phelps, Simone Biles etc.). The advent of digital technologies, however, has afforded broadcasters unprecedented opportunities to deliver comprehensive coverage of the Olympic Games.

New media; old narratives

In 1956, Avery Brundage, then in the early years of his lengthy reign as IOC president, is reported to have said: "The IOC has managed without TV for sixty years and, believe me we are going to manage for another sixty."[41] As a staunch defender of the Olympics' amateur ethos, Brundage feared revenue generated from the sale of television rights would in some way taint the Games. This opinion did not go unchallenged inside the IOC, and, in reality, the Olympics were at the beginning of an ever-closer relationship with television and have become "a standard bearer of innovation in broadcasting".[42]

At the London Games in 1948, the BBC broadcast 64 hours of footage and its coverage "was revelatory, as was the ability to pull athletes straight from their events in front of the cameras for an interview".[43] By 1960, live coverage in Italy of the Rome Olympics was supplemented by video recordings distributed to a further 20 countries. It was the birth of satellite technology, however, that transformed the way in which the Games were broadcast and "enormously increased the potential audience for live coverage".[44] In 1964, the opening ceremony of the Tokyo Olympics was beamed directly to the United States; just four years later, satellite transmissions carried the Mexico Games around the world.

By this stage, the potential of the new technology was obvious. The debate inside the IOC was resolved in favour of those who argued, just as sections of the membership had suggested in the mid-1950s that embracing television coverage could only help the IOC fulfil its objective of spreading the message of Olympism around the globe. Money would also help in this objective, and so the IOC changed its own rules in 1972 to guarantee itself the majority share of television revenues. Since this point, "competition between the networks has driven up the value of rights dramatically".[45]

The advent of digital media has proved to be another watershed moment for Olympic broadcasting. At the London 2012 Games, the BBC covered the most popular events on its main terrestrial channel, but the audience was also able to access other sports that were simultaneously being broadcast online and via the BBC's digital network. The BBC claimed that almost 52 million people in the UK watched at least 15 minutes of the Olympics on television, while 24 million watched coverage on one of the BBC's digital platforms.[46]

The need for broadcasters to diversify their Olympic output was made clear in 2016, when NBC's coverage of the Rio Games saw a marked decline in viewing figures compared with the previous Summer Olympics. The average audience of 27.8 million for the first 10 days of competition was down 17 per cent from London 2012, representing what Andrew Zimbalist termed a "cultural shift" in viewing habits with younger sports fans more likely to stream content than watch on television.[47]

Sensitive to the possibilities opened up by new media, the IOC announced in 2014 that it had begun work on the Olympic Channel, an over-the-top (OTT) streaming service, in addition to the Olympic website and social media presence.[48] Eventually launched in 2016, the channel carries a selection of news, live events, archive material and original series.[49] The rationale behind it was announced in suitably Olympian tones:

We must give our athletes and sports the worldwide media exposure they deserve also between Olympic Games. We must give our many actions in the humanitarian, cultural and social field the attention they deserve. We must give the youth better access to athletes, sport, Olympic History, Olympic Culture and Olympic Values.[50]

The Olympic Channel is, therefore, both a response to the changing media landscape and an attempt to relate to a new generation whose viewership is imperative to the continuation of the Games. Just months after the launch of the Olympic Channel, the IOC proudly announced:

In just four months to the end of 2016, the Channel had already distributed more than 4,000 pieces of video content, resulting in more than 428.5 million video views and 1.588 billion impressions on social media alone. Most significantly, 52 per cent of visitors to the digital platform and 94 per cent of the Channel's Facebook followers are aged under 35.[51]

The Olympic Channel might also be seen as part of the IOC's wider attempts to manage the media narratives that surround the Games. As Christopher Shaw contends, the framing of the

Summer and Winter Games is "carefully constructed".[52] The Olympics may be, above all else, a sporting festival, but the aims of the Olympic movement have never been limited to a two-week window of competition. As the IOC state, the "goal of Olympism is to place sport at the service of the harmonious development of humankind".[53]

Between Games, the Olympic movement continues "to spread and promote the principles of Olympism".[54] But the stories that appear in the media during these periods are not always positive and, while rarely acknowledged by officials, the Olympics are beset by problems. In a rare moment of candour, Bach has "acknowledged that the Olympic Games are mired in crisis".[55] The doping controversies that have engulfed athletics and cycling are a small, but very real, part of the explanation. Similarly, there is concern that young people are uninterested in the Olympics, which helps to explain the IOC's flirtation with eSports.

Yet the real struggle for the IOC is in finding cities willing and capable of hosting an Olympic Games, the cost and size of which seem to grow exponentially. A number of locations touted as possible Olympic hosts – Krakow, Hamburg, Munich, Budapest, Innsbruck, Davos – have seen their citizens vote against plans to stage the Games. Faced with an existential threat, the IOC is turning to nations with poor human rights records, which, at least in theory, contravene the Olympic Charter. In February 2019, Gian-Franco Kasper, who until 2018 was a member of the IOC, said with reference to the 2022 Olympics being held in Beijing: "For us, everything is easier in dictatorships. Dictators can organise events such as this without asking the people's permission."[56]

Kasper's comments were embarrassing for the IOC, but the negative press surrounding the Games would exist without his intervention. It is why, in 2016, the IOC spent $5.9 million on advertising and $25.4 million for "promotion of the Olympic movement".[57] It is why they employ marketing firms to lobby journalists to cover "good-news" stories.[58] In this context, the IOC's digital turn can be seen as an attempt to control both the message and the medium, a way to ensure a continuous stream of Olympism between Olympiads, an online space, as the website proudly announces, "where the Games never end".

Challenging the narrative

The official Olympic message is one of sporting excellence coupled with a belief in the positive social outcomes of staging a Games. In addition, since its inception, a key element of the Olympic narrative has been that the Games are apolitical. The IOC even go so far as to enshrine this in the Olympic Charter, forbidding any kind of political demonstration at the Games.[59] Yet history contains numerous examples of the links between politics, protest and the Olympic Games. Anyone who denies this reality is guilty of either wishful thinking or wilful ignorance.

Basic typologies have outlined the various political actors who have used the Games to spread political messages.[60] First, we can identify nation–states, which have treated the Games as either propaganda exercise or proxy for geo-political conflict (the Nazi Olympics of 1936; the Cold War posturing of the United States and Soviet Union). Second, we could include those athlete–activists who have used the platform of the Olympic Games to make a political statement (Smith and Carlos in Mexico 1968, Cathy Freeman at the Sydney Games of 2000).

Third, there is also a long tradition of political activists using the media attention of an Olympic Games to highlight a specific cause or issue. Examples of this include but are certainly not limited to: the pro-democracy demonstrators at the Mexico Olympics, human rights campaigners protesting against the Chinese government in 2008 and the international condemnation of Vladimir Putin's stance on gay rights during the 2014 Sochi Winter Games.

We must also add those who have actively opposed the staging of the Olympic Games themselves, a history that is increasingly documented by academics and activists alike. While not opposed to sport itself, these anti-Olympic protests have challenged the narrative – advanced by the IOC and assorted Olympic boosters – that staging a Games is an unqualified good for a host nation. Helen Lenskyj, who has written extensively on activism and the Olympic industry, has said: "[D]espite the persuasive rhetoric, most aspects of the Olympics are organized to maximise power and profit rather than to promote the welfare of individuals and groups engaged in sport as a healthy and fulfilling human activity."[61]

The anti-Olympic movement has tapped into a general feeling that the Games have "come to represent promises made, then broken".[62] These protests have grown in frequency over recent years, as David Goldblatt has detailed: "Where domestic conditions allow, variants of the anti-Olympic movements first sighted in the 1980s and 1990s have re-emerged – small in Torino and London, but a real presence at Vancouver 2010 and in the preparations for Rio 2016."[63] The message of these demonstrations may not have matched the glitz and glamour of the Games, but they have attempted to raise important and, at times, awkward questions of the Olympic movement.

In each instance, campaigns have argued there is – in addition to the staggering sums of capital laid out – a considerable human cost to staging an Olympic gaze, one that is hidden from the public view. Across continents and at both Summer and Winter Games, protestors have sought to highlight the cost of the Games, the increasingly commercial nature of the Olympics, infringements on the civil liberties of residents in a host country and the gentrification that accompanies areas of Olympic regeneration.

The question of sustainability is another concern common to each of the anti-Olympic campaigns, reflecting both the growing acknowledgement of the climate emergency and the effects of staging the event. Since the 1990s, the IOC has made strides in this area and now promises to "encourage and support a responsible concern for environmental issues".[64] Yet there appears to be a gap between rhetoric and reality. The most egregious and hypocritical examples of the Olympics impact on the environment – the building of Winter Games venues in Sochi National Park; the oil company BP's position as a "sustainability partner" at the 2012 Olympics – can mask the fact that, from stadia construction to air travel, the Games inevitably come with an environmental cost attached. This disconnect has led some, such as Toby Miller, to accuse the IOC of "greenwashing", presenting itself as "greener" than it really is as part of a public relations exercise.[65]

Anti-Olympic protests have also raised geographically specific issues. Opposition to the Vancouver Winter Games was in part motivated by the concerns of indigenous peoples.[66] Activists were aghast at the militarisation of London in 2012, where surface-to-air missiles, designed to deter terrorist attacks, were placed on top of residential buildings.[67] The citizens of Rio campaigned around the corruption of central government, state violence and the destruction of favelas which lay in the path of Olympic construction.[68]

As with other protest movements, unrelated to sport, anti-Olympic campaigns have included protest, academic-style critique and citizen journalism. In the absence of guaranteed, sympathetic coverage in the mainstream media, campaigners have utilised online spaces, which, as Roberts argues, provide "excellent outlets for modes of activism, dissent and resistance".[69] The anti-Olympic narrative is disseminated through a host of blogs, YouTube channels, social media platforms and podcasts. Since Sydney 2000, "nonaccredited journalists have become a significant component of the Games' journalistic community".[70]

The rise of citizen journalism reflects the argument that mainstream "journalists have frequently failed to fulfil their mandate on Olympic-related issues".[71] Yet at certain points elements of the anti-Olympic critique can be found in newspapers and on television. It has been suggested, for instance, that in "cities and countries which host the Olympic Games, the question of their cost, particularly to the public purse, arguably attracts as much attention from the media, governments and the public as the sporting aspects of the event".[72]

It should also be remembered that there is a fine tradition of investigative journalism exposing the controversial aspects of the Olympic movement, the Games and their supposed legacies. Over the past three decades, Andrew Jennings has produced a body of work, including articles, books and television documentaries, exposing corruption within the IOC.[73] Equally, Jonathan Calvert and the *Sunday Times* Insight investigations team have covered stories ranging from the fate of the Olympic stadium after London 2012 to the ongoing controversy over Russia's state-sponsored doping programme.

While the media can sometimes appear as cheerleaders for the Games, it is also capable of offering coverage to both the Olympic and anti-Olympic messages, serving "the pivotal role as the referee in this discursive battle".[74] In part, the media in its various forms is motivated by the nature of the Games, which have been described as a "vortextual spectacle", an event so large as to suck "attention in with a considerable intensity, temporarily dominating the news agenda".[75] The sheer scale of the media's Olympic operation, and the increased demand for content, ensures a diversity of opinion.

Research conducted by Jules Boykoff also suggests that, despite the misgivings of some activists, opposition voices can help to shape these media narratives. Examination of press coverage in the lead-up to both the Vancouver and London (2012) Games found "critics inside and outside the mainstream media wedged open discursive possibilities. The mass media often reflect and reproduce social relations, but they can also assist activists in their quest to challenge the macroarrangements of power".[76]

In the news stories sampled, 38 per cent featured anti-Olympic activists, a similar number to that of government officials (37 per cent).[77] And, while dissent was not always framed in a positive manner, more than half the stories concerning anti-Olympic protests and concerns were framed, in Boykoff's schema, as "principled grievances".[78] Once the Games begin, however, and the vortextual spectacle is underway, opposition voices are almost entirely absent from the media's Olympic coverage. As Rowe has argued, this is "a conventional occurrence because, when the sports action takes place, and especially after the Opening Ceremony, the specialist sports media (as opposed to the general press) come to the fore".[79]

Once the Closing Ceremony is concluded, the Olympics transition into its next cycle, the Games move to a new host city and the IOC continues its message of Olympism. At this point, the counter-narratives must begin anew, a consequence of the essentially nomadic nature of anti-Olympic protest. Boykoff, assessing the character of the movements that had appeared in Vancouver, London, Sochi and Rio, argues in his book *Power Games*, "In a sense, mobilising to challenge the Games is an activist version of Whack-a-Mole. The Olympics pop up in one city, rearing their head in a different city two years later. Activists then return to their pre-Games protest patterns, refocusing on their central targets and objectives".[80]

Until recently, anti-Olympic protests have seemed to be a series of connected but ultimately discrete campaigns. Each host city produces its own activism in relative isolation, despite the common concerns shared with its predecessors. The internet, however, has allowed a degree of continuity between protests. Digital communication has allowed activists from around the world to connect and share ideas, campaign materials and tactics. In July 2019, activists from campaigns across the world met in Tokyo, the site of the 2021 Summer Games, for the first-ever transnational summit of anti-Olympic protest.

For the IOC, the decentralised nature of modern media can be seen as "simultaneously offering additional avenues to promote the Olympic brand and experience across the globe *and* challenging their capacity to maintain control over Olympic related media".[81] Just as the IOC has used online platforms to promote its vision of the Olympism, so activists have also been able to utilise the connectivities of digital communication to challenge the official Olympic message. The tension between these narratives will undoubtedly be a key aspect at each of the Games in the next decade.

Conclusion

The Olympics are both a sporting and media spectacle, drawing worldwide attention from sports fans, journalists, politicians and multinational corporations. More than anything they have become a television spectacular. Both the IOC and their chosen broadcasters are currently adapting to the changing media environment, exploring the possibilities offered by new, digital technology. Despite periodic concerns, the Games will continue for the foreseeable future, thereby presenting an almost unequalled opportunity for sports journalists to cover sporting competition at the very highest level.

Olympic stories, however, have never been limited to sport. The power of the IOC, and the importance of the Olympics to both the media and commercial interests, mean the staging of a Games is accompanied by huge political, social and economic ramifications, the outcomes of which are hotly contested. Those who cover the Games must make sense of this complex picture. As Boyle and Haynes have argued:

> The challenge for sports journalists working, for example, in the UK is to offer uncomplicit, informative and entertaining journalism against the backdrop of an increasingly commercial and privatized media system. In such an environment the need for some parts of sports journalism to question, investigate and call to account the powerful within sports and its attendant political and commercial culture will become even more acute.[82]

Opposition to the Games is not abating; if anything it is intensifying. Grassroots campaigners continue to protest the negative effects that accompany the staging of an Olympic Games; potential host cities are deterred by rising costs and doubts over the fabled Olympic legacy. The IOC claims to promote "the educational value of good example, social responsibility and respect for universal fundamental ethical principles", so sports journalists have a duty to look beyond the track, ring or pool and, where necessary, hold the Olympics to account.

References

1. Joseph A. Maguire, "'Civilised games?' Beijing 2008, power politics and cultural struggles", in *Power and Global Sport: Zones of Prestige, Emulation and Resistance*, Routledge: London, 2005, p. 146.
2. Garry Whannel, "The television spectacular", in Alan Tomlinson and Garry Whannel (eds.), *Five Ring Circus: Money, Power and the Politics of the Olympic Games*, Pluto: London, 1984, p. 30.
3. John Horne, *Sport in Consumer Culture*, Palgrave Macmillan: Basingstoke, 2006, p. 51.
4. Although Coubertin drew inspiration from the Olympics of ancient Greece, his modern version of the Games differed in several ways. As such, it is more accurate to talk of a renovation than a revival of the Olympic Games.
5. de Coubertin Pierre, *The Olympic Idea: Discourses and Essays*, Carl Diem Institute: Köln, Germany, 1967, p. 9.
6. Holt Richard, *Sport and the British: A Modern History*, Clarendon Press: Oxford, UK, 1989, p. 274.
7. Quoted in Richard D. Mandell, *The First Modern Olympics*, University of California: California, Los Angeles, 1976, p. 157.

8. Quoted in Allen Guttmann, *The Olympics: A History of the Modern Games*, University of Illinois Press: Chicago, IL, 1992, p. 16.

9. Charles Waldstein, "The Olympic Games", *The Times*, 1 April 1896, p. 12. The Times Digital Archive, http://tinyurl.galegroup.com/tinyurl/A6bNQ1, accessed 22 May 2019.

10. "The Olympic Games", *The Manchester Guardian* (1828–1900), 13 April 1896, https://search.proquest.com/docview/483380720?accountid=10472

11. John J MacAloon, "Double visions: Olympic Games and American culture", in Jeffrey Segrave and Donald Chu (eds.), *The Olympic Games in Transition*, Human Kinetics Books: Champaign, IL, 1988, p. 279.

12. Maurice Roche, *Mega-Events and Modernity: Olympics and Expos in the Growth of Global Culture*, Routledge: London, 2000, p. 1.

13. International Olympic Committee, *Annual Report 2016: Credibility, Sustainability and Youth*, IOC: Lausanne, Switzerland, 2016.

14. Kristine Toohey and Anthony J. Veal, *The Olympic Games: A Social Science Perspective* (2nd ed.), CABI: Wallingford, UK, p. 159.

15. Andrew Zimbalist, "The economic legacy of Rio 2016", in Andrew Zimbalist (ed.), *Rio 2016: Olympic Myths, Hard Realities*, Brookings Institute Press: Washington, DC, p. 213.

16. International Olympic Committee, *IOC Marketing Report: Rio 2016*, IOC: Lausanne, Switzerland, 2016, p. 23.

17. Quoted in Inside Left, *Resistance: The Best Olympic* Spirit, 2012, http://insideleft.org/resistance-the-best-olympic-spirit/, accessed 7 July 2019.

18. Jules Boykoff, *Power Games: A Political History of the Olympics*, Verso: London, 2006, p. 246.

19. International Olympic Committee, *Olympic Charter*, 2018, IOC: Lausanne, Switzerland, p. 21.

20. John Hoberman, "Toward a theory of Olympic internationalism", *Journal of Sport History*, Volume 22, Issue 1, 1995.

21. Robert V. Bellamy Jr., "The evolving television sports marketplace", in Lawrence A, Wenner, (ed.), *MediaSport*, Routledge: London, 1998, pp. 84–85.

22. FIFA, *2018 FIFA World Cup Russia: Global Broadcast and Audience Summary*, https://resources.fifa.com/image/upload/njqsntrvdvqv8ho1dag5.pdf, accessed 8 December 2019.

23. FIFA, *Financial Report 2018*, https://resources.fifa.com/image/upload/xzshsoe2ayttyquuxhq0.pdf, accessed 8 December 2019.

24. Garry Whannel, "Television and the transformation of sport", *The Annals of the American Academy of Political and Social Science*, Volume 625, 2009, p. 206.

25. See for example, Raymond Boyle and Richard Haynes, *Power Play: Sport, the Media and Popular Culture* (2nd ed.), 2009, Edinburgh University Press: Edinburgh, UK, chapter 3.

26. Barry Smart, *The Sports Star: Modern Sport and the Cultural Economy of Sporting Celebrity*, Sage: London, 2005, p. 91.

27. Bellamy, Jr., p. 85.

28. Michael Payne, *Olympic Turnaround*, London Business Press: London, 2005, p. 114.

29. Ibid.

30. Murad Ahmed, "Olympics takes gold with $3bn Mengniu Dairy-Coca-Cola deal", *Financial Times*, 24 June 2019, https://www.ft.com/content/11568a4a-95a7-11e9-9573-ee5cbb98ed36, accessed 24 June 2019.

31. International Olympic Committee, *IOC Marketing Media Guide: PyeongChang 2018*, IOC: Lausanne, Switzerland, 2018.

32. John Horne and Garry Whannel, *Understanding the Olympics*, Routledge: London, 2016, pp. 90–91.

33. Owen Gibson, "Olympics coverage to remain on BBC after discovery deal", *The Guardian*, 2 February 2016, https://www.theguardian.com/sport/2016/feb/02/olympics-bbc-discovery-deal, accessed 20 July 2019.

34. International Olympic Committee, *Annual Report 2018: Credibility, Sustainability and Youth*, IOC: Lausanne, Switzerland, 2018, p. 14.

35. Adrianne Blue, *Faster, Higher, Further: Women's Triumphs and Disasters at the Olympics*, Virgo: London, 1998, p. 163.
36. Bill Carter, "On TV, timing is everything at the Olympics", *New York Times*, 24 August 2008, https://www.nytimes.com/2008/08/25/sports/olympics/25nbc.html, accessed 20 July 2019.
37. https://www.obs.tv/home
38. Garry Whannel, *Culture, Politics and Sport: Blowing the Whistle, Revisited*, Routledge: London, 2008, p. 73.
39. Quoted in Centre for Media Literacy (n.d.), *No Two Countries See the Same Olympics*, http://www.medialit.org/reading-room/no-two-countries-see-same-olympics, accessed 9 July 2019.
40. Andrew C. Billings, *Olympic Media: Inside the Biggest Show on Television*, Routledge: London, 2008, p. 23.
41. Wolf Lyberg, *Fabulous 100 Years of the IOC: Facts, Figures and Much More*, IOC: Lausanne, Switzerland, 1996, p. 350.
42. *Royal Television Society, Olympic Broadcast Progress Through Time*, 2015, https://rts.org.uk/article/olympic-broadcast-progress-through-time, accessed 1 July 2019.
43. Richard Haynes, *BBC Sport in Black and White*, Palgrave Macmillan: London, 2016, p. 57.
44. Allen Guttmann, *The Games Must Go On: Avery Brundage and the Olympic Movement*, Columbia University Press: New York, 1984, p. 218.
45. Stefan Szymanski, "Jeux avec Frontieres: Television markets and European sport", in Alan Tomlinson, Christopher Young and Richard Holt (eds.), *Sport and the Transformation of Modern Europe: States, Media and Markets 1950–2010*, Routledge: London, 2011, p. 116.
46. BBC, *London Olympics Give Boost to Media*, 2012, https://www.bbc.co.uk/news/entertainment-arts-19253278, accessed 2 July 2019.
47. Stephen Battaglio, "NBC's Olympic ratings drop while online viewership surges: 'There is a cultural shift'", *Los Angeles Times*, 16 August 2016, https://www.latimes.com/entertainment/envelope/cotown/la-et-ct-olympic-ratings-20160812-snap-story.html, accessed 7 July 2019.
48. International Olympic Committee, *Olympic Agenda 2020: 20+20 Recommendations*, IOC: Lausanne, Switzerland, 2014, p. 5.
49. www.olympicchannel.com
50. IOC, *Olympic Agenda* 2020, p. 5.
51. IOC, *Annual Report* 2016, p. 5.
52. Christopher A. Shaw, *Five Ring Circus: Myths and Realities of the Olympic Games*, New Society Publishers: Gabriola Island, 2008, p. 16.
53. IOC, *Olympic Charter*, p. 11.
54. Ibid., p. 92.
55. Boykoff, *Power Games,* p. 239.
56. Inside the Games, *Kasper Causes Controversy After Claiming Easier for IOC to Organise Olympic Games in Dictatorships*, 2019, https://www.insidethegames.biz/articles/1075192/kasper-causes-controversy-after-claiming-easier-for-ioc-to-organise-olympic-games-in-dictatorships, accessed 15 July 2019.
57. Deadspin, *Where Does the IOC's Money Go?*, 2018, https://deadspin.com/where-does-the-iocs-money-go-1822983686, accessed 15 July 2019.
58. Andy Bull, "Nobody can afford to host the Olympics but at the IOC the largesse never stops", *The Guardian*, 23 October 2018, https://www.theguardian.com/sport/2018/oct/23/olympic-games-host-ioc-money, accessed 15 July 2019.
59. IOC, *Olympic Charter*, p. 93.
60. See Gareth Edwards, "We have nothing to lose but our medals", in Mark Perryman (ed.), *London 2012: How Was It for Us?*, Lawrence & Wishart: London, 2013, pp. 189–200; Jules Boykoff, *Activism and the Olympics: Dissent at the Games in Vancouver and London*, Rutgers University Press: London, 2014, chapter 1.
61. Helen Lenskyj, Inside the Olympic Industry: Power, Politics and Activism, State University of New York Press: Albany, NY, 2000, p. 3.
62. Mark Perryman, *Why the Olympics Aren't Good for Us, and How They Can Be*, OR Books: London, 2012, p. 17.

63. David Goldblatt, *The Games: A Global History of the Olympics*, W.W. Norton & Co.: London, 2016, p. 395.

64. IOC, *Olympic Charter*, p. 17.

65. Toby Miller, *Greenwashing Sport*, Routledge: London, 2018.

66. Shaw.

67. Dave Zirin, *Game Over: How Politics Has Turned the Sports World Upside Down*, The New Media: London, 2013, pp. 53–58.

68. Adam Talbot and Thomas F. Carter, "Human rights abuses at the Rio 2016 Olympics: Activism and the media", *Leisure Studies*, Volume 37, Issue 1, 2018, pp. 77–88.

69. John M. Roberts, *New Media and Public Activism: Liberalism, the State and Radical Protest in the Public Sphere*, Policy Press: Bristol, 2014, p. 11.

70. Andy Miah, Beatriz Garcia and Tian Zhihui, "'We are the media': Nonaccredited media and citizen journalists at the Olympic Games", in Monroe E. Price and Daniel Dayan (eds.), *Owning the Olympics: Narratives of the New China*, University of Michigan Press: Ann Arbor, MI, 2008, p. 320.

71. Helen Lenskyj, *Olympic Industry Resistance: Challenging Olympic Power and Propaganda*, State University of New York Press: Albany, NY, 2008.

72. Toohey and Veal, p. 121.

73. See for instance: Vyv Simson and Andrew Jennings, *The Lords of the Rings: Power, Money and Drugs in the Modern Olympics*, Simon & Schuster: London, 1992; Andrew Jennings, *The New Lords of the Rings: Olympic Corruption and How to Buy Gold Medals*, Pocket Books: London, 1996; Andrew Jennings and Clare Sambrook, *The Great Olympic Swindle: When the World Wanted Its Games Back*, Simon & Schuster: London, 2000.

74. Boykoff, *Activism and the Olympics*, p. 130.

75. Horne and Whannel, p. 223.

76. Boykoff, *Activism and the Olympics*, p. 157.

77. Boykoff, *Power Games*, p. 153.

78. Ibid., p. 143.

79. David Rowe, *Global Media Sport: Flows, Platforms and Futures*, Bloomsbury Academic: London, 2011, p. 125.

80. Boykoff, *Power Games*, p. 250.

81. Brett Hutchins and Janine Mikosza, "The Web 1.0 Olympics: Athlete blogging, social networking and policy contradictions at the 2008 Beijing Games", *Convergence: The International Journal of Research into New Media Technologies*, Volume 16, Issue 3, 2010, p. 281.

82. Boyle and Haynes, p. 183.

24

Football hooliganism

Roger Domeneghetti

"You can talk about police provocation, or other fans causing trouble, but it only seems to happen where the English go." Such was Gary Lineker's reaction on Twitter to clashes between police and England fans in Marseille at the start of the 2016 European Championships (Euro 2016). Ultimately, events at the tournament proved Lineker's assessment to be wide of the mark.

It was quickly shown that organised Russian gangs were indiscriminately targeting English fans and, furthermore, that violence did not only happen where the English went. In fact, Euro 2016 was marred by trouble in seven different host cities involving followers of at least 11 countries other than England. In Lille, German and Ukrainian fans fought each other; in Nice, French and Northern Irish fans clashed; in Paris, French hooligans attacked Turkish fans and there were also fights between French and Portuguese fans; in Cologne, Spanish tourists were attacked by Russian hooligans; in Saint-Etienne, there was violence during the match between the Czech Republic and Croatia; in Lyon, there were clashes between Albanian and Romanian fans; in Marseille, Hungarian fans clashed with stadium stewards.

Yet Lineker's reaction was not uncommon among the wider media's initial response which viewed England fans as a homogenous group, cast football violence as a solely English problem and was dismissive of the notion that there may have been more complex, less immediately obvious causes. For some, the media's response was justified, a fair representation of the type of person who follows England abroad, to others it will have been indicative of an unrepresentative stereotype employed by the media. These contrasting and competing views beg serious questions about the media (re)presentation of football hooliganism: are journalists guilty of amplifying and sensationalising the problem, or are their assumptions about England fans and the nature of hooliganism justified?

Exciting the phenomenon?

Over the years, various scholars have analysed the media coverage of football hooliganism.[1] One of the earliest was Hall,[2] who identified six key themes in the coverage of hooliganism. First, Hall suggested that the media "excites the phenomenon" by prioritising the most sensational stories or most sensational angle within stories, thereby exaggerating their impact. Second, this is in part achieved through the "misleading use of the language of violence". Hall argued that while some incidents deserve dramatic language, "a proper sense of scale and judgement" is required. Third, Hall identified the "dismissive labelling" which likens hooligans to animals, thus removing the possibility of human rationale for their behaviour. He argued, fourth, that this consequently stigmatises hooligans and by association all football fans, while, fifth, preventing meaningful discussion of deeper or plausible explanations. Finally, Hall suggested this leads to the creation of a "moral panic":

> as things get tougher and look bleaker for us all, the temptation grows to deal with any problem, first by **simplifying** its causes, second by **stigmatising** those involved, third by whipping up public feeling into a **panic** about it, and fourth by **stamping hard on it from above**.[3]

Whannel added a separate dimension to this analysis by looking at the way that journalists construct stories, in particular their use of quotes. He noted that "most 'incident' stories consist not so much of descriptions of the incident but reactions to it".[4] These reactions, in the form of quotes, come from six main sources, the first five of which are "official": (1) club sources; (2) game authorities; (3) police and/or magistrates; (4) government and political; (5) transport; and (6) the public – sometimes members of the crowd, but often outraged bystanders. While acknowledging that the use of official quotes was at least partly a consequence of professional convenience (it is easier to ring official sources than to contact eyewitnesses), Whannel argued that this has created a "hierarchy of viewpoints within which the official opinions are privileged".[5] Whannel further argued that this is compounded by the fact that sports journalists have an interest in maintaining good relationships with official sources, and so are likely to accept rather than challenge the official view of football hooliganism. In turn, this official viewpoint is mediated through newspaper production processes which highlight and dramatise key quotes and phrases, thereby creating a common framework within which all subsequent incidents are reported.

Research on the coverage of England fans in the 1990s and early 2000s conducted by Poulton[6] noted that the findings of Hall and Whannel still had resonance. Poulton found that there was a prevailing view of the archetypal hooligan – "shaven-headed, beer-bellied, tattooed, drunk and disorderly young males"[7] – a stereotype which was often challenged by the types of people actually involved in trouble. Poulton also found that there was a tendency to blame all fans for the misdemeanours of a minority, while at the same time there was a lack of serious analysis of the underlying causes of trouble.

The one tournament where this pattern was not followed was during the 2002 World Cup in Japan and South Korea. Poulton noted a "significant shift" in the reporting which now provided a "widespread and positive profile of ordinary England supporters".[8] The fact that the absence of trouble prompted surprise among reporters that not all England fans were hooligans suggests that the reporters only had one frame of reference, or narrative structure, through which to view supporters. Poulton argued that this was a consequence of the fact that there is often a failure among journalists to distinguish between sections of England's support, which in turn leads to the misrepresentation of the majority: "As soon as trouble breaks out, almost all distinctions between the violent, xenophobic minority and non-violent majority is lost in the media coverage that emphasises the behaviour of the former. Consequently, the majority loses all sense of identity, voice and presence."[9]

A brief examination of some of the coverage of the violence involving England fans at Euro 2016 shows this conventional frame of reference still dominates coverage, albeit with contradictory explanations being afforded some space. For example, in a comment piece in the

Daily Mail following the trouble between fans of England and Russia at Euro 2016, Martin Samuel[10] argued that "[t]ear gas is not being randomly fired into other groups of supporters" before suggesting "it is disingenuous to act as if this country sent 35,000 lambs to the port of Marseille". Having reinforced the prevalent notion that hooliganism is an English-only problem and effectively labelled all England fans as hooligans, thereby denying the peaceful majority a distinct identity and voice, Samuel did briefly acknowledge (somewhat grudgingly, it would seem) that, "by the looks of it many innocent England fans were inadvertently caught up in some pretty horrific violence [at the hands of Russian hooligans]". (It is worth mentioning that anecdotal evidence suggests that social media has given fans a tool to present a countervailing view to that presented by traditional media discourse.)

Samuel then identified several complementary underlying causal factors, including: the history of trouble between England fans and Marseille's immigrant youth population; the post-9/11 landscape; the shift to the right in Britain and Europe; Russia's "notorious racist hooligans"; the heat; the late kick-off time that facilitated all-day drinking; and the fact the game was scheduled on a weekend, enabling tens of thousands to travel. Thus, he argued, the trouble would have been "all so avoidable" had UEFA taken it upon themselves to acknowledge the issues and move the game to a more suitable time and venue. Yet this more nuanced approach to the issue was buried at the end of an article which likened England fans to "an occupying army" which "terrif[ies] the world", thereby giving prevalence to the stereotypical approach identified in coverage at previous tournaments. Furthermore, in reporting the arrests of England fans, following the trouble in Marseille, it is notable that the *Daily Mail* highlighted the job titles of two of the fans in particular: "a psychiatric nurse and a trainee engineer".[11] On the same day, the *Daily Mirror*[12] named the six England fans arrested but again listed the occupations of only two: the psychiatric nurse and the engineer. That both papers found these occupations worthy of note suggests they ran counter to the "convenient, but simplistic, stereotype that [the media] has helped to construct" of the English football fan-cum-hooligan.[13]

By contrast, a staunch defence of the coverage of football violence has been offered by journalist-turned-academic Rob Steen.[14] Steen argues that while on the one hand sociological analysis of hooliganism tends to diminish its scale, on the other it blames the media. In particular, he argues that the "space-starved, time-pressed daily newspapers" have been "the prime scapegoats" accused of "wilful, irresponsible hyperbole; in short sensationalism".[15] One of the key criticisms Steen levels at analysis of the media coverage of football hooliganism is that, "[n] one of the authors had interviewed the purported sensationalists – if for no other reason than to give them the chance to defend themselves".[16] This *is* a notable gap in such research, and it is one Steen sought to address by interviewing two journalists who covered football in the 1980s: David Lacey and Guy Hodgson, who both subscribed to the view that the coverage of football hooliganism was justified.

However, Perryman[17] also goes some way to addressing the problem in his account of following England abroad. In a chapter pointedly titled *The Blame Game*, Perryman, echoing Poulton's findings, opined how the coverage of England fans all too often allowed little room for differentiation between the violent minority and the peaceful majority, which in turn created a vicious circle. Thus, he was moved to ask: "If the impression is created that the only way to follow England is to be thuggish, is it any wonder that many are scared off, while some are attracted for all the wrong reasons?"[18] Perryman then went on to ask a range of print and broadcast journalists why coverage was framed in the manner it is. The results were revealing and somewhat at odds with Steen's analysis. For example, Paul Kelso, now a Sky Sports correspondent but at the time writing for *The Guardian*, admitted: "News tends to focus on covering the abnormal, so outbreaks of mindless violence, however unrepresentative, do tend to get covered."[19] Kelso went on to acknowledge that truly balanced coverage required journalists to speak to fans as well as the authorities, in effect requiring fans to be moved up Whannel's "hierarchy of viewpoints".

Chris Skudder, who also works for Sky Sports, as he did at the time, expressed similar sentiments, from a broadcast perspective, in terms of both the type of incidents the media sought out and how the media might produce more balanced coverage. He acknowledged that: "News reporting is all about access … Previously, for 20 years or more, the only fans' story we had access to was trouble. Now it is different and the reports are slowly changing."[20] About the incident in Belgium he added:

> The crews gather where they think there's most likely to be trouble. Charleroi at Euro 2000 was when I was ashamed to be a TV reporter. One small square, cameras pointing at the crowd of fans from every possible vantage point. All waiting for the main event. And, of course, some of the fans, German as well as English, duly obliged us.[21]

These comments were echoed by *The Guardian*'s Charlie Whelan, who wrote about the "distortion" of events in Charleroi created by the TV coverage:

> The TV crews got what they wanted. Violence. Once the telly had the pictures of the Belgian police firing tear gas into pubs and arresting everyone inside, they had their story … The incident with the water cannon that the TV reported actually lasted no more than about 10 minutes, while 15,000 England fans enjoying themselves with Germans in the hundreds of bars around the square received no coverage.[22]

Hillsborough and after

In the final part of his analysis, Steen himself admits that in the past when newspapers had fewer pages "there was clearly a decision to give bad news precedence over any balancing views",[23] a point reinforced by Oliver Holt, now the *Mail on Sunday*'s chief sportswriter, who candidly admitted that "good news isn't usually particularly attractive".[24] Foregrounding bad news at the expense of balanced coverage is as close a definition of sensationalisation as you are likely to get, and this habit reached its apogee in the media's coverage of Hillsborough, which perpetuated the myth that the disaster was caused by the behaviour of the fans for nearly 30 years. There is, as yet, no evidence that any journalists were actively involved in a conspiracy to cover up the police's culpability at Hillsborough.

However, journalistic practice and news production processes, namely (a) the priority given to "official" sources and (b) the focus given to bad news or "extreme" events, coupled with attitudes which meant that "[b]y the late 1970s and early 1980s the hooligan had become a dominant character of British political and social discourse",[25] created fertile ground in which the police lies could take root and grow.

The Sun's infamous front page which purported to tell "THE TRUTH"[26] is often held up as an example of the worst excesses of both the coverage of Hillsborough and Rupert Murdoch's particular brand of tabloid journalism, but the reality is that the majority of the rest of the media was little better. The story, which originated from the Sheffield-based Whites News Agency, led both the BBC and ITV bulletins the night before, and on the same day *The Sun* ran the story; so too did the now-defunct *Today*, *The Times*, *The Telegraph* and the *Daily Express*. Content analysis of coverage of Hillsborough in the immediate aftermath of the disaster undertaken by Coleman et al. highlights how police statements that thousands of drunk, ticketless fans caused a "fatal surge" were reported uncritically and that, "despite all indications to the contrary 'hooligan hysteria' persisted to dominate the coverage and the agenda was set to turn Hillsborough into a public order issue".[27]

This "hysteria" was perhaps born of numerous incidents of violence at matches throughout the 1980s. In a 12-week period in 1985 alone, there was rioting between Chelsea and Sunderland fans at Stamford Bridge, leading to 104 arrests and 40 injuries. Nine days later, Luton and Millwall fans fought each other and the police before, during and after a televised FA Cup sixth round tie at Kenilworth Road, leading to 47 arrests and causing 31 injuries. Less than two months later, a 15-year-old boy was killed when a wall collapsed during a riot between Birmingham and Leeds fans at St. Andrews. These were all quickly overshadowed by the events at Heysel Stadium prior to that May's European Cup final at the dilapidated Heysel stadium in Brussels, where a charge by rioting Liverpool fans led to the deaths of 39 Juventus fans. Fourteen Liverpool fans were convicted of manslaughter as a result. Coleman et al. also found significant evidence that as a result of this latter incident coverage of Hillsborough was also framed by a "Heysel factor" (that is, the erroneous suggestion that because Liverpool fans were involved in violence at Heysel they must necessarily have been involved in violence at Hillsborough).

The narrative framework was in evidence in the "quality" as well as the tabloid press. For example, The Independent's Patrick Barclay suggested that Hillsborough was caused by "the passion that engenders in people who allow excitement to get the better of them". Hammering the point home, he argued that to blame the police, stadium layout or ticket allocation "seems to be missing the central and most painful point … the danger has remained. It is in the way some people behave".[28] It is insightful that one of the few articles cited in Coleman et al.'s study as correctly identifying the cause of the disaster was written by renowned stadium expert Simon Inglis, someone who had the knowledge to provide suitable context but who was not a journalist by profession and as such was not caught up in the hooligan hysteria that influenced so much coverage.

By foregrounding the comments of the authorities at the expense of the fans, the media's coverage of Hillsborough showed the ongoing validity of Whannel's "hierarchy of viewpoints". But the coverage of the tragedy also showed a willingness among some journalists to find blame where none existed – to demonise fans and sensationalise events – and this was a habit which had also been in evidence at another tragedy four years earlier. Following the Valley Parade disaster, which killed 56 fans in 1985, Ian Truman wrote in the Daily Star:

> A smoke bomb caused the tragic Bradford football fire, I am convinced of it, I was sitting only yards away from the seat of the inferno that killed at least 52 fans. I saw everything, every horrifying second, I saw a smoke bomb thrown by hooligans from the stand adjoining the main building and I know the killer who threw it would have escaped.[29]

At the inquest into the tragedy, Truman (an ironic name, given his actions) admitted that he had in fact seen no smoke bomb and had based his story on unattributed sources he spoke to on the pitch. This admission led QC Andrew Collins, counsel for the public inquiry, to chastise Truman for wasting police time and for Lord Popplewell to describe his evidence as "unreliable". Fortunately, the notion that the actions of fans were to blame for the fatal Bradford blaze did not take root in a similar manner to the way in which it did following Hillsborough four years later. However, what this largely forgotten incident shows is that not only did journalists reporting on football in the 1980s regularly view fan behaviour through the prism of hooligan hysteria but some at least would also attribute blame to fans even when none existed, to the extent that they would by their own admission fabricate elements of stories which would subsequently be shown to be wholly without substance.

In *Among the Thugs*, his travelogue following England fans, Bill Buford made similar allegations that such media misrepresentation was evident a year after Hillsborough, during the 1990 World Cup in Italy (Italia '90). Buford described how during a confrontation between English and Italian fans, the English media actively chose not to photograph the violence committed by the Italian fans: "It was the images of the English they wanted ... Italians behaving like hooligans? Unheard of. English behaving like English? *That* was interesting!"[30] Similarly, Pete Davies, who was also at Italia '90 to research his book, *All Played Out*, wrote about repeated allegations fans made of journalists attempting to bribe them to cause trouble. Davies was circumspect about the claims but such was the antipathy he encountered from fans towards a press corps they felt had consistently maligned and misrepresented them, he was moved to ask, "what hope can there be for the press to tell the truth *even if it wants to?*"[31] Perhaps the feeling of the majority of fans in the late 1980s and early 1990s was best summed up by one paragraph in the searing post-Hillsborough editorial in the national fanzine *When Saturday Comes:*

> The implication is that "normal" people need to be protected from the football fan. But we are normal people. "The Football Fan" is not an easily defined social stereotype, whatever the tabloid cartoonists may choose to believe. All manner of people go to football matches. A few of them are intent on unleashing aggressive instincts which are also manifested in wine bars on a Saturday night or in tourist hotels on the Costa Del Sol. Thuggish behaviour is rarely reported in any detail when it can't be directly linked to a football match.[32]

It is perhaps little wonder that by that time fans had already begun to try to take control of their collective identity through both their own publications (the myriad fanzines that sprung up across the country) and by forming the Football Supporters' Association (FSA). Anthony Vickers, now chief sportswriter on the *Middlesbrough Evening Gazette* but in the late 1980s a founder member of the Teesside branch of the FSA, has detailed how he and his colleagues felt it necessary to "educate" sports reporters and invite them along to FSA meetings so they could see "articulate fans discussing the game on a very well-informed level". Furthermore, they made a point of giving their telephone numbers to reporters so "they could get a fan's perspective instead of just getting the police's version of events".[33]

While much progress has been made in the intervening decades, some of those working with fans suggest there is still work needed to change attitudes towards them. Amanda Jacks, a case worker for the Football Supporters' Federation (which grew out of the FSA), is adamant that football fans do not get a fair hearing from the media, arguing that they are "the last group in society that can be demonised without anybody questioning it", and that the narrative that English fans are hooligans "suits an element of the media". Jacks added: "At least four times a season I will deal with incidents involving football fans and police that if they involved protesters, would be on the front page of *The Guardian*. Because it happens with football fans, it goes against the narrative that all fans are hooligans. It's almost as if people don't want to see the other side of it."[34]

Of course, none of this is to suggest that football hooliganism does not exist and is not a problem, nor that it should not be reported. However, there is little justification for the foregrounding of "bad news" regarding hooligans at the expense of balanced reportage of all fans, including the peaceful majority. Along with journalism, academia must shoulder its share of the blame for the focus of research from the 1970s to 1990s on football hooliganism at the expense of comparable analysis of other, non-violent football sub-cultures. That focus, perhaps unwittingly, reinforced the idea that hooligans are representative of the majority of football fans not, as is the case, the minority.

However, more research along the lines that Steen[35] suggests, which seeks to gain an understanding from journalism practitioners of why certain media narratives are constructed, can only enhance our understanding of the coverage of football violence. Yet, while it is important to address Steen's key criticism of the analysis of the coverage of football hooliganism – that journalists are not given a voice – fans must also be heard. If they are not, there is a risk that research will be contaminated by a "hierarchy of viewpoints",[36] which would in turn undermine our understanding of football fan culture.

References

1. For example: Gary Whannel, "Football, crowd behaviour and the press", *Media, Culture & Society*, Volume 1, Issue 4, 1979, pp. 327–342; Murphy, P., Eric Dunning and John Williams, "Soccer crowd disorder and the press: Processes of amplification and de-amplification in historical perspective", *Theory, Culture & Society*, Volume 5, Issue 3, 1988, pp. 645–673; Richard Giulianotti and Gary Armstrong, "Ungentlemanly conduct: Football hooligans, the media and the construction of notoriety", *Football Studies*, Volume 1, 1998, pp. 4–33; Emma Poulton, "Tears, tantrums and tattoos: framing the football hooligan", in Mark Perryman (ed.), *Hooligan Wars: Causes and Effects of Football Violence*, Mainstream: Edinburgh, UK, 2001; Poulton, "New fans, new flag, new England? Changing news values in the English press coverage of World Cup 2002", *Football Studies*, Volume 6, Issue 1, 2003, pp. 19–36; Poulton, "English media representation of football-related disorder: 'Brutal, Short-hand and Simplifying'?", *Sport in Society*, Volume 8, Issue 1, 2005, pp. 27–47.
2. Stuart Hall "The treatment of football hooliganism in the press", in Roger Ingham, Stuart Hall, John Clarke, Peter Marsh, Jim Donovan: *Football Hooliganism: The Wider Picture*, Inter-Action Inprint, London, 1978, pp. 24–36.
3. Ibid., p. 34.
4. Whannel, p. 332.
5. Ibid., p. 332.
6. Poulton 2001, 2003, 2005.
7. Poulton 2005, p. 28.
8. Poulton 2003, p. 32.
9. Poulton 2001, p. 124.
10. *Daily Mail*, 13 June 2016.
11. *Daily Mail*, 14 June 2016.
12. *Daily Mirror*, 14 June 2016.
13. Poulton 2005, p. 28.
14. Rob Steen, "Sensationalists united? Football hooliganism and the English press", *Sport in Society*, Volume 19, Issue 2, 2016, pp. 267–279.
15. Ibid., p. 4.
16. Ibid., p. 3.
17. Perryman, *Ingerland: Travels with a Football Nation*, Pocket Books: London, 2010.
18. Ibid., p. 176.
19. Quoted in Ibid., p. 185.
20. Quoted in Ibid., p. 192.
21. Quoted in Ibid., p. 192.
22. Quoted in Poulton 2005, pp. 32–33.
23. Steen, p. 12.
24. Quoted in Perryman 2010, p. 180.
25. Carlton Brick, "Taking offence: Modern moralities and the perception of the football fan" in Jon Garland, Dominic Malcolm and Michael Rowe (eds.), *The Future of Football: Challenges for the Twenty-First Century*, Frank Cass: London, 2000, p. 170.
26. *The Sun*, 19 April 1989.

27. Phil Scraton, Sheila Coleman and Ann Jemphrey, *Hillsborough and After: The Liverpool Experience; First Report*, Liverpool City Council: Liverpool, UK, 1990, p. 116.

28. Quoted in Ibid., p. 127.

29. Quoted in Oliver Popplewell, *Committee of Inquiry into Crowd Safety and Control at Sports Grounds: Interim Report*, Her Majesty's Stationery Office: London, 1985, p. 5.

30. Bill Buford, *Among the Thugs: Face to Face with English Football Violence*, Arrow Books: London, 2001, pp. 76–77.

31. Pete Davies, *All Played Out: The Full Story of Italia '90*, Mandarin: London, 1991, p. 200.

32. *When Saturday Comes*, 28 June 1989.

33. Roger Domeneghetti, *From the Back Page to the Front Room: Football's Journey Through the English Media* (2nd ed.), Ockley: Huddersfield, UK, 2017, p. 186.

34. John Brewin, "Hooliganism in England: The enduring cultural legacy of football violence", http://www.espnfc.co.uk/blog/espn-fc-united-blog/68/post/2193850/hooliganism-in-england-the-enduring-cultural-legacy-of-football-violence, accessed 28 November 2019.

35. Steen.

36. Whannel.

25

Football managers and the press

Stephen Wagg

At the heart of this essay is the argument I've been pressing for some considerable time – most recently in my inaugural professorial lecture of 2014, "The Football Manager: A Brief History of a Modern Myth"[1] – which is that the football manager has become an on-tap, individualised explanation for the performance of football teams, one which allows us to disregard otherwise self-evident structural factors.

Since the 1980s, in parallel to established patterns in the wider world, wealth has flowed upward to top brand football clubs of Northern and Southern Europe: La Liga in Spain, Serie A in Italy and, most especially, the English Premier League (EPL), founded in 1992. These clubs pay by far the biggest salaries, tend to monopolise the best players and expect to win the various trophies on offer. This is tacitly understood, and quite often – albeit on occasion unintentionally – acknowledged. When, for example, in 2015 a comment I made to the effect that the EPL was not a competition at all but "a global television spectacular and a showcase for the top six brands [as the half-dozen richest clubs – Manchester City, Chelsea, Manchester United, Arsenal, Liverpool and Tottenham Hotspur were now generally known]" was printed in a national British newspaper, it passed without any perceptible comment. I was told later that the journalist whose article quoted my remark simply agreed with me and had had nothing to add.[2] Nonetheless, the media insistence that the manager (and not manifest wealth differentials) is either the sole or the determining factor in a team's performance has become ever more relentless.

The manager is now, effectively, a paradigm, within which explanations for team performance are now commonly sought; that's to say it's become virtually impossible to discuss the outcome of contemporary elite football matches without citing team managers as the key variable. This chapter analyses the development of this paradigm and then considers what ramifications it has for the contemporary relationship between football managers and the media. In regard to the latter discussion, the chapter will draw on events at Leicester City FC between 2014 and 2018, which seem to me in several ways to illustrate important elements in that relationship.

The football manager: History and mythology

An estimated 10.1 million people illegally downloaded the video game Football Manager 2013,[3] one indication among so many that football managers have become part of the popular cultural air we breathe. The football manager floats, in a taken-for-granted way, through our consciousness and daily discourse. He (hitherto, it has almost always been a "he"[4]) constitutes a myth – "myth" in the sense employed by the French cultural theorist Roland Barthes, namely something rendered as natural and therefore incontestable.[5] At the core of this myth is the notion that the football manager is the decisive (often the sole) variable in his team's performance: if they do well, he is tactically astute; if they do not, he is a bungler and must depart. Needless to say, this was not always so.

In their early years, the football clubs that we follow today were run by committees, usually of local businessmen, who selected the players and minded the finances. But a number of factors increased their preparedness, at least on the face of it, to delegate responsibilities for team affairs to a third party. These included the time-consuming chore of finding good players and, importantly, the growing identification of local people with the team and correspondingly growing expectations, prompting pitch invasions and other sometimes violent expressions of discontent when team performances were poor.[6] The men now given nominal responsibility for team affairs were generally called "secretaries" or perhaps "secretary–managers" – a designation that survived well into the 1950s. From the early 20th century, there was also the factor of the incipient professionalism of footballers, requiring someone to act as intermediary between football capital and football labour. Players might want someone to represent their interests at board level or to discuss tactics with them. There was, above all, a growing insistence that this managerial figure should not be someone who had "never played" – that is, was not an ex-professional: public-relations man George Allison, who succeeded Herbert Chapman as manager of Arsenal in 1934, remains one of the few Football League managers never to have played football professionally, becoming a lightning rod for these objections.[7]

The first _de facto_ football manager to be paid was Glaswegian George Ramsay, who had trained as a clerk and captained Aston Villa before being appointed club secretary in 1884, a post he held for 42 years.[8] Although Villa were very successful during his tenure, few people outside Birmingham or the football history fraternity will have heard of Ramsay; this is because in his time, team and managerial performance were seldom equated. Some early managers, though, are now frequently rendered as tacticians: these include William Sudell (Preston North End, 1881–1889), Tom Watson (Sunderland, 1889–1896) and Herbert Chapman (Northampton Town, 1907–1912). It is hard to know what these men actually did, or were allowed to do.

There's been a huge growth of football history in the past 30 years, and club archives and newspaper libraries have been plundered accordingly. The language in which football history has been rendered has sometimes been retrospective: there has been much recourse to phrases such as "he guided them to …". But managers often saw little of the club's players during the week, and sometimes, if a manager left, his club decided not to replace him. Managers were seldom seen or referred to. They wore suits, waistcoats and watchchains, and they identified with the board, to which they were, officially, secretary. They might, like secretaries to the board in other businesses, be in a job for a long time: as we saw, George Ramsay was in his post at Aston Villa for 42 years, and Fred Everiss, secretary manager at neighbouring West Bromwich Albion, lasted 46 (1902–1948). According to one website, "much of his work was administrative and he did not pick the team".[9] Others combined football management with second jobs: Fred Westgarth, manager of Hartlepool United from 1943 until his death in 1957, also ran a betting shop across the street from the ground and for good measure kept hens under the stand.[10]

The football press were, if anything, hostile to the notion of a tactical advisor shepherding a team of professional footballers. Nothing illustrates this better than their treatment of Walter Winterbottom, an ex-amateur with Manchester United (1936–1938) and subsequently a lecturer in physical education at Carnegie College in Leeds, who was appointed the FA's Director of

Coaching (and *de facto* coach to the England team) in 1946. The England players had already begun to have tactical discussions in the 1940s[11] but press commentary took no account of this and regarded Winterbottom, initially, as peripheral.

When the England party travelled to Brazil for the World Cup finals of 1950, the *Daily Herald*, definitely the most cogent of Britain's popular newspapers, barely acknowledged his presence, noting as an apparent afterthought "the [England] party also ... included Mr Walter Winterbottom, team manager". During the tournament they mentioned him only twice, reporting that he'd recommended that the players take an afternoon nap and that he had asked the hotel kitchen if they could cook the English staple of steak and kidney pudding for the squad.[12] Increasingly, however, the English football press mocked Winterbottom, painting a picture (widely rejected by England players in their memoirs) of the England squad sniggering behind their hands as the "boffin" Winterbottom tried to lecture them on what they already knew, intuitively, how to do. When the ex-Tottenham and England player Alf Ramsey succeeded Winterbottom in 1963, the transition was widely rendered as "Muddy Boots" replacing "Chalky Fingers".[13]

At least five factors help to explain the emergence of the modern football manager in England. The first was the inauguration of coaching courses by the FA in 1936. This marked the birth of football as a *technocracy* – government by experts. By the 1970s, clubs, players and supporters alike would harbour the expectation that a football manager would have his coaching badge.

Second, in 1953 England were defeated 6–3 by Hungary at Wembley. Hungary was a communist country and, despite having a rich and longstanding football culture that pre-dated communism, the English press had rendered the game as a metaphor for the political divide between the West and East. Indeed, before the return game in Budapest in 1954 (which England lost 7–1) Bob Ferrier of the *Daily Mirror* insisted that the difference between English and Hungarian football was "as stark as that between the Sovietised State and the eternal freedom of Britain".[14] But, since the sons of "eternal freedom" had come a poor second in both matches and individual virtuosity in these games had come exclusively from the "Sovietised" Hungarians, the match was soon widely seen as boosting the technocratic argument. After the humbling in Budapest, a chastened Ferrier had written: "We must sweep away those plumbers and builders and grocers who select national teams, and give responsibility to men who have played and know the game."[15]

Thus, England, the nation that had purportedly given the game to the world, now needed football coaching. This led to a widening of the "Muddy Boots v. Chalky Fingers" schism in the game. Professionals increasingly embraced coaching, but scorn grew for the men who had initially peddled it – the PE lecturers and others who had "never played": the cry went up around the League clubs – "What did *they* know?"[16]

Third, the maximum wage ceiling for League footballers was removed in 1961, rapidly transforming footballers into expensive assets. This moved managers closer to their players, tending to their needs, often building a family ethos around them and defending them against "outsiders": a number of them now relinquished the hat-tie-and-watchchain ensemble in favour of tracksuits. At the elite level, the leading exemplars were Don Revie at Leeds United (1961–1974) and Alf Ramsey (Ipswich 1955–1963; England 1963–1974). Ramsey, in particular, typified the protective screen that managers were now wont to build around their charges: reportedly relaxed and supportive with his players, Ramsey displayed a sitcom aloofness when dealing with the press, delivering terse answers to their questions while trying (with limited success) to gentrify his Dagenham accent. He personified "What Do *They* Know?" Meanwhile "We Never Saw Him" stories about managers of a previous generation began to abound in the football world.

Fourth, football had become a television show, beginning with BBC's *Match of the Day* in 1964 and the extensive coverage of the World Cup of 1966. Football managers became *known*, as individuals and as a part of the football landscape. By 1970, most people probably knew that Matt Busby managed Manchester United, that Tottenham Hotspur were managed by Bill Nicholson and Liverpool by Bill Shankly; comparatively few could name the previous managers of those clubs.[17]

Fifth, in the 1960s, doubtless due to the proliferation of leisure options open to the paying public, attendances at League matches began to fall: whereas 83,260 people had had attended Manchester United v. Arsenal at Maine Road in January 1948 (a record for the ground), only 8,015 came to watch Manchester City play Swindon there in January 1965 (a record low for a League match). This provoked a growing need on the part of clubs who were unsuccessful to say, "We're under new management." The notion that managers were responsible for results was already being affirmed by new technocratic arguments.

Understandably, football managers readily embraced the mystique which was beginning to form around them. What was their secret? "How does a sculptor make an elephant?" Busby (Manchester United manager, 1945–1969) once remarked. "He gets a block of stone and knocks off the bits that don't look like an elephant," was his enigmatic answer to his own question.[18] The success of Liverpool between the 1960s and the 1980s was invariably attributed to their managers (Shankly 1959–1974; Bob Paisley 1974–1983; Joe Fagan 1983–1985) and to their habitation of the mystical "boot room" below the stand at the club's Anfield ground.[19] In 1976, Alan Mullery was newly installed as manager of Brighton and Hove Albion. The *Match of the Day* cameras arrived to cover a Brighton match, which they won. Afterwards commentator Barry Davies posed the question: "Alan, what kind of a manager are you?" Mullery replied: "A successful one. Obviously."[20]

In recent times, further factors have combined to consolidate our core assumptions about the football manager. One is the growth of supporter activism since the mid-1980s. The Football Supporters' Association was founded in 1985 in the wake of the Heysel Stadium disaster of that year, in which 39 people died in a decrepit football ground in Belgium. This was soon followed by a rapid growth of fanzines, including a national one (*When Saturday Comes*, founded in 1986) and numerous others devoted to individual clubs. These often populist, supporter-derived publications helped, among other things, to bring managers under ever-closer scrutiny and to cement their accountability.

This development was, in turn, further strengthened by the growth of the internet, whereon, by the early 21st century, a multiplicity of websites and chatrooms, many once again dedicated to individual clubs, had begun to flourish. Many of these were run by football supporters, and their stock-in-trade was football gossip, chiefly covering the conjectured transfers of players and, alternately, managerial excellence or culpability. With the advent of satellite television and the establishing of a 24-hour news cycle, this has helped to create an often ferociously competitive market for football news (football being the most newsworthy sport in Britain), and it is, moreover, a market in which demand for news invariably exceeds supply. In this context, the journalistic tools with which football managers have been described have been sharpened, with the number of games rapidly reducing before various outlets announce that a manager is "under pressure" or "must be under threat".

Two further interlocking factors have served to anchor these common-sense assumptions about the football manager. One is the ever-growing redefinition of football as a televised spectacle. Televised football now brings with it a number of tropes, many of which place the manager at centre stage. For example, managers are interviewed both before and after matches, underlining their accountability. This accountability is further affirmed during the match when the camera returns to the manager following each notable incident – when his side score a goal, he exults, fists in the air; a near miss and he grimaces and looks away in anguish. Add to this the way in which, when a team is doing badly, the camera picks out lines of disgruntled supporters heading for the exits, well before full-time, or disconsolate fans weeping in their seats at the realisation that their team has been relegated. These images demand a sacrifice.

The other factor has been the huge capitalisation of football, owing in large part to the access to global television that it offers investors. The big football leagues – La Liga, Serie A and most especially the EPL – attract huge sponsorship. For clubs in the EPL sport sponsorship alone generated £280.8 million in revenue for the season 2017–2018. Of the overall figure, £217 million went to the six top brands: Manchester United (Chevrolet cars, US, £47 million), Chelsea (Yokohama tyres, Japan, £40 million), Manchester City (Etihad airline, United Arab Emirates, £35 million), Tottenham Hotspur (AIA insurance, China, £35 million), Arsenal (Fly Emirates airline, United Arab Emirates, £30 million) and Liverpool (Standard Chartered Bank, UK, £30 million). There was a gap of £20 million between the sixth and seventh clubs.[21]

This has had broadly two important effects on the public representation of the football manager. First, a major investment demands an adequate return and, in the absence of that return, a managerial departure is virtually certain to follow. Second and equally important, however, there is an ever-more heightened insistence that success, too, in an apparently financially distorted market, is nevertheless also the work of the manager. In this way, large sums of money are, figuratively speaking, laundered: that's to say, they are injected into a football club and dissolved into the myth of the football manager, re-emerging as his achievement in guiding the team purchased with the original funds to whatever place they occupy in the table. In 2017, for example, the *Daily Mirror* pointed out that Pep Guardiola, then the most fêted manager in the EPL at Manchester City, had, over his career, not only had some of the world's best players at his disposal, but had been able to spend almost 1 billion euros in acquiring many of them.[22] While occasionally acknowledged, however, the resources available to football managers are never allowed to undermine the managerial myth. The football manager remains, for the most part, a figure who is not allowed to have a context, to inhabit circumstances.

Needless to say, most managers publicly subscribe to this myth: "If I look at what he is doing now at Manchester City, following his incredible work at Barcelona and Bayern Munich, I can only admire him and put him in the highest echelon", said fellow manager Ronald Koeman of Guardiola in the same paper a few months later.[23] Koeman's tribute notwithstanding, by 2017 what many already privately regarded as the financial distortions of the EPL were being openly acknowledged. As long ago as 1999, the leading football sociologist John Williams had pointed to a virtually exact correlation between expenditure and league position.[24] In December 2017, ex-Liverpool and England player Jamie Carragher, now a pundit for Sky television (chief broadcaster of the EPL), declared on air: "The Premier League now is becoming a bit of a joke league, with the top teams being so far ahead of the ones at the bottom."[25] Carragher's blunt summation pointedly excluded managers as a significant – or indeed as any kind of – variable in team performance.

"When a question ain't really a question": The football manager as news item

All this must be borne in mind when considering the relationship between the contemporary football manager and the press. The man who, before football became primarily a television show, was seldom seen or even mentioned, is now centre stage and the assumptions about him locked in. Moreover, the manager's relationship with the media is now in large part structured and compulsory: in the EPL, pre- and post-match press conferences are obligatory, and managers receive reprimands if they do not attend. This enforced confrontation between manager and press has important implications.

First, besides constituting the manager as a living news item (in that whatever he says will become "news"), the microphone poked under his chin or the duty to answer the (largely predictable) questions from the assembled press corps help to underline the *performativity* – that is, making a social script a reality through repetition – of football management.[26] Managers, in other words, become what virtually every facet of their social environment tells them that they are.

Second, the growing inequality of the elite football world has in many cases heightened the presentation of self-adopted by some managers. The managers of the successful clubs are *de facto* celebrities and thus likely to develop a persona that exalts their achievements – the Portuguese manager José Mourinho's self-designation as "The Special One" on being appointed manager of Chelsea in July 2004[27] is a good example here. As the writer Alex Hess wrote perceptively in 2017, "Football, in its modern guise, is a soap opera first and a sport second. Some coaches have long since realised this and accordingly spend each week playing to the cheap seats, fastidiously honing their character in the great Premier League pantomime."[28] As befits a pantomime, the roles and, substantially, the script are known in advance. As the American singer John Prine once wrote, "A question ain't really a question/When you know the answer too,"[29] and managers of winning teams will invariably be indulged with the "How?" question ("How pleased were you with the three points today?"; "How satisfied were you with your back four, who kept another clean sheet?"). These are, needless to say, not really questions at all.

The corollary, however, of the indulgence shown to winning managers is the equally predictable call-to-account shown to losing ones: they have been defeated in, say, nine games out of the last 13 – do they now fear for their jobs? These questions, too, are a well-established facet of the ritual and are usually countered with one of a variety of favoured ripostes – "I'm not thinking about my job. I'm focused on the task in hand"; "I'm confident we'll turn it round. We have good players here"; "We know what we have to do. We just have to keep on working hard on the training field"; or, perhaps, "I am not a quitter." These are examples of role distance – of removing oneself, emotionally, from the professional role being enacted.[30]

The assumptions which underlie this largely ritualised interface between football managers and the contemporary mass media are best revealed when they are in some way disrupted – as in the saga of Leicester City and their managers of the time, during the period 2014 to 2017.

In 2014, Leicester City were promoted to the Premier League as champions, by some margin, of the Championship. In the customary vocabulary of football reportage, Nigel Pearson had "brought them up", "done a great job", proved himself "a master tactician", "a great motivator" and so on. In February of that year, for example, Pearson had been made "Manager of the Month" by a betting firm. In the ultra-populist *Daily Star*, Chisanga Malata's routinely individualised appraisal – "The Foxes boss guided his side to five straight victories which saw them stretch their lead at the top of the Championship to eight points. In the process Pearson set a club record by winning eight games in a row."[31] – was one of many.

Once in the EPL, however, Leicester, despite some creditable performances, were soon bottom of the table. The football press now began to ask the (for them, and for most parties to this ritual) standard question of whether he feared for his job. Pearson's response, along with subsequent events, was revealing in several ways.

First, Pearson failed to establish role distance. Instead, like Ramsey in another era, he sought to interpret questions about his likely dismissal as criticism of his players and to define such remarks as the encroachment upon professional space by unqualified lay judgement, citing mitigating factors in the team's performance. This difference of definition (what were standard questions for press people were undue criticism for Pearson) expressed itself in a memorable exchange between Pearson and an agency reporter called Ian Baker at a press conference in April 2015. With his team beginning to rally, Pearson observed: "To win four games on the spin at any level, but certainly at Premier League level, is difficult and for the players to have to deal with the amount of criticism and negativity they've had to endure over the course of the season has tested us." Baker asked: "What criticism are you talking about?" Pearson replied that Baker must have been on holiday for six months, adding, "Your question is absolutely unbelievable, the fact you do not understand where I am coming from. If you don't know the answer to that question then I think you are an ostrich. Your head must be in the sand."[32] An angry Pearson then left the press conference. Veteran BBC sports reporter Pat Murphy later publicly rebuked Pearson, claiming that the press had been "supportive" of the Leicester players and calling Pearson a "bully".[33]

These events are instructive for several reasons. Professional football is here affirmed primarily as a media event. For the purposes of public information, football managers are what the media say they are and not what they, as professionals, believe themselves to be. What Pearson did and said was the journalistic equivalent of contempt of court. The What-Do-They-Know ideology of the 1970s was no longer viable. Any attempt to adduce mitigating factors (his team's lack of experience in the higher division, the greater resources of other clubs, etc.) was ruled inadmissible to the central discourse. So was the apparent stress Pearson seemed to be under: for instance, his altercation with a disgruntled Leicester supporter, whom he told to "fuck off and die" in December 2014 (and for which he was fined £10,000) and his tussle with Crystal Palace player James McArthur in February 2015 were seen simply as further evidence of his instability.[34] Indeed, for the various media, Pearson became a mini-moral panic – an ongoing media narrative in which Pearson became synonymous with "ostrich-gate". Recent records were trawled for further evidence of his abrasiveness, and the football media fed on responses to its own reporting: "Nigel Pearson ostrich rant: the best memes after the Leicester manager's extraordinary outburst" offered *The Independent*,[35] while the *Leicester Mercury* had researched "Nigel Pearson's bizarre ostrich rant: how the internet reacted".[36]

The incident doubled as a collective admonishment of Pearson for breaches of media protocol and, for the same reason, a welcome news story that briefly raised transactions between football managers and the media above the dreary enunciation of questions that often "ain't questions". Weeks later, Leicester City, seen until recently as certain to fall back into the division below and thus cause Pearson to be dismissed, had earned enough points to stay up. The football media resumed discourse as usual. Pearson was redefined according to circumstance: "Nigel Pearson orchestrates great escape as Leicester survive relegation" declared the ESPN website.[37]

Dilly ding, dilly dong: Claudio Ranieri and the "fairytale"

In June 2015, with the 2014–2015 season now concluded but this so-called orchestration of Leicester City's escape still apparently fresh in the memory, the club's owners against all public expectation dismissed Nigel Pearson. This raised further questions about the political environment in which the elite football manager now worked.

In 2010, Leicester City, having been rescued from financial turmoil by the wealthy Serbian-American entrepreneur Milan Mandaric, had been sold to Asian Football Investments (AFI), a consortium owned by Vichai Srivaddhanaprabha of King Power, a major Thai duty-free retailer, based in Bangkok. It cannot be assumed that this transaction – one of many purchases of English football clubs by international corporations or consortia since the 1990s – was inspired either by a love of football or by a special feeling of benevolence towards the football public of this town in the East Midlands. These deals are driven primarily by the quest for global publicity, now easily acquired through the televising of the EPL across five continents. The club's ground was renamed the King Power Stadium in 2011 and the team duly became *de facto* ambassadors for the owners' empire.

In this capacity, and as recent Great Escapees, the squad had visited Thailand. During the visit three reserve players, one of them Pearson's son, had filmed themselves having an orgy with young Thai sex workers and making racist remarks about them. The film had been mailed to friends and, inevitably, passed on to the tabloid press. The incident was reported with predictable faux disgust (the *Daily Mirror* put the film on its website[38]) and the players were sacked. When Pearson was himself fired some days later, press reports cited this incident as the reason: *The Telegraph*, for instance, stated that the dismissal of Pearson's son was "understood to be a pivotal factor".[39] This explanation lacked credibility – it was, after all, difficult to see how, in the circumstances, Pearson could have quarrelled with the dismissal of his son. Nor could he be – and in all probability he was not – blamed for the presence of sex workers in a hotel owned by the King Power group. It was at least as likely that the club's owners, albeit impressed by his strong relationship with the Leicester players, had nevertheless become concerned about Pearson's fractious relations with the media and had decided to seek a cheerier personality to represent the King Power brand to the world, via football-on-television. Football managers, was the implication, should now be held accountable both for match results and for corporate image by their clubs' seldom-seen owners.

Perhaps it was these publicity criteria that provoked former Leicester and England player and now television football presenter Gary Lineker to describe Pearson's successor, Claudio Ranieri, as "an uninspired choice".[40] Ranieri, by then 63, had played in the Italian league in the 1970s and 1980s and then managed a number of teams across Europe, including Chelsea, Valencia, Parma, Juventus, Roma, Inter Milan and Monaco. Most recently manager of Greece, Leicester was his 16th managerial post. Seldom in a job for more than two years, Ranieri had a low media profile. His stay at Leicester would not exceed his accustomed two years, but his tenure would furnish further insights into the contemporary relationship between the football manager and the press. I'd like to discuss various aspects of this relationship.

First, whereas Pearson had provided terse responses to questions which he regarded as challenging his professional competence, Ranieri, possibly exaggerating his already broken English, responded to journalists' inquiries with a mixture of chivalry and amiable nonsense, giving his press conferences the aura of a children's party. If Leicester had been performing badly, this might easily have been rendered in the press as an irresponsible presentation of self – a failure to take a troubling situation seriously. But, to the continued consternation of a battalion of football pundits, Leicester spent all season at, or near, the top of the Premier League and, in one of the most improbable outcomes in the history of modern sport, won it by 10 points.

This meant that two imperatives in the football manager's relationship with the sport press – manager-as-living-news-item and manager-as-author-of-team-performance – came together. An example: at a press conference, on 3 March 2016, with Leicester still perched at the top of the table and contemplating an away game at Watford, questions were reverential and purported to uncover the secret of Ranieri's current success. One reporter quoted Leicester midfielder Danny Drinkwater as saying that Ranieri has "an imaginary bell", which he rang to gain the players' full attention. Did he have such a bell? Ranieri chuckled: "If Drinky says something, it is true." The reporter then stepped forward to present Ranieri with a reception bell, which he now obligingly tinkled to rouse any reporter who may have dozed off. The reporter persisted: did Ranieri feel he had "the aura of a head teacher" about him? Ranieri, doubtful of this, but warming to the bell theme, responded that, if something seemed wrong in a training session, he would shout "dilly ding, dilly dong, wake up" at the players.[41]

Two things are noteworthy here. First, the inescapable link between managerial behaviour and team performance was once again affirmed: the following day the upmarket *The Independent* had the headline "'Dilly-ding, dilly-dong' – Claudio Ranieri reveals unusual training method to keep players happy" and Ranieri saying, "Every manager is different and has their philosophy, their way. I like to (try to make it so for) my players and myself, everybody can do our job, but with a smile – that is my philosophy. I don't want to see sad people around me. It is important to stay together, smiling."[42] Ranieri's managerial secret, therefore, was spreading happiness.

Second, Ranieri hereby became established as a media celebrity, with the additional accoutrement of a catchphrase: he was now the man who said "dilly ding, dilly dong". This phrase and Ranieri's playfulness now became news items in their own right. In May 2016, the *London Evening Standard* reported the former Chelsea player Gianfranco Zola as stating "that Claudio Ranieri's 'dilly-ding, dilly-dong' song at Leicester is nothing new, with the Foxes boss having used the catchphrase in Italy".[43] The local paper, the *Leicester Mercury*, renamed their regular football podcast "Dilly Ding, Dilly Dong".[44] Leicester players were asked to comment on the phrase.[45] And, by late April 2016, with Leicester now EPL champions, Ranieri knew what was expected of him. "Hey, man," he chided reporters. "We are in Champions League. We are in Champions League, man. Dilly ding, dilly dong!"[46]

When Leicester won the EPL is early May 2016 – something that, given their substantial lead, had been expected for some weeks – news crews began to park outside the King Power Stadium and, between them, local, national and global media generated a blizzard of superlatives. It was pointed out that at the start of the season Leicester had been 5000:1 with the bookmakers to win the league and there was frequent recourse to the word "fairytale".[47] A video appeared on the internet entitled "THE LEICESTER DREAM – The Greatest Sporting Story Ever".[48] Later in the summer, local reporter James Sharpe pondered: "Will Leicester City's Premier League title win ever really sink in?"[49] Premier League chief executive Richard Scudamore said that Leicester's victory had "made mugs of us all".[50]

However, from this ocean of hyperbole, which evoked memories of *How Steeple Sinderby Wanderers Won the F.A. Cup*, JL Carr's comic novel of 1975,[51] important inferences were never drawn. It is precisely in the context of competitions such as the FA Cup, which is open to a huge range of clubs from different strata, that journalists hope to deploy their often well-worn phrases about giant-killing and the pitting of highly paid professionals against part-time footballers who during the working week are butchers, bin men or long-distance lorry drivers. But Leicester had merely been competing in a division and, over a 10-month season, had won it. If this was a "fairytale", as it was almost universally rendered, what did that say about the nature of the division they had won? The inescapable answer appeared to be that it was a division characterised by financial inequalities so wide that to transcend them would be unfeasible – a "fairytale" that would "make mugs of us all" and the reality of which would probably "never sink in". That's to say it was not assumed to be an open competition at all. That being the case, shouldn't an acknowledgement of these inequalities inform the routine press judgements made on football managers, and not simply read off from the current league placings? Alternatively, applying these now common-sense football judgements, was not Ranieri, who had apparently wrought "the greatest sporting story ever" *de facto* therefore football's greatest-ever manager, with a job, surely, for as long as he wanted it?

Conclusion: Fundamentally broken?

In July 2016, French midfielder N'Golo Kante, who had been with Leicester only a year but was widely regarded as the biggest single factor in their winning of the EPL, moved to Chelsea. An established top brand owned and capitalised since 2003 by the Russian billionaire Roman

Abramovich, Chelsea had won the title in 2014–2015 and would do so again in 2016–2017. The following February, with Leicester's thus depleted team now in the bottom half of the table, Ranieri was sacked. Given the momentous events of the previous season, this was a big media story, but it did not disturb the common-sense assumptions which govern press reporting of these (myriad) dismissals. *The Independent* was not untypical in its coverage, allowing several of its writers to address Ranieri's departure from slightly different angles, but within the same paradigm of uninterrogated managerial responsibility. Ian Herbert's opinion appeared beneath a headline invoking football's mythical past, calling Leicester's action a "despicable act of felony which shows how football has lost touch with its soul".[52] His colleague Ed Malyon presented a statistical defence of Ranieri, suggesting that Leicester still had a 78 per cent chance of remaining in the Premier League,[53] while Miguel Delaney, under the headline, "Claudio Ranieri's sacking is sad, but modern football means Leicester could not afford to be romantic: not even that title-winning campaign, the closest thing football has seen to a miracle, could buy the Italian time," remarked simply that something was now "fundamentally broken" in the Leicester team.[54]

In September 2017, Danny Drinkwater, another of the title-winning team, also left Leicester for Chelsea. As with Kante, Leicester were unable to replace him. Leicester's first six EPL fixtures included games against Arsenal, Chelsea, Manchester United and Liverpool – four of the division's top six brands. They lost all four. The club now sacked Ranieri's successor, his former assistant Craig Shakespeare.

Late the following January, League leaders Manchester City attempted to sign Leicester's Algerian international Riyad Mahrez, another member of the title-winning team. Manchester City had been owned and heavily endowed since 2008 by Sheikh Mansour Bin Zayed Al Nahyan, a member of the ruling family of Abu Dhabi with access to his nation's huge oil revenues. The club had spent £215 million on players the previous summer. Leicester declined to do business and Mahrez went on strike. BBC *Match of the Day* pundit Danny Murphy told viewers that Mahrez would go to Manchester City in the summer and "make them stronger", adding that the player had "outgrown Leicester. He's too good for Leicester".[55] Fellow pundit Robbie Savage similarly insisted in the *Daily Mirror* that "Leicester's Riyad Mahrez deserves respect for wanting to play at the highest level after Man City move fell over". These are, of course, not only comments on Mahrez; they are comments on the (tacitly assumed) nature of the Premier League. Murphy states that a player is "too good" for one club and must move to another in the same division. Likewise, Savage defines "the highest level" by club and not by stratum.

Occasionally, managers themselves acknowledge the banal economic realities that underlie the day-to-day media stories of their (successful or failed) helmsmanship. "The top teams in that top six, it might be top seven now, they do have enormous spending power," observed Crystal Palace (and former England) manager Roy Hodgson in February 2018. Such teams "leave people like us looking up there and hoping one day we can get there ourselves", said Hodgson, adding the now-inevitable caveat: "But Leicester have proved it's possible. So that's our hope."[56] Days later, when it was pointed out to Manchester City manager Guardiola that his club had spent £448 million on players during his 19-month tenure as manager, Guardiola replied that it had been "necessary to improve the quality of his entire squad".[57] Few would quarrel with what Hodgson and Guardiola say here – indeed, they appear statements of the self-evident. But they are remarkable for the questions that they raise and which football discourse ordinarily excludes. In a financially distorted competition, why were managers of the less well-endowed, and thus lower-achieving, clubs nevertheless defined as failures? After all, in the EPL, eight managers of these clubs lost their jobs between August 2017 and February 2018. And, if such large sums of money were necessary to improve the quality of the team, surely the manager-as-Svengali paradigm was cast into doubt.

For the press, although these structural factors are invoked from time to time, they do not, generally speaking, have any intellectual impact on the day-to-day rendition of the comings, goings and general practice of football managers. The football manager is, as I have argued, a myth, now of some long standing and subscribed to by all relevant social groups: employers, players, supporters, press people and managers themselves. Punishment awaits a manager who disrupts the ritual engagement between himself and the press. Pearson received his in the form of media-orchestrated ridicule. Then-Sunderland manager David Moyes, who took exception to being asked in March 2017 by BBC reporter Vicki Sparks whether he felt under more pressure that day "because the club's owner, Ellis Short, was watching [his] relegation-threatened side", was fined £10,000 for telling Sparks off-camera that she might "get a slap" if she asked him such a question again. (Because the reporter was female, the incident was rendered as a matter of sexist abuse by Moyes. Sparks' question, drawing as it did on the shared managerial myth of the football world, went unremarked.)[58]

To this extent football reportage merges routinely with PR, and the press pack become apologists for a system of structured inequality for which the men in the dugout are held responsible.

References

1. https://www.youtube.com/watch?v=nNyCDQKTBAc, accessed 18 December 2017. This chapter draws heavily on that inaugural lecture and on my long-remaindered book, *The Football World*, Harvester Press: Brighton, UK, 1984.
2. See Glenn Moore, "FFP was launched with good intentions but served to protect elite clubs. Time for a rethink", *The Independent*, 22 May 2015, http://www.independent.co.uk/sport/football/news-and-comment/ffp-was-launched-with-good-intentions-but-served-to-protect-elite-clubs-time-for-a-rethink-10271380.html, accessed 18 December 2017.
3. Wesley Yin-Poole, "Football Manager 13 illegally downloaded over 10m times", http://www.eurogamer.net/articles/2013-11-14-football-manager-13-illegally-downloaded-over-10m-times, posted 14 November 2013, accessed 10 January 2018.
4. The brief tenure of Portuguese woman Helena Costa as manager of the French Second Division club Clermont Foot 63 and the apparently misogynistic remarks made about her by club officials hint at the difficulties that face women contemplating entering football management. See Kim Willsher and Marie-Helene Martin, "Helena Costa: I walked from Clermont Foot 63 after being sidelined by men", *The Guardian*, 25 June 2014, https://www.theguardian.com/football/2014/jun/25/helena-costa-male-colleagues-football-france, accessed 10 January 2018.
5. See Roland Barthes, *Mythologies*, Paladin: St. Albans, UK, 1974.
6. See Stephen Wagg, *The Football World: A Contemporary Social History*, Harvester: Brighton, UK, 1984, pp. 15, 46–47.
7. Wagg, *The Football World*, pp. 38–39.
8. See Neil Carter, *The Football Manager: A History*, Routledge: Abingdon, UK, 2006, p. 13 and 31.
9. https://www.revolvy.com/main/index.php?s=Fred%20Everiss, accessed 10 January 2018.
10. https://www.hartlepoolunited.co.uk/news/2017/february/from-westgarth-to-mclean-1945-to-1968/, accessed 10 January 2018.
11. See Wagg, *The Football World*, pp. 78–79.
12. See Stephen Wagg, "Naming the guilty men: Football managers and the media", in Alan Tomlinson and Garry Whannel (eds.), *Off the Ball*, Pluto Press: London, 1986, pp 36–53.
13. See Wagg, *The Football World*, pp. 73–100. See also Stephen Wagg, "Pioneer at the Chalk Face [Obituary of Walter Winterbottom]", *When Saturday Comes*, No. 182, April 2002, http://www.wsc.co.uk/the-archive/32-Managers/2914-pioneer-at-the-chalkface, accessed 11 January 2018.

14. *Daily Mirror*, 22 May 1954. Quoted in Ronnie Kowalski and Dilwyn Porter, "Cold War football" in Stephen Wagg and David L Andrews (eds.), *East Plays West: Sport and the Cold War*, Routledge: Abingdon, UK, 2007, pp. 64–81. See also Gellert Tamas, "England v Hungary – a football match that started a revolution", http://www.bbc.co.uk/news/magazine-25033749, 23 November 2013, accessed 31 January 2018.

15. *Daily Mirror*, 24 May 1954. Quoted in Jeffrey Hill, "Narratives of the nation: The newspaper press and England v. Hungary, 1953", in Tony Collins and Jeffrey Hill (eds.), "England 3, Hungary 6", *Sport in History* (Special Issue), Volume 23, Issue 2, Winter 2003–2004, pp. 47–60.

16. See Wagg, *The Football World*, pp. 73–100.

17. It was Walter Crickmer, Jimmy Anderson and Phil Taylor respectively.

18. Geoffrey Green, *There's Only One United: The Official Centenary History of Manchester United*, Coronet: London, 1979, p. 53.

19. See Stephen Wagg, "'No scouse, please. We're Europeans': Liverpool Football Club and the decline of the boot room mystique", in Jon Magee, Alan Bairner and Alan Tomlinson (eds.), *The Bountiful Game: Football, Identities and Finance*, Meyer and Meyer: Aachen, Germany, 2005, pp. 121–141.

20. Wagg, *The Football World*, p. 176.

21. Alex Miller, "Premier League shirt sponsorship deals soar to £281.8m", http://www.sportingintelligence.com/2017/07/24/premier-league-shirt-deals-soar-by-record-rates-to-281-8m-250701/, posted 24 July 2017, accessed 11 January 2018.

22. Mark Jones, "Hey big spender! Pep Guardiola is one transfer away from splashing out one billion euros as a manager", *Daily Mirror*, 26 July 2017, https://www.mirror.co.uk/sport/row-zed/pep-guardiola-transfer-signings-spending-10874946, accessed 17 January 2018.

23. Simon Mullock, "'Best manager on earth' Manchester City boss Pep Guardiola ready to join England's World Cup 2018 challenge", *Daily Mirror*, 30 December 2017, https://www.mirror.co.uk/sport/football/news/best-manager-earth-manchester-city-11772853, accessed 18 January 2018.

24. John Williams, *Is It All Over? Can Football Survive the Premier League*, South Street Press: Reading, UK, 1999.

25. Mark Jones, "Jamie Carragher calls the Premier League 'embarrassing' and 'a joke league' because of negative tactics", *Daily Mirror*, 28 December 2017, https://www.mirror.co.uk/sport/football/news/jamie-carragher-calls-premier-league-11761801, accessed 19 January 2018.

26. The concept of performativity is, of course, most closely associated with the American philosopher Judith Butler – see, for example, Judith Butler, *Excitable Speech: A Politics of the Performative*, Routledge: London and New York, 1997 – but the idea is rooted in longer-standing interaction theory and exemplified in the work of, among others, the Canadian social psychologist Erving Goffman – see, for instance, his *Asylums: Essays on the Condition of the Social Situation of Mental Patients and Other Inmates*, Pelican: Harmondsworth, 1968.

27. See https://www.youtube.com/watch?v=pybQAg2YUxY, accessed 19 January 2018.

28. Alex Hess, "Puel and Pellegrino are often lost on the Premier League's pantomime stage", https://www.tifofootball.com/features/puel-pellegrino-often-lost-premier-leagues-pantomime-stage/, posted 18 December 2017, accessed 19 January 2018.

29. From the song "Far from Me" on his debut album *John Prine*, Atlantic Records: Los Angeles, 1971.

30. A concept most closely associated, once again, with Erving Goffman – see his *The Presentation of Self in Everyday Life*, Pelican: Harmondsworth, UK, 1975. An interesting discussion of the concept by Robert Cohen, "Role Distance: On Stage and On the Merry-Go-Round", first published in 2004, can be read at http://www.robertcohendrama.com/other-writings/role-distance-on-stage-and-on-the-merry-go-round/, accessed 21 January 2018.

31. Unattributed, 7 February 2014, https://www.dailystar.co.uk/sport/football/364306/Leicester-City-s-Nigel-Pearson-named-the-Sky-Bet-Manager-of-the-Month, accessed 21 January 2018.

32. A transcript along with a video clip were published by, among others, *The Guardian*, 30 April 2015, and billed as "Nigel Pearson's rant in full: Leicester manager's 'ostrich' outburst", https://www.theguardian.com/football/2015/apr/30/nigel-pearson-rant-full-leicester, accessed 21 January 2018.

33. This can be heard on YouTube. Posted by BBC 5 Live, 30 April 2018; accessed 21 January 2018.

34. See, for example, "Nigel Pearson: His daft season in review", published on the Short List website. Unattributed and undated, but sometime in mid-2015, https://www.shortlist.com/entertainment/sport/nigel-pearson-his-daft-season-in-review/74257, accessed 21 January 2018.

35. Ian Orr, *The Independent*, 30 April 2015, http://www.independent.co.uk/sport/football/premier-league/nigel-pearson-ostrich-rant-the-best-memes-after-the-leicester-managers-extraordinary-outburst-10214427.html, accessed 21 January 2018.

36. Unattributed, 30 April 2015. Part of this article can be seen at: http://journalisted.com/article/8rtsv, accessed 21 January 2018.

37. Ben Jacobs, "Nigel Pearson orchestrates great escape as Leicester survive relegation", http://www.espn.co.uk/football/club/leicester/359/blog/post/2443891?src=com, posted 26 May 2015, accessed 21 January 2018.

38. See Simon Wright, "Premier League stars' racist orgy shame caught on camera during Thailand end of season tour", *Daily Mirror*, 30 May 2015, https://www.mirror.co.uk/sport/football/news/leicester-city-racist-orgy-video-5794654, accessed 31 January 2018.

39. John Percy, "Nigel Pearson sacked by Leicester City after complete collapse in relationship with owners", http://www.telegraph.co.uk/sport/football/teams/leicester-city/11709435/Nigel-Pearson-sacked-by-Leicester-City.html, posted 30 June 2015, accessed 31 January 2018.

40. "Claudio Ranieri: Leicester City appoint ex-Chelsea manager" http://www.bbc.co.uk/sport/football/33513290, posted 13 July 2015; accessed 31 January 2018.

41. The following day Leicester City put these exchanges on YouTube and they can viewed at https://www.youtube.com/watch?v=hPNzhJQbzJ8, accessed 2 February 2018.

42. Phil Medlicott, "'Dilly-ding, dilly-dong' – Claudio Ranieri reveals unusual training method to keep players happy", *The Independent*, 4 March 2016, https://www.independent.ie/sport/soccer/premier-league/dillyding-dillydong-claudio-ranieri-reveals-unusual-training-method-to-keep-players-happy-34512317.html, accessed 2 February 2016.

43. Vaishali Bhardwaj, "Chelsea legend Gianfranco Zola reveals the origins of Claudio Ranieri's 'dilly-ding dilly-dong' song", *Evening Standard*, 11 May 2016, https://www.standard.co.uk/sport/football/chelsea-legend-gianfranco-zola-reveals-the-origins-of-claudio-ranieris-dillyding-dillydong-song-a3245716.html, accessed 2 February 2018.

44. https://audioboom.com/channel/dilly-ding-dilly-dong, accessed 2 February 2018.

45. See, for example, http://sport.bt.com/video/king-on-ranieris-dilly-ding-dilly-dong-91364058634608, posted 6 May 2016, accessed 2 February 2018.

46. See https://www.youtube.com/watch?v=tw-_54RA_NY, posted 22 April 2016, accessed 2 February 2018.

47. See, for instance, Stuart James, "Leicester City win the Premier League title after a fairytale season", *The Guardian*, 3 May 2016, https://www.theguardian.com/football/2016/may/02/leicester-city-win-the-premier-league-title-after-fairytale-season, accessed 2 February 2018.

48. Published by Vadym Sklyaruk Pictures, https://www.youtube.com/watch?v=SkfTShRBJ68, posted 31 May 2016, accessed 2 February 2018.

49. *Leicester Mercury*, 9 July 2016, https://www.leicestermercury.co.uk/sport/football/football-news/leicester-citys-premier-league-title-211497, accessed 2 February 2018.

50. "Leicester City's Premier League win 'made mugs of all of us' – Scudamore", http://www.bbc.co.uk/sport/football/36192037, posted 3 May 2016, accessed 2 February 2018.

51. JL Carr, *How Steeple Sinderby Wanderers Won the F.A. Cup*, London Magazine Editions: London, 1975.

52. Ian Herbert, "Claudio Ranieri sacked: A despicable act of felony which shows how football has lost touch with its soul", *The Independent*, 23 February 2017, http://www.independent.co.uk/sport/football/premier-league/claudio-ranieri-sacked-leicester-city-sack-premier-league-a7596586.html#commentsDiv, accessed 5 February 2018.

53. Ed Malyon, "It's not just sentiment that makes Leicester wrong to sack Claudio Ranieri, the stats say so too", *The Independent*, 24 February 2017, http://www.independent.co.uk/sport/football/news-and-comment/claudio-ranieri-sacked-leicester-stats-sentiment-new-manager-odds-a7597156.html, accessed 5 February 2018.

54. Miguel Delaney, "Claudio Ranieri's sacking is sad, but modern football means Leicester could not afford to be romantic", *The Independent*, 24 February 2017, http://www.independent.co.uk/sport/football/premier-league/claudio-ranieri-sacked-leicester-city-a7596836.html, accessed 5 February 2018.

55. http://www.bbc.co.uk/sport/football/42898542, posted 1 February 2018, accessed 5 February 2018.

56. Robert Warlow, "Leicester City have given us all hope, but Manchester City, United, Liverpool and Arsenal do have enormous spending power", https://www.croydonadvertiser.co.uk/sport/football/football-news/leicester-city-given-us-hope-1160314, posted 3 February 2018, accessed 5 February 2018.

57. Joe Wright, "Guardiola defends huge City spending as Mahrez rumours emerge", http://www.goal.com/en/news/manchester-city-pep-guardiola-defends-transfer-spending/4mv47c5n5tch1uni58o086bd5, posted 30 January 2018, accessed 5 February 2018.

58. *Guardian Sport*, "David Moyes charged by the FA over female reporter 'slap' remark", 26 April 2017, https://www.theguardian.com/football/2017/apr/26/david-moyes-sunderland-charged-fa-female-reporter-slap-remark, accessed 6 February 2018.

26

Who owns the narrative?

Sam Duncan and Ian Glenn

Setting the sports news agenda and owning the narrative was once a battle between the traditional media and sporting organisations. Historically, traditional media set the agenda and, largely, also set the tone of the broader discussion around the issue. During times of controversy and crisis, sporting organisations would try to manage the message, control the narrative and, in doing so, limit the damage to their organisation.[1] Thus, forming strong relationships with news organisations, reporters and journalists was vitally important for sporting bodies. However, this process has changed.

Traditional, mainstream media and sporting organisations now have to contend with social media for control of the message and narrative.[2] Increasingly, fans on social media are claiming control of the narrative and therefore setting the agenda and, in particular, the tone of the discussion around sport and sports issues. Social media is global in its reach, instantaneous and, often, over-emotional, sensationalist, outraged and, because of this, extraordinarily powerful. Importantly, mainstream media often feed off the emotion and, on other occasions, often add to it with their commentary characterised by sensationalist headlines, clickbait, strong, hardline views and sheer volume of content.[3]

In times of sporting crises, this can create a hostile, emotive, sensationalist and even outraged environment – even more so than in the past.[4] This has challenged sporting organisations, who have lost control of the narrative.[5] Thus, instead of being in control of the discussion around various issues, they are now constantly on the back foot, needing to appease the perceived community angst.

So, it seems when it comes to the narrative of various sporting controversies and the tone in which the story is discussed, the power is with the people. But is this a good thing? And is the emotive, outraged tone of social media, which drives so much mainstream commentary and, ultimately, the actions of sporting organisations, a true and fair reflection of "community sentiment?" Often, it seems, it's not. Indeed, one wonders if social media is the domain of extreme and emotive views, asking "where is the 'sensible centre' in all of this?"

Further, given that sporting organisations are constantly responding to online angst, anger and outrage, it is possible some decisions made by sporting organisations are not always reflective of community sentiment or expectations and thus can been seen as too harsh or extreme. The notion of social media setting the tone and owning the narrative is best illustrated by an analysis of "Sandpapergate" – an Australian ball-tampering cricketing controversy that reverberated around much of the world, but more so, stimulated a rapid, and at times furious, response on social media. This chapter will explore the relationship between social media and mainstream media in setting the agenda, narrative and tone of the discussion surrounding the cricketing crisis and how the generally negative, outraged, angst-ridden social media response influenced the actions and decisions made by Cricket Australia, the governing body of the game there, in responding to the crisis. However, before exploring this case study in depth, it is first necessary to understand the strength, force and influence of social media outrage.

Social media outrage

While social media have given society a platform to discuss and debate important issues, it appears that those who do express their opinions via social media platforms such as Twitter don't necessarily represent the majority. Rather, it seems that while the majority stays silent, or chooses to express their views in the physical world, those with extreme views are more likely to vent online. As Mackay notes, social media are often the domain of the extremes: "People are more motivated to express an opinion if they really like something or if their opinion is strong; so, the majority in the middle, who do not have very strong views, are under-represented."[6]

Further, it appears that these extremes are generally negative, characterised by notions of anger, outrage and sensationalism. A 2013 study by Fan et al., relating to anger expressed on Weibo, a "Twitter like" social media site, found that anger spreads most easily and more rapidly than any other emotion on the social media platform.[7] Joy came a distant second. As Crockett states, "anger begets more anger".[8] This appears to reflect the observations of a growing number of academics and media commentators who believe social media platforms such as Facebook and Twitter generate superficial and chaotic commentary which lacks depth, nuance and an appreciation for the complexity characterising many important issues, including sporting controversies such as Sandpapergate.

Thus, issues and crises can be oversimplified, discussed with outrage and emotion and lacking sophistication and nuance. Many, such as Teddy Wayne of the *New York Times*, believe social media activity is too often "aggressive" and dominated by those "trumpeting their ethical outrage". In 2014, he wrote:

> Bile has been a part of the Internet as long as Al Gore has; peruse any epithet-laced comments section or, worse, a chat room. But the last few years have seen it crawl from under the shadowy bridges patrolled by anonymous trolls and emerge into the sunshine of social media, where people proudly trumpet their ethical outrage.[9]

Markman echoes these sentiments, claiming social media is "extraordinarily aggressive, without resolving anything".[10] *The Guardian*'s Rafael Behr describes the style of social media debate as "pulpit and pillory" and believes "rage is contagious. It spreads from one sweaty digital crevice to the next, like a fungal infection",[11] while conservative English political commentator, Iain Dale, describes Twitter as "a hateful place, an absolute sewer", where complexity is ignored and "Shades of grey have been driven out".[12]

Worryingly, these academics and social commentators are not only highlighting the negativity and vitriolic nature of social media, but also that social media commentary and debate are likely to focus on problems in oversimplified, shallow, superficial ways that are largely unlikely to – or perhaps unable to – consider and discuss meaningful solutions. As such, social media may add to the volume of criticism, anger and outrage, but do little to advance the issue or assist in reaching a suitable resolution.

Furthermore, Crockett[13] writes that the condemnation of others by social media users makes them appear less human. For example, those condemning athletes on social media do not have to deal with the "human" reactions of the sports stars when they are denouncing or abusing them. Social media users do not have to see or hear the athletes respond to their criticism – they don't see their facial expressions, hear the tone of their voice or gauge their emotions in response to being labelled "cheats" or a "disgrace" or an "embarrassment". Thus, angry social media users are more likely to continue to vent their anger anonymously.

Nevertheless, the power of social media commentary cannot be denied, particularly when considering the role of mainstream media in both stimulating social media outrage and responding to it with equal measures of sensationalism. Indeed, in the rapid 24-hour news cycle of the digital age where content is ubiquitous, in order to stand out from the crowd and attract both consumers and advertisers, news outlets are increasingly creating and posting content designed to invoke an emotional response (Chen et al., 2015).[14] Thus, many publishers measure the value of their content by the number of comments it generates and hence monitor social media to determine which topics are resonating more than others, which can guide their editorial decisions. Further, passionate, divisive and controversial issues can even influence the way mainstream media discuss the issue – often turning to anger and outrage to ensure clicks, comments, likes, retweets and sparking further debate online.[15]

As Crockett[16] states, "these observations suggest that digital media transform moral outrage, by changing both the nature and prevalence of the stimuli that trigger it. The architecture of the attention economy creates a steady flow of outrageous 'clickbait' that people can access anywhere and at any time". Crockett goes on to explain that clickbait headlines are often presented alongside "highly distinctive visual icons" that act as cues for people to vent their anger at the click of a button.

Furthermore, Messner and Distaso and Wallsten found that bloggers do in fact influence what journalists choose to write about, which, according to Grzywinska and Batorski, highlights that social networking audiences are "telling the media what to write about instead of the other way around".[17] They also write that "the first empirical studies conducted in this field show that Social Networking Sites (SNS) can indeed become the source of media agendas".[18] This was supported by the research findings of a survey of US journalists by Omnicom Group, which found that "blogs are not only having an impact on the speed and availability of news but also influencing the tone and editorial direction of reporting".[19] Similarly, in a study of Australia's changing media landscape, Wilding et al.[20] found negative effects on the mainstream news cycle, including shorter, more emotive content, can be attributed to social media platforms.

So, just who is setting the agenda? If social media, and by extension social media users, are influencing editorial decisions of mainstream media organisations – from the topic of the news to the tone in which its reported and discussed – it seems the power is with the people. There are, however, still times when mainstream media outlets set the agenda, sparking furious conversation online and then, subsequently, feeding further social media debate by adding additional layers to the story.

Yet, in considering who is setting the agenda – particularly in relation to sporting crises – the broadcasters of sport must also be considered. Undoubtedly, through the combination and order of powerful vision and commentary – both as the events unfold and in the immediate aftermath – a very clear, or subtle, narrative can begin to form in the viewer's mind. Standard conventions of sports commentary dictate that commentators are relatively objective, passive and even "invisible" – after all, they are not the stars of the show – the athletes are. But as this chapter illustrates, by "breaking the rules" and taking a more active role in seeking out transgressions and providing more forthright commentary, broadcasters can play a major role in setting the agenda, forming the narrative and shaping what happens thereafter.

Nevertheless, given the instantaneous response to controversies online, issues can very quickly become a crisis, with organisations at the centre of the controversy helpless to manage the way in which they are spoken about. Before the introduction of digital and social media, as Feezell stresses, the narrative of any sports story was generally controlled and contested by the media and sporting organisations.[21] For positive news, the process was quite straightforward, with sporting organisations keen to engage media to share their good news and communicate the story to their fans and the broader sports community.[22]

For negative stories, the narrative was contested between the sports organisation and the media. In times of issues or crisis management, the sports organisation is likely to want to control the narrative and the information released via the media in order to communicate and reveal what they deem in the best interests of the organisation, athletes, sponsors and fans.[23] Put simply, they want to tell the story in their own words to minimise any subsequent image or reputational damage. In doing so they will want to "play down" the significance of the incident to minimise the newsworthiness of the story.[24] On the other hand, independent media would investigate the full story, highlight its newsworthiness and challenge the sporting organisation about the "truth". Thus, the narrative of a story concerning a sport-related issue, controversy or crisis was largely contested between sporting organisations and the media. Furthermore, following any given sport-related incident or controversy, the sporting organisation generally had some time to respond via a press conference, public statement, interview or media release in the hope of either setting the agenda of what the story's narrative would be, or to wrestle back some control of it.[25]

However, this is quickly changing, with sporting organisations now forced to respond far more hastily than at any point in history due to the rapid-fire response to sport-related issues or crises on social media. As content editor for *Media First*, Adam Fisher notes on *Ragan's PR Daily* website:

> When disaster strikes, you have to respond quickly. The time frame for responding is constantly changing – the latest thinking suggests organizations have just 15 minutes to respond.[26]

Indeed, it seems neither the mainstream media nor sports organisations control the narrative of a sporting controversy, issue or story in today's digital and social media world. Nor do athletes or savvy public relations "spin doctors". Rather, the instantaneous nature of social media means that the moment something controversial occurs, social media is in a spin, often characterised by furious "crusaders" voicing their disapproval, disgust and dismay. Thus, the sentiment and tone of the conversation and narrative around the story are set and it seems the mainstream media, who are closely monitoring what is trending and resonating online, follow suit with their own sensational headlines, news stories and talkback radio segments that stir another round of frantic social media commentary.[27]

The social media outrage and subsequent media coverage thus create a particular sentiment and even expectation about how the sporting organisation or athlete at the centre of the controversy should respond – from expected apologies to penalties fans believe should be given and served.[28] Ultimately this can lead to organisations making decisions based on online, and subsequent mainstream media, commentary and sensationalism, rather than independent, level-headed objective thinking. This means sports organisations can end up giving fans what they presumably want – harsh penalties, long bans, merciless punishments. And, while these decisions could reflect the demands of the majority, it seems they may be simply responding to the extremes.

Understanding the theory of social outrage, how it influences the narrative and tone in which issues are discussed and, importantly, what this means for the decisions organisations make in response to the prevailing narrative, is best understood through the example of the Australian cricket Test team's ball-tampering crisis during their 2018 tour of South Africa.

Sandpapergate

To understand the Sandpapergate controversy and how reactions to it unfolded, one needs a variety of contexts: on the conventions of cricket commentary; on the production of images at sporting events; on the particular context of the Test series in which the incident occurred and the bad blood between the teams; and of the reaction between conventional broadcast images and social media reactions.

From a South African perspective, these contexts suggest that the images produced drove a strong narrative of Australian cheating that international commentators struggled to make sense of as they were driven by a need to maintain what Bourdieu calls the "*illusio*" of a pure sporting combat while local Afrikaans commentators were far more able to interpret and attack the images of ball-tampering. In his study of Bourdieu's use of *illusio*, Costey notes that Bourdieu draws on Huizinga and the etymological links between ludens and illusion, playing a game and being taken in by it.[29] The South African analysis also suggests that social media were heavily influenced by broadcast images – including images displayed on the big screens at the ground – and commentary, while social media forced English language commentators into discussing the problem.

Another major conclusion about the events is that most thoughtful commentators observe that many problematic issues around the events remained unresolved. The role of the three punished Australian players as scapegoats and the reconciliatory comments of South African players after the events allowed a narrative of an exceptional deviation from sporting behaviour rather than a deep examination of the underlying issues. In this, one can see this case as typical of many sporting "scandals" such as match-fixing or drug-taking.

It seems pertinent to offer some technical notes on how cricket commentary works on SuperSport, the South African broadcaster that covered the series. Most international cricket matches are played between English-speaking countries and, by agreement, the typical commentary team will include people from more tan one country. Often a team of three commentators will include one commentator from each competing country and one "neutral" commentator. For example, during an Australia Test match against South Africa, an Australian commentator such as Brendon Julian or Shane Warne would be paired with a South African commentator, such as Graeme Smith or Kepler Wessels, and a "neutral" commentator, Jamaican Michael Holding or Englishman Mark Nicholas, former players all.

One of the intentions of this arrangement is to ensure balanced commentary, if not neutrality, and to accommodate viewers from different nationalities with different loyalties. The strength of this arrangement is that it makes for differing perspectives and national perspectives; the weakness is that it may avoid controversy and lack the sharpness of passionate partisanship.

SuperSport also runs an Afrikaans-language commentary largely for South African viewers. This commentary uses the same visuals, but the commentary team, usually of two commentators, are clearly under less pressure to provide a balanced or neutral perspective as they are speaking to a home audience supporting South Africa.

The decision on what images appear on-screen is determined by a broadcast team, not the commentators. With something like 24 high-definition cameras at the ground, an experienced producer can decide what images to show and provide a narrative through the images. According to an interview with one such, Fanie De Villiers, the commentators, far from the action of the pitch, are as reliant on the television images as spectators at home, though they may look up from the television screen to get a sense of field placings or weather conditions, for example.[30]

What does the producer look for? In some cases, commentators may ask for something to be highlighted during play, but some commentators prefer to socialise with the production team rather than other commentators or players, and this enables them to alert cameramen and producers what to look for in play.

Another question is what spectators at the ground see on the big screens that often provide replays or highlights when there is no action on the field. The decisions on what to show on the big screens are, according to SuperSport production head Alvin Naicker, taken by another company who can decide on which advertisements to show on the screens during breaks.[31]

Ball-tampering

By the time the third Test between Australia and South Africa started at the Newlands Ground in Cape Town in March 2018, relations between the teams were strained, with the first two Tests of the series punctuated with heated clashes and controversies involving players from the competing teams. Thus, emotions were high going to Cape Town.

The ball-tampering issue was rumbling beneath the other more obvious clashes. Tampering with the ball is an illegal act. Under Law 41, subsection 3 of the Laws of Cricket, the ball may be polished without the use of an artificial substance, may be dried with a towel if it is wet, and have mud removed from it under supervision; all other actions which alter the condition of the ball are illegal.[32] It is a breach of the laws to tamper with the ball to gain an unfair advantage by causing an unnatural or manipulated movement of the ball.

South African fast bowler turned television commentator Fanie de Villiers said that the Super-Sport commentary team had noticed that the Australians had managed to get the ball to reverse swing after 20 or 25 overs in the Durban Test, something that experienced observers felt was impossible on that surface unless something had been done to the ball.[33] Indeed, many suspected the Australians had tampered with the ball in first two Tests, with Australian Vice-Captain David Warner, who had been accused of "scuffing" the ball with tape in the previous Test, the prime suspect. Thus, the Australian team were placed under the microscope of many suspicious eyes in Cape Town.

In Cape Town, the *SuperSport* production team were determined to watch for any suspicious behaviour in handling the ball. De Villiers said that he and a few other commentators lunched with the technical team and, as this happened after the interval, it seems likely that they, rather than the English-speaking team who ate elsewhere, were more aware of what the images might show as they knew that cameramen were watching carefully for any ball-tampering.

The cameras picked up Australian fielder Cameron Bancroft's role in manipulating a yellow object and using it to rub the ball, and then putting the object down his trouser front. This might have passed without much commentary except that the decision was made to show the images on the big screens at the ground, drawing the attention of the umpires and the Australian coaching staff.

Naicker said that the decision to show the images on the big screen at the ground, something which probably played a decisive role in what followed, was taken by a different organisation with the rights to show images.[34] Cameras then showed Australian coach Darren Lehmann reacting by sending Australia's 12th man – reserve player – Peter Handscomb onto the field, something which Lehmann later justified as simply trying to find out what was going on but which led to speculation that the Australian coach knew they had something to hide.

The umpires questioned Bancroft, who under pressure lied and said it was only a sunglass cloth that he took out of his pocket. Later, of course, all hell broke loose and, as Geoff Lemon wrote, the internet went feral in its anger.[35]

Almost immediately, the narrative and tone of the discussion surrounding the ball-tampering by the Australians was damning and, justified or not, sensationalised, outraged and emotive. While there was some support for the Australians from fans calling for "level heads", emphasising the notion of giving the players the benefit of the doubt and assuming them innocent until proven guilty, the vast majority of activity on Twitter was particularly hostile towards the perpetrators and, indeed, the rest of the Australian team's "win at all costs" culture.

Indeed, the tone was emotive and perhaps reflective of Mackay's claims that social media often represents the extremes of an issue.[36] However, whether the instantaneous condemnation of the Australian team was reflective of the majority or the "sensible centre" of this issue, remains disputable. Indeed, if Mackay is correct, the majority would not have been as hostile towards the Australians, nor would those supporting the Australians be as defensive.

Of more interest to this study is how the instantaneous eruption of social media activity helped shape the overall narrative and tone around the issue, both online and in the discussions emanating from mainstream traditional news outlets in Australia and South Africa. In particular, did the initial mainstream media spark the social media debate, or did the social media firestorm that immediately followed the incident "force" mainstream media to address the issue and, further, encourage them to report on the issue with the same fervour, emotion, sensationalism, outrage and condemnation that was clearly evident online?

As previously noted, in the digital age, mainstream media increasingly measures the "value" of its content by online metrics including clicks, likes, shares, retweets and comments generated by the article or post.[37] As such, they tend to monitor social media activity for "hot" issues that are trending online and generating heated debate and heightened emotion to develop their stories and ensure they're resonating with their target audience.

Mainstream media can, however, also "feed" social media responses, which in turn can stimulate even more sensationalised headlines and create an overall narrative of outrage or sensationalism.[38] In the case of "Sandpapergate" it seems the social media reaction to the incident may have been both a reaction to and a stimulus of the prevailing narrative around the three Australians at the centre of the storm, and indeed, the entire Australian team. Yet, while it seems social media and mainstream traditional media stimulated each other throughout the ordeal, just which platform shaped the narrative – at least initially – appears to have been different in Australia and South Africa.

To fully understand this, it is necessary to analyse the respective television commentary of the both the Afrikaans- and English-speaking SuperSport commentary teams as the ball-tampering moments unfolded.

The commentary

As the events unfolded on Cape Town's Newlands Cricket Ground, the two different television commentary teams took two very different approaches to describing the events that unfolded before them and discussing the broader issues of ball-tampering and the possibility that this was not the first time the Australians had tampered with the ball during their tour of South Africa. The English-speaking commentary was generally more circumspect than the pro-South African Afrikaans coverage, whose audience was almost exclusively South African. The difference between the commentary (see Table 26.1) and immediate reaction to the vision of Bancroft tampering with the ball are stark, with the Afrikaans commentary (translated for this article) initially far more critical and damning of the Australians, even creating a narrative that the action may not have been the first time the Australians had cheated.

The commentary of the events was as follows (translated Afrikaans commentary in bold text):

Table 26.1 TV commentary

Time and visuals	Comment in different languages
Bancroft rubbing ball with his right hand. He puts something in his pocket.	English commentary: Brendon Julian: He's really working on the ball, trying to get that reverse. The South Africans did it so well yesterday. The older it got. **Afrikaans commentary:** **Fanie de Villiers: There he's hiding something. There is something in his pocket. I want to know, who is that? There was scratching. We are all sitting wondering how they are scratching the ball.** **Jeremy Fredericks: He is going to be caught out!** **F de V: That man is in trouble!**
Facial close-up of Bancroft.	Brendon Julian: It's so important to get that ball to reverse. **Afrikaans commentary:** **F de V: There is something in his pocket. He knows the cameras are filming him. We can watch what he is going to do with that little piece of stuff.** **Fredericks: If it is the case, it is very poor sportsmanship.**
Cut to Lehmann in the dressing room, who is speaking behind his hand on a two-way radio. Cut to Handscomb, who will get message. Then to captain Steve Smith.	English commentary: Shane Warne: General comments on how difficult it is to get wickets. **Afrikaans commentary:** **JF: I think the coach has been told what is happening.** **F de V: Yes, the coach is part of this. There is no question. They are guilty. Radios ... There he is ... guilty.**
Cut to South Africa captain Faf du Plessis watching television in the dressing room. He imitates motion Bancroft made in rubbing the ball. Then cut back to Bancroft.	English commentary: Kepler Wessels: What is happening there? What is happening BJ? BJ: What are you talking about? What is Faf doing? **Afrikaans commentary:** **JF: He [Faf] was also in trouble with the zip and the other case.**
Handscomb runs onto field with helmet. Gives it to wicketkeeper Tim Paine.	English commentary: Inaudible comments about the ball and pockets. **Afrikaans commentary:** **JF: Here comes the message. I am telling you Fanie, they are being watched with eagle eyes. Every movement.**
Umpires confer.	English commentary: BJ: Not sure why, perhaps about the light. Ah no. Not clear where the sound is coming from. **Afrikaans commentary:** **JF: Now they must go see what he has in his pocket.**

(Continued)

Table 26.1 TV commentary (*Continued*)

Time and visuals	Comment in different languages
Cut to Handscomb taking yellow bit of paper from pocket and putting it down front of trousers.	English commentary: No commentary but sounds of "Oh No" and booing as this presumably shown on big screen. **Afrikaans commentary:** **JF: Let us look to see what it is.** **F de V: Sandpaper! Look where he is hiding it. Here comes trouble!**
Umpires approach Handscomb, who takes black sunglass cover from his pocket. Cut to teammates David Warner and then Smith.	English commentary: BJ: The umpires are having a chat to Cameron Bancroft. I think they're asking him about what he had in his pocket. That looks like the cover you put your sunglasses in. That's what the umpires were talking to Cameron Bancroft about. **Afrikaans commentary:** **JF: Here is trouble. Hand it over. Show us from the other side so we can see. No, that is not what he had in his pocket! He hid that away in his trousers. It was a piece of paper, that looks like sandpaper that he put down the front of his trousers. They must tell the umpires the paper isn't there. They must look in his trousers.** **F de V: You can go scratch around there if you want to!** **JF: No!**
Later commentary with no English equivalent.	**Afrikaans commentary:** **F de V: Ah no. He is as guilty as you can be. Lehmann should call him off the field, say it is a toilet break and get rid of the incriminating evidence. He is in trouble, with what is it, 18, no, the producer tells me 24 cameras watching. It is like a soap opera.** **There are rules. He must be banned. There is a big difference between a bit of spit and this.**
Close-up of Bancroft with hands in his pockets, chewing gum.	(English suggestion of rain around in the area) **Afrikaans commentary:** **F de V: Now we know why the ball started reversing so quickly. He can't even chew it, he is being watched so closely. They should have looked closely at the ball to see circular signs.** **There will definitely be an inquiry.** **It is the system. The coach knows, the whole team knows. We got it to swing much later. It's not a pitch for reverse swing.**
Bancroft fielding in slips. Puts his hand on his crotch briefly.	**Afrikaans commentary:** **F de V: That thing is beginning to scratch you in the wrong place. [Laughter.]**

The vastly different commentary from the Afrikaans- and English-speaking commentators raises significant questions of how much the audience of a particular broadcast plays in determining the tone in which sporting controversies are discussed and the prioritisation of various narratives, including the prevailing storyline. Clearly, the Afrikaans commentary is far more critical and damning of the Australians than the English-speaking commentary, which appears more reserved, indeed, at times oblivious about what's playing out on the field in front of them. One reason for this may be because the Afrikaans commentary team consisted exclusively of South African commentators and was tailored for an almost exclusively South African audience who, given their intense rivalry with Australia, would be far more receptive to an anti-Australian narrative than those watching from Australia. Conversely, the mild and somewhat careful commentary from the English-speaking commentary team may have been the result of an Australian, Brendon Julian, commentating at the time and the fact that much of the audience watching the broadcast was from Australia, an audience who may have been more inclined to give the Australians the benefit of the doubt.

Nevertheless, the two starkly different responses from the commentary teams provides an insight into relationship between three major forces: the broadcasters, mainstream traditional media and social media. In particular, it highlights how they react to one another to create a prevailing – often outraged, sensationalist and emotive – narrative. However, exactly which media type initially creates and steers the narrative and tone of discussion can vary from issue to issue and indeed, from country to country.

Who dictated the narrative?

Given the forthright nature of the Afrikaans commentary and reaction to the ball-tampering incident, it is possible that the commentary was responsible for sparking the firestorm of social media that ensued, but the most powerful role was certainly played by the damning images, particularly that of the small yellow square of sandpaper.

The way the incident played out on ESPNcricinfo, the world's leading online cricketing commentary platform, was indicative. The textual reporting at the time of the incident was being handled by an Australian, Daniel Brettig, who at first, like the English television commentators, ignored the evidence. But rapidly online responses from people who were watching the live broadcast and following the website flooded in, forcing Brettig to move from the "I never saw anything" line to a bland claim that "everybody does it".[39] Immediately, several online comments asked whether Brettig was Australian and being partisan. Jocular comments about "Captain Underpants", and condemnation followed with ESPNcricinfo soon having to admit that the incident was likely to overshadow normal cricket coverage.

Outside Australia, the most important early social media comments came from powerful cricket figures, many of them radio and television commentators. Their comments at once amplified the significance of the incident and made it very difficult for the cricketing bodies or broadcasters to sweep it under the table, even if they had wanted to.

Though at this stage it was unclear what the yellow object Bancroft had used to scuff the ball was, South African fast bowler Beuran Hendricks, a marginal figure in the national team, tweeted that it was a particular grit sandpaper.[40] Kevin Pietersen, the South African-born former England player, raised the question, which never was fully settled, of how this could happen without the knowledge and approval of coach Darren Lehmann and captain Steve Smith. South African fast bowler Dale Steyn, injured and out of action, simply said: "Can we talk about this?"[41] India's captain, Virat Kohli, commented on how the disgrace would affect the whole group. The former South Africa captain Graeme Smith, the current South Africa player Tabraiz Shamzi and others weighed in.

In Australia, the ball-tampering events took place close to midnight, meaning the first reactions to the saga took place on social media. As highlighted above, the commentary from the English-speaking SuperSport commentary beaming into Australia was far less inflammatory and critical of the Australian cricketers than the Afrikaans commentary, but much of the instantaneous reaction from cricket fans in Australia venting on social media was not as objective, reasoned and rational as the commentary they were listening to while watching Sandpapergate unfold. Rather, much of the commentary was instantly damning of the Australians, criticising their actions, labelling them cheats and calling for significant – even lifetime – bans for those responsible. Fans venting on social media were particularly hostile towards Steve Smith, who was seen as a key architect of the decision to tamper with the ball and who many Australian cricket enthusiasts believed had been largely responsible for what they saw as a decaying, unsportsmanlike, win-at-all costs culture. Indeed, Smith stated in a press conference after the game that the plan to tamper with the ball was devised by the team's leadership group. This prevailing narrative was matched with an emotive, sensationalist tone of outrage and anger, directed towards the Australian cricket team.

To highlight this, key search terms, including "cricket" and "Australia", were used via the advanced search tool on Twitter. Given the incident occurred close to midnight in Australia, the date range for the sample tweets was set from 24 March 2018 to 25 March 2018. This enabled the initial Twitter responses to Bancroft manipulating the ball to be monitored. The first page of responses was used as a sample of typical tweets, with a random selection chosen to highlight the "typical" response to the saga (see Table 26.2).

The first reactions on Twitter were fuelled by outrage and anger, with fans expressing their shock and disappointment at what they had seen transpire on the cricket field. Examples of this included.

The following morning the criticism of the Australian cricketers extended to the highest offices in Australia, with Prime Minister Malcolm Turnbull stating the actions of Smith, Warner and Bancroft were "completely beyond belief" and "a shocking disappointment" and called for Cricket Australia to take "decisive action soon". This was then posted to social media by Sky News Australia.[42] Similarly, the leader of the Australian Labor Party, Bill Shorten, tweeted: "Like all Australians, I can't quite believe what we saw last night. For the sake of all cricket lovers I hope Cricket Australia make it clear that this behaviour is unacceptable."[43]

Thus, the fans, influential former players, commentators and politicians who first reacted to the incident online had created a powerful narrative, characterising the Australians as "cheats" who had disgraced, embarrassed and brought shame upon the nation. As far as the Australian public were concerned, the cricketers had tarnished Australia's reputation. Many were calling for "heads to roll" and for the perpetrators to be sacked, banned, suspended or to resign. The Australian public felt embarrassed and ashamed and clearly, they were angry and outraged.

But were those the views of a hot-headed few, or was this the prevailing narrative endorsed by the majority? Regardless, the swift reaction on social media was used by the commentary team of the English-speaking broadcast as an excuse, or reason, for addressing the issue during the tea break of the match. After a discussion of the match situation during the tea-break analysis, a notably embarrassed-looking host, Mark Nicholas, remarked to fellow commentators, Shane Warne and Graeme Smith, "There's been another moment this afternoon that's already

Table 26.2 Social media: Immediate reaction

David Brown: (@DavidDbbear) 24 March 2018	They need to send the whole team home ... Ban for life from test cricket those who were orchestrating this horrid act ...
@melbourneminker 24 March 2018	Have never liked the Australian Cricket team. Have always been arrogant wankers now cheats!!! @CricketAus
Avtar Singh: (@aman_avtars) 24 March 2018	Heads must roll. This was a betrayal of the public trust. We want accountability
Sel: (@cooloolaman) 24 March 2018	They have been busted cheating, plain 'n simple, sack all involved, especially the so called leadership group for starters, send a clear message to Australians that we don't need to cheat to win
Annie Seaton: @annieseaton26 25 March 2018	What an awful day for Australian cricket fans. Feeling betrayed #CricketAustralia
Dmac: @dmac_0609 25 March 2018 Replying to @TJch9 @wwos and @SunFootyShow	Here's hoping he [CEO James Sutherland] announces that Cricket Australia are sacking every player in the leadership group immediately following the completion of the test and replacing them with players who don't sook [sic], whinge, complain and play cricket with the highest levels of integrity! #SackThem!
David Bartlett: @Bartlett_DJ 25 March 2018	Shame #CricketAustralia shame.
Diane Saunders: @Scottie_Di 25 March 2018	#CricketAustralia Who does that? Who makes a conscious decision to cheat – then gets the newbie to do it? The captain of the Australian Cricket team thats [sic] who. Whatever Bancroft gets the leadership group should get double.
Robert MacSween: @RobMacAUS 25 March 2018 Replying to @GusWorland @CricketAus and @stevesmith49	That's no longer my Aussie cricket team. To think the Australian Captain @stevesmith49 AND the senior squad contrived this low act has not only damaged Aussie #cricket but I feel tainted the nation on the world sporting arena. #shame #SAvsAUS #cricketaustralia @CricketAustrala
Jane: @janenmortimer 25 March 2018	One of the most squeaky clean sports in Australia has just disgraced the nation. Utter bewilderment how this has single handedly destroyed the integrity of Cricket Australia. #Cricket #AUSvsSA #SandpaperGate #balltampering #Bancroft #cricketaustralia
Robert: @magga123 25 March 2018	#CricketAustralia the leadership group delegating dirty commands to a fringe player is the real disgrace in this
Kate Doak: @katedoak 25 March 2018 Replying to @sarahdaviscc	Heads need to roll, both in the team and in Cricket Australia. This sort of crap doesn't just start within the players, it's also a problem culturally within the wider organisation. If CA doesn't act, the Players Association needs to in some way.

(Continued)

Table 26.2 Social media: Immediate reaction (*Continued*)

Chris Doherty: @TapestryC 25 March 2018	The death of Australian Cricket – perhaps we could burn Steve Smith's cap and put it in an urn, play South Africa with our tails between our legs forever more. #shame #stupid #CricketAustralia
Matthew Thorne: @RiskDiversity 25 March 2018 Replying to @LaTrioli	If Cricket Australia doesn't sack the perpetrators I will happily miss out cricket next summer. It is the time to show the nation who idolise sports people some really basic ethics. Do not cheat.
EMMANUEL ZUNINO: @eezpetit 25 March 2018	Get rid of that captain!!!!! Embarrassing … disgusting … a cheat !!! #CricketAustralia
Matthew Sparling: @MattSparlo 25 March 2018 Replying to @davidgower616	As a proud Aussie I am embarrassed & ashamed. They have tarnished cricket & Australia as a whole. There is no option but to remove Smith as captain & suspend the whole "leadership" group. Disgraceful
Shelby Wright: @hypostrophe 25 March 2018	Don't care how many games we lose for how many years. Everyone involved must be sacked before this sun sets. Steve Smith, I dry retched through your press conference. #BallTamperers #CricketAustralia When you have a cancer, you have to cut it out.
Stephen Wright: @stephendayle 25 March 2018	Being called a cheat is a stain that will NEVER wash out … It's the lowest act that can be performed on a sporting field … The damage caused by this will remain forever … #CricketAustralia
Dasher: @Dasher245 25 March 2018	Australian Cricket Captain Steve Smith and his bunch of "Leadership Group" Arseholes should just get out of the game. They are a fucking disgrace, conspiring to cheat, in order to win. Just fuck off. Cricket Australia should resign en masse.
Natalie Kerr: @NattieKerr 25 March 2018	In the words of my husband these boys have "disgraced the nation!" I can't see how the "leadership team" or Bancroft can survive this #CricketAustralia
King Breezer: @Unclebreezer 25 March 2018	I knew Steve Smith was a piece of shit, see you later Little lord fuck pants #cricketaustralia
Peter Baldwin: @MelbMusings 25 March 2018	Cricket Australia must move swiftly and decisively to sack all of the Australian players and officials who condoned the ball tampering plan #balltampering #fairplay
getRIDofDermottB: @ri_dof 25 March 2018	I've always thought that Smith was a petulant little brat but everyone said he's such a great batsman – he is a good batsman but he's now an embarrassment to cricket & Australia. Shame on those involved by grubbing up our reputation! @CricketAustrala

causing a lot of attention on social media," in reference to the images of the ball-tampering incident. He also remarks that "this is what is interesting people all over the world actually at the moment", leading to a more critical analysis of the incident, which gathers momentum when Warne, the great former Australian spin bowler, states: "I don't care who you are, you can't tamper with the ball" (see Table 26.3). From then on, all the commentators appear to become more critical and expansive.

Table 26.3 Former players' TV comments

Commentator and nationality	Comments
Shane Warne (Australian)	Yeah, look, I don't care who you are, you can't tamper with the ball. We don't know, we can't make accusations, but I don't care if it's Australia or South Africa, you can't do the things that it looks like that we all think it's doing. To me, it will be very disappointing and a lot of the Australian sides I played in never did anything like that so I'd be disappointed. I feel a bit for Cameron Bancroft because I don't think he's taken it upon himself to take something and put it in his pocket. Now, who's told him to do that? Has he said, you're the man who's going to do that? I don't know what that process is so it's important to find out that. Got to get to the bottom of why that has happened. And what was it. You've got to own up, you've been caught, you've got to own up what was it you were hiding. It's as simple as that. You can't have that in the game.
Graeme Smith (South African)	I think Warney is spot on and I think if it is proven that the footage we're seeing is correct you have to ask some tough questions of Steve Smith and Darren Lehmann. They've obviously driven this process. They're the leadership, [Bancroft's] the guy who's played seven or eight test matches, you can't see him just deciding that this is what he's going to do on a given day. It's got to be a decision that was obviously taken behind the scenes. We saw mumblings of this in Port Elizabeth and if it was sandpaper it was really silly and not on.
Mark Nicholas (English)	I know that Smith was very quick to support Faf … It's a different thing if there's an outside agent.
Shane Warne	Yeah, I don't have any issue with anyone if they're sucking on a mint or chewing some gum and that's just natural saliva. Every side does that and every designated shiner would do that so you can let that go. But bringing a foreign object that tampers with the ball, that's got to be seriously looked at. There has to be a process to say, let's get to the bottom of what it was. How did it happen? And it's not fair to nail Cameron Bancroft on it either because I don't think he would have made that decision, as I said, by himself. So, we've got to get to the bottom of it. You know, when you get caught, you've got to own up and be honest. It's as simple as that. The Aussies have to be honest to own up and say well, this is how it happened.
Mark Nicholas	Are you happy with that?
Graeme Smith	Well, I have to be. It doesn't look good. There are a lot of questions that have to be answered and Australia need to answer them and for me, the umpires need to take control. For me, it's obvious that he's doing something with the ball, and I'd like to see the umpires do something about it.

This exchange suggests that the broadcast team, who have been far more reserved in their criticism of the Australians as the events unfolded, had been monitoring social media, and using it as a gauge to detect just how big a deal the incident was. Having noticed that the issue had significantly irked many cricket fans around the world, the commentary team had decided the issue needed to be discussed and explored in more detail.

Perhaps assured that the general public would support a more critical stance on the issue, the commentary team became more negative, expansive and critical of the Australians. Thus, it seems the online tone had been somewhat matched by the broadcasters, creating a dominant narrative that the Australians had transgressed the spirit of the game – or more damning, cheated – in what was one of the most significant incidents in the history of the game. The tone of outrage and anger also included cricket fans demanding action, with the most common theme being that the players must be banned.

Following the day's play, it had become clear to the Australian cricket team, and the players involved, that the issue had become a crisis, and, understanding how important the media would be in shaping the narrative that would follow, Smith and Bancroft held a press conference to explain their actions. The exact details of the lead-up to the press conference remain in dispute. It was reported in the *Sydney Morning Herald* that Smith and Bancroft were insistent that they wanted to face the media to explain what had happened, even though they had been urged by Cricket Australia to "wait a day to consider the ramifications of going public".[44] It was also reported that they were encouraged to say as little as possible, with Smith advised to say he was constrained by what he could inform the media due to the fact that Bancroft had been charged and an investigation was underway. However, the Australian Cricket Association president Greg Dyer stated that he had been "dumbfounded that Smith and Bancroft had been allowed to go public after day three in Newlands".[45]

Whatever the case, the Australian duo did conduct the media conference, expressing their sorrow and emphasising the importance of the game's integrity, with Smith stating: "I'm not proud of what's happened. It's not within the spirit of the game."[46] However, the press conference left many unsatisfied, with fans taking to social media to claim the Australians lacked genuine contrition, and to express anger and disappointment at Smith's revelation that the entire leadership group had discussed and endorsed the plan to tamper with the ball. Whether this is actually true remains disputable as the official board investigation into the incident found that only Smith, Warner and Bancroft knew of the plan.[47] Importantly, Bancroft claimed that he had used yellow tape to scuff the rough side of the ball. Four days later it was reported that he had lied and that the "yellow tape" was, in fact, sandpaper.[48] Nevertheless, the overnight hostile, angry, outraged commentary from fans which punctuated Twitter and other online, social media platforms reverberated throughout the mainstream traditional media headlines that followed, with online news outlets, newspapers and leading radio and television networks echoing the criticisms and condemnation first expressed online.

The *Daily Telegraph*'s front-page headline of "Shame" with an image of the iconic Australian "baggy green" cap was followed with headlines on their website including "Deplorable Smith Should Be Sacked as Captain".[49] Online, News Corp's *The Weekend Australian* led their website with headlines condemning the Australian team and, in particular, captain Smith, including "Blatant Cheating. Disgraceful"[50] and "Smith, you're gone. Now".[51] The *Sydney Morning Herald* also shamed Smith, with their leading online story claiming the scandal was "The worst Australian captaincy crisis since underarm incident",[52] referring to a notorious episode in 1981.

Cricket commentators, former players and columnists in Australia's major media outlets echoed these sentiments. Former Australia batsman Jimmy Maher called it "a national day of shame" for the country "and for the entire cricket world, really".[53] Former Australia wicketkeeper Adam

Gilchrist told BBC Radio 5 Live he was "stunned", "shocked" and "embarrassed". Sports editor of the *Sydney Morning Herald*, Chris Barrett, wrote: "Whatever the label, this is a shameful chapter in Australian cricket and there must be consequences," adding, "What took place at the foot of Table Mountain was dumb and deplorable in equal measure."[54] Fellow *Sydney Morning Herald* columnist Peter FitzSimons was even more pointed and stinging with his criticism, labelling the incident "cold-blooded, premeditated, clear-eyed CHEATING".[55] A sports columnist on Australia's national broadsheet, *The Australian*, Patrick Smith, took aim at the Australian Test team's culture, tweeting: "That Steve Smith has not already stepped down as skipper indicates he still does not know the gravity of his actions. Something awful was always going to be the result of the Aussies continually moving 'the line'." ABC cricket commentator Catherine McGregor also called for Smith to be removed as captain: "One it is culpably stupid but, secondly, it's just an appalling and deliberate systematic attempt to undermine the rules and laws of the game. I think the captain's position's untenable. There's no euphemism left for this, this is cheating."[56]

This, according to Grzywinska and Batorski (2016), is typical of how the modern news cycle operates, with media outlets monitoring social media for insights into "trending" or "popular" issues and feeding tones of outrage and anger to encourage consumers to engage with their content and importantly to stimulate interaction with the content in the form of debates, discussion, likes, retweets, shares and comments. Thus, the cycle continues. Whether it's the mainstream media stimulating fiery social media debates or social media anger and outrage motivating emotive mainstream media commentary, the two forms of media can feed each other to create powerful, emotive and often extreme narratives which may or may not reflect the views of mainstream society and those who choose not to express their attitudes, feelings and views online.

But perhaps more problematic is the fact that the narrative and tone created by social media users and mainstream news outlets can set the agenda for how sporting organisations such as Cricket Australia react and respond to such issues. In truth, Cricket Australia was never on the front foot with this issue. Rather, they were forced to respond to the narrative that was set in the immediate aftermath of the ball-tampering. And, while many agree with the way Cricket Australia responded, many others claim their response was, in fact, unfair, too harsh on the players and not truly reflective of what the "mainstream majority" – in Australia, at least – wanted or deemed necessary.

Cricket Australia reacts

Unable to control the narrative, Cricket Australia responded by acting to satisfy the "community response and sentiment", penalising the guilty players. After their investigation into the incident, the board found that Smith, Warner and Bancroft had breached article 2.3.5 of Cricket Australia's Code of Conduct by engaging in conduct that was "contrary to the spirit of the game, unbecoming of a representative, harmful to the interests of the game, and/or which brings the game into disrepute".[57]

As a result, Bancroft was suspended for nine months from "all international and domestic cricket", and he "will not be considered for team leadership positions until a minimum of 12 months after the conclusion of [his suspension] from international and domestic cricket". Vice-captain David Warner and Smith both received a 12-month suspension from "all international and domestic cricket". Warner's punishment also stated that he "will not be considered for team leadership positions in the future". For Smith, he "will not be considered for team leadership positions until a minimum of 12 months after the conclusion of [his suspension] from international and domestic cricket".

Following the announcement of the player penalties, Bancroft, Smith and Warner returned to Australia, and all conducted individual press conferences. Bancroft and Smith held theirs on the same day, with both tearfully apologising to the cricketing public in a raw, authentic, emotional display of contrition. Smith's father stood behind him during his press conference, putting his hand on his son's shoulder as Smith tearfully expressed his remorse and sorrow.[58]

The revealing press conferences sparked another firestorm on social media, but this time, the tone and attitude were far more supportive of the Australians than in the immediate aftermath of Sandpapergate. Indeed, the narrative had changed dramatically, with many on social media (see Table 26.4) claiming that the treatment of the players during the Cricket Australia investigation was unfair and unwarranted, and that, while the players had erred, they should be forgiven and even congratulated for their heartfelt apology.

Examples of this include:

Table 26.4 Social media: Reaction from Australia after the press conference

Jonathan Green: @GreenJ 30 March 2018	I hope the game looks after Steve Smith. And I hope he has the strength to see this through, and be back. He seems to be a good'un. This whole thing has been many years in the making … not his to shoulder alone.
Alister Nicholson: @AlisterNicho 30 March 2018	If there's a positive to be drawn from the terrible example set by behaviour in South Africa it's the example of Steve Smith yesterday. A clearly broken man, Smith understood the damage caused, accepted responsibility and showed genuine remorse. Restored some faith. #ownedit
Sarah Davies: @Sarah_K_Davies 30 March 2018	#respect for Steve Smith. It's bloody hard to show up & genuinely accept responsibility. Leadership is tough; where we might fail in some aspects, we achieve in others. Authenticity, owing the consequences, taking responsibility & learning – great leadership.
Dr Peter Larkins: @doclarkins 30 March 2018	The Steve Smith media conference was as raw an exposure of human remorse and regret you will ever see – difficult to watch but compelling. We do not support what happened but Steve needs unconditional support now as a broken man whose life has changed forever #healthiseverything
Mathew Mcgrath: @matmcgrath74 30 March 2018	Now today everybody loves Steve Smith, day before everyone wanted murder him and hide his body. You're all a Buch [sic] of weirdo fuckwits, kick the absolute cunt out of someone then say it's ok mate, you'll be right, I love you. Very Fickle & fucked up disgraceful society we Live in.
Matt Thistlethwaite: @MThistlethwaite 30 March 2018	We all make mistakes. Steve Smith did the right thing with his apology. What he needs now is the support of his family, friends and the nation #getbehindSteve

(Continued)

Table 26.4 Social media: Reaction from Australia after the press conference (*Continued*)

Rory Gallery: @rorygallery 30 March 2018	Steve Smith showed more grace and remorse in 1 minute than Lance Armstrong ever did. The crimes are not comparable. He's said sorry now time to move on.
David Evans: @DavidEvans_GGL 30 March 2018	I really hope there is redemption for Steve Smith. He's not a bad person just a 28 year old who made a horrible mistake & who of us hasn't done that? Bigger issue is overall culture that allowed this to happen.
Gaye Cameron: @gayecameron 30 March 2018 Replying to @ChrisReason7	I tip my hat to Steve Smith. He showed true leadership, many of our political leaders and others don't demonstrate. I hope the public give him space and time … take it easy cobber Steve Smith.
Karen Pereira: @pereira2karen 30 March 2018 Replying to @ChrisReason7 and @MarkFerguson_7	Compassion. Empathy. Forgiveness. Its [sic] what comes to mind when you watch the press conference by Bancroft and Smith. Give them space now to rebuild. Let's not forget Warner either.
The Mole: @9_Moley 30 March 2018	All you keyboard warriors who crucified our cricketers, did you not feel like you over-reacted just a LITTLE when you saw poor Steve Smith break down last night?
Mirza Iqbal Baig: @mirzaiqbal80 30 March 2018	It's really sad to see Steve Smith, one of the finest batsman [sic] of this era breaking into tears. He has the courage to accept his blunder, now when he has apologised, leave him at his own.
Shoaib Akhtar (former Pakistan fast bowler): @shoaib100mph 30 March 2018	At least Steve smith has the courage to admit like a man but absolutely gutted to see Steve smith breaking down @ the press conference & also the way people treating him @ Airport & in Australia its sad … leave that poor chap alone now …
Katherine Henderson: @RCEMpresident 30 March 2018	Well done Steve Smith. A leader who made a dreadful mistake and has been brave enough to stand up to say so.
Sanjay Manjrekar (Indian cricket commentator): @sanjaymanjrekar 30 March 2018	Hope in time I can earn forgiveness says Steve Smith. He has already got mine. Cricketers have done worse & never admitted their guilt. #StevenSmith
Neroli Meadows: @Neroli_Meadows 30 March 2018	Yes, the wrong thing happened & it was incredibly disappointing. Darren Lehmann & Steve Smith are thoroughly decent men. I have loved working with them over many years & I will always admire them for the way they handled things in 2014. It's hard not to feel sad tonight.

(Continued)

Table 26.4 Social media: Reaction from Australia after the press conference (*Continued*)

deborah knight: @deborah_knight 30 March 2018	Just spent 20 minutes consoling my crying 9 year old who is a major Steve Smith fan after he watched the press conference. Encouraging him and all kids to write Steve a letter telling him how much you love and admire him.
Georgie Gardner: @GeorgieG 30 March 2018	My 11 year old forgives you @stevesmith49 as do we all.
Julie Snook: @JulieSnook 29 March 2018	Steve Smith is a broken man, a devastated man. He's sorry. We forgive and move on. Let's hope @CricketAus his family & friends rally over the coming days, weeks, months. Enough.
Joel Thompson: @joel_thompson12 29 March 2018	If anyone just watched that Bancroft press conference would agree these guys [sic] mental health & Well being should be a priority now for @CricketAus. He was a broken man, it was so hard to watch
Bill Shorten (leader of Australian Labor Party): @billshortenmp 29 March 2018	No one's perfect. A terrible lapse in judgement but good people make mistakes. Credit to Steve Smith for fronting up. Now let's give him some time and space.
Barnaby Joyce: @Barnaby_Joyce 29 March 2018	Enough is enough. Smith, Warner& Bancroft did wrong, they have paid for it. What are you trying to do? They aren't criminals.
Andrew Flintoff (former England cricketer) @flintoff11	Are people satisfied now? Horrible to watch the lad made a mistake

These views were in stark contrast to the initial social media outrage highlighted above, which lashed out at Smith as, among other things, "a piece of shit", "arsehole" and a "petulant brat". Nevertheless, the sudden outpouring of goodwill towards Smith from many on Twitter was reflected in the columns of Australia's leading newspapers and websites. Following Smith's press conference, *The Australian*'s chief cricket writer Peter Lalor wrote in a column titled "Steve Smith is a broken man, and still one to be proud of":

> We were so proud of Steven Devereux Smith. For some time we thought we were wrong. We were angry and betrayed and stunned. Tonight, as that devastated, broken, young man faced the people he let down there was some comfort in knowing we were right to be proud in the first place.[59]

Yet, in truth, while many sympathised with Smith and his fellow perpetrators, not everyone on social media was as forgiving (see Table 26.5). Many sports fans around the world, perhaps with no emotional ties to Australia, vented their surprise at the sudden sympathy shown towards the Australians:

This was reflected in non-Australian newspapers around the world, who took a more cynical view of Smith's press conference tears. For example, the *Daily Mail* in the UK led with an image of Smith crying at his press conference with the headline "Captain Cry Baby"[60] while

Table 26.5 Social media: Reaction from outside Australia after the press conference

Robert John Stanley: @r_jstanley 30 March 2018	So, Steve Smith, Australia's cricket captain breaks down in tears. Do I care? No! he's only crying because he was caught not because he cheated, PATHETIC!
Kezsa: @kezsajm 30 March 2018	The same people sticking up for Steve Smith are the same people who would cheat on their partner and expect forgiveness because they've admitted it and said sorry
Ian......: @redian77 30 March 2018	Anyone have a bit of sympathy for ex Australian cricket captain Steve Smith after his tears at that press conference? Nope me neither #CheatingCunt #BallTamperingScandal
Dany Grimwood: @Danyfab 30 March 2018	Don't get the sympathy for Steve Smith imagine if it was @KP24. People would want a public execution!
Luke Styman: @lptstyman 30 March 2018	I'm not up for all this sympathy for Steve Smith. Millions of people look up to this guy. He is his country's captain! Honour it! Remember, you had a choice pal

the *Daily Star* featured the same image with the headline "Bawl tampering: Crying shame of Aussie cheats".[61]

Nevertheless, the emotional press conferences had led many in Australia to vocalise their support for the Australian players – particularly Smith – and vent their opposition to the penalties, claiming that they were too harsh (see Table 26.6). According to some, the venom on social media, which continued in mainstream media narratives and played a significant role in the penalties handed to the guilty cricketers, did not seem a true reflection of community sentiment.

Perhaps because of the change in attitude among many cricket fans online, or perhaps coincidentally, the same sentiment was expressed in large sections of the mainstream media, including opposing players and commentators in South Africa.

Shane Warne claimed the public reaction to the incident resulted in excessive penalties being handed down by Cricket Australia,[62] while Mark Nicholas wrote, "Clearly the captaincy had to go, and equally clearly the vice-captaincy. The punishment that has followed has been extremely severe, and I cannot help but think of Smith and Bancroft."[63] This sentiment was shared by the Indian master batsman Sachin Tendulkar, who stated that the Australian cricketers "have dealt with enough criticism", urging the media and cricket fans to spare thoughts for their families and that they should be given some breathing space.[64] Former England captain Michael Vaughan believed the penalties were "too harsh", while Indian commentator Harsha Bhogle went as far as saying: "I honestly do not believe any other country would have handed its captain and lead player a one-year ban for attempted ball-tampering."[65]

Thus, the entire tone and narrative around the three Australians had changed. Suddenly, after days of being the subject of hostile, derogatory criticism in tones of outrage and anger both online and within mainstream media outlets, they had suddenly garnered a level of support, with many claiming they'd been hard done by. Had the "sensible centre" of this debate found their voice? Or was the radical change in attitude fuelled by the extremes of the argument? Had the "other extreme" of the argument rallied and found their voice? Or had those who were baying for blood simply changed their mind?

Whatever the case, Cricket Australia had conducted their investigation in the midst of a social media firestorm characterised by anger and outrage. They had acted to satisfy a disillusioned community, but in doing so may have served to appease the "extreme" minority rather than the quieter more measured majority. For many, the issue remained unresolved, with key questions relating to whether the Australians had tampered with the ball in previous Tests, and exactly

Table 26.6 Social media: Reaction to Smith's ban

akash keyal: @akashkeyal 29 March 2018	The one year ban for Steve Smith is way too harsh and the way he is being treated like a convicted criminal is just not acceptable
HM Jyothish: @hmjyothish14 29 March 2018	Ball tampering has never seen anything more than a two-match ban as a punishment. Why then are Steve Smith and David Warner being made to serve one-year bans? #BallTamperingRow #cricketpolitics
Ejaz Ahmed احمد اعجاز: **@ejazahmed510** 29 March 2018	One year ban for players like Steve Smith & David Warner is too much. There had been many such instances of ball tampering in the past but the punishments were not so harsh. #BallTamperingRow #CricketAustralia #OneYearIsTooMuch #PunishmentDoesn'tFitThe Crime
Anand Srivastha: @Jigarthanda 29 March 2018	Steve Smith did cheat but one year ban too harsh when you consider others getting away with the same so called cheating.
Suresh Pandey: @youandme87 29 March 2018	One year ban on Steve Smith is too harsh. I know he breached the trust of Australian public but still he needs to be given chance for redemption, loss of captaincy could have been enough, main worry now will be his mental health. Hopefully CA will look after it.
Graham Staerk: @GStaerk 28 March 2018	A 12 month ban for Steve Smith is appallingly unjust and a complete over reaction to the mob mentality that's distorted society. I hope he sues for restraint of trade.

how many of the team knew of the plan to tamper with the ball in Cape Town, either ignored or unsatisfactorily answered. Certainly, to a certain degree *illusio* was restored by the penalties handed to Smith, Warner and Bancroft by Cricket Australia.

Conclusion

From analysing Sandpapergate it is clear that the narrative of the ball-tampering incident and its aftermath was emotive and, at times, one of anger and outrage. Perhaps the online discussion around the incident and the tone in which it was discussed was fair and accurate in terms of the severity of the indiscretion, and consistent with the mainstream majority of the cricket community around the world. Perhaps the agenda was set by the active role played by the Afrikaans broadcasters in anticipating the indiscretion and then the instantaneous, clear and critical commentary of Fanie de Villiers and Jeremy Fredericks as the events unfolded before them. Perhaps the first tweets and the mainstream media news and commentary that followed were independent of each other, but equally as critical, reflecting the passion cricket fans have for the game and those who represent their country. Perhaps social media now influence mainstream media headlines and commentary, giving "the people" a power in setting the agenda that they have never previously had. Or perhaps mainstream media are still responsible for creating the news and framing the story, which is often exacerbated and heightened by instantaneous, emotive and, at times, extreme views.

Yet from our analysis it is clear that the powerful unexamined factor here was the role of the broadcasters, who decided before the event that cheating was happening and focused on finding evidence of it, and then presented the chain of events with a powerful logic, amplified by the decision to show the damning images on the big screen at the ground. After that, social media and mainstream media co-created the narratives and agendas, stimulating and feeding off each other to create an increasingly emotive, sensationalist tone.

Whether the media sparks online debate or social media outrage informs editorial decisions and stories, it seems clear that today's media narratives are far more fluid, fluctuating and negative. And, regardless of whether social media users start or merely contribute to the narrative and tone of a story such as Sandpapergate, the reality is they have more power in shaping or setting the agenda than ever before. On the one hand, this is an exciting advance as it democratises the media landscape, giving a powerful voice to the public. However, it also has its consequences.

For one, those venting on social media may not represent the views of the majority. Rather, they may be giving an exaggerated voice to a fringe, extreme minority. Indeed, when it comes to many issues, this notion can too be celebrated, but in times of dealing with complex issues, the debate can, at times, lack nuance, depth and an appreciation for various complications. This tends to dumb down the debate, with reasoned discussion giving way to exaggerated emotion. And, problematically, if mainstream media takes its lead from a community minority on social media, then, in fact, the notion of setting the agenda has not been democratised.

The instantaneous response of social media can hijack important discussions, placing the sporting organisations at the heart of the issue on the back foot. Instead of steering the narrative, they are, in fact, responding to it. If Sandpapergate had happened in the 1990s, before social media were created and used, would the media coverage have been different? Would the penalties handed down by Cricket Australia have been as harsh? Would Cricket Australia and the players have been able to "own the narrative"? And if things would, in fact, have been different in a bygone, pre-social media era, would this be a good thing?

While the analysis of Sandpapergate cannot definitively answer any of these questions, it does highlight the rapid, emotive, volatile and fluctuating nature of the narrative and tone which Cricket Australia were responding to. Furthermore, regardless of whether the penalties handed down by Cricket Australia to Smith, Warner and Bancroft were too soft, too harsh or just right, it seems clear that in the age of social media the formation and fluctuations of the narrative have changed, and so too has the process of sporting organisations responding to controversies. Today, more than ever before, the power is with the people.

References

1. Stoldt, G. Clayton, Dittmore, S. and Branvold, S. (2012)., *Sport Public Relations*, 2nd ed. Champaign, IL: Human Kinetics, Inc.
2. Messner, M. and Distaso, M. (2008). The source cycle: How traditional media and weblogs use each other as sources, *Journalism Studies* 9(3): 447–463; Wallsten, K. (2007). Agenda setting and the blogosphere: An analysis of the relationship between mainstream media and political blogs, *Review of Policy Research* 24(6): 567–587.
3. Crockett, MJ (2017). "Moral outrage in the digital age, *Nature Human Behaviour*. Retrieved at: https://www.nature.com/articles/s41562-017-0213-3, accessed 10 May 2019.
4. Ibid.
5. Briggs, M. (2015). *Journalism Next: A Practical Guide to Digital Reporting and Publishing*, 3rd ed. Washington DC: CQ Press.
6. Mackay, H. (2017). Social media analytics: Implications for journalism and democracy, *Journal of Information Ethics* 25(1): 34–48.

7. Fan, J., Zhao, R., Chen, Y. and Xu, K. (2013). Anger is more influential than joy: Sentiment correlation in Weibo, Preprint submitted to *Elsevier*. Retrieved from https://journals.plos.org/plosone/article?id=10.1371/journal.pone.0110184, accessed 14 May 2019.

8. Crockett, "Moral outrage in the digital age".

9. Wayne, T. (2014). Clicking their way to outrage, *New York Times*. Retrieved from https://www.nytimes.com/2014/07/06/fashion/social-media-some-susceptible-to-internet-outrage.html, accessed 14 May 2019.

10. Cited in Wolchover, N. (2012). Why is everyone on the internet so angry?, *Scientific American*. Retrieved from https://www.scientificamerican.com/article/why-is-everyone-on-the-internet-so-angry/, accessed 10 May 2019.

11. Behr, R. (2017). You can log off, sure. But you can't stop the outrage economy, *The Guardian*. Retrieved from https://www.theguardian.com/commentisfree/2017/dec/27/log-off-stop-outrage-economy-media-dark-side, accessed 13 May 2019.

12. Dale, I. (2018). After a year of poisonous new political lows, is it too much to hope our nation can heed the Queen's call for civility and respect in 2019?, *Daily Mail*. Retrieved from https://www.dailymail.co.uk/debate/article-6539143/IAIN-DALE-hope-nation-heed-Queens-call-civility.html, accessed 5 May 2019.

13. Crockett, "Moral outrage in the digital age".

14. Chen, Y., Conroy, Y. and Rubin, V. Misleading online content: Recognizing clickbait as "false news", *WMDD*, 2015, https://www.semanticscholar.org/paper/Misleading-Online-Content%3A-Recognizing-Clickbait-as-Chen-Conroy/dc049b06ae2a33ea5afe76d7f5136cb7afd5317d, accessed 20 December 2019.

15. Chen et al., "Misleading online content: Recognizing clickbait as "false news"".

16. Crockett, "Moral outrage in the digital age".

17. Grzywinska, I. and Batorski, D. (2016). How the emergence of social networking sites challenges agenda-setting theory, *Konteksty Spoleczne* 4(1:7): 19–32.

18. Ibid.

19. Omnicom Group. (2008). *The state of the news media: An annual report on American journalism*, Report by Omnicom Group. Retrieved from https://www.pewresearch.org/wp-content/uploads/sites/8/2017/05/State-of-the-News-Media-Report-2008-FINAL.pdf, accessed 1 December 2019.

20. Wilding, D., Fray, P., Molitorisz, S. and McKewon, E. (2018). *The Impact of Digital Platforms on News and Journalistic Content*. NSW: University of Technology Sydney.

21. Feezell, J. (2017). Agenda setting through social media: The importance of incidental news exposure and social filtering in the digital era,, *Political Research Quarterly* 71(2): 482–494. http://doi.org/10.1177/1065912917744895, accessed 24 August 2020.

22. Stoldt G. Clayton, Scott E. Branvold, Stephen W. Dittmore and Ross, M. *Sport Public Relations*.

23. Ibid.

24. Ibid.

25. Ibid.

26. Fisher, A. (2019). Crucial parts of holding statements in crisis PR, *PR Daily*. Retrieved from https://www.prdaily.com/crucial-parts-of-holding-statements-in-crisis-pr/, accessed June 16 2019.

27. Feezell, J. "Agenda setting through social media: The importance of incidental news exposure and social filtering in the digital era".

28. Crockett, "Moral outrage in the digital age".

29. Costey, P. (2005). L'illusio chez Pierre Bourdieu. Les (més) usages d'une notion et son application au cas des universitaires, *Tracés. Revue de sciences humaines* (8): 13–27; Bourdieu, P. (1994). *Raisons pratiques: sur la theorie de l'action*. Paris: Éditions du Seuil.

30. De Villiers, F. (2019, 25 November). [Interview with Fanie de Villiers].

31. Naicker, A. (2018, 26 March). *Just Plain Drive: Supersport Head of Production, Alvin Naicker, join us on the topic of Australian Cricket Ball Tampering*. Interviewer: D. Scott, The joy ride, OFM.

32. MCC, Unfair play, *The Laws of Cricket*. Retrieved from https://www.lords.org/mcc/laws/unfair-play, accessed 6 December 2019.

33. De Villiers, F. (2019, 25 November). [Interview with Fanie de Villiers].

34. Naicker, Just Plain Drive.

35. Lemon, G. (2018). *Steve Smith's Men: Behind Australian Cricket's Fall,*. Melbourne, Australia: Hardie Grant Books.

36. Mackay, H. "Social Media Analytics: Implications for journalism and democracy".

37. Chen et al., Misleading online content: Recognizing clickbait as "false news".

38. Crockett, "Moral outrage in the digital age".

39. Cricinfo. "South Africa vs Australia", *ESPN Cricinfo*, 2018, https://www.espncricinfo.com/series/10908/commentary/1075984/south-africa-vs-australia-3rd-test-aus-tour-of-sa-2017-18?innings=3, accessed 15 December 2019.

40. Beuran Hendricks, tweet from Beuran_H13, 24 March 2018, cited in Rob Houwing, "EXPOSED: Ball tampering claims rock Newlands", 24 March 2018, https://www.sport24.co.za/Cricket/Proteas/exposed-whats-gone-down-oz-players-pants-20180324, accessed 20 December 2019.

41. Dale Steyn, tweet from dalesteyn62, 24 March 2018.

42. Tweet from @SkyNewsAust, 25 March 2018.

43. Tweet from @billshortenmp, 25 March 2018.

44. Pierik, J. and Barrett, C. (2018). Smith, Bancroft chose to front Cape Town press conference, *Sydney Morning Herald*. Retrieved from https://www.smh.com.au/sport/cricket/smith-bancroft-chose-to-front-cape-town-press-conference-20180403-p4z7jj.html, accessed 6 December 2019.

45. Ibid.

46. Cricket.com.au (2018). Bancroft, Smith reveal ball tampering plan, *cricket.com.au*. Retrieved at https://www.cricket.com.au/video/cameron-bancroft-steve-smith-press-conference-ball-tampering-tape-australia-south-africa-cape-town/2018-03-25, accessed 3 December 2019.

47. Cricket Australia. (2018). Cricket Australia statement on investigation, *Cricket Australia*. Retrieved fromhttps://www.cricketaustralia.com.au/media/media-releases/cricket-australia-statement-update/2018-03-28, accessed 3 December 2019.

48. Ferris, S. (2018). CA slaps bans on tampering trio, *cricket.com.au*. Retrieved from https://www.cricket.com.au/news/sandpaper-not-sticky-tape-revelation-australia-media-statement-ball-tampering-cameron-bancroft/2018-03-28, accessed 8 December 2019.

49. Lalor, P. (2018). Shame, *Daily Telegraph*. March 26, p. 1.

50. Lalor, P. (2018). Blatant. Cheating. Disgraceful, *Weekend Australian*. March 25, p. 1.

51. Smith, P. (2018). Smith, you're gone. Now, *Weekend Australian*. March 25, p. 1.

52. Barrett, C. (2018). Ball tampering episode the worst Australian captaincy crisis since underarm incident, *Sydney Morning Herald*. Retrieved from https://www.smh.com.au/sport/cricket/ball-tampering-episode-the-worst-australian-captaincy-crisis-since-underarm-incident-20180325-p4z63v.html, accessed 6 December 2019.

53. Graham, C. (2018). "A national day of shame": How Australia reacted to Cameron Bancroft ball-tampering scandal … even Aussie PM wades in, *The Telegraph*. Retrieved from https://www.telegraph.co.uk/cricket/2018/03/25/dumb-deplorable-australia-reacted-cameron-bancroftball-tampering/, accessed 8 December 2019.

54. Barrett, "Ball tampering episode the worst Australian captaincy crisis since underarm incident".

55. FitzSimons, P. (2018). Smith has been stood down, but he must answer these key questions, *Sydney Morning Herald*. Retrieved from https://www.smh.com.au/sport/cricket/smith-must-resign-but-not-before-he-answers-these-key-questions-20180325-p4z641.html, accessed 6 December 2019.

56. Quoted in Graham, C. (2018). A national day of shame, *The Telegraph*, 25 March 2018, https://www.telegraph.co.uk/cricket/2018/03/25/dumb-deplorable-australia-reacted-cameron-bancroftball-tampering/, accessed 20 December 2019.

57. "Cricket Australia statement on investigation", https://www.cricketaustralia.com.au/media/media-releases/cricket-australia-statement-update/2018-03-28, accessed 20 December 2019.

58. Ferris, S. (2018). Emotional Smith breaks down in press conference, *cricket.com.au*. Retrieved from https://www.cricket.com.au/news/steve-smith-press-conference-ball-tampering-scandal-speaks-regret-bancroft-warner/2018-03-29, accessed 3 December 2019.

59. Lalor, P. (2018). Steve Smith is a broken man, and still one to be proud of, *The Australian*. Retrieved from https://www.theaustralian.com.au/news/steve-smith-is-a-broken-man-and-still-one-to-be-proud-of/news-story/4fbecb2d2f078a9aef10818dd9ef8c95, accessed 3 December 2019.
60. "Captain Cry Baby", *Daily Mail*. 30 March 2018, p. 92.
61. "Bawl tampering: Crying shame of Aussie Cheats", *Daily Star*, 30 March 2018, p. 50.
62. Cricket Network, (2018). Warne weighs in on tampering saga, *cricket.com.au*. Retrieved from https://www.cricket.com.au/news/shane-warne-punishment-fit-crime-steve-smith-david-warner-cameron-bancroft-ball-tampering/2018-03-28, accessed 6 December 2019.
63. Nicholas, M. (2018). This is another wake-up call for cricket, *ESPN cricinfo*. Retrieved from https://www.espncricinfo.com/story/_/id/22951414/another-wake-call-cricket, accessed 8 December 2019.
64. Press Trust of India. (2018). Sachin Tendulkar supports cricket Australia ban on Steve Smith, David Warner, *Hindustan Times*. Retrieved from https://www.hindustantimes.com/cricket/right-decision-has-been-taken-sachin-tendulkar-on-steve-smith-david-warner-ban/story-xtQlIRXzHYM-jRkZe50iK6O.html, accessed 6 December 2019.
65. Sportskeeda, Twitter reacts as Steve Smith and David Warner are banned for a year, *sportskeeda,* 2018, https://www.sportskeeda.com/live/twitter-reacts-as-steve-smith-and-david-warner-are-banned-for-a-year-cricket, accessed 8 December 2019.

27

Caster Semenya

John Price

The case of Caster Semenya is an interesting one as it raises questions about some of the fundamentals of sport, such as: What is fair competition? Can sport ever be a level playing field? And, who should compete against who?

Semenya, a South African athlete, made global headlines when she won gold in the 800 m at the World Championships in 2009. She has since gone on to win an 800 m silver medal at the London Olympics in 2012 and a gold at the 2016 Rio Olympics. But she is most often in the headlines for the debates and controversies that surround the nature and definitions of her gender and sex. As a black athlete, issues of race and racism are also often at the heart of her story. At the time of her 2009 World Championship victory, it emerged that Semenya had been subjected to medical tests by the International Association of Athletics Federations (IAAF) to determine her "real" sex. She was suspended from competition for 10 months, but later reinstated with her gold medal intact. However, the controversies, and the headlines they create, continue.

In 2011, the IAAF announced new rules which, in effect, introduced maximum readings of testosterone for female athletes and requiring those affected to take hormones to reduce their levels to "normal". The rule was suspended in July 2015 after being challenged by the Indian sprinter Dutee Chand in the Court of Arbitration for Sport (CAS). The court asked the IAAF to follow procedures that would not exclude athletes who were competing using the natural characteristics of their bodies. In effect, Chand's lawyers argued the rule had been discriminatory against women, because male athletes are not screened for high natural testosterone levels. They also argued that the maximum level of testosterone introduced by the IAAF was an arbitrary one.

Then, in 2018, the IAAF introduced rules that would force female athletes to reduce and limit testosterone levels to a maximum prescribed level if they wanted to compete in events from 400 m to a mile. Semenya challenged the rule through CAS but lost her legal case, meaning she would have to take hormone reduction medication if she wanted to continue competing at her usual, Olympic and Commonwealth Games gold medal-winning distances. Although CAS acknowledged the rule was discriminatory, they accepted the IAAF's argument that it was necessary to maintain "fair" competition in women's sport. The ruling was reported extensively in the sports media, including powerful quotes from Semenya herself and extensive interviews with fellow athletes arguing both for and against the decision. The twists and turns of Semenya's story seem to move as fast as the athlete herself and will no doubt have shifted again by the time of publication. The story is a challenging one for the media – and an important one – as it gets to the heart of what sport is, and should be, about.

This chapter critically discusses the media coverage of Semenya's career to date. It begins with a review of previous academic studies, drawing together some of the core findings and criticisms of the sports media's reporting. A subsequent section then puts some of these criticisms to the test via an analysis of the UK press's coverage of Semenya during the Rio Olympics. Finally, a concluding section provides some overall assessments of the media's role and performance in reporting the story.

The media and Caster Semenya

There is now general agreement among scientists that human bodies do not fit neatly into two distinct categories.[1] This poses a problem for official sport, as it has traditionally upheld the notion that gender and sex are binary in nature, thereby reinforcing a "male or female, masculine or feminine essentialism".[2] For some, the cases of athletes such as Semenya – who may be perceived as "non-conventionally feminine" – have the potential to disrupt and challenge traditional, simplistic notions of sex and gender. The process of sex testing exposes some of the complexities and ambiguities in identifying someone's sex. "This process thus challenges the underlying assumptions that sex/gender difference is inherent, natural and most of all, can be categorically 'known' – all assumptions through which the binary is upheld."[3] However, for others, it is during these moments of potential disruption and challenge that sport is most likely to reaffirm its binary foundations. The media, and sports journalists, have important roles in how this plays out.

A number of academic studies have looked at media coverage of Caster Semenya. Although this research has taken in many different national media and contexts, a core and common set of findings has emerged. First, Semenya is predominantly reported in terms of the debates about her sex, rather than her athletic performance. For example, Boykoff and Yasuoka analysed US and UK media coverage of the 2012 Olympics. They found that Semenya was defined by the controversy surrounding her gender and sex in 63 per cent of stories (89 per cent in US coverage, 52 per cent in UK). The result of this was to make the test the athlete's "defining characteristic. Semenya was not able to define herself outside of the verification test and the grammatical structures used to discuss her".[4] As Farrington et al. have observed: "A world champion being investigated, and potentially stripped of their gold medal, is a genuine news story."[5] However, it is perhaps the extent of the focus on this aspect of Semenya's story that is problematic.

A second and related finding is that media coverage has tended to accept and perpetuate, rather than challenge and question, traditional sex definitions and distinctions in sport. Cooky et al. conducted a content analysis comparing US and South African media coverage of Semenya. They found that both the US and South African media frames reinforced limited, binary definitions of sex and gender and discussed whether Semenya was a "real woman". The US coverage tended to depict sex-testing as a necessary and scientific method of upholding a level playing field in sport. The South African coverage framed it as racist and a lasting effect of colonialism, but did not question the binary segregation on which sport is based. Only 1 per cent of articles raised the possibility of abandoning sex segregation.[6] Gunter produced a similar conclusion after analysing coverage of Semenya in the Swiss German-language print media, finding very little evidence of coverage challenging the binary basis of sports competition. She states: "The binary sex and gender constructs and the 'heterosexual matrix' were not productively destabilized or transformed to suit Semenya's body, but rather rearticulated throughout these Swiss German print publications."[7] What might alternative forms of media coverage involve? Sport is based on a myth that it is a level playing field, while, in reality, it reinforces social inequalities. "There should be a clear recognition and acceptance that sport is not a level playing field. This effectively eliminates the need to sex test athletes, male or female, in the first place. This may be an effective route through which to begin to transform sport and to assist with the eradication of sex, gender, race and sexuality injustice."[8]

A third tendency of media coverage of Caster Semenya has been to focus on the biological basis of her sex identity, rather than on how Semenya might define or experience her own identity. As Billings et al. state: "Sex is most commonly understood as the biological difference between men and women. Gender, meanwhile, is a social category, one that emerges and develops in a given culture."[9] Gender, according to that interpretation, is therefore influenced by society and expressed and performed by individuals in their interactions with others and social institutions such as sport and the media. The media has tended to prioritise a rather narrow view of gender – one largely based on official interpretations. Again, this was partly through the preponderance of official voices in reporting, such as medical and sports science experts. As Young observes: "Utilising such expert testimony privileges medical and scientific knowledge over sociocultural and individual knowledge."[10]

A fourth common observation of studies analysing Semenya's coverage by the media has been to find evidence of "ethnic and racist body hierarchies" in the coverage.[11] For some, her case has similarities to the representations of other non-white athletes, such as Serena Williams, who have had their femininity questioned.[12] As well as being portrayed as naturally gifted, with similar connotations to their male counterparts, black female athletes have traditionally been represented as being masculine. As Carrington has suggested, it could be argued that the pervasive "natural black athlete" stereotype has been more damaging for female athletes, as it has "simply heightened the centuries old discourse that black females were already 'mannish amazons' and hence potential if not actual hermaphrodites. Put another way, whereas black male athletes came to be seen as *hyper*-masculine, black female athletes were seen as not female at all".[13] Young has also observed similarities between the treatment of Semenya and that of Saartjie Baartman, the "Hottentot Venus" whose genitalia were publicly exhibited in the 1800s. She argues: "Having Semenya's body examined by medical professionals to verify her femaleness echoed the Baartman case, again publicly humiliating and dehumanizing an African woman."[14]

All of the above findings are to some extent linked to a further tendency in media coverage of Semenya – the dominance of official, male sources within stories. For example, Boykoff and Yasuoka found that the media relied heavily on official viewpoints, and in doing so perpetuated some problematic official terminology – such as the use of the term "gender-verification". This ignores that gender is how Semenya perceives herself, while her sex is what the IOS is trying to establish. For the authors, by following this official "conflation of sex and gender", the media reinforced antiquated concepts regarding sex and gender.[15] The preponderance of official sources within news stories has also meant that male voices have dominated, while Semenya and her voice have been largely absent.[16]

One potential exception to this was when Semenya responded to media controversy by posing for a cover shoot for the South African *You* magazine in September 2009. The headline read: "WOW, LOOK AT CASTER NOW! WE TURN SA'S POWER GIRL INTO A GLAMOUR GIRL – AND SHE LOVES IT!" A photograph of Semenya dominated the magazine's front cover in which she wears a black dress, jewellery and make-up. She is smiling pleasantly and reclined in a passive posture. As Wade (2009) observes: "The copy and the interview tells the reader that Semenya *likes* dressing up and looking pretty, which is an important indicator of both femininity and non-masculinity." The headline also describes turning her from a "power girl" to a "glamour girl", suggesting that it is not possible to be both powerful and glamorous at the same time. Here is the athlete looking as a woman is "supposed" to look. Young (2015), in a detailed analysis of the magazine cover, concludes Semenya's attempts to convince audiences to see her as a "real woman" were flawed. This, she argues, is partly because the *You* cover was in direct contrast to almost all other imagery and coverage at the time.

Caster Semenya and the Rio Olympics

This section presents the findings of a content analysis of UK press coverage of Caster Semenya during the 2016 Rio Olympics (August 5 to August 21). The LexisNexis news database was used to identify articles in the UK national press in which Semenya was a major focus of the content, producing a total of 75 print and online texts. These stories were then analysed in terms of their news frames, selection of sources and the extent to which they provide space for alternative voices to the official views coming from the world of sport. These issues were selected because they allow a critical discussion of results in relation to some of the significant previous research findings highlighted above.

Just 11 per cent of the stories about Semenya focused exclusively on athletics news; 39 per cent focused on the ongoing controversy about her sex, while 50 per cent used a news frame that combined the two – reporting on her athletic performance while making major reference to the sex row controversy. This supports the findings of previous research suggesting that Semenya is overwhelmingly framed in terms of the debates about her gender and sex, and finds it very difficult to escape these representations when it comes to media coverage.

The few examples of purely athletic frames of Semenya tended to involve stories providing form guides for readers considering placing bets on races. Another rare example was written by the Press Association's Mitch Phillips and published by *Mail Online*:

> Caster Semenya qualified for the Olympic women's 800 metres final with supreme ease on Thursday and, barring a catastrophe, appears nailed on for gold in Saturday's final. The South African, looking as if she was out for a Sunday morning jog, won the third of three semis in the fastest time of the night – one minute, 58.15 seconds – with Britain's Lynsey Sharp chasing her over the line to also advance.[17]

The very "straight" nature of this report may lie in its origin from the Press Association and the fact it was published unsubbed online, without the "spin" that a *Mail* reporter may have given it – given the time.

In terms of sources, only 20 per cent of sources directly quoted during Rio were male, while 80 per cent were female. This directly contradicts previous research suggesting that male voices have tended to dominate in media coverage of Semenya to date. This is partly explained by the extensive quoting of athletes, and former athletes, which was obviously in part due to this coverage being during an Olympic Games, when journalists would have access to athletes before and after races. It was also due to the fact that British athletes, such as Scottish runner Lynsey Sharp, were in direct competition with Caster Semenya in the 800 m and so were regularly quoted giving a British take on her performance.

During the Rio Olympic coverage, 79 per cent of sources quoted were athletes, 11 per cent could be classed as experts while 9 per cent were officials (most often Sebastian Coe in his role as president of the IAAF). Just one source did not fit these categories – Semenya's father. Again, these results contradict previous findings suggesting official voices overwhelmingly dominate media coverage about Semenya. And, again, this may in part be due to the analysis focusing on coverage produced during a major event. However, they show that the media can, at least at times, provide a forum for a range of voices to be heard – in their roles as competitors, friends, rivals and interested onlookers. The results also show that extending the range of voices beyond official sources may not necessarily provide more sympathetic coverage of Semenya. Much of the most vociferous opposition to the notion that Semenya should be allowed to compete during this period can be found in the words of female athletes, and former athletes, such as Paula Radcliffe. For example, *The Guardian's* Andy Bull reported that:

> Radcliffe said that Semenya and the other hyperandrogenic women should either "take the medication to suppress the levels, or they choose to have an operation or they choose not to compete".[18]

One of the most interesting aspects of the analysis of the Rio coverage, though, is that the voice of Semenya herself gets a hearing. She is directly quoted in 19 per cent of the stories, which is at odds with previous research suggesting she has been largely absent from media coverage of her life. Again, this may be a quirk of analysing coverage during the Olympics and the opportunities and requirements for media access that it creates. However, it demonstrates that the media is happy to provide a voice for Semenya and other female athletes when given the opportunities to do so, as in the following example:

> Semenya said: "I've been subjected to unwarranted and invasive scrutiny of the most intimate and private details of my being. God made me the way I am and I accept myself."[19]

One strong criticism of the sports media made by previous academic studies[20] is that it has failed to challenge the status quo in its coverage of Semenya, or provide an alternative to the official, perceived wisdom of how sport could deal with the issues concerned. Analysis of the Rio coverage suggests this criticism is unfair. An alternative view of the issues, either challenging or questioning the status quo in athletics, was presented in more than a quarter of stories which focused on the sex row debate.

Dominic Lawson, for example, writing in the *Sunday Times*, argues that many Olympic and sporting champions have unusual biological and physical attributes that help give them an edge over some of their competitors. For example, he considers American swimmer and multiple gold medal winner Michael Phelps, whose arms extend 80 in from fingertip to fingertip, and whose feet are size 14 and reportedly can bend 15 degrees further at the ankle than those of most other swimmers. This is a physical advantage like those of Semenya, but Semenya's advantages are perhaps more controversial than most because they challenge some of the norms and assumptions on which our sporting contests are based. As Lawson writes:

> Where Semenya differs is that she challenges our idea of what it is to be male or female. Matters of gender are intensely politicised and an eternal source of anxiety. Our anxiety is not diminished by the fact that the more we learn, the less simple the matter becomes.[21]

Fleet Street Fox, writing for *The Mirror*, makes some similar points, arguing that Semenya faces extra obstacles because she challenges conventional views of what a woman should look like, or what her place should be:

> Why should she [Semenya] be the one athlete who must suppress it [her advantage], while all the others are encouraged to exploit it? This is nothing to do with sport – it's to do with a medieval obsession with defining the "right sort" of woman … Women who can run faster than most men? Not allowed. Women who weightlift? Don't make me laugh. Women who fancy other women? Well, all right, but only if it's porn.[22]

The *Mail on Sunday* presents a debate between two experts about whether Semenya should be allowed to compete at the Rio Games. Arguing that she should, Roger Pielke Jr., Director of the Sports Governance Center at the University of Colorado, says her case exposes some of the fundamental flaws in how sport is currently organised:

> It turns out human sexuality is not readily distinguished into two categories. Instead, there is a spectrum, coloured in shades of grey. Distinguishing men's from women's categories means drawing a bright line across that spectrum … If people want sport to be divided into high- and low-testosterone groups, that would be a practical way to divide sport by biological characteristics. But sport is divided into men's and women's categories. And so long as being a man or woman is not entirely characterised by biology, sport must accept that biology alone will not always work to identify who fits where.[23]

These are examples of the sports media not only challenging and questioning the official take on events, but also offering potential alternatives. It is an example of how the media can act as a public sphere in which such ideas can be aired and debated. Based on the evidence here, there are numerous examples of sports journalism performing this function, not only reporting the facts of Semenya's case, but also offering discussion about the wider social issues they raise. Often these discussions can be found in the comment and opinion columns appearing alongside straight, factual reports, but they can also be found in more traditional reporting via the quoting of experts, as in the *Mail Online* example above. Studies analysing media coverage of Semenya need to take account of these types of content to provide a fuller and more balanced account of sports journalism's role and performance on this subject.

There is no doubt that reporting about Caster Semenya offers sports journalists a great story, but also a great challenge. Her story rolls together success, failure, heartache, intrigue, controversy, conflict and more – all ingredients loved by a good sports journalist. However, it also embodies complexity, nuance, sensitivity and the implicit dangers of racism and sexism – all elements that may make a journalist wary, and with which the media does not always deal well.

The sports media has generally been criticised by scholars for the way it has reported on Semenya's story to date. As we have seen, some of the main criticisms have been an undue focus on the sex row aspects of her career at the expense of her athletic achievements; a failure to consider or represent Semenya's own expressions of her identity; a tendency to over-represent the views of officials (usually men) and thereby perpetuate a narrow, binary view of what it means to be a woman; and a failure to report how the story may challenge and question the existing structures of sport or provide alternative views about how these may be organised.

This chapter has sought to provide balance to these criticisms by offering mitigation on some and alternative evidence on others. The media undoubtedly is preoccupied with the controversy that surrounds Semenya's sex and gender, and there is further evidence here that this issue either dominates or features in all but a few of her stories. But it must be remembered that the media have not created this story. It was not the media that chose to medically test Semenya, or ban her from competition, or insist that some female athletes should take hormones to reduce their testosterone levels. This is a genuine and important story, and the media would be more culpable if it flinched from engaging with it.

A potentially more serious criticism against the sports media is that, by over-relying on official lines and comments, they are perpetuating a one-sided view of Semenya's story, ignoring her voice and the voices of others – in particular those seeking to challenge some of sport's entrenched assumptions and structures. This chapter has argued, and provided evidence, to suggest that some of this criticism of the sports media has been overstated. Sports journalists are more than happy to provide a voice for Semenya when she is willing, or allowed, to speak; they do give voices beyond officialdom, such as female athletes, a hearing on these issues; and, through the pages of their publications, they are starting to question some of the foundations on which sport is built. Debates about identity, gender, sex and sexuality are social issues, much bigger than any one sport or athlete. However, sport provides one of the arenas in which some of these issues can be played out. The sports media, for all its flaws, is taking part in this conversation by telling the story, or stories, of Caster Semenya.

References

1. Sandra Gunter, "The illegal transgression: Discourse analysis of the media perception of the transgressive aesthetic of performance and display in top-level sports", *Sport in Society*, vol 19, issue 5, 2016, pp. 626–639.
2. Andrew C. Billings, Michael L. Butterworth and Paul David Turman, *Communication and Sport: Surveying the Field*, London: Sage, 2015, p. 192.
3. Cheryl Cooky, Ranissa Dycus and Shari L. Dworkin, "'What makes a woman a woman?' Versus 'Our first lady of sport': A comparative analysis of the United States and the South African media coverage of Caster Semenya", *Journal of Sport and Social Issues*, vol 37, issue 1, 2013, pp. 31–56.
4. Jules Boykoff and Matthew Yasuoka, "Gender and politics at the 2012 Olympics: Media coverage and its implications", *Sport in Society*, vol 18, issue 2, 2015, pp. 219–233.
5. Neil Farrington, Daniel Kilvington, John Price and Amir Saeed, *Race and Racism in Sports Journalism*, London: Routledge, 2012.
6. Cooky et al., "'What makes a woman a woman?' Versus 'Our first lady of sport': A comparative analysis of the United States and the South African media coverage of Caster Semenya".
7. Gunter, "The illegal transgression: Discourse analysis of the media perception of the transgressive aesthetic of performance and display in top-level sports", pp. 626–639.
8. Cooky et al.
9. Billings et al., p. 189.
10. Stephanie Lynn Young, "Running like a man, sitting like a girl: Visual enthymeme and the case of Caster Semenya", *Women's Studies in Communication*, vol 38, 2015, pp. 331–350.
11. Gunter, "The illegal transgression: Discourse analysis of the media perception of the transgressive aesthetic of performance and display in top-level sports".
12. Billings et al.
13. Ben Carrington, *Race, Sport and Politics: The Sporting Black Diaspora*. London: Sage, 2010, p. 80.
14. Young, pp. 331–350.
15. Boykoff and Yasuoka, pp. 219–233.
16. Cooky et al.

17. Mitch Phillips, "Caster Semenya qualifies for women's 800m final along with Team GB's Lynsey Sharp", *Mail Online*, 19 August 2016, https://www.dailymail.co.uk/sport/othersports/article-3748195/Caster-Semenya-qualifies-women-s-800m-final-Team-GB-s-Lynsey-Sharp.html, accessed 19 November 2019.
18. Andy Bull, "Caster Semenya: Athlete wins Olympic gold but faces more scrutiny as IAAF presses case", *The Guardian*, 21 August 2016.
19. Vikki Orvice, "JUST LOOK KAT HER!: What Russian drug cheat said after losing to gender row Semenya", *The Sun*, 17 August 2016.
20. Such as Gunter (2016) and Cooky et al. (2013).
21. Dominic Lawson, "Semenya is a quirk of nature, like Phelps", *Sunday Times*, 14 August 2016.
22. Fleet Street Fox, "Caster Semenya isn't normal – and that's exactly why she has to run in Rio; she's different, just like you and me", Mirror.co.uk, 15 August 2016, https://www.mirror.co.uk/sport/caster-semenya-isnt-normal-thats-8635541, accessed 19 November 2019.
23. Roger Pielke and Ross Tucker, "So is it fair for her to be competing in Brazil at all?", *Mail on Sunday*, 7 August 2016, https://www.dailymail.co.uk/sport/othersports/article-3727419/Caster-Semenya-compete-women-s-800m-Rio-Olympics-allowed-Sportsmail-asks-experts.html, accessed 19 November 2019.
24. Wade (2009) https://thesocietypages.org/socimages/2009/09/12/semenyas-makeover-gender-as-performance/

28

Lance Armstrong

Peter Bramham and Stephen Wagg

This chapter was commissioned to account for the role of the press in the downfall of the world-renowned professional cyclist Lance Armstrong. A weighing of the evidence makes it questionable as to whether what happened to Armstrong should be characterised precisely as a "downfall". It also suggests that the role of the press in establishing Armstrong as a cheat, though crucial, was probably not decisive; the part played by the press in *delaying* this redefinition of Armstrong was also, arguably, considerable.

We'll discuss briefly the growth and importance of international competitive cycling; note the significance of Armstrong in, and beyond, this context; detail the politics of the Tour de France, world cycling's premier event and the chief source of Armstrong's high profile; note the historic use of performance-enhancing drugs (usually called simply "doping") in professional cycling; outline the configuration of factors that led to Armstrong's fall from grace; and, finally, examine the attempts of Armstrong and his entourage to manage what he himself frequently referred to as "the narrative" of this fall.

Au début: The monuments

Professional cycling has its origins in the late 19th century. Importantly, it began, and substantially has remained, a sport of continental Europe – chiefly France, Spain, Italy and the Netherlands. The most kudos are attached to road races, the most prestigious of which were founded in the 1890s or the early 1900s. These include the Belgian event the Liège–Bastogne–Liège, first staged in 1892, and the earliest of the five "Monument" races, the others being the France Paris–Roubaix (begun in 1896), Giro di Lombardia (1905), the Milan-San Remo (1907) and the Tour of Flanders (1913). The biggest race in the professional cycling calendar, however, is the Tour de France, created in 1903, which annually entails punishing climbs through the Alps and the Pyrenees and a finish along the Champ-Élysées. Until the emergence of Armstrong in the 1990s, the leading figure in the pantheon of great road racers had been a European – the Belgian Eddy Merckx, five times victor in the Tour de France(including four in succession from 1969 to 1972) and one of only three riders to win all five Monuments.

Enter Armstrong

Lance Armstrong was born in 1971 and grew up in a small town in Texas. Initially a triathlete, he turned to cycling, which he claimed only to have noticed in 1986;[1] in his late teens, and in 1992, aged 20, he came 14th in the road race at the Barcelona Olympics. He then turned professional with the Motorola team. The same year, amid much derision from spectators, he finished last in the San Sebastian Classic. His performances picked up, however, and, in 1993, he won the World Road Race Championship in Norway. In 1995, he won a stage in the Tour de France, although he was unable to finish the race. In 1996, he signed a sponsorship contract with Nike, who subsequently, signalling his importance to them as a brand, named a building on their campus after him;[2] they also produced a full range of apparel for Livestrong, Armstrong's cancer research charity.[3]

In the same year came what was probably the defining moment in Armstrong's emergence as a public figure: he was found to have testicular cancer that had spread to his lungs and his brain. Against the odds, Armstrong recovered and returned to the saddle, meanwhile establishing his charity for cancer patients. In 1999, he won the first of what, prior to disqualification, would be seven victories in the Tour de France. This, in turn, became the platform for a bestselling autobiography, published in 2000.[4] The book, with its invocations of self-help ("You're not a quitter, are you?", in the frequent exhortation of his mother, a single parent[5]), surviving a life-threatening disease and winning the toughest bike race in the world, made him a ready icon for the American elite of the post-Reagan era: he was fêted at the White House by President Clinton, described as "awesome" by Clinton's successor George W. Bush[6] and invited to ring the opening bell at the New York Stock Exchange on Wall Street, drawing an ovation from the traders.[7] He happily admitted to a chip on his shoulder and to ignoring the rules of the road in pursuit of victory; he was regarded by many in the cycling fraternity as abrasive.[8]

Armstrong and the politics of the Tour de France

By reputation the hardest challenge in professional cycling, the Tour de France, *la grande boucle*, is annually planned, redrawn and marketed as different locations – nation states, regions, metropolitan centres, cities, towns and villages – submit commercial bids to be included by the race organisers as an *étape* or a stage in the race itinerary. Tour organisers, sponsors and *directeurs* of cycling teams, bicycle manufacturers and the mass media take an intense interest in the design, location and coverage of the Tour.

The Tour de France usually spans 2,500 miles over 21 days with two days' rest or *repos*. By tradition, the race includes mountain stages, individual and team time trials and, as noted, finishes in Paris with a mass sprint finish along the Champs-Élysées. The average rider in the peloton (the main bunch of riders) has to consume at least 6,000 and up to 9,000 calories daily to compete, compared to the average adult recommended intake of 2,000 calories. Historically, the race was introduced by an entrepreneurial newspaper proprietor, Henri Desgrange, as a publicity stunt, or *truc*, to increase temporarily the circulation of the yellow newspaper, the *Auto*, subtitled *Automobile-Cyclisme*. But the race has become a permanent feature of cycling and an iconic ingredient in France's national *esprit de corps*, with French media perpetually keen to endorse and support French cyclists as potential contenders for the various subcategories within the competition – for example, "The King of the Mountains", "The Best Young Rider" and, most importantly, the overall champion in the General Classification.

For the pioneering working-class French professional cyclists of the early 20th century, the sole objectives in the race were to secure its monetary prizes and the coveted *maillot jaune* (yellow jersey) that awaited the overall winner. The Tour de France's primary sponsor, Desgrange, resisted several and sustained attempts by the newly professionalised cyclists to make the challenge safer and less damaging to their health and overall well-being. However, Desgrange's vision of the race was to make cycling so hard that only one person would manage to complete the course and survive the race. He designed rules to this effect: he decreed that riders should carry their own spares and effect running cycle repairs without help from others or else risk disqualification. He resisted the introduction of the freewheel, and later even gearing on the bikes. When riders opted to join and cooperate in national or commercial teams to cycle the race collectively and tactically, Desgrange defined that strategy as the antithesis of his rationale for race design. Route planning was destined to make the competition hard. To this end, Desgrange introduced mountain stages, through the Alps and the Pyrenees, and iconic *étapes* to Puy-de-Dome and Mont Ventoux, even though, at the time, the requisite roads and infrastructure were non-existent: "Someone needs to explain to them that the tour is built on pain and suffering. '*Vous êtes des assassins*,' Octave Lapize screamed at the officials after the Tour's first visit to the mountains in 1910. A century later nothing much has changed … nor should it."[9]

Desgranges' prescriptions called, inevitably, for the fortification of the rider. The American academic John Hoberman has argued powerfully that the early cycle races were "de facto experiments investigating the physiology of stress" and that the ingestion of stimulants was as old as the race itself. "Modern doping begins with the cycling craze of the 1890s," he wrote in 1998, when riders' black coffee was laced with "increasing doses of cocaine and strychnine".[10] The respected cycling commentator Phil Liggett likewise recently asserted that "there's always been doping" in competitive cycling, citing alcohol as the early favoured stimulant.[11] The public, sanitised version of the Tour, however, has been that, as with all other such races, the riders' successes were the fruits of their own efforts alone but secured and sustained by the team's overall strategy and protective tactics during race stages of *domestiques*, who were expected to "bury themselves" for a designated team leader. This account was seriously undermined, however, in 1998 when a masseur of the leading Festina team was found to be carrying a huge quantity of banned substances, including the drug erythropoietin (EPO). The Festina team were expelled from the Tour, the first team to be excluded since the Second World War, and the credibility of the race – and of professional cycling in general – plummeted: Hoberman now called the Tour "a pharmacy on wheels".[12]

The "Festina Affair" greatly enhanced the significance of Armstrong; this charismatic striver and cancer-survivor might restore the good name of the Tour, and recalibrate the sport. Armstrong, unfancied and hitherto "never one for the long races",[13] won. But he did not do so in circumstances likely to repair the damage to the Tour's reputation – the race, billed optimistically as the "Tour of Renewal", was won in an improbably fast time, when the organisers, anxious to banish suspicions of doping, had been hoping for a slow one. Armstrong, moreover, was one of a number of participants who had noticeably bullied the French rider Christopher Bassons, who had spoken out against drug-taking on the Tour.[14]

Myth makers and myth busters: Armstrong, cycling and the press

In the world of cycling journalism, David Walsh, who, when working for the British *Sunday Times*, became Armstrong's chief inquisitor, has suggested that there are many media journalists who, often travelling in convoy with the riders, behave like "fans with typewriters".[15] (This is not, of course, unique to sports writing; journalists working other terrain – politics, for example – are equally constrained to keep good relationships with key informants.) The not-wholly-convincing "Tour of Renewal", Walsh argues, represented a "fork in the road" for cycling journalists on the issue of doping.[16] Walsh, the London-based French journalist Pierre Ballester and others regarded some performances by the top cyclists of the time as unfeasible without the assistance of banned substances and said so. This, in the case of Walsh and Ballester, culminated in the publication in France of their book *L.A. Confidentiel: Les Secrets de Lance Armstrong*.[17] On the other side of the fork stood what appeared to be the majority of the cycling press. Their personal involvement with and commitment to the sport and its resident celebrities invariably rendered them unable to ask detached, objective questions about what was happening in front of them. Journalists have their own careers to pursue and a necessary (though not sufficient) condition for success rests upon the need to cultivate and sustain good relations with professional cyclists, team members and their corporate sponsors. There were several key considerations here.

First, there was the notion of bad publicity – in the case of Armstrong, there was a widespread assumption in the cycling press corps that he was good for the sport, having brought extra money into it by breaking cycling in the American market; this development, it was felt, should not be jeopardised by talk of drugs. Armstrong had strong support in the American sport press: for example, in 2008, long after doping rumours had begun to circulate about Armstrong, George Vecsey of the *New York Times* wrote in unqualified praise of him, even quoting him as saying on the drug question: "I think it's time to recognise we had an issue. You put the bad guys away and keep moving."[18] As Walsh saw it, most riders, while resentful of Armstrong's arrogance, also took this view.[19]

Second, good relations with the riders were self-evidently essential for those writers harbouring thoughts of ghosting a cyclist's autobiography. This perhaps persuaded some writers to err on the side of discretion. For instance, in 2014, William Fotheringham, who wrote on cycling for *The Guardian*, referred to "cycling's lengthy battle with its doping demons" – a handy mediaeval formulation not destined to antagonise the professional cycling fraternity: some months earlier, Fotheringham had ghostwritten the biography of leading British rider Bradley Wiggins.[20] Similarly, John Wilcockson, who worked among others for the BBC World Service and *The Times*, was keen to distance himself from Walsh's inquiries and, to Walsh, showed an "enthusiasm for the company of stars",[21] producing three books about Armstrong, including the eulogy *Lance Armstrong: The World's Greatest Champion*.[22]

Third, the life of sports journalists revolves around the need for interviews, publishable quotes and the meeting of deadlines: cyclists angry about too many doping questions might simply refuse to talk to reporters whom they regarded as rocking the boat. Indeed, much testimony on this now heavily written saga attests to the existence of a code of silence (or *omerta*) among cyclists on the matter of doping. A number of writers will also have been privately aware that non-doping riders were styled as *paniagua* ("on bread and water" in Spanish).[23] In his comeback to the Tour de France in 2009, Armstrong was only prepared to do post-race interviews with Frankie Andreu. It was seen as an exercise of power, not least because Andreu had previously testified against Armstrong and as a consequence suffered ostracism and rejection by the professional cycling world, underscored and orchestrated by Armstrong and his legal team.[24]

Fourth, there was the spectre of legal action. The fans with typewriters had morphed in many cases into publicists with laptops. Adverse commentary about doping might antagonise not only the riders but their sponsors (in addition to Nike, Armstrong was funded by the lager giant Anheuser-Busch and a range of others[25]), race organisers and cycling governing bodies. Armstrong deployed legal teams in several countries and the publication of *L.A. Confidential* in 2004 was met with a hail of writs from Armstrong and his legal advisors. Publication of the book in Britain was prevented, and in 2006 Armstrong successfully sued Walsh, Ballester and the *Sunday Times*, even though all their claims turned out to have been correct. (When Armstrong's doping was later established, Walsh and the paper took legal action to retrieve the

£300,000 damages paid in 2006. The matter was settled out of court.[26]) Powerful interests had invested in Armstrong, not only as a successful sportsman and global celebrity, but as a cancer survivor and founder of the Lance Armstrong Foundation, which was rebranded in 2003 as Livestrong. Challenging Armstrong as a doper or a bully simultaneously cast his good works in a bad light.

Moreover, many cycling journalists are outsiders with no cycling expertise or experience, whereas a handful of ex-professional cyclists, with the aid of ghostwriters, have moved into publishing articles and books. The cheerful, wide-eyed coffee-table reporting and commentaries of journalists such as Graham Watson,[27] Geoffrey Wheatcroft,[28] Ned Boulding[29] and even the established cycling specialist Fotheringham[30] sit in sharp contrast to the (often disgraced) insider accounts of Graeme Obree,[31] Paul Kimmage[32] and David Millar.[33] Nevertheless, all journalists in practice must be sensitive to what Irwin Deutscher[34] referred to as the important difference between "words and deeds" – or between the imaginary social order and the "real" one. This lies at the very heart of press "exclusives", media scoops or items that go viral on digital platforms such as YouTube, Facebook or Twitter. Any disparity between his words and his deeds would be the touchstone of several discourses and compelling narratives about Armstrong, his life in the media and in professional cycling.

Professional cycling has developed over time its own culture, language and argot. Indeed, the language spoken in the peloton was historically French but, with the growing impact of global teams, it is currently English. Both languages provide a nuanced repertoire, a wealth of opportunities for participants to account for themselves and their team's actions and behaviours. Spanish and Italian team riders tend to prefer to speak in their own languages and so rely on media interpreters to fill in subtexts for global media outlets. Within professional cycling culture in the 1990s, it was common knowledge that doping regimes were deemed easier in these two nation states because France was seen as fraught with risks, given the heightened vigilance of French police and border officials.

After the Festina team was thrown out of the 1998 Tour de France for drug use and his victory the following year, Armstrong adopted an increasingly aggressive set of responses towards any journalist who framed questions about doping in his team or within the Tour de France peloton in general. Later Tour de France winners such as Wiggins and Chris Froome expressed tiredness and clearly resented persistent questioning about drug use in post-stage interviews from journalists. During his ascendancy in the Tour de France, Armstrong himself continually denied taking performance-enhancing drugs, but his stock response to queries usually sidestepped the direct question by asserting that he had never failed a drug test. However, that was not quite true, as he did test positive for testosterone in 1999. On that occasion, defensive strategies were mobilised: the Union Cycliste Internationale (UCI), in apparent collusion, warned his US Postal Team of this test failure, stressing that he and US Postal needed to provide a suitable excuse quickly. Armstrong's *soigneur* (masseuse) Emma O'Reilly later admitted that his medical team had scoured the internet, identified a suitable cream to deal with saddle sore and found a doctor prepared to manufacture a predated prescription certificate to validate its use.[35] In California in February 2009, he challenged the credentials of the Irish cyclist-turned-journalist Kimmage by suggesting that he had no right to sit on a chair and attend any cycling press conference;[36] another journalist (Walsh) was labelled a "troll" for assiduously asserting that Armstrong took performance-enhancing drugs. Both journalists were critical of Armstrong and accused him of lies and deception. Armstrong countered that they as journalists should welcome the "clean Tour" of 1999 and do their job properly: "You journalists need fall back in love with cycling."[37]

Managing the Armstrong narrative

Armstrong retired in 2005, ostensibly the winner of seven Tours de France. He returned to cycling in 2009.[38] Why is not clear. Perhaps he simply yearned to wear the yellow jersey once again. Maybe his backers estimated that there was more commercial mileage in Armstrong as a global sport celebrity. Or both. It seems clear, though, that Armstrong's return brought now-historic allegations of doping back into play.

It's important, however, to bear in mind that Armstrong's downfall, such as it was, was triggered not, ultimately, by investigative journalism but by the intervention of state actors. Until 2005, affirmations that Armstrong had used banned substances in his race preparation had come from people in the cycling world, for example, from fellow rider Frankie Andreu and his wife Betsy, who had testified to hearing Armstrong admit as much during his hospital treatment for cancer. Although Armstrong and his legal team had sought to discredit these witnesses, their claims had been bulwarked by the occasional failed drug test and the discovery of doping paraphernalia by police or border officials. It was also known that Armstrong had a close working relationship with the Italian doctor Michele Ferrari, a man known to regard the sporting body as an engine whose performance could be enhanced by scientific means, irrespective of the regulations of international cycling.[39]

However, the turning point in the Armstrong investigations came with a complaint made by SCA, a Dallas insurance firm, with whom Tailwind, a company run by Armstrong and his manager Bill Stapleton, had done business. Tailwind had taken out a policy with SCA, as a result of which SCA had paid Armstrong $10 million in bonuses for winning the Tour de France in 2002, 2003 and 2004. With numerous accusations of doping against Armstrong now in the public domain, SCA had raised the possibility of fraud. This had triggered the involvement of the United States Anti-Doping Agency (USADA), a quasi-government body, and an investigation headed by US Food and Drug Administration (FDA) agent Jeff Novitsky, a specialist in drugs-in-sport inquiries.

Riders had now agreed in some numbers to testify against Armstrong, many of them because, *omerta* notwithstanding, they weren't "going to say no to a federal agent" – especially when told, as in the case of former teammate George Hincapie, that to admit doping would mean a six-month suspension, whereas to deny it would carry a lifetime ban.[40] Others, who had themselves been sanctioned for doping, felt that they had been "thrown under the bus" by managers and administrators more anxious to protect cycling's poster boy.[41] These included American Floyd Landis, who in 2006 had been stripped of his title of winner of the Tour de France after testing positive for synthetic testosterone – the first Tour de France winner to be disqualified since 1904.[42] In 2009, he was denied a place in the Astana team by team *directeur* Johann Bruyneel when Armstrong returned to the Tour de France because he was "tainted".[43] Publicity – not cycling, nor regulation, nor morality – was the governing consideration here, and any rider or cycling ancillary who spoke out against what seems to have been systematic doping was immediately confronted with a platoon of corporate lawyers.

The subsequent USADA report in 2012 confirmed "overwhelming evidence" of doping by Armstrong and his US Postal team.[44] Only now, with Armstrong's professional reputation officially in tatters, did the bulk of the press fully acknowledge this "story". For instance, on the day of the publication of the USADA report, masseuse O'Reilly, whose evidence against Armstrong had been known for several years and who had since left Armstrong's entourage and set up a private practice in the UK, was told by her receptionist that their phone had been ringing solidly for three hours by journalists now wanting O'Reilly to comment.[45]

Armstrong, however, was not without crucial resources. A creature of the postmodern era, he readily recognised himself as a text, or, to use his preferred term, an ongoing "story".[46] Equally readily, and doubtless with expert impression management advice, he deployed those skills best described by the Canadian social psychologist Erving Goffman: the presentation of self and the management of stigma, or "spoiled identity".[47] Thus, Armstrong could try – indeed, he would have been compelled by his backers – to define himself anew. After all, as Stuart Hall has written, "identity is not a set of fixed attributes, the unchanging essence of the inner self but a constantly shifting process of positioning".[48]

Armstrong's chief forum for the management of his spoiled identity was astutely chosen: *The Oprah Winfrey Show*, a hugely popular syndicated daytime talk show on American television. Winfrey's format, as Eva Illouz's perceptive analysis makes clear, was confessional and specialised in "making failure and suffering into acceptable public narratives of the self"; in Illouz's telling phrase it offered its audience "pain and circuses".[49] In his interview with Winfrey, which took place in January 2013, Armstrong answered a straight "Yes" to a series of "Did you …?" questions about the consumption of banned substances but thereafter portrayed himself, consistent with the Winfrey paradigm, as a flawed human being, one who'd made bad choices, but unavoidable choices thrown up by the culture he inhabited. "Was it humanly possible to win the Tour de France without doping, seven times?" asked Winfrey. "Not in my opinion," replied Armstrong. "That generation. I didn't invent the culture, but I didn't try to stop the culture." Thus, ultimately, like so many of Oprah's guests, Armstrong was a victim of circumstance.

Indeed, much of the conversation ranged over the culture and mechanics of doping in cycling, but, at other crucial times, the interview took Armstrong out of this culture and defined him once again as stand-alone cancer survivor and stop-at-nothing striver, locked in a primaeval and unrelenting defence of his territory. At one point Winfrey asked him the apparently leading questions: "How important was winning to you and would you do anything to win at all costs?" He replied: "It was win at all costs. When I was diagnosed [with cancer] I would do anything to survive. I took that attitude – win at all costs – to cycling. That's bad. I was taking drugs before that but I wasn't a bully."[50] This definition of Armstrong, propounded originally and most strongly in his bestselling autobiography *It's Not About the Bike*, retained much credibility: as O'Reilly (whom he had once called a "whore" in an effort to undermine her testimony) observed, Armstrong had "his fists up against the whole world".[51]

The point of all this was to salvage some degree of Armstrong's lucrative celebrity, something shrewdly captured by the Australian scholar David Rowe: "The crafted public confession – in Armstrong's case involving the world's best-known and most reliably empathetic interviewer – maximises publicity for his admission of doping while trying to head off subsequent attempts to pursue the matter in detail. It garners the enormous media coverage that re-confirms the celebrity's newsworthiness and, in the process, creates the potential for post-penitence bankability. It invites sympathy among fellow human beings who also have feet of clay but who have not been subject to the same extraordinary pressures and temptations."[52]

Nor, indeed, was the salvation of Armstrong's celebrity a problem only for Armstrong, as evidenced by the strategic-commercial basis of the broadcast. Winfrey's show went out on the Discovery Channel, and Discovery Communications not only co-owned Winfrey's production company (OWN – Oprah Winfrey Network), they had also sponsored Armstrong and the now-disgraced US Postal team between 2004 and 2007. As part of the deal, Armstrong had made regular appearances on Discovery. They, clearly, had a stake in any possible redemption of Armstrong, the brand.

That interview cut comparatively little ice in the cycling community or among Armstrong's long-term accusers. Some of the latter pointed out that livelihoods had been lost following the

Armstrong camp's attempts to discredit them and their testimony. "Betsy Andreu, the wife of his former team-mate Frankie Andreu, was labelled crazy after she insisted she had heard Armstrong tell a doctor he had doped as long ago as 1996," reported the Press Association. She told CNN: "He's not getting it. What about Greg LeMond's[53] bike company that was completely destroyed? … Other guys who didn't want to do what he wanted them to do not having a career? You can't put a price on opportunity lost and we're not even talking millions of dollars, we're just talking about people who just want to make a living so they can pay a mortgage and save some money after."[54]

Conclusion

Any assessment of the role of the press in the "unmasking" of Lance Armstrong must take account of the social configuration in which Armstrong's reputation was constructed, sustained (in the face of mounting criticism) and finally dismantled. In this configuration, the most decisive players were Armstrong's sponsors, the cycling authorities (and their legal representatives) and state and quasi-state actors in the United States. Ultimately the press played second fiddle to these. The cycling press acted chiefly as publicists for a rider deemed good for the sport and the courageous, against-the-tide foraging of Walsh, Ballester and Kimmage had invariably been curbed by the interventions of Armstrong's aggressive legal team. Armstrong's "designer crash landing" (to borrow Rowe's apposite phrase[55]) may have salvaged his brand to some extent, but the real winner in the FDA investigation and the Winfrey soul-baring was, arguably, the ongoing project of professional cycling.

When all the media and legal dust had settled, the whole saga had been characterised largely as a contention between individuals, heroic and otherwise. Armstrong had become cycling's premier and historic rotten apple, by implication now removed to prevent the decay of the whole barrel. He had been taken down by the good guys – "steroid cop" Jeff Novitsky and crusading reporter David Walsh. Indeed, Walsh, despite being only one of Armstrong's several accusers, was subsequently dramatically reconstructed, rather like the man who shot Liberty Valance,[56] as Armstrong's sole nemesis: *The Program*, a feature film to this effect, made in 2015,[57] drew a legal challenge from Walsh's long-time collaborator, Ballester, who had lost his job at the French newspaper *L'Equipe* because of his part in the investigation, yet received no credit in the film.[58] In this individualising of the issue, the culture of doping of which Armstrong had claimed to be a part, along with Walsh's often-professed dream of a "clean" Tour de France, retired once again to the periphery of cycling discourse. The myth busters remained, in the end, also the myth makers; while Armstrong's beautiful lies had been exposed, the ugly truth of the "pharmacy on wheels" culture was still largely hidden behind the fog of celebrity.

References

1. Lance Armstrong, with Sally Jenkins, *It's Not About the Bike. My Journey Back to Life*, GP Putnam's Sons: New York, 2000, p. 53.
2. Reed Albergotti and Vanessa O'Connell, *Wheelmen: Lance Armstrong, the Tour de France and the Greatest Sports Conspiracy Ever*, Headline: London, 2014, p. 225.
3. Bill Gifford, "It's not about the lab rats", *Outside Magazine*, 5 January 2012, https://web.archive.org/web/20130128142357/http://www.outsideonline.com/outdoor-adventure/athletes/lance-armstrong/Its-Not-About-the-Lab-Rats.html?page=all, accessed 13 December 2019.
4. Armstrong and Jenkins, *It's Not About the Bike*.
5. Armstrong and Jenkins, p. 37.

6. Ian Bishop and Deborah Orin, "Bush praises 'awesome' Lance", *New York Post*, 26 July 2004, https://nypost.com/2004/07/26/bush-praises-awesome-lance, accessed 13 December 2019.

7. Armstrong and Jenkins, p. 266.

8. Armstrong and Jenkins, p. 54.

9. Paul Kimmage, *Rough Ride: Behind the Wheel with a Pro Cyclist*, Yellow Jersey Press: London, 2007, p. 303.

10. John Hoberman, "A pharmacy on wheels – the Tour De France doping scandal", http://www.think-muscle.com/articles/hoberman/tour.htm, posted 1998, accessed 13 December 2019.

11. Alex Gibney (director), *The Armstrong Lie* [documentary film], Sony Pictures Classics: USA, 2013.

12. Hoberman, "A Pharmacy …"

13. Gibney, *The Armstrong Lie*.

14. See Conal Urquhart and David Walsh, "Lance Armstrong: The whistleblowers", *The Guardian*, 26 August 2012, https://www.theguardian.com/sport/2012/aug/26/lance-armstrong-doping-whistleblowers?newsfeed=true, accessed 13 December 2019; David Walsh, *Seven Deadly Sins: My Pursuit of Lance Armstrong*, Simon and Schuster: London, 2013, pp.73–76.

15. David Walsh, "It was obvious to me Lance Armstrong was doping", *Press Gazette*, 11 October 2012, p. 9, http://www.pressgazette.co.uk/david-walsh-it-was-obvious-me-lance-armstrong-was-doping, accessed 13 December 2019.

16. Walsh, *The Seven Deadly Sins*, p. 63.

17. Pierre Ballester and David Walsh, *L.A. Confidentiel: Les Secrets de Lance Armstrong (L.A. Confidential: Lance Armstrong's Secrets)*, La Martinière: Paris, 2004.

18. George Vecsey, "Lance Armstrong, domestique?", *The New York Times*, 24 September 2008, http://www.nytimes.com/2008/09/25/sports/othersports/25vecsey.html, accessed 13 December 2019.

19. Walsh, *The Seven Deadly Sins*, p. 84.

20. Bradley Wiggins with William Fotheringham, *My Time*, Yellow Jersey Press: London, 2013.

21. Walsh, *The Seven Deadly Sins*, p. 69.

22. John Wilcockson, *Lance Armstrong: The World's Greatest Champion*, John Murray: London, 2010.

23. See, for example, William Fotheringham, "Emma O'Reilly: 'My relationship with Lance Armstrong was and still is a human one'", *The Guardian*, 2 July 2014, https://www.theguardian.com/sport/2014/jul/02/emma-o-reilly-lance-armstrong-cyclist-doping, accessed 16 November 2017; Donald McRae, "Tyler Hamilton: 'Now the truth about doping will come out'", *The Guardian*, 24 September 2012, https://www.theguardian.com/sport/2012/sep/24/tyler-hamilton-tour-de-france, accessed 13 December 2019.

24. Gibney, *The Armstrong Lie*.

25. Tom Rotunno, "Armstrong loses eight sponsors in a day", https://www.cnbc.com/id/49462583, posted 13 November 2012, accessed 13 December 2019.

26. Press Association, "Lance Armstrong settles with *Sunday Times*", https://www.theguardian.com/sport/2013/aug/25/lance-armstrong-settles-sunday-times, posted 25 August 2013, accessed 13 December 2019.

27. See, for instance, Graham Watson, *The Tour de France and Its Heroes*, Stanley Paul: London, 1990.

28. See, for example, Geoffrey Wheatcroft, *Le Tour: A History of the Tour de France*, Simon & Schuster: London, 2003.

29. An example is Ned Boulding, *How I Won the Yellow Jumper. Dispatches from the Tour de France*, Yellow Jersey Press: London, 2011.

30. For instance, see William Fotheringham, *Put Me Back on My Bike: In Search of Tom Simpson*, Yellow Jersey Press: London, 2002.

31. For instance, see Graeme Obree, *Flying Scotsman: Cycling to Triumph Through My Darkest Hours*, Velo-Press: Boulder, CO, 2005.

32. Kimmage, *Rough Ride*.

33. David Millar with Jeremy Whittle, *Racing Through the Dark: The Fall and Rise of David Millar*, Orion Publishing: London, 2011.

34. Irwin Deutscher, "Words and deeds", *Social Problems*, Volume 13, Issue 3, Winter 1966, pp. 235–254.

35. George Vecsey, "Armstrong, best of his time, now with an asterisk", *New York Times*, 24 August 2012, http://www.nytimes.com/2012/08/25/sports/cycling/armstrong-best-of-his-time-now-with-an-asterisk-george-vecsey.html?pagewanted=all, accessed 13 December 2019.

36. Kimmage, Armstrong noted, had said "a cancer" had returned to cycling in the form of Armstrong himself. This bitter exchange can be seen at https://www.youtube.com/watch?v=nZgns7CXeUI or in Alex Gibney's film *The Armstrong Lie*. Armstrong was, from time to time, accused of using his cancer charity work to deflect accusations of doping – for a detailed analysis see Gifford, "It's not about the lab Rats".

37. Matt Miller, "The journalist who brought down Lance Armstrong", http://www.esquire.com/entertainment/movies/news/a43121/lance-armstrong-the-program-david-walsh/, posted 18 March 2016, accessed 13 December 2019.

38. Lance Armstrong and Elizabeth Kreutz, *My Comeback: Up Close and Personal*, Yellow Jersey Press: London, 2009.

39. Gibney, *The Armstrong Lie*.

40. Gibney, *The Armstrong Lie*.

41. This view was strengthened in 2002 when a UCI report exonerated Armstrong soon after receiving a $25,000 donation from the rider himself. He made a further gift of $100,000 in 2005. See "McQuaid reveals Armstrong made two donations to the UCI", *Cycling News*, 10 July 2010, http://www.cyclingnews.com/news/mcquaid-reveals-armstrong-made-two-donations-to-the-uci/, accessed 13 December 2019.

42. Pat Malach, "Floyd Landis Q&A: They rearranged the pieces but it's the same game", *Cycling News*, 15 August 2017, http://www.cyclingnews.com/features/floyd-landis-q-and-a-they-rearranged-the-pieces-but-its-the-same-game/, accessed 13 December 2019.

43. Gibney, *The Armstrong Lie*.

44. The report can be read in full here: https://d3epuodzu3wuis.cloudfront.net/ReasonedDecision.pdf, accessed 13 December 2019.

45. Emma O'Reilly and Shannon Kyle, *The Race to the Truth*, Transworld Publishers: London, 2014, p. 268.

46. Gibney, *The Armstrong Lie*.

47. See Erving Goffman, *The Presentation of Self in Everyday Life*, Penguin: Harmondsworth, UK, 1971, and Erving Goffman, *Stigma: Notes on the Management of Spoilt Identity*, Penguin: London, 1990.

48. Stuart Hall with Bill Schwarz, *Familiar Stranger: A Life Between Two Islands*, Allen Lane: London, 2017, p. 16.

49. Eva Illouz, *Oprah Winfrey and the Glamour of Misery: An Essay on Popular Culture*, Columbia University Press: New York, 2003, p. 77 and 222.

50. A full transcript can be read on the BBC Sport website: http://www.bbc.co.uk/sport/cycling/21065539, accessed 13 December 2019.

51. O'Reilly and Kyle, *The Race …*, p. 1 and 6.

52. David Rowe, "Lance Armstrong begins his confession – but why Oprah?", *The Conversation*, https://theconversation.com/lance-armstrong-begins-his-confession-but-why-oprah-11688, posted 18 January 2013, accessed 13 December 2019.

53. California-born, LeMond was the first non-European to win the Tour de France in 1986. He was also an outspoken opponent of doping.

54. Press Association, "Lance Armstrong's victims unmoved by television doping confession", *The Guardian*, 19 January 2013, https://www.theguardian.com/sport/2013/jan/19/lance-armstrong-betsy-andreu-confession, accessed 13 December 2019.

55. Rowe, "Lance Armstrong begins …"

56. *The Man Who Shot Liberty Valance* was directed by John Ford and released by Paramount Pictures in 1962.

57. *The Program* (Director: Stephen Frears), Studio Canal, 2015.

58. Shane Stokes, "Armstrong movie dispute to go to trial", https://cyclingtips.com/2017/10/armstrong-movie-dispute-go-to-trial-ballester-publisher-seek-justice/, posted 20 October 2017, accessed 13 December 2019.

Part III
Trailblazers

29

Frank Keating

Rob Steen

Tomorrow we'll bid our rheumy-eyed goodbyes – as our fond fareweller might have put it in his blushless, inimitable way. The venue, Belmont Abbey, a Benedictine monastery east of the Welsh border, is a Victorian monument to a medieval order: an apt final resting-place for a sportswriter whose cosmopolitan nous was embedded in the fertile soil of history. No journalist ever immersed himself quite so thoroughly in the lessons of all our yesterdays as Frank Keating.

Frank was lucky. He picked up his painterly brush in a less critical era, before technology turned Planet Sport into a goldfish bowl and made cynical, half-knowing bustards of us all. Yes, he worked in TV, but long before it made Johnny-Come- Latelies of the press. And yes, he suffered increasingly from nostalgia, the hallucinatory sickness that prevents us from seeing, and appreciating, the way we are. Then again, by the time he vacated the pressbox, the way we were had changed so rapidly, so drastically, so unnervingly.

Still, he recognised that enduring and defining truth: as the 21st century kicked off, sport not only supplied our joybringers-in-chief; it was also, if not the ultimate meritocracy, then the closest approximation we could reasonably wish for – and far closer than it was in his youth, when gents and players occupied different dressing rooms and shamateurs reigned. What made him so special, so inspirational, was not so much those daring experiments with language but that capacity to locate the resplendent in the present.

Witness *High, Wide and Handsome*, his incomparable account of Ian Botham's slam-bang summer of 1985. Written when Frank was nearing 50, the final words distil to perfection spectator sport's singular power to unite classes, creeds, races and ages: "We would not forget him even if we could (and could not forget if we would), as morning after morning the summer's sun rose for him and he went forth and trod fresh grass – and the expectant, eager cry was sent about the land: *Botham's In!*"

If one paragraph can tell you everything you need to know about its author, Frank's description of his favourite catch does, and handsomely. During a Test match in Brisbane in 1985, Richard Hadlee had gobbled down Australia's first eight wickets when Geoff Lawson sliced a drive:

> The great man hared around to get beneath the steepler. He could have half-tripped, pretended to lose sight of it in the sun, fallen over or, dammit, just let the thing pop out of

his hands after a gallant try. But Hadlee made ground and, on the run, dashingly held the catch to give Brown his first Test wicket – and also, in that one act, to deny himself all ten.

Here was the "no-I-in-team" ethic personified; here was nobility.

Sure, Frank had his *bêtes noir* – racism, greed and privilege, killjoys, snobs and cheats. And when he let fire he emptied both barrels, hunting for the brighter, the fairer, the nobler. Unafraid to rave, he was also a spinner of fabulist fables underpinned by a deeper truth: Aesop meets the brothers Grimm. Embroidery was his schtick, but he still nailed the social value of the competitive arts – and hence their timeless allure – a darned sight more regularly than those ain't-the-world-irredeemably-rotten cynics for whom graceless carping, skin-deep psychoanalysis and deepest, greenest envy are now the numbing norm.

Will another writer ever be so willing, without a scintilla of bashfulness, to salute the awe and the ooh and the aah of sport, the electricity and the humanity, the way – even now, even in the age of naked professionalism – it celebrates courage, invention and style, mateship and manners, self-sacrifice and honour? Barring the extinction of TV, it's bloody hard to picture it.

M'dear

I first met Frank in 1983, having been dispatched to his west London home by *Broadcast* magazine to interview him about his latest book. The nerves fluttered madly. I was on the verge of starting a journalism training course; his reporting for *The Guardian* having been one of my chief inspirations, he was one of the biggest reasons I had even got that far. Happily, warmth oozed from every pore: writer and man, it soon became abundantly clear, were indistinguishable (in my experience, this is rarely the case). Within minutes, to my amazement, he was calling me "M'dear" (only later did I discover, somewhat disappointedly, that he called everyone that). Over the next three decades he proved to be one of my greatest champions, perhaps because he recognised a kindred spirit. This column therefore feels duty-bound to declare its complete and utter lack of disinterest.

In 1983, it was newspapers that counted, newspapers that brought aces, cuts and putts into the lives of those for whom being there was impractical. For Frank's generation that meant being salesman, celebrant, critic and campaigner. Now they transmit every ball, as it happens, broadcasters rule the roost. Yet because their function is to sell the game alongside the ringmasters with whom they have forged such an unholy alliance, they narrow the view. Call them the new romantics. Those who survived the heyday of Spandau Ballet and Duran Duran will know this is not an unmitigated compliment.

Video killed most of the radio stars, but live TV all but murdered romance on the sports pages. By bringing goals, tries and sixes to millions, and to sports desks where editors and sub-editors were closer to the action than those on the spot, the magic began to dissolve; so, to a greater extent, did reliance on the reporter's word, and hence the licence to embroider. True, this was a boon, especially to the delivery of fact. The downside was a knee-jerk reaction to broadcasting's more blinkered salesmanship: a greater desire for interpretation and consequence than action. No bad thing at all. Sadly, what excited reporters and fuelled their descriptive skills became secondary.

The generation gap has never helped. Even for the hardiest and most idealistic of hacks, the older one gets and the higher one ascends the greasy pole, the harder it is to empathise with one's subjects, for sportswriters above all media breeds. Our subjects have the lot: youth and fully functioning bodies, dreams and future – everything we're losing. As we age and they remain in their teens and 20s, so we increasingly hark back to reminders of *our* youth, *our* dreams, *our* future.

We're the Peter Pans of wordsmithery, surfing the tides of time and fashion – and none more so than Frank, a writer who thought nothing of inventing words. Trouble is, beyond the compromised world of PR, trumpeting the good as relief from the bad is no longer hip. Innocence isn't the only price we pay for maturity: in the pursuit of wisdom, have we traded in the wonder that first spurred us to do what we do?

The antidote, nonetheless, lies largely with those editors. Their mantra is plain: leave it to TV to cover the oohs and aahs – give us the whys and the why nots, the what nows and the who's nexts. Regrettably, today's hacks have decreasing access to the players because the players trust the broadcasters infinitely more. With precious few exceptions, producers and eager mic-thrusters portray them in the best possible light, media-trained utterances presented as intended – unedited, unchallenged, religiously uncontroversial.

Exacerbated by the ever-expanding chasm in earnings, the distance between players and scribblers is growing by the season. Tweets are the new quotes. One-on-one interviews, once the norm – particularly for those at what John Lennon would have called the toppermost of the poppermost – are scarce and fleeting; as with film critics, a gaggle will share the same words and the same pauses in the same order, every syllable approved and recorded by a PR flunky, manager, coach or agent – the better to control perceptions. Even Frank, a man for all seasons, might have become a nauseating in-my-dayer.

How he thrived on those one-on-ones. They heightened that natural affection, stirred the novelist in him, the verbal wizard. If he took liberties – and *boy*, did he take liberties, albeit harmless ones – no-one he transported from pitch to page complained. Nor did his readers, a band so numerous that, in one TV ad for *The Guardian*, that luxuriantly larynxed thespian Peter Ustinov read from one of Frank's columns.

If he depicted players in a more articulate, humble and loveable, even Keatingesque light, who cared? He knew they were imperfect, that they cut corners and swung lead like the rest of us, but he also knew they could do what we could never do, that what they felt – if not their precise mode of expression – was the sauce that flavoured the meatiness of their labours. If Frank could be accused of fantasising them, he also humanised them. They weren't gods, but nor were they monsters. Sure, he craftily crammed them into his own template for heroism, but such truth-bending was founded on an unswerving belief that this was what his job primarily entailed: understanding and celebrating the architects of modern wonderment.

So what can be done? The last thing I want my students to do is to revive those sepia-distorted days when every opener walked (hah!) and sledging was something you only did in the snow (hah!). I want them to see through all that PR fluff and puffery, pursue the *full* story, hound the frauds and pariahs, expose and right the wrongs. I also want them to savour – and thus convey – the visual beauty and dramatic intensity of a save, tackle or catch, the spiritual upliftment of the stunning debut, the startling comeback and underdog-bites-back.

Sport does this stuff best because, unlike novels and plays and movies, it's fact, not fiction (so long as we can trust eyes and motives). Revelling in the exploits of sportsfolk means admiring those whose job entails confronting physical pain and public humiliation. That's why governments and billionaires and broadcasters throw so much dosh at the best reality show in town. George Orwell was only half-right: elite sport is war minus the shooting *and* the generals on the hill. The highest earners are on the frontline.

Frankly, then, this column can be tweeted down to a single heartfelt plea to every sports editor out there who has relished skewering Lance Armstrong: keep crucifying the villains but put the glory back up there with the gory, the groans and the gossip. In pursuing truth, let it be meaningful truth. Don't mistake winners for gods, losers for failures or flaws for monstrosities. Let's be gracious out there. Let's be generous out there.

Asked if, at 75, he'd rather give up watching movies or sport, Woody Allen's reply was as instant as it was succinct: movies. Sport, he reasoned, still thrills. And nobody captured and bottled that essential essence more enchantingly or winningly than Frank.[1]

Note

1. This is a revised version of Rob Steen's tribute to Frank Keating, "In search of grace and affection", originally published by ESPNCricinfo, 6 February 2013.

30

Hugh McIlvanney[1]

Kevin Mitchell

Hugh McIlvanney's life as a sports journalist resembled one of his perfectly crafted sentences: long, lyrical and rich with surprises. He was a scrupulous and perceptive witness to what he regarded with reverence as the "magnificent triviality" of sport, and his death, at the age of 84, will be the more keenly felt in a climate of concern about the dwindling integrity of the printed word. He leaves behind a fading image of an era that was more forgiving of boisterous behaviour than the one from which he retired in 2016 after nearly 60 years of excellence.

There might be dissenting, scattered voices, but the consensus among his peers was that McIlvanney was the best sportswriter of his era. It is hard to find argument with that conclusion. His friend and rival, Ian Wooldridge, pushed him close – and was probably more willing to cede first place to him than McIlvanney was the other way around – while near-contemporaries such as Dudley Doust and James Lawton kept him honest. Now they are all gone.

During 30 years at *The Observer* and a concluding stint of 23 years at the *Sunday Times,* McIlvanney accumulated a swag of accolades at home and abroad: journalist of the year on a brief sabbatical from sport, when he returned to hard news for the *Daily Express* at the height of the Troubles in Northern Ireland; sports journalist of the year seven times; awarded the OBE in 1996; a lifetime achievement award at the Scottish Press Awards in 2004; and induction into the International Boxing Hall of Fame in 2009.

Sport and journalism in the UK could not have asked for a better champion than the man who insisted he was a reporter rather than a "writer", a title he felt conveyed too much grandiloquence in the circles in which he moved easily, from ringside to the track and, when the mood took him, the bar.

His searing intelligence and an old-fashioned regard for accuracy, embroidered by a gift for verbal musicality, lifted his work to sometimes operatic heights. Others might have been more concise; none was more precise. He cared with monk-like zeal about the layered subtext of his narrative, as well as hitting the right tone and rhythm in his prose, and packaged it all as Beethoven might put together a symphony. If his work was too labyrinthine for some tastes, perhaps the fault lay with the listener rather than the composer.

Anyone who sat alongside McIlvanney at the multitude of world title fights he covered would confirm he suffered over facts to the point of maddening intrusion. "Excuse me for interrupting, wee man," he began one such whispered inquiry while Mike Tyson was telling us how he was going to rip Frank Bruno's head from his shoulders in their world title rematch in Las Vegas in 1996, "but Ingemar Johansson, is it with one S or two?"

McIlvanney brought a breathtaking level of comprehension and expertise to his work without the benefit – or encumbrance, he might say – of a university education. He did not need paper to lend weight to his words. He was his own toughest examiner. It became obvious watching him at close quarters that the perfection he admired in others who strove for it, from Gabriel García Márquez to Muhammad Ali, was buried in his own soul from a young age.

He was born in the Ayrshire town of Kilmarnock to William, a miner, and his wife, Helen (née Montgomery), parents who gave him, his sister and two brothers, one of whom was the future crime writer William McIlvanney, a priceless grounding in the arts of expression. Hugh began on his hometown paper, the *Kilmarnock Standard*, after impressing during a debate at his school, the Kilmarnock academy, and moved briefly to the Scottish office of the *Daily Express* before joining *The Scotsman*. That newspaper's outstanding editor, Alastair Dunnett, introduced him to the collected essays of [the American boxing writer] AJ Liebling, perhaps the pivotal intervention in his long career. McIlvanney had not even considered becoming a sportswriter, but that moment fixed the path of his calling.

To his surprise, McIlvanney loved Liebling's defining book on boxing, *The Sweet Science*. Like the New Yorker with the Sorbonne education, he was originally an accidental tourist in the under-lit suburb of sport. "I was a bit reluctant at the start," he admitted. He was petrified of ending up "a fitba writer" obsessing about Celtic and Rangers. Self-doubt did not often haunt him thereafter.

While his heart never left Scotland, the core of McIlvanney's working life was played out on the pages of *The Observer*, where he began work in 1962 as deputy sports editor. In surroundings that were unremittingly Dickensian, peopled by literary mavericks to whom he would quickly cleave, McIlvanney impressed. But he knew that his editing and sub-editing work was no more than an entree to a more fulfilling line as a writer. He had a piece in the paper within a fortnight, and there was no doubt he had found his métier.

His style, he accepted, had an undeniable Scottish flavour to it. "I think it can be said without pomposity," he wrote, while straying in that very direction, "that I have a recognisable voice in my writing. I would be surprised if there wasn't some Scottishness there, and certainly an attitude to language. The feeling that you could be quite strongly expressive and still very accurate relates in a way to how I was brought up, listening to a lot of people who were very eloquent – although they might not have been very well educated, but who had a great respect for language, especially in the west of Scotland."

Allied to his great style was McIlvanney's huge admiration for the characters of sport, and he never lost faith in his heroes, however flawed. Nobody gave George Best more rope. And Ali stood tallest for him, even when palsied after a boxing career that lingered too long. There was no doubt in McIlvanney's mind that Muhammad (as he insisted on calling him) was The Greatest, as a human being and an athlete.

"His boxing was totally idiosyncratic," he said, "and technically at a level much lower than that of Sugar Ray Robinson. Muhammad was in a sense the eternal amateur, but he was God's amateur, because the will was so magical, the imagination so magical, that he found a way to beat people."

It was the perfect metaphor for McIlvanney's career: the raw yet refined genius from the north who invariably finished in front, sometimes despite himself. His writing – his reporting, as he would have it – was a triumph of the imagination.

Note

1. This article was originally written by Kevin Mitchell as an obituary of McIlvanney in *The Guardian*, and published on 25 January 2019. Reprinted by kind permission *The Guardian*. Copyright Guardian News & Media Ltd 2020.

31

Vikki Orvice[1]

Steven Howard

It was Saturday 4 August 2012, and London's Olympic Stadium was a crucible of bubbling, patriotic fervour.

Jess Ennis-Hill had just won gold in the heptathlon, and Vikki Orvice and I were furiously putting over our copy knowing Mo Farah was due to start the 10,000 metres in under half an hour.

Then from the other side of the stadium came a huge roar.

"What the **** was that?" I yelled at Vikki alongside me.

"Greg Rutherford has only gone and won the flipping long jump," she shouted back over the din.

Not long after, Farah would make it triple gold – three inside an astonishing 44 minutes. It was the greatest night in British athletics, perhaps the greatest night in Olympic history.

At the time, Vikki was in remission from the cancer that had first struck in 2007 – and which, devastatingly, would return in 2014.

For the last four years she fought valiantly – and with no lack of humour – against the odds, her life a strength-sapping treadmill of chemotherapy at London's Marsden Hospital sandwiched in between her jobs as athletics correspondent and football writer for *The Sun*.

Fittingly, for a daughter of Sheffield, she had a core of steel. But the long, unequal struggle ended this morning when Vikki died aged 56.

The grief engulfing her sportswriter husband Ian Ridley, her family and her many admiring friends is only partially mitigated by the relief it is finally all over.

Not surprisingly, the tributes poured in as news of Vikki's death spread.

Sebastian Coe tweeted: "Vikki has been part of my life for 30 years. She believed in London 2012 long before others and drove *The Sun* support. A cheerleader for women in sport & mentor to athletes & my team to be strong female role models in sport. We owe her so much. She will live on in our [hearts]."

Paula Radcliffe tweeted: "Vikki will be greatly missed. A true trailblazer for women journalists, and women everywhere. Lived her life with integrity and courage, always thinking of others and treading her own path."

Dame Jessica Ennis-Hill wrote: "She was such a genuinely lovely woman. I feel really lucky to have spent so much time with her over the years of my athletic career. Lots of great memories and she will be truly missed. A very sad day. Thinking of you and your family x."

And the Women in Football group said: "We are devastated to learn of the passing of our dear friend and colleague Vikki Orvice. Vikki was a brave, brilliant and extraordinary lady who passionately championed women in football. We will miss her dreadfully, and will continue to stand up for all she believed in."

If she was a fundraiser, arch supporter and poster girl – her own words – for the Marsden, she was also a massive source of encouragement for every young girl who wondered whether they, too, could make it in what was the very male enclave of sports journalism.

Working at the coal face of sports journalism, she was not just a pioneer but a suffragette on the slow, back-breaking march towards equality.

At the end, she would stand at the pinnacle, a vociferous defender of women's rights and ceaseless promoter of their abilities – a director of Women in Football and a significant figure at both the Sports Journalists' Association and the Football Writers' Association.

At the age of 10, she entered a *Daily Express* competition, saying she wanted to be a sports-writer. Her subject? Her beloved Sheffield United. She would finally achieve her ambition in the face of constant prejudice but it was a long journey.

Recalling her early days on national newspapers, she said: "I went to Arsenal v. Norwich on the opening afternoon of the season."

"The main stand at Arsenal had a mural on it and I was basically sent along to write about that because, you know, it was a bit girly and stuff. But it actually turned into a good story because Norwich won.

"I remember somebody came over to the sports desk on the Monday morning saying 'Why did you give that match to HER? I should have been there instead."

"I would later have lunch with the sports editor who said a woman could never do the job full-time. In those days, you didn't even question it."

Then in the summer of 1995 came her mould-breaking move to *The Sun*.

Her all-round talent was quickly recognised, and she would soon become the paper's athletics correspondent, a role which she relished – covering all of Usain Bolt's world records – and in which she would prosper.

She would also strike up enduring relationships with many of the sport's leading lights – chief among them Paula Radcliffe, Ennis and Farah.

During all this, she was a sounding-board for other members of her profession unfortunate enough to themselves be afflicted by cancer.

She was also fundraising – one reference to a charity event with Radcliffe showing both her unquenchable spirit and humour.

She tweeted: "I am walking 5k with Paula in the Race for Life. She has a personal best for the event of 14 minutes 29.11 seconds but is recovering from a broken toe and hence is not running.

"I have a personal best of 19 months in remission from secondary cancer – hence not running, either!"

I met Vikki twice for lunch in the last few months with former *The Sun* sports editor Paul Ridley, the man who not only brought her to Fleet Street, but also gave her the athletics job.

Once when, complete in black wig and showbiz sunglasses, she looked a million dollars – despite the chemo. Then again just before Christmas in Soho when she was obviously struggling a bit.

Dressed in a stunning, full-length, camel overcoat and carrying an elegant black walking-stick, she climbed into a black cab that was to take her to see a concerned Sebastian Coe.

Noticing the anguish in my face, she said: "Don't worry, Steve."

What style. What class. Still thinking about other people to the end.

Note

1. This article was originally written by Steven Howard in *The Sun*, and published on 6 February 2019. Reprinted by kind permission of the author.

32

John Samuel[1]

Matthew Engel

John Samuel, who has died aged 86, was *The Guardian*'s brilliant, eccentric and under-appreciated sports editor for 18 years, between 1968 and 1986. He transformed a department that was lagging behind the rest of the paper into one producing the most distinctive and envied sports pages in the business.

Samuel presided over the operation like an impresario running a music-hall troupe. Detail was never his forte: there was little point because his era coincided with the peak of the paper's Grauniad years, when misprints were a speciality and pictures often resembled inky smudges. But he had a knack for attracting talented performers and allowing them to get on with it.

Sport was starved of space, so the sub-editors dismissed what they always called "groin-strain journalism", and downgraded the northern hockey and lacrosse that lingered on from Mancunian days. Instead, Samuel hired writers with broad sympathies and sharp wit, to reach out way beyond the sports-page-first readership.

Sir Neville Cardus, who vied with Alistair Cooke as the greatest of *The Guardian* names, came back from a lengthy exile to write cricket essays alongside John Arlott as cricket correspondent. After Cardus died, Samuel turned to Ian Peebles, another magnificent memoirist. He maintained a matchless dynasty of golf correspondents, choosing first Peter Dobereiner and then David "Dai" Davies to follow Pat Ward-Thomas.

Football was less of a problem as he was able to promote from within early in his reign, and David Lacey rapidly established a grip on the job that would survive into the next millennium. Samuel's later decision to bring John Roberts from the *Daily Mail* gave the pages a necessary infusion of tabloid street wisdom and energy.

His masterstroke was the transformation of Frank Keating from down-table sub-editor to the most original sports columnist in Fleet Street. Samuel spotted his talent, nurtured it and defended it against the myriad doubters. He also insisted on bringing back horse-racing, which had ceased to be a regular feature of *The Guardian* in late Victorian times. He made the paper's coverage more mainstream yet allowed it to be off-the-wall in a way no rival could match.

Samuel made these crucial decisions while usually leaving the day-to-day dirty work to capable deputies. When he did take a turn on the rota there was often chaos. In those days of typed copy and hot-metal printing, the man in charge of the sports desk had to estimate the space for each piece and draw page plans on paper. All this was art, not science. When "the

Gaffer" was involved, the art tended to be expressive rather than exact. But another of his mysterious gifts was that the story he had forgotten to include would usually be balanced out by the one he had schemed twice.

When I went for my initial interview as a sports sub-editor, Samuel was an hour late. He then offered the job to my Reuters colleague Steve Bierley in what, circumstantial evidence suggested, was a case of mistaken identity. Fortunately for me, and my friendship with Steve, another vacancy arose at once. The next sub to be employed, Ian Ridley, was startled to see his letter of application amid the rubble on Samuel's desk, adorned by a large tea-cup stain and the words, "Found It!!". Samuel's happy-go-lucky sports desk fitted perfectly into *The Guardian* ethos of his era. The paper was organisationally chaotic and money too tight to mention, and yet the circulation just kept growing.

Born in Southwick, West Sussex, John was the son of Jack, who worked in a dried-food factory, and Winifred (née Short), and won a scholarship to Hove grammar school. He began in journalism as a 16-year-old covering VE Day for the Brighton *Argus*. He went back after national service in the RAF, then moved to Fleet Street, first with Reuters and then the *Daily Herald*, another hand-to-mouth left-of-centre paper, where he covered Britain's rare win in the 1957 Ryder Cup "virtually single-handed", while the *Daily Express* had an eight-man team. He rose to be deputy sports editor of the *Daily Herald*, became sports editor of *The Observer* (briefly), then in 1961 arrived at *The Guardian* as deputy before succeeding David Gray seven years later.

He played club cricket for Brighton Brunswick, and was an enthusiastic member of the Press Golfing Society and a zestful skier; winter sports (his own domain) were never knowingly under-reported on his watch.

One of his strengths as an editor was that he would always fight to promote sport internally and usually win. His method was not always popular, since it generally involved banging on in departmental heads' meetings until everyone else gave in.

His reign ended when a triple whammy made a reorganisation inevitable: computerisation was coming, which was never going to suit the Samuel style; *The Independent* was just starting to bump up the competition, and his deputy, Charlie Burgess, had been taken as its first sports editor and was waving a chequebook at *The Guardian* staff. Samuel had a brief afterlife as an assistant editor before embarking on a long and active retirement. When he spoke at the celebration of Frank Keating's life in 2013, he seemed to have changed hardly at all.

Note

1. This article was originally written by Matthew Engel as an obituary for Samuel in *The Guardian*, and published on 19 November 2014. Reprinted by kind permission of *The Guardian*. Copyright Guardian News & Media Ltd 2020.

Part IV
The future

33

A new Golden Age?

Raymond Boyle

The "Golden Age" of any cultural form tends to always be in the past. We can live through these times and be blissfully unaware that some future generation will ascribe this title to a moment in history, which, for those who lived through it, may have felt very much less than golden. In the middle of a maelstrom it's often difficult to chart a course or to see the true direction of travel you may be undertaking. For some, the Golden Age of sports journalism, and journalism per se, lies in the past. In a supposedly simpler, less complex time, where narratives were unambiguous, and the role and place of organisations and individuals were well defined.

However, if we examine this through another lens we can reframe this golden age as a time of collusion, between journalists and players; a time where journalistic and supporter knowledge of sports (with some notable exceptions) beyond Britain was patchy at best, and where organisations could carve up the sporting world often for commercial gain, broadly free from the prying eyes of a largely uninterested sports media, whose eyes were firmly focused on events on the pitch or field of play.

This was the age of supply-led media. Newspapers and strictly limited television and radio outlets provided sports journalism and sports broadcasting to an audience underpinned by the notion of sport existing in its own specific world, away from tawdry areas such as news and current affairs. The exception were often national sporting events, that became part of a wider discourse around national identity and helped provide a symbolic expression of what it meant to be, for example, Scottish, English or British.

In the UK, the 1980s and 1990s witness a change in the relationship between sport, media and journalism, and create new rules of engagement between journalists and sports stars in which collusion is replaced by mistrust and suspicion. The increasingly commercially driven tabloid newspaper wars intensify during these decades and sports coverage, and its on-field stars become embroiled in this battle as celebrity (not of course a recent invention or even one created by sport) becomes an increasingly valuable media commodity in an age that moves from supply-led media to a more demand-led media culture. Sport, and football in particular, moves out of its clearly delineated and limited media space as new media players extend the profile and coverage of sport in a deregulating broadcasting era, and newspapers extend coverage of sport through colour, through supplements and through cross-media promotion with the then new kid on the block, Rupert Murdoch's Sky, soon to be BSkyB and eventually the Comcast-owned Sky UK.

In so doing, sport is transformed and liberated from its often ghetto scheduling or absence on television into a ubiquitous entertainment "product" to be used as a "battering ram" to reshape the media landscape and television consumption habits of a new generation of sporting audiences. The 1980s remain the decade where if I wanted to watch live football on television in a non-World Cup year, then my choice usually extended to the European Cup final, the Scotland v. England Home Championship game (remember that tournament ?), and (for viewers in Scotland) the Scottish Cup final and the Junior Scottish Cup final. Such is the pace of change in this demand-led (if you can afford to pay) sports media culture, that over Christmas 2019 I watched as many matches in one day through an OTT streaming service that around a decade or so ago used to be an online book store.

One unanticipated outcome of this more plentiful supply of sports journalism and broadcasting related content – that has grown from the analogue 1980s and early 1990s and been further enhanced in the contemporary digital platform age – is that the audience(s) now know much more about sport and its wider political and commercial hinterland than it did previously. From sporting scandals and corruption, to knowledge and access to sporting events beyond these shores, the sports journalist and broadcaster has had to up their game, as access to information and coverage of international sport have facilitated a more knowledgeable section of the audience.

The cricket writer and broadcaster (and former news journalist) Richie Benaud, who made his name on the field as captain of Australia, would often recommend that any new broadcaster refrain from telling their television audience "as you can see", his argument being that of course they could see what was on the screen, your job was to tell them about something they couldn't see or couldn't know. While some modern-day presenters (many lacking journalistic training) remain immune to Benaud's words of wisdom, the dominant trend in an era that sees sports journalism and media coverage of sport become more and more prominent across all media platforms, from print to online, is that it's becoming harder for journalists to tell their audience something they don't already know. Reporting what happened in a football or rugby match they have already seen, has become more redundant, so added news value or analysis becomes more important. In an age of always-on sports coverage, looking for other journalistic paths to follow to engage the audience should be a more common practice than it is.

Investigative journalism in sport, traditionally, was driven, on the occasions that it happened, by non-sports journalists. Paradoxically, in an age when sections of the sports audience (not all of it, by any means) are more likely to appreciate investigative material that gets below the surface and takes us backstage, this type of journalism in the newspaper sector remains rare. *The Guardian*'s David Conn is a notable exception, and in many ways his sporting role echoes with the wider investigative culture that has become an important part of that newspaper's brand. The stumbling block in today's media market is usually money and time. Carrying out investigative journalism can be costly (often requiring legal support) and time-consuming at a moment where journalists are producing more copy than any of their generational predecessors.

It is no accident that the popularity in the rise of the sports documentary – ironically, driven not (as you might imagine) by public service media, but rather by the commercial, subscription-funded pay-TV and OTT sports channels with schedules to fill – offers sports fans and more general viewers a behind-the-scenes access that journalism used to promise it was giving. From BT Sport Films to Amazon Prime exclusives such as the *All or Nothing* series or *Resurfaced*, the story of Andy Murray's battle to return to tennis, a new kind of sports journalist, one at home in both understanding the importance of constructing visual content and having an ability to identify sporting news values, is coming to the fore.

These highly visually driven documentaries, of course, juggle that fine line between being driven by journalistic access across all areas and becoming a sanitised promotional video for a club or individual. Yet they provide some form of visual long-form journalism at a time when the written equivalent, while still around, appears to be becoming more and more niche. Yes, it's out there if you want to hunt for it and pay extra for it, yet for younger supporters of sport, brought up in a more visual age than my print-hungry generation of supporters, the new sports film and documentaries are becoming an increasingly important part of the wider journalistic landscape that engages, mediates and makes sense of the complex world of sport.

Sports journalism in all its differing forms and practices will continue to play a role in mediating and making sense of our relationship with sport. It matters because sport matters, of course. But sport, in its modern configuration, matters in part because the media think it matters. In the age of the television box set, the commercial value of televised sport lies in its *liveness* and *immediacy*, hence its value to certain media platforms. You don't pay a subscription to watch a box set of the UEFA Champions League. However, the value of sport has also been in its ability to touch us emotionally and connect us as individuals through shared fandom, and this, in part, is achieved in the telling and re-telling of the stories that surround the events that take place on the pitch or in the stadium. Enter journalism.

Through social media, that post- and pre-sports event chatter may have become more accessible (if at times less restrained), yet journalists writing about sport and the events and circumstances it creates and represents will remain important cultural intermediaries in the process of creating the myths, values and narratives that make sport such an important cultural form. The difference nowadays is that the journalist no longer has the exclusive rights to these narratives that they once enjoyed. Don't be surprised if future generations look back at this moment and reach for the label "Golden Age".

34
Diversity

Carrie Dunn

Welcome to the part of the book where the only balls that count are made of crystal. If we were writing this on 20 March 2006 and we said that in the near future a new website would be launched, a website that would only allow you to write "articles" of no more than 140 characters and we said that it would revolutionise the way we communicate, you'd be well within your rights to question our judgement. But the very next day, that's exactly what happened when Jack Dorsey launched Twitter.

If we were writing this on 8 January 2007, and we said that in the near future, a new piece of technology would be announced that would be a touchscreen device, no bigger than a packet of cigarettes; that would be a pocket computer more powerful than most desktop computers; that would be a combination of a telephone, a web browser, an email server, a camera, an audio recorder and a music centre, you'd probably need more than 140 characters to describe your incredulity. But the very next day, that's what Steve Jobs announced at the Macworld Convention, and on 29 June 2007, the first iPhone was launched.

Predicting the future is a risky business, and if we had a real inside track on what that future might be, we wouldn't be writing this book, we'd be sitting on a beach in maybe Hawaii, rich from the Apple shares we bought in 1976. However, we might not be that smart, but we do have a crystal ball. We can see where the wind is blowing, the way the world is turning. And we can have a guess at what the world of the sports journalist might look like in five years' time. What impact might drones have? What might be the real result of the fall of print? And if all goes well, what new chapters might there be in some future reprint of this book?

I am not a psychic, nor a fortune-teller; I cannot read tea leaves, nor divine the future from runes. I am a sports journalist. I started working in the sports media as a student in 1999, when I started to write features for my local football club's website as the dotcom bubble inflated; I became a freelancer in 2005 when I realised that, despite trying out television production work and staffing a press office, there was no other job I would rather do. Journalists tend to have enquiring minds; I opted to combine my freelancing with a return to academic study, this time focusing on sport and sports media, the world I know best.

For years, doom-mongers mournfully continue their predictions that print is a dying medium. If that is so, it is certainly taking a lengthy time to expire. Magazines and newspapers may close, and circulations may be dwindling, but there is apparently still a place for print to fill, and that particular medium evidently remains valued; there continue to be start-ups proving that in some areas there is still a demand for print coverage, and that it remains commercially viable. More anecdotally, friends and acquaintances continue to attribute value to a byline in a printed publication; seeing my name next to an article I have written in a newspaper will likely generate Facebook messages and texts, while seeing it alongside a column online seems to be merely commonplace.

Print continues to walk on, then, albeit perhaps a touch more slowly than it might have done 30 or 40 years ago. It seems likely, however, that in the coming years there will be more and more media through which sports journalists can tell their stories, and more and more outlets to take advantage of. "Multimedia journalism" is so commonplace now that the excitement and novelty once associated with the nomenclature has been entirely lost. It once meant learning new digital skills, creating online content and in doing so improving one's employability with these niche abilities. Digital teams would sit separately from the newspaper staff, working on the website with little consideration of liaising with those producing the print editions.

Now, convergence is the watchword, and "multimedia journalism" is now essential for any job in sports journalism. Digital and print desks have been combined, and staff work across all platforms. "Multimedia journalism" now also requires the knowledge to work on social media, utilising Periscope and Facebook Live, and this will extend further.

This has happened only over the course of around a decade; it may be a cliché but still worth recording that change happens so quickly. I now teach sports journalism for a few days a week, and my students never fail to laugh when I tell them that when I first started reporting from matches there was no such thing as Wi-Fi coverage at stadia, and I would have to ring in my copy to a special copytaking line, reading out the punctuation, spelling out unusual words or names, and noting where each paragraph break should go. In an era where smartphones are omnipresent and Wi-Fi viewed almost as a human right, phoning in one's copy seems almost inexpressibly archaic. Yet this was in the 21st century – hardly the dark ages. I began my match-reporting career at non-league grounds during my studies, and my on-the-job training there has proved more useful than I could ever have predicted – now I spend much of my time covering the elite women's game in England, where press boxes are not always equipped with plugs or internet connection, and arriving fully prepared with a completely charged laptop and an internet "dongle" makes my life much easier, even if I am glad I no longer have to "phone in" my copy.

Yet the further developments in technology that will come in the future will doubtless put more pressure on sports journalists as their job descriptions change – and more pressure is put on them to deliver more content more quickly in a multitude of ways. When the internet became widespread, veteran journalists were given instructions on how to facilitate a live webchat (I vividly recall spending a morning with a very well-respected columnist of an earlier generation, explaining to him both how a tablet worked and what a webchat was); when social media became more popular, a Twitter account – verified where possible – became essential for all journalists, to deliver news nuggets but also to promote their work. Rarely does a sportswriter file a straight news piece; they will also be filing an audio clip, or sending a stream of tweets with pictures attached. Check any reporter's Twitter feed when they're covering a match – whether they're primarily a radio commentator, or a TV pundit, or a newspaper writer, they will be sending pictures of teamsheets as well as the view from their seat in the press box. It is likely the demands on the journalist's time and skills will increase as the media available expand.

Diversity of the press pack and their coverage

It is my fervent hope that as the media platforms increase, so too does the diversity of the staff using them. It should be an embarrassment to the trade that so few of its practitioners are women. The Sports Journalists' Association, in their evidence to the House of Commons Select Committee in 2013, glossed over the systemic problems that are clearly preventing women from considering a career in sports journalism, instead opting to point to a handful of female exceptions who had succeeded in spite of this. In the same collection of evidence, the National Union of Journalists were rather more realistic, pointing to the lack of women in the Press Gazette's top 50 sports journalists of the year (only two nominees were female), and estimating that only 4 per cent of the membership of the Football Writers' Association were women.[1]

Similarly, very few sports journalists are from a black or minority ethnic background. A 2016 study by researchers at City University indicated that around 6 per cent of journalists in the UK identified as having a black or minority ethnic background, when only 87 per cent of the UK working population were white. This imbalance in representing the UK population as a whole in journalism is neither new nor improving; this is a statistic that was much the same four years prior in an NCTJ survey.

Yet simply noting this demographic imbalance is not enough. Similarly, it is not enough to pay lip service to the desire to attract a more diverse workforce; careers talks to sixth-formers come too late. Action is required imminently if we are to encourage a more diverse – and, yes, more interesting – future for sports journalism. It should also not be forgotten here that class and family background are also a form of diversity, particularly when lengthy unpaid internships are too often seen as the only route into the media; this eliminates young people from lower-income families, who cannot afford to spend months working for free in the hope that a job might transpire at the end of it.

Sports journalism – and indeed journalism as a whole – needs to attract more diverse voices for its own good. The relentless audible bombardment of male, white, middle-class opinions does not make for a lively, thoughtful news media; it makes for a repetitive, homogenous echo chamber, lacking in excitement, freshness and originality.

Not only does it require more diverse voices, it also needs these voices to be covering a wider range of sports. The relentless focus on men's elite football is just as tiresome as the relentless march of the same journalistic voices. This remains a vicious circle; this is the sport that gains the highest viewing figures and most page clicks, and so more resources are poured into it, resulting in high viewing figures and page clicks. Yet it is a self-fulfilling prophecy: no other sport has a chance to assert itself in the shadow of the footballing monolith, and editors rarely want to take a commercial risk in these challenging economic times by giving coverage to a less-safe bet.

Increasing market fragmentation may help with that: with more outlets, particularly those online, there is certainly more opportunity for minority sports to be covered, albeit often by enthusiastic amateurs rather than by professional journalists. It has also been heartening to see the big conglomerates using their commercial heft and ability to bid for broadcast rights to broaden their range of sports covered too, and offering refreshing alternatives: Sky Sports have taken on the broadcast of domestic and international netball, while BT Sport are the official broadcast partner of the FA Women's Super League, the elite level of women's football.

The tiresome repetition of much of the sports media, in terms of content and practitioners, is tricky to challenge, but many are endeavouring to do so. Journalist Leon Mann, for example, runs the D-Word conference, offering a space to discuss the need for greater diversity in sports journalism; the campaigning group Women in Football focus on gender representation in one particular sport; and there is also space for smaller-scale local work. Sport England's *This Girl Can* has encouraged greater participation in sport, but also offers a way for schools, colleges and universities to show sport as a viable career option for women in a number of roles.

As someone who teaches sports journalism in addition to my professional career, the consistency of each intake's demographic has been disheartening, suggesting that a more diverse industry is not imminent. This has led to us running outreach sessions in local schools – ones where applying to university might not be expected of every student, sometimes – but at primary school level as well as secondary. After all, if girls and BAME children are put off sport as a career right from the off, because they do not see anyone who looks like them already doing the job, it is too late to persuade them when they are 18 and looking for work. The neat little phrase "They can't be it if they can't see it" is a truism, but worth considering.

It is my fervent hope that a more diverse body of sports journalists covering a more diverse range of sports will also lead to diversity of the way in which sport is covered. It is important to consider that encouraging and ensuring diversity is not just about the amount of coverage, nor just about the way in which the content is delivered, but also in the tone of the coverage. It may be unfashionable to say it, but sports coverage still finds itself veering into racism, perhaps unthinkingly or unknowingly, but still dangerous. The words that are used to describe black athletes still carry stereotypical overtones; the bodies of black athletes continue to be sexualised in a way that their white equivalents would not be.

It is also hugely sexist. There is still an assumption that the reader or viewer of sports coverage is a man. Sports news channels pair young, conventionally attractive female newsreaders with older male counterparts, hired for gravitas. Men's Twenty20 cricket hires female dancers to mark every single boundary hit. The PDC darts events always hire "walk-on girls" to accompany the male players to the oche. (Interestingly, when Anastasia Dobromyslova has made it to the big televised events, she has found herself accompanied either by a male model, in an effort for some kind of "equality" of objectification, or by the same walk-on girls, waving placards reading "Girl Power!" or similar.)

Why should it be the case that sports coverage – across media – continues to be sensationalised in many different ways? Academic researchers have investigated this over the past half-century. Eric Dunning, Patrick Murphy and John Williams argue that prior to the 1966 World Cup in England, newspapers began to sensationalise their coverage of football in particular, including focusing on crowd disturbances, in order to increase sales. This presented the football ground as a place where violence was commonplace, expected and even acceptable, thus attracting an element who sought a place to fight, making the concept of the "dangerous" ground a self-fulfilling prophecy.[2] Anne Coddington describes the popular perception of the football ground during the 1970s and 1980s as "a haven for racist, sexist thugs", explaining that many women were put off going to football for fear of violence during this period, although this was not the case for everyone.[3] So in the last 30 years, (analysis of) sports media has served to invisibilise female fans; media coverage has tended to reinforce the heterosexist gender binary in which men are imbued with power and play an active role, while women are passive and objectified.

As a female sports journalist, it has never failed to amaze and vaguely disgust me when I have been given editorial guidelines suggesting that if I could find a picture of an attractive woman to accompany a story, that would be helpful. Once I was told to "stop writing so much like a woman" by a national sports editor. It is evident that the sports journalist continues to be assumed to be male, and so is his audience.

Though the percentage of female sports journalists remains depressingly minimal, there are plenty of women consuming sports media. I have often wondered how other women feel about the "laddish" banter and tone of a significant proportion of sports coverage: a TV commentator advising his viewers to ring their wives to say they would be late home as a match went into extra-time; Sky Sports' Soccer AM persisting with their Soccerette; innumerable websites running galleries of the most attractive wives and girlfriends of footballers. Absent from all this are female voices – female reporters, female pundits and female fans.

Despite this, women continue to consume this sports coverage; after all, to keep up with the sports they love, they have little choice. They find themselves negotiating a tricky dilemma – either they ignore the sexism exuded from sports media, or they acknowledge it, making them enjoy their sport just a little bit less. They have to negotiate their identities, as fans and as women, in institutionally sexist sports, reinforced by the media they consume.

This is why I decided to combine my freelance journalism with a research project into the experiences of female fans of men's football – I wanted to know how other women coped with this. Despite the sexism on show, my research[4] indicates that female fans in football have a high level of sports media consumption – primarily focused on their own team, using their club's official website for news and watching highlights of their team's games, but also reading national newspapers and magazines and watching matches in which their team is not involved.

It was clear during this research that often female sports fans find themselves in a conflicted position, participating in a fandom which is institutionally sexist and thus (hetero) sexually objectifies women (who are not generally deemed as part of the fandom). However, they had a range of attitudes and reactions about the representation of gender and female fandom in the media they consumed. Some highlighted examples of what they felt was "inappropriate" female conduct within football, and others chose to ignore examples of highly gendered or sexualised sports media, such as the Soccerette on Soccer AM. Whelehan argues that the woman who happily accepts the gender stereotypes portrayed in the media and participates in them (in this case simply by consumption) also accepts that "women are primarily prized and displayed for their looks", and while women are depicted only in relation to men (as the heavily gendered Soccer AM does) then this undermines "contemporary female assurances that glamour and style are done 'for myself' and not for male approbation".[5]

Yet female football fans are largely very well aware of the gendered nature of some of the media they consume in relation to their football fandom, and they thus create ways to negotiate potential issues. Although Whelehan says that these women are colluding with a hierarchical structure that reinforces gender stereotypes, some of my respondents argued that females who display themselves in a sexualised manner within a sporting context are simply operating under the freedom of choice. Their reaction to the football media is just another way in which my respondents perceive and perform their identity as fans.

My expertise is in female sports fans, but on a cursory glance across the back pages and clicking through to the leading sports websites, I would imagine similar issues might be experienced by fans from BAME backgrounds. For example, at the tail-end of 2016, Raheem Sterling was at the centre of a news story – not for anything he had done on the pitch, nor for anything he had done that calendar year, but because a tweet from two years previously had surfaced, showing him shopping in a discount store. A few months previously, Sterling had been castigated in some media outlets for his expenditure and décor of a new home, intended for his mother. Some journalists and fans suggested on Twitter that for certain demographics of the sports media, a young, wealthy black man would never be able to spend his money in the "right" way; this was beautifully noted by Daniel Harris in the *New Statesman*.[6]

Similarly, fans identifying as LGBTQI often find their concerns ignored or brushed over by the sports media; the repeated debate about the possibility of a male Premier League player "coming out" as gay often triggers this. Certain sections of the sports media – mostly white, male, heterosexual middle-class – take the view that an athlete's sexuality is "unimportant", with one stroke dismissing the arguments put forward by LGBTQI groups that role models are important, and that it is even more important for athletes to feel they can speak honestly and truthfully about their personal lives in a way that heterosexual athletes have always been able to.

The assumptions made about the consumers of sports journalism by its creators are not always good ones; I would argue that these stereotypes put forward over the course of decades have led to a certain amount of insidious, institutional discrimination and prejudice, reinforced by the lack of diversity in the industry. These generalisations have not been challenged; indeed, quite often it appears they are just not noticed. One of the buzzwords of the socially aware on social media is the advice, "Check your privilege" – think about the perspective from which you are speaking, and think about how that might seem to other people. Quite often, this would be useful for the remarkably privileged sports media to do.

The road ahead

Leaving aside my wishes for a more diverse industry covering a more diverse range of sports and understanding the diversity of its audience, I consider that it is reasonably safe to say that there will continue to be a huge demand for sports news – and sports gossip – in the years directly ahead of us.

Degrees in sports journalism have sprung up across the country, many staffed by excellent reporters looking to share their knowledge with the next generation. That said, it has to be noted that there are unlikely to be full-time jobs in sports journalism for every single sports journalism graduate – but then again, that would probably have always been true. Degree courses should – and do – help their students develop transferable skills and support them as they head into the world of work, and many graduates go into the worlds of teaching, PR and – increasingly – club media.

Perhaps the real question for sports journalism and journalists to consider, then, is how sports journalism is actually going to be delivered – and whether sports journalists are essential to that. Media platforms will continue to expand, of course; but I have come to think that the bigger question is whether or not sports news will be delivered by professional sports journalists – or simply enthusiastic amateurs.

With everyone able to publish directly onto the internet, whether via a blog or a social media account, sports journalists are no longer the keepers of "sacred knowledge" remembered by Charlie Lambert.[7] Indeed, sports journalists are now operating in a world where they and their colleagues are viewed as the least trusted professionals, according to nationwide surveys; only politicians are seen as less trustworthy than journalists.[8] It is no wonder that non-professionals can set up their own websites or social media accounts and attract a loyal readership as they build up their own reputations.

The worrying thing here is of course that journalistic work starts to be done for free. This has long been the case; fan-led sites have operated for almost as long as the internet, providing information to other fans as a labour of love. I know of other situations where professional journalists are happy to run their own websites on a niche sport simply because they feel it is important for the reporting to be done, but they have not managed to interest any editors in paying for that work. More and more, though, I hear of and see publications asking for correspondents to write about a club or a sport, and offer nothing in recompense except the vanity of a byline. If one is a passionate fan of a sport or a club, and already has a full-time job to pay the bills, then it is unsurprising that one might choose to do that.

However, the enthusiastic amateur is inevitably going to lack some important skills: objectivity, for example; the bulging contacts book to check a story or a rumour; and the ability to tell a story. They might be able to *write* a story reasonably well, or film a chunk of footage adequately, but they will not have access to the polish a professional would be able to bring. Now, this may sound outrageous to a professional journalist, but commercially an outlet might still prefer the amateur instead of someone they have to pay. For a publication looking to maximise their profits, they might be happy to continue taking a risk on the amateur; a professional might produce better quality work, but would they bring in a bigger audience?

We have already established that sports journalism is an expanding market with more and more potential outlets for information; publications need to carve out their niche, establish a readership, and ensure repeat business in order to survive. The quality of the content they are publishing is some way down the list of priorities for many of these outlets; the term "clickbait" is thrown about as a derisory term, but the principle – encouraging people to click on a link through to a website – is one that applies across the industry. Even with broadsheet newspapers, the print headlines are becoming increasingly sensationalised for the same reason – they want to encourage people to pick up the paper and hand over their cash.

In an increasingly commercialised media battlefield, making money is becoming more important than the quality of the journalism; and so the biggest challenge for sports journalists as we move through the 21st century is perhaps, as we attempt to regain our reputation, to make the case for why our trade and our skills are still important.

References

1. The Select Committee's report into women and sport is fascinating on this, with a certain defensive tone coming from the industry. The full report with minutes is available online - http://www.publications.parliament.uk/pa/cm201415/cmselect/cmcumeds/513/513.pdf
2. Eric Dunning, P. Murphy and John Williams, *The Roots of Football Hooliganism: An Historical and Sociological Study*, Routledge and Kegan Paul: London, 1988.
3. Anne Coddington, *One of the Lads: Women Who Follow Football*. HarperCollins: London, 1997.
4. Carrie Dunn, *Female Football Fans*, Palgrave Pivot: London, 2014.
5. Imelda Whelehan, *Overloaded: Popular Culture and the Future of Feminism*, Women's Press: London, 2000.
6. Daniel Harris, "Racism in British football is clear in our newspapers as well as the stands", *New Statesman*, 13 January 2017, http://www.newstatesman.com/politics/sport/2017/01/racism-britishfootball-clear-our-newspapers-well-stands, accessed 16 December 2019.
7. Charlie Lambert, "Why the press pack must raise its game", *British Journalism Review*, Volume 3, Issue 2, 2012, pp. 32–37.
8. Ipsos MORI, 2016; "Politicians are still trusted less than estate agents, journalists and bankers", https://www.ipsos-mori.com/researchpublications/researcharchive/3685/Politicians-are-stilltrusted-less-than estate agents-journalists-and-bankers.aspx, accessed 16 December 2019

35

Reporting

Toby Miller

We cannot credibly predict the future without some knowledge of history and contemporane-ity. So following a discussion of journalism in particular, and its historic role and its place in the current conjuncture, this chapter examines some key aspects of football journalism's possible future. The topics are nationalism, gender/race and technology/labour. But first – what is foot-ball journalism for? What *does* it do, and what *should* it do?

At its best, journalism in general connects people who would otherwise be out of touch with others' concerns; enables them to scrutinise private and public institutions; highlights social problems; informs debate over values; and animates the public power of reason.[1] In his famous 17th century defence of the freedom (for Protestants) to print the truth without censorship, John Milton avowed that "when complaints are freely heard, deeply considered, and speedily reformed, then is the utmost civil liberty attained".[2] Two hundred years ago, Jeremy Bentham referred to journalism as the "check to arbitrary power … upon the conduct of the ruling few".[3] John Stuart Mill followed by defending it "as one of the securities against corrupt or tyranni-cal government"[4] and Simón Bolívar called for "freedom of the press" to be a cornerstone of Hispanic America's independence from Spain – part of "all that is sublime in politics".[5] These high-minded ideals still animate not-for-profit, public-interest elements of the bourgeois and activist media alike.

Journalism requires research, interpretation, dissemination and mobilisation.[6] For democra-cies to function, journalism must operate without fear or favour. There needs to be regular press coverage of political affairs, with a focus on human rights, public policy, international relations, environment, culture, economy, society, culture, elections, lawmakers' deliberations and judicial review. The idea is to draw citizens into the policy process, ensuring informed public comment and dissent as well as willing consent. Perhaps the most famous example is the link established by Amartya Sen between a free press, multi-party democracy and the avoidance of famine.[7]

But the task is far from simple. Despite the claims made by political theory and economics for the value of the news media to citizenship, reporters have long been regarded as disposable and unworthy. If we go back to the origins of the profession in the 17th- and 18th-century European occupations of the gazetteer and newsman, we find they were derided as unreliable and given to sensationalising. Such complaints indexed their contradictory roles as spokespeople for either traditional sources of ecclesiastical and state authority, or rivalrous emergent bourgeoisies – for the earliest journalists were passionate observers and partisan chroniclers of an urbanising Europe, whether they were anonymous reporters or philosopher–anthropologists named Kant.[8] These writers were describing the Industrial Revolution as it deepened and spread.[9] Inevitably, this attracted opprobrium.

In his famous essay "Politics as Vocation", Max Weber addressed journalism's social standing and found it was "always estimated by 'society' in terms of its ethically lowest representative". Conversely, he admired reporters, because of the extraordinary responsibility that came with their role and the factory-like discipline of deadlines, which both demanded and constrained creativity. This was especially true at times of war and newly arrived peace (Weber was writing in one such period, just after the Great War). Such a mission was very difficult to live up to; journalists were "propertyless and hence professionally bound", their occupation "an absolute gamble in every respect and under conditions that test one's inner security". The sense of being obligated to employers was connected to the priority placed on advertising revenue over true independence and the absence of both "genuine leadership" and "the responsible management of politics".[10] The cataclysmic tumult that ushered in Weber's blend of scepticism and admiration was of course repeated 20 years later.

Those issues of legitimacy and professional and public repute have long been relevant to sports reporters. They occupy what is often tagged as the toy store of the paper, a conceptual and physical area populated by fanboys rather than serious journalists. Their reports appear in the back of the paper or the tail of the news bulletin – something of minor historical and political import. But this is equally true of their typically uncritical approach towards the ontology, epistemology and politics of their objects of engagement: the fanboy approach characteristic of sports reporters has three components – vicarious pleasure that derives from projecting oneself onto the football pitch; enjoyment of others' physical endeavour and aptitude; and the social experience of informal professional networks.[11]

The key change to sports journalism over the past three decades has been democracies' deregulation of the electronic media, such that radio and television need not provide omnibus services, from music to current affairs to weather. The emergence of channels and stations dedicated purely to sport has given greater prominence and power to many sports journalists – no longer must they share newsrooms with those allegedly embarked on a higher calling of greater prestige. As per the freedom enjoyed by Milanese reporters working for *La Gazzetta dello Sport* since the 1890s, or Madrileños faithfully incanting the word from the Bernabeu in *Marca* since the 1940s, no one dare suggest today at ESPN in Buenos Aires, or Sky in Brentford, that football doesn't matter by contrast with the rest of what goes on in the building. But the issues of seriousness and legitimacy remain for football journalists who work in conventional omnibus newsrooms. The sense of marginality can be even greater for online sports reporters within traditional media. They represent the "toy department within the toy department".[12]

Of course, we are often told today that journalism of all kinds is in crisis. This is variously attributed to the folly of newspapers making their copy available free online while charging for it in print; advertisers moving their money elsewhere; the charge of finance-based conglomerates into media ownership, driven by Wall Street stock valuations rather than the public interest; the spread of fake news; the role of aggregating communications firms such as the F- and G-words (Facebook and Google) masquerading as "social" media; and the notion that anyone, anywhere, any time is a reporter, just because they can tap their thumbs: a tweet from AN Other about the offside rule seemingly "matters".

It could be argued that those problems largely affect the Global North. For internationally, this is a golden age of journalism: more and more people around the world are literate and have disposable income. Such increases in literacy and money mean more readership and advertising.

Dedicated sports outlets proliferate across all the major languages, and football is their principal currency, aside from during the summer Olympics/Indian Premier League of cricket, or if they are dedicated to gambling on which whipped horse will obey its slave master most successfully. Sports are also claimed to be relatively immune to macro-economic distress, thanks to long-term broadcasting deals guaranteeing cash flow, although sponsorship contracts may suffer when highly geared entities' greed and incompetence match their wish for self-promotion during a crisis.[13]

So the future looks brighter for some reporters on the football floor of the toy store than others, depending on their platform, their employer and their location. Three issues will definitely stalk them, wherever they are: nationalism, gender/race and technology/labour.

Nationalism

When English and French fans alike sang *La Marseillaise* before their countries met in a football match just days after Paris had been assaulted in 2015,[14] they did so in the presence of the British monarchy, the French presidency, the police and the military. The event was broadcast and celebrated on public television and radio.[15]

The anthem they shared that night is a notoriously bloodthirsty paean to racism and war: "*Qu'un sang impur/Abreuve nos sillons*" [Let impure blood/Water our furrows]. All in all, it is "a pretty nasty song".[16] Was this performance covered as a manifestation of nationalism through military values and symbols, a paean to language, music, hierarchy, conduct, clothing, celebration and propaganda? Did journalists discuss the cultures of these bloodthirsty imperial nations and weapons exporters? Of course not. That night at Wembley was hailed quite differently in the bourgeois media, lauded as an uplifting occasion of loving solidarity, instantly likened to the tear-jerking sequence in *Casablanca*, when Paul Georg Julius Hernreid von Wasel Waldingau, Corinna Mura and Marie Madeleine Berthe Lebeau lead the crowd singing the same anthem in opposition to Nazism.[17]

But Wembley 2015 incarnated something else: nationalism meeting football, via the state presence, the lyrical content, the uniformed imagery, the armed environment, the declaration of war and the stadium setting.[18] It's significant that when Algeria played France in Paris for the first time in 2001, the anthem was booed by a crowd mainly comprised of postcolonial survivors, and the game called off following a pitch invasion.[19] This followed a history of the Front National's leader calling footballers refusing to sing along with *La Marseillaise* "fake Frenchmen". Critical football journalism alert to such cultural politics went missing in coverage of the 2015 lament.

It has not always been so. George Orwell famously described international sport as "war minus the shooting".[20] That pithy observation came from his description of a 1945 "goodwill" British tour by the Soviet football club, commando ДиНáМО МОСкВá [Dynamo Moscow].[21] He feared that such "sporting contests lead to orgies of hatred" because of the competitiveness inherent in football. Orwell's colonial and militia experience of football in Burma, India and Spain was of uncontrolled and passionate derision expressed by one section of a crowd towards another. No surprise, then, that in *Nineteen Eighty-Four*, "the proles" were fascinated by football; it "filled up the horizons of their minds".[22] Of course, he also referred admiringly to the miner who emerged from the pit covered from head to toe by coal dust, then proudly washed and changed into his best clothes in order to attend a match, imagining a socialist future that would sparkle with the pleasure of watching football.[23]

Those antinomies of loathing and loving in the world of football are remarkably robust, regardless of technology and regulation. They should provide the very stuff of that rare breed: critical football writing. But the majority tendency leans towards chauvinism, regardless of the medium in which it is carried. Such partisanship sees more and more punditry by superannuated players and less and less "hard" news and research. A comparison of TV coverage of the 2014 men's football World Cup in Portugal, Ghana, the US and Germany indicates how common this tendency has become, alongside the nationalism that dogs it.[24]

Consider the developing relationship between propaganda and football journalism in Colombia. The sport was popularly celebrated for its political neutrality amid the polarisation of *La Violencia*, a period of virtual civil war that lasted from the 1940s to the 1960s. Journalism played a positive role in helping make football a core part of newspaper reporting, which had largely ignored it until then. And radio coverage installed the sport as the principal source of a national popular by the mid-1970s. The national popular is an everyday concept in politics across the Americas and in social theory. Deriving in part from the work of the activist journalist Antonio Gramsci's pioneering investigations of fascist Italy, it refers to ways of binding nations together across social classes via nationalistic cultural myths. In Latin America, it is used by all sides of politics and has transcended its more academic uses in the Anglo-Saxon world. The national popular can emerge in dialectical form – simultaneously as the property and design of elites seeking to incorporate the population into their projects, and as the joint creation of those very popular classes, via carnival, expressivity and hopes for upward mobility. Football became the monetary property of the elite and the symbolic property of the public.[25]

Journalism's elevation of football to a crucial part of pacific civil society was not sustained, as drug cartels used it to launder money, compete with one another and exhibit their powers on a public stage. When that conjuncture passed, a new militarism emerged, celebrated to the skies by football journalists. The national TV networks RCN and Caracol shared coverage of the 2016 regional Copa América. RCN joined with the Colombian military to produce stirring commercials of joy, nationalism and militarism that were implicit promotions for its billionaire owner and baron of Postobón, a sugar-drinks firm, Carlos Arturo Ardila Lülle, who was also an honoree for services to the armed forces.[26] RCN and the military thereby merged with Radamel Falcao García Zárate, James David Rodríguez Rubio and their compatriots, thanks to dutiful journalism.[27]

The network's five promotional spots for the Copa featured the military under the rubric of the *Himno Copa América Centenario 2016 #YoCreo* [Copa América Centenary Anthem 2016 #IBelieve]. When viewed in combination, the various military versions comprise seven minutes of striking propaganda.[28] For a helicopter and parachute commercial, the setting was an airfield. Soldiers dropped to the ground draped in the slogan's flag. Airforce planes carried the slogan on their fuselage. The navy provided uniformed women and men to play instruments and sing, and a ship to carry a banner alongside the flag. The presidential guard was in 19th-century attire, part of Colombia's mimicry of Prussian uniforms.[29] Nationalism coursed through these ventures. RCN's "journalism" celebrated itself, the team, fans and the armed forces as one, in seemingly endless paeans to these commercials and what they represented.[30]

Of course, Colombia has other associations in the Anglo mind, emblematised by the front page of *The Sun* on the day of England's match against the national team in the 2018 men's World Cup. Troping the name of England's captain, Harry Kane, it depicted him with "GO KANE" in the headline, to the outrage of the Colombian embassy and media.[31]

In response to their complaints, the next day's paper read:

> The front page of yesterday's *Sun* may have given the impression that Colombia is well known for its cocaine trade. This was unfair on the Colombian people, who are far more embarrassed by the way their cheating, fouling, play acting, mean-spirited national football team played last night.
>
> We are happy to set the record straight.[32]

This cheekily adolescent xenophobia/tabloid imperialism is typical trash "journalism" targeted at the country's white, monolingual working-class. It hides a sense of pride in Britain's vicious slaving past that characterises the paper, and is another moment when nationalism over-determines what football journalism might otherwise be.

There is nothing new here, of course, but it represents a continuity with a chauvinistic history that will simply not go away – and suggests some regrettable links to the present that will probably prosper long into the future. The same applies to gender and race, albeit with bright spots leavening the tiresome hegemony of white men reporting football in wealthy countries.

Gender and race

The picture of white male control of football reportage is dismal, and appears likely to remain that way. British football journalism has long been male-dominated, and sports reporting in general is dominated by men across the globe.[33] Newspapers are the most gendered, as TV makes progress towards what it claims to be an open talent search but is really about targeting audiences and advertisers. Content analysis in Britain, Australia and the US of both textual coverage of women's sports and the thousands of publicly available professional opportunities for women in newspapers sports journalism discloses a huge gap and bias. Survey research indicates that male reporters have very negative views about improving the situation.[34]

By contrast with journalism, the international public relations industry is overwhelmingly female, and many female graduates of journalism schools end up working in sports promotion.[35] The trend is dramatic – a move away from critical, public-interest work into promotion – and as that happens, the tendency will probably be for men to move into strategic communications, as it currently likes to be known, thereby further marginalising women.

Beyond association football, it is notable that the US Just Not Sports organisation launched #MoreThanMean in 2016 as a video campaign to highlight online harassment of women sports reporters. It rapidly reached over four million viewers and attracted bourgeois and specialist sports media coverage alike.[36]

This UK Sky Sports maven boasted in 2018 that:

> At recent press conferences for the leading football clubs in the Premier League, Championship and Scottish Premiership we counted 310 reporters covering 25 clubs. Nearly 300 were men; fewer than 10 per cent were women … Sky Sports News, where we have a 24-hour rolling sports news TV channel and digital sports news team [has] a 70/30 gender balance among our team of around 190 journalists. Our recruitment over the past seven years has been 50/50.[37]

But the lamentable British in general have nothing to crow about when it comes to race. Consider these figures: over half a century of the BBC's flagship football show, *Match of the Day*, there has never been a black host, despite the statistically disproportionate number of professional black players by contrast with the population overall, and the proliferation of black pundits among ex-pros bleating and moaning about today's players. The Corporation's Radio 5 Live (known colloquially as "Radio Bloke") offers nearly 30 hours of football coverage a week; just 60 minutes have a minority host. The BBC's domestic sport correspondents are all white, and no staff reporters for one of the busiest web pages in the world are black. The 2018 men's FIFA World Cup saw the British papers dispatch one black journalist out of more than 60, alongside three women from the media overall.[38]

In short, you'd better be a straight white man who's not very good at football if you want to report on it in the UK: of the 338 roles assigned to sports reporters who are failures on the pitch, five go to black folks and seven to South Asians, while almost half the respondents to a survey by Sports Media LGBT said they had been the objects of discrimination or seen it in newsrooms between 2016 and 2018.[39] Similar trends are clear in US journalism covering the NFL: in 2017, 85 per cent of the sports editors, 76.4 per cent of the assistant sports editors, 80.3 per cent of the columnists, 82.1 per cent of the reporters and 77.7 per cent of the copy editors/designers were white.[40]

There is certainly more discourse today about this inequality and bigotry; there are more organisations dedicated to changing the situation; and there is greater targeting of female and minority audiences by the relevant fractions of capital. All that bodes well for change; but it would be charmingly naïve to imagine either the old guard or their boy progeny willingly giving up the hegemonic hierarchies that have delivered affirmative action for straight, sedentary Anglos for such a long, long time.

Technology and labour

We can only hazard a guess at who among workers will benefit from the next innovation likely to line the pockets of media capital: the automatisation of journalism. A survey of BBC, CNN and Thomson Reuters journalists who use "robo-writing software" suggests they are doubtful about the new technology's ability to sense the qualitative import of stories, but certain of its appeal to their employers.[41] Given the current data fetish that is Taylorising[42] all of sport – think of the "expected goals" category that almost trumps, you know, goals scored – it is no surprise that software is growing in popularity. The Associated Press has been using Automated Insights' Wordsmith program for four years to cover fixtures to which it would not otherwise have sent a reporter.[43] Yahoo! Sports does so to generate millions of match reports aimed at Fantasy Football participants, egging on advertisers to feast on "over 100 years of incremental audience engagement".[44]

New technology also holds some significant implications for the visual side of sports reporting. For example, the *New York Times* and the BBC offer virtual-reality news stories as part of their febrile search for "immersive journalism".[45] And while it would be unwise to make too much of virtual reality as a crucial future development in screen drama, because it asks audiences to do what they want done for them and turns everyone into film theorists in the process, it has great application in medicine, the military – and football fetishism. Relatedly, football photojournalists face dual challenges: capitalist property lines are increasingly being drawn around events, thereby limiting their access, even as technology puts paying spectators into play as their rivals.[46]

By contrast, one area that has been thought of as a more significant contribution to critical journalism in the digital era is long-form football writing. It can blend interpretation, background and data to create something of value for more leisurely and in-depth reading than the 24-hour cycle of news allows/encourages. France's *L'Équipe* has specialized in this "slow journalism" approach, challenging cybertarian orthodoxy.[47] For their part, bloggers are generally not seen as a threat by British football writers, but rather as offering something complementary to their own work that has its niche.[48] In Brazil, the *crônica* and short story provide interesting alternatives. The past few years have seen the emergence of the *Microcontos de Futebol* series and the web documentary *Triângulo do Futebol*, on the history of the sport in the Triângulo Mineiro and Alto Paranaíba.[49]

The Associated Press maintains that robot journalism will create new jobs with greater diversity of everything from skills to cultural backgrounds, and it has many reactionary scholars heady with this next cybertarian gift.[50] Entities such as Canada's Postmedia Network of newspapers may also point the way.[51] It has institutionalised round-the-clock digital reportage, but only of the men's major leagues, targeting male readership. In addition, Postmedia relies on outsourced labour and devotedly unoriginal analysis and bloviation.[52]

A longitudinal study of Twitter use by leading football media outlets between 2010 and 2017 reveals that the drive to find content has augmented the number and rapidity of tweets, seemingly infinite duplication and a tendency to concentrate on star clubs, players and managers. Ironically, given cybertarian claims to the contrary, it discloses that Twitter is used as a "one-directional broadcasting medium, where content is increasingly homogenised – and where search engine optimisation and attractive headlines trump journalistic content".[53] And research on the relationships between spokespeople for German Bundesliga clubs and print journalists who cover those teams discloses that each side sees journalists as more dependent on club officials than vice versa, and most reporters anticipate a growth in the pressure exerted on them to write stories with an emphasis amenable to team interests.[54]

Conclusion

We desperately need greater acumen and coverage of football's political economy, as the influence of global money intensifies – take, for example, the dubious business and political dealings of Leicester City's owners, who are laughably celebrated over and over in the bourgeois press and fan fora as ideal proprietors.[55] We need serious investigative reporting of the corruption that is rife in ruling associations, the environmental impact of football,[56] the role of podcasts in supporting the animal slavery and human addiction of gambling, and the systematic human-rights offences by team owners such as the heads of Paris Saint-Germain, Girona and Manchester City – topics that are almost entirely left to one side by the fanboys of the Anglo world's bourgeois press.[57] It will be a far cry from present practice and the exciting world of chronicling the Industrial Revolution with which we began.

References

1. Amartya Sen, *The Idea of Justice*, The Belknap Press of Harvard University Press: Cambridge, MA, 2009, pp. 335–337.

2. John Milton, *Areopagitica: A Speech for the Liberty of Unlicensed Printing*, Harvard University Press: Cambridge, 1909–1914, p. 1.

3. Jeremy Bentham, *The Collected Works of Jeremy Bentham: On the Liberty of the Press, and Public Discussion, and Other Legal and Political Writings for Spain and Portugal*, Philip Schofield and Catherine Pease-Watkin (eds.), Oxford University Press: Oxford, UK, 2012, p. 8, 13.

4. John Stuart Mill, *On Liberty*, 1859, http://www.econlib.org/library/Mill/mlLbty3.html

5. Simón Bolívar, *El Libertador: Writings of Simón Bolívar*, translated by Frederick H. Fornoff, David Bushnell (ed.), Oxford University Press: Oxford, UK, 2003, p. 21, 42, 73.

6. William P. Cassidy, "Variations on a theme: Professional role conceptions of print and online newspaper Journalists", *Journalism & Mass Communication Quarterly*, Volume 82, Issue 2, 2005, pp. 264–280.

7. Amartya Sen, *Development as Freedom*, Alfred A. Knopf: New York, 2000.

8. Michel Foucault, *The Politics of Truth*, Sylvère Lotringer (ed.), translated by Lysa Hochroth and Catherine Porter, Semiotext(e): Los Angeles, 2007, p. 48.

9. Asa Briggs and Peter Burke, *A Social History of the Media: From Gutenberg to the Internet*, Polity Press: Cambridge, UK, 2003.

10. Max Weber, *From Max Weber: Essays in Sociology*, translated and edited by HH Gerth and C. Wright Mills, Free Press: New York, 1946, pp. 96–98.

11. Sada Reed, "'I'm not a fan. I'm a journalist': measuring American sports journalists' sports enthusiasm", *Journal of Sports Media*, Volume 13, Issue 1, 2018, pp. 27–47.

12. Simon McEnnis, "Toy department within the toy department? Online sports journalists and professional legitimacy", *Journalism,* 2019, doi: 10.1177/1464884918797613

13. https://www.economist.com/international/2009/02/12/is-it-recession-proof

14. https://www.youtube.com/watch?v=o6O_8RohRrI

15. Sheena McKenzie, "England vs. France: How singing 'La Marseillaise' became a different war chant", *CNN*, 17 November 2015, http://edition.cnn.com/2015/11/17/sport/paris-attacks-french-national-anthem-football-wembley/, accessed 17 December 2019.

16. Laurent Dubois, "The blood of the impure", in *Africa Is a Country*, March 2013, https://africasacountry.com/2013/03/the-blood-of-the-impure

17. https://www.youtube.com/watch?v=HM-E2H1ChJM

18. https://www.youtube.com/watch?v=tWwkU-CWy9o

19. David Andress, "The song that once unified France is tearing it apart", *Quartz*, 3 July, 2018, https://qz.com/1320059/la-marseillaise-frances-national-anthem-is-causing-tension-once-again/, accessed 17 December 2019.

20. George Orwell, "The sporting spirit", *Tribune*, December 1945, http://www.orwell.ru/library/articles/spirit/english/e_spirit, accessed 17 December 2019.

21. https://www.youtube.com/watch?v=pYFTYanZXiE; Seweryn Dmowski, "Football sites of memory in the Eastern bloc 1945–1991", in Wolfram Pyta and Nils Havermann (eds.), *European Football and Collective Memory*, Palgrave Macmillan: Basingstoke, UK, 2015, pp. 171–184.

22. Orwell, "The sporting spirit".

23. George Orwell, *The Road to Wigan Pier*, Victor Gollancz: London, 1937, p. 3, 11.

24. Thomas Horky, Galen Clavio and Christoph Grimmer, "Broadcasting the World Cup: A multinational comparative analysis broadcast quality in the 2014 World Cup", *Soccer & Society,* Volume 21, 2020. doi: 10.1080/14660970.2018.1448794

25. David Leonardo Quitián Roldán and Olga Lucia Urrea Beltrán, "Fútbol, desarrollo social y patria: La violencia como factor de lo nacional en clave de gol", *Revista San Gregorio* especial no. 2, 2016, pp. 162–170, and "Fútbol, radio y nación (1946–1974): Una visión antropológica de la violencia en Colombia", *Espacio Abierto: Cuaderno Venezolano de Sociología*, Volume 25, Issue 2, 2016, pp. 51–66; Enrique Santos Molano, "Fútbol: Una pasión incontenible", *Credencial Historia*, September 2016, http://www.revista-credencial.com/credencial/historia/temas/futbol-una-pasion-incontenible, accessed 17 December 2019; Rafael Jaramillo Racines, "El fútbol de el Dorado: 'El punto de nflexion que marcó la rápida evolución del "amateurismo" al "profesionalismo"'", *Curitiba: Revista de Asociación Latinoamericana de Estudios Socioculturales del Deporte*, Volume 1, Issue 1, 2011, pp. 111–128.

26. Carlos Rodríguez Romero and Edison Jair Duque Oliva, "Seguimiento a la dinámica competitiva de dos grupos económicos colombianos", *Innovar*, Volume 17, Issue 29, 2007, pp. 137–154; Fabio López de la Roche, "Debate público, guerra y desregulación informativa en Colombia", *Íconos: Revista de FLACSO-Ecuador*, No. 16, 2003, pp. 54–64; Alfonso José Luna Geller, "Armada Nacional al servicio de intereses de Ardila Lülle en la Copa América?", *Las 2 Orillas*, 3 June 2016, http://www.las2orillas.co/armada-nacional-al-servicio-de-intereses-de-ardila-lulle-en-la-copa-america/, accessed 17 December 2019.

27. "El batallón guardia presidencia cree en la selección Colombia", *Noticias RCN*, 3 June 2016, http://www.noticiasrcn.com/videos/tc-dangond-el-batallon-guardia-presidencial-cree-seleccion-colombia

28. https://www.youtube.com/watch?v=2QpdtsP79w4

29. https://www.youtube.com/watch?v=EqQxvthwia4&app=desktop

30. https://www.youtube.com/watch?v=z7myTM35OLU

31. Luke Taylor, "Colombians angry and bemused by the Sun's controversial Harry Kane 'Cocaine' front Page", *The Independent*, 3 July 2018, https://www.independent.co.uk/news/world/americas/harry-kane-england-colombia-the-sun-cocaine-front-page-newspaper-three-lions-a8429756.html

32. Steve Neville, "The Sun newspaper issues 'apology' – of sorts – for controversial Colombia headline", *Irish Examiner*, 4 July 2018, https://www.irishexaminer.com/breakingnews/sport/soccer/the-sun-newspaper-issues-apology-of-sorts-for-controversial-colombia-headline-853035.html

33. Suzanne Franks and Deirdre Neill, "This sporting life. Why so few women sports writers", *Journalism Education*, Volume 6, Issue 3, 2018, pp. 42–52.

34. Hans C. Schmidt, "Forgotten athletes and token reporters: Analyzing the gender bias in sports journalism", *Atlantic Journal of Communication*, Volume 26, Issue 1, 2018, pp. 59–74.

35. Merryn Sherwood, Matthew Nicholson and Timothy Marjoribanks, "Women working in sport media and public relations: No advantage in a male-dominated world", *Communication Research and Practice*, Volume 4, Issue 2, 2018, pp. 102–116.

36. Dunja Antunovic, "'We wouldn't say it to their faces': Online harassment, women sports journalists, and feminism", *Feminist Media Studies*, Volume 19, 2019. doi: 10.1080/14680777.2018.1446454

37. Andy Cairns, "A new chapter in sporting history", *British Journalism Review*, Volume 29, Issue 2, 2018, pp. 28–32.

38. Hugh Woozencroft, "Why BBC sport can't escape sports journalism's problem", *BBC*, 14 December 2018 https://www.bbc.co.uk/sport/46571432, accessed 17 December 2019; Sports Journalists' Association, "BCOMS founder Mann calls for action on diversity, with thanks to Raheem Sterling", 20 March 2019, https://www.sportsjournalists.co.uk/other-bodies/bcoms-founder-mann-calls-for-action-on-diversity-with-thanks-to-raheem-sterling/, accessed 17 December 2019.

39. Sports Journalists' Association, "BCOMS founder Mann calls for action on diversity, with thanks to Raheem Sterling".

40. Richard Lapchick, *Making Waves of Change: The 2018 Associated Press Sports Editors Racial and Gender Report Card*, The Institute for Diversity and Ethics in Sport, 2 May 2018, http://nebula.wsimg.com/e1801a8b96d97c40f57cf3bf7cd478a3?AccessKeyId=DAC3A56D8FB782449D2A&disposition=0&alloworigin=1

41. Neil Thurman, Konstantin Dörr and Jessica Kunert, "When reporters get hands-on with Robo-Writing", *Digital Journalism*, Volume 5, Issue 10, 2017, pp. 1240–1259.

42. Taylorisation refers to the eponym FW Taylor, whose methods of scientific management created modern factory capitalism. The equivalent in the Soviet Union was Stakhanovism.

43. Klint Finley, "In the future, robots will write news that's all about you", *Wired*, 6 March 2015, https://www.wired.com/2015/03/future-news-robots-writing-audiences-one/, accessed 17 December 2019.

44. https://automatedinsights.com/customer-stories/yahoo/

45. António Baía Reis and António Fernando Vasconcelos Cunha Castro Coelho, "Virtual reality and journalism", *Digital Journalism*, Volume 6, Issue 8, 2018, pp. 1090–1100.

46. Richard Haynes, Adrian Hadland and Paul Lambert, "The state of sport photojournalism", *Digital Journalism*, Volume 5, Issue 5, 2017, pp. 636–651.

47. Christopher Tulloch and Xavier Ramon, "Take five", *Digital Journalism*, Volume 5, Issue 5, 2017, pp. 652–72; Meaghan Le Masurier, "Slow journalism", *Journalism Practice*, Volume 10, Issue 4, 2016, pp. 439–447.

48. Simon McEnnis, "Playing on the same pitch", *Digital Journalism*, Volume 5, Issue 5, 2017, pp. 549–566.

49. Rafael Duarte Oliveira Venancio, "Performance no gramado, poética no texto: A crônica e o conto de futebol como jornalismo esportivo alternativo", *Revista ALTERJOR Grupo de Estudos Alterjor: Jornalismo Popular e Alternativo*, Volume 18, Issue 2, 2018, pp. 2–27; https://www.facebook.com/triangulodofutebol/

50. Yair Galily, "Artificial intelligence and sports journalism: Is it a sweeping change?", *Technology in Society*, Volume 54, August 2018, pp. 47–51. doi: 10.1016/j.techsoc.2018.03.001

51. https://www.postmedia.com/

52. Evan Daum and Jay Scherer, "Changing work routines and labour practices of sports journalists in the digital era: A case study of postmedia", *Media, Culture & Society*, Volume 40, Issue 4, 2018, pp. 551–566. Bloviation refers to pompous speech – it has been in journalistic use for a century, supposedly typifying the addresses of President Warren Harding.

53. Jonathan Cable and Glyn Mottershead, "'Can I click it? Yes you can': Football journalism, Twitter and Clickbait", *Ethical Space: The International Journal of Communication Ethics*, Volume 15, Issue 1–2, 2018, pp. 69–80.

54. Christoph G. Grimmer, "Pressure on printed press", *Digital Journalism*, Volume 5, Issue 5, 2017, pp. 607–635.

55. Toby Miller, "Leicester city Cinderella story authored by Thai oligarch", *Asia Sentinel*, 18 May 2016, http://www.asiasentinel.com/econ-business/leicester-city-little-club-oligarch/#frameId=appnext_widget&height=84, accessed 17 December 2019.

56. Toby Miller, *Greenwashing Sport*, Routledge: London, 2018.

57. But see https://www.addiction-ssa.org/commentary/football-and-gambling-an-unholy-matrimony; https://lavdn.lavoixdunord.fr/484416/article/2018-11-08/une-affaire-de-fichage-ethnique-revelee-au-psg;https://medium.com/@NcGeehan/the-men-behind-man-city-a-documentary-not-coming-soon-to-a-cinema-near-you-14bc8e393e06; https://www.abc.net.au/news/2019-12-08/why-paddy-power-pioneer-quit-betting-industry/11777058?pfmredir=sm; and https://www.abc.net.au/news/2019-12-05/bet365-whistleblower-says-winners-given-delays/11768486.

Index

Pages in **bold** refer to tables.

52 Years of Sport: Complete Sporting Record 1896–1948 180
The 69er 91
500-1: The Miracle of Headingley 1981 (Steen and McLellan) 9

Aberdeen 71
ability(ies): athletes 264; athletic 210; benefit of the web 157; to commentate 111–112; commercial heft and 361; to entertain 33; to identify sporting news values 356; niche 360; redemption 6; skills 103, 107; technology 372; which makes cricketer distinctive 38
Abramovich, Roman 247
The Absolute Game 83, 89
abuse *see* sexual abuse
Academy Award 152
Adams, A. 215
Addison, M. 2
Adelaide 181
Adlington, R. 48
The Adventures of Huckleberry Finn (Twain) 161
The Adventures of Tom Sawyer (Twain) 161
Africa 67
African American athletes 210; *see also* athletes
Agence France-Presse (AFP) 61–62, 65, 67, 69
agencies 61–69; fight against other 69; filing by phone 63–65; international 63; international news 61, 64; national news 62; online news 248; press 24; regional newspapers and news 101; specialist sports 62; team play at big events 65–68; worlds apart 68–69
Ahmedabad 63
Alberto, C. 45–46
Alcock, C. W. 28
Alfred, L. 219
Ali, M. 16, 35, 153, 156, 207, 218
Allard, I. D. 76
Allchurch, I. 202

Allen, W. 168, 207, 344
Allerdyce, S. 60
Allie, M. 215
Allison, G. 196, 282
Allison, M. 46
All or Nothing 139, 356
All Played Out (Davies) 92, 278
All-Purpose Pre-Wembley it for Newspapers 163
All the President's Men (film) 152
Alpine Journal 26
alternative facts 152
Altman, R. 162
Alvarenga, D. 123
Amateur Cup (1967) 89
Amazon 106, 125, 139
Amazon rainforests 3
American Academy of Arts and Letters 37
American Academy of Arts and Sciences 37
Among the Thugs (Buford) 278
Andreu, Frankie 332, 334
Andrews, B. 183
Andrews, J. 156
Andrews, P. 75, 78
Angell, R. 36–40
anger/angry: due to manipulation by directors and administrators 87; ethical discord and 11; expression 296, 309; journalists 257; management 5; outrage and 305, 309–310, 314–315; public 305; reporters 54; sectarianism 94; social media 297, 310
Anglophilia 181
Anichebe, V. 129
Animal Farm (Orwell) 90
anti-apartheid 17, 208, 215–216
Anti-Doping Agency, United States 154
Antigua 5
anti-Olympic protests 267–268
antisemitism 208

anxiety(ies): despondency and 131; sports 23; sports journalists 126, 131

Anyone But England: Cricket and the National Malaise (Marqusee) 217

apartheid 14, 208, 210, 214–216, 218–220

AP Formula One 61

Apperley, C. 25

Apple 359

Appleby, Karen 228

Archer, J. 10, 12, 16, 18

Arendse, N. 219

Argentina 201

The Argus 28, 142–143, 202

Arke, E. 102, 105, 107

Arlott, J. 17, 174, 215–216, 351

Armageddon 162

armchair psychoanalysis 7

Armstrong, L. 10, 154–158, 213, 243, 343; cycling press 332–333; doping 329, 331, 332–333, 334, 335, 336; emergence as public figure 330; *It's Not About the Bike* 335; *The Oprah Winfrey Show* 335; testicular cancer 330; Tour de France 329, 330–331, 332, 333, 334, 335; World Road Race Championship 330

Aronson, Amy 227

Arsenal (football club) 40, 43, 47, 52, 58, 91–92, 121–122, 141, 191, 196; Fan TV 139; TV 105; v. Tottenham Hotspur 152

Arsenal Echo Echo 88–89

Arthur, M. 219

The Art of Captaincy (Brearley) 14–15

Ashe, A. 16

The Ashes (tiny terracotta urn) 2

Ashes Roadshow 18

Ashes Test series 6, 11–12

Ashley-Cooper, F. 174

Asia 80

Asia Yahoo 65

aspirations: footballer 111–112; noblest 17; personal 122; sympathy and 40; traditions and nobler 17; Tyler, M. 122

Assam 63

Associated Press (AP) 61–62, 64, 69, 248; Automated Insights' Wordsmith program 372; robot journalism 372–373

Association of Cricket Statisticians 183

Aston Villa 59, 74, 121, 128, 282

Athens Olympics 153, 261–262

Atherton, M. 38

athletes: ability 264; African American 210; Black 211; clubs and 136; coaches and 127; fans and 126; gay male 226; German 64; journalists speaking to 65; Russian 43; salaries 160; status 108

The Athletic 48, 92, 105, 142–143

athleticism 5

The Athletic News 25, 28, 74

The Athletic UK 142

Atkinson, M. 196

Atlantic 28, 34, 37

Attar, Sarah 262

attitudes: club 90–91; columnists 29; of mind 37; positive 96; public 27, 223; racial 29; sporting behaviour 29; writing styles and 89

Atton, C. 94

Auckland 68

Augur 25

The Australasian 28

Australia 173, 175–179, 184–185; Anglophilia 181; defeated by England 2, 47, 165; defeated by Sri Lanka 218; England tour of 5, 116; helmets 11; marauding fast bowlers 8; put in commanding position 155; *The Referee* 27; sporting editor 28; victory against England 9; won the Ashes 12

Australia–India Test series (2014-2015) 251, 253–258

The Australian 254

Australian ball-tampering cricketing controversy *see* Sandpapergate controversy

Australian Broadcasting Company 173

Australian National Library 179

Australia Yahoo 65

Austria 58

Automated Insights' Wordsmith program 372

Averis, M. 38, 149

Azerbaijan 45

Baartman, S. 323

Babel, R. 128

Babes, B. 76

Bach, T. 262, 266

Baddiel, D. 93

The Bad News Bears (Lancaster) 159

Baker, D. 93

Baker, Ian 287

Baksh, V. 208

Balding, Clare 225

Ball, P. 85, 92

Ballester, P. 17, 332

ballgames 160

ball-tampering controversy *see* Sandpapergate controversy

The Ball that Bowled Bradman 183

Balon D'Or (award) 138

Balonne Beacon 180

Balotelli, M. 128–129

Bancroft, C. 300, 301, 304, 305, 309, 310, 311, 314, 315; *see also* Sandpapergate controversy

Bantam Progressivism 90

Barbados 1, 15
Barbados Cricket Association 15
Barcelona 56, 201
Barclay, P. 195–203, 277
Barden, M. 48
Barker, S. 170
Barkham, P. 78
Barnes, S. 178, 182, 199
Barnsley Chronicle 163
Barrington, K. 184
Barron, T. 214
Barry, A. 209
Barthes, Roland 282
Barton, J. 126
baseball: announcer 167; apartheid ban 210; batting average 184; Big League 210; cards 182; clubs 29; cricket and 34; fan 8; hitters 184; locker room 159; North American 209; physical threat 10; pitchers 7; player 161; racial integration 162; racial staus 213; reporter 161; stars 211; steroid abuse 17; *Sunday Mercury* 26
Baseball Encyclopedia 182
Baseball's Great Experiment: Jackie Robinson and His Legacy (Tygiel) 214
Bassons, C. 154, 331
Batchelor, D. 178
Bates, K. 60, 89
Bates, T. 77
Bateson, B. 57, 147–148
Baum, G. 4
Baxter, J. 197
BBC 8, 34, 42, 45, 73, 91–93, 116–117, 119, 127, 149, 174, 185, 215; digital network 265; *Match of the Day* 271, 284; race at 371; virtual-reality news 372
BBC 141
BBC 1 164
BBC2 93
BBC Online 76
BBC Radio 5 Live 103
BBC Sport 102–103, 107
BBC TV Centre 102
Beadle, Gaz "Geordie Shore" 225
Beamon, B. 153
Bebo 125
Beckett, C. 129
Beckham, David 224
Beckham, Victoria 224
Bedser, A. 177, 180
Beeby, M. 4
Behardien, F. 219
Being There (film) 57
beIN Sports 137
Belgium 195, 276, 284
Bell's Life 27–28, 74, 174
Bell's Life in Adelaide 25

Bell's Life in London and Sporting Chronicle 25
Bell's Life in Sydney 25
Bell's Life in Victoria and Sporting Chronicle 25
Bembrey, Sarah 243
Benaud, Richie 356
"Bender it like Beckham" 224, 229
Bend It Like Beckham (film) 224
Benswanger, W. 213
Bentham, Jeremy 367
Bentley, J. 28
Berkmann, M. 159
Berlin Olympics (1936) 208, 211
Berlin Wall 201
Bert Oldfield 11
Best, G. 56, 195, 197
Best of the Fanzines 85
Bewes, R. 115
Beyond a Boundary (James) 208
Beyond the Boundary 94
Bhattacharya, R. 208
Bhogle, Harsha 314
bias: accusations 216; clubs and managers 130; official 128; professionalism 29; public 119; reporting without 142; unreliable and 26, 74
Bierley, D. 91
Big League 210, 212
Billings, Andrew 252
billionaire utility maximisers 247–248
Bindel, Julie 230
Binstead, A. 30
Bird's-Eye View 181
Birley, D. 217
Birmingham 26, 42, 73–74
Birmingham Sports Argus 79
Black America 35
Blackburn Rovers (football club) 45, 74
Blackpool 77
Black Sox scandal 239–240, 241, 242–243
The Black Watch 90, 95
Blair, P. 165
Blake, H. 17
Blatter, S. 138
Bleasdale, A. 88, 149, 191
Blinker, R. 58
The Blizzard 74, 137
Bloggs, B. 155
Bloomberg 64–65
Blowing Bubbles Monthly 95
Blue Print 93
Blundell Blunders 89, 92
Bolam, J. 115
Boland, John Pius 261
Bolívar, Simón 367
Bolton News 137
Bolton Wanderers 137
Born Kicking 90

Bose, Mihir 245, 246, 247
Bosman ruling 244–245
Boston marathon 63
Boswell, T. 36, 166–167
Botham, I. 4, 6, 9, 14, 148, 165, 341
Botox 166
Boulding, Ned 333
boxing: bare-knuckle 160; coverage 160; cricket
     and 47; heavyweight 209; humour
     168–170; newspaper coverage 47
Box Socials (Kinsella) 159
Boy, D. 149
Boycott, G. 9
Boykoff, Jules 268
Boyle, R. 42–43, 94, 103–104, 106, 252
Boys from the Blackstuff (Bleasedale) 88, 149, 191
The Boys of Summer (Kahn) 61
Bradman, D. 11–12, 36, 173–182, 184–185
Bradman, H. 181
Brady, Jim 248
Brathwaite, C. 5
Braves (baseball team) 209
Bray, C. 178
Brazil 3, 43, 45, 191, 198, 200–201, 372
breaking news 126
Brearley, M. 14–16
Breedon Books 92
Brexit 1–2
Brian 89
Bridge, C. 185
Brierley, J. 44
Briggs, L. 11
Brightly Fades the Don (Fingleton) 177
Brighton and Hove Albion (football club) 149
Brighton Argus 197
Brisbane 165
Brisbane Courier-Mail 179
Bristol 7, 112
Bristol Evening World 38
Bristol Rovers (football club) 46
British Asian 207
British Isles 24
British Liberty 27
British Library 179
British Lions tour of New Zealand (1977) 153
British Open 64, 167
British Satellite Broadcasting 111, 117
Broad, S. 7
Broadcast 342
broadcasting: deals 17; interview with Tyler, M.
     111–123; pay-per-view 47; radio 101;
     rights 17, 130; sports journalism and 102,
     104
Broadway 86
Brockmann, O. 62, 64, 69
Bromley, James 240
Brooklyn Dodgers (baseball team) 209, 211, 214

Broun, H. 36
Broussard, Chris 227
Brown, A. 90
Brown, J. 105
Brown, P. 74–75
Brundage, Avery 264
Brunskell, B. 76
Brutus, D. 215
Bruyneel, Johann 334
Bryant, H. 17, 208
BSkyB 80, 355
BT Sport 106, 130, 361
Buchan, C. 196–197
Bucke, T. 89–90
Buford, Bill 278
Bull, A. 2, 4, 6, 325
Bull Durham (Shelton) 159
Burgess, A. 89
Burgess, C. 46, 165, 352
Burton, R. 58
Burton-Nelson, M. 229
Busby, M. 76, 198, 284
Busby Babes 60
Bush, George W. 330
Butcher, T. 59, 85
Butterworth, M. 252, 257
Buzzfeed 142

Caine, M. 195
Calcutta 63
Calgary Winter Games 264
California Spirit of the Times 25
Calvert, J. 17, 268
Cambridge Chronicle 24
Cambridgeshire 202
Camden Courier-Post 61
Campaign, Justin 226
Cannon, J. 160
Can't Anyone Here Play This Game? 164
Cantona, E. 42
Cantrell, F. 4
Cape Times 214
Capital Radio 192
Capote, T. 161
Captain Marvel *see* Robson, B.
Caracol 370
Cardus, N. 33, 35–36, 44, 164, 178, 207, 351
Carlos, J. 16, 153, 156
carpetbaggers 213
Carr, Alan 224
Carr, J. L. 87
Carragher, Jamie 285
Carrington, Ben 323
Carson, W. 47
Cartland, B. 170
Catley, N. 86
Catton, J. 28, 75

Cauldwell, W. 26
Cavanagh, R. 76
CBS Fox 192
Ceefax 102
Celebrant of Beauty 33
Centenary Test (1977) 14
Central News Agency 24
Central Press 24
Chadwick, H. 26, 28–29, 184
Chairboy Gas 89
challenges: ethical 132; money stakes 28; print
        journalism industry 78; sporting 28; sports
        journalists 129–130, 132
Champagne, J. 138
Champions League (1993) 198
Champions League (1999) 56
Chand, Dutee 321
changes: fan ownership 95; humour 160–162;
        organised baseball 28; personnel 53; public
        relations 142–143; social or cultural 86;
        sportswriting 33
The Changing Room (Storey) 159
Channel Four 52
Chapman, B. 12–13, 175
Chapman, H. 89, 196, 240, 282
Chapman, R. 10
Chapus, E. 25
Charles, J. 202
Charlton, B. 45, 88
Charlton, J. 191
Chas 'n' Dave 77
Chauvenet, L. R. 85
Cheers 166
Chelsea FC (football club) 121, 137, 169, 203
Chelsea Independent 89
Chesham United (football club) 84
Chicago 152
Chicago Daily News 242
Chicago Herald and Examiner 241
Chicago Tribune 160–161, 241
childhood memory 72
childless editors 194
China 3
chronology 24
Chucked Around (Griffith) 15
Cincinnati Red Stockings 6, 240–241
citizen journalism 267
City Gent 83–84, 87–91, 93–94
City Limits 191
Civil Rights 208
Civil War 213
Clapton, E. 39
Clarke, G. 226, 236
Clarke, M. 94
claustrophobia 11
Cleveland Indians (baseball team) 210
The Clicking of Cuthbert (Wodehouse) 159

Clough, B. 147
Clough, D. 63, 67, 69
Clubcall 78
club media 137–140
Club Rugby Union 184
Coca-Cola 36
Coddington, Anne 362
codification 101
Coe, S. 135
Cole, C. 199
Coleman, D. 168
Coleman, S. 276–277
Collett, M. 62, 64, 194
Collins, Andrew 277
Collins, Jason 227, 228
Collins, P. 200
Collymore, S. 121
Colman, Mike 252
Colombia, football journalism in 370
Columbia Journalism Review 248
columnists 27–29, 73, 91, 105, 160
The Comet 85
Comiskey, Charles 241
commentary, Sandpapergate controversy 301–310,
        302–303, 308
communication: consultants 136; digital 103,
        125, 132; effective 130; equipment 48;
        influential 136; real-time 125; specialist
        136, 143; top-down model 48
Communist Party: Great Britain 177; United
        States 209
competitive balance 34
Complete Record 92
complicity 214–216
Compton, D. 183, 197
Congress, United States 208
Conn, D. 92, 239, 244, 245, 246, 247, 248, 356
Connell, Ed 226
Connell, Raewyn 224, 227
Conservatives, Great Britain 55
content analysis 43
content creators 137
Contractor, N. 15
Conway Hall, London 217
Cook, A. 66, 173
Cooke, Alistair 351
Copa América 370
Copeland, Charlie 240
Copinger, G. 182
Corbyn, J. 217
Cornwall 127
Coronation Street 58, 116
Corporation's Radio 5 Live 371
corruption 243–244
Corsellis, N. 5–6
Costner, K. 159
Cotton, F. 153

Coubertin, Baron Pierre de 261
Coughlan, S. 185
Country Reporter 38
County Championship 46–47
Courier 212
The Courier-Mail 183, 252
Courtney, V. 185
Court of Arbitration for Sport (CAS) 321
Coutinho, C. 200
Coventry 71
Coventry Telegraph 79
Cowell, S. 184
Cricinfo 183–184
Cricinfo Magazine 216
cricket: aggression 255; Ashes Test series 6,
11–12; Decision Review System 254;
national identity 253–258; Sandpapergate
controversy 295–296, 299–315; Twenty20
cricket 362; *see also* International Cricket
Council (ICC)
Cricket 26, 28
Cricket Archive 183–184
Cricket Country 173
Cricketer 14, 175, 181
Cricket Historians (Wynne-Thomas) 174
Cricket Mad (Parkinson) 163
Cricket South Africa (CSA) 219–220
Cricket's Unholy Trinity (Foot) 39
Cripps, George 240
Crohn's disease 7–8
Cronje, H. 218, 243
Crower, J. 213
Crystal Palace 58, 88, 91, 130, 193
cultural cringe 185
culture of dissent 90
cup matches 24
Curry, S. 58–60
Curtis, T. 159
Cyril Washbrook's Cricket Annual 181

Dacre, P. 58
dailies 26
Daily Dispatch 215
Daily Express 44, 56, 58, 149, 175–176, 202
Daily Graphic 176
Daily Herald 178
Daily Mail 17, 26, 48, 54, 58–59, 148–149, 180,
182
Daily Mirror 42–43, 51, 53–54, 56, 58, 76, 128, 131,
149, 176, 216
Daily News 74, 213
Daily Star 42, 58
Daily Telegraph 27, 43, 89, 193, 216
Daily Worker 176–177, 209–210, 212–213
Daley, Tom 235
Dalglish, K. 117
Dame Fortune 8

Daniels, R. 33
Darke, I. 170
Darling, J. 176
Darwin, B. 44
Dassler, Horst 244
Davies, B. 170, 284
Davies, P. 92, 94, 278
Davies, Steve 235
Davies, T. 83, 91, 97
Davis, C. 159, 184–185
Davis, W. 165
Day, M. 121
The Day Two Teams Died (Cavanagh) 76
DC Thomson (publishing company) 197
Deakin, P. 86
Dean, M. 196
decision-making 17, 132
Decline and Fall of the Roman Empire
(Gibbon) 162
degrees courses in sports journalism 364
Delaney, M. 137, 139
Delle Donne, Elena 228
demographic imbalance 361
Dempster, S. 182
denial and complicity 214–216
de Pfeffel Johnson, A. B. 2
Derby County 80, 92
Derby Evening Telegraph 80
derby games 24
de Saint-Albin, N. 25
Desgrange, Henri 330, 331
despondency 131
Detours Magazine 85
Dettori, F. 47
de Villiers, Fanie 299–300
Dewhirst, J. 87–88, 90–91, 93–94
Dial M for Merthyr 91, 93, 95
Diamond, I. A. L. 159
Dickinson, M. 4, 91
Die Hard 2: Die Harder (Willis) 192
digital communication 103, 125, 132; *see also*
communication
digital media, Olympics and 265–266
digital revolution 102
Digital Sports Journalism 80
digital technology 104
Dillon, Andrew 223, 224
Di Maggio, J. 184, 212
Dirs, B. 128
disbelief 3, 117, 153, 197
dismissive labelling 274
disruption: broadcast news 127; innovation and 125
Di Stefano, A. 197
diversity 359–365; fanzines 96–97
Dixon, K. 85, 90
Dixon, T. H. H. 27
Dobromyslova, Anastasia 362

Dodgers (baseball team) 159, 163
Do I Not Like That (documentary) 52
D'Oliveira, B. 17, 215–216, 218
D'Oliveira Affair 216
The Don 12, 18
Donald Bradman: Challenging the Myth (Hutchins) 184
Donaldson, Mike 224
Doncaster Gazette 27
doping 329, 331, 332–333, 334, 335, 336
Dorsey, Jack 359
Douglas, K. 58
Dowling, V. 25, 28
dreams 189–194; death of newspaper 193–194; establishing an identity 190–192; growing pains 192–193; reverse the tide 189–190
Dripping Pan 196
Drown, W. 61
Dublin 120
Duchatalet, R. 95
Duesseldorf 62
Duke, V. 89
dummy copy 190
Duncan, J. 89
Dunnett, Alastair 346
Dunning, Eric 362
Durban 6
Durham 88
Durocher, L. 213
D-Word conference 361

Eagle Eye 88, 91
Ebersol, Dick 263
Echo 72, 74
Echo Echo 91
Eco, U. 125
Eden Park (stadium) 68
Edgar, C. H. 86
Edinburgh Festival Fringe 1
editing: articles 152, 154; content and flow 155; copy 153; good 157; pleasure 157; process 156; sports 152; task 157; video 108
Editor and Publisher 162
editorial assistant 135
editorial decision-making 17
editors 27; childless 194; columnists and 28; fanzine 91, 93, 95–96; news 127; newspaper 24, 29; professionalism 29; reporters 27, 127; sports 17, 27, 47, 57, 149, 217; writers and 27
Editors' Code of Practice 224
Education Act (1944) 88
Edwards, D. 60
Edwards, H. 39
Edwards, P. 39
Egan, P. 27, 160
Eight Men Out (film) 242

Eintracht Frankfurt (sports club) 200
elder statesman stints 59
Eliot, T. S. 38
Ellington, D. 213
Ellis, D. 59, 88
Ellis & Thompson of Cobham 122
Elmslie Ender 90
El Vino (drinking establishment) 148
Emburey, J. 149
Emmons, B. 48
employment loss 208
The End of the Terraces (King) 85–86
Engel, M. 1, 9, 36, 164–165, 167, 185
England 51–55, 165–167, 174–179, 217; club games 59; cricket 4–9, 47, 63; defeating Australia 2; employment 216; European Championships defeat by Iceland 44; first magazine 25; Golden Generation 57; journalistic ventures 190; journalists 80; Regency period 27; soccer international 28; sportswriter 207; tour to Australia 116; weekly papers 24; working class 191; *see also* FIFA; hooliganism, football
England v. Australia 175
England v. New Zealand 38
English, S. 13
English Football Association 28
English Football League 3
English Premier League (EPL) 67, 281, 285
Ennis-Hill, Jessica 347, 348
Enterprise Allowance Scheme 84
Epstein, J. 3
Eriksson, S.-G. 57
erythropoietin (EPO) 331
ESPN 118, 129, 137, 170, 214
ESPNCricinfo.com 14, 217
Esports 243
Euro '96 55
Europe 23, 101
European Championships 43, 44, 52, 111, 273
European Champions League 47
European Cup (1960) 197, 199
European Cup (1985) 195
European Cup (1993) 201
European Cup-Winners' Cup 200
European Super Leagues 96
European Union (EU) 1–2, 43
Eurosport 68
Evans, A. 91, 95
Evans, C. 170
Evans, G. 177
Evans, M. 91
Evening Advertiser 91
Evening News 189, 190
Evening Standard 151, 189–190, 192
Everiss, Fred 282
Everitt, R. 88, 91, 95

Everton 192
Ewe Tea Bee 96
Express 54, 142, 180
Extinction Rebellion 1
Ezekiel, G. 217

Facebook 72, 79, 106, 125
Facebook Live 130
FA Centenary Match (1963) 197
FA Cup 30, 41, 73
Fairbanks, D. 159
Fairlie, H. 148
fake news 152
Falafel, O. 1
Falklands War 34
The Fall and Rise of Reginald Perrin/Reggie (TV
        program) 166
fan club 141–143
fandom 129
fanmag 85
Fans' Forum 192
Fantasy Football League 93
fanzine(s) 83–97; defined 95; diversity 96–97;
        editors 91, 93, 95–96; punk inspiration
        85–88; "translating articulate spectator
        opinion" 88–93; trusts and 93–96
Fanzine Publishers' Association 84
Farah, M. 208
Farewell to Cricket (Bradman) 181
Farewell to Sport (Gallico) 35, 160
Farjeon, H. 174
Farrington, Neil 322
Fashanu, Justin 225, 226, 227
Fat Fryer 89
FBI 138
fear 1, 10; distribution 190; editorial standards 142;
        sports journalists 136
Federer, R. 39, 151
Feist, H. 25
Felix *see* Horan, T.
Felstein, S. 140–141
Fenway Park 34
Ferdinand, R. 126, 131
Ferguson, A. 45, 56, 60, 76, 198–199
Fernandes, G. 196
Ferrari, Michele 334
Ferrier, Bob 283
"Festina Affair" 331
Fever Pitch (Hornby) 88, 92
The Field 25, 28
FIFA 9, 17, 116, 135–136, 138, 201, 244; World
        Cup (1950) 45, 283; World Cup (1966)
        9, 54, 284, 362; World Cup (1970) 43,
        45, 201; World Cup (1974) 45; World
        Cup (1978) 45, 111, 119; World Cup
        (1982) 111, 119; World Cup (1986) 111,
        117, 119, 200; World Cup (1990) 52, 59,
92, 117, 201, 278; World Cup (1994)
51–54; World Cup (1998) 150; World
Cup (2002) 274; World Cup (2010) 138,
200–201; World Cup (2014) 370; World
Cup (2018) 139, 263, 370, 371; World
Cup (2022) 135, 138
Figo, L. 138
Financial Fair Play rules 248
Financial Times 3, 105, 151, 157, 216, 246
Fingleton, J. 12, 177
Finney, T. 45, 60
Firestarter 6
First World War 179
Fitzgerald, F. S. 2, 162
Fiver 93
The Flashing Blade 90
Fleet Street 51, 55–56, 58, 147–148, 150, 160, 193
Fleet Street Remembered (Gray) 148
Flood, C. 16
Fly Me to the Moon (Nicholls) 83, 88, 93–94
food banks 1
Foot, D. 38, 183
Foot, J. 38
football 26; American 29, 34; British 41,
        46; capitalisation 285; clubs 39, 80;
        correspondent 17; fanzine 86; hooliganism
        86–87, 273–279; parental or peer
        influence 196–197; professional 26;
        profit-maximising owners 247–248;
        Scottish 13; supporters 42; tabloid writer
        55; televised 284–285; variants 12; writer
        76; *see also* FIFA
Football365 93
Football and Its Fans (Taylor) 87
Football Association 41, 43, 55, 57, 74, 91, 107,
        195, 236
football clubs 281, 285
Football Daft (Parkinson) 163
Football Echo 72, 79
Football Fans Census 84
The Football Imagination (Haynes) 85
football journalism industry 142
football journalists 202
Football League 28, 189, 208
The Football Man (Hopcraft) 243
football manager 281–291; history and mythology
        281–285; as news item 285–287; overview
        281; public representation 285; Ranieri,
        Claudio 288–289
Football Manager (video game) 281
Football Monthly 196–197
football news agenda 223
Football Supporters' Association (FSA) 87, 93, 278,
        284
football writers 199–200
Football Writers' Association 86, 361
Footybits.co.uk 84

Fordyce, T. 103, 105, 108
Formula One 47, 107
Forsyth, B. 159
Forte Village 59
Fortune, C. 214–215
Fort Wayne News-Sentinel 242
Foster, Elaine 228
Fotheringham, William 332
Foul 86–87
FourFourTwo 93
"Four-Inch Course" 13
Four Quartets 38
fourth estate 141–143
Fowler, R. 121
Fox, B. 87–88
Fox, R. K. 28
Fox Sports 245, 247
Fragments of Idolatry 39
France 23, 25, 65, 68, 150, 184
Franklin, B. 78
Frayn, M. 148
"Free Gaza" 207
free journalists 141
Freeman, C. 16
Freeman, E. A. 73
"Free Palestine" 207
free press 51
freesheet 78
French Second Empire (1852–1870) 25
Friends Reunited 125
Frith, D. 14, 178
From Ritual to Record (Guttmann) 174
The Front Page (Hughes) 152
Fulham 87, 196
"Full-Back" 75
Fullerton, Hugh 241, 242
FullTime on Sunday 189, 191, 193

G7 meeting 3
Gahill, G. 129
Gallagher Premiership 69
Gallas, W. 169
Gallico, P. 33, 35–36, 62, 160, 163–164
"Gang of Three" players 59
gangsters 242
Garfunkel, A. 184
Gascoigne, P. 53, 59, 191–193
Gatting, M. 215, 217–218
Gauhati 63
Gaustad, J. 39, 83, 91–92
Gay Football Supporters' Network 226
gays *see* homophobia; LGBTQI
Gazza 59
gender 371–372
Gentile, C. 201
Gentles, T. 84
George Polk Award for Commentary 37

Germany 62
Gerrard, Bill 244
Gibbon, E. 162
Gibson, C. 59
Gibson, J. 76, 210–211
Giggs, R. 197
Gillingham v. Maidstone 193
Gilzean, A. 197
Ginola, D. 138
Glanville, B. 195, 199, 203
Glasgow 74
Glasgow Examiner 28
Glasgow Rangers (football club) 13
Gleason, K. 161, 241
Global North 368
global recession 3
Gloucestershire 39
GMK 84
GM Vauxhall Conference 90
The Godfather 12
Goldberg, A. 92
Goldblatt, David 267
"Golden Age" 355–357
Golden Generation 57
Goldstone Ground 202
Golf Association 130
Golf Illustrated 26
Google 125
Googly Bowling 183
Gower, D. 148–149
Grace, W. G. 35, 39
Graham, George 246
Graham Taylor: The Impossible Job (football documentary) 52
Grant, C. 152
Gravengaard, G. 143
Gray, D. 352
Gray, T. 148
Great Britain 1–2, 24, 26, 29, 34, 42, 56, 73, 80, 153; Conservatives 55; national newspaper sales 102; newspaper development 23; newspaper subscription rate 105; print journalism industry 78; punk rock 85; referendum on membership of European Union (EU) 43; sport model 23; sportswriters 199
The Great Coincidence 9
Great Depression 2, 11
Great Intoxicant 17
Great Own Goals 89
Green, G. 41, 47–48, 199
Greenberg, R. 159
Greene, G. 37
Greenslade, R. 42
Green 'Un 71, 79–80
Greenwood, R. 200

Gregory's Girl (Forsyth) 159
greyhounds 192
Griffith, C. 15–16
Grimes, B. 211
Grub Street 160
The Guardian 2–4, 6, 9, 17–18, 38–40, 42, 45, 84,
  88, 91–93, 104, 137, 141–143, 149–150,
  164–165, 168, 195, 197, 198–199, 207,
  216, 278, 332, 342, 351, 352, 356
Guardiola, Pep 285
Guinness Book of Records 182
Gullit, R. 201
Guttmann, A. 174

Hackett, D. 202
Hadfield, D. 86
Hadlee, R. 166
Haigh, G. 4, 173
Hain, P. 216
Hales, A. 5
Hall, E. 57–58
Hall, J. 90
Hall, S. 273–274
Ham, W. 200
Hamed, N. 207
Hamilton, D. 39
Hamilton, L. 18
Hammersley, W. J. 28
Hammond, W. 175–176, 184
Hanahoe, I. 96
hand-eye coordination 5
The Hand That Bowled Bradman (Andrews and
  Foot) 183
Hansmann, A. 105
harassment *see* sexual harassment
Hard Knocks 227
Haringey Borough 96
Harlow College 92
Harold Gimblett: Tortured Genius of Cricket (Foot) 39
Harris, Daniel 363
Harris, M. 4
Harris, Rob 248
Harrison, M. 84
Hart, J. 117–118
Hartford Times 61
Harverson, Patrick 245, 246
Hassett, L. 177
Hauser, T. 218
Havelange, Joao 244
Hawks, H. 152
Haynes, R. 84–86, 89, 91, 94, 252
Hayter, R. 55, 180
Hayters 55, 57
Hayward, B. 76–77
Hazare, V. 181
Headfire, S. 89
Headingley 1–2, 6, 8–9, 11, 18

Headland, J. 86
Headley, G. 181
Heard, T. 215
Heartbeat 90
The Heart of a Goof (Wodehouse) 159
Heath, E. 43
Hecht, B. 152
Helm, J. 120
Hemingway, E. 162
Henderson, A. 214
Henderson, J. 63
Henman, T. 43
Henry, Joseph 240
Henry, O. 218
The Herald 180
Herald Sun 254, 256
Herald-Tribune 160, 213
Hersh, Seymour 248
Hess, Alex 286
heteronormativity 228
Hey, S. 86
Heysel Stadium, Belgium 190, 195, 198, 277, 284
Hibernian v. Heart of Midlothian 151
Hickman, P. 13
High, Wide and Handsome (Keating) 341
Highbury 88
Highgate Cup Horror 89
Hill, C. 182
Hill, D. 247
Hill, J. 52
Hillsborough 88–89, 190, 276–279; *see also*
  hooliganism, football
Himno Copa América Centenario 2016 #YoCreo
  370
Hincapie, George 334
The Hindu 216
Hirst, Keegan 225
His Girl Friday (Hawks) 152
Hitler, A. 213
Hit Racism For Six (pressure group) 217
Hitzlsperger, Thomas 223, 226
Hobbs, J. 175–176, 178, 182, 184
Hoberman, J. 262, 331
Hoch, S. 167
Hockey, J. 117
Hodgson, Guy 275
Hodgson, R. 44–45, 198
Holbrook, K. 137
Holding, Michael 299
Holiday, B. 213
Holland 53, 59
Holley, D. 72, 79–80
Hollies, E. 173–174, 181, 183
Hollywood 86, 152–154, 200
Holme, T. 219
Holmes, K. 153
Holt, O. 131, 276

homelessness 1
homophobia 159, 224, 235–236; British media 224–226; heteronormativity 228–229; Kay-Jelski's interview 235–236; reverse 228–229, 230; US media 226, 227
Hong Kong 3, 68
Hookes, D. 14
hooliganism, football 86–89, 273–279; archetypal 274; Hall on 273–274; Hillsborough and 88–89, 190, 276–279; moral panic 274; Poulton on 274; Samuel on 275; Steen on 275, 276, 279; Whannel on 274
Hooton, P. 86
Hopcraft, A. 136, 243, 246
Horan, T. 28
Hornby, N. 88
Horne, J. 89–90
Horse Feathers (Perelman) 159
horse racing 24–25, 27
House Un-American Activities Committee 162
Hove Albion FC 141
Howa, H. 214
Howard, J. 184
How Steeple Sinderby Wanderers Won the FA Cup (Carr) 87
Hudson, A. 192
Hudson, T. 90, 95
Hughes, H. 152
Hughes, M. 196
Hughes, P. 10, 12, 252, 254, 255, 256, 257
Hughes, Y. 88, 149, 191
Hull 71
Hull Packet 75
humour 159–170; boxing 168–170; changes 160–162; does humour travel 166–168; "A little pleasure, a little entertainment" 162–163; overview 159–160; sly winker 163–165; sportswriter 165–166
Hundley, Heather 252
Hungary 3, 283
Hunt, B. 13
Hunt, L. 61
Hunter, Jack 239
Hunter, N. 117
Hurst, G. 54
Hussain, N. 207
Hussein, A. B. 138
Hutchins, B. 184, 252, 253
Hutton, L. 177–178, 183–184

Iceland 44
identity: establishing 190–192; national 251–258
Iles, M. 137
Ilford 89
Illouz, Eva 335
I'll Spin You A Yarn (Hollies) 183
The Illustrated Sporting and Dramatic News 26

Imperial Cricket Conference (ICC) 15
Ince, P. 53
The Independent 44–47, 86, 137, 142, 165, 169, 193, 195, 198, 200, 226, 352
Independent Broadcasting Authority 90
Independent on Sunday 169
India 3, 9, 63, 65, 175–176, 179, 208, 217–218
Indian Premier League 10, 253, 369
India Today 217
inequality 1
Infantino, G. 138
in-house journalist 135
injustice 86
Inland Revenue 149
innovation and disruption 125
Instagram 67, 105–106, 125, 129–130
international agencies 63; see also agencies
International Association of Athletics Federations (IAAF) 135, 321–322
International Cricket Council (ICC) 107; World Cup (1996) 217, 218; World Cup (1999) 38; World Cup (2015) 219; World Cup (2019) 5–6, 10
international news agencies 61, 64; see also agencies
International Olympic Committee (IOC) 64, 246
The International Rugby League magazine 86
Internet 83–84, 102–103, 153, 199, 207
Interpol 243
Inverness Caledonian Thistle 156
investigative journalism 78, 356
Iosifidis, P. 103
iPlayer, BBC 102
Ireland 1
Irish Protestant (Rangers) v. Irish Catholic (Celtic) conflict 13
Isaacs, D. 215
Islands of the North Atlantic 1
Isle of Man 13
Israel 11
Italia '90 59
It's One Leek for Mankind (comedy show) 1
ITV 77, 89, 91, 102, 111, 116–117, 119

Jacklin, T. 43
Jacks, Amanda 278
Jackson, G. 65, 67
Jackson, R. 168
Jackson, "Shoeless" Joe 242
Jackson, T. 76
Jacksonville Jaguars (American football franchise) 129
James, C. 169, 208, 218
James, S. 38
Japan 65
Jardine, D. 11–12
Jarrett-Bryan, J. 128–129
Jasani, S. 138

Jazz Age anti-hero 2
Jenkins, S. 2
Jennings, A. 17, 268
Jews 207, 241
jobbing journalist 38–39
Jobs, Steve 359
jock culture 227
Joe Robbie Stadium 34
John, E. 58
Johnson, A. 196
Johnson, B. 4
Johnson, J. 208
Johnson, L. 165
Johnson, M. 11, 165
Johnson, P. 59
Johnstone, M. 88
Jones, E. 68
Jones, F. 90
Jones, K. 44, 46, 200
Jones, R. 228
Jordan, C. 15
Jordan Football Association (JFA) 138
Jory, D. 89–90
journalists 23; death 76; football 202; free 141;
        jobbing 38–39; memories 201;
        metaphors 143; print sports 130;
        sporting 29; sports 27–29; trainee
        sports 135; underpaid 29–30;
        unrespectable 29–30
*Juicing the Game: Drugs, Power, and the Fight for the
        Soul of Major League Baseball* (Bryant) 17
Juventus v. Man United 197

Kaepernick, C. 16, 155–156
Kahn, R. 17, 61–62, 65
Kallis, J. 184
Kane, Harry 370
Kansas City Monarchs (baseball franchise) 209, 212
Kartalis, C. 61
Kasper, Gian-Franco 266
Kauffman, G. S. 161
Kay-Jelski, Alex 226, 235–236
Kearney, L. 179–180
Keating, Frank 341–344, 351; catch description
        341–342; *The Guardian* 342, 343; *High,
        Wide and Handsome* 341
Keats, J. 61
Keegan, K. 121
Kelly, M. 93
Kelly, P. 173
Kelly, S. 94
Kelner, M. 168
Kelner, S. 169
Kelso, Paul 275–276
Kennedy, J. 64
Kenopoly 89
Kent Asp 224

Kenyon Review Award for Literary
        Achievement 37
Kessel, A. 108
Khan, A. 207
Khan, I. 9
Kian, E. 251, 252, 253, 254, 257
Kidd, D. 44–45
Kimmage, P. 10, 17, 333
Kimmel, Michael 227
King, A. 85–86, 90
King, B.-J. 16
King, Daniel 248
King Commission 218
King of the Kippax 84, 88, 90
Kingsmead Stadium 6
Kinnear, J. 196
Kinsella, K. P. 159
Kite, T. 167
Knickerbockers (club) 29
Knight, D. 88, 94
Koeman, R. 285
Kolisi, S. 68
Kolkata 5

Labatt's Canadian Lager 192
Lacey, D. 91, 93, 195–203, 275, 351
Lacey, J. 149
Lacey, L. 149
Lacey, M. 85, 88–90
L.A. Confidentiel: Les Secrets de Lance Armstrong
        (Walsh and Ballester) 154, 332
Ladies Professional Golf Association
        (LPGA) 228
LA Dodgers (baseball team) 165
La Gazzetta dello Sport 368
Laker, J. 180
La Liga 281, 285
Lalor, Peter 313
Laloush, N. 159
Lamb, A. 148
Lambert, C. 80, 364
Lancashire 3, 44, 58
Lancashire Daily Post 44
Lancaster, B. 159
Lance Armstrong Foundation 333
Lance Armstrong: The World's Greatest Champion
        (Wilcockson) 332
Landis, Floyd 334
Landis, Kenesaw Mountain 213, 214, 242
Langan, P. 195
Lapize, Octave 331
Lara, B. 6
Lardner, J. 162
Lardner, R. 33, 160–161, 164, 242
Larwood, H. 12
L'Auto 26
La Violencia 370

Lawrence, A. 92
Lawson, D. 325–326
Lawton, J. 200
Leach, M. J. 2, 7–10, 13
League Publications 86
Le Courier Athlétique 26
Ledbrooke, A. 76
Lee, M. 135–136, 138, 214
Lee, S. 88
Leeds City Football Club 239–240
Leeds Mercury 26, 75
Leicester Mercury 165
Leicester University 87
Lemmon, J. 152, 159
Lemon, G. 2
Lennon, John 343
Lenskyj, Helen 267
L'Équipe 372
Lescott, J. 128
Le Sport 25
Levy, D. 198
LexisNexis news database 324
Leyton Orient (football club) 80, 91
Leyton Orientear 83, 88–89
Leytonstone 89
LGBTQI 235–236, 363; British media 223–226;
    female athletes 227–230; reverse
    homophobia 228–229, 230; stereotyping
    229; US media 226, 227; *see also*
    homophobia
Liebling, AJ 346
Life in London and Sporting Guide (Egan) 27
Liggett, Phil 331
Light at the End of the Tunnel 89
Lightbown, C. 86
"Like losing a friend" 80–81
Lindwall, R. 183
Lineker, G. 52, 273
LinkedIn 106
Lipton, M. 248
Liston, S. 153
literacy rates 24
"Little Old Wine Drinker Me" (Martin) 59
Littlewoods Pools 192
Liverpool 47, 73, 76, 80, 84–85, 121, 128
Liverpool Echo 142, 156
Livewire Sport 107–108
Loaded 105
A Load of Bull 83
loathing 1
London 24–26, 38, 63, 69, 102, 121, 136, 148–149,
    151, 189, 208, 217
London Borough 88
London College of Communication 154
London Daily News 189
London EC4 148
London Olympics (1948) 264

London Olympics (2012) 136, 208, 224, 262;
    women in 262
London Stock Exchange 244
Longstop 28
Lord's Cricket Ground 166
Los Angeles Times 165
Lost in Music (Smith) 169
Louis, J. 209, 211, 213
Low, N. 214
loyalty 148
Lukaku, R. 139
Lülle, Carlos Arturo Ardila 370
Lyle, R. 105
Lyon, N. 156
Lyons, A. 84, 86–87, 94

Macadam, J. 44
MacArthur, C. 152
MacBryan, J. 39
Macdonald, M. 45
MacGregor, A. 83
Mack, C. 35
Macnamara, J. 136
Macworld Convention 359
Madison Square Garden 213
The Mag 90
Magpie Group 90
Maguire, Joseph 261
Mail on Sunday 42
Major League Baseball 9, 34
Making the Local News 74
Malbranque, S. 126
Manchester City 77, 96, 120, 139, 196
Manchester Evening News 76, 79
Manchester Football Writing Festival
    (2018) 137
Manchester Guardian 26, 33, 148
Manchester Mercury 23
Manchester United 40, 47, 56, 60, 76, 84, 89,
    117–118, 121, 128, 131, 137, 140, 142,
    192, 201, 245, 246, 247
Mancini, R. 128
Mandela, N. 14
Mann, Leon 361
Mannion, W. 45
Mansour, Sheikh 247
Man U 40
Maori 207
Maradona, D. 195, 197, 200–201
Margolick, D. 209
Marks, V. 4, 38
Marqusee, M. 216–217
Marsh, R. 197
Marshall, R. 93
Martin, D. 59
Martin, R. 177
Marx, G. 161

Marxist cricket writers 217
Marylebone Cricket Club 216
Mary Poppins (musical film) 156
M★A★S★H 162
Mason, R. 120
mass of numbers 180–183
Match 93, 103
match-fixing 218, 243
Match of the Day (BBC) 45, 123, 284, 371
Mather, A. 143
Mathison, D. 13
Mathspig (blogger) 10
Matthau, W. 152
Matthewson, Christy 242
Maxwell, R. 189
McCosker, R. 14
McGhee, F. 56, 200
McGuire, S. 127
McIlvanney, H. 36, 55, 164, 200, 345–346
McJournalism 78
McKeag dynasty 90
McKeown, J. 85
McLaren, B. 170
McLaren, R. 219
McLellan, A. 9
McNair, B. 78
McNulty, P. 76
mea culpa 159
mediatization 224
Mediawatch 93
Meek, D. 76–77
Meer, J.V. 6
Melbourne Age 176
Melbourne Cricket Ground 14
Menon, A. 173
mentality 85
Merckx, Eddy 329
Merriam-Webster 13
Messi, L. 200
Mexico 43, 153
Mexico Olympics (1968) 153, 265
Miami Dolphins (American football team) 155
Miandad, J. 174
Michael Braude Award for Light Verse 37
"Mickey Mouse referee" 196
Microcontos de Futebol 372
Mid-day 254, 256
Middlesbrough 112
Middlesbrough Evening Gazette 278
midlife crisis 7
Midnight in the Garden of Evil Knievel
      (Smith) 168
Mill, John Stuart 367
Millar, David 333
Millennials 72
Miller, D. 213
Miller, K. 183

Miller, Toby 267
Millward, P. 85, 94
Milton, John 367
Miracle of Headingley II 9, 13
Mirror 181
Mitchell, K. 194
MK Dons (football club) 84
Moggi, Luciano 224
Moncur, B. 163
monetisation 104–106
money 237–249; challenging environment
      248–249; overview 237; scandals/crimes
      239–248; shaping sports 238–239
Monroe, M. 184
Montgomery, A. 59
Montgomery, D. 149
Montreal 26
Monty Python 52
Monty Python's Flying Circus, Friends (TV program)
      166
"Monument" races 329
Moonda, F. 208
Moore, B. 111, 117
#MoreThanMean 371
Morning Leader 26
Morris, A. 178
Mortensen, S. 45
Motherwell 88
Mountain Course 13, 16
Mourinho, J. 128, 140, 286
Moynihan, C. 90
MSN 65
Muchnik, I. 209
Muhammad Ali: His Life and Times (Hauser) 218
Mull, M. 160
Mullery, Alan 284
multiplatform journalism 101–108, 360; Internet
      102–103; monetisation conundrum
      104–106; new breed 107–108; "Working
      harder and longer" 103–104; *see also*
      sport(s)
Mumbai Mirror 256
Munich Air Disaster 76
Munich Olympics (1972) 62
Muralitharan, M. 7
Murdoch, K. 180
Murdoch, R. 148, 244, 245, 247, 276, 355
Murphy, Danny 290
Murphy, P. 287, 362
Murray, A. 43
Murray, J. 165
musical prose, sportswriting 35–36
My Favourite Year 86
MySpace 125

Nadal, R. 151
Nally, Patrick 244

National Baseball Committee 28
National Federation 87
National Football League (NFL) 107, 129, 132, 155
National Football Museum 137
National Hunt Festival at Cheltenham 47
national identity 251–258; cricket and 253–258; newspaper coverage 253–258; sport and 251–252
nationalism 369–371
National League South 112
National Magazine Award for Essays and Criticism 37
national news agencies 62; *see also* agencies
national newspapers 125
National Police Gazette 28
National Scapegoatin-Chief 34
National Union of Journalists 361
National Women's Soccer League (US) 228
Navratilova, M. 16, 228–229
Naylor, A. 143
Nazism 208
Neasom, M. 76
Negro League (1936) 209–210
Neighbours (TV program) 164
Netherlands 51
Neville, G. 121, 128
Neville, P. 142
Newcastle 40, 71, 76, 121
Newcastle Chronicle 73, 79
Newcastle Daily Journal 28
Newcastle Morning Herald and Miner's Advocate 180
Newcastle United Football Club 45, 90, 163, 165
"new journalism" 26
Newman, P. 45, 47
New Musical Excess 85
New Republic 85
News Chronicle 176, 178, 181
News of the World 26, 54, 57, 147–148, 178
Newsom, B. 163
newspapers 41–48; in 18th and 19th centuries 23, 25–27; catalogue 44–46; Chicago 152; death of 193–194; future of 42–43; international 64; magazines and 101–102; national 125; North America 160; sport and 25–27; sportswriter 104; tabloids 55; taxes 23; technological innovations 24; threats 136
New Sporting Magazine 25
newsprint rationing 176–177
Newsweek 161–162
New York 24, 28–29, 64–65, 179
New York City 209
New York Clipper 26
New York Daily News 62, 160
New Yorker 36, 161, 170
New York Giants (football team) 161

New York Herald Tribune 34, 61, 160, 162
New York Marxist Jew 216
New York Mets (baseball team) 8, 164
New York Post 160
New York Sportsman 26
New York Times 28, 34, 137, 161–162, 214, 247; virtual-reality news 372
New York Yankees (baseball team) 166
New Zealand 1, 4, 6, 8, 68, 175, 179, 207
niche abilities 360; *see also* ability(ies)
Nicholas, Mark 299, 305, **308**, 314
Nicholls, R. 88, 93
Nicholson, Bill 284
Nicholson, J. 39
Nicholson, S. 89
Nicklaus, J. 184
Nigeria 139
Nike 139
Nineteen Eighty-Four (Orwell) 369
non-white sportsmen 215
No-One Likes Us 84
Norman, G. 167
Norman, P. 16
North America 101, 105, 179
Northampton 165
Northampton Chronicle 165
Northcroft, J. 137, 139, 142
Northern Echo 26, 73, 76, 157
Northern Rugby Football Union (rugby league) 24
North of the Gap 192
North Vietnamese 35
North-west European Archipalego 1
Norway 51, 53
Norwich 89
nostalgia 1
Nottingham Daily Guardian 75
Nottingham Forest 77
Notts County 91
Novick, J. 11
Novitsky, Jeff 336
NOW 57
Nyland, David 226, 228

The Oatcake 83
Oborne, P. 17
Obree, Graeme 333
The Observer 7, 9, 36, 38, 55, 57, 92, 164, 178, 195, 200, 346
O'Dowd, P. 89
Ofcom 129
Off the Ball 87–89, 91–92
Old Carthusians 74
Old Charlie 44
Olden Opener (Angell) 37
Old Etonians 74
The Oldie 164
Old Trafford 122, 137

Oliver, A. 76
Olympic Broadcasting Services (OBS) 264
Olympic Channel 265–266
Olympic Charter 262
Olympics 63, 104, 135, 176, 244, 261–269, 369;
  attraction 263; British press 262; broadcast
  deals 263–264; campaigns/movement/
  protests against 267–268; commercial
  value 263; coverage 261; cultural
  exchange and competition 262; digital
  media 265; Maguire on 261; motto 262;
  national identity and 252; political actors/
  activists 266; popularity 262; sporting
  triangle 263–264; television rights
  263–264; Whannel on 261
One Step Beyond 88
OneValefan.co.uk 84
Onischenko, B. 166
online news agencies 248; *see also* agencies
Only Fools and Horses (TV program) 149
Open Rugby 86
Oprah Winfrey Network (OWN) 335
The Oprah Winfrey Show 335
O'Reilly, B. 176–177, 180
Oriard, M. 29
Orientear 83, 88–91, 94
Ornstein, David 248
Orvice, Vikki 347–349
Orwell, G. 12, 90
Oslo 51, 53
Osmond, E. 64
Other Old Trafford 18
Outside the Lines (ESPN) 227
The Oval 28, 173, 176, 177, 183, 185
over-the-top (OTT) streaming service 265, 356
Owen, M. 45
Owens, C. 242
Owens, J. 208
Oxford English Dictionary (OED) 13, 85–86
Oxford Mail 91
Oxford United 91

Pacific Islander 207
page design 153
The Page Nineteen Round-Up 192
Paige, S. 210–213
pains 192–193
Paisley, B. 46
Pakistan 9, 65, 174, 217
Palmer, C. 52
Panesar, M. 208
Panja, Tariq 248
Panorama 17
Paralympics GB 69
Pardon, J. 90
Parker, C. 39
Parkin, C. 39

Parkin, R. 91
Parkinson, M. 163
Parnell, W. 219
Parry, Steve 62
Parsons, L. O. 162
patriotism 160
Paylor, E. 76
Pearl Harbour 213
Pearman, M. 117
Pearson, H. 39, 92, 159
Pearson, Nigel 286–287
pedestrianism 28
Peebles, Ian 351
Peel, J. 85
Pegler, Westbrook 242
PEN/ESPN Lifetime Achievement Award for
  Literary Sports Writing 37
penny press 25
The People 26
The People's Game 58
Perelman, S. J. 159
Perera, K. 6
performance-enhancing drugs *see* doping
performativity 286
Periscope 130
Perryman, Mark 275
personality 37
Perth Times 185
Peter, T. 219
PGA Championship 167
PGA Tour 130
Phelps, Michael 325
Philadelphia 29
Philadelphia Bulletin 61
Philadelphia Phillies (baseball team) 211
Philadelphia Police Gazette and Sporting Chronicle 26
Phillips, E. 44
Phillips, Mitch 324
Phoenix Open 130
photojournalists 372
physical violence 12
Pickford, M. 159
The Pie 91
Pietersen, K. 67
Piggott, L. 47
Pilling, R. 74
Pinder, S. 190–194
The Pink 71, 73, 80
Pink 'Uns 80, 189
Pinterest 106
Pitt, N. 35
Pittsburgh Courier 209
Pittsburgh Pirates (Baseball team) 213
Plaid Cymru 95
Planet Sport 12, 341
Platini, M. 138, 195
The Players' Tribune 139

Playfair Book of Cricket Records (Webber) 176, 182
Playfair Cricket Annual 175
Pochettino, M. 140
Poland 53
"Politics as Vocation" (Weber) 368
Port of Spain 36
Portsmouth 63, 76
Portsmouth Evening News 63
Portsmouth Sports Mail 79
The Post 167
Post-World Cup euphoria 191
Potter, H. 90
Poulton, E. 274, 275
Powell, E. 177
Powell, J. 59
power 5; "Like losing a friend" 80–81; paradox
        141; regional newspapers 73–80; shift 137
Power Games (Boykoff) 268
Premier League 4, 42, 47, 54, 79, 86, 95, 106–107, 111,
        126, 129–131, 136, 139, 141–142, 190, 200
Premier League Record 184
press agencies 24; *see also* agencies
Press Association (PA) 24, 62–63, 65, 69, 191, 336
Press Box Red (Silber) 209, 214
Press Complaints Commission (PCC) 224–225
Preston, H. 180
Preston North End (football club) 74
Priestley, J. B. 207
Prince, A. 3, 218
"Prince of men" 13
Prine, John 286
Pringle, D. 38
print sports journalists 130
Pritchett, T. 76
Private Eye 86, 168
prize fighting 101
professional identity 86
professionalisation/professionalism 74, 101
profit-maximising owners 247–248
The Program (film) 336
Propaganda Games *see* Berlin Olympics (1936)
psychoanalysis *see* armchair psychoanalysis
psychosis 218
public attitudes 27
public relations 135–143; changes 142–143;
        club media 137–140; fan club 141–143;
        fourth estate 141–143; sport media's
        puppetmasters 135–140
Puerto Rico 212
pugilism 27
punk inspiration, fanzines 85–88
punk rock, Great Britain 85
Puskas, F. 198

Qasim, I. 13–14
Qatar 135
Queens Park Rangers (football club) 156

race/racism 17, 207–220, 371–372; apartheid
        218–220; denial and complicity 214–216;
        overview 207–208; "Press Box Red"
        209–214; stereotyping 217
Racing Post 189, 193
Radcliffe, Paula 325
Rage On 84
Raging Bull 91
Rain Men (Berkmann) 159
The Rams 80
Ramsay, George 282
Ramsey, Alf 283
Rand Daily Mail 214
Rapinoe, M. 16
rationing *see* newsprint rationing
Raynes Park, London 189
RCN 370
Real, Michael 264
Really Annoying People You Meet at Football 89
Real Madrid (football club) 57, 137, 198,
        200–201
Real Rangers Men 13
*Redemption Song: Muhammad Ali and the Spirit of the
        Sixties* (Mike) 218
Redhead, B. 197
Red Issue 84, 90
Redknapp, H. 60, 198
Red Sox (baseball team) 209
Red Tops 51
Reed, L. 140
Reeve, C. 152
The Referee 26, 27
referees: criticism 198–199; tabloids 53–54
regional newspapers 71–81; power 73–80; threat
        78; *see also* newspapers
Reid, M. 167, 228
Reid, P. 60
Reilly, R. 170
relations *see* public relations
Reporter (Hersh) 248
reporters 137; anger/angry 54; aspiring sports
        141; editors 27, 127, 208; freelance 48;
        news agency 69; newspaper 41; racist 208;
        sports papers 29
resigned tolerance 91
resilience 131
Rest of the World 184
Resurfaced 356
"retire hurt" 11
reverse homophobia 228–229
Revie, Don 283
Reynolds, B. 152
Reynolds Newspaper 26
Rhett Butler Theory 35
Rhodes, W. 184
Rice, G. 36
Rice, T. 86

Richards, H. 194, 218
Richardson, M. 38
Richardson-Walsh, Helen 228
Richardson-Walsh, Kate 228
Rich Guy 84
Rickey, B. 209
Ridley, Ian 347, 352
Ridley, Paul 348
Rights Holding Broadcasters
    (RHB) 264
Ring: A Biography of Ring Lardner (Yardley) 161
Rio Olympics (2016) 42, 43, 262; Bach on 262;
    media personnel 262; NBC's coverage
    265; Semenya and 324–327
riots 3
Rippon, A. 80
Robben Island 215
Robbins Report 88
Roberts, A. 14
Roberts, C. 48
Roberts, E. 175
Roberts, J. 351
Robertson-Glasgow, R. 38–39, 178, 180
Robinson, J. 16, 85, 89, 92, 209, 214
robot journalism 372–373
robo-writing software 372
Robson, B. 46, 52, 59–60
Roche, Maurice 262
Rodney, L. 17, 209–213, 214
Roebuck, P. 39, 185
Rogers, K. 76
Rogers, N. 183
Rogers, R. 225
Rohrbaugh, J. 229
Rome, Jim 228–229
Rome Olympics (1960) 265
Ronaldo, Cristiano 224, 243
Ronay, B. 84–85, 92
Rooney, W. 126
Roosevelt, F. 213
Root, J. 4, 47
Rosen, A. 111–123
Rosenwater, I. 182
Ross, A. 36
Roth, V. 199
Rothstein, Arnold 242
Rowe, D. 136, 252, 268, 335
Royle, J. 77
Rub of the Greens 89
rugby 26; women in 229–230
Rugby Football Union 229
Rugby League World 86
Rugby World Cup 4
Rule, R. 208
Runyon, D. 33, 36
Russell, R. 152
Russian gangs 273

Ruth, B. 35, 179, 210
Ryder, J. 185
Ryder Cup 64

SA Council on Sport (Sacos) 215
Salazar, A. 208
Sam, Michael 227
Sambrook, R. 127
Samiuddin, O. 208
Samson, A. 219
Samuel, John 351–352
Samuel, Martin 275
Sanders, Richard 239
Sandomir, Richard 245, 247
Sandpapergate controversy 299–315; commentary
    301–310, **302–303, 308**; Cricket Australia
    on 305, 309, 310–315; overview 295–296;
    social media 299, 301, 304–305, 308–314,
    311–313
San Francisco 49ers 155
San Marino 54
SA Non-Racial Olympic Committee (Sanroc) 215
San Sebastian 92
Sarandon, S. 152
Sardinia 59
The Saturday Evening Post 161
Saturday Football Final 73
Saudi Arabia 3
Saunders, D. 198
Scargill, A. 217
Schmeling, M. 209
Schofield, M. 117
Schwarz, A. 179, 183
Scoggins, D. 127
The Scone Advocate 180
Scotland 26, 151, 170
Scotland on Sunday 151
The Scotsman 346
Scott, A. 123
Scottish Cup 156, 197
Scottish Premier League 192
Second City 13
The Second of May 90
Second World War 12, 34, 92, 208
self-censor 141
Sellers, P. 57
Selvey, M. 38
Semenya, Caster 321–327; London Olympics
    321; media and 322–324; Rio Olympics
    321, 324–327; sex identity 323; World
    Championship 321
Sen, Amartya 367
Serie A 281, 285
sex 237
sexism 363
sexual abuse 17
sexual harassment 43

sexuality 223–231; British media 223–226; heteronormativity 228–229; homophobic labelling 228; US media 226, 227
Seymour, Harold 241
Shaherkani, Wojdan 262
Shankly, B. 198, 284
Sharpe, G. 39
Sharpe, L. 52
Sharpeville massacre 214
Shaw, C. 265–266
Shaw, P. 83–85, 88
Shearer, A. 45
Shearman, R. 191, 193
Sheffield Daily Telegraph 28
Sheffield Evening Telegraph 24
Shelton, R. 159
Shepherd, R. 195
Sheppard, D. 14
Sheth, D. 140
Shine, O. 66, 68
Shoot! 93
Shultz, B. 102, 105, 107
Sid the Surrealist 89
Silber, I. 209, 211
Sinatra, F. 58
sine qua non 152
Singapore Yahoo 65
Sing When We Fishing 89
Sing When You're Fishing 92
Sit Down and Cheer (Kelner) 168
skills: ability 103, 107; football writing 59; journalistic 94; prodigious 11
Skinner, D. 217
Skinner, F. 93
Skudder, Chris 276
Sky Sports 59, 86, 104, 106, 111, 129, 131, 245, 247; FA Women's Super League 361
Sky Sports Package (app) 106
Sky TV 106, 192
Slater, Matt 248
Slipless in Strettle (Pearson) 159
sliver of ice 37
Sloane, Peter J. 241
Slot, O. 193
Slow Turn (Marqusee) 217
slum sport 87
Smith, A. 52, 121
Smith, Giles 168–170
Smith, Graeme 299, 305, **308**
Smith, M. 64
Smith, R. 34–35, 37, 137, 160
Smith, S. 10–12, 16, 18, 155, 304, 309, 310, 311, 313, 314, 315; *see also* Sandpapergate controversy
Smith, T. 16, 153
Smith, W. 17, 162, 208–209, 212
Smokey *see* Wood, J.

Smyth, R. 7
Snapchat 106
Sniffin' Glue 85
Snipe 87
soccer 24
Socialist Unity Party of East Germany 90
social media 295, 368; control of narrative 295; outrage 296–299; Sandpapergate controversy 299, 301, 304–305, 308–314, **311–313**
Society of American Baseball Research 242
Society of Cricket Statisticians 175
Soljskaer, O. G. 56
Somalia 208
Some Like It Hot (Wilder and Diamond) 159
Soneji, P. 107–108
Souness, G. 88
South Africa 1, 6, 175, 179, 208, 214, 216, 219
South African Cricket Association 214
South African Cricket Board of Control (SACBOC) 215
South African rugby tour of the UK (1969–1970) 214
Southampton 45, 71
Southern Daily Echo 79
Southern Evening Echo 77
Southgate, G. 121
South London 91
South Pacific 214
South Yorkshire Times 163
Sparks, V. 123
specialist sports agencies 62; *see also* agencies
specimen copy 190
The Spectator 262
Spence, Louie 224
Spilius, A. 193
Spinal Tap 52
Spirit of the Times: A Chronicle of the Turf, Agriculture, Field Sports, Literature and the Stage 25
sport(s): in 18th and 19th centuries) 25–27; anxieties 23; codification 101; editor 17, 27–28, 47, 57, 147–152, 191, 217; insiders 127; journalism industry 143; media puppetmasters 135–140; model in Great Britain 23; nationalisation 26; newspapers and 25–27; professionalisation 101; spectatorship 24; violence 13
Sport-Informations-Dienst (SID) 62, 69
Sporting Chronicle 25
sporting journalists 29
Sporting Life 25, 28–29
Sporting Magazine 25, 27
Sporting News 160, 210, 213, 241
Sporting Pink 42
Sporting Review 25
Sporting Times 30

sports journalism: in 18*th* and 19*th* centuries
23–30; broadcasting and 104; England
cricket 4–9; fan 9–17; importance 17;
mid-20th century 101; occupants 2;
relationship with Twitter 125–126;
time-honoured sports page 18; *see also*
multiplatform journalism
sports journalists 101–102, 126; in 18th and 19th
centuries 27–29; audition 141; fear 136;
guidance 33; white media and 215
Sports Argus 42, 73
Sportsbeat 68
Sportsbeat in Britain 62
Sports Echo 72, 80
Sports Illustrated 139, 170, 227
Sports Journalists' Association 80, 361
Sportsman 26
The Sportsman 25
Sports Media LGBT 372
Sports News Lobby 248
Sportspages 83, 85
The Sports Paper For Londoners 193
Sports Personality of the Year (TV program) 169
Sports Report 73
sports rights 244
sportswriters 27, 34, 148, 207; Great Britain 199;
humour 165–166; newspapers 104;
United States 199
sportswriting 33–40, 105, 159; Angell, R. 36–40;
musical prose 35–36; priorities 33;
transatlantic connections 33–34; typing
34–35
Spotify 106
Spurs 148
The Square Ball 89
Squires, D. 92
Sri Lanka 2, 6, 217–218
Stamp Act 23–24
STANDamf 83–84
statisticians 183–185
statistics and records 173–185; importance
174–176; mass of numbers 180–183;
newsprint rationing 176–177; overview
173–174; rise of statisticians 183–185
Stead, W. T. 74
Steele, D. 47
Steen, R. 9, 24, 275, 276, 279
Stein, J. 198
Steinbrenner, G. 166
Steptoe and Son/ Sanford and Son (TV program) 166
stereotypes 219
Sterling, R. 16, 139
Sterling, Raheem 363
steroid abuse 17
Stills, K. 155
Stockholm Olympics (1912) 208
Stockholm Syndrome 40

stock markets 244
Stoke City 83
Stokes, B. 2, 4
Stokes, G. 4–10
Stones, J. 129
Stop Press 73
Storey, D. 159
strained bed fellowship 136
Strait Times 67
The Strand 148
The Street of Shame 160
Stride, C. 86
stupidity 1
Sturgeon, N. 2
sub-editor 151–158; Armstrong, L. 154–158; do
no harm 157–158; importance of flow
154–156; mistakes 157; overview
151–152; stereotyped by Hollywood
152–154; *Sunday Times* 154–158; visual
aids 156–157; *see also* editors
Sudell, William 282
Sugar, A. 55
Sugden, J. 137
Sullivan, J. L. 28
The Sun 13, 42, 51–54, 58, 127, 139, 156, 210, 223,
224, 370
Sunday Chronicle 26
Sunday Express 42
Sunday Independent 127
Sunday Mercury 26
Sunday People 185
Sunday Telegraph 59, 195
Sunday Times 17, 26, 35, 55, 57, 59, 86–87, 92, 137,
142, 154–158, 163, 178, 191, 214, 245,
246
Sunderland 40, 89, 117, 129
Sunderland, H. 179
Sun God 2
Sunshine, Sixes and Cider (Foot) 39
Supercalifragilisticexpialidocious (song) 156
Supporters Club 87, 94
Supporters' Trust 93
Surrey County Cricket Club 28
Surrey v. Middlesex 175
Sussex 216
Sussex Express 149, 196
Sutcliffe, H. 182
Sutton, A. 93
Swain, B. 76
Swansea City's League Cup (2013) 97
Swanton, E. W. 175, 177, 178, 216
Sweden 52
The Sweet Science (Liebling) 346
Swindon Town 91
Switching Channels (film) 152
Sydney 12, 27, 68
The Sydney Morning Herald 4, 176, 178–179, 183

Syed, M. 199
Syria 3

tabloids 51–60; Curry, S. 58–60; journalism 51, 276; newspapers 55; papers 56, 191; referee 53–54
"Tabloid War" 51
Tabor, S. 90
Take Me Out (Greenberg) 159
"Take Me Out to the Ballgame" (song) 34
TalkSPORT 59
Tallon, D. 178
Tanzania 95
Tatchell, P. 223, 224
Tate, S. 28
Taylor, D. 17, 142
Taylor, G. 51–55, 60, 226
Taylor, H. 181
Taylor, L. 39–40
Taylor, P. 181–182
Taylor, R. 87
technocracy, football as 283
technology 372–373; ability 372; change 94; innovations 24
Tel, E. 55
The Telegraph 59, 141, 175, 193, 198
Tendulkar, S. 184, 314
Test and County Cricket Board 14
Test Match Cavalcade 1877–1946 (Roberts) 175
Test Match Special 38
testosterone for female athletes 321
That Peter Crouch Podcast 103
This Girl Can (Sport England) 361
Thomas, A. A. 176
Thomas, G. 225, 235
Thomson, J. 11–12, 28
Thomson, S. P. 76
Thomson Reuters 61–66, 68–69, 372
Thorpe, J. 208
threats 78, 136
Through the Wind and Rain (Kelly) 94
Ticher, M. 84, 87
Tiger, Meet My Sister… And Other Things I Probably Shouldn't Have Said (Reilly) 170
'Til Death Us Do Part/All in the Family (TV program) 166
Timeo Danaos et dona ferentes 57
The Times 2, 4, 26, 41–42, 47, 74, 114, 131–132, 139, 143, 168, 193, 195, 199
The Times of India 254
Tired and Weary 89
Tityrus 75
Today 51, 54, 149, 195
Tokyo Olympics (1964) 69, 265
Tomlinson, A. 137
Toney, J. 68–69
Tongue, S. 86

Tottenham Hotspur 77, 152, 244
Tour de France 26, 136, 154, 329, 330–331, 332, 333, 334, 335
Tourette's Syndrome 1
Touring the Caribbean (1962) 15
Tourist Trophy (TT) motorcycle races 13
trainee sports journalists 135
The Tranny Man 89
transatlantic connections, sportswriting 33–34
"translating articulate spectator opinion" 88–93
Triângulo do Futebol 372
Trinidad 36
Trinidadian Marxist 208
trolling 130
Trove 179, 183
Trueman, F. 164, 184
Trump, D. 3
trusts and fanzines 93–96
Truth 183
Tuck, C. 72
Turner, K. 152
TV rights 244
Twain, M. 161, 168
Twenty20 cricket 362
Twickenham 68
Twitter 41, 48, 54, 60, 66–67, 106, 125–132, 359; acquisition 132; architecture 129; decision-making 132; emphasis 125; fans 130–132; football media outlets 373; opinions 129–130; reliable or unreliable sources 127–129; spread of rumour 126–127; transparency 127
Tydfil, M. 95
Tygiel, J. 214
Tyldesley, C. 170
Tyler, M. 111–123; aspirations 122; broadcasters 118; broadcasting 114–115; as commentator 116–117; covering England international matches 119; cribbing 113–114; daft moment 114; diversity 123; embarrassing moment 114; favourite co-commentator 120–121; memorable game 121; preparation done before game 113; regret 114; training 112–113; Woking football club 112, 118–119
typing, sportswriting 34–35

UEFA 136
Ugra, S. 208, 217, 253, 257
ul-Haq, I. 174
The Umpire 26
un-American discrimination 210
underpaid journalist 29–30
Unholy Trinity 39
Union Cycliste Internationale (UCI) 333
United Press International (UPI) 62–64, 69

United States 25–26, 29, 45, 53, 62, 64, 80,
   118, 208; Anti-Doping Agency 154;
   Communist Party 209; Congress 208;
   social media 106; sportswriters 199;
   trade war with China 3; Trump election
   campaign 55
United States Anti-Doping Agency (USADA) 334
University of Brighton 141
University of Loughborough 141
unrespectable journalist 29–30
Upton Park 95
US "Dream Team" 244
US Food and Drug Administration (FDA) 334
US Just Not Sports 371
US Open Golf Championship 43
US Postal Team 333, 334, 335
Ustinov, Peter 343
utility maximisation 241
utility maximisers 137

Valley Parade 88, 90
Van Dyke, D. 156
Vanity Fair 209
Van Persie, R. 43
van Praag, M. 138
Vardy, J. 43
Vaughan, M. 314
Vecsey, George 332
Veeck, B. 167
Venables, T. 55, 57
Vernon, O. 129
Vero Communications 136, 138
Verwoerd, H. 215
Vice, T. 215, 218
Vice Sports 142
Victoria Falls 8
Vietnam War 156
Vincent, J. 251, 252, 253, 254, 257
violence *see* hooliganism; physical violence
Virgin Atlantic 192
virtual-reality news stories 372
visual aids 156–157
Voges, A. 184
Voice of the Valley 88–89, 91, 93, 95
Vorster, J. 215

Waddell, S. 170
Waddle, C. 59
Wagg, S. 86
Waldstein, C. 262
Walker, D. 76
Walker, E. 202
Wallace, D. 88
Wallace, S. 90
Wall Street Journal 248
Wally Hammond: The Reasons Why (Foot) 39
Walsh, D. 10, 16–17, 154, 331–333, 336

Walsh, P. 57
Wanderers 74
War Minus the Shooting (Orwell) 217
Warne, S. 166, 299, 305, 308, **308**, 314
Warner, D. 300, 305, 309, 310, 311, 315
Warner, P. 39
War of the Monster Trucks 89
Washington, DC 8
Washington Nationals (baseball team) 8–9
Washington Post 161, 208
Watkins, A. 178
Watson, D. 185
Watson, G. 333
Watson, T. 167
Wayne, J. 200
Webb, H. 128
Webber, R. 176, 181–182
Weber, M. 368
Weekes, E. 182
Weekly Dispatch 26
Weekly Times 26
Wei, S. 130
Weibull distribution model 184
Weigall, A. 175
Weller, P. 60
Wenger, A. 122
Western Australian 176
Western Gazette 38
Western Mail 176–177
Westgarth, Fred 282
West Ham 73, 95
West Indies 5, 38, 166, 175, 179, 208, 217
West Indies v. Bristol World Cup (1999) 38
West Side Story 90
Whannel, Gary 261, 274, 276
What a Load of Cobblers 93
Whatever Happened to The Likely Lads (comedy
   series) 115
Wheatcroft, Geoffrey 333
Whelan, Charlie 276
Wheldon, K. 89
Whelehan, Imelda 363
When Saturday Comes 83–84, 86–94, 96, 278
When Skies Are Grey 95
White, C. 178
White Friar 178
White Hart Lane 77
white media and sports journalists 215
"White Rose" 75
Whitington, R. S. 215
Whitlock, Jason 227
Who Dares Wins (school of philosophy) 5
Wide World of Sports (TV program) 208
Wilcockson, John 285, 332
Wilder, B. 152, 159
Wilkie, W. 213
Wilkinson, F. C. 28

William Hill Prize 39
Williams, C. 173
Williams, H. 219
Williams, J. 362
Williams, R. 45–46
Williams, T. 162
Williamson, M. 14
Willis, B. 9, 14, 116, 148, 192
The Willow Wand (Birley) 217
Wills, H. 160
Wilson, J. 137, 139
Wilson, P. 216
Wilson, S. 62–64
Wimbledon 64, 107, 191
Winter, H. 41, 48, 108, 131
Winterbottom, Walter 282–283
Wisden 174–175, 182, 184
Wisden 1949 180
Wisden Asia 216
Wisden Cricketers' Almanack (Engel) 164, 175, 207
Wise Men Say 89
With Bat and Ball 39
Witherow, John 225
Wodehouse, P. G. 159
Woking football club 112, 118–119
Wolstenholme, K. 54
Wolverhampton Wanderers (football club) 24
women: basketball players 228; consumer 362–363; golf players 228; hockey players 228; rugby players 229–230; tennis players 228–229
women sports reporters 361, 362; harassment of 371
Women's Sport and Fitness Foundation 230
Wood, J. 37
Woodfull, C. B. 11–12
Woods, T. 130
Woodward, S. 35
Wooldridge, I. 34, 149, 345
Woolf, V. 161
Woolmer, B. 69
Worker 178
"Working harder and longer" 103–104
World Athletics Championships 62
World Cup (cricket) *see* International Cricket Council (ICC)

World Cup (football) *see* FIFA
World Rugby 107
World Series (baseball) 121, 163, 165, 240
World T20 5
World War I 136
World Wide Web (WWW) 10, 156
World XIs 184
Worrell, F. 16, 182
Wrexham University 170
Wright, B. 203
Wright, Harry 240–241
Wright, I. 52–53, 58, 193
www.cardiffcity.com 84
www.codalmighty.com 85
www.widthofapost.com 85
Wynne-Thomas, P. 174, 182

xenophobia 1, 159–160, 371
XIII Winters 86

Yahoo 65
Yahoo! Sports 372
Yankee Stadium 212
Yardley, J. 161
Yawkey, T. A. 162
Ye Olde Cock Tavern 148
Yokohama Stadium 68
York Herald 23
Yorkshire 159, 163–164
Yorkshire County Cricket Club 1
The Yorkshire Evening Post 142, 240
Yorkshire Post 240
You Know Me Al (Lardner) 161, 164
Young, C. 184
YouTube 47, 60, 69, 104–106, 139
YouTubers 139

Zaltzman, A. 168
zero-hours contracts 1
Ziegfeld Follies 161
Ziegler, Martyn 248
Zimbabwe 1
Zimbalist, Andrew 265
Zimmerman, R. 9
Zine Awards (2007–2008) 84
Zirin, D. 17, 209–210, 262